CONTRACTING FOR SPACE

Contracting for Space

Contract Practice in the European Space Sector

Edited by

LESLEY JANE SMITH

Leuphana University Lueneburg and Weber-Steinhaus & Smith, Bremen, Germany

INGO BAUMANN

BHO Legal, Cologne, Germany

Routledge
Taylor & Francis Group
LONDON AND NEW YORK

First published 2011 by Ashgate Publishing

2 Park Square, Milton Park, Abingdon, Oxon OX14 4RN
711 Third Avenue, New York, NY 10017, USA

Routledge is an imprint of the Taylor & Francis Group, an informa business

First issued in paperback 2016

British Library Cataloguing in Publication Data
Contracting for space : contract practice in the European space sector.
1. Space law--European Union countries. 2. Space vehicle construction contracts--European Union countries. 3. Space industrialization--Law and legislation--European Union countries. 4. Artificial satellites in telecommunication--Law and legislation--European Union countries.
5. Astronautics and state--European Union countries.
I. Smith, Lesley Jane. II. Baumann, Ingo.
343.2'40786294-dc22

Library of Congress Cataloging-in-Publication Data
Smith, Lesley Jane.
Contracting for space : contract practice in the European space sector / by Lesley Jane Smith and Ingo Baumann.
p. cm.
Includes index.
ISBN 978-1-4094-1923-5 (hardback) -- ISBN 978-1-4094-1924-2 (ebook)
1. Space law--Europe. 2. Astronautics and state--Europe. 3. Aeronautics--Law and legislation--Europe. 4. Outer space--Exploration--Government policy--Europe. 5. Research and development contracts--Europe. I. Baumann, Ingo. II. Title.

KJC6925.S65 2011
341.4'7094--dc22

2011009549

ISBN 978-1-4094-1923-5 (hbk)
ISBN 978-1-138-24783-3 (pbk)

Contents

PART IV: SPECIFIC ASPECTS OF SPACE INDUSTRY CONTRACTS

PART V: SPECIFIC ASPECTS OF SATELLITE SERVICES CONTRACTS

PART VI: CONCLUSIONS AND OUTLOOK

List of Figures and Tables

Figures

Tables

List of Contributors

Dr Philippe Achilleas is Vice-Dean of the Faculty Jean Monnet (University Paris-Sud 11, France). He is director of the Institute of Space and Telecommunications Law and of the Master's Degree in Law of Space Activities and Telecommunications at the University Paris-Sud 11.

Timiebi U. Aganaba, MSc (Strasbourg, France), BL (Nigeria), LLB (Leicester, UK), Member of the Nigerian Bar is Directors' Assistant – International Institute of Space Commerce, Isle of Man and Researcher for the Space Security Index. Currently a student of Air and Space Law at McGill University, Montreal, she previously served as: a legal practitioner at Kayode Sofola & Associates, Lagos; Teaching Associate at the International Space University, Strasbourg, France; and Trainee Legal Officer (Legal Services and International Co-operation) at the National Space Research and Development Agency, Federal Republic of Nigeria.

Cristian Bank studied Aerospace Technology at Stuttgart University (Dipl.-Ing.), and Business and Labour Law at Hagen Fernuniversität. He worked at the European Space Technology Centre (ESTEC) in Noordwijk, and at Aeritalia, now Alenia, in Turin, later joining DASA, now EADS, in 1992 in Ottobrunn, and moved to Rostock as Head Environmental Services. He joined the COLUMBUS development programme at Astrium in Bremen in 1996 as a subcontractor manager. In 2003, he became Head of Department for ISS Extension Programmes and for Crew Transport and was appointed Head of Astrium ST Improvement Implementation in 2010.

Dr Ingo Baumann is a partner in the law firm BHO Legal in Cologne, Germany. He studied law in Muenster and Cologne and wrote his doctoral thesis on the international law of satellite communications at the Cologne Institute for Air and Space Law. As an attorney, he then advised small and medium-sized companies from the satellite communications industry. Having worked for seven years as a legal advisor within the German Aerospace Center (DLR), Dr Baumann has wide experience in all types of space industry contracts. Before establishing BHO Legal, Dr Baumann was Head of the DLR Galileo Project Office and CEO of the DLR Space Applications GmbH, the operating company of DLR for the German Galileo Control Centre.

Dr Tare C. Brisibe currently serves as Director, Legal Regulatory Affairs with the Geneva based Société Internationale de Télécommunications Aéronautiques (SITA) /AIRBUS joint venture, OnAir Switzerland sarl. A member of the Nigerian Bar, he previously served as Deputy Director (Legal Services & International Co-operation) National Space Research and Development Agency, Nigeria, and was a former Regulatory Information Officer at Inmarsat PLC (the privatized International Maritime Satellite Organization – INMARSAT). He publishes regularly and is a frequent presenter at national and international conferences. Dr Brisibe is a member of the Permanent Court of Arbitration Advisory Group of Experts on Optional Rules for Arbitration of Disputes Relating to Outer Space. He is a Visiting Fellow at the Graduate Institute for International Studies, Geneva, and appointed to hold the Office of the Chairman of the Legal Subcommittee of the United Nations Committee on the Peaceful Uses of Outer Space for the period of 2012–2013.

Philippe Clerc is the Head of the CNES's Legal Department, where he is responsible for all legal issues concerning the organisation's programme and activities, including international and European affairs. He is currently preparing CNES for its new responsibilities under the 2008 French Space Operation Act (FSOA). He was Deputy Director at the Space Department of the Ministry of Research (1998–2003) and Head of the Central Legal Affairs Office at Arianespace (2003–2006). Since 1999 he has played a major role in the FSOA law-making process. Philippe Clerc is a member of the executive board of the ADDEF (Association for the Development of Space Law in France) and a member of ECSL (European Center of Space Law) and IISL (International Institute for Space Law). He has guest lectured on Space Law, Policy and Strategy at several universities. He passed the *concours* at the 53rd Course of the French 'National Defense High Studies Institute' (2000).

Dr Mireille Couston is a Professor of Law at the University of Lyon 3, Director of the Centre of Space Law and Development, Vice-President of the French Society of Air and Space Law, Vice-President of the Scientific Committee of the French Review of Air and Space Law, and Member of the Academy of Air and Space. She is laureate of the universities of Paris and laureate of the special prize 2010 of the University of Lyon and Rhône Alpes region.

Dr Matthias Creydt studied law at Universities in Germany and the UK. He was a visiting scholar at the Tulane University (USA) for his PhD thesis in the area of private international law and space law. He previously worked for the German Aerospace Agency as an attorney at law and as corporate counsel in the automotive industry. He is currently the Head of Export Control Germany for Astrium, an Aerospace company belonging to the EADS Group.

Hans Dodel lectures at the Carl Cranz Academy in Munich on communications, navigation, and radio regulations. He also runs his own consulting company DodelSatelliteCommunications, contracting with commercial clients and governments in ITU affairs, satellite filings and Earth station coordination. Hans Dodel has attended World Radiocommunications Conferences (World Radio Conferences for Space Telecommunications) since 1971, and, as an expert contractor to the European Commission, has been particularly active in the ITU filing of the European Galileo satellite system.

Catherine Doldirina is currently completing her PhD at the Institute of Air and Space Law at McGill University, Montreal and specialises in copyright and intellectual property law issues in space. She has a number of publications in the field, and is a member of the International Institute of Space Law.

Frans von der Dunk currently occupies the Harvey and Susan Perlman Alumni / Othmer Chair of Space Law at the University of Nebraska-Lincoln, United States, with the world's only LLM Programme on Space and Telecommunications Law. He is Director of the Black Holes space law and policy consultancy in the Netherlands. Prior to his appointment in Lincoln, he worked for many years in various capacities related to space law and public international law at the University of Leiden, in the Netherlands. He has acted as an advisor to many governments, intergovernmental organisations and space companies on issues of space law and policy, and was awarded the IISL Distinguished Service Award in 2004 and the IAA Social Science Award in 2006.

Mustapha Elriz is the CEO of Southern Aerospace & Telecom Consulting (SATConsult) and supports the development of space infrastructure in emerging countries. He belongs to a network of high-level independent technical, regulatory and financial experts for due diligence studies, auditing, specifications, support for procurement or satellite and ground construction monitoring. He has lead important projects and interacted with various telecommunications and satellite operators, satellite and ground manufacturers, regulators, governments, financial backers and development agencies. He is a graduate from the French National School of Telecommunications and holds an MBA. He is a lecturer at the French Institute for Aeronautical and Space in Toulouse.

Dr Michael Gerhard is a legal adviser to the European Aviation Safety Agency (EASA), working in the field of international aviation law, EU law, European administrative law and enforcement. Prior to this, Dr Gerhard worked at the German Aerospace Center (DLR) as a legal adviser where he was mainly occupied with matters of public international law and administrative law. Dr Gerhard lectures in Space Law to students studying Aerospace Technologies at the Aachen University of Applied Sciences. He has published a book on the topic of national space legislation and more than 40 articles on space law and policy.

Kamlesh Gungaphul-Brocard studied European and international law and completed a post-graduate degree in the law of space activities after being a Manfred Lachs Moot Court finalist. She has contributed to several articles on space law and policy. She has worked mainly in the field of international private law and has recently joined the Swiss Space Office as scientific advisor.

Dr Oliver Heinrich is a partner of the law firm BHO Legal with offices in Cologne and Munich. He studied German and Anglo-American law at the Universities of Trier and Cologne. His doctoral thesis focused on legal questions of national and European research funding and possible conflicts with competition and procurement law. Dr Heinrich specialises in the legal management of large-scale projects and in national, European and international (WTO) procurement law. He was a project manager for Galileo at DLR, legal advisor to the Board and authorised officer of TeleOp for the Galileo Concession negotiations.

Dr Kay-Uwe Hörl has worked in the aircraft and space divisions of the European Aeronautic Defence and Space Company (EADS). He is currently heading the Legal and Procurement Department of EADS EFW in Dresden, Germany. Previously, he was Head of Contracts at EADS ASTRIUM in Munich, Germany. Dr Hörl's research interests are the interfaces between aeronautics, space activities and the law.

Oliver Huth is Senior Legal Counsel working for SES in Betzdorf in the Grand Duchy of Luxembourg. Betzdorf is home to the headquarters of SES, a global satellite operator. Before joining SES, he practised as a lawyer in a law firm in Luxembourg. He completed his law studies at the universities of Bonn, Freiburg im Breisgau and Paris XI, and his practical clerking experience (*Referendariat*) in Cologne.

Sylvia Kainz-Huber holds a master's degree in communications, international law and economics from the Ludwigs-Maximilians-Universität in Munich. She worked as a journalist until she joined the European Commission in 1995. Since 2007, she has been Deputy Head of Unit responsible for space policy and coordination at the Commission's Directorate-General for Enterprise and Industry.

Eleni Katsampani joined the European Space Agency (ESA) in 2005 as Contracts Officer and supports in this capacity mainly the Solar Orbiter Mission, the ExoMars Programme, the Lunar Lander Mission and the activities of the AURORA Mars Robotic Exploration Programme and Core Exploration Programme. In parallel to her operational duties, Eleni has been seconded to the ESA Rules and Procedures Office, as a member of the team responsible for the Reform of the General Clauses and Conditions (GCC) for ESA Contracts, which was successfully completed in June 2010. Before joining ESA, Eleni supported for seven years (1998–2005) as in-house lawyer the Greek shipbuilding and maritime group 'NEORION GROUP' specialising in Greek and international company law, contracts law and public procurement law for procurements in the defence sector (military vessels). Eleni graduated from the Faculty of Law of the University of Athens, Greece, in 1997 and received her LLM in European and International Company and Commercial Law from the University of Heidelberg, Germany, in 1998. She is a qualified lawyer in Greek jurisdiction and Member of the Athens Bar Association. Since October 2008, Eleni has been studying Engineering in the Faculty of Technology at the Open University UK with the aim eventually to qualify as an Arbitrator in technological disputes.

Romain Loubeyre is a law student from the Faculty Jean Monnet (University Paris-Sud 11, France) specialised in International and European Law, as well as in Space and Telecommunication Law.

Dr Leopold Mantl is a legal expert with the European Commission. He has worked in the Galileo and GMES programmes and was responsible for the legal framework of the European launchers as a legal administrator with the European Space Agency. He is a member of the IISL and the ECSL and has published several articles on space law and policy.

Martin J. Mittelbach is an attorney at law. As Legal Advisor at the Deutsches Zentrum für Luft- und Raumfahrt e.V. DLR (German Aerospace Center), Cologne, he acquired substantial experience in all types of complex international, European and national projects and R&D contracts.

Philippe Montpert is Managing Director at Willis Inspace, a leading space insurance broker. He graduated from ESTACA, an aerospace engineering school in France and started his career as an engineer at the European Space Agency in the Netherlands. He then moved to the insurance domain, first as an insurer and later as a broker. He has delivered contributions at many international conferences.

Peter E. Newman is President of Pensat Consulting Ltd., a consulting company that specialises in satellite and launch vehicle contract negotiations for satellite operators and government organisations. He was previously employed by Telesat, a Canadian satellite operator and consulting company. He has negotiated in excess of 60 satellite contracts, with all major satellite manufacturers, and over 20 launch vehicle contracts on behalf of Telesat and other clients for a period of 32 years. He also supports legal and financial institutions on matters related to satellite and launch vehicle contractual disputes.

Deirdre Ní Chearbhaill, LLM Eur., is a solicitor in the asset finance group of McCann FitzGerald Solicitors, Dublin. Prior to joining McCann FitzGerald, she worked for Astrium in its satellites division in the UK. She is a member of the Law Society of Ireland.

Claude-Alain du Parquet graduated in Paris from the Paris I (Panthéon-Sorbonne) University of Law where he obtained a master's degree in international law (1974) and a Diplôme d'Etudes Supérieures (DES) in European and International law (1975). After graduating he joined the legal department of Sodeteg, a French engineering company of the Thomson Group, currently known as Thales. In 1985 he joined Arianespace's legal department and has, since then, been involved in the preparation and negotiation of launch services agreements.

Walter Peeters is Professor of Space Business and Management at the International Space University (ISU) and Director of the International Institute of Space Commerce (IISC), a think-tank established in the Isle of Man. Previously, he worked at ESA and was involved in various project control and coordination functions. He is the author of the book *Space Marketing* and has published articles in the field of project management, contract types and space commercialisation.

Dr Laurence Ravillon is a Professor of Private Law at the University of Burgundy, and Dean of the School of Political Science and Law of Dijon (France). She teaches at other institutions in France and abroad. Her doctoral thesis dealt with private law and space activities, and she has organised several conferences on space law. She has published several books and numerous articles, presentations, and chronicles on space law and on international commercial law.

Rafaël Roelandt has been working in the space sector for over 15 years and his current position is Senior Legal Counsel at SES ASTRA in Luxembourg. Previous employers include the European Space Agency and EUMETSAT. He studied law at the University of Leiden with a focus on air and space law and holds a master's degree from the International Space University in Strasbourg.

Ines Scharlach, attorney at law and member of the German bar, is currently legal counsel to Astrium GmbH Services, Munich. She has worked within various remits, including as Contract Policy Manager for Astrium Supply Chain Management. Prior to this she was legal counsel to BetaDigital Company for Digital Transmission Services mbH, Munich.

Dr Bernhard Schmidt-Tedd joined the German Aerospace Center (DLR) in 1987 and is currently Head of the Legal Support for DLR Space Agency Affairs. As an author of a number of articles, he lectures on space law and mentors practice-oriented doctoral theses. He is co-editor of the Cologne Commentary on Space Law (CoCoSL). Membership: IAA, Corresponding Member of the Russian Academy for Cosmonautics, IISL, ECSL and DGLR.

Dr Kai-Uwe Schrogl is the Director of the European Space Policy Institute (ESPI), Vienna. Prior to that, he was Head of the Corporate Development and External Relations Department of the German Aerospace Center (DLR). He is Honorary Professor at the Institute of Political Science at Tübingen University. He is editor of the series *Yearbook on Space Policy* and *Studies in Space Policy* (both Springer) and a member of the editorial boards of *Acta Astronautica*, *Space Policy* and the *German Journal for Air and Space Law*.

Dr Lesley Jane Smith, LL.M. is a Professor of Law at the Leuphana University of Lueneburg, Germany and Professor and former Rector at Riga Graduate School of Law, University of Latvia. She is a Member of the Law Society of Scotland, and also admitted to practice at the Hanseatic Bar of Bremen, where she acts as legal consultant. She has published widely on various aspects of European law, and contributed to several works on commercial space law, as well as the Cologne

Commentary on Space Law (CoCoSL). Dr Smith lectures in various academic and professional contexts on the subject of commercial space law, including at the ISU. She is a member of the editorial board of the *Space Law* series published by Brill Publishers, Netherlands and a member of ECSL, IISL and the IAA.

Gunilla Stjernevi is Head of the Contractual Rules and Procedure Office in the Procurement Department of the European Space Agency.

Dr Gisela Süß completed her education with one year of studies at the Paris Ecole Nationale d'Administration after studying law in Germany. She practised as a lawyer for more than 10 years in several international law firms in Paris. She joined the European Space Agency in 2001 and the Agency's Legal Service in 2005, where she is in charge of Earth Observation Programmes.

Jean-Jacques Tortora currently serves as the Secretary General of ASD-Eurospace, which is the trade association of the European Space Industry. From 2004 to mid 2007, he was head of the French Space Agency (CNES) office in North America and the Attaché for Space and Aeronautics at the Embassy of France in Washington, D.C. Previously he was Deputy Director for Strategy and Programs, responsible for the Industrial Strategy of CNES, the French Space Agency. From 1998 to 2000, Mr Tortora was adviser to the French Ministry of Research for Industrial Policy and France's representative in the ESA Industrial Policy Committee and Joint Communication Board. From 1990 to 1998, he was appointed by Arianespace as Ariane 4 Operations Quality Manager first in Kourou (French Guiana), then in Evry (France).

Richard John Tremayne-Smith is the former Head of International Relations and the Space Environment at what is now the UK Space Agency. He is a Chartered Engineer and a Member of the Institution of Engineering and Technology. He has contributed to UN-related activities to improve the implementation of the Outer Space Treaties and Principles and assisted with the drafting of Principles and Resolutions over the past 20 years. He currently runs a small consultancy concentrating on the space environment, space debris and NEOs, and space authorisation activities.

Christophe Venet is a PhD candidate at the Institute for Political Science at Tübingen University, and a Research Associate at the Institut Français des Relations Internationales (Ifri). He was a co-editor and co-author of *Yearbook on Space Policy 2008/2009* and has published several articles on various aspects of space policy, including space commerce, space strategy and space security. He is a peer reviewer for the journal *Acta Astronautica*.

Dr Dietrich Weber-Steinhaus, LLM is senior partner of Weber-Steinhaus & Smith, a specialist law practice that focuses on international and national commercial litigation and commercial advisory work. Dr Weber-Steinhaus is a member of the Hanseatic Bar of Bremen and Notary Public. He is an accredited specialist in commercial and company law. Dr Weber-Steinhaus is the long-standing legal advisor to the Bremen Cotton Exchange and a lecturer at the University of Applied Sciences in Bremen. He is a member of the German Institution of Arbitration (DIS) and has been involved in numerous national and international arbitration proceedings, both as an attorney and an arbitrator.

Dr Vasilis Zervos is Associate Professor in Economics and Policy at the International Space University (Strasbourg, France) and former lecturer in industrial economics focused on the aerospace, space and defence industries at the University of Nottingham (UK). His work is widely published in refereed journals, books and news articles and he has contributed to several projects, reports and forums related to space, aerospace and defence economics and policies. Key areas of teaching and research include: economics of procurement, international trade and strategic trade analysis, industrial economic analysis and foreign direct investment studies.

Foreword

As in other fields where both public and private funds are used to implement projects, space has a spectrum of contractual mechanisms and practices, which also vary widely with geographic and cultural differences. Some sectors of space have well-developed and accepted contractual environments for procurement and execution, such as the institutional space science projects within ESA, infrastructure projects through the EU, and the now routine commercial geostationary communications services.

In my role as leader of the SSTL group of companies for the last 25 years, I have been involved in many contractual negotiations for space projects with customers across the spectrum of space-faring nations – from ESA and US institutions, Russian and Chinese commercial companies, to Asian and African national space agencies. In particular, emerging space nations and the implementation of new service models enabled by technological advances, especially miniaturisation of spacecraft, have required a flexible and imaginative contracting approach based more upon partnership than contractual rigidity and self-protection.

From these negotiation experiences I have learned to appreciate the importance of understanding the risks involved in delivering complex space projects and the problems encountered in defining risks in a contractual document. I have also learnt that in cases of cross-cultural negotiations with new customers you should not be surprised to discover that what is important to you may be of very minor importance to them and vice versa – and that the meaning of an 'agreed contract' may likewise be perceived very differently – from a legally binding and fixed relationship to simply an expression of mutual understanding intent at the outset of a project!

I therefore believe that the contributors to this book have provided us with a very useful insight into the European space contracting environment and the forces and issues that incentivise the players in this particular environment to act in certain ways that are specific to the European space industry – and also to enable the reader to use this as a touchstone when dealing with other space business cultures.

Sir Martin Sweeting

List of Abbreviations

AEMG	Autorisation d'Exportation des Matériels de Guerre
APE	Agence des Participations de l'Etat
AL	Ausfuhrliste (German Export List)
ANFR	Agence Nationale des Fréquences (France)
API	Advanced Publication Information (ITU)
ARRA	Agreement on the Rescue of Astronauts, the Return of Astronauts and the Return of Objects launched into Outer Space 1968
ARTA	Ariane Research and Technology Accompaniment
ASAR	Advanced Synthetic Aperture Radar
ATV	Automated Transfer Vehicle
AVMSD	Audiovisual Media Services Directive
AWG	Aussenwirtschaftsgesetz (Foreign Trade and Payments Act)
AWV	Aussenwirtschaftsverordnung (Foreign Trade and Payments Regulation)
B2B	Business to Business
B2C	Business to Customer
B2G	Business to Government
BAFA	Federal Office of Economics and Export Control (Germany)
BAFO	Best and Final Offer
BERR	Department of Business, Enterprise and Regulatory Reform (UK)
BGB	Bügerliches Gesetzbuch (German Civil Law Code)
BGH	Bundesgerichtshof (German Federal Court of Justice)
BIS	Bureau of Industry and Security (US)
BIS	Department for Business, Innovation and Skills (UK)
BNSC	British National Space Centre
BR	Radiocommunications Bureau (ITU)
BSS	Broadcasting Satellite Service (ITU)
CASTLE	Clusters in Aerospace and Satellite Navigation Technology Applications Linked to Entrepreneurial Innovation
CCL	Commercial Control List
CCN	Contract Change Notice
CDMA	Code Division Multiple Access
CDRL	Contract Data Requirement List
CEA	Atomic Energy Commissariat
CENELEC	European Committee for Electrotechnical Standardisation
CEO	Chief Executive Officer
CEPT	European Conference of Postal and Telecommunications Administrations
CERN	European Organisation for Nuclear Research
CERP	European Conference of Postal and Telecommunication Administration (CEPT)
CIEEMG	Commission Interministérielle pour l'Etude des Exportations de Matériels de Guerre

CNES	Centre Nationale d'Etudes Spatiales (France)
CoCom	Coordinating Committee for Multilateral Export Controls
COPOUS	Committee on the Peaceful Use of Outer Space (UN)
COTS	Commercial off the Shelf
CP-FP	Ceiling Price Converted into Fixed Price
CPAF	Cost-Plus-Award-Fee
CPFF	Cost-Plus-Fixed-Fee
CPIF	Cost-Plus-Incentive-Fee
CPPF	Cost-Plus-Percentage-Fee
CS	Constitution (ITU)
CS	Commercial Service (Galileo)
CSG	Centre Spatial Guyanais
CTL	Constructive Total Loss
CV	Convention (ITU)
CWL	Cross Waiver of Liability
DARPA	Defence Advanced Research Agency (US)
DBS	Direct Broadcasting Satellite
DDTC	Direction of Defense Trade Control
DESCA	Development of a Simplified Consortium Agreement (EU Framework Research Programme)
DESO	Defence Export Services Organisation
DGA	Délégation générale pour l'armement (France)
DoC	US Department of Commerce
DoD	US Department of Defense
DoS	US Department of Security
DoS	US Department of State
DRS	Data Relay Satellite
DSL	Digital Subscriber Line
DTH	Direct to Home
DVB	Digital Video Broadcasting Standard
EADS	European Aeronautic Defence and Space Company
EAR	Export Administration Regulations
EASA	European Aviation Safety Agency
EBU	European Broadcasting Union
EC	European Community
ECA	European Common Allocation Table (CEPT)
ECC	Electronic Communications Committee (CEPT)
ECJ	European Court of Justice
ECO	Export Control Organisation
ECP	Engineering Change Proposal
ECSL	European Centre of Space Law
ECTRA	European Committee for Telecommunications Regulatory Affairs (CEPT)
EDF	Electricité de France
EEA	European Environment Agency
EEA	European Economic Area
EERP	European Economic Recovery Plan
EGNOS	European Geostationary Navigation Overlay System

ELDO	European Launcher Development Organisation
EMITS	Electronic Mail Invitation to Tender Service (ESA)
ENCADRE	European Network of Clusters for Satellite Applications Development
EO	Earth Observation
EPA	Etablissements publics à caractère administratif
EPIC	Public Industrial and Commercial State Organization
ERA	European Research Area
ERC	European Radiocommunications Committee (CEPT)
ERO	European Radiocommunications Office (CEPT)
ESA	European Space Agency
ESA-PR	European Space Agency Procurement Regulation
ESDP	European Security and Defence Policy
ESINET	European Space Incubators Network
ESOA	European Satellite Operators Association
ESP	European Space Policy
ESPI	European Space Policy Institute
ESRO	European Space Research Organisation
ETO	European Telecommunications Office (CEPT)
ETSI	European Telecommunications Standards Institute
EU	European Union
EU FR	European Union Financial Regulation
EU-FRIR	European Union Financial Regulation and Implementation Rules
EUMETSAT	European Organisation for the Exploitation of Meteorological Satellites
EUSC	European Satellite Centre
EUTELSAT	European Telecommunications Satellite Organisation
EVMS	Earned Value Method System
FCC	Federal Communications Commission (USA)
FCO	Foreign and Commonwealth Office
FFP	Firm-Fixed-Price
FOC	Full Operational Capability (Galileo)
FP	Framework Programme (EU)
FPE	Fixed-Price-with-Escalation
FPI	Fixed-Price with Incentive
FSOA	French Space Law on Space Operations
FSS	Fixed Satellite Service (ITU)
FSTEK	Federal Service for Technical and Export Control
GA	General Assembly
GAC	GMES Advisory Council
GALILEO	European Global Navigation Satellite System
GAO	Government Accountability Office
GATS	General Agreement on Trade in Services (WTO)
GATT	General Agreement on Tariffs and Trade (WTO)
GBT	Group on Basic Telecommunications (WTO)
GCC	General Clauses and Conditions (ESA)
GCS	Ground Control System (Galileo)
GEO	Geostationary Orbit (also GSO)
GEOSS	Global Earth Observation System of Systems

GHz	Gigahertz
GJU	Galileo Joint Undertaking
GLONASS	Global Navigation Satellite System (Russia)
GMDSS	Global Maritime Distress and Safety System (IMO)
GMES	Global Monitoring for Environment and Security
GMPCS	Global Mobile Personal Communications by Satellite
GNC	Guidance Navigation and Control
GNSS	Global Navigation Satellite System (International)
GOCE	Gravity Field and Steady-State Ocean Circulation Explorer
GPA	Agreement on Government Procurement (WTO)
GPS	Global Positioning System (USA)
GS	General Correspondence
GSA	GNSS Supervisory Authority
GSC	Guiana Space Centre
GSC	GMES Space Component
GSM	Global System for Mobile Communications
GTO	Geostationary Transfer Orbit
HDTV	High Definition Television
HSPG	High Level Space Policy Group
IAA	International Academy of Astronautics
IADC	Inter Agency Space Debris Coordination Office
IAP	Integrated Applications Promotion
IATA	International Air Transport Association
ICAO	International Civil Aviation Organisation
ICC	International Chamber of Commerce
ICD	Interface Control Document
ICSS	International Commission on Intervention and State Sovereignty
ICT	Information and Communication Technologies
ID	Identification
IGA	Intergovernmental Agreement
IGO	Intergovernmental Organization
IISL	International Institute of Space Law
ILS	International Launch Service
IMEI	International Mobile Equipment Identity
IMF	International Monetary Fund
IMO	International Maritime Organisation
IMSI	International Mobile Subscriber Identity
IMSO	International Mobile Satellite Organisation
INMARSAT	International Maritime Satellite Organisation
INSPIRE	Infrastructure for Spatial Information in the European Community
INTELSAT	International Telecommunications Satellite Organisation
INTERSPUTNIK	International Organisation of Space Communication
IoM	Isle of Man
IOV	In-Orbit-Validation
IP	Internet Protocol
IPC	Industrial Policy Committee (ESA)
IPO	Initial Public Offering

IPP	Industrial Procurement Plan
IPR	Intellectual Property Rights
ISDN	Integrated Services Digital Network
ISL	Inter-Satellite Links
ISO	International Organisation for Standardisation
ISP	Internet Service Provider
ISPA	International Society of Parametric Analysts
ISPM	International Solar Polar Mission
ISS	Inter-Satellite Service
ISS	International Space Station
ISU	International Space University
IT	Information Technology
ITA	Information Technology Agreement (WTO)
ITAR	International Traffic in Arms Regulation
ITR	International Telecommunications Regulations (ITU)
ITSO	International Telecommunications Satellite Organisation
ITT	Invitation to Tender
ITU	International Telecommunication Union
ITU-D	ITU Development Sector
ITU-R	ITU Radiocommunications Sector
ITU-T	ITU Telecommunications Standardisation Sector
KIS	Knowledge Intensive Services
KIS4SAT	Knowledge Intensive Services in the Satellite downstream application
KPI	Key Performance Indicators
LCC	Life Cycle Costing
LEA	Law Enforcement Agency
LEO	Low Earth Orbit
LIAB	Convention on International Liability for Damage Caused by Space Objects, 1972
LMI	Lead Market Initiative
LSA	Launch Service Agreement
LSP	Launch Service Provider
LTP	Long-Term Space Plan (ESA)
MEO	Medium Earth Orbit
METI	Ministry of Economy, Trade and Industry (Japan)
MFF	Multi-Annual Financial Framework (EU)
MFN	Most Favoured Nation (WTO)
MFR	Master Frequency Register (ITU)
MHz	Megahertz
MID	Ministerstvo Innostrannich Del (Russian Ministry of Foreign Affairs)
MINEFE	Ministry of Economy, Industry and Employment (France)
MMSS	Maritime Mobile Satellite Service (ITU)
MoD	UK Ministry of Defence
MOON	Agreement Governing the Activities of States on the Moon and other Celestial Bodies, 1979
MoU	Memorandum of Understanding
MSISDN	Mobile Subscriber Integrated Services Digital Network

MSS	Mobile Satellite Service (ITU)
MSS	MilSat Services GmbH
MTCR	Missile Technology Control Regime
NASA	National Aeronautical and Space Administration (USA)
NATO	North Atlantic Treaty Organisation
NDA	Non-Disclosure Agreement
NGSO	Non-Geostationary Satellite Orbit
NGSO-FSS	Non-Geostationary Satellite Orbit Fixed Satellite Service
NGSO-MSS	Non-Geostationary Satellite Orbit Mobile Satellite Service
O&U	Operation and Utilization
ODTC	US Office of Defense Trade Controls
OECD	Organisation for Economic Cooperation and Development
OGEL	Open General Export Licence
OIEL	Open Individual Export Licence
OMB	Office of the Management of the Budget
OOSA	Office for Outer Space Affairs (UN)
OS	Open Service
OSCE	Organization for Security and Cooperation in Europe
OST	Outer Space Treaty
OTA	US Office of Technology Assessment
PC	Personal Computer
PECS	Plan for European Cooperating States
PPP	Public Private Partnership
PRM	Programme Review Meetings
PRS	Public Regulated Service (Galileo)
PSI	Public Sector Information
R&D	Research and Development
R&T	Research and Technology
REG	Registration Convention
RFP	Request for Proposal
RNSS	Radio Navigation Satellite Service (ITU)
RR	Radio Regulations (ITU)
RRB	Radio Regulations Board (ITU)
RT	Technical Regulation
S-PCS	Satellite-Personal Communication System
SAR	Synthetic Aperture Radar
SAR	Search and Rescue Service
SDA	Space Data Association
SES	Société Européenne des Satellites
SGDN	Secrétariat Général de la Défense Nationale (France)
SIB	Space Industrial Base
SIEL	Standard Individual Export Licence
SLA	Service Level Agreement
SME	Small- and medium-sized Enterprises
SMOS	Soil Moisture and Ocean Salinity
SNG	Satellite News Gathering
SOA	French Space Law on Space Operations

SoL	Safety-of-Life Service (Galileo)
SOW	Statement of Work
SSA	Space Situational Awareness
SSO	Sun Synchronous Orbit
TAA	Technical Assistance Agreement
TAP	Transfer Account Procedure
TBD	to be decided
TEA	Technical Exchange Agreement
TED	Tenders Electronic Daily
TEN	Trans-European Networks (EU)
TEU	Treaty on European Union
TFEU	Treaty on the Functioning of the European Union
TGI	Court of first instance of General Jurisdiction (France)
TIMS	Technical Interface Meetings
TIP	Tender Information Pack
TKG	Telekommunikationsgesetz (D)
TRIPS	Trade Related Aspects of Intellectual Property Rights (WTO)
TT&C	Tracking Telemetry and Control
TTCP	Technology Transfer Control Panels
TV	Television
UHD	User Help Desk
UI	Underwriting Information
UKSA	United Kingdom Space Agency
UMTS	Universal Mobile Telecommunications System
UN	United Nations
UNCITRAL	United Nations Commission on International Trade Law
UNCOPUOS	United Nations Committee on the Peaceful Use of Outer Space
UNGA	United Nations General Assembly
UNIDROIT	International Institute for the Unification of Private Law
US(A)	United States (of America)
USD	US Dollar
USML	US Munitions List
USTR	US Trade Representative
VAT	Value Added Tax
VOP	Variation of Price
VSAT	Very Small Aperture Terminal
W-LAN	Wireless Local Area Network
WARC	World Administrative Radio Conference (ITU)
WHO	World Health Organisation
WIPO	World Intellectual Property Organisation
WMD	Weapons of Mass Destruction
WMO	World Meteorological Organisation
WPA	Warfare and Assimilated Products
WRC	World Radio Communication Conference (ITU)
WTAC	World Telecommunications Advisory Council (ITU)
WTO	World Trade Organisation
WTPF	World Telecommunications Policy Forum (ITU)

WTSA	World Telecommunication Standardisation Assembly (ITU)

Chapter 1
Introduction

Lesley Jane Smith and Ingo Baumann

Significant developments have taken place across the European space sector over the last decade. Among them, the Lisbon Treaty now provides the European Union with specific space competence (Art. 4(3), TFEU) and mandates coordination in space exploration and exploitation (Art. 189(1) TFEU) as well as cooperation between the EU and the European Space Agency (ESA) (Art. 189(3), TFEU). This has heralded an increase in the European Union's space-related initiatives and, particularly, in moves towards formulating a European Space Policy (Art. 189(1) TFEU). All these developments combine to impact on business and, in turn, the growth of a body of national and European commercial space law that is relevant across the Europe Union and its Member States.

It seems only appropriate to mark these developments with an accompanying publication that analyses and assesses the legal issues and key factors influencing the space sector in Europe. It was with this goal in mind that the editors decided in early 2009 to collaborate on this compendium *Contracting for Space: Contract Practice in the European Space Sector*. This publication is designed as a guide to the complex regulatory background of space projects and an analysis of typical legal problems to be solved by drafters and negotiators in their daily work.

Among the specific significant developments over the past decade are Galileo and GMES, the major flagship programmes of the new European Space Policy (ESP), providing Europe with long-term capabilities in the fields of satellite navigation and earth observation. Galileo is the first system worldwide designed to provide a set of commercial navigation services. A further development is the growing ESA membership, with more Eastern European states being offered the opportunity of joining ESA through its specially created Plan for European Cooperating States (PECS). In addition, ESA has undergone substantial reform, which has resulted in new financial, procurement and contract regulations. These reforms are set to have considerable influence on the European space sector. The main European states have recently enacted national space legislation or are in the process of doing so.

New actors, such as the European Defence Agency, the European Union Satellite Centre, the European Maritime Safety Agency and the European Air Safety Agency, are involved in space activities in their respective field of responsibility. The former international satellite organisations, Inmarsat and Eutelsat, have successfully been privatised, with remaining international bodies ensuring the fulfilment of certain public service obligations. While European military space activities lag behind the United States, the efforts in the military sector have increased considerably, with national Departments of Defence (DoD) procuring a large number of communications and earth observation satellites, sometimes under the model of public private partnerships.

The greater part of space activities in Europe continues to benefit from public funding, albeit to varying degrees, and this balance does not stand to alter in the short term. Nevertheless, commercial space activities have grown considerably over the last years. The global space sector is estimated to constitute a market in excess of EUR 120 billion per annum across its entire value chain, with European companies securing around 40 per cent of the commercial market for satellite manufacturing, launch and satellite services. European companies are among the world leaders in these activities. Since its creation in 1980, Arianespace has launched 277 payloads, accounting for more than one-half of the commercial satellites now in service. SES Global, Eutelsat and Inmarsat are among the world leading operators of commercial satellite communications systems. They account for a significant portion of the overall industry revenues. EADS and Thales are the leading companies for the manufacturing of commercial communications and earth observation satellites.

The markets for satellite manufacturers, launchers and operators build the entry level into a long value chain that supports other industry elements, ranging from satellite system operators, ground station operators, receiver and set-top box manufacturers, through to producers of content for distribution by satellite. Space-related products and applications now form a fast-growing market in which small and medium-sized enterprises (SMEs) are able to develop innovative products and services. Whereas communication and broadcasting once constituted the main sectors for commercial space services, earth observation and navigation now stand to shape business development for the future within the European space community.

The space policy of the European Union focuses on space applications and their potential support to other fields of European policy, including road, rail and maritime transport, intelligent transport systems, environmental protection and climate change, knowledge-based society, telemedicine and much more. The different satellite applications are increasingly converging with other technologies, creating huge potential for new products and services, such as location based services combing mobile communications with geo-information products and navigation aids.

The challenges for the practitioners are significant. Space law and other fields of public international law, the law of ESA and of manifold other international organisations, the law of the European Union, national laws, especially national space legislation and procurement regulations, and finally the entire corpus of international commercial law and practice, form the background to the various types of contracts within an individual space project.

The book aims to address the status of this complex legal framework and to provide a valuable contribution to the further development of a coherent contract practice for the European space sector. Within this particular background, the recent amendments to European Union law and the reform of the European Space Agency's procurement rules are given particular attention.

Contracting for Space offers an overview of the stakeholders, regulators and business interests within the space sector in Europe. The volume delivers an up to date review of the complex regulatory aspects of Europe's space activities and examines substantive issues of law specific to launchers, satellite manufacturers and space service providers. In this context the major issues of risk allocation, liability and insurance are discussed, alongside the contracts between stakeholders at operational level.

One caveat is, however, necessary: the work is not designed as a contract style book. By nature, contracts concluded by the actors for certain projects are highly confidential, especially where strategic or military interests are at stake. The terms and conditions used for certain types of contract are often commercial secrets. Those looking for contract prototypes, boilerplates and styles will therefore not be totally successful in their search.

In preparing this book, the editors have been fortunate in being able to rely on the collaboration of leading experts and practitioners in the field of European space law and policy. The authors expended great effort to submit their contributions and collaborate with the editors, in addition to their normal daily work and responsibilities. We remain grateful to all authors for their substantial contribution of time and energy in making this publication possible.

The European Centre of Space Law (ECSL) has continuously ensured an open forum for the legal community that enables constructive dialogue and exchange. Full recognition and thanks are accorded by the editors to this organisation. The network formed by ESCL has made it possible to gather the leading experts for our book project.

Thanks go too to all those who have supported the book in its development phase. The editors would like to express particular thanks to Dr Bernhard Schmidt-Tedd, Senior Legal Advisor, German Space Agency, Cologne, together with Professor Hans-Jörg Dittus, German Space Agency, Bremen, as well as to their support staff Annika Hasselblatt and Sabine Lindemann in managing the book's pre-publication conference that was held in Bremen on 26/27 November 2009.

Further thanks go to those institutions and companies that, through their generous support, enabled the Bremen conference to take place.

Special warm thanks go to our language editor, Dr Susan-Gale Wintermuth, Hamburg/Lüneburg for her attention and care in reading the manuscripts, to Antje Kautz, Bremen, without whom the text could not have been so readily compiled, and to Angeline Asangire Oprong.

The editors have aimed to ensure that the work reflects the state of the law as of 1 December 2010. Any errors and omissions remain their responsibility.

Lesley Jane Smith and Ingo Baumann
Bremen/Lueneburg and Cologne/Munich

PART I
Introduction

Chapter 2
The Impact of the European Space Policy on Space Commerce

Kai-Uwe Schrogl and Christophe Venet

The Setting

This chapter provides an overview of the impact the policy framework for space activities has on commercial space activities in Europe. It shows that the development of a space policy framework on the European level has, from the beginning, aimed at furthering commercial space activities and strengthening the European space industry.

The chapter first looks at efforts on the European level to strengthen space commerce, before the adoption of the European Space Policy (ESP) by the 4th Space Council in May 2007. Then it details the relevant provisions in the European Space Policy (ESP) and, finally, looks at the most recent policy objectives regarding space commerce developed in response to the financial and economic crises, in particular the European Economic Recovery Plan (EERP) and its call for a European Plan for Innovation of December 2008. The last part is the most substantive – reflecting on the latest decisions by the 4th Space Council of May 2009.

The increasing importance of the economic and commercial aspects within the ESP has an evident impact on contract practices in the European space sector. However, this chapter is intended to set the scene for the following chapters and, therefore, does not go into any regulatory detail; rather it primarily outlines the policy framework for the theme of the book. It does, however, mention and indicate the issues that are investigated in the book, whenever they appear in the policy documents.

The Economic Aspect of Space Policy

Today, space is understood by policy-makers, as well as the public, as being multi-dimensional. Space activities can be justified by a whole range of striking reasons, from the most down-to-earth utilitarian approaches to the most high-minded trans-utilitarian approach. Thus, the spectrum is filled with notions from the creation of jobs and the use of satellite applications for serving various policy areas – from agriculture to security. The other end of the spectrum is taken by fascination, the broadening of our horizon to bringing the youth closer to science.

When we look specifically at space commerce, within this spectrum, we are clearly located in the area of 'utilitarian' aspects of space activities. Here the rationale for investment and engagement in space is based on the creation of wealth, trade, technology and jobs. This set of objectives has always played a role in space policies in Europe. Indeed, the early impetus for space activities, the establishment of national space policies, and later the creation of the European Launcher Development Organisation (ELDO) and the European Space Research Organisation (ESRO) – and later on their merger into the European Space Agency (ESA) – were driven by science: the creation of an industrial base for European engagement in space played an important role in this context.[1] As a consequence, industrial policy for space – epitomised in the famous '*juste retour*' – became one of the key elements in the founding document of ESA in 1975.[2]

The following decades then saw the further elaboration of the industrial policy into a market development policy in particular for space applications. And today we are at a point where we regard the space economy or space commerce as a pyramid, with manufacturing as a rather tiny top, a broader slice of operations and services, and a huge basis of downstream markets for space-related products. Consequently space policies in Europe (by single States and by international organisations) have come to focus on the two priorities of strengthening the manufacturing industrial basis in the space sector, and creating, fostering and supporting broad and substantive downstream markets. The size of the space economy in 2008 was estimated by the *Space Report* at USD 257,220 million.[3]

The rise in importance of space commerce as a component of space policy has been documented throughout the past two decades in various ways. It has continuously been highlighted in very prominent ways since the first Communication of the European Commission on space in 1988[4] – up to its most recent documents. It has, moreover, achieved a very particular signification with regard to the organisation and governance of space policy: while in the first four decades of space activities in Europe, this issue area was usually governed by science or research ministries, there has been a trend in the past decade to instead locate space activities on the national level at ministries for economics. The European Commission became part of that trend, when it moved the responsibility or the coordination function for space from research (first in the Joint Research Centre, then in the Directorate General for Research), to industry (now Directorate General for Enterprise and Industry).

The policies and instruments that have been employed in Europe to reach the two policy goals of a strong manufacturing base and a broad downstream market have developed in parallel. The communiqués of ESA Councils, as well as those of the 4th Space Council (which was established following the agreement between ESA and EC in 2003 to set up a new framework), evidence this in the recent years, as do the concomitant meetings of the Council of the European Union and the ESA Council at Ministerial Level. These policies and instruments became increasingly more user-driven and service-oriented, in particular through the establishing and shaping of the two flagship projects, Galileo and GMES. Space commerce thereby has become the lead mover for large-scale space activities.

In addition, space-related research funded by the European Commission in its Framework Programme (FP) became almost fully focused on these two projects and their goals.[5] ESA and

---

1 ESA 2000. A History of the European Space Agency 1958–1987, ESA Doc. SP-1235; Madders, K. 1997. *A New Force at a New Frontier*. Cambridge: Cambridge University Press; Gante, H-J. 2007. 'Zwischen Konzentration und Europäisierung: Die Luft- und Raumfahrtindustrie in der Bundesrepublik', in *Ein Jahrhundert im Flug. Luft- und Raumfahrtforschung in Deutschland 1907–2007*, edited by H. Trischler and K-U. Schrogl. Frankfurt/New York: Campus, 295–320.

2 ESA Convention 1975, Art. VII and Annex V. '*Juste retour*' is, basically, the principle that the amount of contracts awarded within a Member State should reflect the funds subscribed by the Member State.

3 Space Foundation 2009. *The Space Report 2009*. Colorado Springs, CO: Space Foundation.

4 European Commission 1988. Communication from the Commission, The Community and Space: A Coherent Approach, COM(88)417 final of 26 July 1988.

5 European Commission 2007b. Work Programme 2008, Cooperation, Theme 9, Space, COM(2007)5765 of 29 November 2007; European Commission 2008a. Work Programme 2009, Cooperation, Theme 9, Space, COM(2008)4598 of 28 August 2008.

Member States, however, have maintained over time their own balance between space applications and other space activities.[6] This balance naturally depends on programme developments with peaks and lows, but an important point to be noted was that non-applications are, and will not be, adversely impacted by increases in funds for projects like Galileo and GMES, which have mostly been secured through sources other than research budgets – like transport budgets.

The European Space Policy and Space Commerce

A major step forward in coordinating and focusing European space endeavours was achieved with the adoption of the European Space Policy (ESP) at the 4th Space Council, which took place on 22 May 2007 at Brussels. The detailed outline of ESP is given in a Communication by the European Commission, which was prepared together with ESA;[7] a concise set of essentials and further actions is provided through the Resolution of the Council accompanying the adoption of ESP.[8] Both documents, the Communication and the Resolution, therefore relate to each other, but vary in their character due to the way they are drafted.

The Communication presents in detail the need for a competitive European space industry and points out that an industrial policy has to cover many factors, including regulations, public procurement, and research and development. It then looks at the regulatory environment and highlights issues like the standardisation, inter-operability between national and European space and ground-based systems, data access policies, export and import policies, as well as pan-European licensing of services, spectrum and content that are needed, as well as a more flexible, market-based regime for allocating radio spectrum. In a second paragraph, it looks at public investment in space. There it states that space is a lead market in which public authorities can create conditions for industry-led innovation. The efficient and cost-effective aggregation of public policy needs for space is said to be essential and urgent to secure the potential economic benefits and attract further public and private investment. Following this, the role of small and medium-sized enterprises (SMEs) is characterised as being crucial to innovation and to exploration of new market opportunities.

The relevant passage of the Resolution is quoted here in full, because it lays out the authoritative approach in Europe to industrial policy:

> G INDUSTRIAL POLICY
> 14. RECOGNISES that ESA has a flexible and effective industrial policy based on cost-efficiency, competitiveness, fair distribution of activities and competitive bidding, which secures adequate industrial capacities, global competitiveness and a high degree of inner-European competition for

6 Three examples: in France, the competence for space shifts regularly between ministries but such shift has no real consequence for keeping a stable balance and quest for leadership. While the importance of the economic aspects was signified also in Germany by moving the responsibility for space from the Federal Ministry of Education and Research to the Federal Ministry of Economics and Technology, non-applications have not been concerned and the balance following the transition four years ago was stronger than in shorter periods of time, when different ministers in the previously responsible ministry tried to change priorities in the 1990s. In another way, the UK has been so far the most 'one-sided' advocate for space applications but is actually now starting to create a balance with other areas of space activities.

7 European Commission 2007a. Communication from the European Commission to the Council and the European Parliament, European Space Policy, COM(2007)212 final of 26 April 2007.

8 Council of the European Union 2007. Council Resolution on the European Space Policy, Doc. 10037/07 of 25 May 2007.

> efficient European cooperation on joint space projects, thus providing the basis for the successful development of space in Europe,
> EMPHASISES in this context in particular the political and economic dimension of ESA's 'fair return' principle; and the importance to assess and improve, when necessary, the implementation of the 'fair return' principle in view of the future challenges for industry to remain competitive in a changing environment worldwide while maintaining, and possibly increasing, Member States' motivation to invest in space,
> 15. EMPHASISES the crucial role of SMEs and the supplier industry for innovation and the exploration of new market opportunities,
> 16. INVITES the European Commission to develop adequate instruments and funding schemes for Community actions in the space domain, addressing notably the issues listed in Annex 2, taking into account the specificities of the space sector, the need to strengthen its overall and its industry's competitiveness and the necessity of a balanced industrial structure.

These three sub-paragraphs reflect ESA's industrial policy, the '*juste retour*', the crucial role of SMEs, and invite the EC to develop adequate instruments and funding schemes. This last point is connected with the '*juste retour*' in that the principle of '*juste retour*' remains untouched, although its implementation is considered improvable. The top priorities of ESA's industrial policy as reflected here is the strengthening of the industry's competitiveness, its balanced structure, and the maintenance of governmental motivation to invest in space, priorities which may be reached under whichever industrial policy regime may be in place. The text of the entire Resolution can also be seen as the outcome of a debate among countries that might fare better under an industrial policy regime based on pure competition rather than '*juste retour*'. However, the result of this debate has been the remaining of the '*juste retour*'.

Industrial policy and the reflection of space commerce in times of the ESP are therefore guided by the principle of strengthened competitiveness of European industry without changing the basic regulatory principle of '*juste retour*'. Throughout the ESP text in the Communication, as well as in the Resolution, the importance of the industrial base and the downstream markets is visible and guiding. This is particularly true for all components related to Galileo and GMES, but also when it comes to the regulatory environment and international relations. With ESP, the arguable dominance of space commerce has found its clear manifestation. As has been said before, a balance with regard to programmatics has still to be maintained, but ESP is breathing life into this new, predominantly economic approach. The developments since then, and in particular the financial and economic crisis exploding in 2008, have even accelerated this trend.

Recent Policy Developments Regarding Space Commerce

The economic and financial crisis acted as a strong incentive for political initiatives in the field of space commerce. Indeed, decision-makers realised that space, as an R&D-intensive sector, is an investment in the future. It also became increasingly clear that the space sector represents a major contribution to the Lisbon strategy, which has the overarching goal of making Europe the most competitive and dynamic knowledge-based economy in the world.

In line with these new orientations, a focus was put on space applications and on the creation of new markets for SMEs, mainly within the framework of the two European flagship programmes, Galileo and GMES, but also in the field of telecommunications. In parallel with the long-standing support granted to the European space industrial base, which is directed towards the strengthening of the upstream market, these initiatives aim at creating a European downstream market for satellite applications. As a whole, the stimulating effect of the economic crisis created a political momentum that might still lead to the implementation of an even broader European framework favouring space commerce.

The Political Framework

In 2008 and 2009, a series of official documents issued by the EU and by ESA laid down a broad political framework for space commerce. While the Council Resolution 'Taking Forward the ESP' from 26 September 2008,[9] and the Resolutions adopted at the ESA Ministerial Council on 26 November 2008,[10] indicate general ways to increase competitiveness and innovation in the European space sector, the Brussels European Council on 11–12 December 2008,[11] and the 6th Space Council on 29 May 2009,[12] deal specifically with the consequences of the economic crisis. The 5th Space Council, which took place on 26 September 2008, adopted a Resolution entitled 'Taking Forward the ESP', which identifies four new priorities within the ESP.[13] One of them is the contribution of space to the Lisbon strategy. It states:

> [S]pace, as a high tech R&D domain and through the economic exploitation of its results, can contribute to reaching the Lisbon goals so as to fulfil the economic, educational, social and environmental ambitions of the EU [...] to achieve the objectives for growth and employment by providing new business opportunities and innovative solutions for various services.[14]

The Resolution further recalled that space has been included as a thematic chapter in the Community Seventh Framework Programme for Research, Technological Development and Demonstration (FP7), therefore becoming a priority sector in which to build a European knowledge-based society. It also highlights that space applications in the fields of navigation, telecommunication and earth observation constitute substantial market opportunities, especially for SMEs, and finally calls for the inclusion of space in the Lead Market Initiative (LMI).[15]

The two Resolutions adopted at the ESA Ministerial Council on 26 November 2008 are along the same line, recalling the four new priorities identified by the 5th Space Council. These Resolutions also highlight the necessity for the European space sector to be able to compete effectively in

9 Council of the European Union 2008a. Council Resolution Taking Forward the European Space Policy, Doc. 13569/08 of 29 September 2008.

10 ESA 2008. Resolution on the Role of Space Delivering Europe's Global Objective, Doc. ESA/C-M/CCVI/Res.1 (final).

11 Council of the European Union 2009a. Brussels European Council. 11 and 12 December 2008. Presidency Conclusions, Doc. 17271/1/08 of 13 February 2009.

12 Council of the European Union 2009c. Council Resolution. The Contribution of Space to Innovation and Competitiveness in the Context of the European Economic Recovery Plan and Further Steps, Doc. 10500/09 of 29 May 2009.

13 Council of the European Union 2008a. Council Resolution Taking Forward the European Space Policy, Doc. 13569/08 of 29 September 2008.

14 Council of the European Union 2008a. Council Resolution Taking Forward the European Space Policy, Doc. 13569/08 of 29 September 2008.

15 The LMI was launched with a Communication from the European Commission from 21 December 2007 (European Commission 2007c). It aims at entering fast-growing world-wide markets with a competitive advantage. Six promising emerging markets were identified in the first place, excluding space. A review of the LMI took place in the second half of 2009 (European Commission 2009d).

global markets and place an emphasis on the central role of SMEs in these markets. As a whole, the Resolutions clearly make the link between the potential of space to tackle global challenges and the economic aspects associated with this endeavour. Indeed, 'space by its nature provides global solutions and creates global knowledge'.[16]

These two Resolutions also testify to the increasing integration of economic aspects into the ESP and the rise in awareness that space is not only a useful tool for tackling a wide range of issues, but also an important present and potentially huge market. The reference to the Lisbon strategy in these documents allows articulation of the idea that space can generate economic and social benefits by providing solutions to global challenges, such as environmental degradation, climate change, mobility issues and global security. However, the Resolutions were adopted before the full scope of the financial and economic crisis was acknowledged. When the depth and seriousness of the crisis became clearer, European decision-makers decided to use it as an asset to boost innovation in the space sector. Important decisions were made in this respect at the European Council of 11–12 December 2008 and during the 6th Space Council, which took place on 29 May 2009.

One of the central topics discussed at the Brussels European Council on 11–12 December 2008 was the common European answer to the crisis. In this respect, the Council adopted the European Economic Recovery Plan (EERP) which will represent 1.5 per cent of the GDP of the EU (about EUR 200 billion). The Council further called for the launch of a European plan for innovation and for the development of the European Research Area (ERA). Within these two initiatives to boost innovation, and therefore to support economic growth, the Council identified space technologies and services as one of the main technologies for future investment.[17]

While the European Council set up the general orientations, the 6th Space Council on 29 May 2009 focused on the concrete contribution of space to innovation, competitiveness and economic recovery, building on the decisions of the Brussels Council.[18] In order to maximise the use of funds allocated to the space sector for economic recovery, the Council called for an approach that would ensure a cross-fertilisation of knowledge, innovation and ideas between space and non-space sectors, and between space industry and leading research organisations and universities. In particular, the Council recommended that space should be considered in the fund allocation for the EERP, that it should be included in the Lead Market Initiative and that it should become part of the EERP initiative 'Factories of the Future'.[19] It further highlighted the potential of satellite communications technologies to promote future economic growth in Europe, and called for an integration of these technologies into future broadband projects.[20]

---

16 ESA 2008. Resolution on the Role of Space Delivering Europe's Global Objective, Doc. ESA/C-M/CCVI/Res.1 (final).

17 Council of the European Union 2009a. Brussels European Council. 11 and 12 December 2008. Presidency Conclusions, Doc. 17271/1/08 of 13 February 2009.

18 Council of the European Union 2009c. Council Resolution. The Contribution of Space to Innovation and Competitiveness in the Context of the European Economic Recovery Plan and Further Steps, Doc. 10500/09 of 29 May 2009.

19 The 'Factories of the Future' is one of the three public private partnerships (PPPs) included in the EERP. This research programme intends to support the manufacturing industry in the development of new and sustainable technologies (European Commission 2009e).

20 Council of the European Union 2009b. Brussels European Council. 19 and 20 March 2009. Presidency Conclusions, Doc. 7880/1/09 REV 1 of 29 April 2009.

Focus on Downstream Markets

Both the Brussels European Council of 11–12 December 2008 and the 6th Space Council of 29 May 2009 laid down an overarching political framework for space commerce at the macroeconomic level. On the one hand, they clearly emphasise the interconnectedness between social and economic benefits derived from space assets, by including space in the Lisbon strategy. On the other hand, the crisis was seen as a challenge, but also as a chance to invest in space technologies. The strategy chosen to boost space commerce at the microeconomic level was to focus on the creation of new markets for downstream services, mainly for SMEs.

However, the need for a clear distinction between upstream activities (space asset manufacturing and launching) and downstream activities (space applications) was highlighted in the Organisation for Economic Co-operation and Development publication *Space 2030: Tackling Society's Challenges*.[21] The report stated that the downstream sector already offers better prospects for space commerce, as the upstream sector suffers from chronic over-supply with higher launch capacities than annual launches, thus maintaining high launch costs. The European Commission had already come to the same conclusion in 2004.[22]

The recent progress made towards the operational phase of the two European flagship programmes, Galileo and GMES, offers new perspectives for space commerce. Indeed, the creation of European-wide downstream markets based on space applications in the fields of earth observation (for example GMES), navigation and positioning (Galileo for instance), represents a central component of the two programmes. In this respect, recent EU policy documents place a stronger emphasis on these economic aspects.

A further sector known for the creation of downstream markets is the field of satellite communications. In addition to the efforts of the EU to support the development of end-user markets, ESA also placed a strong emphasis on space applications at the ESA Ministerial Council on 26–27 November 2008.[23] One of its main priorities in this respect is to develop space applications serving public policies, but also the citizenry and enterprises. The Integrated Applications Promotion (IAP) Programme was launched to reach these goals.[24]

Finally, it should be noted that while the economic potential of the upstream segment is not as important as for the downstream sector, the satellite manufacturing and launching industry are nevertheless an important part of the European space commerce sector and a technology driver for Europe's high-tech competence as a whole.

To summarise, four sectors are particularly promising as potential markets: satellite navigation, telecommunication applications, earth observation and space launchers. These four areas have already been identified by the Europe Innova Space Innovation Panel as potential candidates for lead markets in space in 2006.[25]

---

21 OECD 2005. *Space 2030: Tackling Society's Challenges*. Paris: OECD.

22 Europe Innova 2009b. *Sectoral Innovation Foresight Aeronautics and Space*. Interim Report.

23 ESA 2008. Resolution on the Role of Space Delivering Europe's Global Objective, Doc. ESA/C-M/CCVI/Res.1 (final).

24 ESA 2010. What is Integrated Applications Promotion (IAP)?

25 Europe Innova 2006. *Innovation Watch, Sectoral Innovation Panels: Space. Report from the Second Panel Meeting*. [Online, 29 November 2006]. Available at: http://archive.europe-innova.eu/ [accessed: 11 September 2009].

Galileo and GMES: towards new applications

The two programmes, Galileo and GMES, are seen as opportunities to strengthen the downstream market. To foster these markets, a user-driven approach has been adopted: not only businesses directly involved in space should be supported, but also end-users of space technologies and applications. A focus is on SMEs, as these are the main actors able to convert innovative research and ideas into successful commercial products. The aim of the European initiatives in these fields is to support the development of new markets based on satellite applications.

A study requested by the European Parliament's Committee on Industry, Research and Energy and completed in September 2008 identifies the main markets for the two applications: GNSS (road traffic, the transport segment comprising rail, maritime and commercial aviation, personal location based services) and earth observation (energy, agriculture and food security, natural hazards, ocean and maritime and air quality).[26] It should finally be noted that both programmes also support the upstream sector, but that the demand in this sector is predominantly institutional and dependent on public funding, therefore, not tied to the existence of a vast potential market.

Several policy documents highlight the economic potential of GMES and Galileo. The ESP Progress Report first was released by the European Commission on 11 September 2008. It states that 'Galileo and GMES initiatives will create significant opportunities for user-driven applications and services and contribute to the emergence of new European downstream markets'.[27] Similarly, the Council Resolution 'Taking Foreword the ESP' calls for the emergence of an appropriate regulatory framework to allow the emergence of innovative and competitive downstream services.[28]

A particular focus was put on the GMES programme when the first pre-operational services started in 2008. However, the programme was still facing problems, in particular concerning its financing and institutional setup. The 5th and 6th Space Councils stressed the need for a GMES action plan, including aspects of governance, sustainable funding and data policy. Following the Resolution of the 5th Space Council, the EC issued a Communication on 12 November 2008 defining an action plan to reach the operational phase and announcing a legislative proposal for a GMES programme that would be user-driven and public-driven.[29] The economic benefits to be reaped from earth observation applications play a central role in the definition of such a programme.

The EC Communication 'We Care for a Safer Planet' dubbed GMES 'a public investment for growth' destined to increase innovation within the SME sector.[30] The Council conclusions on GMES adopted on 26 November 2008[31] identified the stimulation of the downstream sector as one of the key orientations of the programme. In this respect, it called for the implementation of appropriate measures and instruments to enable:

---

26 Polyakov, E., Bremmer, M., Lieshout, M. and Roso, M. 2008. *EU Space Policies and its Potential for EU Industrial Sector Competitiveness*. Brussels: European Parliament.

27 European Commission 2008b. Commission Working Document. European Space Policy Progress Report, COM(2008)561 final of 11 September 2008.

28 Council of the European Union 2008a. Council Resolution Taking Forward the European Space Policy, Doc. 13569/08 of 29 September 2008.

29 European Commission 2008c. Communication from the Commission to the European Parliament, the Council, the European Economic and Social Committee and the Committee of the Regions. 'Global Monitoring for Environment and Security (GMES): We Care for a Safer Planet', COM(2008)748 final of 12 November 2008.

30 *Ibid.*

31 Council of the European Union 2008b. Council Conclusions on Global Monitoring for Environment and Security (GMES): 'Towards a GMES Programme', Doc. 16267/08 of 26 November 2008.

> integrating the GMES information and creating innovative value-added services in major socio-economic sectors (such as energy, health, agriculture, water management, transport) [...] supporting R&D activities for reaching sustainable business models, but also networking and clustering of public and private sectors (and in particular SMEs) for federation of user needs.

Finally, the EC proposal for a regulation on GMES[32] and its initial operations issued on 20 May 2009 states that one of the general objectives of GMES is to create opportunities for greater private sector use of information sources and to facilitate market take-up by value-adding service providers.

As a whole, the downstream earth observation (EO) sector in Europe is still fragmented and composed of small-sized companies, therefore increasing the exploitation costs. This situation, in turn, makes it difficult for downstream companies to offer integrated solutions to customers. In this regard, one of the main policy objectives is to support value-chain integration. Recent cross-sector acquisitions and mergers in the European EO sector contribute to this consolidation of the downstream sector and approach this goal.[33]

The two GNSS programmes, Galileo and EGNOS (European Geostationary Navigation Overlay Service), on their side were marked by an important re-profiling in 2008/2009. Following a switch towards full EU public funding in 2007, a regulation was released on 9 July 2008 addressing all the issues at hand: the different phases of Galileo, funding, the compatibility and interoperability of both systems, ownership and the public governance of both programmes.[34] The procurement for the first constellation of Galileo satellites was also launched in July 2008 and the first contracts were signed in June 2009. Therefore, the economic aspects of the Galileo programme rather focused on the upstream sector at this time.

However, increasing efforts were also dedicated to the expansion of downstream markets through two main streams of activity. First, innovation was promoted through research and technological development activities within FP7. A second call for proposals was launched in December 2008 covering GNSS applications. This initiative draws on the application projects launched within FP6, which aimed at demonstrating the added value of EGNOS and Galileo and identifying the main areas of interest for the user communities. Second, preparatory work for a Commission Action Plan for fostering the development of new GNSS applications and services continued. The strategic aim of this initiative was to create a framework of promotion and support measures in order to accelerate the emergence of high-value GNSS-related markets.[35]

As a whole, the GMES and Galileo programmes are expected to generate high-value downstream markets in a wide range of new applications. Even if strategic considerations, such as independence in areas as critical as navigation and earth observation, played a driving role in the development of both programmes, the economic aspects became increasingly important. Besides

---

32 European Commission 2009b. Proposal for a Regulation of the European Parliament and the Council on the European Earth Observation Programme (GMES) and its Initial Operations (2011–2013), COM(2009)223 final of 20 May 2009.

33 Polyakov, E., Bremmer, M., Lieshout, M. and Roso, M. 2008. *EU Space Policies and its Potential for EU Industrial Sector Competitiveness*.

34 European Parliament and Council of the European Union 2008b. Regulation of the European Parliament and of the Council on the Further Implementation of the European Satellite Navigation Programmes (EGNOS and Galileo), Doc. 683/2008 EC of 9 July 2008.

35 European Commission 2009c. Report from the Commission to the European Parliament and the Council on the Implementation of the GNSS Programmes and on Future Challenges Pursuant to Article 22 of Regulation (EC) No. 683/2008, COM(2009) 302 final of 26 June 2009.

EO and navigation/positioning, a third space application, satcom technologies, is considered to have the potential to generate economic growth.

Satcom technologies: bridging the broadband gap

Satellite communications technologies have the potential to bridge the broadband gap between rural and urban areas and thereby promote entrepreneurship and create economic growth. As a consequence, the 6th Space Council called for the inclusion of satellite communications technologies in the European broadband strategy, elaborated in the framework of the EERP.[36]

On 3 March 2009, the Commission issued a communication entitled 'Better Access for Rural Areas to Modern ICT'.[37] Given the fact that efficient use of information and communication technology (ICT), in particular high-speed internet (broadband) access, can raise productivity and stimulate innovation, a better access to ICT can help unlock the potential of rural areas. The EERP already recognised the importance of broadband communications for modern economies, and the Commission proposed an additional funding of EUR 1 billion to bridge the broadband gap. The development of ICT access in rural areas is also in line with the Lisbon strategy. It can contribute to enhancing the competitiveness of farm businesses, but also act as a catalyst for SMEs and micro-businesses in rural areas.

The Brussels European Council of 19–20 March 2009 recalled the agreement reached on broadband internet in the framework of the EERP and highlighted the fundamental role of telecommunications and broadband development in terms of European investment, job creation and overall economic recovery. It finally invited the Commission to develop a European broadband strategy by the end of 2009.[38] Building on these decisions, the 6th Space Council underlined the potential of satellite communication technologies to reach these objectives. It called on the Commission, ESA and Member States to consider integrating satellite technologies into future broadband projects. It also identified fields in which satellite communication services could help fulfil an institutional demand, such as transport, energy and security.[39]

In line with these priorities, the European Commission also completed the process of attributing licences to operate S-band MSS (Mobile Satellite Services) in Europe in 2008 and 2009. The goal is to provide video, audio and data transmission services to even the most remote areas, while ensuring their viability. Indeed, MSS can cover a large territory and reach areas where such services were not economically viable before. The EC decision setting up the selection procedure entered into force on 5 July 2008.[40] On 14 May 2009, the Commission announced that Inmarsat

36 Council of the European Union 2009c. Council Resolution. The Contribution of Space to Innovation and Competitiveness in the Context of the European Economic Recovery Plan and Further Steps, Doc. 10500/09 of 29 May 2009.

37 European Commission 2009a. Communication from the Commission to the Council and the European Parliament. 'Better Access for Rural Areas to Modern ICT', COM(2009)103 final of 3 March 2009.

38 Council of the European Union 2009b. Brussels European Council. 19 and 20 March 2009. Presidency Conclusions, Doc. 7880/1/09 REV 1 of 29 April 2009.

39 Council of the European Union 2009c. Council Resolution. The Contribution of Space to Innovation and Competitiveness in the Context of the European Economic Recovery Plan and Further Steps, Doc. 10500/09 of 29 May 2009.

40 European Parliament and Council of the European Union 2008a. Decision of the European Parliament and of the Council on the Selection and Authorisation of Systems Providing Mobile Satellite Services (MSS), Doc. 626/2008 EC of 30 June 2008.

and Solaris Mobile were selected, and that each operator received 2×15Mhz of S-band spectrum and an 18-year licence.

As a whole, the recent initiatives to boost space commerce in the field of satellite communication technologies are in line with the latest orientations decided at the European level. They highlight the link existing between contributing to EU policies and creating economic growth through space applications. In addition, they stress the need to invest in innovation and promising future technologies to overcome the economic crisis. As such, the contribution of space to the broader European broadband strategy has to be understood under the double umbrella of the Lisbon strategy and the EERP.

A final trend that has to be mentioned is the development of public private partnerships (PPP) in the field of satellite communications. On the background of the financial crisis putting increasing constraints on public budgets and making access to capital for private actors more difficult, PPP could benefit both the upstream and the downstream segments.

Upstream markets: reducing costs to maintain a strategic advantage

In the upstream segment, commercial activities do not follow the same logic as in the downstream segment, in particular in the area of launchers. Indeed, the launch market is narrow, has little expansion potential and is therefore always threatened by overcapacity. Launch costs remain high, due to the small series and the high fixed costs of production, mainly in R&D. Due to these structural constraints, no launch operator could survive on the international market without governmental subsidies.[41] In this regard, the European political priority in the field of launchers is not to promote growth or to support the creation of new markets, but to reduce costs and to maintain an independent access to space.[42]

Arianespace, the European launch provider exploiting the Ariane-5 heavy launcher, is currently dominating the commercial launch market. In 2008, Arianespace earned an estimated USD 700 million, representing 35 per cent of the total annual worldwide launch revenues, and launched 40 per cent of the total commercial mass launched into GTO (geostationary transfer orbit).[43] However, the international competition is increasing with Russia, China, India and Japan showing increasing ambitions to enter the commercial launch market, and with the rise of private launch operators such as Orbital Sciences or SpaceX.[44] In this regard, it is far from assured that Europe will maintain its dominant position in the market.

To reach the two goals of reduced costs and independent access to space, Europe continues to work towards the completion of a competitive launcher family. In the near future, the European launcher family will be composed of three complementary launch systems: Ariane-5 for heavy payloads; Soyuz for intermediate payloads, launched from the GSC (Guiana Space Center); and the new Vega launcher for smaller missions. In this regard, ESA and Arianespace signed a framework contract for the procurement of launch services in June 2009, as part of a new legal framework for

41 Bigot, B., d'Escatha, Y. and Collet-Billon, L. 2008. *L'Enjeu d'une Politique Européenne de Lanceurs: Assurer Durablement à l'Europe un Accès Autonome à l'Espace.*

42 Polyakov, E., Bremmer, M., Lieshout, M. and Roso, M. 2008. *EU Space Policies and its Potential for EU Industrial Sector Competitiveness.*

43 Rathgeber, W. 2009. *Space Policies, Issues and Trends 2008/2009.* ESPI Report 18.

44 Bigot, B., d'Escatha, Y. and Collet-Billon, L. 2008. *L'Enjeu d'une Politique Européenne de Lanceurs: Assurer Durablement à l'Europe un Accès Autonome à l'Espace.*

launcher exploitation. Its main purpose is to maximise the use of the three launch systems and to ensure competitive launch prices for ESA missions.[45]

There is a strong link between the strategic goal of independent access to space and the economic dimension of the launch industry. Indeed, in order to guarantee a high level of reliability for institutional launches, which is a central condition for an autonomous and sustainable access to space, a minimum launch rate is required every year. The European institutional launches alone are not sufficient to reach this minimum launch rate and, therefore, Arianespace has to be active in the commercial market as well.[46] In this respect, guaranteeing the profitability and the competitiveness of the European launchers in the commercial market is not solely motivated by economic reasons, but is a vital strategic necessity.

In this context, the reduction of the cost of access to space has become an absolute priority. Reflections were launched in this direction, among others by a report on a European launcher policy prepared in France by the Director of the Atomic Energy Commissariat (CEA), the President of CNES (Centre National d'Etudes Spatiales) and the General Delegate for Armament, released on 18 May 2009.[47] The report calls for a better coordination within the European industrial base and for more transparency in the industrial processes.

Boosting Innovation: Prizes and Networks

Besides establishing a broad political framework encouraging the development of space commerce, the EC and ESA also created two concrete tools to foster innovation policies: prizes and networks. The central goal of these initiatives is to tackle the main obstacles to innovation and to create incentives for SMEs to invest in promising satellite applications.

The European Satellite Navigation Competition was launched in 2004 by the Free State of Bavaria, Germany. It rapidly evolved into a network of European high-tech regions, and is now supported by the GSA (GNSS Supervisory Authority). The goal of the competition is to stimulate research, entrepreneurship and innovation in the area of satellite navigation applications. Besides the main prize, the competition comprises a series of special topic prizes, sponsored by industrial and institutional partners, and regional prizes. The winners of the different prizes receive a grant in money and the possibility to realise their project within an institutional incubation programme or with the help of industrial partners.

Examples of prizes for 2009 include an award for the most innovative applications for use in the public and health sectors, sponsored by T-Systems; a special topic prize for civil protection, life support, and other safety-critical applications, supported by the Madrid region; and the most promising EGNOS application idea, awarded by GSA. This initiative perfectly fits within the broader goal of strengthening downstream markets, as it intends to develop the market for navigation applications.[48]

The second tool used by the EC and ESA is represented by networks. The main space-related initiatives were launched by DG Enterprise and Industry of the EC, within the framework of the Europe Innova initiative. Two types of networks were launched in 2006 as laboratories for the

---

45 ESA 2009. ESA and Arianespace Sign a Frame Contract for the Procurement of Launch Services.

46 Bigot, B., d'Escatha, Y. and Collet-Billon, L. 2008. *L'Enjeu d'une Politique Européenne de Lanceurs: Assurer Durablement à l'Europe un Accès Autonome à l'Espace*.

47 *Ibid.*

48 European Satellite Navigation Competition 2009. European Satellite Navigation Competition website. [Online]. Available at: http://www.galileo-masters.eu [accessed: 20 September 2009].

development and testing of new instruments in support of innovation: cluster networks and financing networks. These structures bring together public and private innovation support providers, with the aim of tackling the two main weaknesses of European space entrepreneurship, namely financing and cross-fertilisation among different actors.

Two pilot projects were launched within FP6. First was INVESat, a financing network, which was active between 2006 and 2008. It focused on emerging markets for satellite applications in the area of ICT (information and communication technologies) and bridging the gap between innovative enterprises and financial investors. Second was FinanceSpace (Finance Innovation Network Addressing New Commercial Enterprises using Space), also a financing network. Its goal was to increase investment activity in innovative space companies and projects, and it operated from December 2005 to June 2008.

Currently, there are three cluster networks active in the space area, bringing different actors together. ENCADRE (European Network of Clusters for Satellite Applications Development) was established in April 2009 and intends to become the key European network for SME-oriented funding and service-support action. CASTLE (Clusters in Aerospace and Satellite Navigation Technology Applications Linked to Entrepreneurial Innovation) brings together three European regional clusters and focuses on satellite navigation applications. KIS4SAT (European Innovation Platform for Knowledge Intensive Services in the Satellite downstream application) is the last of these networks, focusing on satellite downstream applications more broadly in order to enable entrepreneurs and knowledge intensive services (KIS) ventures to seize new market opportunities in this field.[49]

ESA also launched two initiatives to boost innovation and foster entrepreneurship in the space sector. ESINET (European Space Incubators Network) first was launched in 2002 as a platform for the transfer of knowledge and technology. It intends to help launch new companies using innovative technologies in the field of satellite applications.[50] The ESA Investment Forum then was launched in 2007 to bring together start-up companies using space applications with the finance and investment communities.[51]

These concrete steps, undertaken by the two main institutional actors in space, to foster space commerce in general and downstream markets in particular are in line with the new political framework recently set up. They are directed mostly towards SMEs; however, they cover the whole spectrum of satellite applications and support the development of economically viable downstream markets, rather than create an artificial demand through technology push.

Challenges Ahead for a European Policy on Space Commerce

Recently, a series of political decisions taken during high-level meetings (European Council and 5th and 6th Space Councils) paved the way for an enhanced European policy on space commerce. The economic potential of space was recognised, not only with regards to the industrial base and the upstream markets, but also concerning the downstream markets of satellite applications. The economic and financial crisis accelerated this trend, and the progress made in the two flagship projects, Galileo and GMES, accompanied these developments. However, despite promising steps,

49 Europe Innova 2009a. Europe Innova website. [Online]. Available at: http://www.europe-innova.eu/web/guest [accessed: 20 September 2009].

50 ESINET 2009. [Online: European Space Incubators Network]. Available at: http://www.esinet.eu/ [accessed: 20 September 2009].

51 ESA Investment Forum 2009. ESA Investment Forum website. [Online]. Available at: http://www.congrex.nl/08c04/ [accessed: 20 September 2009].

a series of obstacles and challenges is still ahead of us in the field of space commerce – so what are the main issues to be tackled in the near future?

The first challenge lies in the need to find an adequate institutional framework for the cooperation between the main actors of the ESP: ESA and the EC. This is a general policy imperative, which is regularly highlighted in EU policy documents, but it is also true for space commerce, in particular for the harmonisation of procurement rules. The two flagship programmes, Galileo and GMES, have suffered from the absence of such an institutional framework, and the need to elaborate a single cooperation model between the EC and ESA seems necessary to avoid negotiating every new programme from scratch.[52]

A second issue is the need to reconcile the commercial and societal aspects of space.[53] Indeed, space applications are at the service of public policies, such as the Lisbon strategy. GMES, for example, is considered a public service, as is access to ICT in rural areas through satellite communication. As such, these initiatives have to be funded with public money. Similarly, the independent access to space is a strategic necessity for Europe and has to be supported through institutional funding. At the same time, however, the development of a downstream market is only possible if a demand exists and if these markets function according to the classical rules of economic competitiveness. As for the upstream sector, the recent French report on the future of European launchers clearly indicates that, despite the need for institutional support for the European launch sector, there is a need to reduce costs.[54]

A third and further challenge concerns space legislation and regulations dealing with commercial space activities. Indeed, space legislation can contribute either to raise or to remove market barriers. A first concern in this respect is represented by the conditions for authorisation for commercial space activities, which might be equated to market barriers. A second concern is the reasonable implementation of liability regimes, as its absence could impede the development of commercial markets. In this regard, a harmonisation of legislation concerning liability for commercial space activities at the European level is essential in order to guarantee a level-playing field.[55]

A fourth and final obstacle exists for European Member States regarding space industry and space application markets. Indeed, certain countries, such as France and Germany, have a long tradition in space and have a dense network of large space companies as well as SMEs able to use space technologies. In other countries, in particular in the newest Member States of the EU, such conditions are not a given. As a consequence, European policies aiming at fostering innovation and entrepreneurship in the space sector run the risk of benefitting only a few countries.[56]

Apart from these challenges, it must again be stressed that space has during the past year 'matured' in a considerable way: in the policy area, where it was traditionally regarded as a technological field, it has now turned into an instrument for applications in numerous issue areas; it is also now one of the areas focused upon to lend considerable support to Europe's economic

52 Nardon, L. 2009. 'Galileo and the Issue of Public Funding', in *Yearbook on Space Policy 2007/2008: From Policies to Programmes*, edited by K-U. Schrogl et al. Vienna: Springer, 125–37.

53 Steffens, H. 2009. *Europe's Plan for Innovation: How Can Space Technology Contribute to Solve the Economic Crisis?* ESPI Perspective 24.

54 Bigot, B., d'Escatha, Y. and Collet-Billon, L. 2008. *L'Enjeu d'une Politique Européenne de Lanceurs: Assurer Durablement à l'Europe un Accès Autonome à l'Espace.*

55 Sánchez Aranzamendi, M. 2009. *Economic and Policy Aspects of Space Regulations in Europe. Part I: The Case of National Space Legislation – Finding the Way between Common and Coordinated Action.* ESPI Report 21.

56 Steffens, H. 2009. *Europe's Plan for Innovation: How Can Space Technology Contribute to Solve the Economic Crisis?* ESPI Perspective 24.

recovery after the crisis. This is a high expectation, but also a most welcomed opportunity for space to prove its multi-faceted potential.

List of References

Bigot, B., d'Escatha, Y. and Collet-Billon, L. 2008. *L'Enjeu d'une Politique Européenne de Lanceurs: Assurer Durablement à l'Europe un Accès Autonome à l'Espace*.

Council of the European Union 2007. Council Resolution on the European Space Policy, Doc. 10037/07 of 25 May 2007.

Council of the European Union 2008a. Council Resolution Taking Forward the European Space Policy, Doc. 13569/08 of 29 September 2008.

Council of the European Union 2008b. Council Conclusions on Global Monitoring for Environment and Security (GMES): 'Towards a GMES Programme', Doc. 16267/08 of 26 November 2008.

Council of the European Union 2009a. Brussels European Council. 11 and 12 December 2008. Presidency Conclusions, Doc. 17271/1/08 of 13 February 2009.

Council of the European Union 2009b. Brussels European Council. 19 and 20 March 2009. Presidency Conclusions, Doc. 7880/1/09 REV 1 of 29 April 2009.

Council of the European Union 2009c. Council Resolution. The Contribution of Space to Innovation and Competitiveness in the Context of the European Economic Recovery Plan and Further Steps, Doc. 10500/09 of 29 May 2009.

ESA 1975. Convention of the European Space Agency, ESA Doc. SP-1300.

ESA 2000. A History of the European Space Agency 1958–1987, ESA Doc. SP-1235.

ESA 2008. Resolution on the Role of Space Delivering Europe's Global Objective, Doc. ESA/C-M/CCVI/Res.1 (final).

ESA 2009. ESA and Arianespace Sign a Frame Contract for the Procurement of Launch Services.

ESA 2010. What is Integrated Applications Promotion (IAP)?

ESA Investment Forum 2009. ESA Investment Forum website. [Online]. Available at: http://www.congrex.nl/08c04/ [accessed: 20 September 2009].

ESINET 2009. [Online: European Space Incubators Network]. Available at: http://www.esinet.eu/ [accessed: 20 September 2009].

Europe Innova 2006. *Innovation Watch, Sectoral Innovation Panels: Space. Report from the Second Panel Meeting*. [Online, 29 November 2006]. Available at: http://archive.europe-innova.eu/ [accessed: 11 September 2009].

Europe Innova 2009a. Europe Innova website. [Online]. Available at: http://www.europe-innova.eu/web/guest [accessed: 20 September 2009].

Europe Innova 2009b. *Sectoral Innovation Foresight Aeronautics and Space*. Interim Report.

European Commission 1988. Communication from the Commission, The Community and Space: A Coherent Approach, COM(88)417 final of 26 July 1988.

European Commission 2007a. Communication from the European Commission to the Council and the European Parliament, European Space Policy, COM(2007)212 final of 26 April 2007.

European Commission 2007b. Work Programme 2008, Cooperation, Theme 9, Space, COM(2007)5765 of 29 November 2007.

European Commission 2007c. Communication from the European Commission to the Council, the European Parliament, the European Economic and Social Committee and the Committee of the Regions, A Lead Market Initiative for Europe, COM(2007)860 final of 21 December 2007.

European Commission 2008a. Work Programme 2009, Cooperation, Theme 9, Space, COM(2008)4598 of 28 August 2008.

European Commission 2008b. Commission Working Document. European Space Policy Progress Report, COM(2008)561 final of 11 September 2008.

European Commission 2008c. Communication from the Commission to the European Parliament, the Council, the European Economic and Social Committee and the Committee of the Regions. 'Global Monitoring for Environment and Security (GMES): We Care for a Safer Planet', COM(2008)748 final of 12 November 2008.

European Commission 2009a. Communication from the Commission to the Council and the European Parliament. 'Better Access for Rural Areas to Modern ICT', COM(2009)103 final of 3 March 2009.

European Commission 2009b. Proposal for a Regulation of the European Parliament and the Council on the European Earth Observation Programme (GMES) and its Initial Operations (2011–2013), COM(2009)223 final of 20 May 2009.

European Commission 2009c. Report from the Commission to the European Parliament and the Council on the Implementation of the GNSS Programmes and on Future Challenges Pursuant to Article 22 of Regulation (EC) No. 683/2008, COM(2009) 302 final of 26 June 2009.

European Commission 2009d. Commission Staff Working Document, Lead Market Initiative for Europe Mid-term Progress Report, SEC(2009)1198 final of 9 July 2009.

European Commission 2009e. Communication from the European Commission to the Council, the European Parliament, the European Economic and Social Committee and the Committee of the Regions. 'Mobilising Private and Public Investment for Recovery and Long-term Structural Change: Developing Public Private Partnerships', COM(2009)615 final of 19 November 2009.

European Parliament and Council of the European Union 2008a. Decision of the European Parliament and of the Council on the Selection and Authorisation of Systems Providing Mobile Satellite Services (MSS), Doc. 626/2008 EC of 30 June 2008.

European Parliament and Council of the European Union 2008b. Regulation of the European Parliament and of the Council on the Further Implementation of the European Satellite Navigation Programmes (EGNOS and Galileo), Doc. 683/2008 EC of 9 July 2008.

European Satellite Navigation Competition 2009. European Satellite Navigation Competition website. [Online]. Available at: http://www.galileo-masters.eu [accessed: 20 September 2009].

Gante, H-J. 2007. 'Zwischen Konzentration und Europäisierung: Die Luft- und Raumfahrtindustrie in der Bundesrepublik', in *Ein Jahrhundert im Flug. Luft- und Raumfahrtforschung in Deutschland 1907–2007*, edited by H. Trischler and K-U. Schrogl. Frankfurt/New York: Campus, 295–320.

Madders, K. 1997. *A New Force at a New Frontier*. Cambridge: Cambridge University Press.

Nardon, L. 2009. 'Galileo and the Issue of Public Funding', in *Yearbook on Space Policy 2007/2008: From Policies to Programmes*, edited by K-U. Schrogl et al. Vienna: Springer, 125–37.

OECD 2005. *Space 2030: Tackling Society's Challenges*. Paris: OECD.

Polyakov, E., Bremmer, M., Lieshout, M. and Roso, M. 2008. *EU Space Policies and its Potential for EU Industrial Sector Competitiveness*. Brussels: European Parliament.

Rathgeber, W. 2009. *Space Policies, Issues and Trends 2008/2009*. ESPI Report 18.

Sánchez Aranzamendi, M. 2009. *Economic and Policy Aspects of Space Regulations in Europe. Part I: The Case of National Space Legislation – Finding the Way between Common and Coordinated Action*. ESPI Report 21.

Space Foundation 2009. *The Space Report 2009*. Colorado Springs, CO: Space Foundation.
Steffens, H. 2009. *Europe's Plan for Innovation: How Can Space Technology Contribute to Solve the Economic Crisis?* ESPI Perspective 24.

Chapter 3

The Relationship between the EU and ESA within the Framework of European Space Policy and its Consequences for Space Industry Contracts*

Bernhard Schmidt-Tedd

European Space Policy

For more than three decades the European Space Agency (ESA) has been elaborating and implementing a long-term European space policy for space research, technology and their space applications.[1] Talking about the European Space Policy (ESP)[2] in the context of the relationship between the EU and ESA refers to the document which was adopted by the European Space Council in Brussels on 22 May 2007. The European Space Council and the ESP are in turn both based on the Framework Agreement between the European Community and the European Space Agency,[3] which entered into force in May 2004.

For a decade the European Union has made major efforts to become the driver for a coherent approach to a European space policy.[4] The years before were characterised by difficult attempts at cooperation between ESA and the EU.[5] In 1999 European Ministers called on ESA and the European Commission to elaborate a coherent European strategy for space.[6] On the basis of a common effort by both institutions, the Commission published the strategy paper 'Europe and Space: Turning to a New Chapter', as a communication to the Council and the Parliament.[7] In 2000 the 'wise men report'[8] presented ESA perspectives 'Towards a space agency for the EU'. For

---

* This chapter is based on reflections presented at the Contracting for Space Workshop held in Bremen on 27–28 November 2009. The opinions expressed in this chapter are entirely those of the author and do not engage organisations with which he is affiliated.

1 According to Article II of its Convention, approved by the Conference of Plenipotentiaries in Paris on 30 May 1975, de facto functioning from 31 May 1975 and formally into force since 30 October 1980.

2 Resolution on the European Space Policy, ESA BR 269, 22 May 2007.

3 Framework Agreement between the European Community and the European Space Agency, OJ L 261, 6 August 2004, 64–8.

4 Historical background: Schmidt-Tedd, B. 2001. 'Rechtliche Implikationen der gemeinsamen ESA/EU- Raumfahrtstrategie', *ZLW*, 2001, 202; Hobe, S., Schmidt-Tedd, B. and Schrogl, K.-U. 2003. *Project 2001 Plus, Legal Aspects of the Future Institutional Relationship between the European Union and the European Space Agency*. Cologne: LIT Verlag.

5 In detail see Hobe, S., Kunzmann, K. and Reuter, Th. 2006. *Rechtliche Rahmenbedingungen einer zukünftigen kohärenten Struktur der europäischen Raumfahrt*, Münster: LIT Verlag, 64–92.

6 Resolution ESA Council at Ministerial Level, Brussels, 11/12 May 1999; 2112th EU Council Meeting Research, Brussels, 2 December 1999.

7 COM (2000) 597 final, Brussels, 27 September 2000.

8 Report Carl Bildt, Jean Peyrelevade and Lothar Späth to ESA Director General, ESA Press Release No. 65-2000, Paris 26 October 2000.

the programmatic and policy discussion, the Commission developed in 2003 a Green Paper on European Space policy[9] which was afterwards transferred to a White Paper.[10] New elements in this comprehensive space policy approach were an orientation towards 'benefits for markets and society through a demand-driven exploitation of the technical capabilities of the space community',[11] the related flagship projects GALILEO and GMES, and common European Security and Defence Policy aspects, the last of these not being part of the mandate of the ESA.[12]

This development was accompanied by some important institutional decisions. The draft of a European Constitution – the abandoned precursor of the Lisbon Treaty – as adopted in 2003[13] contained for the first time a new space competence for the European Union. Furthermore, ESA and the EU established a taskforce for the implementation of their common strategy paper.[14] This was the first step towards the Framework Agreement of 25 November 2003. Its duration was prolonged in 2007 until 2012.[15]

Article 1 describes two essential aims of the Framework Agreement. '1. The coherent and progressive development of an overall European Space Policy …' and '2. The establishment of a framework providing a common basis and operational arrangements for an efficient and mutually beneficial cooperation between the Parties …'. On the one side, it is clearly stated that for the implementation of the Agreement each party shall undertake the required actions '… in compliance with its own prerogatives, legal instruments and procedures …'.[16] On the other side, it is fixed under EU-prerogatives that under no circumstances shall the European Community be bound to apply the rule of 'geographical distribution'[17] contained in the ESA Convention.[18]

The fields of cooperation include all relevant sectors of space activities. As methods of cooperation, the agreement lists some characteristic non-concluding forms, especially (a) the management by ESA of European Community space-related activities, (b) the participation by the European Community in an optional programme of ESA and (c) the carrying out of activities which are coordinated, implemented and funded by both parties.[19] For the coordination and facilitation of cooperative activities, Article 8 of the Agreement establishes the 'Space Council', regular joint and concomitant meetings of the Council of the European Union and the Council of ESA at Ministerial Level. The decisions of this Space Council are legally non-binding; formal decisions have to be confirmed under the procedures of both institutions. Therefore in practice the Council of ESA and the EU legitimise formal decisions. The meetings of the Space Council are prepared by the Secretariat and the High Level Space Policy Group (HSPG), representing the Member States of both institutions.

---

9 COM (2003) 17 final, Brussels 21 January 2003.

10 White Paper, Space: A New European Frontier for an Expanding Union, An Action Plan for Implementing the European Space Policy, Commission of the European Communities, COM (2003) 673, Brussels, 11 November 2003.

11 COM (2000) 597 final, 3.

12 ESA Convention, Preamble, Article II: '… for exclusively peaceful purposes …'.

13 Text of the Constitutional Treaty in OJ C 310 of 16 December 2004, prepared by the Convent between 28 February 2002 and the final report of 18 July 2003, CONV 850/03.

14 See COM (2001) 718 final, 5.

15 Prolongation according to Article 12 of the agreement, due to a non-termination by either party.

16 Article 4 (1.) Implementation.

17 See Chapter 8 of the present volume.

18 Article 5 (3.) Joint initiatives.

19 Article 5 (1.) Joint initiatives.

The major outcome of the first four sessions, starting with the first session on 25 November 2004,[20] followed by two further sessions in 2005[21] and the decisive fourth session on 22 May 2007 – which involved intensive consultations – is the European Space Policy (ESP). The focus is now on policy. At the first session the vision was to formulate a European Space Programme. In the following discussions, the European programme on this level was seen to be realised by GALILEO and GMES, while the concrete European space programme planning was identified as a domain of ESA. Finally the ESP was submitted by ESA and the Commission in April 2007[22] and endorsed at the 4th Space Council.[23]

The Resolution on the ESP covers eight topics: (1) GALILEO/GMES, (2) security and defence, (3) access to space, (4) ISS and space exploration, (5) science and technology, (6) governance, (7) industrial policy and (8) international relations. For the institutional relationship between ESA and the EU, the resolution confers upon ESA the role of the Commission's technical expert and procurement agent for its projects. The independent role for ESA's self-financed programmes was confirmed. The prolongation of the framework agreement in 2007 fits into this context. While in the years before, models of a further integration of ESA under EU-structures had been discussed,[24] the decisions of 2007 confirmed the model of two independent international organisations with their specific tasks.[25]

A fifth Space Council took place in September 2008, further developing the strategy for a 'Vision for Europe in Space'.[26] Prepared under the French presidency with an informal meeting of ministers for space affaires in Kourou,[27] the updated policy formulated the aim for Europe to become a leading global actor in space. The synergies between civil and defence space programmes became the centre of interest. Key points in this context are the creation of a European Space Situational Awareness capacity, the continuous availability of data by long-term funding of GMES by the EU, and the initiative of a 'structured dialogue' between the European Defence Agency (EDA), ESA, the Commission, the EU Council's General Secretariat for the European Satellite Centre (EUSC) and Member States.[28]

The European Space Policy made substantive progress during the last decade with ESA and the EU as independent actors – and by involving new partners. On the implementing side, there are still a number of open issues, a result of the different characters of those institutions. ESA represents a form of intergovernmental cooperation and a specific industrial policy. The borderline between an

---

20 For the resulting 'First Orientations on the Preparation of the European Space Programme', see: EU Council Doc. 15000/04 of 19 November 2004.

21 Second set of orientations of the 2nd Space Council 7 June 2005 in Council Press Release, 2665th Council meeting Competitiveness, Council Doc.9501/05, 15–19, the 3rd Space Council was focused on Orientations on GMES.

22 Communication from the Commission to the Council and the European Parliament, European Space Policy, COM(2007) 212 final, Brussels, 26 April 2007.

23 Council Doc. 10037/07 of 25 May 2007, published in OJ C 136 of 20 June 2007, 1–5.

24 The Commission's White Paper proposed the integration of ESA into the EU framework after the entering into force of the Constitutional Treaty, see COM (2003) 673, 36.

25 Compare Hobe, S., Heinrich, O. and Kerner, I. 2009. *Entwicklung der Europäischen Weltraumagentur als 'implementing agency' der Europäischen Union: Rechtsrahmen und Anpassungserfordernisse*, Münster: LIT Verlag, 12 (Engl. Summary pp. 346 ff).

26 See Resolution 'Taking forward the European Space Policy', Council Doc. 13269/08 of 29 September 2008, OJ C 268, 23 October 2008, 1; the 6th Space Council took place in Brussels on 29 May 2009.

27 Kourou 20–22 July 2008; informal continuation of the dialogue of the 4th Space Council.

28 See Progress Report, COM (2008) 561, 8.

intergovernmental and a communitarised approach, the sharing of competences between Member States and the EU is now in principle defined in the Lisbon Treaty.

EU Space Competence under the Lisbon Treaty

With the Treaty of Lisbon[29] entering into force on 1 December 2009[30] the European Union gained a new explicit space competence, which has to be interpreted in the context of the treaty structure and the different forms of competence. According to Article 1 of the Treaty on European Union (TEU),[31] the Union is founded on that Treaty (TEU) and on the Treaty on the Functioning of the European Union[32] (TFEU) – a revised form of the former EC Treaty. The wording 'EC Treaty' is replaced by 'Treaty on the Functioning of the European Union' and the 'European Community' (EC) is replaced and succeeded by the 'European Union' (EU).

Specific EU-competences related to special policy areas, such as trans-European networks (GALILEO), which to date have been the legal basis for space-related EU-activities, remain untouched.

The Treaty of Lisbon is a reform treaty, following the Treaty of Amsterdam (1997)[33] and the Treaty of Nice (2001),[34] amending and changing former EU[35] and EC treaties, without replacing them. As such the Lisbon Treaty cannot be read as an autonomous text; reference has to be made to the consolidated versions[36] of the two treaties, TEU and TFEU, as amended by the Treaty of Lisbon.

For the question of intergovernmental cooperation, it is worthwhile to first review the new internal setting of the Union. Until the entry into force of the Lisbon Treaty, the former European Union was based on a structure of three pillars:

---

29 Treaty of Lisbon amending the Treaty on European Union and the Treaty establishing the European Community (hereafter Treaty of Lisbon), Lisbon, done 13 December 2007, entered into force 1 December 2009; OJ C 306/1 (2007).

30 The Treaty – signed on 13 December 2007 by the Heads of State or Governments of the European Union – entered into force the first day of the month following the last ratification (Deposition of the Czech ratification instrument in Rome on 13 November 2009).

31 In the version of the Treaty of Lisbon.

32 Treaty establishing the European Community as amended by the Treaty of Lisbon amending the Treaty on European Union and the Treaty establishing the European Community (hereafter Treaty on the Functioning of the European Union), Lisbon, done 13 December 2007, entered into force 1 December 2009; OJ C 115/47 (2009).

33 Treaty of Amsterdam Amending the Treaty on European Union, the Treaties Establishing the European Communities and Certain Related Acts (hereafter Treaty of Amsterdam), Amsterdam, done 2 October 1997, entered into force 1 May 1999; OJ C 340/73 (1997).

34 Treaty of Nice amending the Treaty on European Union, the Treaties establishing the European Communities and certain related acts (hereafter Treaty of Nice), Nice, done 26 February 2001, entered into force 1 February 2003; OJ C 80/1 (2001).

35 Treaty of Maastricht, formally Treaty on European Union, done 7 February 1992, entered into force 1 November 1993; OJ C 191 (1992).

36 See Provisional Consolidated Versions of the Treaty on European Union (TEU) and of the Treaty on the Functioning of the European Union (TFEU) in: Council of the European Union 6655/08, Brussels, 15 April 2008 OJ C 306/2007, 17 December 2007.

1st pillar: European Communities (EC and Euratom, and until 2002 the Coal and Steel Community);
2nd pillar: Common Foreign and Security Policy (CFSP); and
3rd pillar: Police and Judicial Cooperation in Criminal Matters (PJCCM).

The Treaty of Lisbon integrated the pillar structure into one Union. Internally, the matters of the former 1st and 3rd pillars[37] are communitarised (respectively had already been communitarised), while Common Foreign and Security Policy (2nd pillar) remains intergovernmental following Title V of the Consolidated version of the Treaty on European Union (Articles 21–46 TEU). Space matters in this area should therefore be realised under intergovernmental forms.

The Treaty on the Functioning of the European Union mentions twice the subject 'space': firstly under the categories of EU competences[38] and secondly in Article 189 under Title XIX 'Research and Technological Development and Space'. The substantive Article 189 TFEU formulating the new space competence is worded as follows:

> 1. To promote scientific and technical progress, industrial competitiveness and the implementation of its policies, the Union shall draw up a European space policy. To this end, it may promote joint initiatives, support research and technological development and coordinate the efforts needed for the exploration and exploitation of space.
> 2. To contribute to attaining the objectives referred to in Paragraph 1, the European Parliament and the Council, acting in accordance with the ordinary legislative procedure, shall establish the necessary measures, which may take the form of a European space programme, excluding any harmonisation of the laws and regulations of the Member States.
> 3. The Union shall establish any appropriate relations with the European Space Agency.
> 4. This Article shall be without prejudice to the other provisions of this Title.

Two elements of this Article need to be highlighted. Firstly, the exclusion of any harmonisation of the laws and regulations of the EU Member States and secondly, the reference to the European Space Agency (ESA) as the pre-existing international organisation for European space cooperation.[39] Hereby ESA is recognised with its own mandate in the format of intergovernmental cooperation. The establishment of appropriate relations with ESA presupposes a separate legal entity, in contrast to a subordinated part of the Union. Despite the supranational character of the Union there is no hierarchy between the two international organisations. Competences of ESA derive from its Member States, the borderline of competences is therefore Member States/ESA on the one side and the EU on the other side.

The text of Article 189 TFEU makes a remarkable differentiation between the European Space Policy, which shall be drawn up (sub-paragraph 1), and measures which may take the form of a European space programme – without any form of harmonisation – (sub-paragraph 2). A European space programme is only an option. The outcome of the discussion of ESP, as shown above, confirms the distinction.

Article 189 TFEU has to be seen in the general context of Title XIX of that Treaty (Research, Technological Development and Space). The whole area of research, technological development and space follows the regime of Article 4(3) of the TFEU, defining an atypical sub-category of the

37 Euratom is only linked by certain provisions.
38 See Title I, Art. 4(3) TFEU.
39 This paragraph 3 was introduced in 2005 in the former draft Article III-254.

general rule of shared competence, which does not prevent EU Member States from legislative action in case the Union exercises its competence. In the regular case of a shared competence, Member States cannot exercise competence in areas where the Union has done so.

The three different categories of EU competences are defined in Title I of the Treaty on the Functioning of the European Union:

> Exclusive EU-competence (Articles 2(1) and 3);
> Shared competence between the European Union and Member States (Articles 2(2) and 4); and
> Competence to support, coordinate and supplement the actions of Member States (Articles 2(5) and 6).

In the field of exclusive competence, Member States are only able to legislate or to adopt legally binding acts if empowered to do so by the Union.[40] In case of the shared competence, Member States shall exercise their competence to the extent that the Union has not exercised its competence.[41] For the third category, the Union has competence to carry out actions to support, coordinate or supplement the actions of the Member States, without thereby superseding their competence in these areas.[42]

Space is an atypical sub-category of the shared competence under Article 4(3) TFEU: 'In the areas of research, technological development and space, the Union shall have competence to carry out activities, in particular to define and implement programmes; however the exercise of that competence shall not result in member states being prevented from exercising theirs.' In fact, this is a parallel competence.[43] As a practical result Member States and ESA will remain relevant independent actors in programme definition and with regard to contract terms and conditions.

Implementing Questions and Industrial Policy

One crucial point for the sometimes difficult cooperation and interaction between the EU and ESA is the partly divergent industrial policy between ESA, as a primary research and technology organisation, and the EU as a regional integration organisation with major economic goals. This leads to concrete questions of governance, project-financing and procurement.

ESA operates with the differentiation between mandatory programmes (science, infrastructure, administration and some additional subjects) and optional programmes (78 per cent of the programmes[44]). The special investment in space by Member States is correlated with expectations of a 'fair return' in respect to geographical distribution. Programme definition is an intensive interaction process with the later programme participants and investors. The common understanding is unity in diversity between the participation in various programmes under self-defined priorities. The overall benefit is nevertheless for all Member States.

The EU, by contrast, is defined by an integration and harmonisation approach. Policies and programmes are financed by central budgets. The functioning of the internal market, establishing of competition rules and a common commercial policy are essentials of the exclusive competences

40 See Art. 2(1) TFEU.

41 See Art. 2(2) TFEU.

42 See Art. 2(5) TFEU.

43 A similar parallel competence is formulated for development cooperation and humanitarian aid, as per Article 4(4) TFEU.

44 Budget figure 2011, representative also for the average of the previous years.

of the EU[45] and basics for its self-consciousness. It is not surprising that the EU industry policy approach contains the key-topics: regulation and standardisation, procurement policy and internal market.[46]

Space policy is a cross section subject which serves quite different policy areas. A unilateral market and competition approach is not adequate for the complexity of space policy. There are some positive statements in the ESP approach, which reflect that the message that a differentiated approach is needed has reached its addressees. The 4th Space Council[47] states, for instance, 'the need for a targeted approach for the development of strategic components, concentrating on selected critical components, for which dependency of European industry on international suppliers should be avoided, in order to achieve the optimum balance between technological independence, strategic cooperation with international partners and reliance on market forces'. Even the essence of ESA's 'fair return' principle is recognised: 'ESA has a flexible and effective industrial policy based on cost-efficiency, competitiveness, fair distribution of activities and competitive bidding, which secures adequate industrial capacities …'.

In some other cases there are still fundamental discrepancies between external realities and internal reflections. A typical example can be found in the ESP. Under the subject 'public investment in space'[48] the ESP states:

> … EC is increasing its expenditure on space. During 2007–2013, it will dedicate over € 2.8bn to space applications and activities. Community funds, including those managed through ESA programmes, are governed by the EU Financial Regulation on the basis of open competition. Member States invest a little under € 3bn annually through the ESA, and a similar amount in national programmes. The ESA programmes are governed by the industrial policy principles established in the ESA Convention, in particular by exploiting competitive bidding while distributing industrial contracts in proportion to funding from Member States ("fair return").

The method to compare annual figures with the summarised financing of a seven-year period gives the wrong impression of similar amounts of investment, namely EUR 2.8bn EU (application and activities) under strict market conditions and EUR 3bn ESA programmes under its special industrial policy. In reality the EUR 2.8bn EU are contrasted with about EUR 21bn ESA and a comparable additional amount of Member States, which means about 93 per cent intergovernmental and national space investment compared to 7 per cent EU. It is obvious that the motivation and mechanisms for financing the overwhelming part of Europe's space programme should not be questioned. Furthermore its competitiveness is proven by a 40 per cent share in the heavy lift launcher and the satellite market with one-sixth of the US space budget. A major part of the 93 per cent financing is dedicated to science and technology, far away from concrete market applications (extra-terrestric, exploration and basic science for example) and by nature inadequate to standard competitive bidding. The corresponding space projects are in many cases realised under international cooperation with national, respectively intergovernmental (ESA) contributions according to accepted R&D excellences and not according to actual market conditions.

45 Article 3 TFEU.

46 Communication from the Commission to the Council and the European Parliament, European Space Policy – Preliminary Elements, Brussels, 12 May 2005, Chapter Industry Policy.

47 Council Press Release, Resolution on the European Space Policy, 4th Space Council, Brussels, 22 May 2007, No. 11, 14.

48 Communication from the Commission to the Council and the European Parliament, European Space Policy, COM (2007) 212 final, Brussels, 26 April 2007 under chapter 5.2.

The EU investment in space can fulfil a catalyst function in preparing space applications and real markets, but is not capable of financing the existing space programmes or even an additional single exploration mission. It would neither be its mission. The EU should focus on space-based applications contributing to its policies. In addition, nothing prevents the EU from preparing real user-driven applications under established policy areas with the related dedicated budgets. The framework programme is, anyhow, not the most adequate framework for sustainable forms of application.[49]

The budget figures are correlated to distinctions in substance, such as strategic, institutionally-driven or market-oriented. It makes no sense to insist constantly on a certain concept of open market and competition as a matter of principle in areas which are different in character. It is time to implement also under EU regulations a space-specific industrial policy. The series of ad hoc rules for the implementation of GALILEO and GMES were helpful neither for a smooth management of the programmes nor for the industry concerned. The EU could easily rely on the non-commercial space sector's three decades of ESA experience were the EU to differentiate and adapt its industrial policy.

During the last years ESA has implemented its procurement reform,[50] in order to bring its instruments – as far as possible under its mission – closer to the EU-system. Now it is for the EU to demonstrate its adaptability.

Future Developments

After the entry into force of the Lisbon Treaty, the EU continued different kinds of activities for the further development of ESP. In May 2010 a Conference on Governance of European Space Programmes took place in Segovia, Spain. The Commission is preparing a Roadmap initiative under the title 'Commission Communication on the Future Involvement of the European Union in Space'.[51] For October 2010 a conference on Space Policy at the European Parliament is on the agenda. The 7th Space Council is scheduled for November 2010.

With the momentum of the Lisbon Treaty there were some EU expectations to become in a comprehensive way involved in all types of space programmes.[52] In the view of Member States, the priority areas are still GALILEO, GMES and Space Situational Awareness (SSA).

There is a natural division of tasks between the two international organisations, either research-and-technology-oriented or application-oriented. ESA is the implementing organisation also for EU programmes, in order to avoid a duplication of existing structures. The EU procurement rules remain a critical point of industrial policy. In case of a greater EU involvement in space, the lacking counter-measures would lead to increasing concentration of industry. A prerequisite for a more flexible cooperation with ESA is an appropriate EU industrial policy for the space sector. If the procurement rules would remain as they are, Member States would concentrate even more on an

49 Concerning the limitations of the 7th Framework Programme related to financial instruments for GMES see: Hobe, S., Heinrich, O. and Kerner, I. 2009. *Entwicklung der Europäischen Weltraumagentur als 'implementing agency' der Europäischen Union: Rechtsrahmen und Anpassungserfordernisse*, 247.

50 Finalisation of the ESA Procurement Reform, ESA/C(2010)44, Paris, 31 May 2010.

51 http://ec.europa.eu/governance/impact/planned_ia/docs/59_entr_involvement_in_space_en.pdf [accessed: 2 December 2010].

52 See Questionnaire and Background Paper of the Conference on Governance of European Space Programmes which took place under the Spanish Presidency in Segovia, Spain, 3–4 May 2010.

intelligent division of tasks between ESA and the EU. One reference model could be the transfer of operational tasks from ESA to EUMETSAT.

The programmatic engagement of the EU is not an obligation under the new space competence (Article189 TFEU), but rather a possibility to be decided upon on a case-by-case basis. The willingness of Member States to support a further engagement will depend inter alia on the adaptation of EU procurement rules and industrial policy to the space sector. The results of the related discussions are still open.

List of References

Bildt, C., Peyrelevade, J. and Späth, L. 2000. 'Wise Men Report', Report to ESA Director General, ESA Press Release No. 65-2000, Paris 26 October 2000.

Communication from the Commission to the Council and the European Parliament, European Space Policy, COM (2007) 212 final, Brussels, 26 April 2007.

ESA Convention CSE/CS (73) 19, rev.7; UNTS Vol.1297 (1983), I No. 21524.

Europe and Space: Turning to a New Chapter, COM (2000), 597 final, Brussels, 27 September 2000.

First Orientations on the Preparation of the European Space Programme, EU Council Doc. 15000/04 of 19 November 2004.

Fourth Space Council Doc. 10037/07 of 25 May 2007, published in OJ C 136 of 20 June 2007, 1–5.

Framework Agreement between the European Community and the European Space Agency, OJ L 261, 6 August 2004, 64–8.

Green Paper on European Space Policy, COM (2003) 17 final, Brussels 21 January 2003.

Hobe, S., Heinrich, O. and Kerner, I. 2009. *Entwicklung der Europäischen Weltraumagentur als 'implementing agency' der Europäischen Union: Rechtsrahmen und Anpassungserfordernisse*. Münster: LIT Verlag.

Hobe, S., Kunzmann, K. and Reuter, Th. 2006. *Rechtliche Rahmenbedingungen einer zukünftigen kohärenten Struktur der europäischen Raumfahrt*. Münster: LIT Verlag.

Hobe, S., Schmidt-Tedd, B. and Schrogl, K.-U. 2003. *Project 2001 Plus, Legal Aspects of the Future Institutional Relationship between the European Union and the European Space Agency*. Cologne: LIT Verlag.

Provisional Consolidated Versions of the Treaty on European Union (TEU) and of the Treaty on the Functioning of the European Union (TFEU) in: Council of the European Union 6655/08, Brussels, 15 April 2008 OJ C 306/2007, 17 December 2007.

Resolution on the European Space Policy, ESA BR 269, 22 May 07.

Resolution 'Taking forward the European Space Policy', Council Doc. 13269/08 of 29 September 2008, OJ C 268, 23 October 2008, 1.

Roadmap, Commission Communication on the Future Involvement of European Union in Space, DG ENTR/H6. [Online]. Available at http://ec.europa.eu/governance/impact/planned_ia/docs/59_entr_involvement_in_space_en.pdf [accessed: 2 December 2010].

Schmidt-Tedd, B. 2001. 'Rechtliche Implikationen der gemeinsamen ESA/EU-Raumfahrtstrategie', *ZLW*, 2001, 202.

Treaty establishing the European Community as amended by the Treaty of Lisbon amending the Treaty on European Union and the Treaty establishing the European Community (hereafter Treaty on the Functioning of the European Union), Lisbon, done 13 December 2007, entered into force 1 December 2009; OJ C 115/47 (2009).

Treaty of Amsterdam Amending the Treaty on European Union, the Treaties Establishing the European Communities and Certain Related Acts (hereafter Treaty of Amsterdam), Amsterdam, done 2 October 1997, entered into force 1 May 1999; OJ C 340/73 (1997).
Treaty of Lisbon amending the Treaty on European Union and the Treaty establishing the European Community (hereafter Treaty of Lisbon), Lisbon, done 13 December 2007, entered into force 1 December 2009; OJ C 306/1 (2007).
Treaty of Maastricht, formally Treaty on European Union, done 7 February 1992, entered into force 1 November 1993; OJ C 191 (1992).
Treaty of Nice amending the Treaty on European Union, the Treaties establishing the European Communities and certain related acts (hereafter Treaty of Nice), Nice, done 26 February 2001, entered into force 1 February 2003; OJ C 80/1 (2001).
White Paper, Space: A New European Frontier for an Expanding Union, An Action Plan for Implementing the European Space Policy, Commission of the European Communities, COM (2003) 673, Brussels, 11 November 2003.

Chapter 4

Toward a European Space-Specific Procurement Policy?

Jean-Jacques Tortora

Introduction

Industrial policy is again of concern to European institutions and Member States across all domains of activities. Space is not an exception, although the driver might be of a different nature.

Overall, European institutions are worried by the trend toward de-industrialisation, which is particularly sensitive in some Member States. They feel the need for public bodies to take a more active role in regulations or research and technology (R&T) funding with the general aim of providing support for the competitiveness of European industries so that they can better face global challenges.

Space Commercial Market

In the area of space, this obviously applies to the commercial market. Unlike its international competitors, the European space industry relies heavily on the commercial market, where it makes a significant, although highly variable, share of its turnover. However, it must be remembered that this so-called commercial market is roughly limited to civil space telecommunications with some 20 to 40 heavy geostationary satellites yearly purchased globally by a handful of private operators. It also includes the related share of the launch services market. In all, both in satellite manufacturing and launch services, the European industry demonstrates its efficiency and manages to maintain a share of about one-half of the global market. These results can be saluted but the stakes for European space industry in this area must not be underestimated.

Member States and European institutions are generally aware that, however satisfying, this situation remains tense with a potential aggressive return of the US private industry in this area, since US public funds for military programmes are becoming scarce, or with the future emergence of newcomers like India or China, which might become fierce competitors once major national objectives assigned to their space industries have been fulfilled.

In this respect, public support should continue to accompany the evolution of the European sector.

Space Institutional Markets

Despite its commercial performances, the European space industry remains mostly reliant on public markets.

First, the space telecommunications business is so fluctuant that it cannot, by itself, properly ensure a stable and continuous workload for a highly qualified and specialised work force. Institutional programmes are thus necessary to preserve the critical mass of the industrial base.

Second, institutional programmes are key drivers for the development of new technologies, be it in the field of earth sciences, astronomy, space exploration or security and defence. No commercial market can sustain the level of investment required to keep up with the evolution of technical requirements in these areas, and only institutional programmes can bear the level of risk associated with the in-orbit qualification of the new technologies at stake.

The fact that industry needs a sustained institutional market is undisputable. The corollary is that institutions must assume the major role they play in the structuring of the space industry through adequate industrial policies.

From Industrial Policy to Procurement Policy

In the initial phase of the development of space activities in Europe, this role was fully endorsed by public bodies. The European Space Agency (hereafter ESA or Agency) Convention acknowledges since its inception the prominent role to be played by the Agency in shaping the European space sector.

Most of the major European space companies were at that time publicly owned and Member States then had full control of the situation – from the determination of budgets, the elaboration of technical requirements, to the distribution of industrial activities, first among involved countries, and ultimately within industry.

The results achieved in a couple of decades have been spectacular and with budgets one order of magnitude smaller than their US counterparts, European space agencies have managed to promote the emergence of a fully-fledged space industry able to compete on the global scene in terms of capabilities (although not in terms of capacity).

The development of the sector came with new challenges with which to cope, and a multitude of conflicting interests with which it must properly deal regarding the emergent commercial markets. It also gave birth to an increasing competition among Member States deriving from industrial, political and strategic stakes.

At the same time, the European space industrial sector was deemed mature enough to allow for the lesser involvement of governments, and there was a broad shift toward the privatisation of the *quasi* totality of European space industries.

Once governments were deprived of their full control over industry, 'industrial' policy quickly turned into 'procurement' policy. In this new paradigm, the overarching rule has been to formalise a clear customer/provider relationship between public bodies and industry and to rely to the largest extent on open and transparent competition processes, within the limits of the 'Geographical Return' obligations as far as ESA is concerned (see following section).

Geo Return as a Stimulus for Public Investment

The Geographical Return rule is a direct and inevitable consequence of the principle of voluntary contributions from Member States on which the funding of ESA's optional programmes is based. It has provided Member States with an efficient grip over the procurement process of the Agency and has thus allowed for an initial increase in its budget. It has proven to be highly efficient in an overall collaborative framework, and most of the ESA's achievements demonstrate its relevance to sustain scientific and technological objectives.

The Limits of the Model

However, it must be highlighted that the ESA budget has been at best stagnating over the last 10 to 15 years despite the constant efforts made by its successive director-generals to give the Agency a new impetus. On the contrary, some Member States tend to keep their contributions to ESA flat, while significantly increasing their national space budgets. The question can thus reasonably be raised whether this model has not reached its limits.

Another challenge is the current enlargement process of the Agency. From a political standpoint, it appears a necessity to give access to the Agency to all of the EU Member States. On the other hand, some of them will not provide the substantial additional resources necessary for the Agency's enlargement. Beyond the inherent difficulties in managing an effective decision-making process with a growing numbers of stakeholders, at the industrial level, the integration of newcomers into a sector with overcapacity – and in a depleting budgetary context – generates a lot of frustration.

The Return to an Industrial Policy

The renewed interest of governments in industrial matters, along with the growing involvement of the European Union in the space sector, is the occasion to revitalise reflections on the merits of a sound industrial policy at the European level.

Of course, this concept is considered cautiously by 'liberals', who heavily suspect it is intended to give governments the means to choose the winner in bidding processes. Reference to the Soviet model is often made to definitely conclude that, 'No industrial policy is the best industrial policy'.

However, rather than the Soviet model, one could have a closer look at the other side of the Atlantic Ocean. Successive US administrations have always demonstrated their determination to fight against any risk of decrease in the industrial and technical competitiveness of their national industries. Public action can translate into law – for example, governmental satellites can only be launched from US soil – and regulations or procurement practises favouring the development of new products and processes, such as anchor tenancy.

This action can target some specific sectors or scientific challenges, leading to the concentration of public funds on just a few promising projects. This is, for instance, the sense of the action of DARPA (Defence Advanced Research Agency). DARPA was created in 1958 to set concrete technological objectives and to manage directly the development of projects in industry. Its role is not limited to the early stages of the development of new technologies, but to their 'maturation' to help identifying unpredicted applications, thus strongly promoting innovation. Although a military agency, it works in close relation with major US academia and is at the origin of many applications that ultimately found large commercial outlets for civil applications, the most famous being the Arpanet network, which gave birth to the internet.

Although considered as a reference model and mentioned at length in all the reports and studies dealing with technology development, we still cannot find any equivalent or similar structure in Europe.

The Limits of the European Domestic Market

As compared with the situation of other space-faring nations, one of the characteristics of the European institutional market is its limited size. This is partly due to the absence of major military programmes.

Several factors contribute to this situation among which the most prominent ones are the national based defence structure of Europe and the absence of a Europe-wide defence doctrine justifying large-scale space-based systems.

This is particularly obvious when we compare the situation of the US and European space sectors. To a lesser extent since the end of the Cold War, this is also true as compared to the situation in Russia. Next comes China which is already ahead of Europe in terms of launch record capacity, and whose dynamic development leaves little doubt about the evolution of their relative positions in the near future.

The Absence of Growth

Actually, the European space industry, thanks to the continued R&T support of Member States and ESA, maintains a world-class technological level. These capabilities position Europe at the forefront of space and earth sciences and empower the European industry on the commercial markets.

However, neither the commercial nor the European institutional markets have been able to provide any prospect of growth over the last decade:

- The major driver for the development of the commercial market is TV broadcasting. The emergence of private operators has triggered the setting up of worldwide open competitions. From this standpoint, the space telecommunications sector is an exception, and in all the other areas of space applications, major procurements are most often awarded at a regional level. However, regarding space telecommunications, no new application arises to give it a new impetus and it seems to be durably limited to the replacement of satellites reaching the end of their life.
- The institutional market, notably in the ESA framework, has been mostly driven by scientific objectives. Member States have recently seen no reason to decrease their efforts there, which is a good point, but neither did they see any reason to increase them substantially.

Basically, in a context of absence of growth, the development of the European space industry, fuelled by the continued R&T support of Member States, leads to a situation of structural overcapacity.

The European space industry, now privately owned, adapts to this situation through greater consolidation and, subsequently, concentration.

Work with Monopolies

Antagonist forces are, however, at work:

- on one hand, institutions seek a multiplicity of potential sources to stimulate competition for the benefit of their future procurements;

- on the other hand, in a limited and flat – if not depleting – market, where major long-term procurements are scarce, industry, in an attempt to keep the critical mass and ensure the continuity of the workload in its critical skills, tends to concentrate.

In some areas, the ratio between the level of investment required and the recurring accessible market is so high that the possibility of maintaining some intra-European competition is not even mentioned. Among those, the domain of launchers is probably the most emblematic, but the same problem is encountered in other highly specialised areas.

This actually raises the issue of the capability of European institutions to deal with an industry that is in a monopolistic or quasi-monopolistic position. This is common in the defence domain, for instance. It requires that public bodies keep and maintain a high level of expertise, comparable to the one of industry itself. ESA is prepared for such situations and is, for instance, currently reinforcing its internal skills in the field of launchers with the perspective of the development of the future generation of European space transportation systems.

Regarding the European Commission, its ability and legitimacy to develop and maintain internally high-level engineering expertise is questionable. Further arrangements will thus have to be concluded, for instance with ESA, to set an adequate framework for properly coping with such a situation.

From Manufacturers to Capacity Providers to Service Providers

Beyond hardware manufacturing, space business developed downstream and gave birth to a set of space operators who now play a decisive role along the value added chain. In turn, space operators are actually capacity providers and are key customers of the space manufacturers. The most prominent ones are found in the telecommunications business like Eutelsat, SES Americom, Hispasat or Paradigm, or in meteorology like Eumetsat.

Today, through the implementation of several application programmes, like GMES or Galileo, the ambition of European institutions is to trigger the development of a new set of players, such as the service provider, which will process the data delivered by space systems and thereafter reach end users by bringing adequate added value to the data for them.

The potential development of this sector is promising. What remains to be seen is the positioning of established capacity providers that might see an opportunity to enlarge their business base by capturing a substantial part of this emerging sector.

Space Infrastructures Paradigm

In any case, the sustainability of services can only be ensured by the long-term guarantee of availability of space infrastructures. This raises the question of the most efficient way for public bodies to ensure such sustainability:

- owning the infrastructures implies procuring them and overseeing their operations: this requires a strong and long term involvement in industrial processes;
- relying on the private sector for the development, deployment and exploitation of future European space infrastructures could be done in a PPP (public private partnership) framework where the private sector invests in space systems against long-term

commitments from European institutions to purchase services and/or data for the fulfilling of 'public services'.

After a long and painful procurement process, Galileo and GMES are managed and publicly owned. Some successful examples like Paradigm in Europe, or NextView in the USA, show that the second hypothesis is somewhat relevant. However, this requires from institutions first the capacity to actually commit beyond current budgetary perspectives and, second, to be able to actually define long-term needs and adhere to them.

ESA and EU: Two Different Procurement Approaches

ESA procurement policy takes into account the origin of the funds in awarding contracts through the Geographical Return rule. It also integrates key objectives of industrial policy, such as preserving the industrial base or targeting R&T development for the potential needs of its future programmes.

On the other hand, the European Union has not established specific objectives for the procurement process; rather, it is fully based on an open and transparent competition for fulfilling the needs of the European Union. This in turn presupposes the existence of multiple potential providers in order to actually enable open competition, and ignores formal Geographical Return rules or industrial policy objectives.

ESA procurement policy has proved to be successful in many respects and is not challenged for scientific and technological optional programmes based on the willingness of Member States to join resources to achieve ambitious objectives. It shows its limits, however, when it comes to the development and deployment of operational infrastructures raising commercial, industrial, political and/or strategic stakes. This is where the EU timely and opportunely steps in. For a while Europe will most likely live with the coexistence of these two bodies – the EU and the ESA procurement procedures.

The key question is to assess whether EU rules by themselves are adapted to achieve such important political objectives as the preservation and enhancement of the industrial autonomy of Europe in the space sector and the certainty of the supply of critical items.

Need for a Space Specific Procurement Approach

At least ESA and EU approaches should not be in conflict and, in many respects, EU rules should be adapted to better cope with the specificities of the space sector and serve overarching political goals. Its procurement process should thus be based on a dedicated industrial policy aiming at:

- strengthening the competitiveness, efficiency, and reliability of the European space industry;
- enhancing the European technological non-dependence in the space sector
- building on existing European leading-edge industrial and technological capabilities; and
- contributing to a balanced industrial development across EU Member States.

Moreover, future European public procurements should start with a trade-off to assess whether the benefits of competition balance the drawback of scattering an institutional market which sometimes fails to be sufficient to sustain a sound industrial base and allow the emergence of world-class European champions.

Based on such principles, ESA and EU procurement policies, although different by nature, should at least be compatible and serve common purposes.

PART II
The Legal Framework for Space Projects in Europe

Chapter 5

The Principles of International Space Law and their Relevance to Space Industry Contracts

Lesley Jane Smith

Introduction

'The activities of non-governmental entities in outer space', as commercial space activities are described in Article VI Outer Space Treaty 1967, owe their existence and legitimacy to public international law. International space law is a part of public international law and developed over a relatively short space of time, largely in response to the launching of the Sputnik in 1957. This historical event brought recognition across the scientific and international community that outer space can bring benefits to society, but also requires a regulatory environment to govern activities taking place there. Since then, governments, the United Nations, along with the scientific and technical community, have come together to deliberate on the content of international space law.[1] This formative period of space law also saw the United Nations Committee on Peaceful Uses of Outer Space (UNCOPUOS) emerge as the designated regulatory forum for matters relating to outer space at international level.[2]

Unlike other areas of public international law, international space law predicted and catered for the regulation of the private or commercial space sector from the outset,[3] with the state, the main subject of international law, serving as regulatory anchor over commercial space activities and assuming the financial burdens for breaches of international law on behalf of this sector. This central position does not stand to change, but there are risks of erosion through divergent state practice, notably a lack of coordination where more than one launching state is involved and correspondingly low rate of registration of space objects.

Ongoing developments in space-related technology are now such that, coupled with the interest of states to participate in new business models, commercial space activities are a reality, even if they serve a predominantly public sector market. International space law, supported by demands of private and public customers, including intergovernmental organisations, has been the catalyst

---

1 Galloway, E. 2009. *Cologne Commentary on Space Law, (CoCoSL)*, vol. I, Outer Space Treaty, Preface, edited by S. Hobe, B. Schmidt-Tedd and K.-U. Schrogl. Cologne: Heymanns.

2 Vereschetin, V.S. 2009. 'The Law of Outer Space in the General Legal Field (Commonality and Particularities)', in *Proceedings of the 52nd Colloquium on the Law of Outer Space*. Washington, DC: International Institute of Space Law/American Institute of Aeronautics and Astronautics, 3–15. The post-war era has been referred to as the 'golden age' of outer space law, see Lyall, F. and Larsen, P. 2009. *Space Law: A Treatise*. Aldershot: Ashgate, 37.

3 The Soviet delegation to COPUOS was at first opposed to extending outer space activities to the commercial sector, see Gerhard, M. 2009. *Cologne Commentary on Space Law (CoCoSL)*, vol. I, Article VI Outer Space Treaty. Further, Mulunczuk, P. 1997. 'Actors: States, International Organisations, Private Entities', in *Outlook on Space Law over the Next 30 Years*, edited by G. Lafferanderie and D. Crowther. The Hague: Kluwer, 23–36.

for development of the commercial sector in what was once an area of activities open exclusively to states.[4]

This chapter outlines the key principles imposed by the international law of space, with a view to highlighting their effects at the commercial level. After a brief examination of the structure of the rules of law and principles, the chapter focuses on what is the unique interaction between the public international law of space and commercial contracts in this field.[5]

The Enhancement of Commercial Space Activities through International Space Law

International space law is made up of a varied body of rules composed of UN treaty law, UN Principles, Recommendations and Declarations, and latterly, regulatory documents and guidelines, generally of government or space agency origin.[6] The sources of international law are defined in Article 38 Statute of the International Court of Justice (ICJ) as those legal rules, listed in order of priority, from treaty through to customary law as evidenced by state practice, including the works of leading publicists.[7] Among its sources, international space law counts rules of law that stem from all four categories enumerated in Article 38. At the same time, there is a marked tendency to include certain 'soft law' elements among the growing body of regulatory provisions relevant to outer space activities.[8] This is a direct result of the growth in commercial space activities. Whilst not sources of international law in the traditional sense of Article 38, soft law rules can no longer be overlooked.[9]

Security and safety are paramount to all space activities and dictate the degree to which technical standards, international standardisation and cross-compatibility of systems apply to all space activities, irrespective of whether or not they are commercial. The global nature of the space market dictates the need for adherence to recognised standards and structures across an industry that participates in space projects at international level. These developments have led to an alteration in the type of regulatory measures applying to space activities from the classic principles

4 Public international law has always recognised that sovereign states have an interest in conducting commercial affairs, hence the differentiation drawn in state immunity between acts of government as *ius acta imperii* and acts of a commercial nature, *ius acta gestionis*, the latter denying immunity from jurisdiction, see Brownlie, I. 2008. *Principles of Public International Law*, 7th edition. Oxford, Oxford University Press, 344.

5 Within this chapter, the term 'commercial' is used to cover space activities carried out with a view to profit, irrespective of whether public funding is involved. 'Private' is used in the context of space activities which are exclusively funded through private capital. Few space activities, certainly in Europe, are carried out without some form of public funding, and therefore technically fall under the 'commercial' rubric.

6 Lyall, F. and Larsen, P. 2009, *Space Law*, 50–52.

7 The Statute of the International Court of Justice provides in its Article 38(1)a–d that the various sources of international law are: lit a) international conventions; lit b) international custom, as evidenced by state practice; lit c) general principles of law, recognised by civilised nations, and lit d) judicial decisions and teachings of publicists, as a subsidiary means. There is some acceptance of the view that space law may include some sources not named in Article 38, see Lyall, F. and Larsen, P. 2009. *Space Law*, 31.

8 Lyall, F. and Larsen, P. 2009. *Space* Law, 52. 'Space law, whether formal hard law or less formal soft law, is a vibrant field.' Further, Ferrazzani, M. 1997. 'Soft Law in Space Activities', in *Outlook on Space Law*, edited by G. Lafferanderie and D. Crowther.

9 Lyall, F. and Larsen, P. 2009. *Space Law*. 'Soft space law provides a framework for space activities which supplements the hard space law of the treaties and other formal international agreements.'

of international law, to now include rules such as space debris mitigation guidelines, and latterly Codes of Conduct to enhance the '"rules of the road" for outer space'.[10]

Sources of International Space Law

Treaty Law

There are five UN treaties regulating space activities. The Outer Space Treaty of 1967 (OST), preceded by the UN Declaration of Legal Principles in 1963,[11] was the first of the five UN space treaties to form the basis of the UN-inspired *corpus iuris spatialis*.[12] The Outer Space Treaty lays down the general rules for outer space activities (*lex generalis*), and these are expanded within the subsequent specialist treaties (*lex specialis*).[13] Article I Outer Space Treaty provides for the freedom of exploration and use of outer space for the benefit for mankind, freedom of access to all areas of celestial bodies, providing at all times that the activities are undertaken in accordance with international law (Article 1 para 2 OST).[14] The Outer Space Treaty was followed by the

10 Krepon, M. 2007. 'A Code of Conduct for Responsible Space Faring Nations', in *Celebrating the Space Age: 50 Years of Space Technology, 40 Years of the Outer Space Treaty – Conference Report*, United Nations Institute for Disarmament Research, UNIDIR, 170; Lyall, F. and Larsen, P. 2009. *Space Law*, 38. There is a complex body of standardisation, recommendations and procedures including working arrangements around the technical sides of regulation, such as the Inter-Agency Operations Advisory Group (IOAG – www. ioag.org). Further mention can be made of the Space Frequency Coordination Group (SFCG – www.sfcg-online.org) and the Inter-Agency Space Debris Coordination Committee (IADC – www.iadc-online.org). In the field of telecoms, there are further Memoranda of Understanding relating to Global Mobile Personal Communication by Satellite (GMPCS). The EU adopted the draft Code of Conduct for Outer Space Activities on 27 September 2010. This list is by no means exhaustive and reference is made to the organisations themselves and specialist compendia for a full appreciation of the subject.

11 Declaration of Legal Principles Governing the Activities of States in the Exploration and Use of Outer Space, United Nations General Assembly Resolution 1962 (XVIII) of 13 December 1963.

12 The 1967 Treaty on Principles Governing the Activities of States in the Exploration and Use of Outer Space, Including the Moon and other Celestial Bodies (OST), (610 UNTS 205). The use of the term 'Magna Carta' in relation to the Outer Space Treaty, while recognising its use as common parlance, does not find full favour with leading publicists, largely for historical reasons, see Lyall, F. and Larsen, P. 2009. *Space Law*, 53–4. The remaining four treaties are: The Agreement on the Rescue of Astronauts, and Return of Astronauts and the Return of Objects Launched into Outer Space, 22 April 1968 (672 UNTS 119); the Convention on International Liability for Damage Caused by Space Objects, 29 March 1972 (961 UNTS 187); the Convention on Registration of Objects Launched into Outer Space, 12 November 1974 (1023 UNTS 15); the Agreement Governing the Activities of States on the Moon and other celestial Bodies, 5 December 1979 (1363 UNTS 3).

13 Despite calls for modernisation or reformulation of some of their principles, the treaties are still seen to constitute a vital level of international agreement regarding the peaceful use of outer space. See Lyall, F. and Larsen, P. 2009. *Space Law*, 560, with further references. Benkö, M. and Schrogl, K.U. 1997. 'Article I of the Outer Space Treaty Reconsidered after Thirty Years', in *Outlook on Space Law*, edited by G. Lafferanderie and D. Crowther, 67.

14 Further principles relate to outer space as the province of mankind (Article I para.1), and include a corresponding ban on nuclear activities in outer space (Article IV OST). The Moon Agreement uses the term 'common heritage of mankind', see Article 11 MOON. This idea reflects the status of outer space, where there is no state jurisdiction over the area, see further Hobe, S. 2009. *CoCoSL*, vol. I, Article I Outer Space Treaty, no. 44.

Agreement on the Rescue of Astronauts, the Return of Astronauts and the Return of Objects launched into Outer Space 1968 (ARRA). This latter treaty laid down a state's duty to rescue and return astronauts, independent of whether or not it was a space-faring nation.[15] In the early stages of the international legal regime for space activities, the predominant concern was – and remains – to ensure the utmost safety of those involved in outer space activities.[16]

In establishing an effective liability regime for damage resulting from space objects, it was recognised that states, as subjects of international law, were best placed to assume the burden of the duty to compensate for damage occurring from space activities. The Convention on International Liability for Damage caused by Space Objects, 1972 instated a regime of strict state liability for damage to earth caused by space objects (Article II LIAB) and a fault-based regime for damage occurring in outer space (Article III LIAB).[17] The Convention on Registration of Objects Launched into Outer Space 1975 (REG) subsequently introduced a system under which space objects were to be registered by virtue of Article II REG in a national space registry. This allows the attribution of a space object to a launching state, imposing a duty on the state of registry under Article IV REG to notify the UN Secretary-General about objects launched.[18] Finally, the treaty marking the end of the international space law-making era was the Agreement Governing the Activities of States on the Moon and other Celestial Bodies, 1979 (MOON). This Agreement contains similar prescriptions to those of the Outer Space Treaty regarding the freedom of access, freedom of scientific investigation, non-discrimination, peaceful and non-military use in relation to the Moon. However, the Moon Agreement goes one step further, by providing for the international community to establish a regime to govern the exploitation of the Moon's natural resources under its Article 11.5. This did not come to fruition.

Of all the space treaties, the Moon Agreement has been subjected to the greatest criticism. This is partly attributable to the low number of ratifications, and partly to the limitations imposed by the same principles that exclude appropriation and claims to sovereignty over the Moon (and other celestial bodies), and its natural resources, as specified in Article II Outer Space Treaty.[19] The lack of international interest in cooperating towards creating a special regime for the Moon's resources is evident. However, independent of the degree to which the MOON Treaty is seen to contain binding rules, the foregoing general principles laid down by the Outer Space Treaty are at least now seen to have acquired the status of customary international law.[20]

---

15 Astronauts are envoys of mankind in terms of Article V Outer Space Treaty, although there is no definition given in the treaties. The notion of envoy of mankind first appeared in the UNGA Resolution 1962 (XVIII) of 1963 (The Declaration of Principles' Resolution) prior to the Outer Space Treaty. Space tourists are not seen to fall into the category of envoy of mankind; the term of 'space flight participant' is the term used in US law and for non-crew members within the International Space Station (ISS).

16 Kerrest, A. and Smith, L.J. 2009. *CoCoSL* vol. I, Article VII Outer Space Treaty.

17 *Ibid.*

18 For a discussion of the alternative registration system available prior the Registration Convention under the UNGA Resolution 1721B (XVI) of 20 December 1961 for those states which have not acceded to the Registration Convention, see Schmidt-Tedd, B. and Mick, S. 2009. *CoCoSL*, vol. I, Article VIII Outer Space Treaty.

19 The Treaty is currently only signed by 13 parties. Details of treaty signatory status is available via the UNOOSA offices. [Online]. Available at: http://www.unoosa.org/oosa/en/SpaceLaw/treatystatus/index.html [accessed: 20 June 2011], currently as of 2010.

20 Lyall, F. and Larsen, P. 2009. *Space Law*, 54.

UN Resolutions on Principles of International Space Law

Further statements relating to international space law are to be found in important resolutions on principles requiring states to comply with their obligations in outer space activities. These resolutions are traditionally drafted within the Legal Subcommittee of UN COPUOS and presented to the General Assembly within the annual COPUOS report, to be adopted as resolutions, generally by consensus.[21] On the one hand, they contain important principles relating to space activities, latterly including recommendations on private or commercial activities in outer space. On the other, they remain a challenge to the hierarchy of space law.[22] While technically non-binding, resolutions are now joining the ranks as accepted rules within the corpus of international space law.[23] Although their effect as a source of law is controversial, they cannot be overlooked as a source of guidelines and interpretation. Criticism has nevertheless been forthcoming that resolutions are inapplicable to the private or commercial sector.[24] This has had a negative impact on fields of activity, such as remote sensing, which are developing into clear commercial sectors, at the expense of the community of states, notably those without access to remote sensing facilities. The provisions were formulated with a view to making data available to sensed states on reasonable cost terms under Principle XII. As a matter of international law, these cannot, however, be leveraged directly against commercial companies.[25]

There are various primary sets of Principles of international space law, all adopted within the framework of UN resolutions that relate to the use of outer space.[26] These have facilitated the opening up of outer space to commercial use and mapped out its subsequent development: the Remote Sensing Principles (1986), The Direct Broadcasting Principles (1982), The Principles on the Use of Nuclear Power (1992), and the UN Declaration on Principles of International Cooperation in Exploration and Use of Outer Space (1996). The major areas of commercial space or satellite based activities are to be found in satellite telecommunication, satellite broadcasting and latterly, mobile satellite telephony. These sectors have benefited most from the legitimacy of non-governmental space activities, from developments in space-based technology, as well as from the various phases of market de-regulation, particularly within the European telecommunication sector.[27]

---

21 *Ibid.*, 20. The membership of UNCOPUOS has grown from 24 in 1959 to 69 as of today.

22 Of the various resolutions pre-dating the Outer Space Treaty, the Declaration of Legal Principles governing the Activities of States in the exploration and Use of Outer Space, UNGA Res. 1962 (XVIII) of 1963 is seen to belong to the highest form, given that it was adopted by consensus.

23 Lyall, F. and Larsen, P. 2009. *Space Law*. 48. 'For a variety of cogent reasons, including the method of voting, these Resolutions stand at least in future to be treated as sources of international space law.'

24 Jakhu, Ram S. 2003. 'International Law Regarding the Acquisition and Dissemination of Satellite Imagery', *Journal of Space Law*, 65.

25 Various international cooperation agreements exist such as the Disaster Charter, available at http://www.disastercharter.org, and the UN Space-based Information system for Disaster Management and Emergency Relief (UN SPIDER), available at http://www.un-spider.org that provide for satellite imagery to be made available.

26 The UN Principles and Declarations are available via the website of the offices of the United Nations Office for Outer Space Affairs, with headquarters in Vienna, http://www.unoosa.org.

27 For full details of de-regulation within the European telecommunication market, see Achilleas, P. (ed.) 2009. *Droit de l'espace:* télécommunication, observation, navigation, défense, exploration. Paris: Larcier. Further, Rapp, L. 1997. 'Satellite Communication and Global Information Infrastructure', in *Outlook on Space Law*, edited by G. Lafferanderie and D. Crowther, 373.

Interface between the Law of Outer Space and Commercial Space Activities

General

Space law is therefore one of the few areas of public international law where the activities of non-governmental entities are clearly regulated. Article VI OST provides the essential link between the state responsible under international law for the activities of its non-governmental or private entities subject to its jurisdiction.[28] International law provides the key to assessing how such responsibility arises. Firstly, a state may have jurisdiction by virtue of the nationality of the space activities in question in terms of Article VI OST. Secondly, jurisdiction may be founded under the traditional categories of personal or territorial links, and extend to include jurisdiction over space objects registered within that state's national space register.[29]

In the context of space activities, Article VI OST imposes a clear duty on the state to license, monitor and otherwise supervise the space activities of its private commercial sector.[30] Although not formulated as an explicit duty to legislate, a state's responsibility under Article VI has led to many states installing systems of licensing and regulation of domestic space activities at domestic level.[31] Ensuring regulation of private space activities at national level is a key to ensuring maintenance of the international space law regime. It is also a key to ensuring successful commercial operations at national level.

Commercial Space Activities

Commercial space activities began to develop in the 1980s, largely with government support, and continue to serve a strong public market. They have undergone particular growth in certain countries such as the United States through legal and policy decisions that allowed certain space segments such as remote sensing to operate fully as commercial activities.[32] Developments in space technology have also enabled downsizing of systems and payloads, so that new growth areas for commercial activities continue to develop. The traditional commercial areas of space activities such as satellite telecommunications law and direct broadcasting have now been joined by demands for services such as global satellite navigation, positioning and timing.

Traditionally, the space agencies have generated the space business and the contracts to support it. Space programmes provide for scientific missions, and may include commercial aspects, but

28 Articles IX Outer Space Treaty lays down the principle of international cooperation and mutual assistance, while Article XI Outer Space Treaty foresees notification and intimation of activities that are planned in outer space.

29 As there is no concept of ownership in outer space, Article VIII Outer Space Treaty is used as a basis for creating a link between jurisdiction and property, notable in the context of intellectual property rights, see Schmidt-Tedd, B. and Mick, S. 2009. *CoCoSL*, vol. I, Article VIII Outer Space Treaty.

30 There is no definition of non-governmental entities. They have been referred to as 'natural and legal persons of private law, as well as universities and research organisations (even where they are run as public statutory corporations)', see Gerhard, M. 2009. *CoCoSL*, vol. I, Article VI Outer Space Treaty.

31 For a detailed country by country review of national space legislation, see Jakhu, Ram S. (ed.) 2010. *National Regulation of Space Activities*. Wien/Berlin: Springer.

32 For details of the historical development of US space law, including the development of the Land Remote Sensing Policy *Act* of 1992 and subsequent statutes, see Gabrynowicz, J.I. 2010. 'One Half Century and Counting: The Evolution of US Space Law', *Harvard Law and Policy Review*. [Online]. Available at: http://hlpronline.com/2010/06/gabrynowicz_space/ [accessed: 20 June 2011].

with the exception of telecommunications and broadcasting, are not generally revenue bringing. Now, broader user spectrums are developing, with markets emerging in response to demand for downstream applications and services such as digital satellite broadband. Commercial applications for space signals and data are now joining the range of space products and services that can be supplied. These extend beyond satellite navigation systems to include geo- and environmental information systems, applications for administering civil society such as traffic management, monitoring water quality, satellite secure tracking systems, and much more. Where communication and broadcasting once constituted the main sectors of space services, earth observation, positioning, navigation location and timing now stand to shape the development of business for the future.

At the same time, the growth in the number and capabilities of increasingly small satellites deserves attention. Satellite frequency filing with ITU is an important economic asset attributed to states, with corresponding entitlements for states to register their satellites under the ITU frequency filing rules.[33] The radio frequency spectrum is a natural resource, and states have legal and ethical duties under international law, not only to its equitable use, but also its preservation. Now, with the growth market in small satellites and the (generally unauthorised) use of amateur frequencies for new generations of nano satellites, the international regulatory system is seen to be in danger of being undermined.[34] This is one of the areas where international space law faces challenges in requiring states to control developments at commercial and university research level.

The Key Principles of Outer Space Law and their Effect on Space Activities

General

The principles and rules of international space law are therefore to be found in the combined rules of public international law, including the law of international organisations,[35] private international law, alongside national law, together with supplementary rules deriving from international agreements and particularly in the case of international projects such as the International Space Station, Memoranda of Understanding,[36] through to the body of UN Resolutions that has grown with time.[37] Regulatory control over the commercial sector takes place at national level through the domestic licensing system.[38] The move towards national regulation of space activities has been encouraged by the COPUOS, latterly in its Resolution 59/115 of 10 December 2004

33 The Constitution, Convention of the International Telecommunications Union and its Radio Regulations (ITU-RR) (2002) are available at www.itu.org.

34 There are ongoing discussions about integrating university sponsored small satellites into the regulatory structure. These are often launched as unregistered space objects, see 'The New Age of Small Satellite Missions, 25th IAA/ IISL Joint Scientific Legal Round Table, 2010', in *Proceedings of the 53rd Colloquium on the Law of Outer Space*, Washington, DC: IISL/AIAA, forthcoming.

35 The provisions of the Outer Space Treaty apply to intergovernmental organisations, see Article VI sentence 3. .

36 The Intergovernmental Agreement on the International Space Station (ISS) is available in Space Law – Basic Legal Documents D.II.4.

37 Lyall, F. and Larsen, P. 2009. *Space Law*, 37. 'A MoU is more formal than a gentleman's agreement but less than a contract.'

38 On the potential risks of 'forum shopping' with a view to developing space services in low regulatory jurisdictions, see Lyall, F. 2006. 'Small States, Entrepreneurial States and Space', in *Proceedings of the 49th Colloquium on the Law of Outer Space*. Washington, DC: IISL/AIAA, 382.

recommending the international space community to pass national space legislation in order to ensure the coherency between the content of national and the international space regulation.[39] It has also lead to the passing of a UN Resolution recalling the duties of sovereign states to register space objects, particularly where these take place as commercial launches where more than one state could qualify as a launching state.[40]

Impact of General Responsibility

From the perspective of states, the greatest impact of international law on commercial space activities is the overriding general and, with this, financial responsibility of states for the activities of their commercial enterprises. In the event of failure to follow its duty to authorise and monitor the activities of its nationals, a state may incur its general financial responsibility. Failure to monitor the commercial sector's operations in terms of Article VI OST may constitute a breach of international law which in turn leads to a duty to provide financial compensation. Article VI OST and Article VII OST interact to ensure that, whether a state fails to uphold its duties of responsibility in law or is acting as a launching state in a case where damage occurs, there is more than one basis for duty to compensate for loss. It is governments, not the private sector that primarily bear the risks of outer space activities.[41]

From the perspective of the commercial industry, the financial burden borne by responsible states operates as a business incentive, and may take the form of a security or government guarantee in favour of the private space sector. This provides coverage for the risk involved, over and above the amount insured by the operator.[42] Such a system may follow the model introduced by the United States with its Commercial Space Launch Act, now 2004,[43] and its European counterpart, the French law on Space Operations which was modelled on the US system. The French statute operates with a top-up state guarantee, allowing France to assume the additional financial burden

39 Resolution 59/115 of December 2004, Application of the Concept of Launching State; Resolution 62/101 of 17 December 2007, Recommendation on Enhancing the practice of States and international intergovernmental organisations in registering space objects. 'Noting that the changes in space activities since the Registration Convention entered into force include the continuous development of new technologies, an increase in the number of states carrying out space activities, an increase in international cooperation in the peaceful uses of outer space and an increase in the activities carried out by non-governmental entities, as well as partnerships forged from more than one country, *Recommends* … that (a) States that have not yet ratified or acceded to the Registration Convention should become parties to it in accordance with their national law ….'

40 Resolution 62/101 of 17 December 2007. Recommendations on enhancing the practice of States and international government organisations in registering space objects, at 3. *Further recommends* … that (d) States should encourage launch service providers under their jurisdiction to advise the owner and/or operator of the space object to address the appropriate States on the registration of that space object.

41 The international responsibility of a state that authorises space activities means, firstly, that it is externally or internationally responsible, and possibly internationally liable, for the activities of its private sector. This is the rationale behind the European inter-governmental declaration of acceptance of responsibilities towards European launchers, see Declaration by certain Governments on the Launchers Exploitation Phase of Ariane, Vega and Soyuz from the Guiana Space Centre, 26 November 2009, reproduced in Cmnd 7700 (2009), HMSO, London.

42 Art. 13 French Loi relative aux Operations Spatiales, JO n 129 of 4 June 2008. See, Chapter 26 (Couston, M.).

43 See Hancock, R. 2005. 'Provisions of the Commercial Space Launch Act (CSLA)', *Space Policy*, 21, 227.

beyond the compulsory insurance ceiling limit.[44] While international law regulates the international responsibility for the activities of nationals, the question of whether a state subsequently chooses to claim indemnification from its private sector at national level depends on the degree to which the State party sees such a guarantee as an incentive to supporting commercial operations.[45]

Liability and the Launching State

State liability is imposed by virtue of Article VII OST on the launching state for damage caused by its space objects, and is regulated by further provisions of the Liability Convention 1972 (LIAB). Liability – in contrast to responsibility – attaches to any one of the categories of launching state defined in Art I LIAB.[46] The international law of space presents a very different pattern of state liability to that otherwise known to international law. There is no limitation on the liability of states under the law of outer space. This will have an influence on the type of space activities that states are willing to licence, and impact on the arrangements for commercial services and launch sectors which may operate as consortia across different jurisdictions. Any one of the categories of launching state may become liable under Article VII OST and Articles II and III LIAB.

There are concerns that certain states are approaching the issue of liability at national level with a view to demarcating and restricting their external position *vis-à-vis* the private sector. This takes place when national space legislation makes a distinction in its unlimited international state liability arising from the activities of non-governmental entities. Any attempts by states to reject their international liability for their commercial space sector could effectively destabilise the application of the international space rules.[47] While compulsory insurance coverage technically alleviates the liability burden, international state liability remains the basis of the international regime for space operations. Civil liability claims may nevertheless still be raised at national level against the launchers and satellite owners for fault or negligence arising during launching, operations and extend to manufacturer's product liability.[48] They are not excluded by the international liability regime. Claims need not be exhausted at national level before the Claims Commission Procedure is called into place under Article XI LIAB. The rationale for unlimited liability imposed on states is to ensure that there is an effective system of compensation for damage beyond the ceiling limit insured. The international system relies on the compliance with these principles by states.

Jurisdiction and Registration

International registration prescribed by the Registration Convention 1975 is a compulsory measure that enables identification of a space object and attribution to its launching state. Where there

44 *Ibid.* See Chapter 26 (Couston, M.).

45 Financial risk guarantees may be a consideration making certain jurisdictions attractive for commercial space operations, see Chapter 13 (Aganabe, T.).

46 The categories of launching state are prescribed in Article 1 Liability Convention and Article I Registration Convention. Four categories of launching state are recognised. A launching state is either one which carries out the launch or procures the launching of a space object or a state from whose territory or facility a space object is launched.

47 Lyall, F., Kerrest, A. and Smith, L.J. 2009. *CoCoSL*, vol. I, Article VII Outer Space Treaty.

48 Ravillon, L. (ed.) 2005. *Le droit des activités spatiales à l'aube du XXIe siècle*, CNRS, CREDEMI. Paris: Litec, 24. Insurance is generally compulsory by virtue of national legislation. See n. 41, above for the provision of government liability agreements in relation to European launchers.

is more than one launching state, as with international cooperation projects, or where launching services of another state are being used by a non-resident customer, there should be agreement as to which state party is to register the space object under Article II(2) REG. The system is designed to ensure that there is only one state of registration. Registration under Article VIII OST is a non-delegable duty, implying that the commercial sector must be subject to the superior control of the launching state.[49]

In practice, this may leave states with options when it comes to regulating foreign space operations. Launches undertaken by a state or its nationals should lead to registration in the national register.[50] In some cases, notably the United States, launches from non-US operators from US territory are not registered by the US.[51] This requires coordination between states from which launch services are operated and the 'own state' requirements under national space law, in accordance with international law.

The Convergence of Systems – the 'Privatisation' of Space Law

General

While national space law is steadily emerging to secure regulatory structures for space activities at domestic level, certain aspects of international trade law and private international law are gaining importance in the field of commercial space activities: space activities are by nature without boundaries. Exposure to foreign law and jurisdiction may easily arise through participation in international space projects, through the use of foreign commercial space services such as launching, or through the operation of space services out of foreign states. Despite the confidentiality attached to commercial space contracts and the influence of agency rules which impose their own applicable law, questions such as the proper law of the particular space contract and the law applicable to damage arising from space accidents require consideration when addressing risk management from a contract perspective.[52]

Various legal rules applicable to the space sector derive from attempts to harmonise law at international level through international unification bodies such as United Nations Commission on International Trade Law (UNCITRAL), the World Trade Organisation (WTO), the European Union (EU) and UNIDROIT, the International Institute for the Unification of Private Law. These range from creating uniform law for the international sale of goods under the UN Convention on the law of international sales (CISG) 1980, to considerations as to the applicability of international procurement rules (GPA) under WTO rules to European Global Navigation Satellite System Galileo, and the continuing work on the current draft UNIDROIT Protocol on Registration of Interests in Mobile Assets.[53]

49 See Schmidt-Tedd, B. and Mick, S. 2009. *CoCoSL*, vol. I, Article VIII Outer Space Treaty.

50 This is the situation under the US legislation, see Schmidt-Tedd, B. and Mick, S. 2009. *CoCoSL*, vol. I, Article VIII Outer Space Treaty, nos 54–8.

51 Hancock, R. 2005. 'Provisions of the Commercial Space Launch Act'.

52 Smith, L.J. 2009. 'Facing Up to Third Party Liability: Some Reflections', in *Proceedings of the 52nd Colloquium on the Law of Outer Space*. Washington, DC: IISL/AIAA, 255–64; Smith, L.J. and Doldirina, C. 2010. 'Jurisdiction and Applicable Law in Cases of Damage from Space in Europe: The Advent of the Most Suitable Choice, Rome II', *Acta Astronautica*, 66, 239–44.

53 See Chapter 18 (Weber-Steinhaus, D. and Ní Chearbhaill, D.).

In essence, space law and contracts are exposed to various influences extending beyond public international law to include private and international private aspects of the law as well. This does not signify any more than the interdependencies between the various disciplines of the law where different actors are involved. It should not be taken to imply a fragmentation of international space law but the interaction between the international and the domestic level.

Commercial Contracts for Space

Commercial space contracts cover a wide variety of activities, largely relating to the manufacture, supply and delivery of systems and services, components, objects and structures to be used in space projects. From the outset of a project through to its final implementation, the various elements are brought together within an 'architecture' of main and subcontracts. The structure of the contracts is not dissimilar to those found in large construction or high technology projects, with various levels of contractors and subcontractors working to fulfil delivery orders to specific key dates and performance levels, generally under the supervision of a main or general contractor, within what is generally referred to as a prime contract. In terms of contract law, such contracts do not differ greatly from other commercial contracts, in that provision is made for performance, non-performance, consideration, IP retention, confidentiality, to name but a few. Technical provisions figure high within this contract structure.

The areas where international law exercises its greatest influence relate to technical rules and risk allocation provisions. In essence, the space agency or customer will ensure that risks are capped at each level of responsibility, and that risks are allocated between all partners. The predominant areas of interest within space contracts reflect elements similar to certain provisions of the treaties. These relate to authorisation, reporting mechanisms, ownership of IP, liability, dispute settlement and ultimately public law influenced rights of agencies to 'overrule' or impose alterations on the contract itself, almost as a prerogative right.

Cross-waivers and flowdown

Of the principles of space law outlined, those dominating the commercial sector relate to state responsibility and liability.

Contracts relating to commercial space activities, be they between satellite manufacturers, operators, space agencies, launchers and other contractors, therefore generally reflect the rationale of international space law. This is reflected in the clauses relating to both cross-waiver and flowdown of responsibility and liability.

The cross-waver of liability is a regular standard contract clause that entitles parties to carry their own risk, thereby relieving other project partners from the additional financial burden of direct liability in contract and tort for damage arising towards partners. Each state, and with this concept of cross-waiver, each commercial operator, assumes liability for its own damage, including its personnel.[54] This is the same position as that contained in Article VII (a) LIAB whereby nationals and foreigners participating in the operation of the space object are excluded from the Convention's ambit.

The consequences of financial risks governed by cross-waivers are generally alleviated through compulsory insurance imposed as part of the licensing regime. In certain growth areas, for example, with space tourism, a field involving elements of clear voluntary assumption of risk, the

54 Article 16 International Governmental Agreement (IGA) on the International Space Station.

combination of *volenti non fit iniuria* together with the cross waiver will be linked to compulsory insurance. These developments are currently being debated in Europe on the level of which regime of law is the most appropriate to accompany such ventures. Air law rather than space law appears, at least in the case of suborbital flights, to find favour.[55] The international rules of space law apply equally to intergovernmental organisations, for example, the European Space Agency. As of 2009, three intergovernmental organisations, the European Space Agency, EUMETSAT and EUTELSAT have made declarations of recognition of their obligations under international law.[56]

Further down the division of responsibilities for space projects between prime and subcontractors, techniques such as flowdown of responsibility and liability are used to achieve what is effectively the same result as the cross-waiver or limitation of liability at each level involved. Each contractor remains responsible for its own level of authority and no superior claims may be raised other than by the customer (generally the Agency) which is empowered to exercise standard contractual rights to performance and damages, generally measured in relation to the contract volume.

Conclusion

The foregoing highlights the extent to which public international law provides an essential platform for commercial space activities. The advent of commercial space activities was not an unexpected development, but the relationship between the non-government entity and the state is unique: the state remains responsible within the international context. In addition, unlimited liability may be allocated to those countries acting as launching states in the case of damage caused by space objects. The commercial sector, however, has no right to undertake commercial activities in outer space. Space operations within the private or commercial sector are at all times accessory and subsidiary to the interests of the state responsible in international law. This should not be overlooked.

Today, there is a distinct need for a systematic alignment of national legislation to ensure the regulatory and legal stability for the community and environment affected by space activities. Ensuring that the universal aspects of outer space are maintained in commercial practice requires constant monitoring and reporting, both at national and international level. Space agencies and international organisations are fully aware of these responsibilities. While the task of balancing the communality of interests falls to those institutions funding space activities, it is paramount that the commercial actors too strive to maintain the principles of international law imposed. This can be achieved at one level through contract drafting and negotiation, by ensuring that the project partners, lawyers and engineers operate within the above parameters. For the remainder, it is important to ensure that commercialisation does not become synonymous with low standards that have been witnessed in other areas of international law, notably through the effects of outflagging in the maritime sector. Active and responsible solutions are demanded from the community of space faring nations, and extend to the younger space states which are entering the commercial

55 The current ESA position paper on suborbital flights available at their website indicates an interest in supporting these developments and a clear tendency to see suborbital flights as airflights, falling within the remit of the European Aviation Safety Agency.

56 It is open to international organisations to make declarations of acceptance of their responsibilities under the Rescue and Return Agreement (ARRA), the Registration Convention (REG) and the Liability Convention (LIAB). Of the European organisations, the European Space Agency, ESA, and EUMESAT have as of January 2009 made declarations of acceptance of all three treaties, ARRA, LIAB and REG, while EUTELSAT has done so for LIAB.

market, whether by attracting new forms of space-based services and industries or encouraging more earth-based space activities.[57]

For the future, the perceived bifurcation[58] within the law of space may well continue. International space law is moving from a field once dominated by international law alone, to one of a complex matrix of rules, formal legal norms, voluntary codes and recommendations that apply to state and commercial space activities alike. Earlier predictions describe how it may fork between the categories of exploration-linked and earth-based activities.[59] Be this as it may, those participating in space activities within the international community are ethically and legally bound to strive for coherency and convergence within the structures created by the international conventions. This can be done in a variety of ways: through enacting national space legislation, through implementing international obligations, applying space law at domestic level and ensuring that contract practices and procedures are based on the rules of space law.

List of References

Achilleas, P. (ed.). 2009. *Droit de l'espace:* télécommunication, observation, navigation, défense, exploration. Paris: Larcier.

Benkö, M. and Schrogl, K.U. 1997. 'Article I of the Outer Space Treaty Reconsidered after Thirty Years', in *Outlook on Space Law Over the Next 30 Years*, edited by G. Lafferanderie and D. Crowther. The Hague: Kluwer, 67.

Böckstiegel, K-H. 2002. *'Project 2001': Legal Framework for the Commercial Use of Outer Space.* Cologne: Heymanns.

Bownlie, I. 2008. *Principles of Public International Law*, 7th edition. Oxford: Oxford University Press.

Buhlmann, U. and Martinez, L. 2007. 'Fly Me to the Moon, Legal and Political Considerations of the Space Exploration Initiatives', in *Proceedings of the 49th Colloquium on the Law of Outer Space*. Washington, DC: International Institute of Space Law/American Institute of Aeronautics and Astronautics, 117–30.

Diederiks-Verschoor, I. 2008. *Introduction to Space Law*, 3rd edition, edited by V. Kopal. The Hague: Kluwer.

Ferrazzani, M. 1997. 'Soft Law in Space Activities', in *Outlook on Space Law, Over the Next 30 Years*, edited by G. Lafferanderie and D. Crowther. The Hague: Kluwer, 429–48.

Gabrynowicz, J.I. 2010. 'One Half Century and Counting: The Evolution of US Space Law', *Harvard Law and Policy Review*. [Online]. Available at: http://hlpronline.com/2010/06/gabrynowicz_space/ [accessed: 11 January 2011].

Galloway, E. 2009. *Cologne Commentary on Space Law, (CoCoSL)*, vol. I, Outer Space Treaty, Preface, edited by S. Hobe, B. Schmidt-Tedd and K.-U. Schrogl. Cologne: Heymanns.

Gerhard, M. 2009. *Cologne Commentary on Space Law (CoCoSL)*, vol. I, Article VI Outer Space Treaty, edited by S. Hobe, B. Schmidt-Tedd and K.-U. Schrogl. Cologne: Heymanns.

Hancock, R. 2005. 'Provisions of the Commercial Space Launch Act (CSLA)', *Space Policy*, 21, 227.

---

57 See Chapter 13 (Aganaba, T.). Lyall, F. 2006. 'Small States, Entrepreneurial States and Space', 382.

58 Lyall, F. and Larsen, P. 2009. *Space Law*, 559.

59 Buhlmann, U. and Martinez, L. 2007. 'Fly Me to the Moon: Legal and Political Considerations of the Space Exploration Initiatives', in *Proceedings of the 49th Colloquium on the Law of Outer Space*. Washington, DC: IISL /AIAA, 117.

Hobe, S. 2009. *Cologne Commentary on Space Law (CoCoSL)*, vol. I, Article I Outer Space Treaty, Cologne: Heymanns.

Jakhu, Ram S. 2003. 'International Law Regarding the Acquisition and Dissemination of Satellite Imagery', *Journal of Space Law*, 29 (2 and 3), 65.

Jakhu, Ram S. 2006. 'Legal Issues Relating to the Global Public Interest in Outer Space', *Journal of Space Law*, 31.

Jakhu, Ram S. 2010. *National Regulation of Space Activities*. Berlin/New York: Springer.

Kerrest, A. and Smith, L.J. 2009. *Cologne Commentary on Space Law (CoCoSL)*, vol. I, Article VII Outer Space Treaty. Cologne: Heymanns.

Krepon, M. 2007. 'A Code of Conduct for Responsible Space Faring Nations', in *Celebrating the Space Age: 50 Years of Space Technology, 40 Years of the Outer Space Treaty – Conference Report*. United Nations Institute for Disarmament Research, UNIDIR, 170.

Lyall, F. 2006. 'Small States, Entrepreneurial States and Space', in *Proceedings of the 49th Colloquium on the Law of Outer Space*. Washington, DC: International Institute of Space Law/ American Institute of Aeronautics and Astronautics, 382.

Lyall, F., Kerrest, A. and Smith, L.J. 2009. *Cologne Commentary on Space Law (CoCoSL)*, vol. I, Article VII Outer Space Treaty. Cologne: Heymanns.

Lyall, F. and Larsen, P. 2009. *Space Law, A Treatise*. Aldershot: Ashgate.

Mulunczuk, P. 1997. 'Actors: States, International Organisations, Private Entities', in *Outlook on Space Law Over the Next 30 Years*, edited by G. Lafferanderie and D. Crowther. The Hague: Kluwer, 23–36.

Rapp, L. 1997. 'Satellite Communication and Global Information Infrastructure', in *Outlook on Space Law Over the Next 30 Years*, edited by G. Lafferanderie and D. Crowther. The Hague: Kluwer, 373.

Ravillon, L. 2005. *Le Droit des activités spatiales à l'aube du XXIe siècle*, CNRS, CREDEMI, vol. 25. Paris: Litec.

Schmidt-Tedd, B. and Mick, S. 2009. *Cologne Commentary on Space Law (CoCoSL)*, vol. I, Article VIII Outer Space Treaty. Cologne: Heymanns.

Smith, L.J. 2009. 'Facing Up to Third Party Damage: Some Reflections', in *Proceedings of the 52nd Colloquium on the Law of Outer Space*. Washington, DC: International Institute of Space Law/American Institute of Aeronautics and Astronautics, 255–64.

Smith L.J. and Doldirina, C. 2010. 'Jurisdiction and Applicable Law in Cases of Damage from Space in Europe: The Advent of the Most Suitable Choice, Rome II', *Acta Astronautica*, 66, 239–44.

Vereschetin, V.S. 2009. 'The Law of Outer Space in the General Legal Field (Commonality and Particularities)', in *Proceedings of the 52nd Colloquium on the Law of Outer Space*. Washington, DC: International Institute of Space Law/American Institute of Aeronautics and Astronautics, 3–15.

Chapter 6
The Impact of National Space Legislation on Space Industry Contracts*

Michael Gerhard and Kamlesh Gungaphul-Brocard

Introduction

Private entities engaging in space or space-related activities operate under an intricate legal framework. This framework is made up of general local laws regulating the nationals' activities and, since recently in some countries, of specific national space legislation.

Different from other areas of law, the legal framework applicable to private entities engaged in space or space-related activities is very much interlinked with the international treaties.[1] Those apply in the first place to states – but private entities should also be familiar with them: international treaties contain certain provisions requiring states to implement domestic legislation applicable to private entities engaging in space-related activities. In addition, some of the international treaties create responsibilities for states, irrespective of whether they themselves or their nationals engage in space activities. Consequently states may want to alleviate this responsibility by introducing (additional) requirements for private entities within their domestic legislation.

Several states have implemented national space legislation to varying degrees, indicating that the role of the non-governmental space sector is acknowledged and predicted to become more significant. The international treaties provide that states should at least authorise and supervise the non-governmental activities in outer space under their jurisdiction[2] and establish a registry of space objects.[3]

There are, however, more certainty and transparency required on authorisation and registration if states wish to foster their private space sector. Gerhard and Schrogl (2002) note that by addressing

---

* This chapter does not in any way reflect the views of the authors' employers or organisations with which they are associated.

1 The Treaty on Principles Governing the Activities of States in the Exploration and Use of Outer Space, including the Moon and Other Celestial Bodies [adopted by the General Assembly in its resolution 2222 (XXI)], opened for signature on 27 January 1967, entered into force on 10 October 1967 (96 ratifications and 27 signatures. Hereinafter referred to as the Outer Space Treaty or OST). The Agreement on the Rescue of Astronauts, the Return of Astronauts, the Return of Astronauts and the Return of Objects Launched into Outer Space (the 'Rescue Agreement', adopted by the General Assembly in its resolution 2345 (XXII), opened for signature on 22 April 1968, entered into force on 3 December 1968 (87 ratifications and 26 signatures). The Convention on International Liability for Damage Caused by Space Objects, adopted by the General Assembly in its resolution 2777 (XXVI), opened for signature on 29 March 1972 (81 ratifications and 26 signatures. Hereinafter referred to as the Liability Convention). The Convention on Registration of Objects Launched into Outer Space, adopted by the General Assembly in its resolution 3255 (XXIX), opened for signature on 14 January 1975. Hereinafter referred to as the Registration Convention. The Agreement Governing the Activities of States on the Moon and Other Celestial Bodies, opened for signature on 19 December 1979.

2 Art. VI of the Outer Space Treaty.

3 As stipulated in the preamble and in Art. II (1) and III of the Registration Convention.

certain key elements, national space legislation can provide the required transparency, which is needed for private actors to manage their potential risks of liability, positively impacting contracts.[4]

Relevant Legal Framework

The commercialisation of space activities is not in itself problematic under the space law regime.[5] It is, however, the 'privatisation' of these activities which challenges the provisions of the space treaties. Private parties engaging in space activities do so by entering into contracts under their own negotiated terms. However, regardless of the contractual elements between the parties, it is the state – if party to the international space treaties[6] – that remains internationally responsible and liable under the OST. As a result, the legal framework directly or indirectly applicable to the negotiated contracts governing industrial relationships for private activities is a mix of international private law, national space legislation and public international law.

International Law

The OST bears provisions imposing international responsibility on states for activities carried out in outer space. These, contained respectively in Art. VI, VII and VIII, include: the obligation of the state to authorise and continuously supervise all such activities carried out by non-governmental entities; the imposition of liability on the state for damages caused by space objects (even if the space object is operated by a private party); and the obligation of the state to exercise jurisdiction and control over space objects.

The 1972 Liability Convention's main provisions, and as stipulated at Art. IV, impose on the launching state absolute liability for damage caused by its space object on earth or to aircraft in flight, and fault-based liability for damage caused in outer space.

Art. II (1) and III of the 1975 Registration Convention call for the establishment of a national registry for space objects as well as for registration of such objects with the United Nations General Secretary. The national registry contains details of the space objects for which the state is effectively taking responsibility and for which this state assumes jurisdiction and control.

National Space Legislation

National legislation enables states to implement these international law obligations, while also responding individually to the requirements and needs of the local private sector. Faced with increased private participation in launching or satellite operations, the state must seek to enact such national laws.

As such, the state will have to enact requirements and procedures for the authorisation of launching activities, as well as for the operation of satellites and other space objects, by non-governmental (for example private) entities. Procedures and means to carry out the necessary

4 Gerhard, M. and Schrogl, K-U. 2002. 'Report of the "Project 2001" Working Group on National Space Legislation', in *Project 2001: Legal Framework for the Commercial Use of Outer Space*, edited by Karl-Heinz Böckstiegel. Cologne: Heymanns, 529, 530.

5 Couston, M. 1994. *Droit spatial économique: régimes applicables à l'exploitation de l'espace*. Courtenay: Sides.

6 The significant number of states having ratified the main treaties establishes the principles as customary international law.

supervision of such activities will have to be implemented by the state, while at the same time the state will have to establish requirements and procedures to register space objects in its national registry.

In doing so, a key aspect for the state to consider is how to balance, on one hand, the requirement to bind the private sector to comply with those obligations and, on the other, the need to foster the private space sector. National space legislation can help generate increased legal certainty for private actors, especially in the spheres of licensing, promoting participation and investment.

Simultaneously, in implementing national space legislation, the state must ensure protection of the global public interest. National law can be drafted to include reimbursement mechanisms through which the state, if it has had to pay compensation following its international obligations as a liable launching state, can take recourse against the private entities that caused the damage. It is fair to say that all existing domestic space legislations seek to achieve this balance between ensuring compliance with the international space treaties and promoting the domestic space sector. However, private entities need the states to go further in harmonising the finer elements – such as ceiling amounts for liability and licensing regimes.

International Private Law

Private space ventures are more often than not a multinational effort of private companies, as a result of the nationality of the investors, the experts and the operators.[7] The relationship between the participating private parties is governed by the contracts they agree to, containing the commercial commitments they see fit, as well as by the laws of their individual state when it is party to the international space treaties.

The challenges to compliance with space law become more evident in determining the 'launching state', the allocation of responsibility, and the allocation of liability in case of damage caused by a space object that cannot be identified in spite of the registration requirements – or of a change in ownership or lease of the space objects. Space industry markets being more trans-national than national would benefit from more regulatory harmonisation, and efforts to this effect are under way.[8]

Liability

The liability for damage caused by private actors is taken on by the state under international law and passed on to the former under the applicable national (space) laws. Clarifying the different aspects of potential liability in the contractual document governing their space activities and industrial relationship is fundamental in ascertaining the potential financial repercussions for the parties. For the investors, launch operators and part-manufacturers/subcontractors alike, the exposure to the whole spectrum of potential risks is daunting in an industry in which the lack of predictability itself could impede contractual relationships. Recognising this, national laws have

7 Brachet, G. 2008. *Long-term Sustainability of Space Activities*. [Online: UNIDIR]. Available at http://www.unidir.org/pdf/activites/pdf2-act363.pdf [accessed: 23 March 2010].

8 Smith, L.J. and Doldirina, C. 2010. 'Jurisdiction and Applicable Law in Cases of Damage from Space in Europe: The Advent of the Most Suitable Choice-Rome II', *Acta Astronautica*. [Online], 66 (2010), 239–44.

developed requirements that private operators need to fulfil in addition to those imposed by the specific research and launch contracts.[9]

The implementation of national space legislation establishes the legal framework within which private space activities take place.[10] The increased certainty is desirable for the private actors in the space industry: they can make informed decisions and take more calculated risks when investing in research and development. Equally, if not more importantly, it enables the state to implement mechanisms to shift the financial burden it would unduly shoulder and recoup costs from private entities. Shifting the financial burden to the private sector is a move which must be balanced against not hindering the industry. Hence, certain states have included ceiling amounts in their national space laws, enabling operators to work out their maximum financial liability in case of damage[11] and manage costs, including those of mandatory insurance policies.

Insurance and liability questions pose legitimate serious concerns to private participants. By definition, any third party subjected to damage from a space activity and seeking compensation from the participants would not be party to any of the binding contractual agreements in place. The private actors responsible for the damage caused would be facing actions under traditional tort rules. For the tort system to function, insurance coverage, from which a successful claimant can be paid, must be in place. To complicate matters further, the question of conflict of laws would be almost always unavoidable, given the transnational provision of services by operators. Adding to the legal uncertainty is the necessary determination of jurisdiction and choice of law and the recognition and enforcement of foreign judgments.

A welcome relevant development, although not designed for space activities specifically, is the Rome II Regulation.[12] Its purpose is to lay down a uniform code that EU Member States' courts must apply to determine, in situations involving a conflict of laws, the law governing non-contractual obligations (such as torts) between parties in civil and commercial matters. The Regulation applies to actions within the Member States, limiting the potential conflict between the national rules that could apply in cross-border claims. A similar alignment exercise could be envisaged by states, at least in reference to obligations arising in tort or from other non-contractual bases, among private space actors and third parties.

The French and US legislators have made the grant of licence or authorisation and state guarantee subject to third-party insurance cover. These requirements ensure the survival and viability of the space insurance market. While an entity looking for insurance may be able to shop around to obtain the coverage best suited to its needs, the prospect of having to cover the full extent of damages in the event of a space accident may not make business sense for an insurer, who could refuse to extend coverage to the sector. The result so far has been that legislation imposes the requirement of obtaining insurance for third-party liability to the 'maximum probable loss', or 'in accordance with the insurance market'.[13]

---

9 For example, Australia, Belgium, France, South Africa, the Netherlands, the UK, Ukraine the US have provisions related to insurance with either ceiling amounts specified or to be decided on a case-by-case basis.

10 Some national space legislations take recourse against private entities, sometimes only under certain conditions, for example if not properly authorised or if acting in contradiction to the licence.

11 Assuming there is no intentional wrongdoing.

12 Regulation (EC) No. 864/2007 of the European Parliament and of the Council on the law applicable to non-contractual obligations.

13 See for example, Sec 48 of the Australian Space Activities Act 1998.

Cross Waiver of Liability and Limitation Clauses

The cross-waiver is a common principle incorporated into the space industry's agreements, whereby the parties agree to an inter-party waiver of liability – between and among the customers, the (sub) contractors and the launch provider. In fact, amongst the national space laws, only the French and US laws include specific provisions related to cross-waiver arrangements,[14] while others provide for action either against the insurer or the responsible party. These contractual tools are a means to enable and promote business by the non-governmental sector in these high-investment/high-risk activities. Incorporating waivers of liability and limitation clause requirements in the specific national laws would increase harmonisation between the applicable legal frameworks, which would in turn lead to increased competition in the international space ventures market. Commercial operators are inclined to prefer legal frameworks that afford the most legal certainty and leave less for the courts to decide in the event of a dispute.

Probably one of the most referred-to working examples of the cross waiver of liability arrangement is the agreement applicable to inter-party damage on board the International Space Station (ISS).[15] Essentially, the activities being carried out by the numerous partners of the ISS needed a legal framework that could be relied upon to regulate matters of liability among the actors and not just between the participants and third parties. This arrangement ensured that the international endeavours would as far as possible be free from disputes[16] among the partners and, more importantly, preserve and foster the character of international cooperation.

While the example of the ISS is not the trigger for cross-waiver agreements in contracts in the space industry, it is a signal that such an arrangement can be adapted to the specificities and needs of private enterprise, when the issue of liability in space law refers essentially to damage to third parties. A cross-waiver of liability inclusion in a contract is not the ideal solution for private investors in any given activity. However, faced with the high investments and high risks inherent to launch, payload and operations, participants view the cross-waiver of liability as the next best arrangement in conducting business.

Limitation-of-liability clauses in space ventures represent an essential and attractive contractual instrument for private operators. States that have implemented national space laws have done so while taking into account the existing commercial practices. A working example is that of the Ariane Declaration, which specifies the ceiling amounts Arianespace must reimburse the French Government, if the latter is required to pay for claims for damages as a result of a launch from the Guiana Space Centre.[17] French national space legislation is one of the few providing for state guarantee beyond ceiling amounts, which can be transposed into contracts as a limitation of liability for the parties.

Faced with the possibility of unquantifiable claims for damages, insurance premiums can be astronomical and, therefore, unaffordable by some private space operators. Limitation clauses pave the way for private launch and satellite operators to secure insurance at affordable premiums for

---

14 See Articles 19 and 20 of the Loi no. 2008-518 du 3 juin 2008 relative aux opérations spatiales and 49 USC 70112 – Sec. 70112. Liability insurance and financial responsibility requirements.

15 Article 16 of the Intergovernmental Agreement (IGA). The IGA establishing the International Space Station cooperative framework, has been signed by 14 governments: the United States of America, Canada, Japan, the Russian Federation, and 10 Member States of the European Space Agency (Belgium, Denmark, France, Germany, Italy, the Netherlands, Norway, Spain, Sweden and Switzerland).

16 With the exception of intellectual property rights protection and actions in the remit of criminal law.

17 The Guiana Space Centre (GSC) being French territory.

their space activities, since most risks remain identifiable.[18] The formalisation of these arrangements in a couple of the major space faring states reinforces their legitimacy in contracts among private parties. Thus, national space legislation provides the means to incorporate clauses that will prove acceptable and economically sound to those affected. The possible open question is what would happen in the absence of legislative backing for cross-waiver liability arrangements? The most probable scenario is that contractual partners would include these in their space activities-related contracts, without the reassurance that the clause cannot be invalidated in a dispute.

Jurisdiction

Under Art. VIII OST, the State of Registry retains jurisdiction and control over an object while it is in outer space. 'Jurisdiction and control' means the legislation and enforcement of laws and rules in relation to the object. Thus, it defines the rights and powers of the State of Registry towards an object registered in its national registry.[19]

Jurisdiction and control over an object in outer space applies, despite outer space being an international territory, meaning a territory not subject to national appropriation.[20] The concept of, on the one hand, 'jurisdiction and control' over an object in outer space and the concept, on the other hand, of 'non-appropriation' of outer space do not contradict each other. The State of Registry can exercise its sovereignty over such object, without appropriating outer space.[21]

'Jurisdiction and control' therefore defines the law applicable to space objects as well as the rules applicable to the supervision of compliance with such laws.[22] It follows that the national laws of the State of Registry apply to such space objects.[23] This concerns, for example, intellectual property rights laws, an area of definite interest during a space mission. Consequently, private operators of, for instance, a satellite may have an interest that a certain jurisdiction applies to the satellite while in outer space. There is a certain margin to influence which state becomes the State of Registry. The State of Registry, which retains such jurisdiction and control, is the state in whose registry the object is carried, see Art. I (c) REG. Only a launching state can register an object in its national registry, see Art. II (1).This means that only a launching state can become the State of Registry – and retain jurisdiction and control over the object.[24]

A launching state is a state that launched the object, procured the launching of the object, or from whose territory or facility the object is launched, see both Art. VII OST and Art. I (a) REG. Considering the definition of the term 'launching state' it is obvious that for a single object several states can be launching states: for instance, for a Swedish state-owned satellite launched from French Guiana, Sweden as well as France are launching states. But only one state can be the State

18 Except for those activities for which data is not readily available due to dual-use nature and sensitive research and development.

19 Bittlinger, H. 1988. *Hoheitsgewalt und Kontrolle im Weltraum*. Cologne: Heymanns.

20 Meaning outer space is not subject to national appropriation by claim of sovereignty etc., cf. Art. II OST.

21 Schmidt-Tedd, B. and Mick, S. 2009. Art. VIII, in *Commentary on Space Law*, edited by S. Hobe, B. Schmidt-Tedd, K-U Schrogl. Cologne: Heymanns, 44; Vereshchetin, V.S. 1981. 'International Space Law and Domestic Law: Problem of Interrelations', *Journal of Space Law*, 9 (1 and 2), 32.

22 Schmidt-Tedd, B. and Mick, S. 2009. Art. VIII, in *Commentary on Space Law*, 48.

23 Schmidt-Tedd, B. and Mick, S. 2009. Art. VIII, in *Commentary on Space Law*, 59.

24 Mick, S. 2007. *Registrierungskonvention und Registrierungspraxis*. Cologne: Heymanns, 16 et seq.

of Registry – and retain jurisdiction and control. In cases where there are two or more launching states, they shall jointly determine which one of them shall register the object, see Art. II (2) REG.[25]

As a result, in order to influence which state's jurisdiction applies to a space object, a private operator can first influence which state becomes a launching state, specifically by determining the state from whose territory or facility the object is launched. Secondly, the private operator may want to ensure that the launching states conclude an agreement, stipulating which one of them enters the object in its national registry. Thirdly (if the launching states are in favour of such agreement), the private operator may also try to impose its view on which state would be best to exercise jurisdiction and control, convincing the launching states to stipulate accordingly.

Licensing

To complete the picture, the issue of licensing has to be mentioned. Licensing in the context of the present chapter means any licence, approval or authorisation issued by the competent authority to authorise an activity undertaken in outer space. International cooperation projects, multinational industries or start-ups at a very early stage may have the possibility to influence which national legislation will apply to such licensing.

Licensing requirements, established in various national legislations, are based upon Art. VI OST. According to this article, contracting states have to authorise and continuously supervise national activities of non-governmental entities in outer space. About a dozen states have transposed this international obligation into proper national space legislation.[26] Other states may authorise national activities in accordance with other, more general procedures, or based upon individual measures.

In order to understand the sphere of personal application of such national legislation, the international obligation of states should be briefly described. States are responsible to authorise and continuously supervise national activities of non-governmental entities in outer space for which one of them is the appropriate state to bear such responsibility. Unanimously, all scholars are of the view that a state is the appropriate state to bear such responsibility, if this state has the jurisdiction over such activity. However, it is contested under which circumstances a state has jurisdiction

---

25 Although the launching states have to agree which of them shall register the object – and thus retain jurisdiction and control – they can conclude appropriate agreements on jurisdiction and control over the object. However, these agreements only affect the launching states.

26 USA, 49 USC 701 Commercial Space Launch Activities, CFR 14 III 400 Commercial Space Transportation, Land Remote Sensing Policy Act, Communications Act, Commercial Space Launch Act, etcetera; Norway, Act on Launching Objects from Norwegian Territory etc. into Outer Space, 1969; Sweden, Act on Space Activities, 1982, Decree on Space Activities, 1982; UK, Outer Space Act, 1986; South Africa, Space Affairs Act, 1993 as amended; Russian Federation, Law about Space Activity, 1996 as amended, Statute No. 403 Licensing Space Operations, 2006; Ukraine, Ordinance on Space Activity, 1996 as amended, Decree No. 798 on Licensing Private Entities undertaking Space Activities; Australia, Space Activities Act, 1998 as amended, Space Activities Regulations, 2001; Hong Kong, Outer Space Ordinance, 1999; Brazil, Administrative Edict No. 27, 2001; Belgium, Law on the activities of launching, flight operations or guidance of space objects, 2005, Royal Decree implementing the Law of launching … – draft; South Korea, Space Exploration Promotion Act, 2005; the Netherlands, Rules Concerning Space Activities and the Establishment of a Registry of Space Objects, 2006; France, Bill Nr. 2008-518 relating to space operations, 2008. In addition part wise regulations on aspects of authorisation in Canada, on registration in Argentina and Spain, as well as on aspects of liability in Italy.

over an activity.[27] Following the majority of scholars, a state has jurisdiction over an activity in outer space, if the activity is either undertaken from the territory or undertaken by a national of such state.[28] Some scholars add that a state also has jurisdiction over an activity if such activity is undertaken from an object registered within the registries of such state (for example a launch vehicle launched from a platform in the high seas, if the platform is registered in such state). In line with this majority view, all states have defined the applicability of their respective national legislation. With minor differences,[29] such national legislation typically applies to activities undertaken from the territory or by nationals of the respective state. In case of legal persons, the nationality is sometimes specified, for example, by way of holding the controlling interests (see for example US 14 CFR 401.5 and Sweden's *Regeringens* Proposition 1981/82:226, p. 8 et seq.).

As a consequence of falling within the sphere of certain national laws, the national licensing requirements and procedures apply. Although all national laws transpose the international obligations of states and, therefore, are comparable, such laws differ when it comes to details. This is particularly true for the licensing procedures. The duration of issuing a licence varies from a few weeks to six months or longer. Some states issue licences for free while others impose licensing fees. Some states require the operator to hold third-party liability insurance, other states do not. The measures established to supervise activities differ a lot, including fines and penalties for not complying with the terms of the licence. Finally, some (but not all) states impose on the licence holder the obligation to apply for approval of a transfer of ownership, if the licence holder decides to sell the space object – with which the activity in outer space is undertaken – to another owner.[30]

In addition, if the responsible state is at the same time a launching state,[31] this state will also impose requirements aimed at avoiding the occurrence of any damage for which this state can (also) be held liable. Some states will also take recourse for any damage they had to pay as a liable launching state: some of them opt for full recourse, while others limit the recourse to a certain amount, typically the amount that is (compulsorily) insured for by the licence holder. Finally, the requirements under which such state takes recourse differ.[32]

As a consequence, it is not only important to know which national legislation applies to a certain activity in outer space, but it is also important to use all possible means to influence which legislation is applicable, for example by determining where a satellite is launched into orbit or

27 Gerhard, M. 2009. Art. VI, in *Commentary on Space Law*, edited by S. Hobe, B. Schmidt-Tedd, K-U Schrogl. Cologne: Heymanns, 40 et seq.; Gerhard, M. 2002a. *National Weltraumgesetzgebung – Völkerrechtliche Voraussetzungen und Handlungserfordernisse*. Cologne: Heymanns, 45 et seq.

28 It is necessary to differentiate between on the one hand the jurisdiction over an activity in outer space, as treated here, and on the other hand jurisdiction and control over a space object, as treated in the precedent chapter. A minority view only is of the view that the state which is appropriate to exercise its responsibility over an activity in terms of Art. VI OST is the State of Registry, having the jurisdiction and control over the space object in terms of Art. VIII OST.

29 Gerhard, M., 2009. Art. VI, in *Commentary on Space Law*, 47.

30 Gerhard, M., 2009. Art. VI, in *Commentary on Space Law*, 87; Gerhard, M. 2002b. 'Transfer of Operation and Control with Respect to Space Objects: Problems of Responsibility and Liability of States', *Zeitschrift für Luft- und Weltraumrecht*, 51, 571 et seq.

31 A launching state is a state that has launched the object – with which the activity in outer space is undertaken – into outer space, that procured the launch or from whose territory or facility the object was launched.

32 Gerhard, M. 2002a. *National Weltraumgesetzgebung*, 90 et seq.; Gerhard, M. 2005. 'National Space Legislation: Perspectives for Regulating Private Space Activities', in *Current Problems and Perspectives for future Regulation*, edited by M. Benkoe and K-U. Schrogl. Utrecht: Eleven International, 75 et seq.

where the principal place of business of the entity being responsible for undertaking the activity (which is to operate and control, for example, the satellite) is established.

Conclusion

Under general international law, a state is not internationally responsible for the activities of its nationals, unless it endorses the said activities. International space law, however, introduces both implicitly and explicitly that the state party to the agreement endorses international responsibility for space endeavours undertaken within its jurisdiction. In addition, it is the launching state that will be held liable, and it is up to the harmed state to present its claim. However, the private entity will be – in addition – responsible and liable under the applicable national law, depending upon the national rules and regulations and space legislation, if any. Private participants in the space sector can find their contractual agreements and activities subjected to a law regime different to their own, or to the one they expected, by virtue of the nationality of their satellite operators or launch providers, giving rise to added uncertainty in the allocation of risks and the effects of contractual limitation or exclusion of liability – and the prospect of unlimited liability does not enable sound financial risk management.

Faced with this commercial reality, and backed by the absence of aligned elements such as registration, licensing, financial liability caps or state guarantee in existing national space legislation, private actors can attempt to shop for a preferred jurisdiction. This 'alternative' method of liability risk management would not foster the global private industry, but rather contain the activities to a selected few. Measures that have developed as a matter of commercial and industry practice, such as contractual cross-waivers of liability, now a common feature of launch agreements, must be adopted at the national level. In addition, internationally aligned mechanisms in national space legislation for state recourse to indemnification, for instance, through requirements for operators to obtain liability insurance, could further clarify the liability question for the private industry.

List of References

Aust, A. 2007. *Modern Treaty Law and Practice*, 2nd ed. Cambridge: Cambridge University Press.

Bittlinger, H. 1988. *Hoheitsgewalt und Kontrolle im Weltraum*. Cologne: Heymanns.

Brachet, G. 2008. *Long-term Sustainability of Space Activities*. [Online: UNIDIR]. Available at http://www.unidir.org/pdf/activites/pdf2-act363.pdf [accessed: 23 March 2010].

Couston, M. 1994. *Droit spatial économique: régimes applicables à l'exploitation de l'espace*. Courtenay: Sides.

Gerhard, M. 2002a. *National Weltraumgesetzgebung – Völkerrechtliche Voraussetzungen und Handlungserfordernisse*. Cologne: Heymanns.

Gerhard, M. 2002b. 'Transfer of Operation and Control with Respect to Space Objects: Problems of Responsibility and Liability of States', *Zeitschrift für Luft- und Weltraumrecht*, 51, 571 et seq.

Gerhard, M. 2004. 'The State of the Art and Recent Development of National Space Legislation', in *Towards a Harmonised Approach for National Space Legislation in Europe: Proceedings of the Project 2001 Plus Workshop*, edited by S. Hobe, B. Schmidt-Tedd, K-U. Schrogl. Cologne: DLR.

Gerhard, M. 2005. 'National Space Legislation: Perspectives for Regulating Private Space Activities', in *Current Problems and Perspectives for future Regulation*, edited by M. Benkoe and K-U. Schrogl. Utrecht: Eleven International, 75 et seq.

Gerhard, M. 2009. Art. VI, in *Commentary on Space Law*, edited by S. Hobe, B. Schmidt-Tedd, K-U Schrogl. Cologne: Heymanns.

Gerhard, M. and Schrogl, K-U. 2002. 'Report of the "Project 2001" Working Group on National Space Legislation', in *Project 2001: Legal Framework for the Commercial Use of Outer Space*, edited by Karl-Heinz Böckstiegel. Cologne: Heymanns, 529, 530.

Kerrest, A. and Smith, L.J. 2009. Art. VII, in *Commentary on Space Law*, edited by S. Hobe, B. Schmidt-Tedd, K-U. Schrogl. Cologne: Heymanns.

Mick, S. 2007. *Registrierungskonvention und Registrierungspraxis*. Cologne: Heymanns.

Schmidt-Tedd, B. and Mick, S. 2009. Art. VIII, in *Commentary on Space Law*, edited by S. Hobe, B. Schmidt-Tedd, K-U Schrogl. Cologne: Heymanns.

Smith, L.J. and Doldirina, C. 2010. 'Jurisdiction and Applicable Law in Cases of Damage from Space in Europe: The Advent of the Most Suitable Choice-Rome II', *Acta Astronautica*. [Online], 66 (2010), 239–44.

Vereshchetin, V.S. 1981. 'International Space Law and Domestic Law: Problem of Interrelations', *Journal of Space Law*, 9 (1 and 2), 31 et seq.

Chapter 7
The Legal Framework for EU Activities in the Space Sector, with a Particular Focus on GMES*

Leopold Mantl and Sylvia Kainz-Huber

Introduction

The purpose of this chapter is to provide an analysis of the different legal and contractual instruments used to implement European Union (EU) activities in the space sector, starting from an overview of the overall legal framework for the European Space Policy.

In the last decades, Europe has become a major space power. It contributes to the International Space Station (ISS), has developed world-class launchers and is a leader in space applications. Initially, these activities were carried out on a national level, or through intergovernmental organisations, including the European Space Agency (ESA) and the European Organisation for the Exploitation of Meteorological Satellites (EUMETSAT). From the late 1980s, the EU[1] started playing an increasingly active role in the European space sector and has not only become a major contributor to ESA programmes, but also fully finances the further implementation of the European satellite navigation programmes (EGNOS and Galileo). The 7th Framework Programme for research, technological development and demonstration activities (FP7) contains for the first time a theme dedicated to space, marking the increasing importance the EU attaches to playing an independent role in space.

The FP7 space theme includes space-based applications built for the benefit of European citizens, with a focus on the Global Monitoring for Environment and Security (GMES) initiative, exploration of space, space research and space technology development. Additionally, support for earth observation activities within the framework of GEOSS, and for Galileo and EGNOS, is covered by the environment and transport themes within FP7. With the entry into force of the Lisbon Treaty, the competence of the EU to carry out space activities is now explicitly provided.

In addition to examining the different legal and contractual instruments used to implement EU activities, the flagship programme GMES will be analysed. Finally, a brief overview concerning the situation after the entry into force of the Lisbon Treaty, and the preparation of a European space programme will be given. The chapter concentrates on areas in which the EU carries out its own programmes, rather than the manifold horizontal EU activities of a regulatory nature (including for example competition policy, standardisation, IPR policy, electronic communications policy and export control).

---

* The chapter reflects exclusively the personal opinion of the authors.

1 For the purpose of this chapter, the term EU (see Article 1 of the EU Treaty) also encompasses legal persons under previous Treaties, including the European Economic Community and the European Community.

Legal Framework for the EU Space Policy

Before the entry into force of the Lisbon Treaty on 1 December 2009, the EC Treaty did not contain an explicit reference to outer space. This is one of the reasons why the EU did not play a significant role in the space sector before the 1980s. As outlined in its first Communication relating to space,[2] the entry into force of the Single European Act on 1 July 1987 constituted a pivotal point for two reasons.

First, the EU acquired far reaching competences in the field of research and development (R&D). Secondly, the preparation for the completion of the internal market in 1992 had a major impact on many industries, including the space industry. The 1988 Communication already outlined the main contributions the EU could make in the space sector within this framework, namely (i) providing political leadership and democratic legitimacy, (ii) creating a favourable regulatory environment for space activities in Europe, and (iii) financing programme activities, in particular with a view to ensuring the exploitation of space applications following their development.

To this end, the European Commission commenced financing projects in the field of earth observation.[3] Additionally, the EU contributed to the launch of EGNOS, then Galileo and GMES. It was not problematic to find a legal basis for these activities, and the bases included Article 166 of the EC Treaty[4] (research and technological development), Article 156 of the EC Treaty[5] (trans-European networks) and Article 308 of the EC Treaty.[6]

In parallel, the EU intensified work on an overarching European Space Policy, together with the European Space Agency.[7] Key milestones in this regard include[8] the Council Resolution on a European space strategy of 16 November 2000,[9] the 2003 White Paper of the European Commission,[10] and the Resolution of 21 May 2007 on the European Space Policy.[11] Further, it was necessary to clarify the relationship with ESA.[12] A framework agreement between the European Community and the European Space Agency[13] (the 'Framework Agreement') was concluded in 2003 and entered into force in 2004. It is based on a model of cooperation between the institutions

2 Commission Communication 'The Community and Space: A Coherent Approach', COM(88) 417 final of 26 July 1988 (the '1988 Communication').

3 See Brachet, G. 2004. 'From Initial Ideas to a European Plan: GMES as an Exemplar of European Space Strategy', *Space Policy*, 20 (1), 8.

4 Article 182 TFEU.

5 Article 172 TFEU.

6 Article 352 TFEU.

7 A detailed overview of early documents on the European space policy (up to the White Paper of 11 November 2003) can be found in Van de Wouwer, J.L. and Lambert, F. 2008. *European Trajectories in Space Law*. Brussels: Bruylant, 104–26.

8 A more complete list of documents can be found at http://ec.europa.eu/enterprise/policies/space/documents/esp-background_en.htm [accessed 30 April 2011] and http://www.espi.or.at/index.php?option=com_content&task=view&id=261&Itemid=45 [accessed 16 June 2011].

9 Resolution C 371/2 of 16 November 2000.

10 White Paper 'Space: A New European Frontier for an Expanding Union: An Action Plan for Implementing the European Space Policy', COM (2003) 673 of 11 November 2003.

11 See Council Resolution 2007/C 136/01 (the 'Resolution on the European Space Policy'), adopted at the 4th Space Council meeting.

12 For more details concerning the ESA-EU relationship, see Chapter 3.

13 See OJ L 261 of 6 August 2004, 64.

and introduces an institutional novelty, the Space Council.[14] The Lisbon Treaty has introduced an explicit space competence for the EU, which will be discussed in the last section of this chapter. The legal and contractual boundary conditions for existing programmes will be analysed in more detail in the following sections.

Legal and Financial Instruments for the Implementation of EU Space Activities

Before describing the specific programmes and initiatives of the EU in the space sector, it is useful to give an overview of some of the basic legal instruments of relevance. This section focuses on binding legal acts, as opposed to non-binding documents, including Resolutions of the Council and the European Parliament. The latter are very important to define the political framework for a space activity, but cannot as such form the basis for budget implementation in the space sector.

EU Financial Regulation

The basic rules for the implementation of the EU budget are defined in the EU Financial Regulation[15] and, for the Commission, in the implementing rules.[16] Part 1 chapter 2 of Title IV (methods of implementation) is of particular relevance in this context. According to Article 53 of the EU Financial Regulation, the Commission implements the EU budget either on a centralised basis, by shared[17] or decentralised[18] management, or by joint management with other international organisations.[19] Centralised management is either performed directly by Commission departments, or indirectly through the bodies listed in Article 54 (2) of the EU Financial Regulation, including agencies, and national and international public sector bodies.[20]

The EU Financial Regulation also contains rules for procurement[21] and grants.[22] Procurement covers public contracts, which are defined as:

14 The Space Council is a joint and concomitant meeting of the Council of the EU and the ESA Council meeting at ministerial level, in line with Article 8 of the Framework Agreement.

15 Council Regulation 1605/2002 of 25 June 2002 on the Financial Regulation applicable to the general budget of the European Communities, OJ L 248 of 16 September 2002, 1, as amended (the 'EU Financial Regulation'). The Financial Regulation is currently being revised.

16 Commission Regulation 2342/2002 of 23 December 2002 laying down detailed rules for the implementation of Council Regulation 1605/2002 on the Financial Regulation applicable to the general budget of the European Communities, OJ L 357 of 31 December 2002, 1, as amended (the 'Implementing Rules').

17 This means that budget implementation tasks are delegated to Member States in accordance with Article 53b of the EU Financial Regulation.

18 Decentralised management means that budget implementation tasks are delegated to third countries in accordance with Article 53c of the EU Financial Regulation.

19 See Article 53d of the EU Financial Regulation, which is the legal basis for the GMES agreement concluded between ESA and the EU.

20 The agreement dealing with the delegation of budget implementation tasks to ESA for the Galileo deployment phase is based on Article 54.

21 A more detailed description of EU procurement rules can be found in Chapter 16.

22 See Titles V and VI of Part I of the EU Financial Regulation.

> contracts for pecuniary interest … in order to obtain, against payment of a price paid in whole or in part from the budget, the supply of movable or immovable assets, the execution of works or the provision of services.[23]

Conversely,

> [g]rants are direct financial contributions, by way of donation, from the budget in order to finance: (a) either an action intended to help achieve an objective forming part of a European Union policy; (b) or the functioning of a body which pursues an aim of general European interest or has the objective of forming part of a European Union policy.[24]

A detailed description of grant and procurement rules under the EU Financial Regulation and the different management modes is beyond the scope of this chapter. Nevertheless, some general remarks of relevance for the space sector can be made.

First, it is important to note that the Framework Agreement does not modify the financial, accounting and procurement rules of ESA and the EU.[25] For this reason, thus far the application of these rules to jointly financed programmes was decided on a case-by-case basis. In practice, up to 2008, all major EU investments took the form of the participation by the European Community in an optional programme of ESA.[26] This participation was based on diverse legal instruments, including a series of grant agreements in the case of EGNOS, the channelling of EU funds through a joint undertaking set up under Article 171 of the Treaty (now Article 187 TFEU)[27] for Galileo and the conclusion of a delegation agreement under Article 53d of the EU Financial Regulation for GMES. With the end of the development phases of Galileo and GMES, the situation is now changing. In particular, the financial envelopes under Regulation 683/2008[28] are implemented by ESA outside the framework of an optional programme in accordance with Article 5.1(a) of the Framework Agreement.

This leads to a second observation. As shown above, the framework for EU involvement in navigation and earth observation programmes depended on the programme phases in question, including design, development and exploitation (system operation and service provision). This means that, up to now, for each phase specific rules applied. In the case of Galileo, these included the participation in an ESA optional programme for design and development and ESA management of EU funds according to EU rules for the deployment phase. The framework for the exploitation

23 See Article 88 of the EU Financial Regulation.

24 See Article 108 of the EU Financial Regulation.

25 According to Article 5.3 of the Framework Agreement, 'Any financial contribution made by one Party in accordance with a specific arrangement shall be governed by the financial provisions applicable to that Party.'

26 See Article 5.1.(b) of the Framework Agreement. For EGNOS, the relevant ESA programme was the ARTES-9 programme, for Galileo the GalileoSat programme and for GMES the GMES Space Component programme. Research projects of a smaller scale carried out under the EU Framework Programmes were and are managed outside ESA optional programmes.

27 See Council Regulation 876/2002 of 21 May 2002 setting up the Galileo Joint Undertaking, L 138 of 28 May 2002, 1, as amended (the 'GJU Regulation').

28 Regulation 683/2008 of the European Parliament and of the Council of 9 July 2008 on the further implementation of the European satellite navigation programmes (EGNOS and Galileo), OJ L 196 of 24 July 2008, 1 (the 'GNSS Regulation').

phase remains to be determined.[29] It has not been possible yet to define the legal and financial framework for the EU space programmes, from system design to the dismantling of the relevant installations, from the outset. The main reason for this is that financial planning beyond the multi-annual financial frameworks (MFF)[30] of the EU is difficult.

Thirdly, it is interesting to note that in the past decisions on the financing of EU space activities were taken independently from a specific governance framework defined in legislative acts. For example, at the moment of the adoption of GJU Regulation in 2002 and the Regulation on the management structures of Galileo and EGNOS[31] in 2004, significant funds from the Trans-European Networks (TEN-T) and the research framework programmes had already been committed for Galileo and EGNOS. In the case of GMES, the decision on FP7[32] provided for significant funding of the second EU flagship programme, whereas no specific governance framework was in place.

Legally speaking, this is not problematic. In the absence of a specific framework, the general rules governing, for example, research or TEN-T budgets, and the EU Financial Regulation, apply. Nevertheless, in the Communication 'Progressing Galileo: Re-profiling the European GNSS Programmes',[33] the Commission underlined that the dissociation of financing and governance framework is not always an optimal solution.

In this context, it is clear that the governance framework established for a specific EU space activity needs to take into consideration the boundaries of Article 57 of the EU Financial Regulation. In particular, the Commission cannot entrust tasks to private sector entities where the exercise of public authority or the use of discretionary powers of judgment is involved.

Finally, it should be underlined that Part 2 of the EU Financial Regulation (special provisions) does not contain specific rules concerning the space sector. Special provisions currently only exist for certain funds (including the European Agricultural Guarantee Fund and Structural Funds), research, external action, European offices and administrative appropriations. Nevertheless, it is possible to define 'sector-specific' financial rules in Basic Acts which complement the EU Financial Regulation. Additionally, it is possible to define 'sector-specific' rules in Basic Acts[34] which complement the EU Financial Regulation. Examples include the FP7 Rules of Participation,[35]

29 The Commission will make proposals concerning the exploitation phase, in line with Article 4.3 of the GNSS Regulation.

30 These are defined in Interinstitutional Agreement between the European Parliament, the Council and the Commission. The current MFF is contained in the Interinstitutional Agreement on budgetary discipline and sound financial management of 17 May 2006, OJ C 139 of 14 June 2006, 1, as amended. The last two MFF had a duration of seven years, but this duration is not obligatory. According to Article 312 TFEU, the MFF will be adopted as a Regulation.

31 See Council Regulation 1321/2004 on the establishment of structures for the management of the European satellite radio-navigation programmes, OJ L 246 of 20 July 2004, 1, as amended. Regulation 1321/2004 has been replaced by Regulation 912/2010 of 22 September 2010, OJ L 276 of 20 October 2010, 11.

32 See the Decision 1982/2006/EC of the European Parliament and of the Council of 18 December 2006 concerning the Seventh Framework Programme of the European Community for research, technological development and demonstration activities (2007–2013), OJ L 412 of 30 December 2006, 1 (the 'FP7 Decision').

33 COM(2007) 534 final of 19 September 2007, 11.

34 According to Article 49(1) of the EU Financial Regulation, a Basic Act 'is an act adopted by the legislative authority and may take the form of a regulation, a directive, a decision within the meaning of Article 249 of the EC Treaty or a decision *sui generis*'. The adoption of a Basic Act is normally a precondition for the use of appropriations entered in the EU budget.

35 Regulation 1906/2006 of the European Parliament and of the Council of 18 December 2006 laying down the rules for the participation of undertakings, research centres and universities in actions under the

TEN-T rules and the specific procurement rules defined in the GNSS Regulation. Some of these examples are discussed in the following sections.

The EU Research Framework Programmes

As set out in section 2, the reinforcement of the research competence of the EU in the Single European Act was an important factor for the EU involvement in space. In the absence of a specific legal base for space in the treaties, many of the space activities of the EU were financed through EU research framework programmes, including the Fifth Framework Programme (FP5),[36] the Sixth Framework Programme (FP6)[37] and the Seventh Framework Programme (FP7).[38] These framework programmes are implemented through specific programmes, which lay down objectives and rules for participation.[39] The technical content of the different areas covered by the specific programmes is defined in work programmes, adopted by the Commission under a comitology procedure.[40] Additionally, the EU adopted a regulation on horizontal rules for participation,[41] including provisions on the composition of research consortia, the evaluation and selection of proposals and the award of grants, consortium agreements, the EU financial contribution, and intellectual property rights (IPR). One important principle of the FP7 IPR rules is that results, including information, generated by an indirect action,[42] are normally owned by the participant

Seventh Framework Programme and for the dissemination of research results (2007–2013), OJ L 391 of 30 December 2006, 1, (hereinafter the 'FP7 Rules of participation').

36 See the Decision 182/1999/EC of the European Parliament and of the Council of 22 December 1998 concerning the fifth framework programme of the European Community for research, technological development and demonstration activities (1998–2002), OJ L 26 of 1 February 1999, 1.

37 See the Decision 1513/2002/EC of the European Parliament and of the Council of 27 June 2002 concerning the sixth framework programme of the European Community for research, technological development and demonstration activities, contributing to the creation of the European Research Area and to innovation (2002–2006), OJ L 232 of 29 August 2002, 1.

38 See the Decision 1982/2006/EC of the European Parliament and of the Council of 18 December 2006 concerning the Seventh Framework Programme of the European Community for research, technological development and demonstration activities (2007–2013), OJ L 412 of 30 December 2006, 1 (the 'FP7 Decision').

39 See Article 3 of the FP7 Decision.

40 See for example Article 7.2 of the Council Decision 2006/971/EC of 19 December 2006 concerning the specific programme 'Cooperation' implementing the Seventh Framework Programme of the European Community for research, technological development and demonstration activities (2007–2013), OJ L 54 of 22 February 2007, 30 (the 'Decision on the specific programme "cooperation"'). Comitology means that the Commission is assisted by a committee of Member States when adopting implementing measures. Procedural details are defined in Council Decision 1999/468/EC of 28 June 1999 laying down the procedures for the exercise of implementing powers conferred on the Commission, OJ L 184, 17 July 1999, 23 (the 'comitology decision'), which was amended in 2006 through Council Decision 2006/512/EC of 17 July 2006, OJ L 200, 22 July 2006, 11. These comitology rules have been replaced following the entry of the Lisbon Treaty, which contains new rules on delegated acts and implementing acts in Articles 290 and 291, respectively.

41 The 'FP7 Rules of participation'.

42 Indirect actions are actions other than those carried out directly by the Joint Research Centre of the Commission ('direct actions', see Annex III in fine of the FP7 Decision).

and not by the Commission.[43] Finally, the Commission adopted a number of additional documents, including IPR guidelines and other guidance documents.[44]

The bulk of space activities outside the GNSS programmes is financed under the 'space theme' in the specific programme 'co-operation' in FP7, with a budget of EUR 1,430 million.[45] According to the work programme for the space theme,[46] around 53 per cent of this budget will be used for space infrastructure development and access to third-party data. The rest is earmarked in particular for GMES service projects, satellite communications, space surveillance technologies, space exploration, and space science and technology.[47] It should be underlined that some space activities are covered by other areas of FP7, including earth observation[48] and GNSS.[49]

Two legal aspects merit a specific discussion in this context. In the first place, the FP7 rules for participation are not meant to replace, but to complement, the EU Financial Regulation. This is made clear in recital 16 and Article 1 second paragraph of the FP7 Rules for Participation. This means, in particular, that the Commission may use legal instruments not referred to in the FP7 rules for participation, including the delegation of budget implementation tasks under Articles 53d and 54 of the EU Financial Regulation. The delegation agreement concerning GMES is a case in point. In practice, however, grant agreements remain the most important instrument for implementation of the FP7 budget, and most of the guidance documents concern grant rules.

Secondly, the EU contributions to a joint undertaking or any other structure set up pursuant to Article 171 of the Treaty[50] do not fall within the scope of the FP7 rules for participation.[51] A comparable rule was also contained in the FP 6 rules for participation.[52] On this basis, the Galileo Joint Undertaking set up under the GJU Regulation could adopt its own financing and procurement rules in a relatively flexible way. It is interesting to note, however, that currently neither of the two major space programmes of the EU is managed as a joint technology initiative,[53] although this possibility was explicitly foreseen for GMES.[54]

---

43 See Article 39.1 of the FP7 Rules for participation.

44 These are available at the website of the Commission at http://cordis.europa.eu/fp7/find-doc_en.html [accessed: 4 June 2010].

45 See Annex II of the FP7 Decision. Administrative expenditures of the Commission must not exceed 6 per cent according to Article 3 of the Decision on the specific programme 'co-operation'.

46 Contained in Commission decision C(2010) 4900 of 19 July 2010.

47 See section I.9 of Annex I of the FP7 Decision.

48 See section I.6 of Annex I of the FP7 Decision (environment, including climate change).

49 See section I.7 of Annex I of the FP7 Decision (transport, including aeronautics).

50 Now Article 187.

51 See recital 26 of the FP7 rules for participation.

52 See Regulation 2321/2002 of the European Parliament and of the Council of 16 December 2002 concerning the rules for the participation of undertakings, research centres and universities in, and for the dissemination of research results for, the implementation of the European Community Sixth Framework Programme (2002–2006), OJ L 355 of 30 December 2002, 23.

53 Joint technology initiatives are defined in section I of Annex I of the FP7 Decision. In the case of Galileo, the tasks of the GJU were taken over either by the GNSS Supervisory Authority, or by the Commission itself. For GMES, it was decided to conclude an agreement with ESA under Article 53d of the EU Financial Regulation, instead of setting up a joint undertaking.

54 See Annex IV of the Decision on the specific programme 'co-operation'.

Specific Basic Acts

The legal framework for EU space activities may also be defined in legislative acts that are adopted specifically for a given space initiative or programme. The first legislative acts of this kind were the GJU Regulation, and then the Regulation 1321/2004,[55] which contained a governance framework for budgets that were based on other legal acts. The GNSS Regulation is the first piece of secondary EU legislation that not only contains governance rules, but also constitutes a basic act for significant budget appropriations. The GNSS Regulation, and, in particular, its chapter III (public governance of the programme) do not only complement the EU Financial Regulation, but in some cases also derogate from it, in particular regarding the '6 + 2 rule' defined in Article 17(3)(c) of the GNSS Regulation.

A second basic act dedicated to a space initiative was adopted at the end of 2010, namely the proposal for a Regulation on the European earth observation programme (GMES) and its initial operations (2011–13).[56] During the legislative procedure, the legal basis was changed from Article 173 TFEU (ex Article 157 TEC) to Article 189 TFEU. This means that the GMES Regulation is the first legal act adopted on the basis of the new space competence of the EU.

An overview of the legal and contractual framework for GMES is given in the following section.

European Earth Monitoring Programme (GMES)

Programme Overview

Global Monitoring for Environment and Security (GMES) is an earth monitoring initiative led by the EU. Together with the Galileo satellite navigation programme, GMES constitutes the second flagship space programme of the EU. Earth monitoring consists of the collection of information about the earth's physical, chemical and biological systems, or, more generally, the monitoring of the natural environment. GMES is based on both space-based (for example satellites) and non-space-based facilities, including airborne, seaborne and ground-based installations (such installations are generally referred to as 'in situ infrastructure'). Data collected through satellites and in situ infrastructure is processed to enable the provision of GMES services. This will allow, for example, a more efficient management of natural resources and biodiversity, monitoring of the state of the oceans and the chemical composition of our atmosphere – important factors for climate change – a more efficient response to natural and man-made disasters, and more effective border surveillance.[57]

---

55 See footnote 31.

56 See the Regulation 911/2010 of 22 September 2010 on the European Earth monitoring programme (GMES) and its initial operations, OJ L 276 of 20 October 2010, 1, hereinafter referred to as the 'GMES Regulation'.

57 See the Commission Staff Working Document accompanying the Proposal for a Regulation of the European Parliament and the Council on the European Earth observation programme (GMES) and its initial operations (2011–2013), Impact Assessment and Ex Ante Evaluation, SEC(2009)639 of 20 May 2009 (the '2009 GMES Impact Assessment'), 5. More detailed information on GMES can be found at http://ec.europa.eu/gmes.

Earth observation activities have been carried out on a national level for several decades.[58] At the end of the last millennium Europe possessed some of the best experimental earth observation satellites worldwide, operational[59] meteorological satellites managed by EUMETSAT and operational imaging missions on a national level (both in the civil and military sector). Nevertheless, at the European level, no coherent framework for the exploitation of environmental satellites and the provision of operational Earth monitoring services existed. Such an operational and user-driven framework is essential for the EU to obtain sufficient information on the state of the environment, climate change and security issues. GMES was created to respond to this need.[60]

It is possible to determine different stages of GMES, on the basis of the legal and financial framework, namely: (i) pre-operational activities lasting up to the end of 2013, financed by the EU through FP5, FP6 and FP7, and ESA, (ii) GMES initial operations (2011–13), financed mainly on the basis of the regulation proposed by the Commission on 20 May 2009, and (iii) the fully-fledged exploitation of GMES post-2013, which will continue to be accompanied by research activities.[61] The legal basis for the exploitation phase of the GMES programme post 2013 will be defined in a basic act in the framework of the preparation of the next financial framework.[62]

Within FP 6, the EU has spent EUR 100 million on GMES projects, whereas ESA invested another EUR 100 million in the GMES Service Elements projects. In the space theme of the specific programme 'cooperation' of FP7, the EU will make available approximately EUR 430 million for GMES information service projects between 2007 and 2013. Additionally, EUR 624 million from the space theme of FP7 will be used to contribute to the development of the ESA Space component programme.[63] The EU also finances the procurement of space data from third-party missions, which are used for GMES service projects. The in situ component will remain to a large extent a responsibility of the Member States. The EU could contribute to co-ordination activities, where appropriate, to support the development of in situ infrastructure, notably by encouraging both pan-European and globally co-ordinated data collection and exchange.[64]

The GMES Regulation is the basis for a transformation of GMES into a fully-fledged EU programme with its own legal framework. According to Article 2 of the GMES Regulation, GMES consists of a service component, a space component and an in situ component (for example airborne, seaborne and land-based sensors). The service areas within the GMES service component include land, marine and atmosphere monitoring, monitoring of climate change, and emergency and security information. The latter services provide support in the event of emergencies and

58 For more details concerning the history of GMES, see Mantl, L. 2009. 'The Commission Proposal for a Regulation on the European Earth Observation Programme (GMES) and its Initial Operations (2011–2013): A Major Milestone for GMES', *ZLW*, 3/2009, 405–12.

59 The term 'operational' can have different meanings from a technical perspective. For the purpose of this article, and also in Commission documents published thus far, the term 'operational' is used for activities that go beyond research projects and are therefore financed by other budgets than research budgets (including budgets foreseen for the framework programmes for research and technological developments of the EU).

60 See the Impact Assessment accompanying the Communication 'Global Monitoring for Environment and Security (GMES) – Challenges and Next Steps for the Space Component', SEC(2009) 1440 of 28 October 2009, (the 'Impact Assessment accompanying the GSC Communication'), 8.

61 See Mantl, L. 2009. 'The Commission Proposal for a Regulation on the European Earth Observation Programme (GMES) and its Initial Operations (2011–2013)', 409.

62 See the 2009 GMES Impact Assessment, 6.

63 See the 2009 GMES Impact Assessment, 5.

64 See the Communication 'GMES: We Care for a Safer Planet', COM(2008) 748 final of 12.11.2008, 7.

humanitarian aid needs, in particular to civil protection authorities, and accurate information on security-related aspects (for example maritime surveillance, border control, global stability).[65]

Unlike in the Galileo programme, the programmatic management of GMES has not been entrusted to external entities, for example, joint undertakings pursuant to Article 187 TFEU, or regulatory agencies. In the beginning, GMES was managed through ad hoc structures agreed with ESA and EUMETSAT, including initially a GMES support team, a GMES Steering Committee, and a GMES Forum.[66] An ad hoc expert group was created in 2004 following the Action Plan (2004–2008),[67] the GMES Advisory Council (GAC). In 2006, the Commission established the GMES Bureau, a unit in the Enterprise and Industry Directorate which coordinates GMES-related activities in the Commission.[68]

The following section analyses in more detail the contractual framework for the three components of GMES. The section focuses on the current pre-operational activities and the development of space infrastructure.

Contractual Framework

The technical implementation of the GMES space component is delegated to ESA. Activities focus on coordinated access to space data and space infrastructure development in cooperation with ESA. In addition to a grant covering data access,[69] the Commission contributes to five space missions (the 'Sentinels') developed specifically for GMES in the framework of the optional GMES space component (GSC) programme of ESA[70] with total costs of EUR 2,246 billion (at 2008 economic conditions).[71] The legal basis for the transfer is a delegation agreement according to Article 53d of the EC Financial Regulation which was concluded between ESA and the Community on 28 January 2008 and amended twice thereafter (the ESA-EU GMES Agreement).[72] The ESA-EU GMES agreement foresees that ESA manages the GSC programme (including the EC contribution) according to ESA procurement[73] and financial rules, with the main exception that ESA must not apply its 'fair return'[74] rules for activities financed by the EU. The ESA-EU GMES agreement

---

65 See Annex I of the Impact Assessment accompanying the GSC Communication.

66 Commission Communication entitled Global Monitoring for Environment and Security (GMES) - Outline GMES EC Action Plan (Initial Period: 2001–2003), COM(2001) 609 final of 23 October 2001, 12–14.

67 See the Communication Global Monitoring for Environment and Security (GMES): Establishing a GMES capacity by 2008 – (Action Plan (2004-2008)), COM(2004) 65 final of 3 February 2004, 16.

68 Decision C(2006)673 of 8 March 2006. The mandate of the GMES Bureau was initially limited to 31 May 2009, but has been prolonged until 2013.

69 According to this grant agreement, ESA will procure data from contributing missions (for example missions other than the Sentinel missions that collect data or relevance for GMES) for GMES service projects. After the expiry of the grant at the end of 2010, data access activities will be covered by the delegation agreement referred to further below in this paragraph.

70 For an overview of the content of the Sentinel missions see Liebig, V., Aschbacher, J., Briggs, S., Kohlhammer, G. and Zobl, R. 2007. 'GMES – Global Monitoring for Environment and Security: The Second European Flagship in Space', *ESA Bulletin*, 130, 14–15.

71 See the 2009 GMES Impact Assessment, 5.

72 See also Froehlich, A. 2008. 'ESA-EU-Vereinbarung zur Umsetzung des gemeinsamen GMES-Projektes', *ZLW*, 03/2008, 354–66.

73 For an overview of ESA procurement rules, see Chapter 16.

74 The 'fair return' rules are based on Article VII(1)(c) and Annex V of the ESA Convention and oblige ESA to ensure that the share of contracts awarded to companies under the jurisdiction of a State participating

constitutes an innovation, as Article 53d of the EC Financial Regulation was used for the first time to delegate budget implementation tasks in the space sector.[75]

Regarding the GMES service component, the Commission finances collaborative projects that will develop pre-operational services in key service areas (land, marine and atmosphere monitoring, emergency services, security services and climate change).[76] Additionally, some projects of a smaller scale are carried out, in particular in the field of downstream services. These projects are managed in line with standard FP7 rules, on the basis of calls for proposals and grant agreements.[77]

In the in situ component, a grant agreement[78] has been concluded with the European Environment Agency (EEA).[79] The EEA will assist the Commission in the co-ordination of the in situ component, which mainly remains in the remit of the Member States. This includes an analysis of existing data policies.

IPR Rules and GMES Data and Information Policy

In this section, two aspects will be covered, namely the rules concerning IPR for intangible assets developed in the framework of the GMES space component programme, and the policy for GMES data and information.

Regarding the first aspect, it should be underlined that according to Article 3 of the ESA-EU GMES Agreement, ESA rules apply, unless provided otherwise in this agreement. According to the ESA rules concerning information, data and intellectual property, the contractor becomes owner of the IPR developed in an ESA optional programme. ESA and its Member States have the right to use this IPR under the conditions defined in the rules concerning information, data and intellectual property. Article 11 of the ESA-EU GMES agreement states that the usage rights of ESA and the states participating in the GMES space component programme are extended to the EU and its Member States.

The policy for the distribution of information produced by GMES services and data collected through GMES infrastructure is dealt with in Article 9 of the GMES Regulation. Article 9(1) of the GMES Regulation contains a list of objectives of the GMES data and information policy, namely (i) the promotion of the use and sharing of GMES information and data, (ii) full and open access, subject to security restrictions,[80] (iii) the strengthening of earth observation markets in Europe, (iv) contributing to the sustainability of GMES data and information provision and (v) a support to European research communities. The objective of full and open access, which was underlined

---

in a given ESA programme corresponds to the share of contribution of this state to the financial envelope of the programme.

75 See Mantl, L. 2009. 'The Commission Proposal for a Regulation on the European Earth Observation Programme (GMES) and its Initial Operations (2011–2013)', 410–11.

76 Including the GEOLAND2, MYOCEAN, MACC, SAFER and G-MOSAIC projects.

77 An overview of the different projects can be found at also http://cordis.europa.eu/.

78 This grant was awarded without a call for proposal pursuant to Article 168.1.(e) of the Implementing Rules because the EEA was identified as a pre-defined beneficiary in the work programme for the space theme.

79 The EEA is a regulatory agency established by Council Regulation (EC) No. 401/2009 of the European Parliament and of the Council of 23 April 2009 on the European Environment Agency and the European Environment Information and Observation Network, OJ L 126, 21 May 2009, 13–22. For further information see http://www.eea.europa.eu/.

80 These restrictions were analysed by the GMES data security subarea of the Council Security Committee.

already in section 3 of the Communication 'GMES: We Care for a Safer Planet', was selected for several reasons.[81]

First, the principle of full and open access is contained in section 5.3 of the 10-Year Implementation Plan of Earth Observation System of Systems, which has been endorsed by the EU at the Third Earth Observation Summit on 16 February 2005.[82] Further, it would be contrary at least to the principles of existing environmental legislation, including the INSPIRE Directive[83] if GMES data and information was sold with a view to maximising third-party revenue. Finally, full and open access to GMES data and information is therefore expected to give the earth observation sector the boost that is one of the main objectives of GMES.[84]

According to Article 9(2) of the GMES Regulation, the Commission may adopt delegated acts pursuant to Article 290 TFEU in order to (i) establish registration and licensing conditions for GMES users and (ii) define criteria for restricting access to GMES information and data. In doing so, the Commission will take into consideration the data policies of data providers, without prejudice to rules and procedures applicable to national infrastructure.

Outlook

With the entry into force of the Lisbon Treaty, the EU has now a clear legal basis to implement the new priorities of the European Space Policy, with a view 'to promote scientific and technical progress, industrial competitiveness and the implementation of its policies.'[85] Space can thus be considered a key domain for the implementation of the EU 2020 strategy. The EU 2020 strategy refers, in particular, to the need to ensure the implementation of GMES and Galileo.[86]

Building on the existing European Space Policy, the Council Resolutions from 2007 and 2008 and the provisions of Article 189.1, the European Commission is now preparing the EU's future involvement in space. The 2008 Space Council Resolution defines priority areas in addition to Galileo and GMES to include space and climate change, the contribution of space to the Lisbon strategy, space and security, and space exploration. These priorities were further developed in the Commission Communication 'Towards a space strategy for the European Union that benefits its citizens', COM(2011) 152 final of 4 April 2011.

It is currently foreseen that climate change will be dealt with mainly through the climate change service in the GMES programme.

Regarding security, a difference needs to be made between 'security from space', and 'security in space'. As concerns 'security in space', proposals for concrete actions focus on space situational awareness (SSA) activities. The Resolution on 'The contribution of space to innovation and competitiveness in the context of the European Economic Recovery Plan, and further steps',

81 For a more detailed discussion of these reasons, see section 4.2.3 of the 2009 GMES Impact Assessment.

82 The Resolution and the 10-year implementation plan are available on the website of the Group on Earth Observation (http://www.earthobservations.org/), which is coordinating efforts to establish an Earth Observation System of Systems.

83 Directive 2007/2/EC of the European Parliament and of the Council of 14 March 2007 establishing an Infrastructure for Spatial Information in the European Community (INSPIRE), OJ L 108 of 25 April 2007, 1.

84 See section 4.2.3 of the 2009 Impact Assessment.

85 Article 189.1 TFEU.

86 Communication from the Commission 'EUROPE 2020 – A Strategy for Smart, Sustainable and Inclusive Growth', COM(2010) 2020 of 3 March 2010, 15.

adopted at the 6th Space Council meeting on 29 May 2009, made reference to the adoption of a ESA preparatory programme, while recalling that the EU will take, in liaison with ESA and their respective Member States, an active role to set up progressively a European capability for SSA and an appropriate governance structure. The 6th Space Council Resolution also reaffirmed

> the need to assess the possibilities offered by European Union policies to embed space exploration in a wider political perspective and, recognising that space exploration has the potential to provide a major impact on innovation.

Corresponding legislative proposals may be tabled in 2011.

List of References

Brachet, G. 2004. 'From Initial Ideas to a European Plan: GMES as an Exemplar of European Space Strategy', *Space Policy*, 20 (1), 7–17.

Commission Communication. 'The Community and Space: A Coherent Approach', COM(88) 417 final of 26 July 1988.

Commission Communication. 'Global Monitoring for Environment and Security (GMES) - Outline GMES EC Action Plan (Initial Period: 2001–2003)', COM(2001) 609 final of 23 October 2001.

Commission Communication. 'Progressing Galileo: Re-profiling the European GNSS Programmes', COM(2007) 534 final of 19 September 2007.

Commission Communication. 'GMES: We Care for a Safer Planet', COM(2008)748 of 12 November 2008.

Commission Communication. 'EUROPE 2020: A Strategy for Smart, Sustainable and Inclusive Growth', COM(2010) 2020 of 3 March 2010.

Commission Decision creating a Bureau for Global Monitoring for Environment and Security, C(2006)673 of 8 March 2006.

Commission Regulation 2342/2002 of 23 December 2002 laying down detailed rules for the implementation of Council Regulation 1605/2002 on the Financial Regulation applicable to the general budget of the European Communities, OJ L 357 of 31 December 2002, 1, as amended.

Commission Staff Working Document accompanying the Proposal for a Regulation of the European Parliament and the Council on the European Earth observation programme (GMES) and its initial operations (2011-013), Impact Assessment and Ex Ante Evaluation, SEC(2009)639 of 20 May 2009.

Council Decision 2006/971/EC of 19 December 2006 concerning the specific programme 'Cooperation' implementing the Seventh Framework Programme of the European Community for research, technological development and demonstration activities (2007-013), OJ L 54 of 22 February 2007, 30.

Council Regulation 876/2002 setting up the Galileo Joint Undertaking, L 138 of 28 May 2002, 1, as amended by Council Regulation 1943/2006 of 12 December 2006, OJ L 367 of 22 December 2006, 21.

Council Regulation 1321/2004 on the establishment of structures for the management of the European satellite radio-navigation programmes, OJ L 246 of 20 July 2004, 1, as last amended by Regulation 1942/2006 of 12 December 2006, OJ L 367 of 22 December 2006, 18.

Council Regulation 1605/2002 of 25 June 2002 on the Financial Regulation applicable to the general budget of the European Communities, OJ L 248 of 16 September 2002, 1, as amended.

Council Resolution on a European space strategy of 16 November, 2000C 371/2 of 31 December 2000.

Council Resolution of 21 May 2007 on the European Space Policy, 2007/C 136/01.

Decision 1999/468/EC of 28 June 1999 laying down the procedures for the exercise of implementing powers conferred on the Commission, OJ L 184, 17 July 1999, 23 as amended by Council Decision 2006/512/EC of 17 July 2006, OJ L 200, 22 July 2006, 11.

Decision 1982/2006/EC of the European Parliament and of the Council of 18 December 2006 concerning the Seventh Framework Programme of the European Community for research, technological development and demonstration activities (2007-013), OJ L 412 of 30 December 2006, 1.

Directive 2007/2/EC of the European Parliament and of the Council of 14 March 2007 establishing an Infrastructure for Spatial Information in the European Community (INSPIRE), OJ L 108 of 25 April 2007, 1.

Framework Agreement between the European Community and the European Space Agency, OJ L 261 of 6 August 2004, 64.

Froehlich, A. 2008. 'ESA-EU-Vereinbarung zur Umsetzung des gemeinsamen GMES-Projektes', *ZLW*, 03/2008, 354–66.

Impact Assessment accompanying the Communication 'Global Monitoring for Environment and Security (GMES) – Challenges and Next Steps for the Space Component', SEC(2009) 1440 of 28 October 2009.

Interinstitutional Agreement on budgetary discipline and sound financial management of 17 May 2006, OJ C 139 of 14 June 2006, 1, as amended.

Liebig, V., Aschbacher, J., Briggs, S., Kohlhammer, G. and Zobl, R. 2007. 'GMES – Global Monitoring for Environment and Security: The Second European Flagship in Space', *ESA Bulletin*, 130, 11–16.

Mantl, L. 2009. 'The Commission Proposal for a Regulation on the European Earth Observation Programme (GMES) and its Initial Operations (2011–2013): A Major Milestone for GMES', *ZLW*, 3/2009, 404–22.

Proposal for a Regulation of the European Parliament and the Council on the European Earth observation programme (GMES) and its initial operations (2011-013), COM(2009)223 of 20 May 2009.

Regulation 2321/2002 of the European Parliament and of the Council of 16 December 2002 concerning the rules for the participation of undertakings, research centres and universities in, and for the dissemination of research results for, the implementation of the European Community Sixth Framework Programme (2002-006), OJ L 355/23 of 30 December 2002.

Regulation 1906/2006 of the European Parliament and of the Council of 18 December 2006 laying down the rules for the participation of undertakings, research centres and universities in actions under the Seventh Framework Programme and for the dissemination of research results (2007-013), OJ L 391 of 30 December 2006, 1.

Regulation 683/2008 of the European Parliament and of the Council of 9 July 2008 on the further implementation of the European satellite navigation programmes (EGNOS and Galileo), OJ L 196 of 24 July 2008, 1.

Regulation (EC) No. 401/2009 of the European Parliament and of the Council of 23 April 2009 on the European Environment Agency and the European Environment Information and Observation Network, OJ L 126, 21 May 2009, 13.

Regulation 911/2010 of the European Parliament and of the Council of 22 September 2010 on the European Earth monitoring programme and its initial operations (2011-2013), OJ L 276 of 20 October 2010, 1.

Regulation 912/2010 of the European Parliament and of the Council of 22 September 2010 setting up the European GNSS agency, DJ L 276 of 20 October 2010, 11.

Van de Wouwer, J.L. and Lambert, F. 2008. *European Trajectories in Space Law*. Brussels: Bruylant.

White Paper 'Space: A New European Frontier for an Expanding Union: An Action Plan for Implementing the European Space Policy', COM (2003) 673 of 11 November 2003.

Chapter 8
The Geographical Return Principle and its Future within the European Space Policy*

Bernhard Schmidt-Tedd

The Geographical Return Principle and its Context in the ESA Convention

Experience of the Past and Purpose of the Agency

The geographical return principle, sometimes also called 'fair return' or '*juste retour*', is an element of the complex industrial policy of the European Space Agency (ESA or 'Agency'). The substance of this principle has to be analysed by taking into account the purpose of the Agency and its industrial policy in general.

The ESA Convention[1] was approved by the Conference of Plenipotentiaries held in Paris on 30 May 1975 and entered formally into force on 30 October 1980. According to Resolution No. 1 of the conference the ESA began to function *de facto* on 31 May 1975. Its purpose is defined in Article II of the ESA Convention.[2]

The institutional consolidation of the European space sector was driven by the goal of preparing Europe for an autonomous and self-defined role in international space cooperation,[3] and by some negative experiences with European dependencies and the lack of independent access to

---

* This chapter is based on reflections presented at the Contracting for Space Workshop held in Bremen on 27–28 November 2009. The opinions expressed are entirely those of the author and do not engage organisations with which he is affiliated.

1 CSE / CS (73) 19, rev. 7; UNTS Vol. 1297 (1983), I No. 21524.

2 The article reads as follows:
'Article II: PURPOSE
The purpose of the Agency shall be to provide for and to promote, for exclusively peaceful purposes, cooperation among European States in space research and technology and their space applications, with a view to their being used for scientific purposes and for operational space applications systems:
a. by elaborating and implementing a long-term European space policy, by recommending space objectives to the Member States, and by concerting the policies of the Member States with respect to other national and international organisations and institutions;
b. by elaborating and implementing activities and programmes in the space field;
c. by coordinating the European space programme and national programmes, and by integrating the latter progressively and as completely as possible into the European space programme, in particular as regards the development of applications satellites;
d. by elaborating and implementing the industrial policy appropriate to its programme and by recommending a coherent industrial policy to the Member States.'

3 Lafferranderie, G. 2005. *European Space Agency, Intergovernmental Organizations – Suppl. 20*. The Hague, 17.

space.[4] The classical example is the limitation of the French-German telecommunication satellite SYMPHONIE to non-commercial use, according to the NASA launch service contract.[5] The failure of launcher development under the European Organisation for the Development and Construction of Space Vehicle Launchers (ELDO), a predecessor of ESA, also had commercial impacts. Without a certain degree of autonomy, there is no access to critical products and services. In space, strategy and policy decisions always prevail. Reality had proven that a unilateral dependency on so-called space markets is a weak position.

Consequently, the ESA was founded to build up the necessary competencies, through cooperation among European states, in space research and technology, and space applications for scientific and operational space applications. Creating a coherent industrial policy appropriate to ESA's programmes was an important part of this. The coordinated development of space assets serves the interests of Member States, hence the set-up of the European infrastructure is the result of intergovernmental cooperation and not of market developments. Indeed, as far as the operational sector is concerned – the potential basis for market developments – the ESA can initiate promotional activities under optional programmes, but cannot decide on its own to enter the operational sector.[6]

Two examples of exceptionally successful and in the long term sustainable promotional activities are the Ariane promotion series and the Meteosat Operational Protocol, leading to the Arianespace launcher business and the European Meteorological Intergovernmental Organisation (IGO) EUMETSAT.

The first step for operational activities, whether private, public or semi-public, remains the technological basis set-up and support by European space programmes.

Ten years after the *de facto* start of the ESA, the European Long-Term Space Plan (LTP)[7] was adopted at the ministerial level at the ESA Council in Rome in 1985 and confirmed in 1987 in The Hague.[8] It laid down a comprehensive space programme. Basic principles were coherence of the programme, adequate balance between science, infrastructure and application, and European autonomy and presence in all relevant space activities. The mandatory science programme formulated in ESA's 'Horizon 2000' was complemented by major optional programmes (Ariane V, Columbus, Hermes and DRS).

4 See Kaiser, K. and Welck, S. Frhr. v. 1987. *Weltraum und internationale Politik.* München: R. Oldenbourg, 294, 487 f.

5 Contract between the US NASA and the CNES and GFW for satellite launching and associated services to be furnished by NASA in connection with the launching of SYMPHONIE satellites (No. SYS -07-73-/73-CNES-115). Art. XVI, sect. 1: 'It is understood and agreed between the parties that the fundamental purpose of the programs of use for Symphonie satellites to be launched under this contract are and will continue to be experimental in character.'

6 Lafferanderie, G. 2005. *European Space Agency*, 42.

7 ESA Council Resolution ESA/C-M/LXVII/Res. 1 adopted on 31 January 1985 and ESA/C-M/LXXX/Res. 1 adopted on 10 November 1987 on the European Long-Term Space Plan and Programmes in: *Space Law: Basic Legal Documents*, edited by K.-H. Böckstiegel and M. Benkö. Dordrecht: Martinus Nijhoff, 1990–, under C.I.2; overview by Spude, M. 1991. 'Integrierte Zusammenarbeit. Die europäische Weltraumorganisation ESA', in *Handbuch des Weltraumrechts*, edited by K.-H. Böckstiegel. Cologne: Heymanns, 667.

8 Schmidt-Tedd, B. 1994. 'Revidierte LTP-Planung, Etablierung der Europäischen Union: Fragen zur ESA-Standortbestimmung', *ZLW*, 38.

Industrial Policy and Geographical Return

A new element of the ESA Convention was the introduction of a specific industrial policy as formulated in Article VII – by cross-reference to Article II d – and further specified in Annex V.[9] The ESA industrial policy is – derived from its basic goals – a well-balanced set of principles counterbalancing some partially conflicting elements, such as European requirements, world-wide competitiveness, equitable participation according to a state's financial contribution, and the option of later defined additional objectives. Sub-paragraph 2 addresses the preference for the maximum use of external contractors without denying a certain internal capability for preparation and supervision. This aspect is also a decisive element of the ESA industrial policy. If only market rules applied, there would be an understandable tendency to safeguard key technologies developed in-house by national institutions.

The specific elements of equitable participation according to geographical distribution are specified in Article IV of Annex V[10] of the industrial policy and the resulting procedural questions in Articles V and VI of the same Annex. As a result, the geographical return principle is only one

9 The article reads as follows:
'Article VII: INDUSTRIAL POLICY
1. The industrial policy which the Agency is to elaborate and apply by virtue of Article II d. shall be designed in particular to:
a. meet the requirements of the European space programme and the coordinated national space programmes in a cost-effective manner;
b. improve the world-wide competitiveness of European industry by maintaining and developing space technology and by encouraging the rationalisation and development of an industrial structure appropriate to market requirements, making use in the first place of the existing industrial potential of all Member States;
c. ensure that all Member States participate in an equitable manner, having regard to their financial contribution, in implementing the European space programme and in the associated development of space technology; in particular the Agency shall, for the execution of its programmes, grant preference to the fullest extent possible to industry in all Member States, which shall be given the maximum opportunity to participate in the work of technological interest undertaken for the Agency;
d. exploit the advantages of free competitive bidding in all cases, except where this would be incompatible with other defined objectives of industrial policy.
Other objectives may be defined by the Council by a unanimous decision of all Member States. The detailed arrangements for the attainment of these objectives shall be those set out in Annex V and in rules which shall be adopted by the Council by a two-thirds majority of all Member States and reviewed periodically.
2. For the execution of its programmes, the Agency shall make the maximum use of external contractors consistent with the maintenance of the internal capability referred to in Article VI, 1.'

10 The article reads as follows:
'Article IV (Annex V: Industrial Policy)
The geographical distribution of all the Agency's contracts shall be governed by the following general rules:
1. A Member State's overall return coefficient shall be the ratio between its percentage share of the total value of all contracts awarded among all Member States and its total percentage contributions. However, in the calculation of this overall return coefficient, no account shall be taken of contracts placed in, or contributions made by, Member States in a programme undertaken:
a. under Article VIII of the Convention for the establishment of a European Space Research Organisation, provided that the relevant Arrangement contains provisions to this effect or that

of several elements of the ESA industrial policy. Exploitation of the advantages of free competitive bidding[11] is also a basic rule, as well as the improvement of world-wide competitiveness.[12]

With the present system of space cooperation, Europe has gained a 40 per cent share of the global heavy lift launcher and satellite market, proving that the European space industry is highly competitive and efficient. Moreover, the European Commission has recognised that ESA, with its first generation space programmes, has achieved its objective of securing for Europe a major role among the space-faring nations and that the establishment of the management organisations, ARIANESPACE, EUMETSAT and EUTELSAT, was a success.[13]

Adjustments and Results

In implementing ESA's industrial policy, the Council keeps the industrial potential and industrial structure in relation to the Agency's activities (general structure, degree of specialisation, coordination of national policies, interaction with other international bodies, production capacity, potential markets, and the organisation of contacts within the industry) under review.[14] Furthermore, the industrial policy includes a preference rule for ESA Member States.[15] Moreover, geographical distribution can be influenced in principal *ex ante* in the preparation of an optional programme or *ex post* by adjustments after an evaluation period. The procedure is formulated in Articles V and VI of Annex V ESA Convention.[16]

---

all participating States subsequently unanimously so agree; b. under Article V, 1 b of the present Convention provided that all original participating States unanimously so agree.

2. For the purpose of calculating return coefficients, weighting factors shall be applied to the value of contracts on the basis of their technological interest. These weighting factors shall be defined by the Council. Within a single contract having a significant value, more than one weighting factor may be applied.

3. Ideally the distribution of contracts placed by the Agency should result in all countries having an overall return coefficient of 1.

4. The return coefficients shall be computed quarterly and shown cumulatively for the purpose of the formal reviews referred to in paragraph 5.

5. Formal reviews of the geographical distribution of contracts shall take place every five years, with an interim review before the end of the third year.

6. The distribution of contracts between formal reviews of the situation should be such that, at the time of each formal review, the cumulative overall return coefficient of each Member State does not substantially deviate from the ideal value. At the time of each formal review, the Council may revise the lower limit for the cumulative return coefficient for the subsequent period, provided that it shall never be lower than 0.8.

7. Separate assessments shall be made, and reported to the Council, of the return coefficients for various categories of contract to be defined by it, in particular advanced research and development contracts and contracts for project-related technology. The Director General shall discuss these assessments with the Council, at regular intervals to be specified, and in particular at the interim review, with the aim of identifying the action needed to redress any imbalances.'

11 Article VII 1 d.

12 Article VII 1 b.

13 The Community and Space: A Coherent Approach, Communication from the Commission, COM (88) 417 final, Brussels, 26 July 1988.

14 Article I, Annex V ESA Convention.

15 Article II (1.), Annex V ESA Convention.

16 The articles read as follows:

'Article V

Statistics and reviews on industrial return include weighing factors according to the technological value of the contract. The lower limit of the overall return was adjusted during Council meetings at the ministerial level a couple of times, for example, increasing between 1990 (0.90) and 1995 (0.96). Further, in December 1988, new statistics on industrial return per programme were introduced and published on a quarterly basis.[17] During the Edinburgh Council meeting at the ministerial level (2001), Articles IV and V were adapted with formal reviews for a five-year period and a lower limit of 0.8 for the cumulative return coefficient. The last formal review of the geographical distribution of contracts took place in 2010 for the period 2005–2009.

The geographical return principle has always been a special instrument for European integration and motivation for additional national investments. Nevertheless, the political influence in detail should be reduced to an adequate level. The positive effect of geographical return should not be foiled by exaggerated expectations of a 100 per cent return per programme and the overall goal of creating a valid technical and scientific basis should not be lost from sight.[18]

If, between two formal reviews, a trend is identified indicating that the overall return coefficient of any Member State is likely to be below the lower limit defined according to Article IV, 6, the Director General shall submit to the Council proposals in which the need to remedy the situation takes precedence over the Agency's rules governing the placing of contracts.'

'Article VI

Any decision taken on industrial policy grounds which has the effect of excluding a particular firm or organisation of a Member State from competing for the Agency's contracts in a particular field shall require the agreement of that Member State.'

17 Lafferranderie, G. 2005. *European Space Agency*, 108 f.

18 See Morel de Westgavers, E. and Imbart, P. 1989. 'Le "juste retour": contrainte ou instrument d'intégration européene?', *ESA-Bulletin*, 59, 62 (69) with a positive, differentiated vote.

Geographical Return and EU/EC Law

Decades of Discussion

EU/EC[19] engagement in space began after the entering into force of the Single European Act (SEA) 1 July 1987,[20] which introduced a new article on research and technological development.[21] With the SEA, the interface between ESA and the EU, and especially questions of industrial policy and procurement, came under discussion. It became evident that the EC had developed ambitions of new processes of integration, including in the field of research and development (R&D).

In 1991, the report 'The European Community – Crossroads in Space'[22] was published. The ESA itself analysed the consequences of the SEA and finalised the respective report in December 1991.[23] In addition the ESA engaged Euroconsult in 1990/91 to study 'The Competitiveness of the European Space Industry'. This study included opinion poll results and feedback from inside the industry.[24] Other legal reports, *inter alia* those of Micklitz and Reich, under contract from Eurospace (Paris), and Prof. Börner from Germany, analysed, from a legal standpoint, the compatibility of the geographical return principle with EC law.[25] The subject was further discussed at an international colloquium of the European Centre for Space Law (ESA/ECSL) in October 1993 in Florence under the title 'The Implementation of the ESA Convention – Lessons from the Past'.[26]

Narjes, Vice-President of the Commission at the time, states that the EU arguments for engagement in space ranged from 'lacking comprehensive European space policy'[27] to the need 'to

---

19 The Treaty establishing the European Economic Community (EEC), the so-called Treaty of Rome, was signed in March 1957. In 1993, by the Treaty of Maastricht, the EEC Treaty was renamed the Treaty Establishing the European Community (EC Treaty) and, with the Lisbon Treaty of 2009, the Treaty on the Functioning of the European Union (TFEU). The European Union (EU) was formally established when the Maastricht Treaty came into force on 1 November 1993; Treaty of Lisbon amending the Treaty on European Union and the Treaty establishing the European Community (hereafter Treaty of Lisbon), Lisbon, done 13 December 2007, entered into force 1 December 2009; OJ C 306/1 (2007); Provisional Consolidated Versions of the Treaty on European Union (TEU) and of the Treaty on the Functioning of the European Union (TFEU) in Council of the European Union 6655/08, Brussels, 15 April 2008.

20 The Single European Act was the first major revision of the EC Treaty / Treaty of Rome, with the objective to establish a Single Market by 31 December 1992. After the Maastricht Treaty (1993) a further consolidation was reached with the Treaty of Amsterdam (1999), followed by the Treaty of Nice (2003); Treaty of Amsterdam Amending the Treaty on European Union, the Treaties Establishing the European Communities and Certain Related Acts (hereafter Treaty of Amsterdam), Amsterdam, done 2 October 1997, entered into force 1 May 1999; OJ C 340/73 (1997); Treaty of Nice amending the Treaty on European Union, the Treaties establishing the European Communities and certain related acts (hereafter Treaty of Nice), Nice, done 26 February 2001, entered into force 1 February 2003; OJ C 80/1 (2001).

21 Title XV (Art. 130 f–q) EC Treaty, Title XVIII (Arts 163–73) Treaty of Amsterdam.

22 Reflected in: KOM (92) 360 final of 23 September 1992.

23 ESA/C (91) 99, Paris 2 December 1991; preliminary studies (ESA/C (89) 85) in 1990 a Working Group under the mandate of the Council was established (ESA/C (90) 11, Annex 11).

24 ESA/C-WG/SEA (91) 2, Paris, 30 January 1991.

25 Micklitz, H.W. and Reich, N. 1989. *Legal Aspects of European Space Activities*. Baden-Baden: Nomos; Börner, B. 1989. *Gutachten ESA und EWG*, see references in ESA/C-WG/SEA/MIN/2 of 24 October 1990 and ESA/C-WG/SEA (90) 4 of 19 September 1990.

26 Conference Report by Kayser, V. 1994. 'International Colloquium, The Implementation of the ESA Convention: Lessons from the Past, Florence, 25–26 October 1993', *ZLW*, 68.

27 Narjes, K.-H. 1989. 'Space and the European Community', *Space Policy*, February, 59 (61 f.).

put the full weight of its democratic legitimacy behind the new ambitious ESA programmes …'. With the Community taking on potential new roles, Narjes also mentions typical market-oriented points, such as '… to frame policies that help establish favourable conditions for the development and exploitation of space applications: for example, the completion of the Community's internal market …' and '… to ensure that the activities of those involved in the space industry remain consistent with Community law with regard to competition policy, trade policy …'.

These points characterise the approach still relevant now. Not a specific space approach, but a conformity with other areas of Community competence is the focal point of all considerations. This basic difference remains unchanged today. With good cause; ESA and the EU are still autonomous, independent international organisations with their own respective regulations.

The question of incompatibility of the ESA geographical return principle and EU/EC law was discussed with regard to membership in both IGO's. In this respect, the study of Micklitz and Reich refers to general treaty principles. Article 5 of the EC Treaty of Rome[28] states:

> Member States shall take all appropriate measures, whether general or particular, to ensure fulfilment of the obligations arising out of this Treaty or resulting from action taken by the institutions of the community. They shall facilitate the achievement of the Community's tasks. They shall abstain from any measure which could jeopardise the attainment of the objectives of this Treaty.

The complained of incompatibility was seen to exist between, on the one hand, the geographical return principle, which attempted to award contracts in an approximate relationship to the state's contribution and thus its accompanying restrictions on competition, and, on the other hand, the principle of the unrestricted exchange, and hence free movement of, goods (Arts 30 to 36 EC Treaty)[29] and services (Art. 59 EC Treaty).[30]

Further, conflict was seen in the competition rules (Arts 85 and 86 EC Treaty)[31] and state aid (Art. 92 EC Treaty).[32] In this regard, the question posed is if EC Member States that are also ESA Member States would be obliged to work towards abrogation of the geographical return principle. It was argued that EC Member States have special obligations to correct incompatibilities, according to Article 234 of the Treaty of Rome,[33] but this article concerns only former treaties, from the period before the EC. Factually, none of these argumentations were fully settled before the Framework Agreement.[34] Incidentally, Micklitz and Reich's report assumes an EU competition law that is not even partially adaptable.[35] On the contrary, Börner emphasises that the ESA is not

28 EC Treaty of 25 March 1957, UNTS Vol. 298, 11, EU-Doc No. 1 1957 E; Art. 10 Treaty of Amsterdam of 2 October 1997.

29 Arts 28–30 Treaty of Amsterdam, now Arts 34–6 TFEU.

30 Art. 49 Treaty of Amsterdam, now Art. 56 TFEU.

31 Arts 81 and 82 Treaty of Amsterdam, now Arts 101 and 102 TFEU.

32 Art. 87 Treaty of Amsterdam, now Art. 107 TFEU.

33 Art. 307 Treaty of Amsterdam, now Art. 351 TFEU.

34 Framework Agreement between the European Community and the European Space Agency, Council of the European Union, Brussels 7 October 2003, Council Decision 12858/03 and ESA Council …; see Reuter, Y. 2004. 'The Framework Agreement between the European Space Agency and the European Community: A Significant Step Forward?', *ZLW*, 56.

35 Micklitz, H.W. and Reich, N. 1989. *Legal Aspects of European Space Activities*, p. 17: 'The analysis has clearly shown that exemptions from the basic economic freedoms can be justified for non-economic reasons only.'

an international organisation with an economic character, but rather one with mainly a scientific character and, thus, there is no conflict with the EU. Some authors justify the compatibility directly by citing the exemption clause of Article 36 EC Treaty,[36] despite a formal conflict with Articles 28 and 29 EC Treaty.[37]

Generally, a fundamental asymmetry between the EC – with its aim to remove trade and other barriers, thereby forming a single internal market, bottom-up – and the ESA – creating pan-European industrial structures through R&D space programmes, top-down – needs to be recognised.

Independent of formal legal positions, the fundamentally different starting point of the EU, which is the establishment of a single internal market and the gradual harmonisation of the economic policies of the Member States, persists. This basic understanding leaves little room for constructive interventions that act on the assumption of equitable participation according to national financial contributions.

In 2003, the Framework Agreement between the European Community and the European Space Agency[38] was concluded. With regard to the discussion on industrial policy, a *status quo* was defined in Article 5 (joint initiatives) as follows:

> 3. Any financial contribution made by one Party in accordance with a specific arrangement shall be governed by the financial provisions applicable to that Party. Under no circumstances shall the European Community be bound to apply the rule of 'geographic distribution' contained in the ESA Convention and especially in Annex V thereto. Compliance with the rules relating to financial control and auditing of the Party contributing to the joint initiatives, or of both Parties in case of joint contribution, shall apply to any joint activity.

EU Procurement Experience GALILEO

GALILEO, the European satellite navigation system, is the first flagship project to emerge from EU/EC involvement in space. The project was justified by the need of a self-determined, independent European system, following negative experiences with dependency on the GPS signal. This open, and originally not guaranteed, signal is a product of the US military navigation system set up as a public investment. Regardless of a certain degree of imponderability *vis-à-vis* civil uses,[39] GPS initiated an enormous market for end user products of this free signal.

Europe's investment in its own satellite navigation system was not market-driven, but a strategic investment aimed at European autonomy. The challenge was to establish, despite the existence of the cost free GPS signal, an alternative civil system with a differentiated user community – using a range of applications from civil to security – partially cost free but also partially against payment. In a second step this European system had to be integrated on an equal footing into a global network of cooperation pertaining to existing navigation systems. This had to be done based on political decisions about partners and the form of cooperation, and not according to unspecified market decisions. GALILEO is not a limited investment in infrastructure or end user products.

---

36 Art. 30 Treaty of Amsterdam, now Art. 36 TFEU.

37 Arts 28 and 29 Treaty of Amsterdam, now Arts 34 and 35 TFEU; see Grillo, W. 1993. 'Die Vereinbarkeit der ESA-Konvention mit europäischem Gemeinschaftsrecht am Beispiel des juste retour', *Zeitschrift für Recht und Verwaltung der wissenschaftlichen Hochschulen*, Beiheft 10 Rechtsfragen der Forschung, March 1993, 63 (72 f.).

38 *Official Journal of the EU* (OJ) L 261 of 6 August 2004, 64.

39 Spradling, K., 'The International Liability Ramifications of the U.S.' NAVSTAR Global Positioning System', in *IISL-Proceedings Dresden 1990, AIAA Washington 1991*, 93.

However, while it was expected that investment in GALILEO would have been determined by these basic criteria, instead of concentrating on the timely completion of an autonomous European navigation system, GALILEO became, to a large extent, a test-bed for EU/EC procurement rules in space.[40]

The first concepts for GALILEO can be found in a Memorandum of the EC of 12 February 1999.[41] After two publicly funded phases (1. Definition and 2. Development and In-Orbit-Validation, IOV), the third phase of Full Operational Capability (FOC)[42] was prospected as a form of public private partnership (PPP). This PPP included the establishment of an industrial consortium for the construction and operation of the system. In return for the financial contribution of this consortium, a 20-year concession for the exploitation of the system was offered. On the public side, the Galileo Joint Undertaking was established as a common approach of ESA and the EU according to Article 171 EC Treaty.[43]

In practice EC competition and procurement rules interfered constantly with ESA industrial policy; the project and ESA as procurement agent had to follow EC regulations. On the industrial side, bidding for the deployment phase ended after different intermediate stages, resulting in a merged consortium, reflecting more or less the industrial interests of the contributing Member States. Following the EC procurement process and the Brussels Agreement of 5 December 2005, hopes were then focused on the consortium. But for the concession contract, no consensus about the allocation of financial and liability risks could be reached. In June 2007 the concession process was terminated and in November 2007 the Council decided to continue with an exclusively publicly funded deployment phase.[44] Besides all the internal issues, the biggest setback was the time lost while further development and upgrade of the United States' GPS system continued.[45]

EC procurement rules are further complicated by the WTO Agreement on Government Procurement (GPA).[46] By contrast, the ESA is not a party to the GPA. Consequently, the Agreement is not applicable to ESA's procurement procedures. This would likewise be the case if ESA could conduct the procurement for EU (respective ESA/EU) space projects according to its own procedures. The conceptual alternative to the present situation, therefore, with ESA as the EU's procurement agent, would be a comprehensive ESA management as implementing agency.

---

40 For further details see Hobe, S., Heinrich, O. and Kerner, I. 2009. *Entwicklung der Europäischen Weltraumagentur als 'implementing agency' der Europäischen Union: Rechtsrahmen und Anpassungserfordernisse*. Münster: LIT Verlag; Hobe, S., Heinrich, O., Kerner, I. and Schmidt-Tedd, B. 2009. 'Ten Years of Cooperation between ESA and EU: Current Issues', *ZLW*, 49; and Kerber, M.C. 2009. *Das Großvorhaben Galileo auf dem Prüfstand des Europäischen Wettbewerbs- und Vergaberechts*. Berlin: TU Berlin.

41 COM (1999) 54 final.

42 According to COM (2000) 750 final, 24 originally scheduled for the beginning of 2008.

43 Council Regulation (EC) No. 876/2002 of May 2002 setting up the Galileo Joint Undertaking OJ L 138, 28 May 2002, 1 ff.

44 Council press release 16090/07 and 15231/07 (preliminary) of 23 November 2007.

45 See PricewaterhouseCoopers: Inception Study to Support the Development of a Business Plan for the Galileo Programme, TREN/B5/23-2001Executive Summary, 20 November 2001, 4, 12.

46 See Hobe, S., Heinrich, O. and Kerner, I. 2009. *Entwicklung der Europäischen Weltraumagentur als 'implementing agency' der Europäischen Union*, 214 ff.; Hobe, S., Heinrich, O., Kerner, I. and Schmidt-Tedd, B. 2009. 'Ten Years of Cooperation between ESA and EU', 49, 61 ff.

The actual situation is based on the GNSS Regulations as formulated in 2008.[47] In the resulting Tender Information Pack (TIP) two special rules[48] are implemented in order to guarantee widespread distribution of the contract volume. According to the two-out-of-six rule, one independent legal entity 'may bid for the role of prime contractor for a maximum of two of the six main work packages'. According to the 40 per cent rule, at least 40 per cent of the aggregated value of the activities has to be subcontracted by competitive tendering at various levels to companies other than those belonging to the groups of the prime. Obviously special arrangements outside standard procurement were necessary.

Reflecting on a decade of Galileo procurement, one wonders if the classical approach – with the system being set up by ESA and the operational phase transferred to a dedicated European organisation[49] – would not have been more efficient. An undisputed role for the EU, though, is certainly the creation of a legal framework for the application of the various services, including the responsibility and liability scheme. However, many unresolved issues remain.[50]

Recent Developments

As discussed, a European Space Policy has existed at least since the ESA Long-Term Space Plan (LTP) of 1985/87. Talking today of the European Space Policy, this would refer to the document of 21 May 2007 and its further development.[51] Implementation of the ESA-EU Framework Agreement is supported by the informal institution 'Space Council', which means the common meetings of the ESA Council and the EU Council.[52] After three meetings with a list of 'orientations', the European Space Policy was published as a political recommendation under the wording 'resolution'.[53] After the entry into force of the Lisbon Treaty, the major question is the distribution of programme initiatives between Member States/ESA and the EU under the new parallel space competence. Industrial policy and procurement rules have an indirect influence on those decisions.

ESA Procurement Reform

Under the weight of the perennial discussion regarding procurement and industrial policy, the ESA took the initiative with an international symposium, Developing Trends in Public Procurement and Auditing,[54] and made a major effort to obtain a general comparative overview of the worldwide landscape of different methods of public procurement.

---

47 Supplement of the *Official Journal of the EU*, 1 July 2008: B-Brussels: supply and services contracts for the Galileo full operational capability (FOC) procurement 2008/S 125-165928.

48 TIP, page 6.

49 Compare the EUMETSAT example.

50 See Schrogl, K.-U. and Sanchez, A. 2009. 'Policy Aspects of Third Party Liability in Satellite Navigation', *ESPI Report*, 19 (July 2009).

51 Council Doc. 10037/07 of 21 May 2007, published in ABI. C136 of 20 June 2007, 1–5.

52 The sessions are prepared by the High Level Space Policy Group and a secretariat, see Hobe, S., Kunzmann, K., Reuter, T. and Neumann, J. 2006. *Rechtliche Rahmenbedingungen einer zukünftigen kohärenten Struktur der europäischen Raumfahrt*. Münster: LIT Verlag, 246.

53 For the non-binding character see Hobe, S., Heinrich, O. and Kerner, J. 2009. *Entwicklung der Europäischen Weltraumagentur als 'implementing agency' der Europäischen Union*, 59 f.

54 Arnold, I. and Plingen, C. 2007. 'International Symposium: Developing Trends in Public Procurement and Auditing. Noordwijk, the Netherlands, 14–16 May 2007', *ZLW*, 627.

In 2008 ESA, through its Council on Ministerial Level, decided on a reform to update the existing procurement procedures and thereby also to minimise differences with regard to EU procurement rules. The reform comprised evolution of procurement procedures for large procurements over EUR 20,000,000, enhancement of the procurement policy and reform of ESA's Contracts Regulations and the General Clauses and Conditions (GCC).[55] The reform was finalised mid 2010. The Procurement Regulations were approved December 2008 and entered into force on 1 June 2010.[56] The ESA Procurement Regulations have incorporated a certain number of articles deriving from the EC Financial Regulations Implementing rules, regarding for example conflicts of interest, qualification and registration of economic operators, administrative penalties, time limits for tendering periods.[57] They have, however, been adapted to the ESA situation.

Some elements of the ESA procurement process resulting of the peculiarities of the space sector and its long-term projects should remain, though, such as the 'preliminary authorisation to proceed', some flexibility in renegotiation, prolongation and follow-up contracts and internal conflict management and arbitration. A useful instrument, after the competition phase, is the 'Core Team Selection Process', which ESA can initiate. This process aims at preventing the too great involvement of one single integrator and too high a degree of verticalisation.

The ESA Industrial Ombudsman, established in 1999, has now received additional functions. The role ensures that the prime contractors conduct their procurement activities on a fair and equitable basis and, should a case of conflict arise between ESA and prime contractors, going to the ombudsman is a mandatory step before recourse to arbitration.[58] Furthermore, the procurement reform established a Procurement Review Board, independent of ESA, for disputes relating to decisions taken by the Agency under the procurement regulations. After 20 years of the former procurement regulatory framework, ESA has adapted its procurement procedures to actual needs by a broad evaluation of external developments.

Space-related EU Industrial Policy

The 4th Space Council invited the European Commission to develop adequate instruments and funding schemes for Community actions in the space domain, taking into account the specificities of the space sector.[59] In May 2009 the 6th Space Council recalled this need to develop adequate EU financial and procurement instruments for the space sector. Until now the Commission seems not to have made major efforts to respond to those demands.

The European space manufacturing industry has become highly concentrated following a number of rounds of consolidation. Unmodified EU procurement rules have therefore led to an even higher degree of concentration. Consequently, counter-measures preventing the emergence of monopolistic structures and a higher degree of verticalisation, which means a concentration of all activities within the prime company, are necessary.

---

55 ESA/C (2010) 44, Paris 31 May 2010.

56 ESA/C(2008) 202 Procurement Regulations, approved by 207th Council ESA/C(2009)135 on 17 December 2008.

57 ESA/C(2010) 44, 11; this document contains in the annex, p. 13 a comparison between EU and ESA regulations and the remaining differences.

58 For further details see ESA web portal: 'How To Do Business with ESA, Industry Portal'. [Online]. Available at: http://www.esa.int/SPECIALS/industry_how_to_do_business/SEMJFO6H07F_0.html [accessed: 23 August 2010].

59 4th Space Council, Brussels 22 May 2007, Resolution on the European Space Policy, No. 16.

The need for counter-measures was finally accepted in the procurement regulations for GALILEO Full Operational Capability,[60] but this should be considered as only a first step towards a general approach. In this space sector of strategic investments, the public side should be more reserved, for example in the decision about double sourcing. In the case of large-scale projects, consideration should always be given to the possible negative impacts of procurement decisions on the industrial structure as such. To build up enabling technologies and then not consider their sustainable development makes no sense. The same is true for component-autonomy established despite market conditions.

A further matter to be considered is the geographical distribution principle. It is an essential factor in motivating Member States to invest in space. Furthermore, it guarantees a minimum geographical distribution of space investments in Europe. In R&D programmes the EU also takes care to ensure an adequate geographical distribution between different project partners. But with a central budget this cannot logically be related to differentiated financial contributions, as in ESA programmes.

Summary

Space is and remains a strategic topic. Programme decisions are oriented to that baseline which is also therefore a relevant part of the 'market' for which industrial policy and procurement rules are defined. Commercial space markets in this public-oriented domain are always interdependent. Realistically and rightfully, every space-faring region will have to be entitled to strategic assets and the required degree of autonomy. Consequently, this leads to the need for a space-specific industrial policy with related procurement rules.

Such a policy should be distinct from the indifference of a global market and uncontrolled open competitions. In order to prevent monopolistic situations or a lack of independence, counter-balancing measures are necessary. Following concrete past experiences with a lack of autonomy, the ESA has found its way to an industrial policy in which geographical return is an essential and still indispensable factor. The detailed concept has been readjusted to the changing environment during the last decades.

Based on its macro-economic, market-oriented approach, the EU/EC has developed its first major space project (GALILEO) under its own leadership. Today, the lack of a space-specific industrial policy under EU regulations – which takes into account the positive experiences of the ESA – is obvious. Only by this means, will it be possible in the future to define joint ESA/EU projects as topic-oriented and not tactically-oriented to aspects of the respective financial regulations. In addition, a solution needs to be found on the EU side whereby it can comprehensively authorise the ESA to be the implementing agency for European space projects, without the present restrictions of the framework agreement, excluding any form of geographical return for non-ESA financing.

List of References

Arnold, I. and Plingen, C. 2007. 'International Symposium: Developing Trends in Public Procurement and Auditing. Noordwijk, the Netherlands, May 14–16 2007', *ZLW*, 627.

EC Treaty of 25 March 1957, UNTS Vol. 298, 11, EU-Doc No. 1 1957 E.

60 GALILEO Regulation (EC) No. 683/2008, Article 17.

ESA Convention CSE / CS (73) 19, rev. 7; UNTS Vol. 1297 (1983), I No. 21524.

European Space Policy, Council Doc. 10037/07 of 21 May 2007, published in ABl. C136 of 20 June 2007, 1–5.

Framework Agreement between the European Community and the European Space Agency, Council of the European Union, Brussels 7 October 2003, Council Decision 12858/03; *Official Journal of the EU* (OJ) L 261 of 6 August 2004, 64.

Grillo, W. 1993. 'Die Vereinbarkeit der ESA-Konvention mit europäischem Gemeinschaftsrecht am Beispiel des juste retour', *Zeitschrift für Recht und Verwaltung der wiss. Hochschulen*, Beiheft 10 Rechtsfragen der Forschung, 63.

Hobe, S., Heinrich, O. and Kerner, I. 2009. *Entwicklung der Europäischen Weltraumagentur als 'implementing agency' der Europäischen Union: Rechtsrahmen und Anpassungserfordernisse.* Münster: LIT Verlag.

Hobe, S., Heinrich, O., Kerner, I. and Schmidt-Tedd, B. 2009. 'Ten Years of Cooperation between ESA and EU: Current Issues', *ZLW*, 49.

Hobe, S., Kunzmann, K., Reuter, T. and Neumann, J. 2006. *Rechtliche Rahmenbedingungen einer zukünftigen kohärenten Struktur der europäischen Raumfahrt*. Münster: LIT Verlag.

Kaiser, K. and Welck, S. Frhr. v. 1987. *Weltraum und internationale Politik.* München: R. Oldenbourg.

Kayser, V. 1994. 'Conference Report, International Colloquium, The Implementation of the ESA Convention: Lessons from the Past, Florence, 25–26 October 1993', *ZLW*, 68.

Kerber, M.C. 2009. *Das Großvorhaben Galileo auf dem Prüfstand des Europäischen Wettbewerbs- und Vergaberechts*. Berlin: TU Berlin.

Lafferranderie, G. 2005. *European Space Agency, Intergovernmental Organizations – Suppl. 20.* The Hague.

Micklitz, H.W. and Reich, N. 1989. *Legal Aspects of European Space Activities*. Baden-Baden: Nomos.

Morel de Westgavers, E. and Imbart, P. 1989. 'Le "juste retour": contrainte ou instrument d'intégration europóene?', *ESA-Bulletin*, 59, 62.

Narjes, K.-H. 1989. 'Space and the European Community', *Space Policy*, 59.

Provisional Consolidated Versions of the Treaty on European Union (TEU) and of the Treaty on the Functioning of the European Union (TFEU) in Council of the European Union 6655/08, Brussels, 15 April 2008.

Reuter, T. 2004. 'The Framework Agreement between the European Space Agency and the European Community: A Significant Step Forward?', *ZLW*, 56.

Schmidt-Tedd, B. 1994. 'Revidierte LTP-Planung, Etablierung der Europäischen Union: Fragen zur ESA-Standortbestimmung', *ZLW*, 38.

Schrogl, K.-U. and Sanchez, A. 2009. 'Policy Aspects of Third Party Liability in Satellite Navigation', *ESPI Report*, 19.

Spradling, Kevin K. 1990. 'The International Liability Ramifications of the U.S.' NAVSTAR Global Positioning System', in *IISL-Proceedings Dresden 1990, AIAA Washington 1991*, 93.

Spude, M. 1991. 'Integrierte Zusammenarbeit. Die europäische Weltraumorganisation ESA', in *Handbuch des Weltraumrechts*, edited by K.-H. Böckstiegel. Cologne: Heymanns, 667.

The Community and Space: A Coherent Approach, Communication from the Commission, COM (88) 417 final, Brussels, 26 July 1988.

Treaty of Amsterdam Amending the Treaty on European Union, the Treaties Establishing the European Communities and Certain Related Acts (hereafter Treaty of Amsterdam), Amsterdam, done 2 October 1997, entered into force 1 May 1999; OJ C 340/73 (1997).

Treaty of Lisbon amending the Treaty on European Union and the Treaty establishing the European Community (hereafter Treaty of Lisbon), Lisbon, done 13 December 2007, entered into force 1 December 2009; OJ C 306/1 (2007).

Treaty of Nice amending the Treaty on European Union, the Treaties establishing the European Communities and certain related acts (hereafter Treaty of Nice), Nice, done 26 February 2001, entered into force 1 February 2003; OJ C 80/1 (2001).

Chapter 9

Regulatory Framework for Authorising Satellite Applications: The Case of Telecommunications

Philippe Achilleas and Romain Loubeyre

Introduction

Since the launch of the first satellite 'Sputnik 1' by the Soviet Union, 4 October 1957, development of space activities has not slowed. Nowadays it is one of the most important components of the so-called 'Global Village'.[1] More than a need, the use of satellite systems is becoming a necessity in every aspect of society and, at the same time, virtually erasing boundaries. Correlatively, the space industry is rapidly becoming a more private market. These two facts, the proliferation of space applications and their privatisation, in parallel with a scarcity of resources, have made an efficient regime of authorisation and licensing a priority – at the international, regional and national levels. An efficient regime is necessary in order to ensure the consistency and viability of such activities.

However, this necessity appears to be of greater importance concerning two applications, specifically telecommunication[2] and broadcasting by satellite, since they are largely already privatised and generate the greatest commercial benefits,[3] whereas remote sensing and positioning by satellite remain mainly public activities and less profitable (in the economic sense of the word).

This chapter will thus focus on authorisation and licensing of satellite telecommunication, leaving broadcasting for another day. The chapter starts with preliminary remarks on the regime of authorisations and licences concerning the space operation itself. It then focuses on authorisations and licences for telecommunications by satellite.

---

1 McLuhan, M. 1962. *The Gutenberg Galaxy: The Making of Typographic Man*. Toronto: University of Toronto Press.

2 Telecommunication refers to the remote transmission of any kind of information by using an electronic system. Most of the telecommunications are now performed by using a combination of ground and space-based stations and networks, especially when it comes to international telecommunications. Television broadcasting is the activity to distribute audiovisual content to customers, which can also be performed using telecommunication satellites in order to directly reach the end-user without passing through a ground-based network, thanks to small dishes installed at home, or to transport of the content from one ground station to another over a large distance, which will then disseminate the content to the customers using the ground networks.

3 The fixed satellite sector (FSS) grew both in terms of transponder demand (+5.3 per cent) and revenue reaching $ 10.3 billion revenue in 2009. Around 26,000 channels were broadcast by satellite in 2009, increasing by 3,000 each year.

Preliminary Remarks: Authorisations and Licences Concerning Space Operations

Most space-faring nations have established a system of control of space operations conducted by private entities, in application of Article VI of the Treaty on Principles Governing the Activities of States in the Exploration and Use of Outer Space, including the Moon and Other Celestial Bodies[4] (OST). This puts the weight of international responsibility for the activities of private entities on the state, giving the latter control and jurisdiction over these activities in outer space. For this reason a procedure is normally set up that has to be undertaken by the satellite operator in order to be able to launch its satellite. Most states require only the operator to comply with an authorisation/licence procedure for the launch operation itself, as for example the Australian Space Activities Act of 1998[5] or the US Commercial Space Launch Act,[6] whereas some other states have applied a stricter interpretation of the Article VI OST by asking for authorisations for in-orbit operations of the satellite, such as the UK Outer Space Act of 1986.[7]

The French Law on Space Operations of 2008,[8] effective10 December 2010, appears as the stricter legal framework for satellite operators since it requires, in its Article 2, the operator to obtain a general licence for space operations and a special authorisation for each specific operation,[9] the issuance of which being the responsibility of an administrative authority, the minister in charge of space[10] that will verify the moral, financial and professional guarantees of the applicant and the conformity of the systems and procedures that will be used with the technical regulation, especially in the interest of the security of people and goods and the protection of public health and of the environment.[11]

The authorisation to operate a space object in orbit must be obtained for all the relevant and necessary technical operations, such as manoeuvres to place and maintain in orbital position, the necessary orbital manoeuvres (in case of collision with space debris for example) and de-orbit

4 Treaty on Principles Governing the Activities of States in the Exploration and Use of Outer Space, Including the Moon and Other Celestial Bodies, 27 January 1967, 18 UST 2410, TIAS No. 6347, 610 UNTS 205 (effective 10 October 1967), Article 6: 'States Parties to the Treaty shall bear international responsibility for national activities in outer space, including the moon and other celestial bodies, whether such activities are carried on by governmental agencies or by non-governmental entities, and for assuring that national activities are carried out in conformity with the provisions set forth in the present Treaty. The activities of non-governmental entities in outer space, including the moon and other celestial bodies, shall require authorization and continuing supervision by the appropriate State Party to the Treaty.'

5 Australian Space Activities Act no. 123 of 1998 as amended by Statute Law Revision Act no. 8 of 2010.

6 USC Title 49, Subtitle IX, chapter 701.

7 UK Outer Space Act of 1986, c.38 of 18 July 1986, Article 5 (2) d) 'requiring the licensee to obtain advance approval from the Secretary of State for any intended deviation from the orbital parameters, and to inform the Secretary of State immediately of any unintended deviation'.

8 French Law on Space Operations no. 2008-518, entry into force on 10 December 2010, 0J no. 129 of 4 June 2008; for an unofficial English traduction of the text, read *ESPI Perspectives*, 11 of 20 August 2008 on the new French Act relating to space activities.

9 Such as the launch phase, the in-orbit operation of the satellite, the transfer of the authorised satellite to a foreign national and the transfer to a French national of a non-authorised satellite.

10 As provided by the decree no. 2009-643 of 9 June 2009 published in OJ of 10 June 2009, the minister in charge of space is advised by the Centre National d'Etudes Spatiales for the decision making in the authorisation process.

11 French Law on Space Operations no. 2008-518, Article 4.

manoeuvres of the satellite.[12] Thereby, as of 10 December 2010, Eutelsat SA as a French satellite operator company has had to obtain a general licence for its activities concerning space operations and specific authorisations each time it launches a new satellite (through a launch company that must also obtain an authorisation) and manoeuvre a satellite in orbit (even if it has been launched before the entry into force of the law and its decrees). As stated by Article 5 of the law, a number of obligations are binding on the licensed operator.[13]

Moreover, the minister in charge of space can perform multiple controls[14] and take relevant measures to protect public safety, security of people and goods, public health and environment, the interests of national security and the respect by the state of its international obligations, such as the withdrawal of the licence or refusal of an authorisation. In case of false information transmitted by the operator or lack of compliance with the above-mentioned obligations, sanctions can be imposed by the minister, such as the withdrawal of the licence or authorisation or the imposition of a fine of maximum EUR 200,000.[15]

Provision of Telecommunication Networks and Services

Satellites are more and more involved in telecommunications[16] by completing terrestrial infrastructures, but also by entering into competition with ground networks. Telecom operators using satellite systems have to comply with a regime of authorisations and licences designed to regulate the exploitation of electronic communications networks in their ground segment and the provision of electronic communications services. Moreover, they are subject to specific authorisations for using limited resources that are frequencies, orbits and phone numbers.

The International Telecommunications Union defines telecommunications as 'any transmission, emission or reception of signs, signals, writing, images and sounds or intelligence of any nature by wire, radio, optical or other electromagnetic systems'.[17] This term has been replaced in the European Union by the expression 'electronic communications'[18] in order to consider the evolution

12 Decree no. 2009-643, Article 13.

13 Such as obtaining enough insurance coverage or financial guarantees to cover: third party liability within a limit legally fixed at EUR 60 million; the states and its administrations; the European Space Agencies and its Member States; and finally the launch operator, the satellite manufacturer, their respective partners and subcontractors; French Law on Space Operations no. 2008-518.

14 These rules are contained in the Decree no. 2009-643 Title III.

15 French Law on Space Operations no. 2008-518, Articles 9 and 11.

16 Even though the European Union uses the terms electronic communications instead of telecommunication since 2002, we will use both terms in this chapter since telecommunication is still mostly used by the international instances, the actors of the market and the customers.

17 Constitution of ITU of 1992: Annex – Definition of Certain Terms Used in this Constitution, the Convention and the Administrative Regulations of the International Telecommunication Union, no. 1012.

18 Directive EU no. 2002/21/EC of the European Parliament and of the Council of 7 March 2002 on a common regulatory framework for electronic communications networks and services (Framework Directive), OJ L.108, 24 April 2002, 33–50, Art. 2 a): 'electronic communications network means transmission systems and, where applicable, switching or routing equipment and other resources which permit the conveyance of signals by wire, by radio, by optical or by other electromagnetic means, including satellite networks, fixed (circuit- and packet-switched, including Internet) and mobile terrestrial networks, electricity cable systems, to the extent that they are used for the purpose of transmitting signals, networks used for radio and television broadcasting, and cable television networks, irrespective of the type of information conveyed'; and Art 2 c): 'electronic communications service means a service normally provided for remuneration which

of the market by encompassing the extreme variety of activities consisting in the provision of networks and services enabling the remote delivery of any kind of signals, regardless of the content which is carried.[19]

At the international level, setting apart the procedures governing the use of the radio frequencies spectrum established by the ITU, telecommunication activities are governed by the principles of the World Trade Organisation (WTO). Most significantly, the Reference Paper[20] is setting regulatory principles that are legally binding for Member States which have committed to it by appending the document, entirely or not, to their schedules of commitments. This latter document is the most important concerning authorisations and licences of telecommunication activities since it established the four basic principles in this matter, which have been implemented by the European Union though the 'Telecoms Package' of 2002: promotion of competition (§ 1), transparency in the criteria to obtain licences and statements of reasons for a refusal (§ 4), establishment of an independent national authority in charge of regulating the telecommunications market (§ 5) and finally repartition and use of limited resources according to an objective, opportune, transparent and non-discriminatory procedure (§ 6).

At the European level, the Telecoms Package is the legal framework for electronic communications networks and services within the European Union. The directive 2002/20/EC[21] of the European Parliament and the Council of 7 March 2002 on the authorisation of electronic communications networks and services (Authorisation Directive) sets up rules and conditions to become an operator of electronic communications within Member States. The two major objectives of this directive were harmonisation of the regional procedures and significant simplification of the administrative procedures for becoming a licensed operator. To be fully operational, the Authorisation Directive had to be implemented within Member States of the European Union by the mean of national legislation. Since all national legislation has the same basis,[22] only the example of the French system will be described hereafter.

Authorisations for Satellite Telecommunication Activities

Procedure to obtain the status of telecom operator According to Article 3 of the Authorisation Directive, which has considerably simplified the procedure to become a telecom operator, the establishment and exploitation of electronic communications networks is open to the public and

---

consists wholly or mainly in the conveyance of signals on electronic communications networks, including telecommunications services and transmission services in networks used for broadcasting, but exclude services providing, or exercising editorial control over, content transmitted using electronic communications networks and services; it does not include information society services, as defined in Article 1 of Directive 98/34/EC, which do not consist wholly or mainly in the conveyance of signals on electronic communications networks'.

19 Example: internet access is included in the expression electronic communications.

20 WTO Reference Paper on Basic Telecommunications, signed on 15 February 1997 (GATS XVIII).

21 OJ L 108, 24 April 2002, 21.

22 Considering the obligation of Member States to implement European Directives into their national law. Even though they are free to choose the form of this implementation, they are obliged by the content of the directive, as it is stated by Article 18 of the Authorisation Directive stating: 'Member States shall adopt and publish the laws, regulations and administrative provisions necessary to comply with this Directive by 24 July 2003 at the latest.'

governmental control should only take the form of a general declaration[23] of the national regulatory authority (NRA) that must be performed by the future operator. This declaration, according to Article 3.3, shall contain the expression of the operator's intention to provide electronic communications networks or services and the minimum level of information allowing the NRA[24] to keep records of the declared electronic communications operators over its territory. The company becomes legally an 'electronic communications operator' from the date the declaration has been recorded and the receipt delivered by the NRA.

Article 4 of the Authorisation Directive establishes the list of rights to which operators are entitled, which include the necessary rights to install facilities considered in accordance with Article 11 of Directive 2002/21/EC (Framework Directive), to negotiate interconnection with and where applicable obtain access to or interconnection from other providers of publicly available communications networks and services covered by a general authorisation anywhere in the Community,[25] and finally be given an opportunity to be designated to provide different elements of a universal service and/or to cover different parts of the national territory.[26]

Licences and authorisation to use limited resources Any emission and reception of data by a satellite from and to earth implicate the use of radio waves[27] notably characterised by their frequencies, the spectrum[28] of which being a key resource for satellite applications considering that it is the only method used to transport information on earth via outer space. The ground segment of telecommunications (when performed wireless) is subject to the same conclusion. Yet, the radio spectrum is not an unlimited resource since emissions on identical frequencies, or frequencies that are not sufficiently differentiated, can affect the quality of communications, or even engender jamming, if they are performed in the same area. The same issue applies to orbital positions, especially concerning geostationary earth orbits (GEO) that are limited to a certain number of available positions, and also to the most important orbits in satellite telecommunications. Two different systems of regulation on the use of limited resources are coexisting and completing each other to form a coherent and efficient structure, one being designed for the use of frequencies and their associated orbital positions with space stations and the other for the use of frequencies with ground stations and numbers.

---

23 Authorisation Directive Article 3.2: 'The undertaking concerned may be required to submit a notification but may not be required to obtain an explicit decision or any other administrative act by the national regulatory authority before exercising the rights stemming from the authorisation.'

24 In France, since the 'loi relative aux communications électroniques et aux services de communication audiovisuelle' of 9 July 2004 and according to the Article L. 33-1 of the Code des postes et communications électroniques, the general authorisation is performed by the Autorité de Régulation des Communications Electroniques et des Postes (ARCEP).

25 Under the conditions of and in accordance with Directive 2002/19/EC of 7 March 2002 on access to, and interconnection of, electronic communications networks and associated facilities (Access Directive), OJ L.108 of 24 April 2002, 7.

26 In accordance with Directive 2002/22/EC of the European Parliament and of the Council of 7 March 2002 on universal service and users' rights relating to electronic communications networks and services (Universal Service Directive), OJ L.108, 24 April 2002, 51.

27 ITU Radio Regulations Volume 1, Article 1, no. 1.5: 'Electromagnetic waves of frequencies arbitrarily lower than 3 000 GHz, propagated in space without artificial guide.'

28 The radio spectrum can be defined as the part of the electromagnetic spectrum containing the full range of radio frequencies (in other words, frequencies under 3,000 GHz), which are used in telecommunication and broadcasting.

Concerning the use of frequencies through the space station, in order to avoid situations of jamming and to protect the quality of telecommunications, there is a set of rules enforced at an international level, promulgated by the International Telecommunication Union,[29] to promote and support coordination between states concerning the use of frequencies and their associated orbits, to prevent harmful interference[30] and conflicts and to keep lines of communication open. These rules are contained within three documents established by ITU: the Constitution of ITU of 1992, the Convention of ITU of 1992[31] and the Radio Regulations, the last of these being the most important for coordination in frequencies allocation. The ITU recognises through these documents[32] the scarcity of frequencies and associated orbital positions and, therefore, establishes a number of mechanisms designed to satisfy the needs of every state. The international regime of the ITU would not be effective without a national framework that allows each state to perform a first level of management concerning the assignments of frequencies/orbits between its national entities and to coordinate with foreign states, when necessary, under the auspices of ITU-R, via the Radiocommunication Bureau[33]

Within each state a national authority is competent to deliver the administrative authorisation (called 'assignment'[34]) concerning the use of frequencies with the satellite. In France, the satellite operator must obtain the authorisation from the minister in charge of electronic communications.[35] However, this authority cannot deliver the authorisation in case of a potential risk of harmful interference at an international level (if a system used by another state could be jammed), which is almost always the case in satellite telecommunication and broadcasting. To solve this problem and obtain international protection of the desired frequencies, an agency will be responsible for the

29 As it defines itself, 'ITU is the leading United Nations agency for information and communication technology issues, and the global focal point for governments and the private sector in developing networks and services'.

30 ITU Radio Regulations, Article 1, section IV no. 1.169: 'harmful interference: Interference which endangers the functioning of a radionavigation service or of other safety services or seriously degrades, obstructs, or repeatedly interrupts a radiocommunication service operating in accordance with these Regulations.'

31 Constitution and Convention of the International Telecommunication Union concluded at Geneva on 22 December 1992, United Nations, Treaty Series, vol. 1825, No. 1-31251.

32 In Article 33 of the Convention and Article 42 of the Constitution of the ITU.

33 As defined by the ITU, the Radiocommunication Bureau (BR) is the executive arm of the Radiocommunication Sector. Its missions are to: provide administrative and technical support to Radiocommunication Conferences, Radiocommunication Assemblies and Study Groups, including Working Parties and Task Groups; apply the provisions of the Radio Regulations and various Regional Agreements; record and register frequency assignments and also orbital characteristics of space services, and maintain the Master International Frequency Register; provide advice to Member States on the equitable, effective and economical use of the radio-frequency spectrum and satellite orbits, and investigate and assist in resolving cases of harmful interference; coordinate the preparation, editing and dispatch of circulars, documents and publications developed within the Sector; provide technical information, organise seminars on national frequency management and radiocommunications, and work closely with the ITU Telecommunication Development Bureau in assisting developing countries.

34 ITU Radio Regulations Volume 1, Article 1, no. 18, Assignment (of a radio frequency or radio frequency channel): 'Authorization given by an administration for a radio station to use a radio frequency or radio frequency channel under specified conditions'.

35 It can be the ARCEP, the Conseil Supérieur de l'Audiovisuel, the Ministry of Defence or the Agence Nationale des Fréquences.

international notification of the project by transmitting files to the ITU in order to start the process of international coordination and registration of frequencies.[36]

The ITU is then the vehicle for negotiations between any concerned states in order to reach an agreement. The process will continue until the states have reached an agreement.[37] Once it is achieved, or if no risk of jamming is created by the project, the ITU will register the frequencies and the associated orbital position in the Master International Frequency Register,[38] which will entitle the operators to obtain international protection for the future of the space resources utilised by their systems. The registration is performed on a first-come, first-served basis, but this rule has been partly limited by the frequencies allocation and allotment systems[39] of the ITU and by obliging the operator to start using the frequencies within five years.[40] Moreover, under the principle of due diligence, the national agency will have to transmit any document proving the reality of the project to the ITU.

Once the registration is performed by the ITU, the national authorisation should be given concerning the exploitation of the frequencies protected at an international level via the ITU procedure. It should be remembered that this procedure is only applied to 'non-planned bands', considering that, when the project implies the use of frequencies that have been allocated to the state through the planning of frequency bands performed by the ITU, there is no need to obtain the international protection since no other state could legitimately use these frequencies.

Concerning the use of frequencies with ground stations, Article 5 of the EU Authorisation Directive sets up a regime of special authorisations to be obtained on an individual basis by the operators in order to gain access to limited resources for electronic communications, which are radio frequencies[41] and numbers. These individual rights must be granted for a limited period of time,[42] after an open, transparent and non-discriminatory procedure. The choice of the authority to contact depends on the system established by the state, meaning that the same regulator can be competent for both telecommunication and broadcasting applications, for example in the United States with the Federal Communication Commission (FCC). In the European Union, as provided

36 In France, this duty has been given to a specific agency, the Agence Nationale des Fréquences (ANFr). Since 21 June 2004, the system was instituted by the 'loi n° 2004-575 pour la confiance dans l'économie numérique' (LCEN), implemented by the Code des Postes et des Communications Electroniques (CPCE), Articles L. 97-2 and following, and by the decree no. 2006-1015 of 11 June 2006 implemented by the CPCE Articles R.52-3-1 and following.

37 It is important to consider that the negotiation phase can take years to achieve an agreement and thus jeopardise a project of satellite telecommunication or broadcasting. This risk has to be acknowledged by the operators and should be avoided, when it is technically possible, during the project development by choosing secure frequencies.

38 Radio Regulations *no. S8.3.*

39 Radio Regulations Volume 1, Article 1.16: the allocation is the 'entry in the Table of Frequency Allocations of a given frequency band for the purpose of its use by one or more terrestrial or space radiocommunication services or the radio astronomy service under specified conditions. This term shall also be applied to the frequency band concerned'; Article 1.17, allotment (of a radio frequency or radio frequency channel): 'Entry of a designated frequency channel in an agreed plan, adopted by a competent conference, for use by one or more administrations for a terrestrial or space radiocommunication service in one or more identified countries or geographical areas and under specified conditions'.

40 Up to seven years in exceptional cases such as a delay in the satellite delivery or a launch failure.

41 See also the Decision No. 676/2002/EC of the European Parliament and of the Council of 7 March 2002 on a regulatory framework for radio spectrum policy in the European Community (Radio Spectrum Decision).

42 Article 5.2 of the Authorisation Directive, the duration shall be appropriate for the service concerned.

by the Authorisation Directive, the operator who obtained the general authorisation must apply for individual rights to the NRA, which is the specific authority for frequencies concerning electronic communications activities, another entity being then in charge of broadcasting. To obtain an individual right to use frequencies or numbers, a company must apply according to the rules of the national numbering plan or frequencies allocation, as applicable.

In the usual case, the satellite operator would only obtain the individual rights to use frequencies with the space station, since it is the telecommunication operator's responsibility to obtain the rights to use frequencies with the ground stations. However, the contract concluded between both entities can transfer the responsibility to perform the emission or reception with the ground station directly to the satellite operator, which will then be in charge of obtaining both administrative authorisations. Certain situations might be more complicated, requiring three different authorisations. This is the case for example when the telecommunication operator in charge of the emission from the ground station to the satellite is different from the operator in charge of the ground station receiving data from the satellite. In this situation, each telecommunication operator must apply for the individual right to use frequencies with its own ground station to the competent authority (which might be different), while the satellite operator must obtain the authorisation to exploit the frequencies filing with its satellite.

Obligations Due under Authorisation Regimes

Description of the obligations The directive states a number of obligations attached to the general authorisation and the individual rights that can be included by Member States in their national legislation in parts A, B and C of its Annex, keeping in mind that these conditions shall 'be objectively justified in relation to the network or service concerned, non-discriminatory, proportionate and transparent'.[43] Concerning the general authorisation, Member States are free to choose the ones they consider the more appropriate considering the local situation including: participation in the financing of the universal service, administrative taxes, interoperability of services and interconnection of networks, requirements in matters of environmental protection, urban planning and land management, protection of privacy or maintaining networks integrity.

For the operator, the usual obligations linked to the individual rights are to use the frequencies efficiently, to respect the technical specificities attached to the concerned frequencies, to limit risks of jamming and to assist the administration in the implementation of the radio regulations, especially in the case of a demand arising from the minister in charge of telecommunications to stop any harmful interference caused by the satellite systems. Administrative charges can be established by Member States according to Article 12 of the Authorisation Directive for the treatment of files by the national administration in an 'objective, transparent and proportionate manner which minimises additional administrative costs and attendant charges'. Moreover, a fee can be demanded by Member States to the electronic communications operators for the use of limited resources and the installation of facilities.[44]

Obviously, as an electronic communications operator, the obligations contained in the other texts of the Telecoms Package must be respected. Moreover, the procedures of general authorisation and individual rights do not exempt the operators from obtaining authorisations arising from

43 Authorisation Directive Article 6.

44 Authorisation Directive Article 13: 'Member States may allow the relevant authority to impose fees for the rights of use for radio frequencies or numbers or rights to install facilities on, over or under public or private property which reflect the need to ensure the optimal use of these resources.'

other regimes, such as space telecommunication and broadcasting rules. It would be the case, for example, of a satellite operator to provide not only a service of communications routing but also one or more television or radio channels to customers.

Control of compliance and sanctions incurred As provided by Article 10 § 1 of the Authorisation Directive, the NRAs have the power to control compliance with the obligations associated with the general authorisation and the individual rights by the operators under their jurisdiction. In order to perform their task, and according to Article 11 § 1 b), the NRA can ask for any relevant information from the operators to prove their compliance, on a case-by-case basis, if they receive a complaint, have reason to suspect a lack of compliance from an operator, or on their own initiative during an investigation they are conducting. According to Article 11 § 1 a), an NRA can systematically, or on a case-by-case basis, verify compliance with the conditions linked to financial participation in the universal service and to the payment of fees and administrative charges.

As provided by Article 10 of the Authorisation Directive, in case of non-compliance with one or more obligations, the NRA will inform the offending company of the facts that are reproached and give 'a reasonable opportunity to state its views or remedy any breaches within: one month after notification, or a shorter period agreed by the undertaking or stipulated by the national regulatory authority in case of repeated breaches, or a longer period decided by the national regulatory authority'. If the case is not solved within the appropriate period of time, the NRA shall take any 'appropriate and proportionate measures aimed at ensuring compliance', which could be financial penalties if the Member State granted this power to the NRA, the necessity to comply within a certain period of time with the obligations, and in the worst case the partial or total suspension, reduction or even permanent withdrawal of the authorisation. In the case of 'serious and repeated breaches', it may be decided to 'prevent an undertaking from continuing to provide electronic communications networks or services or suspend or withdraw rights of use'. However, in any case, the operator that is subject to measures provided by Article 10 has the right to appeal the decision of the NRA in accordance with the procedure referred to in Article 4 of Directive 2002/21/EC (Framework Directive).

Conclusion

The proliferation of space applications and their privatisation, along with scarcity of the necessary resources, have forced formulation of a regime of authorisation and licensing at the international, regional and national levels in an attempt to ensure the consistency and viability of such activities. This is particularly important concerning telecommunications since they are largely already privatised and generate some of the greatest commercial benefits.[45] The authorisation and licensing of satellite telecommunication outlined in the chapter should always be reassessed for improvement, but as it stands today offers a workable and cooperative regime for authorisations and licences for telecommunications by satellite.

45 The fixed satellite sector (FSS) grew both in terms of transponder demand (+5.3 per cent) and revenue reaching $ 10.3 billion revenue in 2009. Around 26,000 channels were broadcast by satellite in 2009, increasing by 3,000 each year.

List of References

Achilleas, P. 2004. 'Le régime juridique des assignations de fréquences relatives aux systèmes satellitaires', *Communication – Commerce électronique*, 30–34.

Achilleas, P. 2005. 'La diffusion de programmes illégaux par satellite – l'affaire Al Manar', *Communication – Commerce électronique*, 2, 39–42.

Achilleas, P. 2009. *Droit de l'espace:* télécommunication, *observation, navigation,* défense, *exploration, collection droit des technologies*. Bruxelles: Editions Larcier.

Agence Nationale des Fréquences. [Online]. Available at: http://www.anfr.fr/ [accessed: 30 April 2011].

Australian Space Activities Act no. 123 of 1998 as amended by Statute Law Revision Act no. 8 of 2010.

Autorité de Régulation des Communications Electroniques et des Postes. [Online]. Available at: http://www.arcep.fr/ [accessed: 30 April 2011].

Constitution and Convention of the International Telecommunication Union concluded at Geneva on 22 December 1992, United Nations, Treaty Series, vol. 1825, No. 1-31251.

Convention for the Protection of Human Rights and Fundamental Freedoms, 213 U.N.T.S. 222, entered into force 3 September 1953.

Decision No. 676/2002/EC of the European Parliament and of the Council of 7 March 2002 on a regulatory framework for radio spectrum policy in the European Community (Radio Spectrum Decision).

Directive no. 2002/21/EC of the European Parliament and of the Council of 7 March 2002 on a common regulatory framework for electronic communications networks and services (Framework Directive), OJ L 108, 24 April 2002.

Directive 2002/20/EC of the European Parliament and the Council of 7 March 2002 on the authorisation of electronic communications networks and services (Authorisation Directive), OJ L 108, 24 April 2002, 21.

Directive 2002/19/EC of 7 March 2002 on access to, and interconnection of, electronic communications networks and associated facilities (Access Directive), OJ L.108 of 24 April 2002, 7.

Directive 2002/22/EC of the European Parliament and of the Council of 7 March 2002 on universal service and users' rights relating to electronic communications networks and services (Universal Service Directive), OJ L 108, 24 April 2002, 51.

'ESPI Perspectives 11' of 20 August 2008 on the new French Act relating to space activities.

EUR-Lex. [Online]. Available at: http://eur-lex.europa.eu/ [accessed: 30 April 2011].

European Conference of Postal and Telecommunication. [Online]. Available at: http://www.cept.org/ [accessed: 30 April 2011].

European Space Policy Institute. [Online]. Available at: http://www.espi.or.at/ [accessed: 30 April 2011].

French law no. 86-1067 of 30 September 1986 on freedom of communication as modified and supplemented, JORF No. 177 of 2 August 2000, 11903, last modification by law no. 2009-258 of 5 March 2009 on audiovisual communication and new television public service.

French Law on Space Operations no. 2008-518, entry into force on 10 December 2010, 0J no. 129 of 4 June 2008.

International Telecommunication Union. [Online]. Available at: http://www.itu.int/ [accessed: 30 April 2011].

McLuhan, M. 1962. *The Gutenberg Galaxy: The Making of Typographic Man.* Toronto: University of Toronto Press.

Ravillon, L. 2004. 'Droit des activités spatiales, adaptation aux phénomènes de commercialisation et de privatisation', in *Université de Bourgogne – CNRS, Travaux du Centre de recherche sur le droit des marchés et des investissements internationaux*, Volume 22, Edition LexisNexis Litec.

Treaty on Principles Governing the Activities of States in the Exploration and Use of Outer Space, Including the Moon and Other Celestial Bodies, 27 January 1967, 18 UST 2410, TIAS No. 6347, 610 UNTS 205 (effective 10 October 1967).

United Kingdom Outer Space Act of 1986, c.38 of 18 July 1986.

United States Code, Title 49, Subtitle IX, chapter 701.

WTO Reference Paper on Basic Telecommunications, signed on 15 February 1997 (GATS XVIII).

Chapter 10
Reforming National Licensing and Agency Structures: A Current Overview of the UK Space Agenda

Richard Tremayne-Smith

Introduction

This chapter will focus on the national licensing practices relevant to contracting for space and will do so within the current scope of the 1986 Outer Space Act as administered by the UK Space Agency (UKSA). The United Kingdom has now set up a space agency; the UK Space Agency was officially launched on 23 March 2010,[1] while the former British National Space Centre (BNSC) became UKSA on 1 April 2010. In the short term, licensing practices will remain the same[2] with UKSA taking over responsibility for the licensing activity related to the UK Outer Space Act of 1986. The option remains open to outsource further aspects of the licensing process, but the final stage of the process that issues a licence with whatever qualifications and caveats that may be required will remain an official function carried out on behalf of the Secretary of State.

The background to the UK licensing process, the 1986 Outer Space Act its intent and current scope of application will be covered. As part of this background, the post-2000 review of the implementation of the Outer Space Act is introduced and the subsequent changes that resulted in the implementation process. A further public review of the implementation is still a possibility.

Apart from simple changes to process, the changes made to the implementation of the Outer space Act, in order to better cover the developing industrial landscape and its range of activities, is also covered. This includes the licensing of ground stations involved in controlling operational satellites or, more generally, the licensing of spacecraft operations separately from the licensing of spacecraft ownership – due to the potential for liability to the state.

Some comparison with ongoing US and developing European practice is used to indicate areas for future consideration when supporting industry in contracting for space activities.

Background and Scope of UK Licensing

With a background in commercial space applications and manufacturing of space systems, the UK had an early need to regulate the activities carried out by its nationals in manufacturing and procurement of space systems and services. From the early space communications systems through small satellites for a range of countries to major capability in navigation and earth observation, the UK has had to address the licensing of many dozens of space systems and related services.

1 http://www.ukspaceagency.bis.gov.uk/About-Us/Transition-plans/13736.aspx [accessed: 27 August 2010].

2 http://www.ukspaceagency.bis.gov.uk/OSA+Licensing/11936.aspx [accessed: 27 August 2010].

The 1986 UK Outer Space Act brings the UK space treaty obligations into national legislation and primarily covers the Treaty on Principles Governing the Activities of States in the Exploration and Use of Outer Space, including the Moon and Other Celestial Bodies (the Outer Space Treaty, 1967), the Convention on International Liability for Damage Caused by Space Objects (the Liability Convention, 1972) and the Convention on Registration of Objects Launched into Outer Space, 1976. However, the general scope of the 1986 Act, conferring licensing and 'other powers', can also be considered to cover the Agreement on the Rescue of Astronauts, the Return of Astronauts and the Return of Objects Launched into Outer Space.

In addition the UK has clearly taken into account the Principles adopted by the UN General Assembly, in particular the Principles Governing the Use by States of Artificial Earth Satellites for International Direct Television Broadcasting and the Principles Relating to Remote Sensing of the Earth from Outer Space. The UK Act does this in a general way with an emphasis on controlling the state liability by evaluating and thus managing the risk associated with an activity and ensuring that financial recompense is available to the state. The indemnity to the state can be via company support, insurance or for a research or state actor notified to the UK Treasury as a contingent liability by the relevant government department.

The flexibility of the Act has been demonstrated over time, as a significant change in the utilisation of space has occurred. This change has occurred with the move from predominantly government and international treaty organisations utilising space to the current position where, as for many other countries, space is primarily a commercial activity.

The Inmarsat satellites provide a good example of the change in licensing practice. All Inmarsat satellites now appear on the UK Registry and have been notified to the UN Office of Outer Space Affairs (OOSA), which maintains the UN Registry[3] required under the Registration Convention. As an international treaty organisation, Inmarsat had no agreement on who should register the satellites, in part because the majority of its Member States were not a party to the relevant Registration Convention. Now it is a commercial operation and UK-based, the registration requirements are clear.

In addition, the UK Registry has recorded debris items as well as items launched into space that have now re-entered the earth's atmosphere and decayed from orbit. This demonstrates a positive move beyond just listing details of satellites or other items at the time of launch. This activity is consistent with the work of the UN working group on registration practices and the resulting General Assembly (GA) Resolution.[4]

On liability, the UK view is that if a person or UK-based organisation is operating a satellite, such that it has supervision and control of the satellite, then it can be deemed to be liable for any action it takes with regard to the satellite. This is not just for an owner operator, where the position is fairly clear and obvious, but also where a person provides a backup control function or carries out the pre-operational testing and commissioning activity. In addition any UK ground station transmitting control information based on decisions made by an operator based on UK territory would have such control and that ground station function would typically need to be licensed.

The act of procuring a launch, rather than owning a satellite, is also potentially a licensable activity and this can occur in partnership with a delivery in orbit contract. Here a licence would be required by the UK entity but the state of ownership would be expected to register the satellite, as it would ultimately own and operate the system and have liability through de-orbiting or correct re-orbiting at the end of the system's life. The state of final ownership is the one which effectively

3 http://www.unoosa.org/oosa/en/SORegister/index.html [accessed: 27 August 2010].

4 A/AC.105/C.2/L.266 and A/RES/62/101.

procured the system and is thus responsible for the satellite having been launched – and so is effectively the 'Launching State'.

Each real case is slightly different so no hard and fast rules can be given, but for industry there is a clear need for early and continuing discussion with the licensing authorities to ensure conditions are met and approval is available before critical dates occur. Due to late applications and slow reactions to requests for information from the licence applicant, it is not unknown for a licence to be issued very close to the launch date for a new satellite.

The Licensing Process and its Coverage of the Obligations

In this chapter we have now made the link between the UK Outer Space Act and the UN General Assembly Treaties and Principles, and given some idea of the scope of the Act. We will now look more specifically at the process of checking the compliance of applications by considering some of the major system classifications. More general matters on conformance issues when applying for a licence are introduced. These areas directly relate to the requirements placed on industry or commerce when applying for a licence and to the contract terms for customers, which are covered in the next section.

Overall conditions vary by orbit and the final use of the system. For a communications satellite in geosynchronous earth orbit (GEO), an application will require an International Telecommunications Union (ITU) approved slot and frequency allocation as part of the licence application process. Details of the filing and its conformance with the overall application will be checked during the technical evaluation that is part of the licensing process. Initial space environment issues are also checked at this time supported by the fact that the ITU has implemented its own space debris mitigation standards that are compatible with the GEO requirements of the Inter Agency Space Debris Coordination (IADC[5]) committee guidelines on space debris mitigation.

For an earth observation satellite system, whether in low earth orbit (LEO) or GEO, the special aspect of a licence application is the need to have a data policy for the satellite(s) that clearly demonstrates the compliance of the system with the Principles Relating to Remote Sensing of the Earth from Outer Space. It is particularly important to demonstrate the method of access to remote sensing data for sensed states. Where access is not clearly open but specific international details are required on who is responsible for the access and other details of the satellite capability, this information would typically be found on the website of the company responsible for exploitation of the data. A good example is the UK TopSat satellite where the data policy was the responsibility of the European company Infoterra.[6]

Earth observation systems are becoming increasingly commercial, which is a major change from the previous situation where earth observation and remote sensing were either for military applications or scientific research. It is important for commercial operators to understand the obligations of the Remote Sensing Principles and a published data policy is a good way to demonstrate this understanding. The licensing process should provide the necessary route to complete such a process to a level acceptable to all involved parties in the operation and utilisation of the satellite.

LEO satellites have to exist in a much more densely populated region than satellites in GEO or medium earth orbit (MEO), so debris migration procedures become even more critical in order to

5 Details at http://www.iadc-online.org/index.cgi [accessed: 27 August 2010].

6 http://www.infoterra.co.uk/data_sat_topsat.php [accessed: 27 August 2010].

maintain the many important orbits, such as the sun synchronous orbit (SSO), so that they can be kept open for further utilisation. The 25 years to de-orbit after the end of the satellite's operational life is a way to provide a reduction in the orbiting population that, when it was devised, would keep the population stable. However, with the many recent collision events, starting with the 2007 Chinese Anti Satellite (ASAT) test, the population will continue to grow even with no new satellite launches, so more significant action is required. 'Remediation' of the LEO debris problem, as the action has been named, will require active de-orbiting of satellites to reduce the collision risk and help prevent a runaway event that could leave critical orbits such as SSO unusable for hundreds of years. It will be in the interest of all the users to keep these orbits open for business, but it will take government action – and probably a number of governments acting in concert – to achieve the necessary remediation action. Industry as well as governments can be expected to become involved in this activity, which should start as soon as is reasonably possible.

Licensing of satellites in LEO should not only check if the proposed orbit for operation is viable, with the ever degrading environment, but also ascertain the value to the world at large of the proposed system to be launched. It may be that simple student satellites should not be allowed in higher LEO regions, while coordinated research satellites for monitoring the earth and its climate would be given priority due to their unique capability. Licensing of satellites will increasingly have to address these issues. While it was once reasonable to check the effect of adding a new satellite to LEO and setting a threshold for the level of the risk of impact, it is now essential in the more crowded LEO regions to also look at the effect of any new launch through the operational life and disposal phase of the mission. Even a relatively small impact in the future could have a more significant effect than a previous large impact event, due to the increasing debris population.

The orbit characteristics and related technical issues of the satellite are essential checks to ensure the safe operation of launched systems in the ever more crowded space environment. The related technical issues will include propulsion for orbit change and end-of-life procedures. This is coupled to the need for system reliability to give a high confidence of the required avoidance manoeuvres or end-of-life procedures being carried out successfully. General technical issues, such as no explosions and no parts degrading, for example paint flakes or thermal insulation degradation, can be significant causes of pollution. It is also important that the type of propellant used by a satellite or upper rocket body that is part of the delivery to orbit needs to be appropriate for the trajectory and orbit position where it is used, for example, solid propellant rockets that can create particles should not be used in long lifetime orbits. In addition the orbital manoeuvring procedures such as those used to place a satellite into its operational orbit need to be checked, for example to ensure where possible that any part of the launcher additional to the operational satellite is correctly disposed of if it is separated from the operational system. All these measures have some sort of associated cost and can add to system complexity but their implementation is essential if space is to be kept *open for business*. ESA, NASA and others have developed detailed procedures covering these issues and many more, the International Standards Organisation (ISO) is also developing a range of relevant implementable space standards[7] in a process involving national agencies and industry that will support improved debris mitigation.

7 http://www.iso.org/iso/catalogue_detail.htm?csnumber=42034 [accessed: 27 August 2010].

The Implications for Industry and Commerce

One of the implications for industry is the need to track the evolving standards and requirements in order to remain compliant. This is best covered by an involvement in national and international standards work where industry has the opportunity to affect both the work that is to be standardised and its priority, as well as the detail of specific standards. National standards activity is necessary to remain informed of the priorities of the international standards activity and thus to influence the voting process towards sensible and viable activities.

Future satellites will need to be more capable and many will require more manoeuvrability from more capable propulsion systems, for example for de-orbiting or collision avoidance. The capability will be orbit dependant, but will also vary within an orbital region depending on the size and exact location of the proposed system.

It is to be expected that nearly all future systems launched into space will require propulsion or a de-orbiting device, if they are in LEO, or active end-of-life propulsion capability for MEO and GEO orbital regions. Clearing orbital slots in GEO will have a significant element of self interest for the high revenue communications and broadcasting systems deployed there and collaboration among competitors is already evident. A commercial system of space surveillance data sharing has been established on the Isle of Man (IoM) and is known as the Space Data Association[8] (SDA). This organisation was established by Intelsat, Inmarsat and SES with the majority of other interested parties operating in the region also expected to join in due course.

Conclusions

While looking at operations in near-earth space, doing one's best and hoping was once considered a good idea by some, it is now very clear that future contract practice in the space arena will require significant activity in the area of analysing the future of the near-earth space environment and only allowing future near-earth space utilisation when it has significant value to the community at large and the 'through life risk' of any new launch is consistent with maintaining active use of near-earth space. Like it or not, remedial action in LEO is already a necessity if we are not to lose certain critical orbits for centuries.

In GEO, good practice derived from enlightened self interest is certainly a move in the right direction and the SDA and more general sharing of critical information between commercial competitors and government agencies shows that long-term sustainability is a possibility. However, even in GEO more needs to be done before the next accidental collision – not after it happens.

In addition, the GEO disposal orbit concept is still not fully understood by some. The current minimum disposal height has been chosen so that the disposal orbit has a collision probability that is very low, but many users just take the formulae and go to the minimum height, or just below, thinking this is OK. For the long-term sustainability of space we need each end-of-life manoeuvre to take the satellite as far away from the active GEO region as possible. If the current disposal orbit becomes too crowded then the next disposal orbit will be much higher and need even more fuel to reach. Many operators already go as high as possible with the available fuel at end of life (for example 850 km instead of 300 km above GEO). This practice and its long-term advantage for all current and future users of GEO should be better understood.

8 http://space-data.org/sda/ [accessed: 27 August 2010].

As to the new UK policy; time will tell, but what is clear is that as a major user of space applications and the host to many innovative and forward looking space companies and users, the UK will continue to keep in touch with the developments in the area of the space environment and be sensitive to the effect of the updates to the implementation of the Outer Space Act 1986 for industry, both the supply side and the user community.

For the future, it is clear that increased harmonisation of worldwide activities related to the regulation of space activities is required, and a good start will be to make appropriate moves for them in the European space sector. Contract practices required for licensing compliance and international standards will form a major part of the harmonisation process. In particular, a common database of standards and guidelines, compiled such that their relevance to specific projects can be easily identified, would be a good starting point. The UK has already compiled such a list[9] for use in the UK licensing process.

In addition, all countries should ensure that there is also common treatment of general liability and insurance issues, without such action unfair commercial regimes would develop and activity contrary to best practice could emerge. National licensing practices should be updated as the state of the space environment evolves. As an example, the increased number of objects in orbit at a height of 800 to 1,000 km will require that new launches to the SSO should only be allowed where there is a common benefit for the global community. Current operations are already compromised by the rapidly deteriorating environment in that region of space and because of its significant physical characteristics, that support remote sensing for the benefit of all, this orbital regime must be protected.

---

9 http://www.bis.gov.uk/assets/bispartners/ukspaceagency/docs/osa/dtbofstnds2010.pdf.

Chapter 11

Consequences of the French Space Law on Space Operations (FSOA) on CNES's Mission as a Contracting Space Agency*

Philippe Clerc

Introduction

France adopted domestic legislation on Space operations on 3 June 2008.[1] The act entered into force on 10 December 2010. In a few words, the general purpose of this French Space Operation Act (hereafter FSOA or SOA) is to set up a coherent national regime for authorisation and control of space operations under the French jurisdiction and/or for which the French government bears international liability either under UN Treaties (namely the 1967 Outer Space Treaty, the 1972 Liability Convention and the 1976 Registration Convention) or in accordance with its European commitments with ESA and its Member States (for European launchers such as Ariane).

The governmental authority (FSOA Arts 2 and 4.2) responsible for granting space operation authorisation, and for controlling its implementation, is the Ministry of Research, as Ministry in charge of Space Affairs, according to the Authorisation Decree[2] (Art. 1).

The Centre National d'Etudes Spatiales (CNES) on its side has been delegated by law full authority for the technical instruction of authorisation applications (FSOA Art. 28 g).

This chapter focuses on the effects of such legislation on CNES's missions, in particular risks of conflicts of interest between its traditional space agency missions, for example space programme management (including those in relation with ESA[3]) and technical centre activities, and its newly delegated responsibilities and duties consisting in attesting and monitoring, on behalf of the French government, the compliance of private systems (and their operating procedures) with the FSOA's technical regulations provisions being set forth for the safety of persons and property, the protection of public health and the environment. One may consider that such a role for CNES basically does not differ that much from those resulting from its former involvement in Ariane production monitoring or qualification maintenance since 1980 as 'design authority' (*autorité de conception*), on behalf of the French government or in its ARTA mission (Ariane Research and Technology Accompaniment) for ESA. The main differences now are that CNES's role under the FSOA is on the one hand to be limited to the assessment of space systems' compliance with technical regulation

* All opinions expressed herein are the personal views of the chapter author and do not bind those of his employer.

1 French Space Operations Act 3 June 2008, no. 2008-518, *French Republic Official Journal* (JORF) 4 June 2008, cited as FSOA.

2 Decree no. 2009-643 on the authorisations dated 9 June 2009, *French Republic Official Journal* (JORF) 10 June 2009, in accordance with French Act no. 2008-518 of 3 June 2008 relative to space operations, cited as 2009 Authorisation Decree.

3 European Space Agency.

provisions, but not to propose any complementary technical support or remedies, and on the other hand to exclude any contractual relations with the controlled operator.

The issue discussed in this chapter also includes CNES's missions at the Guiana Space Centre (GSC), the European Launch Base for Ariane, Soyuz and Vega, where CNES's President has been entrusted by FSOA with a special authority over the general safety, security and base management ('administrative police' in French law). Here also, CNES's President, FSOA's police mission, is not an *ex nihilo* creation, but a formal and belated translation into national legislation of previous French governmental responsibilities, delegated to CNES, in the frame of an international agreement with the European Space Agency dealing with the GSC and its associated services signed on 5 May 1976, and constantly renewed and currently in force.

Under this Agreement:

> ESA recognises the French government's delegation to CNES of its responsibilities concerning the general safety, security and base management at the GSC.
>
> France and ESA shall establish the rules for the sharing of the burden of the liability for damages caused by launchers operated from GSC: ESA shall be liable for damages caused by its own launcher programmes (for example Ariane 1 development, before its qualification flight, or nowadays VEGA maiden flight) or if its satellite is the cause of the damages. France shall be liable for any other damage (in particular after 1980, for damages caused by Ariane launches during its production/exploitation phase).
>
> France and ESA share the financial burden of the GSC launch base maintenance cost on a respective proportion of 1/3 to 2/3.

FSOA Principles and their Consequence on CNES Missions

CNES's Statute and Missions before FSOA

The French space agency was created by Act of 19 December 1961[4] under Charles de Gaulle's presidency in order to design and implement the French government's space policy. CNES's founding fathers, in particular Professor René Auger, were also those who supported, at the same time, around 1962, the constitution of both European space organisations, ESRO and ELDO, precursors of the present ESA organisation. The rationales were to provide France with an autonomous body to carry out national research and international and European cooperation and to develop a domestic space capacity in the field of science, industry and space applications. CNES's

---

4 CNES Constitutive Act, 19 December 1961, no. 1961-1382, codified by Ordinance 11 June 2004, no. 2004-545, into the French Research Code (hereafter RC), Articles L 331-1 to L 331-6, the whole being amended by Articles 21 and 28 of French Space Operations Act 3 June 2008 adding Articles L 331-7 and 8, hereafter cited as CNES Constitutive Act.

CNES organisation and functioning is regulated by decree no. 84-510 of 28 June 1984, 'relating to the Centre National d'Etudes Spatiales'. [Online]. Available at: http://www.legifrance.fr [accessed: 30 April 2011]. This 1984 decree was amended following FSOA issue by Decree no. 2009-644 issued on 9 June 2009, *French Republic official Journal* (JORF) 10 June 2009, hereafter cited as CNES Amended Decree.

mission as a space agency, according to its constitutive act (RC Article 331-2 a to e provisions, before FSOA's Article 28 addition)[5] is very comprehensive concerning:

> a proposal for the government's final decision on space development programmes (in the fields of science, technology, innovative operational systems, satellites or launcher systems), such programmes being achieved as the case may be on a national or European scale or in the frame of international cooperation;
>
> management and implementation of such programmes, as contracting authority, or through cooperation or partnership, or through its technical centres' expertise (Toulouse Space Centre for orbital systems, science and space application, Launcher Directorate for launch systems);
>
> international space cooperation with other national space agencies;
>
> publication, promotion, education and other actions encouraging the development of space activities and applications.

CNES has a legal personality (RC Article L331-1), distinct from that of the French state. That means CNES disposes, under general authorisation of its board, of an independent budget, can sue or be sued by third parties in courts, and is solely responsible and liable in connection with its actions. In other words CNES, as compared with NASA for example, is not a branch of the government.

As another specificity resulting from its constitutive law, CNES has been embodied as an 'Industrial and Commercial State Organisation' (EPIC), such status traditionally reserved at this time to operational monopolistic public utilities such as EDF (Electricité de France), the national electricity power supplier, or SNCF, the state-owned French railways company.

A difference between CNES and state operators, which are mainly financed by funds generated by the public services provided to users, is that CNES's financial resources are mainly provided by the National Research Budget (Finance Yearly Act, nos 191 and 193, defence and civil items) and contracts or mandates from ministry or other public agencies, included ESA (at GSC for example).

5 Le Centre national d'études spatiales a pour mission de développer et d'orienter les recherches scientifiques et techniques poursuivies en matière spatiale. Il est notamment chargé : a) De recueillir toutes informations sur les activités nationales et internationales relatives aux problèmes de l'espace, son exploration et son utilisation ; b) De préparer et de proposer à l'approbation de l'autorité administrative les programmes de recherche d'intérêt national dans ce domaine; c) D'assurer l'exécution desdits programmes, soit dans les laboratoires et établissements techniques créés par lui, soit par le moyen de conventions de recherche passées avec d'autres organismes publics ou privés, soit par des participations financières; d) De suivre, en liaison avec le ministère des affaires étrangères, les problèmes de coopération internationale dans le domaine de l'espace et de veiller à l'exécution de la part des programmes internationaux confiée à la France; e) D'assurer soit directement, soit par des souscriptions ou l'octroi de subventions la publication de travaux scientifiques concernant les problèmes de l'espace; f) (FSOA, Article 28) D'assister l'Etat dans la définition de la réglementation technique relative aux opérations spatiales; g) (FSOA, Article 28) D'exercer, par délégation du ministre chargé de l'espace, le contrôle de la conformité des systèmes et des procédures mis en œuvre par les opérateurs spatiaux avec la réglementation technique mentionnée au f; h) (FSOA, Article 28) De tenir, pour le compte de l'Etat, le registre d'immatriculation des objets spatiaux.

CNES has also never developed any 'commercial' permanent activity on its own, at least within the meaning of the French commerce or tax codes. CNES's capacity to undertake commercial activities is then limited to the necessary transition period before the transfer of the activities to the private sector (as a kind of incubation) or when a default of a private offer or capacity occurs. In any case, such potential competitive activities (operations or downstream applications) have been conceded, through a framework agreement, to a dedicated stock company, Arianespace SA for launch services[6] or Spot Image for spot satellite's data worldwide distribution.

The advantages of the EPIC status, in terms of flexibility, as compared to traditional state administration, or other public organisational status, in particular Public Administrative Organisations (Etablissements publics à caractère administratif: EPA)[7] are:

autonomy of governance by an independent board of directors and *ad hoc* consultative committees;

management by a president, named by the French Republic President (Minister Council decree), with chairman and CEO authority like in a private company;

an '*a posteriori*' control by budget authorities on many decisions;[8]

and, last but not least, a private staff regime. CNES's employees are not subjected to a civil servant regime but to a specific one.

From missions described in CNES's 1961 Constitutive Act, as described here above, some additions or developments were made before FSOA:

management of the Guiana Space Centre, as a result of the launch base establishment, under CNES responsibility pursuant to Decree 65-388, of 21 May 1965 and French government-ESA Agreement on GSC, as above mentioned;

creation and/or stockholding[9] in a civil or commercial company, to extend or spin off its programmes' achievements, the major ones being:

- Arianespace SA, launch service provider (since 1980)

6 The Ariane production (and exploitation) scheme was originally defined by the 'Ariane Inter Governmental Production Declaration' adopted on 14 January 1980, between the associated Ariane Programme European Participating State, and implemented through the ESA-Arianespace convention or arrangement. This organisation has not been changed to date. It is important to underline further that under said Declaration (still in force as renewed on 30 March 2007), the French Government is the sole state responsible (as a Launching State as referred to in the 1972 U.N. Liability Convention) for indemnifying any accident victims caused by Ariane Launch services performed under Arianespace responsibility from the GSC.

7 Such as METEO France, IGN (Institut Géographique National) the national geography agency, state museums, universities and high schools, official academies and agencies in France.

8 Decree no. 84-510 of 28 June 1984 relating to the Centre National d'Etudes Spatiales, Article 5.

9 As an application of CNES' constitutive Act, CR Article L331-2 c 'CNES is entrusted: … (c) to ensure implementation of such programmes, either in laboratory and technical establishments created by itself, or by means or research convention settled with other public or private organisations, or financial share (stock holding).'

- Intespace SA, space environment ground facility testing (1983, now controlled by Astrium)
- Spot Image SA, space remote sensing data distribution (1983, controlled exclusively by Astrium since July 2008)
- Simko, a private-public building estate company to support Kourou city development in Guiana, following the implantation of the GSC launch base (set up in 1976)

French government representation on the ESA and programme boards since its constitution in 1973 (effective in 1975)[10] in association with the Ministry for Foreign Affairs;

participation at the European Union's space dedicated boards and committees, following its inclusion in space affairs policy and programmes since the 1990s;

defence programmes on space-segment responsibility (satellite platform or bus, except their sensitive payload). Cooperation with the Ministry of Defence was reinitiated in the 1980s with the Helios Programme, a Defence Earth Observation Satellite utilising the derived platform of the CNES's SPOT civil satellite. Following the lesson learned from the first Gulf War in 1991, the French government decided to develop and strengthen a coherent Defence Space Policy. In this view, CNES's 1984 Functioning Decree was modified in 1993[11] to add to the Ministry of Research in charge of Space Affairs, the Ministry of Defence as co-responsible for Governmental Space Policy, in particular for CNES's governance and funding. Nowadays, the average defence contribution in CNES programmes and budget is about 20 per cent;

in line with (or as an extension of) its research programme responsibilities, CNES has been entrusted with the following 'operational' activities without any special formal statutory decision (law or decree):

- government or private not standard satellite in-orbit positioning and control service provider
- outer-stratosphere balloon launch and operation on behalf of the scientific community, at national scale or through international cooperation.

---

10 The text of the ESA Convention elaborated by the VI° CSE on 31 July and 20 September 1973 (Ref. CSE CS(73)19, rev.7) was approved by the Conference of Plenipotentiaries held in Paris on 30 May 1975. The Convention was signed after this Conference by all Member States of the European Space Research Organisation and of the European Organisation for the Development and Construction of Space Vehicle Launchers (ESRO and ELDO) and opened for signature by the Member States of the European Space Conference.

The European Space Agency functioned de facto from 31 May 1975. The ESA Convention entered into force on 30 October 1980. Date of deposit of instruments of ratification. A Cooperative Agreement between ESA and Canada as associated member entered into force on 1 January 1989.

11 Decree no. 93-277 dated 3 March 1993 amending CNES's Decree no. 84-510 of 28 June 1984.

FSOA's Main Feature

Persons and space activities subjected to FSOA The FSOA is only applicable to space operations together with space operators. The definition of which is given by Article 1:

> The term 'space operator' (hereafter operator): means any natural or juridical person carrying out a space operation under its responsibility and independently.
>
> The term 'space operation' means any activity consisting in launching or attempting to launch an object into outer space, or of ensuring the commanding (control) of a space object during its journey in outer space, including the Moon and other celestial bodies, and, if necessary, during its return to earth.

Under Article 2, the following persons are required to obtain an authorisation from the Administrative Authority (the Ministry in charge of Space Affairs according to the 2009 Authorization decree, namely the Ministry of Research at the present time):

1. *Any operator, whatever its nationality*, intending to proceed with the launching of a space object from the national territory or *from means or facilities falling under French jurisdiction*, or intending to proceed with the return of such an object onto the national territory or onto facilities falling under French jurisdiction (for example space object launching or return services from or onto the French territory or jurisdiction);
2. *Any French operator intending to proceed with the launching* of a space object from the territory of a foreign state or from means or facilities falling under the jurisdiction of a foreign state or from an area that is not subject to the sovereignty of a state, or intending to proceed with the return of such an object onto the territory of a foreign state or onto means and facilities falling under the jurisdiction of a foreign state or onto an area that is not subject to the sovereignty of a state (for example space object launching or return services occurring outside the French territory or jurisdiction, but performed by a French citizen, and then involving French Government indemnification under the 1972, liability convention);
3. Any natural *person having French nationality* or juridical person whose headquarters are located in France, whether it is an operator or not, *intending to procure the launching of a space object* or any French operator *intending to command such an object* during its journey in outer space (for example any French company, space operator or not, that intends (1) to procure a launch service for its satellite or/and (2) to operate such satellite in orbit).

Consequently, any foreign operator that procures a launch of a space object using the services of a French launch operator (Arianespace for example) shall not be subjected to FSOA (as a non-French citizen as referred to in Article 2 § 3 here above). The authorisation for the launch shall only be applied for by the relevant French launch service operator according to Article 2 § 1, and only for the launching phase.

According to Article 3, the *transfer of the control of a space object* also requires a governmental authorisation (Article 3) in the following conditions:

the transfer (*by selling or any other means*) to a third party of the control of a space object which has been authorised pursuant to FSOA is subject to prior authorisation;

any French operator intending to take control (*by purchase or any other means*) of a space object whose launching or control has not been authorised under the present act (*for example a foreign satellite*) shall obtain to this end a prior authorisation.

Condition for granting authorisation (FSOA Article 4) Authorisation to launch, to command or to transfer the commanding of a space object or to proceed with its return to earth is granted by the administrative authority (the Ministry of Research as Ministry in charge of Space Affairs under the 2009 Authorisation Decree) upon a showing:

of moral, financial and professional guarantees of the applicant, and if necessary from its shareholders;

that systems and procedures to be implemented are compliant with the Technical Regulations (TR) set forth for the safety of persons and property, the protection of public health and the environment. Such Technical Regulations shall be issued by the Ministry in charge of Space Affairs, following CNES proposal, under FSOA Art. 4 §1 and 28 f.

Authorisation shall not be granted if the operations or the systems intended to be implemented are likely to jeopardise national defence interests or the respect by France of its international commitments.

A licence system (for example a global framework authorisation for a determined period of time to given operators for given operations) is set up to facilitate authorisation application for experienced operators, at different scales, namely:

licences certifying that a space operator complies with moral, financial and professional requirements

licences attesting the compliance of given systems or procedures with the Technical Regulations

licences equivalent to authorisations for standard satellite operations

The 2009 Authorisation Decree sets forth the terms of application of FSOA Article 4. It specifies in particular:

the information and documents to be provided to support applications for authorisation, as well as the application procedure for these authorisations;

the conditions under which the licences equivalent to authorisation may be granted, and

the conditions under which the beneficiary of such licences shall inform the administrative authority of the space operations it undertakes.

A specific and simplified regime is reserved by FSOA Article 4 § 4 for operations (such as launching services) that are to be procured by an applicant, under Article 2 § 3, from the territory of a foreign state or under a foreign jurisdiction. Such activities, despite the fact they are to be performed and controlled outside the French jurisdiction, are likely to involve French liability and indemnification duty as a launching state under the NU 1972 Liability Convention (specifically as the state 'which procures the launching of a Space Object'). In such case, the Administrative Authority may exempt the applicant from all or any part of the present technical compliance assessment, provided that such foreign country national and international commitments as well as its legislation and practices include sufficient guarantees, regarding the safety of persons and property and the protection of public health and the environment, and regarding liability matters.

FSOA's liability regime FSOA's liability regime rationale is to concentrate the burden of liability on the sole operator for any damage caused by its space operations to third parties (in case the French jurisdiction is competent). This indemnification regime (FSOA Art. 13) is largely derived from the UN 1972 Liability Convention, which imposes:

absolute liability for damages on ground and in air space

liability on a fault basis for damages caused in outer space

FSOA provides, however, specific waiver or limitation of liability for the authorised space operators, except in the event of wilful misconduct, as follows:

- *Limited period of liability*. An operator's liability obligation ends in any case when the requirements set out in the authorisation for its own phase of responsibility (for example the 'launching phase' for a space launch operator, or the 'in-orbit commanding phase' for a satellite operator), are fully fulfilled, or at the latest one year after the date on which these obligations were deemed to be fulfilled according to such authorisation. The government's obligation then supersedes the operator's indemnification obligation for any damage occurring after this period.
- *Liability allocation between the French government and space operators* has been construed in the form of an indemnification ceiling, wherever the claim may arise from (FSOA Articles 14 to 19). Should any FSOA authorised operator (or exceptionally one of its sub-contractors) being sued and condemned by a domestic court or by a foreign court, or should the French government being obliged, under the UN 1972 liability convention, to indemnify any foreign victim for damages on the ground caused by any authorised operations under FSOA, the French state guarantee (ceiling) is granted to such operator for any indemnification payment exceeding approximately EUR 60 million (the 2008 Fiscal Act ['Loi de finances rectificative' 30 December 2008 no. 2008-1993, JORF no. 0304 31 December 2008 article 119] set up a bracket between EUR 50 and 70 million, but due to the Intergovernmental European Launchers Exploitation Declaration, this amount is being frozen at EUR 60 million for Ariane, Vega and Soyuz).
- *Cross waiver of liability and hold harmless clause*. FSOA Article 20 confirms the validity of, and establishes, a 'by default' cross-waiver contractual regime between the associated parties to the space operations:

  - no claim between the participants to an authorised space operation (launch service operator, customer with its associated contractors, launch base operator, manufacturers, sub contractors);
  - this provision shall be self-enforceable and mandatory between the participants;
  - sole legal exception: if otherwise expressively provided for in a contract between participants to the in-orbit command of a satellite.
- This concentration of the liability on the operator along with the enforced cross-waiver of liability provisions shall hold harmless an operator's contractors and subcontractors from being sued by third parties and thus limit their need of an insurance coverage.
- *Insurance.* As an equitable counterpart of the state's guarantee here above, the operator is required by Article 6 to obtain insurance coverage for damages to third parties below the aforementioned ceiling (i.e. EUR 60 million) or to secure equivalent financial guarantees. This shall benefit namely the government, ESA, the operator and the persons having taken part in the space operation or in the production of the space object.

Mission Entrusted to CNES and to the CNES's President by FSOA and the Question of Potential Conflicts of Interests

It is to be underlined that through FSOA the French government delegated to CNES and its president the whole of its technical responsibility for authorising and monitoring space operations under its jurisdiction. This delegation scheme was originally proposed in April 2006 by the State Council (Conseil d'Etat) itself in its preliminary study report entitled 'A Legal Policy for Space Activities' (here above referenced). In this report (pp. 77 and 78), the State Council assumes that it is not necessary to create an independent authority to regulate the space sector, as previously done in other economic sectors, such as telecommunications and energy. It suggests that the FSOA's future implementation decree appoints the Ministry of Space Affairs as the Administrative Authority in charge of delivering authorisation.

Meanwhile it recommends, due to the unique nature of CNES's technical expertise, especially in the launcher area, and the lack of resources and means of the Ministry of Space Affairs in such technical fields, to delegate to CNES the assessment of compliance of the space systems and procedures with the Technical Regulations.

It is to be underlined that the State Council especially points out the risk of 'conflicts of interest' between new CNES FSOA missions and its previous missions (under RC Article L 331.2), in particular as contracting authority, operator (in-orbit positioning and manoeuvres) of private satellites, and as shareholder of Arianespace SA and Spot Image SA. It does not retain, however, any legal impediment, provided that CNES separates its activities into two different sectors (FSOA and non-FSOA activities), ends any supply of commercial services and transfers its shareholdings in business companies to another governmental agency, such as the State Participation Agency (APE 'Agence des Participations de l'Etat'). Such legal opinion from the State Council (by its Study and Report Section), and endorsed by its Plenary Assembly, was very helpful for FSOA's law-making process, given the fact that despite its legal advisory and assessment role on regulatory matters on behalf of the government, the State Council acts as well *in fine* as the French Supreme Administrative Court.

On its side, Claudie Haigneré the Minister for Space Affairs, in a 2002 preliminary report drafted by her Space Department ('Space Law Evolution in France'), urges the strengthening of CNES missions, under the future space legislation, by entrusting it with a technical authority in certifying, controlling and holding registries of space activities. The content of this report also analyses the risk of conflicts of interest and proposes remedies (pp. 42–5).[12]

Henri Revol's report on behalf of the Senate Economics Affairs Commission, (report no. 161 here above mentioned, pp. 42 and 43) also recommended to legitimate such CNES technical authority for FSOA's purposes and, noting possible conflicts of interest, called for an unquestionable disengagement of CNES from any activity and stock-holding incompatible with the exercise of its new legal responsibilities. A special annex to this report (annex II pp. 93–5) makes a comprehensive inventory of CNES's current interests in competitive activities, distinguishing on the one hand CNES's commercial activities with a description of its situation and remedies already taken or to be taken and, on the other hand, CNES's shareholding situation and remedies taken or to be taken. The text suggests that CNES abandon any in-orbit services for private companies and commercial satellites and that it withdraw from Arianespace and Spot Image stock.

Last but not least, The European Commission, in consultation with the French government in April 2007, on the basis of EC Treaty Article 88 § 3 (State Liability Ceiling Conformity / E.C. Public Aid Legislation) takes note of 'measures undertaken by French authorities in order to prevent any conflict of interest between CNES's technical control of space operations and its commercial activities directly or by means of its participations'. Mention was made that the governance of CNES guarantees sufficient independence through the traditional framework convention between ESA and Arianespace since 1980, as renewed following the 2007 Intergovernmental Launcher Declaration on European Launchers Exploitation.

Mission entrusted to the CNES as a legal body FSOA CNES's missions focus on the assessment of technical compliance of space operations with the Technical Regulations and on the Registration of French Space Objects as set forth in FSOA Article 28 and translated in Article L. 331-2 of the Research Code f), g) and h):

> f) To assist the Government in the definition of the technical regulations relating to space operations;
>
> g) To certify, by delegation of the minister in charge of space, that the systems and procedures implemented by the space operators comply with the technical regulation mentioned in paragraph f);
>
> h) To hold the register of the space objects on behalf of the Government.

Mission entrusted to CNES's president personally FSOA CNES's 'president authority' is legally qualified as an 'administrative police mission', able to exercise, for example, a set of preventive measures to avoid any regulatory infringements, as opposed to the 'judicial police', whose purpose is to stop and punish any infringement.

Such CNES president authorities are set forth in FSOA Article 21 and translated in Article L. 331-6 of the Research Code as follows:

---

12 Ministry for Research and New Technology in charge of Space Affairs, 2003, Study report from 'Evolution of Space Law in France', Colloquium on 13 March 2003. [Online]. Available at: http://www2.enseignementsup-recherche.gouv.fr/rapport/droitespace/synthesea.pdf [accessed: 4 November 2010] and http://www2.enseignementsup-recherche.gouv.fr/rapport/espace_environnementjuridique.pdf [accessed: 4 November 2010] (summary available in English).

At the GSC

CNES's president exercises on behalf of the French government the Special Exploitation Police at the facilities of the Guiana Space Centre. As such, the president is in charge of a general mission of safeguard consisting of controlling the technical risks related to the preparation and carrying out of the launches from the Guiana Space Centre in order to ensure the protection of persons, property, public health and the environment, on the ground and during the flight, and set out to this end the specific regulations applicable. Basically, CNES's president would delegate most of this 'administrative police' competence to the head of the GSC.

In addition, CNES's president, under the authority of the government representative in French Guiana, coordinates the implementation by companies and other entities settled in GSC of measures taken in order to ensure the security of the facilities and of the activities undertaken therein, and checks that those companies and agencies fulfil their obligations in this respect.

For emergency measures

More generally in case of emergency, CNES's president, under FSOA Article 21 III provisions translated into RC Article L. 331-7, may take for any space operation, by delegation of the Minister in charge of Space, the necessary measures to ensure the safety of persons and property, as well as the protection of public health and the environment.

CNES's Traditional Activities Dealing with FSOA's Delegations

CNES's missions under FSOA dealing with the assessment of compliance with the Technical Regulations must be exercised in a independent, objective and impartial way, without interference from any relationship or interest. In this regard, a survey was made in 2009 by CNES of its business interests in relation to potential applicants (private operators) for authorisation, in order to assess the potential risk of conflicts of interest and to propose remedies as the case may be. Three fields of activity have been affected in this survey.

CNES's Activities as Space Programme Agency

As a procurement agency for the needs of its space programmes (new launcher satellite assets or services purchases, R&D contracts awards), CNES is subject to the Ordinance no. 2005-649 of 6 June 2005 relating to contracts concluded by certain public and private establishments not being subject to the Public Procurement Contracts Code.[13] Such ordinance is derived from EC directives[14] on the same subjects. It requires that contract awards respect the principles of freedom of access to procurement, equal treatment of candidates and transparency of procedures. These principles call for prior definition of the procuring entity's needs, compliance with the publication and competition requirements and selection of the economically most advantageous tender. On this basis, the risk of conflicts of interest can be reasonably diverted for such procuring mission.

CNES's policy in favour of new technology promotion and incubation is no more impaired as a result of FSOA.

---

13 Public Procurement Contracts Code 31 March 2006 Date of the last known amendment: Decree no. 2005-1737 of 30 December 2005. *Official Journal* of 31 December 2005.

14 Council directives 89/665/EEC, 21 December 1989 and 92/13/EEC 25 February 1992 – Council and Parliament directives 2004/17/EC and 2004/18/EC 31 March 2004.

CNES's Activities as Technical Centre and Space Operator

In addition to its main missions at the technical centre in Toulouse (satellites, science, space applications), Evry (launcher programmes) or GSC (launch base management, security and safety) CNES is allowed to supply services, grant access to its facilities and give expertise support to private companies, on a non-discriminatory basis and at a reasonable cost (between the real cost and the market price), provided that this activity does not jeopardise its main missions (according to CR Art. L331-2 a to e).

As a consequence, the following activities for CNES will not be affected by FSOA implementation :

in-orbit operation for governmental entities (including ESA, EUMETSAT, inter-governmental or agency cooperation)

marginal utilisation of testing facilities, computing facilities, station network (2GHz) …

payload preparation facilities, physics and chemical measures laboratories managed by CNES at GSC

On the other hand, CNES shall end any questionable supply activity, such as:

in-orbit operation for private entities, French or not (Eutelsat, SES Astra, etc.), or for governments if awarded in an international or competitive call for tender;

any supply contract (as sub-contractor) on behalf of a prime manufacturer or a space operator for a space system (satellite or launchers) potentially subject to FSOA's authorisation or control regime. The same applies towards European competitors of the above mentioned manufacturers or operators in order to avoid any interference in the European market competition;

quality support, computing services (trajectory optimisation) for Arianespace.

CNES's Stock Participations and Partnerships with Private Companies

The authorities consulted during FSOA's lawmaking process, including the State Council, National Assembly, Senate, French government and European Commission, unanimously underlined that CNES should abandon its shareholdings in Arianespace SA and Spot Image SA, before FSOA's entry into force.

CNES sold in July 2008 the whole of its stockholding in Spot Image SA to Astrium SAS (an EADS subsidiary in satellite sector).

For Arianespace SA, it has been suggested to transfer CNES's shares to an independent French public body (such as the 'Public Participation Agency'). Such a transfer would have to be made as soon as possible through an appropriate process taking into account current commitments resulting from ESA, its Member States and such company share holders and decisions to be taken by 2011 on Arianespace governance.

New Rules for CNES's Staff

CNES must guarantee, for itself and for its agents, that any data or information transmitted to it by operators or any private company for the needs of the authorisation's application or monitoring process or for the needs of GSC's regulations shall be kept confidential and strictly used for the purposes defined by FSOA.

This confidentiality obligation shall apply:

to any third party, to any data, information – and not only proprietary information, for any form of communication. For example, the dissemination of information about a minor failure in a system, whether or not sensitive from a technological or safety point of view, can have considerable consequences on the value of the relevant space operators stock quotation and business and must be avoided.

to any other CNES activities or staff, in particular: CNES staff involved in missions and systems development projects, upstream technical or technological research (in other words activities performed under CR Article L 331-2 a to e).

CNES's Staff Rules for the Assessment of Compliance and for the GSC Special Police Regime

Three categories of personnel are involved in SOA's activities. All this staff is subject to a specific regime as refers to hierarchy, confidentiality and deontology rules.

FSOA controllers (FSOA Article 28) CNES FSOA's controllers – appointed by CNES's President for a given period of time (three years normally) – shall check and assess that systems and procedures implemented by the operator comply with the FSOA's Technical Regulations. They intervene during the authorisation application process or after, during the preparation phase of the space operation or its carrying out.

This staff, assigned exclusively on FSOA's technical compliance responsibilities, is not allowed to work in any other CNES field of activities (and reciprocally), for the duration of their controller's mandate. Controllers shall subscribe to specific deontology and confidentiality commitments.

Commissioned officers The commissioned officers are empowered to engage the necessary controls (only after the granting of authorisation, during the preparation and implementation phases of the space operation) in order to ascertain that the special requirements (if any under Article 5) mentioned in the authorisation are fulfilled.

As part of their assignment, commissioned officers shall have access at any time to the buildings, premises and facilities where space operations are conducted and to the space object itself. They can request any document or useful item, irrespective of the *medium*. They can make copies and gather any necessary information and justification, *in situ* or upon notification.

The operator is informed at the latest when the controlling operations begin that it may attend the operations and be assisted by any person of its choice, or that it can be represented for that purpose.

The commissioned officers are bound by professional confidentiality under the conditions and penalties set out by Articles 226-13 and 226-14 of the Penal Code.

They are appointed and dismissed by the Ministry in charge of Space Affairs under proposition of CNES's President (FSOA Article 7 I. 1° and 2009 FSOA's Authorisation Decree Arts 19, 21, 22 and 23).

Sworn officers (judicial police) Sworn officers are commissioned officers with judicial police powers. In addition to their ability to have access at any time to the buildings, premises and facilities where space operations are conducted and to the space object, sworn officers are authorised, in accordance with the Code of Criminal Procedure, to investigate and record any breaches of FSOA's requirements, in particular facts that give rise to a fine of EUR 200,000, pursuant to Article 12 or, pursuant to Article 10, entails a withdrawing or a suspension of the granted authorisation.

Sworn officers record these breaches in reports which are considered authentic unless the contrary is proved. Such reports are sent to the Procureur de la République (Head of the Prosecution Department at courts of first instance of general jurisdiction), who decides either to sue or not the infringer.

Sworn officers take an oath, after endorsement by the Head of the Prosecution Department, at the Court of first instance of General Jurisdiction (TGI) under FSOA's Authorisation Decree Arts 19, 21, 22 and 23.

Conclusion

The assessment made by CNES, of its business with private operators potentially subject to the FSOA authorisation and control regime, in order to assess conflict risks, has not revealed any critical impediment. This appraisal has contributed to identifying a set of 'acceptance (or no) criteria' and a pricing policy for supply activities, mainly on the basis of the French Public Service Legal Doctrine or Case Law,[15] in accordance with the European law, specifically:

> continuity of service, transparency, non-discrimination, pre-defined pricing policy based on real costs, no subordination links with a private company, activities in close relation with a public investment or facility, priority given on CNES traditional missions, no commercial or competitive activities.

Accordingly, solutions and remedies to avoid any conflicts of interest and to ensure legal compatibility among CNES's various missions as a fully competent space agency, and pursuant its FSOA responsibilities, can be summarised as follows:

> CNES must abandon any commercial or competitive activity or interests in private companies;
>
> CNES is however, allowed to supply remunerated services in a 'public service' contract framework;
>
> CNES's organisation must set up a 'Chinese wall' between its traditional missions (RC L331-2 a to e) and its new FSOA responsibilities (RC L331-2 f to h and L 331-6 and 7).

Respect of the above requirements will allow CNES to hold off risks of conflict of interest between its FSAO responsibilities and its activities in selling services. Moreover such conditions will help CNES to preserve its main capacities as a contracting space agency so as to continue to undertake

15 Conseil d'Etat, 'Quelle tarification pour les services liés à l'usage des infrastructures', Dossier documentaire, Les entretiens du Conseil d'Etat, Paris 16 December 2009.

innovative space programmes with the private sector for the mutual benefit and competitiveness of industry and general interest of government space policy.

List of References

CNES Constitutive Act, 19 December 1961, no. 1961-1382, codified by Ordinance 11 June 2004, no. 2004-545, into the French Research Code (cited as RC), Article L. 331-1 to L331-6, the whole being amended by Article 21 and 28 of French Space Operations Act, 3 June 2008 adding Article L 331-7 and 8 (cited as CNES Constitutive Act).

Couston, M. 2008. 'Commentaires sur la loi française relative aux opérations spatiales' [Comments on the French Space Operation Act], *Revue française de droit aérien*, 1 July 2008, 3, 327–32.

Decree no. 2009-643 on the authorisations issued on 9 June 2009 in accordance with French Act no. 2008-518 of 3 June 2008 relative to space operations (cited as 2009 Authorisation Decree).

Decree no. 2009-644 issued on 9 June 2009 amending decree no. 84-510 of 28 June 1984 relating to the Centre National d'Etudes Spatiales (cited as CNES Amended Decree).

French Space Operations Act, 3 June 2008, no. 2008-518 (cited as FSOA).

Ministry for Research and new technology in charge of Space affairs: Study report 'Evolution of Space Law in France', February 2003, MRNT, Technology Directorate Space and Aeronautics Department (synthesis available in English), edited by Ministère délégué à la Recherche et aux Nouvelles Technologies. (Available on request from the Département de la communication via email at secretariat-communication@recherche.gouv.fr.)

National Assembly (Assemblée nationale): Mr Pierre Lasbordes's report, on behalf of the Economics Affairs Commission, 2 April 2008, no. 775.

Rapp, L. 2008. 'Une loi spatiale française' [A French Space Law], ADJA, *Actualité Legislative*, 29 September 2008, 1755.

Schmidt-Tedd, B. and Arnold, I. 2008. 'The French Act Relating to Space Activities: From International Law Idealism to National Industrial Pragmatism', for European Space Institute, *ESPI Perspective*, 11.

Senate: Mr Henri Revol's report, on behalf of the Economics Affairs Commission, 15 January 2008, no. 161 and no. 328 (2007–2008).

State Council (Conseil d'Etat): Appraisal Studies, 6 April 2006, 'A Legal Policy for Space Activities' [pour une politique juridique des activités spatiales], edited by La Documentation Française, Paris, 2006.

Chapter 12
The Complexities of International Space Industry Contracts

Cristian Bank

Introduction

This chapter provides an insight into the management challenges – including potential legal problems – associated with institutional space projects when embedded in an international collaborative environment extending beyond the Member States of the European Space Agency (ESA), for example to the USA, Russia, or other space-faring nations, such as Brazil, China, India, Russia, South Africa or South Korea. All these nations have established national space programmes and therefore are factual or potential partners in collaborative international or European space programmes. The chapter also provides suggested procedures for minimising the problems associated with those challenges.

While programmes with a commercial origin follow international commercial rules, governmental programmes, especially those in a collaborative environment, involve specific risks for the space agencies as well as for the industry. These risks may be commercial, legal or technical. However, the advantages of international agreements are that they create business opportunities that would not exist on a national level, bring together technological competencies from all partners, and provide some protection against an easy swing of opinion among the governmental decision makers often resulting in cancellation of the activity by one participating state.

Usually the political intention of intergovernmental or inter-agency agreements is translated into public procurement contracts with a complex technical system of implementation requiring the exchange of very specific and sometimes sensitive information, which may either be subject to export regulations or is considered intellectual property by industry. When funding is provided by public sources, the budget may need to be confirmed annually; furthermore, when technical results are obtained with public funding, they may also need to be published. As these rules may apply during the early phases of establishing the core team or the shortlist of potential bidders in a restricted competition, the conclusion of a governmentally approved Technical Exchange Agreement (TEA) or a Non-Disclosure Agreement (NDA) is often mandatory.

The selection of industrial team members is often subject to administrative intervention in order to enforce the underlying national industrial policy or to apply the geo-return principle. This may undermine efficiency of the team and put existing strategic industrial alliances at risk. On the other hand, it may allow new entrants to join the activity, to strengthen a competence or a company, to implement an industrial policy goal, or to pool technologies, all of which are often the decisive reason for a state to join a collaborative programme. Furthermore, agreeing on the applicable international and national space law, and handling general terms and conditions, always requires careful consideration, but in politically motivated space programmes, it is sometimes pursued under political considerations rather than with a view to the underlying real project situation.

Also other risks affecting the commercial aspects require mitigation. These include the proper formulation of mission and system requirements and their translation into technical specifications. Interface definitions and reasonable programmatic planning are usually considered as purely technical aspects, yet they are key to commercial success and always part of the legal project framework. Unclear definition of applicable standards for dimensioning, safety, parts, materials and processes, as well as for test and verification, may not seem urgent in the early phase of the project, but such inattention may result in a significant additional management and legal effort in the later stages of implementation. As documentation can be changed easily, it is tempting to change interfaces, specifications or processes that had previously been agreed. When this happens, while the technical change may be minor, the process of analysing its consequences, negotiating who is to bear it, and agreeing on its legal implementation, may take very long, adding uncertainty and consequential costs to either party.

Legal considerations tend to emphasise late or faulty delivery, which could result in anything from a nuisance to a mission loss. But the effects on the project can be counteracted by cautious and proactive project management. Less easy to overcome from a project point of view are consequences of relying on a single source abroad or facing a qualified component running out of production. And when technology finally works, the confirmation of payment milestones, price escalation and contract closeout provide for more hurdles in collaborative programmes.

In conclusion, potential contract partners cannot fail to identify the specific benefits of each case of collaboration and weigh them against the risks. Furthermore, the contracting partners must not only make sure that precautions are taken to assure success, but each must also formulate an exit strategy. In these respects, space is no different from any collaborative activity in the high technology or research domain.[1]

Public vs. Commercial Origin

What opportunities and risks do public collaborative programmes embody as opposed to typical commercial space activities?

While space programmes with commercial origin follow economic constraints and a long-established international commercial legal framework,[2] governmental programmes, especially those in a collaborative environment, often are based on political will transformed into project specific intergovernmental agreements (IGA).[3] Within ESA, all Member States participating in such an optional[4] programme need an IGA[5] ratified by their executive bodies (usually the national parliaments of the participating states).[6] When an IGA is ratified, it expands the multilateral legal framework defined by both common public law and international space law: it thus links the political intention with rules that have a direct impact on the industrial implementation. By defining major rights and obligations, how to share the inherent risks, how to enact, and how to

1 BMBF. 2009. *Umgang mit Know-how in internationalen FuE-Kooperationen – Ein Leitfaden für Forschungsinstitute und Hochschulen*. BMBF (ed.). Bonn/Berlin.

2 For example procurement of equipment for commercial telecommunication satellites, provision of launch services or remote sensing data.

3 Inter-agency agreements are often concluded as 'Memoranda of Understanding' (MoU).

4 This is in contrast to the obligatory ESA activities, especially the science programme.

5 See for example the ratification process of the ISS IGA in the participating European states.

6 OTA. 1986. Space Stations and the Law: Selected Legal Issues; OTA Report OTA-BP-ISC-41 / LCCCN 86-600569.

modify the agreement, the IGA provides the political guidelines for detailed practical agreements among the implementing entities. A well known current IGA on a specific non-commercial space project is the IGA on the International Space Station (ISS)[7] accompanied by bilateral MoUs (see *supra* n. 3) between NASA and all other participating space agencies,[8] but there are a multitude of others since the early days of space activities.[9]

This chapter concentrates on collaborative programmes implemented under space agency contracts.

The general characteristics of such activities under public procurement are described in Chapter 16 'Procurement in the Space Sector'.

The main differences between such politically motivated collaborative programmes, reflected in agency participation, and commercial activities, specifically with respect to their legal and industrial implementation are:

> agency participation provides unique mission definitions[10] and system specifications, as well as management processes for development, production, and operation, instead of standard missions,[11] commercially available equipment and tools, and best-practice oriented processes;
>
> agency participation involves commercial standard contracts based on a fee-for-service principle, instead of implementing the programme by bartering items and services, leading to an exclusion of exchange of funds between the industrial partners (as may be required for example for indemnification of additional effort);
>
> the initially unclear legal regime, especially regarding which legal status the specific agreement has,[12] the influence and application of national law,[13] which courts are competent

7 ISS IGA. 1998. Agreement among the Government of Canada, Governments of the Member States of the European Space Agency, the Government of Japan, The Government of the Russian Federation, and the Government of the United States of America Concerning Cooperation on the Civil International Space Station.

8 The Russian Roskosmos, the European ESA, the Japanese JAXA and the Canadian CSA.

9 Intelsat. 1971. Agreement Relating to the International Telecommunications Satellite Organization (INTELSAT) with Annexes and Operating Agreement; Inmarsat. 1976. Convention on the International Maritime Satellite Organisation (INMARSAT) with Annex and Operating Agreement; as amended 1985; with Protocol; 1981; Interkosmos. 1973. Agreement on Cooperation in the Exploration of Outer Space for Peaceful Purposes; signed on 13 July 1973, proclaimed on 25 March 1977; or Spacelab. 1973. Agreement Between the Government of the United States of America and Certain Governments, Members of the European Space Research Organisation, for a Cooperative Programme Concerning the Development, Procurement and Use of a Space Laboratory in Conjunction with the Space Shuttle System; Agreement done at Neuilly-sur-Seine 14 August 1973, entered into force 14 August 1973.

10 For example for scientific missions (astronomy, planetary exploration).

11 Telecommunication in geo-stationary orbit or an earth observation mission in sun-synchronous orbit for instance.

12 In some countries, for example in Europe, Canada or Japan, IGAs are ratified by parliament, in others like the USA they are treated as executive agreements without developing a legally binding character; see Staudt, B. 1992. *Die transatlantische Raumstationskooperation – Der rechtliche Rahmen einer langfristigen multinationalen Zusammenarbeit*, Europäische Hochschulschriften, Reihe II, Bd. 1248. Frankfurt: P. Lang.

13 During the development phase, industry is mostly concerned with tort law, while for operation also criminal law between individuals of an integrated team may become an issue; see OTA 1986.

and how jurisdiction can actually be imposed. This situation affects particularly questions of liability, but also typical industrial issues like warranty, acceptance, standards, terms of payment, intellectual and physical property law, etc.; and

restriction or limitation of exchange or export of technology, information, or any product developed in the frame of the collaborative programme by national law,[14] international agreements[15] or political decisions.[16]

The US Office of Technology Assessment (OTA) described this situation in a background paper[17] on legal issues connected to an international space station:

> Between sovereign nations, 'choice of law' and 'conflict of law' questions may not be particularly important since the resolution of an issue is likely to be accomplished by diplomatic negotiation. These questions will be much more important to private firms whose business decisions may be predicated on an understanding of the liability and financial risks of a given space venture.

The above differences lead to a situation where well-established and practical ways of solving issues between industrial partners in commercial programmes, even in an international environment, are not applicable when dealing with an inter-governmental case. For example, a purely barter-based implementation quickly leads to a separation of cause and effect from its indemnification, which can arise when one side considers changing an interface or a test programme and the other partner is forced to implement the resulting change on its side.

This does not mean that such governmental programmes are pursued outside of any defined legal framework; it is just pointed out that here the interpretation of public law, the hierarchy of the legal systems and their impact on commercial processes interfere with established practices in commercial activities when it comes to the interaction between the industrial teams of the participating states. The fact that international collaborative programmes rely much more on inter-agency interaction and diplomacy than on coded law leads to the situation that industrial entities, in many cases, refrain from claiming additional remuneration and instead quote up-front with a large 'safety margin' or risk provision to mitigate the inevitable extra effort.

This situation is a direct result of the liability regulations of the Outer Space Treaty,[18] which considers and covers liability only as a result of damage caused by space objects between states, but not of damage caused in space activities by and between individuals or companies. To avoid complex ex-ante regulations, the USA often implemented a cross waiver of liability (CWL) in

---

14 A typical example is national export restrictions with reference to regulations concerning goods of dual use.

15 Especially launcher-related technology may fall under the international Missile Technology Control Regulations (MTCR), see footnote 23 below. However, the application of national export control regimes may be in contradiction to the original political intention to foster international collaboration, as for example the application of ITAR regulations is clearly against the ISS IGA which establishes a much more liberal approach for exchange of information and technology.

16 Rather than any obvious blocking of goods, a state may temporarily act indirectly through taking items into custody in customs, refusal of visa for foreign personnel, by blocking formal communications or declaring sites as being of military relevance and not accessible to foreigners.

17 OTA 1986, p. 8.

18 OST. 1967. Treaty on Principles Governing the Activities of States in the Exploration and Use of Outer Space, including the Moon and Other Celestial Bodies, Article VI and IX.

its collaborative activities,[19] covering not only the participating agencies, but also the involved industrial contractors. This practice culminated in the CWL contained in the ISS IGA of 1996, which thence precludes any claim, not only between the international partners on an agency level, but also among their respective industries.

The above particularities of the collaborative environment affect mainly the prime contractor. Within the participating states, the situation is much more standardised, as the space agencies entrusted with the implementation of the respective programme share instead an industrial team through public procurement, often organised under the lead of a system prime contractor, which in turn involves subcontractors[20] or suppliers. While the former are involved through contracts reflecting the boundary conditions of both the collaborative programme and the public procurement process, the latter may be contracted through commercial contracts.

Reflecting on the above, one sometimes wonders what drives companies to strive for such contracts. However, the advantage of internationally agreed programmes is that they provide some protection against changing public opinion in a single participating state, since in the political domain, the international obligations undertaken by ratifying an IGA often form a strong anchor against domestically motivated moves to withdraw.[21] Hence such activities, once contracted, provide a stable environment, sometimes over decades, rarely found in the commercial domain.

Export Control

How do international, politically motivated, collaborative space programmes blend with national and international regulations of export control?

Usually the political intention of intergovernmental or inter-agency agreements is translated into public procurement contracts of a technical system requiring the exchange of detailed, often very specific and sometimes sensitive, information and goods between European and foreign countries, which may be subject to export regulations. Space technology is, in most cases, considered a dual-use technology and even information about space products is considered core technology know-how. Present arms control regulations may apply even now to single electronic parts, embedded software used in avionics equipment or even to test software used in ground test equipment. Export control has hence become a subject of high relevance in both private as well as public space programmes. A detailed introduction into export control issues is given in Chapter 24 'Export Control Issues in Space Contracts'.

For European companies, national and international regulations that are in force now include the Missile Technology Control Regime (MTCR) and the Wassenaar Agreement,[22] both intended to provide higher transparency in the transfer of arms and dual-use technology. The Wassenaar Agreement not only covers arms export control, but also control of dual-use items[23] and the

19 For example between NASA and ESA in the Spacelab Agreement of 1973 (Spacelab 1973), or with any foreign entity concerning Space Shuttle launches, payloads, and operations; see OTA 1986, p. 48.

20 For the legal definition of subcontractor and its specific working environment see http://definitions.uslegal.com/s/subcontractor/ [accessed: 3 November 2010].

21 Which does not mean that this would never happen. In the past the USA withdrew from a number of internationally agreed collaborative programmes, such as ISPM (later 'Ulysses') or the X-38 development.

22 Wassenaar. 1996. Compilation of basic public documents. [Online]. Available at http://www.wassenaar.org/ [accessed: 30 April 2011].

23 Wassenaar. 2003. Statement of Understanding on Control of Non-Listed Dual-Use Items; agreed at the 2003 Plenary.

installation of intangible transfers of technology controls.[24] While the decision on transfer, or denial of transfer, resides with each participating state, the Wassenaar Agreement foresees mutual participation on such decisions. The participating states agreed on a List of Dual-Goods and Technologies with two annexes, one for 'sensitive' and one for 'very sensitive' items. The Agreement provides guidelines (as 'Best Practices'), definitions, procedures, forms of statement of compliance and end-user declarations, and 'advisory questions for industry' intended to clarify the reason for getting in contact with national arms control authorities in case of technology export. The space equipment, software and machinery used for the production of space hardware that need an export licence is also listed.

The Missile Technology Control Regime (MTCR)[25] addresses specifically weapons of mass destruction, in particular missile technology in the broadest sense: from complete systems down to microcircuits, software, avionics, propulsion, materials, 'guidance, navigation, and control' (GNC) equipment, sensors, test and modelling equipment and related drawings, diagrams, handbooks and operational know-how are subject to the regulations of this treaty, for example basically all know-how, technology and products employed in space technology.

European space product companies are often affected by the US International Traffic in Arms Regulations (ITAR) under control of the Department of State's Directorate of Defense Trade Controls.[26] ITAR Parts 120 to 130 contain the US Munitions List (USML) and define the items falling under the regulation, offshore procurement, required registration and export licensing procedures, and penalties for violation; it is regularly and frequently updated. Items include not only products (for example communication satellites) and any parts of them (for example transponders, thrusters), but also other know-how or services – like training, repair or maintenance, and even mock-ups or models revealing any relevant technical detail.

Unlike other regulations, an ITAR approval does not depend upon the end use of the item. However, a statement by the end user of the exported item about its final use is nonetheless required to obtain clearance. ITAR addresses the transfer of know-how to any foreign person or entity, whether in the USA or outside. It, however, excludes information for marketing purposes, generally accessible academic know-how or general descriptions of systems. Also excluded from ITAR is foreign technical data being returned to the original source from where it was exported. However, as soon as this information becomes part of a US document, it falls under ITAR again. This happened, for example, in the development of the International Space Station, when European technical documentation was re-issued as a NASA document and thus became restricted information, inaccessible to the originators in Europe.

A major difference between ITAR, on one hand, and some other national laws (French export regulations for instance) and regulations of more export-oriented nations (for example Germany), on the other, is that the former requires an explicit clearance for all products, even those not on the list of critical technologies, while the latter consider all products not explicitly listed as cleared for export. Furthermore, what makes ITAR particularly difficult to handle is that it does not foresee any means of appeal from the denial of clearance, which is often politically motivated, while other countries allow the standard means of appeal as would be taken from any other administrative decision. As such, ITAR has developed much more of a political character and is used as an instrument for industrial and foreign policy. These export control regulations are often encountered

---

24 Wassenaar. 2006. Best Practices for Implementing Intangible transfer of Technology Controls; agreed at the 2006 Plenary.

25 MTCR. 1987. Compilation of detailed information.

26 ITAR. 2009. Compilation of recent regulations.

during the first talks within industry, when US employees are reminded that even revealing orally any detailed information about the intended project is prohibited without a specific licence, which in turn often leads restrictions on the presentations and discussions that are preliminary to any technical exchange or assistance agreement (TEA/TAA, see below).

Only US citizens or US-based companies may obtain licences or approvals for export. And, it typically takes several weeks to months to obtain such a licence; hence timely application by the US partner is required. The required licences cover at least the following authorisations:

> Technical Assistance Agreement (TAA), which authorises a US supplier to deliver services and to transfer technical data to the authorised signatory parties, to be obtained not later than 6 months after start of the activity
>
> Export Licence (DSP 5) to export hard-/software from the USA, to be obtained prior to shipment
>
> General Correspondence (GS) for the re-transfer of USML items already under custody of a non-US entity

The European partner should support the US supplier in this application process by providing the required information on the end use of the item, according to the applicable US forms. Often successfully obtaining the governmental authorisations is a contractual obligation for subcontractors and part of a specific payment milestone.

It is beyond the scope of this chapter to discuss the practical implications of the ITAR interpretations by the US administration after 11 September 2001 on such matters as the collaboration on the ISS, but suffice it to say that the current practice is not compatible with the original intention of the ISS IGA negotiated in 1998.

In the meantime, similar regulations exist in Russia, which undertook a considerable effort in 2000–2002 to modernise the previously Soviet legislation on export control and to adapt it to the needs of its export-oriented arms industry in accordance with the international treaties. This effort concentrated on establishing a list of controlled items and technologies, streamlining approval procedures and internal compliance programmes, and the enforcement of the Federal Law.[27] Subject to the export regulation now is also the transfer of know-how to a foreigner while in Russia, as well as transfer by intangible means, for example orally in direct talks or on conferences, via e-mail, in teaching or any other communication channel with foreign access. On the other hand, the licensing process has been streamlined and general licences may be obtained for dual-use goods.

The effect of this enforced Russian law is similar to the US ITAR regulation, as the formerly rather open discussion with Russians on space projects or products is now much more restricted, and Russian companies take precautions not to run any risk of violating the Federal Law on Export Control. West European partners still tend to underestimate the time and effort required to obtain clearance, even for technical discussions and collaboration at a very early stage, and a number of European-Russian collaborative initiatives have failed due to ignorance of the issue.

Although this chapter concentrates on the complexities of contracting with third states regarding space projects, the topic of export control requires mention of the fact that similar restrictions still exist also within Europe and between the ESA Member States, especially where space projects are

27 MID. 2008. Compilation of recent regulations; unofficial translation dated 5 September 2002; background information, NTI. 2009. Russia: Export Control Legislation.

said to have benefited from national weapons development. Recent examples include the export of control software for the new European launcher VEGA from France to Italy, or the transfer of test and simulation software for the European cargo vehicle ATV from France to Germany, which both claimed to be based on, or to incorporate, know-how from nuclear missile development. Again, the timely start of the procedure is mandatory; Table 12.1 shows typical durations for obtaining the various licences.

Table 12.1 Typical duration of export licensing procedures

Licence	Authority	Duration (months)
TAA	DoS (US)	4–6
ITAR licence and GS	DoS (US)	~ 4
EAR licence	DoS (US)	~ 2
EAR modification	DoS (US)	~ 1
Export licence	METI (J)	~ 2
Export licence	MID (RU)	3–6
Dual use licence	MINEFE (F) / BAFA (D) / BERR (UK)	0.5–3
Military licence	MoD (UK)	~ 2
Military licence	BAFA (D)	~ 2
AP	CIEEMG (F)	~ 3
AEMG	DAS (F)	~ 2

Public Funding

How does funding from public sources interfere with, or support, commercial interests?

Funding in governmental space business is provided by public budget lines, which in some countries and programmes may need to be confirmed annually, and technical results obtained under public funding may be declared public domain or may be required to be published. Collaborative programmes in ESA are usually optional for its Member States, and the financing scheme is passed for each programme phase (0, A, B, C/D, E) until its nominal end (either by a design review, the product's acceptance, its launch or the end of its nominal operation / utilisation). Hence European space industry is less affected by annual administrative budget planning cycles than other international partners whose work share in the collaborative activity may be subject to administrative approval cycles affecting most frequently the financing.[28] In such cases, European

28 For example NASA may cancel its work share in collaborative programmes prematurely if the US budget share is not annually approved by the US administration, as happened for ISPM/Ulysses for instance.

partners need to take precautions to avoid a premature delivery of European know-how or product to the partner, if the European benefit or return on investment comes only at the end of the programme (through integration, test or operation of the jointly-developed product). Instead, European partners may want to seek a collaborative scheme, for example in which both sides agree to contribute mutually to earlier integration stages or test models of the final product[29] or to make available a defined know-how, service or a specific test facility as compensation for premature programme cancellation.

While public funding (or non-funding) may lead to stabilisation or cancellation, many R&D activities under governmental funding or sponsorship are meanwhile required to publish the results[30] or make them available to other companies, if the originally funded company decides to withdraw from, or cancel its involvement in, the activity. The risk associated with such a situation is typical for R&D with public subsidies and is not specific to space activities, but with a view to the often strategic interests of the involved administration in the technology or know-how in question and the sometimes limited alternatives of suppliers, the publication and transfer of technology may become a major schedule and programme risk driver. Hence opt-out or termination clauses need to cover more than just the obvious financial consequences.

Further reading about R&D financing and financial provisions of the European Union can be found in Chapter 19 'Research and Development Contracts'.

Industrial Team Building

Why is industrial team building so important in international space ventures, and how do the new European procurement regulations relate to industrial practice?

Industrial team building in the space sector is a complex endeavour and needs to be approached according to the type and complexity of the product, the political boundary conditions and the procurement authority in charge. Due to the long-term nature of space programmes, the team set-up determines the fate of participating (and even more – non-participating) companies for quite some time.

For ESA contracts, the team is usually a result of geo-return requirements,[31] historically developed competence from previous activities in the domain and a certain degree of competition between lower level subcontractors. With the application of the ESA 'Best Practices',[32] more competition for the selection of the subcontractors takes place. The prime contractor may be set by the level of budget subscription by a large Member State or, if two or more states have subscribed to a similar level of funding, an arrangement between the potential prime contractors about collaboration and work share is expected. Alternatively, especially in early phases of a new activity, two prime contractors together with their respective teams may be asked to work in concurrent engineering teams.

---

29 NASA and ESA conducted early drop tests with the X-38 model incorporating a parafoil with European GNC software. Although the programme was later cancelled by NASA prematurely, the drop tests provided both partners with valuable test results which prevented the European investments up to that point in time from being in vain.

30 OECD. 2007. OECD Principles and Guidelines for Access to Research Data from Public Funding.

31 The 'geo-return' principle is addressed and explained elsewhere in this chapter and in other chapters of this book.

32 ESA. 2005. ESA Best Practices for the Selection of Subcontractors by Prime Contractors in the frame of ESA's Major Procurements; ESA/IPC(2005)34, rev. 3.

In collaborative projects with third states outside of ESA, a similar arrangement must be found at the beginning, as the respective prime contractors are usually set – proceeding on the assumption that a 'classical' arrangement between the space agencies is installed: no exchange of funds, negotiation on 'equal footing'[33] and so on. In such an environment, the European prime contractor has to establish quickly and often informally at least a list of potential competent level 1 subcontractors[34] in order to introduce the European technological competence and strategic interests properly into the international work share negotiations, and to stand up against claims for the same work share by non-European suppliers.

This informal part of the team building process has to take place much earlier than the later formal bidding process, which, according to the ESA 'Best Practices' rules, is initiated only after formal endorsement of the Industrial Procurement Plan (IPP). The IPP is part of the prime contractor's formal bid and hence comes after the formal initiation of the programme by the agencies, based on their agreement on the large-scale work share.[35] It could then happen that the 'Best Practices' lead to the involvement of a competent supplier of another partner, other than the one which had been assigned with the task. A suitable process to handle such potential conflicts is the compilation of shortlists of potential suppliers, which can be discussed with, and endorsed by, all involved agencies before the IPP is finalised and the formal procurement process is started.

The compilation of a suitable industrial team has become a more complex and time-consuming issue[36] since ESA introduced its 'Best Practices', which were conceived to strengthen the position of ESA and smaller companies *vis-à-vis* the large multi-national European industrial groups, EADS and Thales-Alenia, and with a view to harmonising ESA programme procedures with the more commercially oriented procurement rules of the EU. The rather formal process, with multiple release cycles by the agency, will inevitably lead to weakening the European industrial position in the start-up of the programme, when important procedural and work share agreements on the working level are developed.

More on the formal aspects connected to the public procurement process can be found in Chapter 16 'Procurement in the Space Sector' and Chapter 3 'The Relationship between the EU and ESA within the Framework of European Space Policy and its Consequences for Space Industry Contracts'.

The formalisation of the 'political agreements' on the collaboration, including the intended development work share, cost and risk allocation, rights and obligations of system operation and utilisation, etc. leads to different contract types. Since this aspect is not specific to international collaboration, it is not discussed in greater detail here; more on contract types can be found in Chapter 14 'Typology of Contracts in the Space Sector'.

---

33 The expression 'equal footing' in ESA terminology is usually used to describe a formal agreement reached during the early stages in which the parties agree that in case of conflict during programme execution, the decision making process between the participating agencies (and subsequently also between the potential industrial partners) is conducted with all parties having the same rights and obligations or 'weight', no matter what the actual role, contribution, or work share of each partner in the cooperation is. This approach is similar to decision-making processes within certain ESA bodies or the EU, where each Member State has one vote, no matter its financial contribution, know-how, number of inhabitants etc.

34 'Level 1 subcontractors' are direct subcontractors to the prime contractor, while suppliers and subcontractors to those are 'level 2 subcontractors'.

35 At the time of writing, the ESA 'Best Practices' have not yet been applied to any collaborative programme, and they leave ample space for interpretation and tailoring. It is hence not clear to which extent the 'Best Practices' can and will ever be applied to collaborative programmes.

36 The lead times will become an estimated four months longer than under the former regulations.

In the early phase of a programme, the conclusion of a Non-Disclosure Agreement and an industrial Technical Exchange / Assistance Agreement[37] is mandatory, both for the protection of intellectual property as well as to comply with export control issues. More on security of intellectual property and confidentiality aspects can be found in Chapter 28 'Negotiating the Security Aspects of Satellite Communications Services Contracts'.

Industrial Policy

How does industrial policy influence the implementation of international collaborative programmes?

In all large projects financed with public money, whether they are national or international, the selection of industrial team members is of particular interest for the administration. In the EU, like in many regions of the Western world, most areas of economic activities are liberalised and follow commercial rationale and the public procurement standards set forth by the EU.[38] However, public procurement in the space sector addresses different policy goals than in other areas, for example civil engineering. Details on the specific aspects of public procurement in the space sector are described in Chapter 14 'Typology of Contracts in the Space Sector' and Chapter 16 'Procurement in the Space Sector', while recent developments in the European space policy are described in Chapter 2 'The Impact of the European Space Policy on Space Commerce'.

Within Europe there are mechanisms to accommodate national interests and specific know-how or strategic goals in space projects, the geo-return principle and the voluntary participation in the optional ESA programmes for instance. One of the participating states may foster the involvement of a specific domestic company, a domestic product or a key technology to enforce a strategic goal pursued by its participation, for example to acquire a certain technology or experience or to prevent other participants from acquiring this know-how.

Over time and through the spectrum of the manifold ESA activities, European states and industries manage to balance their participation and to achieve, at least on an average and over time, a level of know-how and experience that corresponds to the national strategic goals. The nature of the geo-return principle, its practical implementation, and the resulting effects in Europe are described in Chapter 8 'The Geographical Return Principle and its Future within the European Space Policy'.

However, in large space programmes extending beyond the ESA framework, the achievement of such equilibrium may not be possible. International collaborative programmes, due to their complex nature, are much less frequent than national programmes. Also, they are usually long-term and imbalances between the partners imposed at the beginning are difficult to compensate elsewhere and, as a result, may determine the industrial and technological balance between the industries of the partners for decades. An example of such a risk is the former cooperation between Russia and Europe in the CSTS programme, in which Russia intended to provide the re-entry element, and Europe the orbital service module.[39] If this work share had been maintained, it would

37 See explanations above on export control.

38 EU. 2004. Directive 2004/18/EC of the European Parliament and of the Council of 31 March 2004 on the coordination of procedures for the award of public works contracts, public supply contracts and public service contracts.

39 See ESA. 2009. Human Spaceflight, Microgravity and Exploration Programme Board – Status Report on CSTS; ESA/PB-HME(2009)21, 28 April 2009; and Bank, C. 2008. 'Legal Issues in Future Cooperative Human Spaceflight Projects', in *Proceedings of the IAC 2008 IAC-08-1.7*, C. Bank, L.J. Smith and A. Böhm. Glasgow.

have precluded Europe from acquiring any significant experience in re-entry capsule design and operation for the next decades, and would have constrained Europe to an even lower level of technology and know-how than that which was achieved with ATV.

But also in collaborative programmes with a much more balanced share on the top level, the actual implementation on the industrial level may significantly constrain the industry of one partner for a long time. Typical examples of this resulted from the political imbalance between the USA and its international partners in the ISS programme[40] as determined by the ISS IGA,[41] and even more by the respective MoUs,[42] which were later mirrored on the industrial implementation level, namely:

> Interface definitions and their changes were often determined by the US industry, while the non-US industries had to take the risk of either implementing these moves before they were formally finalised and endorsed by the agencies, or waiting for the formal approval and facing higher costs and late changes.
>
> Test, verification, safety and acceptance criteria were unilaterally defined by the US side which rarely took note of existing processes and standards abroad, which led to additional efforts and costs.
>
> Items declared as 'common items' to be used throughout the ISS were usually furnished by US industry[43] with all the problems associated with single sources.
>
> Seemingly minor items furnished by single sources of one partner[44] could become the critical path and hence drive the development, integration and test schedule of all international partners.

Finally the result of the procurement and industrial team-building process may lead to industrial constellations that do not correspond to previously established strategic alliances with technological cooperation and agreed long-term work shares for commercial activities. Apart from being detrimental to the development of long-term cross-border cooperation, this could lead to problems of protecting IPR, Non-Disclosure Agreements, technology transfer, export licensing and sourcing agreements. It could also diminish the efficiency of the industrial team and lead to a costly start-up phase.

Programme Implementation Risks and Mitigation

What are the specific opportunities and challenges of international collaborative space endeavours for the implementing industry, and how are the risks mitigated?

---

40 This is particularly true for the 'small' Western partners, Europe, Japan and Canada; only Russia with its decades of experience in designing and operating the man-rated orbital stations Salyut and Mir managed to negotiate a more or less similar level of responsibility and influence in the ISS programme.

41 ISS IGA 1998.

42 ISS IGA 1998. For an evaluation of the imbalances between the space agencies see Staudt. 1992. *Die transatlantische Raumstationskooperation.*

43 ISS 'common items' in Western modules are for example the lighting units, the grapple fixtures, windows or the inter-element hatches, all provided by US companies.

44 Typical items of this category are hi-rel harness connectors or EEE parts.

Once the programme intention, scope and framework of collaboration are defined, industry is supposed to start working on the contractual basis established between each partner's agency entrusted with the programme's implementation and its prime contractor. The primes rarely have an integrative contractual relation with each other. Instead, to procure specific common items or parts, one prime contractor may become a supplier of the other in a supply contract that is, however, part of the overall agency-prime contract.[45] Often joint work to define basic interface requirements and definitions or to coordinate integrated testing and integration is, again, for each partner separately, part of the overall agency-prime contract. This lack of overarching interrelation makes it difficult (or costly) to manage all the elements that are key to the (commercial) success of a project.[46]

The proper formulation of mission and system requirements, and even more their translation into (viable) technical specifications and interface definitions, determines to a large extend the development and operations costs. Without contractual relations, one partner may be tempted to ease for example performance requirements on its own work share at the expense of more effort on another partner's contribution. This could later introduce claims of the latter towards its customer without the customer being responsible for the increased effort.

Reasonable programmatic planning is not a mere 'contractual promise' to the customer, but the basis for resource planning and activity coordination within the industrial team. Changing key planning milestones by one prime could severely affect the activities of another partner's industrial team, again raising claims by that team to its own agency.

Unclear definitions of applicable standards for dimensioning, safety, parts, materials and processes, as well as for test and verification, may not seem urgent in the early phase of the project, but such lack of attention may result in significantly greater effort in the final stages of implementation, especially when such standards form the basis for requirements verification, safety reviews, product acceptance, launch readiness reviews and so forth. Imposing national standards of one partner on the other partners could lead to invalidating parts of their original industrial proposal, which may have been established on the basis of own standards.[47]

Often the above mentioned technical changes first appear in informal engineering documentation or minutes of meetings. As such documentation can be changed easily, it may be tempting for one side to change agreed interfaces, specifications or processes, especially at the beginning of a programme when new results of technical analyses come in and earlier definitions need to be changed. While the change may be minor, the process of analysing its consequences, negotiating who is to bear these consequences and agreeing on the change implementation may take very long,[48] adding uncertainty and consequential costs in case of retroactive changes. The mechanisms provided by the typical agency-industry contract to date lead to further budget claims, schedule

45 For example Boeing, prime for the US segment of the ISS, was supplier to Thales-Alenia Space Italy, co-prime for COLUMBUS, to provide some hardware items for COLUMBUS which are common to all Western ISS modules.

46 Even in a project not driven primarily by competitive market considerations, industry needs to assure that it delivers 'on time, on quality and on cost', as most governmental programmes today are implemented in a fixed firm price environment and political support may dwindle over time.

47 A typical example is the discussion on metric and imperial system of units between the USA and other 'metric' Western partners, or the comparability of definitions of the European ECSS standards system with Russian industrial standards in joint programmes with Russia.

48 Typical times for such negotiations are several months up to more than one year.

slip or additional risk provisions, which are the inevitable and observable effects in almost all large programmes.[49]

More details on the subsequent change and claim management processes between industry and customer, as well as the effects of delays and cost overruns can be found in three chapters of this book: Chapter 22 'Cost Overruns in Space Contracts: Mitigation Methods and Strategies', Chapter 11 'Consequences of the French Space Law on Space Operations (FSOA) on CNES's Mission as a Contracting Space Agency', and Chapter 20 'Contract Management'.

The consequences of a qualified component running out of production can severely affect an ongoing programme. In a national programme, the decision to cease production of a component is usually made in a coordinated process between customer, prime contractor and supplier that addresses also the impact on the programme, for example whether to start a qualification process for a substitute, to replace the item by a new product, or to produce a dedicated batch in order to have sufficient spares. In a collaborative programme, external partners may not be involved in this discussion and would learn about the decision only from a 'last order' call by the supplier, which leaves little time to consider future alternatives, especially if the supplier is a single source for the item. Agencies feel uncomfortable with such a situation and tend either to avoid buying a critical item from a foreign supplier or to start a development programme to establish a second source within its own perimeter, which in turn leads to the detrimental effect of what was originally intended by the collaboration – to save costs and time and make specific know-how or a certain capability of one partner available to all partners.

In practice, joint operation and utilisation (O&U) of a system can either be established by installing a joint team in one place,[50] or requiring a complex coordination between independent entities of each partner.[51] Since the later system's operations costs and the benefit of utilising it determine to a large extend the life cycle cost and benefit of the endeavour, agreeing on the O&U scheme is the most complex task in establishing an overall agreement, since naturally each partner tends to obtain the maximum benefit for the least investment.

This issue has to be solved often before the system is properly defined, its operations cost assessed, its termination and disposal agreed and its utilisation potential fully understood. To evade the problem of quantitative (monetary) evaluation, partners tend to define services or success criteria instead. But unrealistic assumptions about the future O&U situation result in obligations that may be perceived as unbalanced by one partner, and due to the long-term nature of such systems, may lead to profound disenchantment and depreciation of collaborative projects by decision makers. For the ISS, a distribution scheme was founded among the partners[52] that has little connection to any measurable quantity like the actual work share, development effort, etc. Although the fact that an agreement was established was probably decisive for the successful implementation of the IGA, it was politically imposed and it is virtually impossible to implement higher efficiency, reduce cost or ease commercial access.

49 For a 'customer view' on the issue see for example GAO. 2009. Assessment of Selected Large-Scale Projects; GAO-09-306SP March 2009.

50 Like for example the joint long-term operation of the Hubble Space Telescope or other astronomy missions.

51 Like the O&U planning of the ISS for instance.

52 ISS IGA 1998, Article 15.

Despite being discussed since the very first Space Station plans in the West, and being fostered by all participating space agencies in dedicated programmes, the commercial utilisation of the ISS remains negligible, mainly due to difficult access and unsatisfactory IP protection.[53]

As in all good partnerships, there may come a time that one partner decides to withdraw or the community agrees to terminate the programme. Unfortunately, not all agreements on collaborative endeavours provide proper exit or termination mechanisms. In case of unilateral withdrawal, there should be no opportunity for the remaining partners to be able to continue the programme, especially if the withdrawing partner has a dominant role in the collaboration. This may be due to a missing key element[54] of the system, too high completion or operations costs for the remaining group of partners, or lack of political determination. As mentioned above, in the case of an item running out of production, equitable partners would tend to install alternative sources to be able to run the system, even in case of withdrawal of one partner, or insist on setting up the system in a way that it is not endangered in case one partner does not deliver.[55] This results, however, in the system being rather a collection of self-standing parts than an integrated system, lacking the once targeted advantage of joint development and O&U – cost reduction, schedule shortening, process simplification etc.

If a second source outside of a withdrawing partner's premises does not exist, and the remaining partners intend to continue O&U of the system, the required technology or production facility should be transferred. Here again, export control regulations may impede the transfer (or be used as an excuse not to do it) and the monetary evaluation of the effort and value of the transferred technology or facility is difficult. To date no such regulations have ever been applied to space programmes, although there are such mechanisms described in some large European programmes.[56]

Conclusion

The challenge in agreeing on the implementation of an international collaborative space programme often proves to be so complex that, as a result, more brilliant initiatives fail due to this aspect than due to technical problems. Collaboration on 'equal footing' is rare, as many implementation rules cannot be deduced from technical analysis, but sometimes must be imposed by a leading party and accepted by the followers, either on a political or on industrial level – just like in any national activity. And even if successfully implemented, it is not a certainty that collaboration saves money or time.

---

53 For example HoR-CST. 2008. U.S. House of Representatives Committee on Science and Technology, Subcommittee on Space and Aeronautics: Hearing Charter – NASA's International Space Station Program: Status and Issues; 24 April 2008.

54 'Missing element' encompasses not only parts of the flight segment, but also production, integration, test, operation and other infrastructure means on ground.

55 For the ISS, both the Russian and the US segment are able to operate for themselves without the other one's segment, and the US segment can be operated without the contributions of any other Western partner. For the post-Apollo collaboration between the USA and Western Europe, the European contribution 'Spacelab' was defined in a way that allowed the US part, the Space Shuttle, to operate without it. In turn, in both cases the European part would have been useless if the US would have decided to withdraw from the activity.

56 Typically in joint military systems development agreements like Eurofighter/Typhoon, Tornado and so forth, but also ESA contracts contain such regulations in case one company withdraws from the industrial team.

Collaboration works if, and only if, there is a political will to define, implement and achieve the ultimate objective for the mere purpose of political success, and if there is a clear structure with a prime contractor and direct contractual relations in the industrial team. While the ISS development is a great example of technical, organisational and political success, and the IGA is certainly a remarkable example for future collaborative programmes, European scientists have meanwhile used twice their allocated resources for experiments and its programmatic record is less enchanting. Against this backdrop, it may take many years until a similar collaboration can be established to, for example, launch an international collaboration to explore the Moon or Mars.

List of References

Bank, C. 2008. 'Legal Issues in Future Cooperative Human Spaceflight Projects', in *Proceedings of the IAC 2008 IAC-08-1.7*, by C. Bank, L.J. Smith and A. Böhm. Glasgow.

BMBF. 2009. *Umgang mit Know-how in internationalen FuE-Kooperationen – Ein Leitfaden für Forschungsinstitute und Hochschulen*. BMBF (ed.). Bonn/Berlin.

ESA. 2005. ESA Best Practices for the Selection of Subcontractors by Prime Contractors in the frame of ESA's Major Procurements; ESA/IPC(2005)34, rev. 3.

ESA. 2009. Human Spaceflight, Microgravity and Exploration Programme Board – Status Report on CSTS; ESA/PB-HME(2009)21, 28 April 2009.

EU. 2004. Directive 2004/18/EC of the European Parliament and of the Council of 31 March 2004 on the coordination of procedures for the award of public works contracts, public supply contracts and public service contracts.

GAO. 2009. Assessment of Selected Large-Scale Projects; GAO-09-306SP March 2009.

HoR-CST. 2008. U.S. House of Representatives Committee on Science and Technology, Subcommittee on Space and Aeronautics: Hearing Charter – NASA's International Space Station Program: Status and Issues; 24 April 2008.

Inmarsat. 1976. Convention on the International Maritime Satellite Organisation (INMARSAT) with Annex and Operating Agreement; as amended 1985; with Protocol; 1981.

Intelsat. 1971. Agreement Relating to the International Telecommunications Satellite Organization (INTELSAT) with Annexes and Operating Agreement.

Interkosmos. 1973. Agreement on Cooperation in the Exploration of Outer Space for Peaceful Purposes; signed on 13 July 1973, proclaimed on 25 March 1977.

ISS IGA. 1998. Agreement among the Government of Canada, Governments of the Member States of the European Space Agency, the Government of Japan, The Government of the Russian Federation, and the Government of the United States of America Concerning Cooperation on the Civil International Space Station.

ITAR. 2009. Compilation of recent regulations.

MID. 2008. Compilation of recent regulations; unofficial translation dated 5 September 2002.

MTCR. 1987. Compilation of detailed information.

NTI. 2009. Russia: Export Control Legislation.

OECD. 2007. OECD Principles and Guidelines for Access to Research Data from Public Funding.

OST. 1967. Treaty on Principles Governing the Activities of States in the Exploration and Use of Outer Space, including the Moon and Other Celestial Bodies.

OTA. 1986. Space Stations and the Law: Selected Legal Issues; OTA Report OTA-BP-ISC-41 / LCCCN 86-600569.

Spacelab. 1973. Agreement Between the Government of the United States of America and Certain Governments, Members of the European Space Research Organisation, for a Cooperative Programme Concerning the Development, Procurement and Use of a Space Laboratory in Conjunction with the Space Shuttle System; Agreement done at Neuilly-sur-Seine 14 August 1973, entered into force 14 August 1973.

Staudt, B. 1992. *Die transatlantische Raumstationskooperation – Der rechtliche Rahmen einer langfristigen multinationalen Zusammenarbeit*, Europäische Hochschulschriften, Reihe II, Bd. 1248; Frankfurt: P. Lang.

Wassenaar. 1996. Compilation of basic public documents. [Online]. Available at http://www.wassenaar.org/ [accessed: 30 April 2011].

Wassenaar. 2003. Statement of Understanding on Control of Non-Listed Dual-Use Items; agreed at the 2003 Plenary.

Wassenaar. 2006. Best Practices for Implementing Intangible transfer of Technology Controls; agreed at the 2006 Plenary.

Chapter 13
Developing Space Markets in Small Jurisdictions: The Case of the Isle of Man

Timiebi U. Aganaba

Introduction

In the context of this chapter, the term 'small jurisdictions' refers to states that have classically sought to benefit from their status as a territorial or dependent state to attract business. They enable capital flows to and from major countries (particularly a parent state) and increasingly from emerging economies. In the small state space market, the case of the Tongasat company is often discussed where the infamous state of Tonga was the first small jurisdiction to create a market for commercial access to geostationary orbital slots. This lucrative market capitalises on the fact that access to orbital slots can be a long and difficult procedure. Access to favourable slots determines the market potential of the operation and, as spectrum is a limited resource, securing fast, convenient and efficient filing of orbital slots is a vital part of all satellite business planning.

The issue becomes that entrepreneurs who approach small states with proposals for business may do so with the realisation that in small states they may not be as rigorously supervised as they might be elsewhere. In the European context, few small states have been put in the spotlight and it is acknowledged that, for the most part, 'the supervision of commercial dealings is considerable'.[1] Nevertheless, doubt still exists about the extent to which these small jurisdictions can fulfil the duties and responsibilities bestowed by international law with respect to activities of private commercial entities, particularly where the real ownership of some of these companies could be hidden. The state of Tonga gained notoriety because, despite the gentlemen's agreement that countries only register for slots that they are actually going to use, Tongasat, on its own initiative, submitted and locked up several satellite network filings with the International Telecommunication Union (ITU) that they would then try to lease for profit, thereby creating the problem that became known as 'paper satellites'.[2]

Following the Organisation for Economic Co-operation and Development (OECD) initiatives and harsher focus on offshore jurisdictions as unscrupulous tax havens, the spotlight is fiercely on small jurisdictions to ensure transparency in operations.[3] Though it could be said that classically many of these small entrepreneurial states may have served as little more than post boxes for companies registered in their domain, now the move is towards creating incentives to benefit the local environment and to raise the international profile of the jurisdiction, such that it is seen as an able location, sufficient to support local business in its own right.

---

1 Lyall, F. 2006. 'Small States, Entrepreneurial States and Space', in *Proceedings of the 49th Colloquium on the Law of Outer Space*. Washington, DC: AIAA, 382–90.

2 Thompson, J.C. 1996. 'Space for Rent: The International Telecommunications Union, Space Law, and Orbit/Spectrum Leasing', 62 *J. Air L. & Com.* 279.

3 Levin, M. 2003. *The Prospects for Offshore Financial Centres in Europe*. Centre for European Studies Research Report, August 2003.

Following the Isle of Man's recognition by the G-20 and the OECD as a top 40 global jurisdiction – and not a 'tax haven'–[4] and by the International Monetary Fund (IMF) as a leading and well regulated 'International Finance Centre',[5] the focus of this chapter is on how the Isle of Man has sought to become a real player in the space market. With the huge capital costs of satellite and space activity, the Isle of Man promotes itself as a jurisdiction where substantial cost savings can be made by establishing corporate structures, operational or leasing subsidiaries of space companies in its domain. The Isle of Man space strategy is highlighted to show how space initiatives in small jurisdictions can benefit the local environment, whilst addressing international markets and abiding by international conventions.

A Space Strategy for a Small State

The Isle of Man is a British crown dependency in the British Isles and as such maintains a unique status with respect to its relationship with the UK. Though the UK has the power to legislate for the Isle of Man for matters of mutual concern (including defence and international relations), and is responsible for overall good government of the island, the Isle is internally self governing and contributes to the UK for provision of these services.[6] Increased self determination is encouraged, but the Isle's strategy is to align itself with the UK when the stance is strategically beneficial and to differentiate itself where and when it can provide better services. The effect is that the Isle of Man is greatly enhanced and protected by its relationship with the UK and works hard to ensure that Isle of Man business adds value to the UK through the maintenance of a hub-and-spoke-style relationship.

The initiative to create a space industry on the Isle of Man came in 1998 by a private company called ManSat Ltd. ManSat's vision was that by utilising Isle of Man orbital slots, increased business would flow to the Isle of Man as the orbital revenue cycle would open up. ManSat's proposal was accepted by the Isle of Man Government, which began to market itself as a jurisdiction for orbital filings. To ensure that orbital slots applied for through the Isle of Man would be allocated with speed and efficiency, the Isle of Man granted, via commercial contract, sole and exclusive rights to ManSat for all its orbital applications and as such ManSat became the first commercial company to have filing rights at the ITU.[7]

The Island's foray into the space sector has since grown and what makes the Isle stand out from other small jurisdictions is the articulation of a dedicated strategy to make a mark in the space sector. The *Isle of Man Government Strategy on Space*[8] is essentially focused on monitoring the changing climate of space commerce and ensuring that the Isle of Man is placed to attract and receive space and space related business, most importantly by working with and supporting that

4 OECD 2009. *A Progress Report on Jurisdictions Surveyed by the OECD Global Forum in Implementing the Internationally Agreed Tax Standard.* [Online: Organisation for Economic Co-operation and Development]. Available at: www.oecd.org/dataoecd/38/14/42497950.pdf [accessed: 30 April 2011].

5 IMF 2009. *Isle of Man: Financial Sector Assessment Program Update – Financial System Stability Assessment.* [Online: International Monetary Fund]. Available at: http://www.imf.org/external/pubs/cat/longres.cfm?sk=23266.0 [accessed: 30 April 2011].

6 Solly, M. 1994. *Government and Law in the Isle of Man.* Castletown: Parallel Books.

7 ManSat Ltd 2008. 'Introduction to International Space Law', *ITU and Geostationary Orbits.* [Online: Mansat Ltd]. Available at: http://www.mansat.org/lectures.htm [accessed: 30 April 2011].

8 Isle of Man Treasury 2008. *Isle of Man Government Strategy on Space.* Provided by Mr Tim Craine, Director of Space Commerce, Space and Satellite Division, Isle of Man Treasury.

business, in essence, to build a regulatory and market hub that will allow global space businesses to thrive, and which gives the space industry 'freedom to flourish'. It highlights the aim of the Government with respect to the specific space and space-related areas, including:

- ensured level playing fields in national and international regulation: the 'level launch pad' approach
- privatised approach to space development with government working hand in hand with industry
- increased national awareness and understanding of space markets
- creation of effective enabling legislation
- focus on education and training
- utilisation of specialised financial and legal services sector
- watching developments in new space markets while working in the established market of satellite communications

The uniqueness of the strategy is that, unlike most other jurisdictions, it was initially spearheaded by a partnership of industry interests working in cooperation with the Space Commerce division of the Isle of Man Treasury; note that this is unlike others in that it is not a department of industry or a science agency. In recent times, while the Director of Space Commerce still oversees the strategy, it is now being implemented within the Business Development Agency of the Department of Economic Development. This unique and strong statement ensures that 'space' on the island is seen both as a commercial and financial endeavour and as a tool for sustained economic development of the Isle. The space strategy has attracted satellite and space-related business, promoting the Isle as a host site for satellite networks and orbital applications, and a host of other activity as highlighted by Futron's 2011 study assessing the "spaceisles" policy and results.[9] The 'Space Isle' marketing campaign brings together the core Isle of Man space expertise by providing for marketing of the island's expertise internationally under one banner, through sponsoring and partnering at events such as Euroconsults' World Satellite Business Week, Satellite Finance, the Space Frontier Foundations' Newspace conference, sponsorship of the X Prize Foundation, and others.

The island's space expertise is maintained through the establishment of the Isle of Man Space Industry Group, where members work in collaboration as a one-stop shop service to the space industry. The public private group is comprised of the Isle's leading insurance firms, tax and accounting firms, legal offices, corporate service providers, banks, satellite companies and space-related businesses, as well as relevant government departments. Whilst the space industry group is an informal committee, it is an extremely useful initiative to keep interested businesses united in the effort to encourage business sharing and networking. The marketing initiative and industry group is led by ManSat Ltd, which also offers a bespoke filing and consultancy service for Isle of Man registered companies wishing to undertake any activity in outer space. Under the leadership of ManSat, and in partnership with the government, the Isle of Man space support services industry aims to provide an efficient and holistic service to its customers who include satellite companies, small technical companies, research institutions and new space companies.

9 Futron Corporation 2011 Innovative Strategies for Space Competitiveness: Assessing the Space Isles Policy and Results [Online: Futron] .Available at http://www.futron.com/upload/wysiwyg/Resources/Whitepapers/Innovative_Strategies_for_Space_Competitiveness_0111.pdf [Accessed 30 April 2011].

Local Benefits

The Isle of Man space strategy seeks to create a space hub within the Isle of Man itself, even if the majority of business takes place outside the island. Appreciable local benefits from the space strategy to date include:

1. Innovative diversification of the economy:
   By January 2008,[10] with an accumulated expenditure of approximately £1.5 million to market the Isle as a centre of excellence for the space industry, it is reported in the Tynwald Hansard Parliamentary debate record that the satellite industry on the Isle was worth more than 25 million pounds during the three year period (2005–2008).
2. Increased specialist and high-paying new jobs for the economy.
3. Increased international profile and marketing benefit.
4. Increased opportunity for educational 'out-reach' for scholarships and studies and educational 'in reach' into schools and curriculum for inspiration of student body. Educational opportunity focus enhanced by increased local awareness through events such as:
   a. scholarship programme each year for sixth-form students via an essay competition, for which the winner attends NASA's International Space School in Houston
   b. industry and government sponsorship for executives to attend the International Space University (ISU) Executive Space Course
   c. ManSat scholarships for ISU students
   d. ManSat post-graduate fellowship programmes at the Lunar Planetary Institute and others
   e. Cains Space Law Prize for ISU masters students
   f. establishment of the ISU International Institute of Space Commerce located at the International Business School (IBS) Isle of Man
   g. astronaut and cosmonaut visits to schools
   h. enhanced support for astronomy and astrophysics programmes
   i. Heinlien Foundation sponsored space suit tour of flown Russian 'Sokol KV-2' space suit; tour of all high schools including educational materials matched to curriculum for teachers
   j. SES Satellite Leasing Limited (Isle of Man) sponsorship of the ISU executive space MBA programme. Beginning in January 2009, SES SL supports a five-year plan to establish and manage the programme. With a EUR 30,000 initial investment, plus an additional EUR 50,000 per year from 2009 to 2013, including one SES SL scholarship
   k. government and industry-supported scholarships from high school through post-graduate fellowships for international studies in space
5. General public programmes on space awareness and education:
   a. NASA moon rock to national museums
   b. Postage stamp collection – 'Man in Space; the Future'
   c. Isle of Man space coin series

10 Isle of Man Government 2008. Summary of Proceedings in the Council of Ministers January 2008 Part I Decisions made by Council. [Online: Isle of Man Parliament – Tynwald]. Available at: http://www.gov.im/government/council/proceedings/proceedings_2008.xml [accessed: 30 April 2011].

The Isle is still working on developing its local space-related infrastructure and is seeking partnerships to develop the Tromode Earth station and teleport that is currently underutilised. Development of this local infrastructure will certainly add to the local benefits by bringing operational space business to the Island.

A legal framework for feasible space activities

Licensing

Economic development is the primary objective of the Manx government's strategy with limited focus on engaging directly in space science or exploration. That notwithstanding, the creation of effective enabling legislation is a vital part of ensuring increased business and supporting the space industry. Space activities on the Isle of Man are governed by the Outer Space Act 1986 (Isle of Man) Order 1990, which extends to the Isle of Man all the provisions (as amended) of the UK's Outer Space Act 1986. As a crown dependency, Isle of Man registered companies wishing to undertake any type of space activity must apply to the UK Secretary of State via the UK Space Agency (UKSA) for a launch and operations licence.

Here Isle of Man companies are treated exactly the same as UK companies. A sharing arrangement has been reached between the Isle of Man and the UK with respect to potential liability in case of damage whereby Isle of Man applicants need only take out a single insurance policy in the name of the Isle of Man Government to indemnify both the UK and Isle of Man. The Isle of Man has in addition taken out its own policy to indemnify the UK government in case damage goes above and beyond what is covered by the applicant's policy. This risk sharing arrangement evidences the emphasis that is placed on ensuring that Isle of Man business operates in a manner that is in line with international standards. To further maintain this high standard of regulation, the Isle of Man has also adopted the UK's regulatory process for launch and operational licences. While this has the added effect of minimising any additional administrative burden on satellite operators wishing to operate from the Isle of Man, it also maintains and ensures compliance with the UK's standards.

The Isle of Man has appointed a commercial due diligence and risk management service provider experienced in space insurance to further examine the risk element as it may apply to the Isle of Man Government in regards to the licensing process and third party liability. Here the only additional requirement being this third party insurance element of the application to the UKSA must also be sent to the Isle of Man risk management service provider where a review will be performed for Isle of Man liability exposure. Here the Isle of Man employs a market safeguard or 'health check' in addition to the regulatory process.

The Isle of Man always seeks parity with other small jurisdictions, such as Gibraltar, with respect to the ability to license space activities, to ensure that Isle of Man businesses can benefit from the convenient access to local decision makers: the 'level launch pad' approach. The Isle of Man Space and Telecommunications Bill aims to vest regulatory powers for space activities for the Isle of Man on the Manx Communications Commission.[11] Under the bill, after consultation with the UK Secretary of State, the Communications Commission may regulate launch, procurement and/or operational activities or any other activities in outer space. The draft bill itself is based upon

11 Isle of Man Communications Commission 2009. *Communications Commission Service Delivery Plan 2009*. [Online: Communications Commission]. Available at:_www.gov.im/lib/docs/government/servicedeliveryplan2009.pdf [accessed: 30 April 2011].

that presently used by Gibraltar. Importantly, from this action the Isle will be free to maintain its own space register in any format so long as it complies with UK international obligations. The space register would aim to emulate the success of the Isle of Man corporate jet and super yacht registers and take its place as the world's first commercial space register.

Attracting Technical Expertise

Whilst focus is primarily on promotion of the isle as a base for the "financial engineering of space," the space strategy initially highlighted a desire to diversify the type of space business on the island, including attracting more technical expertise, to boost the existing space manufacturing base in the form of small technical space companies, and also exploring ways in which Isle of Man businesses can constructively engage with the European Space Agency (ESA).

A recent initiative on the Isle of Man, which can serve as a case study and example of how to develop a technical base, is the Isle of Man Aerospace Cluster. Since inception of the initiative, the individual companies of the Aerospace Cluster have experienced increased growth and are now more in tune with the changing face of aerospace business. By acting as a united front, they are able to compete better on global markets. This type of initiative coupled with the idea of space business incubation could be the key to attracting more space-related technical expertise to the island. The management team of the Isle of Man innovation centre, which forms part of the European Business and Innovation Center Network, indicated an interest in such a proposal and creating a package specifically geared towards the space industry, if the demand could be proved. If connected to the ESINET network (Europe's dedicated programme of space business incubators), Isle of Man registered start up businesses would be placed at a greater advantage.

With respect to participation in ESA contracts, the Isle of Man does not directly contribute to ESA through a mandatory contribution, but according to ESA[12] the Isle of Man is a part of the UK. As such, an Isle of Man company that would reply to an ESA Invitation to Tender, and win the competition, could be awarded an ESA Contract. The UK view[13] is that, though the Isle of Man is *not* a part of the UK, the British Government would not stand in the way of an Isle of Man company that won an ESA bid. The Isle of Man Government now has an understanding in place to pay a proportional amount of any '*juste retour*' for any Isle of Man company winning an ESA contract. However, despite these official viewpoints, further analysis would be necessary as to the true viability and economic effect of increased participation of Isle of Man registered companies in ESA space contracts, bearing in mind the indirect method of contribution to the ESA budget.

Conclusion

The Isle has sought to attract all manner of space business from satellite to the new space industry to space academia. While this strategy has proven successful thus far, other small similar jurisdictions like Bermuda and Gibraltar have chosen to focus on creating a regulatory environment adequate for the satellite telecommunications industry, and are also successfully attracting business.[14] Space interests on the Isle of Man are unique in that the Isle has chosen to outsource through commercial

12 ESA 2008. Email communication dated 7 July 2008 between author and Bernard Zufferey, ESA Manager in charge of European Cooperating States.

13 BNSC 2008. Email Communication dated 13 August 2008 between author and Andrew Lunnon, BNSC Regulatory Manager.

14 Snowdon, C. 2006. 'The Right Orbit', *Satellite Finance*, 44, 41–2.

contract much of the commercial aspects to the private sector, to ensure little bureaucracy and fast and efficient handling of business.

It is this unique combination of industry working together with government, this partnership, that is the island's driving strength. With efforts driven by the market and not dictated by government policy, the relationship is based on a true value situation. This ensures that society, industry and government work together for mutual benefit. That said, government still has a strong role to play towards the increased growth of space markets, particularly so where there are high risks and long development periods, which are still characteristic of the space business. Incentives must be continuously provided to industries to develop new markets and spin-off technologies through maintaining a space commerce friendly jurisdiction, where market access factors such as open and non-bureaucratic licensing policies, a competitive landscape and risk sharing are essential goals of increased private sector participation. The Isle of Man Government has sought to provide such a landscape to the international community through its initiatives and has also recently commissioned a cost benefit analysis of its financial investment in the development of the space industry to ensure that its own development goals are simultaneously being met. The 'Space Isle' continuously seeks the input of the private sector as to what more is needed to develop the space market.

List of References

BNSC 2008. Email Communication dated 13 August 2008 between author and Andrew Lunnon, BNSC Regulatory Manager.

Cains 2008. Isle of Man Government News Release. 'A Busy Week in Space for the Isle of Man', 21 August 2008. [Online: Cains Advocates]. Available at: http://www.cains.co.im/library/news/2008/ [accessed: 30 April 2011].

ESA 2008. Email communication dated 7 July 2008 between author and Bernard Zufferey, ESA Manager in charge of European Cooperating States.

House of Commons 2007. *Science and Technology – Seventh Report*, 4 July 2007. [O: House of Commons, United Kingdom Parliament]. Available at: http://www.publications.parliament.uk/pa/cm200607/cmselect/cmsctech/66/6602.htm [accessed: 30 April 2011].

IMF 2009. *Isle of Man: Financial Sector Assessment Program Update – Financial System Stability Assessment*. [Online: International Monetary Fund]. Available at: http://www.imf.org/external/pubs/cat/longres.cfm?sk=23266.0 [accessed: 30 April 2011].

Isle of Man Communications Commission 2009. *Communications Commission Service Delivery Plan 2009*. [Online: Communications Commission]. Available at:_www.gov.im/lib/docs/government/servicedeliveryplan2009.pdf [accessed: 30 April 2011].

Isle of Man Government 2006. Tynwald Order Paper (2006) PP2/06. [Online: Isle of Man Parliament – Tynwald]. Available at: www.tynwald.org.im/papers/orders/2005-2006/to17012006.pdf [accessed: 30 April 2011].

Isle of Man Government 2008. Summary of Proceedings in the Council of Ministers January 2008 Part I Decisions made by Council. [Online: Isle of Man Parliament – Tynwald]. Available at: http://www.gov.im/government/council/proceedings/proceedings_2008.xml [accessed: 30 April 2011].

Isle of Man Treasury 2008. *Isle of Man Government Strategy on Space*. Provided by Mr Tim Craine, Director of Space Commerce, Space and Satellite Division, Isle of Man Treasury.

Levin, M. 2003. *The Prospects for Offshore Financial Centres in Europe*. Centre for European Studies Research Report, August 2003.

Lyall, F. 2006. 'Small States, Entrepreneurial States and Space', in *Proceedings of the 49th Colloquium on the Law of Outer Space*. Washington, DC: AIAA, 382–90.

ManSat Ltd 2008. 'Introduction to International Space Law', *ITU and Geostationary Orbits*. [Online: Mansat Ltd]. Available at: http://www.mansat.org/lectures.htm [accessed: 30 April 2011].

OECD 2000. *Towards Global Tax Cooperation; Progress in Identifying and Eliminating Harmful Tax Practice*. [Online: Organisation for Economic Co-operation and Development]. Available at: www.oecd.org/dataoecd/25/27/44430257.pdf [accessed: 30 April 2011].

OECD 2009. *A Progress Report on Jurisdictions Surveyed by the OECD Global Forum in Implementing the Internationally Agreed Tax Standard*. [Online: Organisation for Economic Co-operation and Development]. Available at: www.oecd.org/dataoecd/38/14/42497950.pdf [accessed: 30 April 2011].

Snowdon, C. 2006. 'The Right Orbit', *Satellite Finance*, 44, 41–2.

Solly, M. 1994. *Government and Law in the Isle of Man*. Castletown: Parallel Books.

Thompson, J.C. 1996. 'Space for Rent: The International Telecommunications Union, Space Law, and Orbit/Spectrum Leasing', 62 *J. Air L. & Com.* 279.

PART III
General Aspects of Space Industry Contracts

Chapter 14
Typology of Contracts in the Space Sector

Laurence Ravillon

With the commercialisation of outer space, aspects of private law, in particular of contract law, have become more prominent. They fit into a framework of national and international public law, which stems from national space legislations, from European texts and from international treaties.

Contracts of the space industry, which encompass a wide range of agreements, are not completely new contractual figures: they borrow pre-existent moulds and do not differ from contracts in other domains. However, contractual practice innovates in order to answer new needs created by high technologies and high technology adds important features to these contracts because there is a substantial attendant risk inherent in these contracts (the satellite is at risk throughout its entire lifetime). These sophisticated contracts look very much alike, and contain the same clauses, regardless of the governing law and the language in which the contract is drafted.

The contracts of the spatial sector are manifold: they can concern the manufacturing, the launching and the operation of the satellite; they can be intellectual property contracts (exclusive patent licences, and technology transfer agreements); they can be contracts relating to the proper functioning of the satellite (contracts on ground station telemetry, tracking and command equipment, and software; positioning operations contracts); or they can relate to the transmission[1] and the sale of satellite pictures, collaborative agreements or back-up agreements between launch carriers.

We will see that, in terms of typology, some contracts are national, others are international; some contracts are commercial contracts, others are institutional contracts.

This chapter studies contracts related to the satellite: satellite purchase contracts, satellite launch contracts and transponder agreements. They concern manufacturers of satellites, launchers of satellites, owners and operators of satellites, lessors of transponder capacity and providers of services delivered by satellite. Financial institutions and investors, as well as insurers, are also very important in the space sector and in space contracts.

Satellite Purchase Contracts

Satellite purchase contracts are concluded by the manufacturers of satellites (Boeing, Lockheed Martin, Space Systems/Loral and Orbital Science Corporation in the United States, EADS Astrium Satellites and Thales Alenia Space in Europe) and their customers. The manufacturing of satellites reveals a complex contractual scheme, reflecting the tasks shared between the equipment suppliers, the subcontractors and the manufacturer who integrates and tests the sub-units.

First the buyer establishes some specifications, mentioned in an invitation to tender, which is sent to the selected manufacturers. These manufacturers then submit proposals (technical, financial,

1 Salin, P. 1992. 'Analysis of Several Bilateral Remote-Sensing Contracts between Satellite Operators and Ground-Stations', *IBLJ*, 2, 219–34.

contractual) from which the buyer chooses. The buyers can be international organisations, national agencies or private customers. Moreover, the contents of contracts of satellite purchase may vary according to the nature of the co-contracting parties and their bargaining power in the negotiation process.

The satellite purchase contract covers 'the design, construction, testing and delivery'[2] of one or several satellites (scope of work). The manufacturer supplies the staff, the material, the equipment, the services and the installations necessary for the execution of its obligations (manufacturing of the satellite, performances of the spacecraft). The buyer undertakes to pay the price.

The intensity of the obligations pressing on both parties depends on the characterisation of the contract related to the spatial object to be made. The satellite purchase contract can be regarded as a sales contract. Nevertheless, as it also involves the supply of services, it could also be characterised as a supply services contract.

In French law, to help choose between these two characterisations, of sales contract and contract for the provision of services, at first the economic criterion or *accessorium sequitur principale* can be applied. This examines the respective importance of both constituents of the contract, the supply of the work, of the material, and the *accessorium* following the fate of the main component. If the space object has a value superior to that of the services (training of the staff of the buyer, installation of the satellite on the launcher, and so on), then the satellite purchase contract will be a sales contract. But if this criterion is replaced by the criterion of design, then the contract will be a sales contract if the manufacturer alone conceived the product, and a supply of services contract if the manufacturer follows the wishes of the customer.[3] In the latter case, the satellite purchase contract would be closer to a supply of services contract because it corresponds to a unique supply, for the satisfaction of the needs of the customer. This does not correspond to mass production (even if mass production in the field is increasingly common, in particular in the manufacturing of satellite platforms[4]).

However, the contract can also be qualified as a supply of services contract only if the customer plays an essential role in the design of the product (specifications and technical means to be used), not if the customer merely describes the objectives of the product, as the French Supreme Court reminded us in its 6 March 2001 decision[5] concerning the supply by Alcatel of a cable with optical fibres unfit for the use for which it was intended.

The satellite purchase contract can also be a 'delivery in orbit' contract. This contract, which appeared in the second half of the 1980s, covers all the services to be delivered during the life of the satellite (manufacturing, launching, functioning in orbit), services which are all incumbent upon the manufacturer.[6] The contractual process is simplified in favour of the buyer, because the buyer only has one interlocutor: the manufacturer of the satellite. On the other hand, for the latter, the risk associated to this type of contract is high: indeed, the manufacturer has to demonstrate good capacities of coordination, and has to bear all the risks, from the design of the satellite to its construction, its launch and its functioning in orbit.

---

2 Common wording used in satellite purchase contract, after the Proposed FOS Model Contract with (Contractor) for Intelsat FOS Spacecraft and Associated Equipment and Services.

3 Cour de cassation, chambre commerciale, 4 juill. 1989, *Dalloz*, 1990, p. 246.

4 For example the structure of the satellite which contains all the equipment of support for the payload: acquisition of the final orbit, the correction of the orbit, the control of the attitude of the satellite, the supply in energy, thermal control, telemetry, remote control.

5 Cour de cassation, chambre commerciale, *JCP*, 2001, 10564.

6 Chappez, J. 1992. 'Le contrat de livraison en orbite', in *L'exploitation commerciale de l'espace, Droit positif, droit prospectif*, edited by Ph. Kahn. Paris: Litec, 183–201.

As the manufacturer builds the spacecraft, arranges for the launch and bears the launch risk, in this type of contract services are very important. Consequently, we can think of the contract as a supply services contract. This characterisation is strengthened by the notion of public private partnerships (PPP), in which the manufacturer supplies a service, and not equipment, and becomes an operator.

The Paris Court of Appeals rendered a decision on 15 June 1988, in a dispute between Aérospatiale and Eutelsat and several insurers.[7] In this decision, the Court decided that Aérospatiale was a 'seller-manufacturer' of the satellite, without explanation, and that Aérospatiale had to be aware of the possible defects and, in accordance with Article 1645 of the Civil Code, the company could not exclude or limit the '*garantie des vices cachés*' (liability defects).

The bargaining power acquired by customers of the manufacturer – satellite operators – has sometimes been used to press the manufacturer not only to deliver a satellite, but also to provide the frequencies and the geostationary positions, as well as to provide support in case of a complaint by the operators to their insurers in the event of a failure of the satellite, most of these activities being traditionally within the competence of the operator. All these obligations favour the characterisation of the contract as a supply of services contract. But characterisation could differ in other states: for example, in the United States, where manufacturers have adopted mass-production assembly line techniques in order to speed up and standardise the manufacturing process, qualification as a sales contract is more obvious.

With satellite purchase contracts being very detailed, characterisation could be considered unimportant. Nevertheless, just the opposite could be the case, in particular when the validity of clauses excluding or limiting liability must be measured, depending on the nature of the contract and the governing law.

In satellite purchase contracts, manufacturers usually only guarantee that the satellite will be free of defects at the time of launch, when risk is transferred to the purchaser. When a manufacturer has to deliver several satellites to a customer, if the first does not operate according to the contractual specifications, the manufacturer has to take corrective measures for the subsequent satellites to ensure they will be free of defects (Clause: Corrective Measures in Unlaunched Satellites and other Deliverable Items). Furthermore, the purchaser may include in the contract an incentive payments clause (or performance payments) to be paid to the manufacturer if the spacecraft works properly in outer space.

The Launch Services Agreement

In the space launch market, competition is tough. Arianespace, the European launch company, which has for a long time been in a monopoly position in commercial launches, is now widely challenged, not only by American and Russian companies, but also by Chinese, Japanese, Indian and Brazilian ones. Arianespace launches the Ariane 5 rocket from the Guiana Space Centre.

This competition is organised through various forms of cooperation. As a consequence, Arianespace is part of a joint venture, Starsem, with, among others, the Russian space agency, whose goal is to place satellites in low or medium orbit with the launcher Soyuz. International Launch Services (ILS) is a joint venture constituted by Lockheed Martin and the manufacturers of the Russian rocket Proton, which intends to commercialise the American launch vehicles, Titan and Atlas. The Sea Launch consortium launches the Zenit rocket from a converted offshore platform,

7 1988. Revue française de droit aérien et spatial, 203.

off the coast of California.[8] Finally, Boeing and Lockheed Martin formed a joint venture, United Launch Alliance, authorised by the Federal Trade Commission and by the European Commission. The cooperation also results in back-up agreements set up between launch companies, such as the agreement between Arianespace, Boeing Launch Services and Mitsubishi Heavy Industries, which guarantees customers the availability of a rocket: Ariane 5, or Sea Launch, or H-2 in Japan.

The launch is the cornerstone of spatial activities. The subject of the launch services agreement 'is the Launch of a satellite supplied by Customer at the Launch Base for the purpose of accomplishing the Launch Mission in accordance with the terms and conditions of this Agreement'.[9] Thus the launch company, for their part, prepares the launch (that is, prepares the launch site, the payload and the integration of the satellite to the launcher). The customer, for their part, delivers the satellite, in compliance with the contractual specifications, in due time, pays the price of the satellite according to a payment schedule, respects rules related to the export of goods, and respects the confidentiality agreement.

The contract includes the following provisions: recitals, definitions, services to be provided, launch schedule, launch postponements, replacement launch, price, method of payment, representations and warranties, reciprocal waivers of liability, insurance, *force majeure*, authorisations, termination, arbitration, applicable law, assignment, language, entire agreement, entry into force and confidentiality.

The launch services agreement is a supply services contract because the main obligation of the launch company is to supply the launch. The launch is defined in the contract as 'the event from which the operations become irreversible',[10] but the exact definition can vary according to the technical specificities of each rocket.

The launch services agreement is an international contract, because it takes place in an international space – outer space – and involves operations of design and manufacture taking place in several countries. Moreover, in a court decision of the Paris Court of Appeals (10 May 2007), *Caisse centrale de réassurance v. Arianespace*,[11] concerning a space reinsurance contract, it was specified that the dispute is international if the operation does not involve a single state. The activity covered by the reinsurance contract was not exclusively French, but at least European, so the arbitration was international according to Article 1492 of the French Code of Civil Procedure.

The launching entity promises to use its best efforts ('diligently working in a good and workman-like manner, as a reasonable, prudent manufacturer of launch vehicles and provider of launch services'[12]), for example, for the preparation of the launch vehicle and of the payload interfaces, for the execution of its obligations, to grant a replacement launch slot in case of failure of the initial launch, and so on.

The contract contains cross-waivers of liability between launch participants; the satellite customer and launch provider 'flow down' the waiver to their respective contractors and subcontractors involved in the launch. These clauses, which correspond to a commercial space industry practice, result in the simplification of the allocation of risk.

8 In June 2009, the company was placed under the protection of Chapter 11 of the US Bankruptcy Code.

9 Excerpt from a launch services agreement. This type of clause was originally drafted by NASA.

10 Du Parquet, Cl.-A. 2005. 'La gestion des risques dans les contrats de services de lancement', in *Le droit des activités spatiales à l'aube du XXième siècle*, edited by L. Ravillon. Paris: Litec, 183.

11 Mourre, A. and Pedone, P. 2007. 'Sommaires de jurisprudence des cours et tribunaux', *Gazette du Palais*, 13 au 17 juillet, 44.

12 Excerpt from a launch services agreement.

Satellite Operation Contracts

A contract for operation of a satellite allows the client to obtain the available capacity on the satellite in the case of communications satellites, to obtain data and images in the case of remote sensing satellites, and to obtain localisation data in the case of navigation satellites.

With regard to telecommunications satellites, contracts allow the satellite operator (for example Intelsat, Eutelsat, Inmarsat, SES), the owner of the satellite, to market the capacity available on the satellite. In these contracts, the operator lets to its customers, who are telecommunications service providers, the transponders aboard the satellite over a certain number of years.[13] Transponders are a set of elements that receive a signal from a ground station (up-link), transfer it to a different frequency and amplify it for broadcast towards another ground station (down-link).

In the rental agreement of capacity contract, the satellite operator supplies capacity on a satellite as well as certain services allowing use of the satellite by the customer against payment over certain periods. There are various types of contracts for attribution of capacity: the degree of priority of the services chosen by the customer distinguishes them, as do pre-emption and restoration rights (protected or restorable transponder or unprotected or non-restorable transponder).

Concerning characterisation, a contract without right of pre-emption is very close to a contract of lease, because the owner of the satellite grants to its client the use of a spacecraft, a transponder, for a period of time, for a determined price. But the contract could be regarded as a supply services agreement[14] because the operator provides access to the capacity of the satellite thanks to a certain number of services intended to monitor the control, the location and the good functioning of the satellite, and the ground stations (provision of facilities and services), for the customer's benefit. Furthermore, '(the) operator of the satellite can oblige at any time his customer to end the use of the transponder for reasons connected to the functioning of the satellite'.[15]

In this case, the customer is deprived of the free use of the spacecraft, which characterises the lease contract. Furthermore, the operator has police power to ensure the coexistence of various users, which allows the operator to intervene to maintain and to protect the performance of the satellite and to suspend the access of any party not respecting the procedures. The contract can also say that 'if the maintenance and the protection of the overall performance of the Satellite requires lessor to interrupt lessee's use of the transponder, ... lessor shall do so only to the extent necessary and for the shortest possible time'[16] or that 'lessor shall have the right to suspend lessee's access to the transponders and the satellite in the event that lessee breaches any of the operations procedures during such time as any breach continues'.[17]

In transponder agreements, the provision concerning the respective rights and obligations of the parties, in the event of an interruption of service or total satellite failure, plays an essential role. Contracts can provide for outage and/or degraded service credits and specify the backup capacity switching rights. They can specify if degraded service or service outages constitute a ground for premature termination, or for a refund or a reduction of fees. Financial adjustment and the right of termination are the customer's sole remedies in avoiding the risk of liability for profit losses, for example.

---

13 Eadie, C. 1994. 'Satellite Transponder Agreements', *Telecommunications and Space Journal*, 1, 315–25; Hermida, J. 1996. 'Transponder Agreements', *Journal of Space Law*, 24 (1), 35–42.

14 Hermida, J. 1996. 'Transponder Agreements', 37.

15 Loquin, E. 2008. 'Le partage des risques dans les contrats de location de transpondeurs', in *Gestion et partage des risques dans les projets spatiaux*, edited by L. Ravillon. Paris: Pedone, 11.

16 *Ibid.*

17 *Ibid.*

Concerning tele-observation satellites, we can take the example of Spot Image distribution agreements: Spot Image provides Spot Scenes – standard products being the object of a basic treatment (choice of the level of pre-treatment; colour images or black and white) – or SpotView – exploitable cartographic background images with a geographical information system or software for cartography. Any order and/or supply of Spot products are governed by the general conditions of supply of products of satellite imaging,[18] for the order of products referenced in the catalogue or not (in that case, the satellite has to be the object of a specific programming). Any use of Spot products is governed by Spot licences.[19] These can be standard licences (which indicate the use of the Spot product for the internal needs of the end user) or multi-licences (which concern the sharing of the product between several end users for a common project), for Spot images, for Spotmaps products (mosaics produced from Spot images), or for 3D products.

A dispute concerning the legal categorisation of the sale of satellite images was judged by a French court. In this dispute, concerning the regime of payment of VAT for the delivery of goods made by Spot Image, the company claimed that the sales it realises must be likened to a supply of services, the execution of which is the generative fact of the VAT. The tax authorities claimed it was the delivery of possession, the liability for VAT thereby being based upon the delivery of the goods. The Administrative Court of Toulouse judged that Spot Image delivered goods, because the company buys satellite images, transforms them and sells a new product derived from the acquired image.[20]

The company appealed. The judgment was affirmed by the Administrative Court of Appeals of Bordeaux, which considered that the sale of satellite images must be qualified as delivery of goods (purchase of the goods, adaptation, transformation, packaging of the goods, and marketing of a new product), in spite of the fact that part of the activity of the company involved intellectual creation. Hence, fiscal definitions are different from the definitions of contract law.[21]

For navigation satellites, the situation in the United States differs from that in Europe. In the United States, GPS operation is coordinated by the Department of Defense, which set up a free system. In Europe, however, Galileo is a civil programme placed under civil control, though it can, at the same time, be used for military purposes. Galileo involves the European Space Agency (ESA) and the European Union, which have already concluded study contracts (feasibility studies, global architecture of the system, market studies, interoperability, legal and economic aspects studies) and technical contracts. In contractual matters, the European Commission published on 25 June 2008 an Invitation to Tender No. TREN / G3 / 318-2008 Advisors Contract to the European Commission on the European GNSS Schedules (Programs). On 1 July 2008, ESA, acting in the name of and for the European Commission, published Tender Information Package for the Phase of Deployment of the System. The first contracts were signed by ESA at the beginning of 2010.

In the matter of navigation satellites, in Europe, some contracts will be made with the system operator for some services[22] (other services, like the Open Service, will be delivered free of charge,

18 www.spotimage.com/CGF.htm [accessed: 4 November 2010].

19 www.spotimage.com/licence.htm [accessed: 4 November 2010].

20 29 décembre 1998, Société Spot Image. 1999. *Revue de jurisprudence fiscale*, no. 549.

21 La vente d'images satellitaires reconditionnées est-elle une livraison de biens ou une prestation de services?, sous CAA Bordeaux, 20 mars 2003. 27 septembre 2004. *Petites affiches*, 6.

22 Galileo will offer a variety of services: Open Service – timing and positioning signals; Safety of Life Service (SoL) – for means of transport where lives could be endangered in case of bad functioning of the service; Commercial Service – greater accuracy; Public Regulated Service (PRS) – for state authorities: police, customs, coastguard; Search and Rescue Service (SAR).

and therefore without a contract, as in the United States). But the operator of the system is not yet determined.

As we have seen, there are a variety of contracts (sales, lease, supply agreements) but their legal characterisation has rarely been submitted to courts. This characterisation depends on the governing law and the choice of governing law may affect the interpretation of the contract provisions. A national law can be chosen.[23] The Unidroit Principles of International Commercial Contracts are sometimes referred to.[24]

At the same time, the content of contracts is being discussed increasingly in national or arbitral courts.[25] An examination of the nascent space case law proves that private companies hesitate less and less to submit disputes to state courts or arbitral tribunals. However, case law is related to the content of space contracts and not to their categorisation. Disputes brought to courts are insurance disputes, disputes concerning the performance, or rather the non-performance, of the contracts (late delivery of the satellite, anomaly in the functioning of the satellite, problem with a launcher), and are related to the clauses limiting or excluding the contractors' liability.

Arbitration is preferred because of the flexibility and confidentiality of arbitral proceedings. In this domain, the issue of evidence is highly important and complex. Moreover, it necessitates the hearing of numerous experts and witnesses, and cooperation among lawyers and engineers because of the technical complexity of the matter.

List of References

Chappez, J. 1992. 'Le contrat de livraison en orbite', in *L'exploitation commerciale de l'espace, Droit positif, droit prospectif*, edited by Ph. Kahn. Paris: Litec, 183–201.

Couston, M. 2008. *Fascicule 1600 Jurisclasseur Transports: Droit spatial, – Etude sur le cadre juridique du lancement spatial et du transport spatial.*

Du Parquet, Cl.-A. 2005. 'La gestion des risques dans les contrats de services de lancement', in *Le droit des activités spatiales à l'aube du XXième siècle*, edited by L. Ravillon. Paris: Litec, 179–86.

Eadie, C. 1994. 'Satellite Transponder Agreements', *Telecommunications and Space Journal*, 1, 315–25.

Gaubert, C. 2009. 'Risques et assurances dans les activités d'accès à l'espace', in *Droit de l'espace*, edited by Ph. Achilleas. Bruxelles: Larcier, 123–40.

Hermida, J. 1996. 'Transponder Agreements', *Journal of Space Law*, 24 (1), 35–42.

Hermida, J. 2004. 'Commercial Space Launch Service Contracts in France and in the United States of America', *Uniform Law Review*, 3, 537–46.

Kronke, H. 2005–2006. 'The UN Sales Convention, the Unidroit Contract Principles and the Way Beyond', *Journal of Air Law and Commerce*, 25, 451–65.

23 For example, in a launch services agreement, we can read that: 'The rights and duties of the parties hereto under this agreement shall be governed by the law of France' and waiver of the immunity of jurisdiction.

24 Kronke, H. 2005–2006. 'The UN Sales Convention, the Unidroit Contract Principles and the Way Beyond', *Journal of Air Law and Commerce*, 25, 455; Arbitral Award, 15.V.2002. 2003–2004. Arbitration Court of the Lausanne Chamber of Commerce and Industry (Switzerland), *Unif. L. Rev.*, 986–8; Arbitral Award, 31.I. 2003. 2003–2004. Arbitration Court of the Lausanne Chamber of Commerce and Industry (Switzerland), *Unif. L. Rev.*, 990–92.

25 Mourre, A. 2005. 'Arbitration in Space Contracts', *Arbitration International*, 21 (1), 37–53; Ravillon, L. 2003. 'Arbitral Disputes in the Space Activities Sector', *IBLJ*, 7, 825.

Loquin, E. 2008. 'Le partage des risques dans les contrats de location de transpondeurs', in *Gestion et partage des risques dans les projets spatiaux*, edited by L. Ravillon. Paris: Pedone, 11–20.

Mourre, A. 2005. 'Arbitration in Space Contracts', *Arbitration International*, 21 (1), 37–53.

Mourre, A. and Pedone, P. 2007. 'Sommaires de jurisprudence des cours et tribunaux', *Gazette du Palais*, 13 au 17 juillet, 44.

Peyrefitte, L. 2002. 'Les contrats de ferroutage et les contrats de lancement spatial sont-ils des contrats de transport?', in *Etudes offertes à B. Mercadal*. Paris: Ed. F. Lefebvre, 493–502.

Ravillon, L. 1998. 'Les contrats spatiaux: quelques thèmes récurrents', *RFD aérien et spatial*, 35–62.

Ravillon, L. 2003. 'Arbitral Disputes in the Space Activities Sector', *IBLJ*, 7, 801–29.

Ravillon L. (ed.). 2004. *Droit des activités spatiales. Adaptation aux phénomènes de commercialisation et de privatisation*. Paris: Litec.

Ravillon, L. (ed.). 2005. *Le droit des activités spatiales à l'aube du XXIe siècle*. Paris: Litec.

Ravillon, L. 2007. 'The Adaptation of Contract Law to Technological Innovations: the Example of Data-Processing and Space Sectors', *International Business Law Journal*, 4, 453–77.

Ravillon, L. (ed.). 2008. *Gestion et partage des risques dans les projets spatiaux*. Paris: Pedone.

Ravillon, L. 2009. 'Le cadre contractuel des activités de lancement', in *Droit de l'espace*, edited by Ph. Achilleas. Bruxelles: Larcier, 109–22.

Ravillon, L. 2010. *Fascicule 141-30 Jurisclasseur Droit international: Espace extra-atmosphérique – Aspects contractuels*.

Salin, P. 1992. 'Analysis of Several Bilateral Remote-Sensing Contracts between Satellite Operators and Ground-Stations', *IBLJ*, 2, 219–34.

Wells, C. 2008. 'Les spécificités des contrats d'assurances d'objets spatiaux', in *Gestion et partage des risques dans les projets spatiaux*, edited by L. Ravillon. Paris: Pedone, 51–66.

Chapter 15

Space Contracting within the Framework of the European Space Agency*

Gunilla Stjernevi and Eleni Katsampani**

Introduction

This chapter addresses the general topic of contracting with the European Space Agency, but focuses specifically on the evolution that occurred with regard to the general clauses and conditions for ESA contracts in the context of its recent reform.

An Historical Perspective

European space-related cooperation reached an institutional dimension through the foundation of the European Space Research Organisation (ESRO).[1] The convention establishing this organisation was laid before an intergovernmental conference in Paris in June 1962.[2] The 10 founding states were Belgium, Denmark, France, Germany, Italy, the Netherlands, Spain, Sweden, Switzerland and the United Kingdom. Austria and Norway also participated in the deliberations to establish ESRO, but did not at that time join the organisation.

The institutional founding of ESRO was considerably influenced by the European Organisation for Nuclear Research (CERN) and its convention. Major contracts were awarded competitively, the successful bidder being the one who made the lowest offer satisfying the laboratory's technical and delivery requirements.

By 1964, two different European agencies had been established; ESRO and the European Launch Development Organisation (ELDO), the latter with a mandate to develop a European launch capacity.

ESRO established itself as a leader in space exploration during its first and only decade of existence, whilst ELDO was dealing with technical problems, cost overruns and political disputes. The idea of a new single European space organisation was discussed in the early 1970s leading to the founding of the European Space Agency (ESA or the 'Agency') in 1975, through the merger of ESRO and ELDO. The main features of ESRO were adopted for the new organisation, both from an institutional point of view and in terms of content of the convention and other regulatory documents, such as the general clauses and conditions for ESA contracts.

---

* Special acknowledgment to Ms Monika Breider for her valuable contribution to this chapter. Monika Breider is a lawyer working as a contract procedures officer in the European Space Agency.

** The authors are lawyers working in the Procurement Department of the European Space Agency. This chapter reflects exclusively the personal opinion of the authors. Any IPR infringement is not intentional and the authors will be happy to rectify such upon notification.

1 Krige, J., Russo, A. and Sebesta L. 2000. SP- 1235, *A History of the European Space Agency, 1958–1987*. Noordwijk: European Space Agency.

2 The text is available via the United Kingdom's treaty series – No. 56 (1964).

The contracting practice in this early period of the Agency reflected a situation of generous programme budgets and research, laboratory and integration capacity available within the Agency itself. Contracts were placed predominantly under cost reimbursement conditions and the responsibility of the prime contractor was to deliver the (sub-) system developed under its responsibility, whilst the overall integration was left to the Agency which either contracted this under a separate contract or performed the integration itself.

The Agency's Procurement and Contracting Practices

Fundamental key factors in the Agency's procurement and contracting practices were and remain driven by the need to achieve technical success with a consequent focus on risk management.

Procurement practices

Procurement procedures

The primary procurement method of ESA is open competition and this is true for smaller research and development type contracts as well as for large projects. Such large projects are procured and contracted for in a step-by-step approach where knowledge and concepts are gradually maturing and the requirements of the subsequent phase are firmed up. This approach is necessary, in order to ensure maturity of the requirements and thereby a gradual reduction of the technical risks.

Procurement in direct negotiation is also possible in cases where there is but a sole source of the supply or in cases the follow-on of an activity is dependent on a single source, due to technical, scientific or financial reasons.

Considerations of industrial policy may exceptionally influence the choice of procurement method.

Industrial build-up

The Agency has introduced a gradual build up of the industrial team in its large projects through the 'Code of Best Practices'. The Agency requests, when applying this code, a proposal that is fully committing in all aspects and covers the complete scope of work, but does not include all subcontractors. It would, at submission, typically include the prime contractor and some key subcontractors responsible for major subsystems or instruments. The lower level subcontractors are then selected in competition under the responsibility of the prime contractor, with the involvement of ESA reviewing and accepting the bid-packages and participating in the evaluation and selection of subcontractors. This build up of the industrial team is done during the definition phase. It's primary objective is to ensure fairness of the competitions at subcontractor level but it also reduces the technical risk in the implementation phase because it forces early, detailed review of subsystems and unit design, which leads to a timely consolidation of requirements at lower level.

Contracting practices The Agency's contracts are based on the ESA General Clauses and Conditions (GCC), which is a regulatory document aiming to be self-standing and, hence, requiring limited tailoring. However, there have been areas where practice has been developed starting from, but reaching beyond, the GCC.

Price type practices

In the early days of the European Space Agency and space activities in Europe, the primary price type of major development contracts was cost-reimbursement. In the latter part of the 1990s this changed to more frequent use of fixed price contracts. Reasons for this were several: the maturity of the large space companies; their experience having done business with ESA for more than 20 years; and the experience of the major system integrators, which allowed them to shoulder a higher degree of risk under a fixed price scheme. A number of key technologies, for example in the area of platforms, were also considered mature and qualified, such that they could be procured by fixed price. Another reason was the toughening of the economic climate, leading to pressure to achieve higher efficiency and more results in exchange for the financial contributions made by Member States.

Fixed price is the dominant price type of ESA contracts today; it remains, however, a decision taken on a case-by-case basis and the Agency also concludes cost-reimbursement contracts when considered more cost-effective.

Incentive/penalty schemes

Contracts for major projects nominally include incentive/penalty schemes depending on the nature of the work. These vary between simple schemes where, as an incentive, a lump sum amount is due upon achievement of certain functional criteria, for example at the commissioning review a few months after launch, to complex solidarity schemes where the prime contractor and its key subcontractors participate jointly in the incentive scheme and they, as well as ESA, invest in the scheme and may earn double or lose their investment.

Reform of ESA's Procurement Rules and Contracts Conditions

Important goals of this reform undertaken in 2008 have been to reflect the regulatory evolution that has taken place both in and outside of ESA, but also to address evolving market conditions, new customer partnerships and contracting practices, as well as changes in the industrial landscape. The Agency's regulations related to procurement have been revised within the framework of the procurement reform to reflect this regulatory evolution and also to encompass new procurement techniques, such as two-stage tendering. The reform has touched upon both procurement and contracting rules and practices, including the General Clauses and Conditions for ESA Contracts (hereinafter called GCC Reform).

Intellectual Property Rights Regime

The first rules to undergo revision were those related to intellectual property rights (IPR).

The revised conditions concerning IPR for ESA study, research and development contracts were introduced in 2003 (Part II of the General Clauses and Conditions for ESA contracts, Revision 6).

A salient feature of the Agency's IPR regime (both before and after the reform) is that the contractor remains the owner of the IPR resulting from an ESA contract. Important changes were, however, introduced in the area of the licensing schemes of such IPR. The old regime granted the Agency, participating states and persons and bodies under their jurisdiction a free of charge licence to use the IPR developed under an ESA contract for all space applications. Whilst being more restrictive, the rules introduced in 2003 confirm the access and use of the IPR by the Agency (including the right to grant royalty-free sub-licences) in ESA space programmes free of charge. The use of IPR for other purposes is, however, available under the following conditions: IPR resulting from an ESA contract, which is used for a national public programme, is available under favourable conditions to participating states and persons and bodies. IPR resulting from an ESA contract is available for other purposes (for example commercial purposes), also under market conditions, to any third party, but the contractor may refuse the granting of a licence, if the access and/or use by the third party are contrary to its legitimate commercial interest.

The new rules introduced a strengthening of the Agency's position in situations where the contractor does not register generated IPR or wishes to abandon previously registered IPR. The Agency may require the contractor to assign its rights for registration and exploitation to a third party on favourable conditions. If the Agency does not find a suitable party, the Agency itself may register the IPR. In this case, the contractor, participating states and persons and bodies have a free of charge licence for their own purposes.

Under the old regime, the contractor had to announce the use of background IPR prior to the contract being placed. Upon agreement to use such background IPR, the Agency's dissemination right, as well as right of usage, was restricted and limited to specifically identified circumstances.

Under the new regime, the contractor has no obligation to identify the background IPR prior to the contract being placed, but may do so at any time during contract execution. The Agency has the right to use such background IPR free of charge for the project specified in the contract. A third party requesting to use this background IPR shall be granted a licence at favourable conditions, if the third party performs an activity within the framework of the same project specified in the contract, and at market conditions for any other project unless this would be contrary to the contractor's legitimate commercial interest. This applies also to a company performing an activity under another ESA programme.

The Ministerial Council in November 2008[3] paved the way for a wide reaching reform by approving a number of fundamental procurement-related principles. These principles are linked to the need to better control cost and scheduling of major programmes and to the securing of competition at all levels.

Procurement Practices

Four-step approach in large procurements Procurements of major programmes, for example with a forecasted cost at completion above EUR 20 million, are now organised in four steps:

1. The early phase of the project (feasibility and design assessment) shall be carried out in parallel with two contractors in competition.
2. At the end of this preparatory phase, a procurement proposal is submitted to the Agency's committee at delegate level for industrial policy matters (IPC). The procurement is approved by the IPC if a double simple majority, meaning the majority of participating states representing more than one-half of the contributions to the programme in question, votes in favour of it.
3. A contract proposal is presented to the IPC after the competition has taken place. The proposal is approved by the IPC if a simple majority of the participating states vote in favour.
4. The programme can be stopped by the responsible programme board (which is also composed of delegates from the ESA Member States) at the end of the preliminary definition phase (Phase B) and before going into the detailed definition/production phase (Phase C/D). Such decision can be made if the contract price has increased at this stage compared to the value decided in the IPC and if it is decided by a double two-thirds majority of the participating

3 This ESA Council meeting at ministerial level took place in The Hague in November 2008.

states (two-thirds of the participating states representing two-thirds of the contributions to the project).

The aim of this four-step procedure is to reinforce the competitive procurement method, to increase the role of the main contributors to the programmes of ESA, and also to be more transparent concerning the evolution of the cost of ESA programmes.

Review procedure A fundamental feature of the new procurement regulations is the introduction of a review procedure allowing companies with a direct interest in a procurement action to appeal against a breach of the procedural rules governing the tendering process.

The introduction of the review procedure seeks to fully ensure the right to an effective remedy and fair hearing to all economic operators that have demonstrated direct interest in an Agency's procurement.

ESA is an intergovernmental organisation with immunity from jurisdiction and execution.[4] As a result of this, the ESA convention states that contracts placed by the Agency shall provide for arbitration. However, prior to the introduction of the new procurement regulations, there was no possibility of a hearing for the pre-contractual stage within the rules of the Agency.

The new review procedure provides the right of a hearing with the purpose of guaranteeing access to justice in line with international rules of law. The right of review stipulated in the procurement regulations[5] is, therefore, strictly restricted to procedural aspects.

Claims shall be submitted to the head of the Agency's procurement department and unless resolved by mutual agreement, the claim may be submitted to the ESA industrial ombudsman. The ombudsman is independent in the performance of his/her functions. After consultation with the parties, the ombudsman issues a written recommendation. If this recommendation is not accepted by the parties, the claim may be brought to a procurement review board consisting of six members external to the Agency and that are not members of delegations of ESA Member States, associate Member States or cooperating states. The decision of the procurement review board is final and binding on the parties.

The review process provided in the procurement regulations does not delay the entry into force of any resulting contract. Compensation, below a financial ceiling, may be granted by the procurement review board for the loss or injury suffered due to a procedural breach of the procurement regulations.

General Clauses and Conditions Reform

The major procurement contracts placed by ESA comprise for example the development and production of an innovative satellite, and the smaller procurement contracts result typically in a technological achievement in the form of a study report and/or of a preliminary hardware (breadboard). There is no standardised production line which is updated from time to time with newly developed technical improvements or design innovations. Each satellite contracted is individually developed, designed and produced. And even though one could argue that there is a focus on receiving the satellite at the end of the contract and, therefore, an element of a sales contract, the main focus is not on the purchase of the satellite, but on the result and the service

4 ESA Convention, Annex 1, Article IV.

5 ESA/REG/001, Part VI.

provided by the contractor throughout this development. Therefore, these ESA contracts have to be considered work contracts, also known as manufacturing contracts.

The unlimited liability foreseen in the General Clauses and Conditions for ESA contracts (GCC) were de facto limited due to the non-involvement of industry in assembly, integration and testing of satellites as previously described in this chapter. This equilibrium changed when companies developed their own facilities for satellite integration and testing. Then, industry started bearing more risk and consequently the liability scheme foreseen in the GCC created an uneven sharing of risk between the Agency and the European space industry.

The main areas that the GCC reform touched upon are the following:

Liabilities CISG[6] as well as the Unidroit principles[7] have the same approach with respect to the liabilities for damages: they introduce the general principle of full compensation with the restriction, however, that the damage needs to be foreseeable and certain. This implies an exclusion of liabilities for indirect damages, as the damage which is too indirect, will usually also be uncertain as well as unforeseeable. Article 5 of the CISG provides that losses arising from death or personal injury are excluded from the convention's coverage. In general, the regulation or limitation of damages for death or personal injury by virtue of contractual clauses has been disputed by jurisprudence. However, the interparty cross-waiver of liability for injury or death to persons has been acknowledged as a valid liability-sharing scheme in space activities at the international level (with a mandatory flow-down to the private law entities involved in the space activities),[8] as well as at the national.[9] The interparty cross-waiver of liability has been selected as the liability-sharing scheme included in the standard contract conditions of professional associations.[10]

Revision 6 of the ESA GCC makes reference to the applicable law and introduces the strict liability of the contractor for damage to goods covered by the contract. In practice, liability caps were introduced in a non-consistent way as a result of negotiation.

As the European space industry currently undertakes development risks under the ESA contracts, it was deemed necessary to cap open-ended commitments and risks in order to foster innovation and technology development and to render the Agency a reliable partner. As the procurement approach of the Agency is success-driven, performance related liabilities remain unlimited. Liability for third parties claims or ex delicto liabilities remain unlimited as they may not be limited by contractual means. The interparty cross-waiver of liability has been introduced for damages to goods and injuries to persons as follows:

- Damages to Goods:
- Revision 6 of the ESA GCC makes reference to the law declared as applicable in the contract with no limit of liability for damage to goods owned by the parties.
- The scheme of the new GCC foresees the cross-waiver of liability for damage to goods owned by the parties, with the following exclusions: third-party claims, gross negligence,

6 CISG (United Nations Convention on Contracts for the International Sale of Goods) 1980, Vienna: UN, Articles 74–7.

7 UNIDROIT Principles of International Commercial Contracts 2004, Rome: UNIDROIT, Article 7.4.1–7.4.3.

8 Space Station Intergovernmental Agreement (IGA), Article 16. par. 3 (a), (b) and (c), available at http://lois.justice.gc.ca/en/C-31.3/ [accessed: 30 April 2011].

9 E.g. French Space Law No. 2008-518 dated 3 June 2008 (Article 20).

10 Fédération Internationale des Ingénieurs-Conseils (FIDIC). 1999. *Conditions of Contract for Plant and Design-Build.* Geneva: FIDIC Publications, Article 17.

wilful misconduct as well as damage to goods arising from the use of ESA testing facilities or equipment (given the different schemes already in place regulating the operation of the ESA testing facilities) and damage to deliverables and customer-furnished items for which a different liability scheme has been agreed with the European space industry (see paragraph below).

- The waiver of the insurers' subrogation rights in case of damage to goods on a reciprocity basis is the pre-requisite for the applicability of this scheme.
- Damage to items covered by the contract:
- Revision 6 of the ESA GCC foresees the strict unlimited liability of the contractor till the time specified in the contract for damage to items covered by the contract (deliverables and customer-furnished items).
- The liability of the contractor in the new ESA GCC for damage to deliverable items is limited to the contract price, and for the customer-furnished items is limited to the value of the item agreed by the parties in the contract.[11]
- Damages to persons:
- Revision 6 of the ESA GCC makes reference to the law declared applicable in the contract with no limit of liability for injury to persons.
- The new scheme agreed with the European space industry, represented by Eurospace and SME4Space, foresees the cross-waiver of liability combined with reciprocal hold-harmless agreements for injury to persons involved in the execution of the contract under the control of the parties, with the following exclusions: third-party claims, gross negligence, wilful misconduct as well as injury to persons arising from the use of ESA testing facilities or equipment.
- The reciprocal waiver of the insurers' subrogation rights in case of personal injury and the mandatory flow-down of such scheme to all levels of contracting are preconditions for the applicability of this scheme. The cross-waiver of liability for damage to goods and injury to persons was selected as the most appropriate scheme in order to facilitate the dispute settlement and render it an insurance issue.[12]
- Consequential/indirect damages:
- Revision 6 of the General Clauses and Conditions for ESA contracts does not regulate the issue of consequential (or 'indirect') damages.
- In the new scheme, the parties agree not to hold each other liable for consequential damages, specified in a non-exhaustive list as follows: rental expenses, losses of contract, income or revenue, profit, interests, financing, loss of customers, loss of availability and use of facilities, employees' productivity or loss of services of such persons.[13]
- Damages resulting from the use of the goods covered by the contract after acceptance by the Agency.
- Revision 6 of the ESA GCC foresees the unlimited liability of the Agency for damages resulting from the use of the goods covered by the contract after acceptance by the Agency,

---

11 European Space Agency (ESA). 2010. Clause 18.2: Damage to Deliverables, Clause 11.5: Liability for Damage, General Clauses and Conditions for ESA Contracts. [Online]. Available at: http://emits.esa.int/emits/owa/emits.main [accessed: 4 November 2010].

12 European Space Agency (ESA). 2010. Clause 18: Damage to Staff and Goods, General Clauses and Conditions for ESA Contracts.

13 European Space Agency (ESA). 2010. Clause 19: Liability for Consequential Damage During the Execution of the Contract, General Clauses and Conditions for ESA Contracts.

with the exception of damage attributable to the contractor's gross negligence or wilful misconduct.

- Such scheme remained unchanged in the new GCC, with the exception that the contractor could be held liable by the Agency for product liability claims in case the parties agree at contract conclusion that the delivered products (identified as such under the relevant legislation) shall be commercialised.[14]
- This change became necessary due to the recent developments in product liability, which were hardly in focus at the time of the establishment of Rev. 6 of the ESA GCC. Furthermore the Agency's activities changed, while previously such claims could not arise due to the nature of the business, nowadays this is possible.
- Performance-related liabilities:
- Revision 6 of the ESA GCC foresees unlimited performance liability.
- The new GCC foresees unlimited liability of the contractor for non-performance or bad performance during the contract execution. However, such liability is capped at 100 per cent of the contract price, however linked with increased enforceability of the Agency's cancellation right (see below under 'Termination').
- The capping of the contractor's liability towards the Agency was balanced in the execution clauses of the ESA GCC, which were updated with the aim to preserve high professional standards and high quality in the execution of ESA contracts as follows:

Delays/penalties When looking beyond the ESA regulations, one notices that the CISG[15] as well as the Unidroit principles[16] have the same approach for late or non delivery. The essence of these principles is to foresee an additional time period for the seller to cure a non-performance, which includes also a late performance.

In case of a successful cure, the buyer is not entitled to claim compensation instead of taking delivery, but remains entitled to compensation for damage suffered because of the delay.[17] However, after the expiry of an additional reasonable time period, the buyer is entitled to terminate the contract.[18]

With respect to penalties, the situation is more diverse. The common law only recognises liquidated damages,[19] while under civil law penalties are allowed to different extents.[20] Whether or not the aggrieved party is entitled to claim damages for additional damage is also dealt with

14 European Space Agency (ESA). 2010. Clause 20: Liability After Acceptance, General Clauses and Conditions for ESA Contracts.

15 CISG (United Nations Convention on Contracts for the International Sale of Goods) 1980, Vienna: UN Articles 45, 46, 47.

16 UNIDROIT Principles of International Commercial Contracts 2004, Rome: UNIDROIT Article 7.1.4.

17 UNIDROIT Principles of International Commercial Contracts 2004, Rome: UNIDROIT, Article 7.4.2; CISG (United Nations Convention on Contracts for the International Sale of Goods) 1980, Vienna: UN Article 47 II.

18 UNIDROIT Principles of International Commercial Contracts 2004, Rome: UNIDROIT, Article 7.1.5.

19 Dunlop Pneumatic Tyre v. New Garage & Motor Co Ltd [1915] AC 79 at 86.

20 France: Article 1226–33 Code Civil; Germany: §§ 339–45 BGB; Spain: Article 1154 Código Civil.

differently; namely, the Unidroit principles only foresee the general idea of introducing liquidated damages/penalties to a contract.[21]

In order to enforce timely delivery, ESA applies through clause 17 of the ESA GCC[22] so-called penalties to its contracts, which do not go beyond what is allowed under the common law principle of liquidated damages. For this principle the crucial factor is the content of the actual clause, not what the title of the clause is. Even a clause titled 'penalties' can still be valid under common law as long as the content of the clause declares a sum payable that is a genuine pre-estimate of the damage and that is not extravagant or unconscionable. A missed launch opportunity might mean damage for ESA that could go significantly beyond the contract price. Nevertheless the calculation of the so called penalty is based on a fraction of that amount. Therefore the approach chosen by ESA is within the boundaries of common law even though the term 'penalty' is used.

The principles for delays and penalties contained in Revision 6 of the ESA GCC were expanded and elaborated in detail in the new GCC as follows:

As the standard approach to a delay in delivery, clause 14.2 of the ESA GCC[23] foresees granting an extension in case the delay is not due to fault or negligence of the contractor; or granting a respite in any other case. In case the contractor still does not deliver at the extended point in time, clause 17 of the ESA GCC foresees a penalty which constitutes, according to clause 17.1.5 of the ESA GCC, the sole remedy for delay. In clause 17.1.5 of the ESA GCC, ESA also reserves the right to terminate in accordance with clause 32 of the ESA GCC.[24] This right of termination is not comparable to the right a buyer would have under the framework of the CISG or the Unidroit principles, where the right to terminate would be considered a remedy in case of non-performance or the consequence of non-performance after the expiry of an additional time period for delivery. Under clause 32 of the ESA GCC, ESA only has the right to terminate the contract in case the delay in delivery would seriously jeopardise the performance of the contract.

Due to the highly innovative technology for which ESA is contracting, and the scarceness of suppliers in this domain, the interest of ESA in being able to terminate a contract in case of delay is limited. Therefore, the right to terminate as a remedy for late performance is only foreseen as the last option and only under the additional requirement of a serious jeopardy of the contract. The success of the mission and, likewise, the delivery of the functioning satellite is the highest priority; therefore, a convenient termination right is not the main focus, but having the means to force the contractor to deliver on time and in accordance with the requirements, which is achieved by the combination of the clauses 14, 17 and as a final measure clause 32 of the ESA GCC.

For the first time, the ESA GCC now also foresee the option to introduce performance penalties to a contract. Specific kinds of contracts, for example service contracts, do not have a specific end date by which an item has to be delivered. Instead, those contracts require a consistent high-level performance. Until now no remedy was foreseen within the ESA framework in case such contracts were not performed to the required standards other than termination under very specific conditions. As ESA's main interest is to receive either the contracted items or the services, the new framework allows the introduction of this more useful tool, foreseen in clause 17.2 of the ESA GCC.

---

21 UNIDROIT Principles of International Commercial Contracts 2004, Rome: UNIDROIT, Article 7.4.13.

22 European Space Agency (ESA). 2010. Clause 17: Penalties/Incentives, General Clauses and Conditions for ESA Contracts.

23 European Space Agency (ESA). 2010. Clause 14.2: Delay in Provision of Deliverables or Services – Respites, General Clauses and Conditions for ESA Contracts.

24 European Space Agency (ESA). 2010. Clause 32: Termination with Fault of the Contractor, General Clauses and Conditions for ESA Contracts.

Force majeure The extent to which cases of force majeure are recognised varies a lot and often interferes with what can be considered hardship. The International Chamber of Commerce (ICC) provides a principle in the ICC Publication No. 650,[25] which has been taken into account when drafting the ESA provisions on force majeure.

In Revision 6 of the ESA GCC, *force majeure* was not specifically regulated and was left to the applicable law. It was deemed necessary to regulate this gap, in particular in view of the diversified approach regulating the *force majeure* in the various national laws.

The new GCC provides a definition of *force majeure* in Annex IV.[26] Even though such a definition is often integrated into the body of the text itself, here it was more efficient to make it a proper definition, as two different clauses (clause 14.3 and clause 33) of the ESA GCC refer to the term.

Specifically, clause 14.3 of the ESA GCC[27] details the procedure to be followed in case of a *force majeure* event. The important feature here is that the party affected by the *force majeure* event has to report the consequences of the event (e.g. the factory collapsed because of an earthquake) within one week to the other party. Furthermore it has to prove the existence, duration and consequences of the *force majeure* (contractual consequences such as delay in delivery) to the other party within one month. In case the affected party followed these procedures and the delay caused by the *force majeure* exceeds three months, both parties are entitled to terminate the contract in accordance with clause 33 of the ESA GCC.[28]

Alternatively the parties can agree to modify the contract. Under some Agency programmes, a delay cannot be accommodated due to restraints set by the Member States or cooperating organisations. Therefore, ESA has to also reserve the right to terminate the contract in case the delay would not exceed three months.

The financial consequences of such a termination are settled in clause 33.5 in connection with 31.2 and 31.4 of the ESA GCC. Anything already effected under the contract will be paid for, any material that is undamaged that has been acquired for the execution of the contract will be paid for, but no compensation for the loss will be paid.

Force majeure on the subcontractor level is not automatically considered *force majeure* for the prime contractor. The contractor has to prove that the delay of its subcontractor because of *force majeure* had an unavoidable impact on its own final delivery date.

Transfer of ownership Article 4 (b) CISG excludes the transfer of ownership from the applicability of the CISG, which only covers the formation of the contract and the parties' obligations arising from it. At which point in time ownership transfer is regulated in a very diverse way throughout national legislation. In general it is open for contractual negotiations and a popular approach is

---

25 ICC Force Majeure Clause 2003 and ICC Hardship Clause 2003, ICC Publication No. 650.

26 '*Force majeure*' means an event which is, unforeseeable, unavoidable and external at the time of contract signature, occurs beyond the control of the affected party and renders the performance of the contract impossible for the affected party, including but not limited to: acts of God, governmental administrative acts or omissions, consequences of natural disasters, epidemics, war hostilities, terrorist attacks.

27 European Space Agency (ESA). 2010. Clause 14.3: Delay in Provision of Deliverables or Services due to Force Majeure, General Clauses and Conditions for ESA Contracts.

28 European Space Agency (ESA). 2010. Clause 33: Termination in Special Cases, General Clauses and Conditions for ESA Contracts.

to take incremental ownership in correspondence with instalments of the payment of the contract price.

As mentioned above,[29] the regulatory framework of ESA has been influenced significantly by the framework of CERN. The CERN regulations foresee the transfer of ownership upon the acceptance of the supplies, which occurs either with a written notice of acceptance by CERN or at payment of the full price, whichever is earlier.[30] This approach has been reflected in Revision 6 of the ESA GCC. However, in large procurement contracts resulting in the delivery of flight systems, there have been in practice systematically deviations from the above approach, foreseeing the transfer of ownership at lift-off.

When looking at the pure amount and not the value of contracts placed by ESA, the majority of contracts are not for a satellite (also known as flight system) but for smaller items and research and development. The ESA GCC distinguishes in clause 15.4[31] between flight systems, intellectual property rights and other deliverables. The general approach is similar to the approach chosen by CERN, to transfer the ownership with acceptance, with the difference that, according to clause 16.3 of the ESA GCC, ESA does not provide an acceptance procedure as CERN does, but only agrees such a procedure with the contractor once the requirements for such a procedure become evident. Also the payment of the full contract price by ESA does not necessarily mean that ownership is transferred.

Intellectual property rights are dealt with under Part II of the ESA GCC and are not covered by Clause 15.4 of the ESA GCC.

Clause 15.4 of the ESA GCC foresees for the transfer of ownership for flight systems to be regulated in the contract. Due to the high value of such a flight system, the insurance for it is a major factor. During the development of the flight system, the contractor's insurance covers the satellite. The policy of ESA is to take ownership of a satellite at lift-off, which leaves the insurance obligation with the contractor. Since the prime contractor remains in physical control of the satellite until it is launched, such arrangement is the most favourable one from a financial point of view.

In case of a termination of a contract, the priorities are different. For such cases clause 30 of the ESA GCC[32] foresees ESA taking ownership for any items it has paid for. In the event of termination, ESA aims to own what it has paid for and the contractor has no interest in keeping parts that have been specifically developed for ESA and that cannot be used for any other purposes.

Warranty Even though the EU established specific rights for consumers in Directive 99/44/EC for warranty claims in case of defective goods, there is no such unified document for commercial transactions. Therefore the warranty obligations vary significantly and can even be limited to financial compensation.

As a successful mission and not financial compensation is the main priority of ESA, warranty rights are of major importance. ESA needs to be able to launch the satellite at the end of a contract and not to reimburse its Member States their contributions to the programme. Therefore, financial compensation for a defective deliverable would not be sufficient. ESA needs the contractor to repair or replace such a defective deliverable. Revision 6 of the ESA GCC regulated warranty at a high level without distinguishing between hardware and software and, in practice, there systematically

29 Section 1A.

30 CERN. General Conditions of CERN Contracts, CERN/FC/5164-II, Clause 21.

31 European Space Agency (ESA). 2010. Clause 15.4: Transfer of Ownership and Risk General Clauses and Conditions for ESA Contracts.

32 European Space Agency (ESA). 2010. Clause 30: General Rule, General Clauses and Conditions for ESA Contracts.

have been deviations from the standard clause, especially in large procurements, in order to cover the warranty requirements of these procurements in a detailed manner. Clause 21.2 of the new GCC[33] distinguishes between warranty for hardware and software. Defective hardware has to be removed by the contractor and at the cost of the contractor, and the contractor can choose whether it wants to replace or repair the defective hardware at its own cost. In case of defective software, the warranty obligation of the contractor is restricted to correcting any defect at its own cost.

Items developed under ESA contracts are innovative and therefore have to go through extensive testing. In case of a defect of the original deliverable, new tests become necessary for the repaired or replaced item. These are also covered by the contractor's warranty.

Another special feature of the warranty required by ESA is laid down in clause 21.3 of the ESA GCC, the warranty for a defect of a systematic nature. If a defect is found in, for example, a component, identical components have to be replaced under the warranty commitment without the same defect having been proved in the other individual components.

Revision 6 of the ESA GCC foresees that the duration of the warranty is one year from the delivery of the item. Taking into account, however, the time lapse till the integration of the item in the overall system, there systematically have been deviations from the above approach foreseeing that the warranty is granted for one year from the acceptance of the item. According to clause 22 of the new GCC,[34] the contractor is under a warranty obligation for one year from acceptance for non-flight items, including hardware and software.

For flight items the situation is different. ESA also insists on a one-year warranty as a nominal approach, but with the difference that here it is either one year or until lift-off, whichever is earlier. A post-launch warranty is different in nature from a nominal warranty. Therefore a clear cut has to be made at launch and an additional post-launch warranty has to be introduced to the contract. This is why clause 22.3 of the ESA GCC foresees an additional warranty to be negotiated in the contract in case a post-launch warranty is required in an individual case.

Termination The Unidroit principles foresee in Article 7.3.1 a right to terminate a contract in case of a fundamental non-performance by the other party, this principle is also reflected in the Articles 49 and 64 of the CISG.

The ESA GCC also foresee in clause 32[35] a similar right for ESA to terminate a contract for a 'material breach', but with the additional requirement that this material breach seriously jeopardises the performance of the contract.

Under revision 6 of the ESA GCC, the material breach still had to jeopardise the programme. In the early days of space activities in the framework of ESA, the programme was understood to be the satellite programme whilst today the programmes are often significantly larger in scope and more complex (for example the Galileo programme). With the new GCC this is now consequently reduced to the contract itself.

Because of this relaxation of termination requirements, the clause is more effective and offers a tool for the Agency in case of serious lack of performance by the contractor. The exposure of

---

33 European Space Agency (ESA). 2010. Clause 21: Scope of Warranty, General Clauses and Conditions for ESA Contracts.

34 European Space Agency (ESA). 2010. Clause 22: Warranty Period, General Clauses and Conditions for ESA Contracts.

35 European Space Agency (ESA). 2010. Clause 32: Termination with fault of the Contractor, General Clauses and Conditions for ESA Contracts.

the contractor in case of termination for fault is, under the new GCC, limited to the contract price whilst it was unlimited in revision 6.[36]

In addition to the above in clause 31 of the ESA GCC,[37] ESA also reserves the right to terminate the contract at any time without the fault of the contractor. This rather unusual right to terminate a valid and properly executed contract is a necessary reservation by ESA because of the specific political and programmatic conditions ESA is operating under as an intergovernmental organisation. Such termination would not be due to any fault of the contractor and clause 31.3 of the ESA GCC foresees consequently a compensation right for the contractor, which is capped by clause 31.4 of the ESA GCC at the contract price.

The reforms of ESA contracting rules entered into force for contracts concluded on or after 18 December 2008. The practices that develop as from then will give the Agency and its contractors greater practical insight into their operation. It appears that the reforms have been well received. However, forthcoming experience will be required in order to assess their full impact.

List of References

CISG (United Nations Convention on Contracts for the International Sale of Goods) 1980. Vienna: UN.

European Space Agency (ESA) 2010. General Clauses and Conditions for ESA Contracts. [Online]. Available at: http://emits.esa.int/emits/owa/emits.main [accessed: 4 November 2010].

Fédération Internationale des Ingénieurs-Conseils (FIDIC). 1999. *Conditions of Contract for Plant and Design-Build*. Geneva: FIDIC Publications.

Krige, J., Russo, A. and Sebesta L. 2000. SP- 1235, *A History of the European Space Agency, 1958–1987*. Noordwijk: European Space Agency.

UNIDROIT Principles of International Commercial Contracts 2004. Rome: UNIDROIT.

36 Except in cases of gross negligence or wilful misconduct of the Contractor.

37 European Space Agency (ESA). 2010. Clause 31: Termination Without Fault of the Contractor, General Clauses and Conditions for ESA Contracts.

Chapter 16
Procurement in the Space Sector

Oliver Heinrich

Activities in the space sector are for the greater part still the domain of states. Over the years space projects have evolved into an important tool for implementing economic goals. In the beginning of the new millennium the EU realised the potential of space activities for the implementation of numerous policies. The development of an EU space policy was the decisive step that elevated space projects to a new economic level.

Under the ESA procurement regulation the most dominant aspect of procurement is the implementation of the required geographical return quota. Procurement for implementation of the EU space policy is, however, subjected to the strict EU procurement rules. The first project to come into contact with such procedures was Galileo – Europe's highly ambitious undertaking to establish its own independent global satellite navigation system. The Galileo procurement process may well be the most complicated procurement undertaking one could possibly envisage as the premiere for applying EU procurement rules to space projects and may herald a new era for public procurement in the space sector.

Introduction – Three Elements of a Successful Tender

Success in a procurement process consists of three main elements: first, awareness of the upcoming procurements in due time; second, knowing and – more important – understanding the procurement procedure and the applicable rules; third, putting it all together in a competitive and compliant tender for goods, services or works. In sum, each element turns out to be crucial for placing a successful offer, while each requires a different amount of effort and can be more or less easily achieved.

The main focus of this chapter is to provide a basic understanding of the complex rules of public procurement.

First Element: Awareness of Upcoming Procurements

Nothing is more painful than a missed chance, the worst kind being a chance of which one was unaware.

Both ESA and the EU are employing the internet in order to inform interested parties about upcoming procurement procedures. For ESA there is EMITS (Electronic Mail Invitation to Tender Service)[1] and for the EU there is Tenders Electronic Daily (TED)[2]. Both services offer the possibility of content-sensitive search by keywords.

---

1 Internet Link to EMITS: http://emits.esa.int/emits/owa/emits.main.

2 Internet Link to Tenders Electronic Daily: http://ted.europa.eu/.

It is advisable for any economic operator to scan frequently the information systems for keywords connected to areas of its economic interest. In addition, there are numerous free public and commercial providers offering a general or even customised search and update service of upcoming procurement projects on a more or less regular and timely basis.

Awareness of an upcoming procurement process is, however, not sufficient for participation in ESA procurement procedures. Under the ESA Procurement Regulation (ESA-PR)[3] a prerequisite for acquiring the relevant procurement documents and subsequently for participation in a procurement process is the registration in ESA's open, but mandatory, supplier list. Entering into the list is possible for any interested economic operator from any country worldwide through registration on ESA's EMITS homepage. Finalisation of registration unlocks access to the ESA tender documents applicable for participation in open competitive procedures. The registration process may take some time and therefore should ideally be initiated well before any procurement project of interest to the respective economic operator is published.

It is also important to note that an economic operator may be excluded from participation in procurements for ESA projects due to industrial policy considerations. This first and foremost applies to the economic operators not belonging to a state legitimating it to participate in the ESA procurement.[4] Concerning the criteria necessary to determine whether the tenderer belongs to a state legitimating it to participate in ESA procurements, Article 18 no. 1 (a) ESA-PR makes reference to Article II.3 of Annex V of the ESA Convention.[5] Unfortunately, Article II.3 of Annex V of the ESA Convention fails to provide any particular guideline for fulfilling these requirements. Doubtful cases are left to the ESA Council to decide.

In contrast, the EU procurement rules currently do not require economic operators to register in any supplier list. Participation in EU procurement procedures depends entirely on the procurement process applied.

Second Element: Knowing and Understanding the Procurement Process

Public procurement procedures follow specific rules laid down in the respective procurement regulations. Familiarity with these regulations is a precondition for acting with competence in a procurement process and for delivering a compliant tender. It is also important for spotting mistakes made by the contracting authority and for applying legal remedies.

---

3 See Article 18 No. 2 ESA-PR.

4 See ESA Procurement Regulation, PART III INITIATION OF TENDER, ARTICLE 18 – QUALIFICATION AND REGISTRATION OF ECONOMIC OPERATORS '1. All economic operators who are considered to belong to one of the Member States, Associate Member States or Cooperating States of the Agency are eligible to participate in a tendering procedure of the Agency provided: a) they satisfy the requirements set under Article II.3 of Annex V to the Convention; […].'

5 Article II.3 of Annex V of the ESA Convention: '3. The question whether an enterprise should be considered to belong to one of the Member States shall be settled in the light of the following criteria: location of the enterprise's registered office, decision-making centres and research centres, and territory on which the work is to be carried out. In doubtful cases the Council shall decide whether an enterprise shall be considered to belong to one of the Member States, or not.'

The EU and ESA operate under different procurement regimes. While ESA may be acting as procurement agent of the EU[6] in specific programmes like Galileo, it is important to note that nevertheless the EU procurement rules apply.[7]

EU Procurement Regime

Identifying the correct procurement regime The EU procurement rules are divided into two main sections depending on the legal identity of the contracting authority. All procurements performed by contracting authorities of the EU Member States are regulated by the directives on the coordination of public procurement 2004/18 EC[8] and 2004/17 EC.[9] In contrast, all procurements performed by EU bodies have to follow the procurement rules of the EU financial regulation[10] and implementation rules.[11] While these regulations make frequent reference to the above mentioned directives, they are an independent set of rules.

Nevertheless, in case of uncertainty about specific rules of the regulations, it can be helpful to consult the directives and the corresponding judgements of the ECJ on their implementation in order to gain a better understanding of the provisions in the regulations. As the ESP is implemented by EU bodies, the mentioned financial regulation and implementation rules are the correct procurement regimes and must be followed for procurements of the EU in space projects. These

6 Concerning GMES see COM(2008) 748 final, Brussels, 12 November 2008, Communication from the Commission to the European Parliament, the Council, and the European Economic and Social Committee, and the Committee of the Regions: 'Global Monitoring for Environment and Security (GMES): We Care for a Safer Planet', '[...] For new space component infrastructure, that might be necessary to fill gaps for the provision of GMES services, again ESA should be assigned the role of procurement and, where applicable, development agent, for and on behalf of the EU', p. 8; concerning Galileo/EGNOS see Regulation (EC) No. 683/2008 of the European Parliament and of the Council of 9 July 2008 on the further implementation of the European satellite navigation programmes (EGNOS and Galileo), OJ 2008 L 196, 1, there Article 17 (1) and Article 18.

7 See COM(2005) 208 final, Brussels, 23 May 2005, Communication from the Commission to the Council and the European Parliament, 'European Space Policy – Preliminary Elements' '[...] The EU industry policy will incorporate: [...] (b) Procurement policy, cost-efficient, adapted to the new EU industrial environment and consistent with relevant Community law will be applied. This will be a consequence of space systems, integrated with in-situ monitoring and other terrestrial systems, becoming driven and eventually paid for by user policies [...]', p. 9.

8 Directive 2004/18/EC of the European Parliament and of the Council of 31 March 2004 on the coordination of procedures for the award of public works contracts, public supply contracts and public service contracts, OJ 2004 L 134, 114.

9 Directive 2004/17/EC of the European Parliament and of the Council of 31 March 2004 coordinating the procurement procedures of entities operating in the water, energy, transport and postal services sectors, OJ 2004 L 134, 1.

10 Council Regulation No. 1605/2002 amended by Council Regulation No. 1995/2006 – Financial Regulation applicable to the general budget of the European Communities, OJ 2002 L 248, 1 (hereinafter referred to as EU-FR).

11 Commission Regulation No. 2342/2002 last amended by Commission Regulation No. 478/2007 laying down detailed rules for the implementation of the Council Regulation (EC, EURATOM) 1605/2002 on the Financial Regulation applicable to the general budget of the European Communities, OJ 2002 L 357, 1 (hereinafter referred to as EU-FRIR).

rules have been amended a number of times. The latest versions of the regulations can be found on the internet from the EU website on Financial Programming and Budget.[12]

Understanding the general procurement principles Public procurement under the EU rules is based on five general principles:

equal treatment
non-discrimination
mutual recognition
proportionality and
transparency[13]

These principles derive from the EU Treaty itself, namely the principle of freedom of movement of goods,[14] the principle of right of establishment[15] and the principle of freedom to provide services.[16] Consequently, these principles have to be adhered to throughout any procurement process and therefore have considerable influence.

The principles of equal treatment and non-discrimination
The principle of equal treatment is based on the idea that equal characteristics have to be treated equally. Under this rule, the procurement regulations have to be applied equally to all candidates/tenderers. This is especially important in situations where the contracting authority offers, for example, clarifications to one candidate or when negotiating under certain conditions with one candidate or when excluding one candidate/tenderer for failing to fulfil certain requirements. In these instances, all other tenderers/candidates have to be treated in the same way. Clarifications have to be given to all other candidates, negotiations have to be held under the same conditions with all other candidates, and all other candidates/tenderers who failed to fulfil the specific requirements have to be excluded.

The principal of non-discrimination goes one step further. It means that even when there are some aspects of differentiation between candidates or tenderers and tenders, these differences may not be taken into account but instead have to be disregarded in a procurement process. Typical examples are the participation of tenderers with different ethnic or social minority backgrounds or different national places of origin of offered products.

The principle of mutual recognition
The principle of mutual recognition guarantees free movement of goods and services without the need to harmonise EU Member States' national legislation. Goods that are lawfully produced in one Member State cannot be banned from sale on the territory of another Member State, even if they are produced according to different technical or quality specifications. The only exceptions

---

12 See http://ec.europa.eu/budget/documents/financial_regulation_en.htm#table-1_1 [accessed: 30 April 2011].

13 See Article 56 No. 2, 89, 99 EU-FR; Article 43 No. 6 a) EU-FRIR; see also recital No. 2 Directive 2004/18/EC.

14 See Policy for the principle of movement of goods: Articles 26 No. 2; 28 et seq. TFEU.

15 See Policy for the principle of right of establishment: Article 49 et seq. TFEU.

16 See Policy for the principle of freedom to provide services: Articles 26 No. 2; 45 et seq. 56 et seq. TFEU.

allowed (however subject to strict conditions) are those of overriding general interest such as health, consumer or environmental protection. The same principle applies to services.[17]

Transferred to a public procurement scenario, this means that the contracting authority generally has to recognise requirements and standards for products and services established in one EU Member State as equivalent to those of another EU Member State.

The principle of proportionality

The principle of proportionality can be considered a result of the buyer power that contracting authorities regularly have. This buyer power may put the contracting authority in a position to direct demands at the tenderer exceeding the procurement need, and which otherwise would not be accepted in the open market. The principle of proportionality forbids such excessive requests. Instead, the contracting authority may only require from the tenderers what is strictly necessary in order to fulfil the particular procurement need.[18]

Consequently the demand to fulfil additional policy considerations without particular connection to the procurement need is highly restricted. According to the judgment of the Court of Justice, it is first to be differentiated between personal requirements including selection criteria, on the one hand, and award criteria on the other hand. Policy aspects in personal requirements and selection criteria are generally discriminating, if they are not strictly a requirement for the fulfilment of the contract.[19] Even then the requirements should be limited to the criteria for qualitative selection explicitly mentioned in the respective procurement rules. The Court of Justice decided in a number of judgments[20] concerning the procurement directives[21] that the therein listed personal requirements are exclusive and may not be extended by the Member States.

Concerning award criteria, the Court of Justice in line with the procurement directives leaves it to the contracting authority to choose the criteria on which it proposes to base the award of the contract. The contracting authorities' choice may, however, relate only to criteria aimed at identifying the economically most advantageous tender.[22] The criteria themselves have to be linked to the subject matter of the contract, and all such criteria must be expressly mentioned in the

---

17 http://europa.eu/legislation_summaries/internal_market/internal_market_general_framework/l21001b_en.htm [accessed: 30 April 2011].

18 See Judgment of the General Court (Third Chamber) of 2 March 2010 – Evropaïki Dynamiki – Proigmena Systimata Tilepikoinonion Pliroforikis kai Tilematikis AE v European Maritime Safety Agency (EMSA), (Case T-70/05) paragraph 129.

19 Judgment of the Court (Fourth Chamber) of 20 September 1988 – Gebroeders Beentjes BV v State of the Netherlands (Case C-31/87) paragraph 18, 35; Judgment of the Court of 26 September 2000 – Commission of the European Communities v French Republic (Case C-225/98), paragraph 51.

20 Judgment of the Court of 3 June 1992 – Commission of the European Communities v Italian Republic (Case C-360/89), paragraph 18; Judgment of the Court of 26 April 1994 – Commission of the European Communities v Italian Republic (Case C-272/91), paragraph 18.

21 Articles 45 to 52, Directive 2004/18/EC.

22 Judgment of the Court (Fourth Chamber) of 20 September 1988 – Gebroeders Beentjes BV v State of the Netherlands (Case C-31/87) paragraphs 18, 35; Judgment of the Court of 28 March 1995 – The Queen v Secretary of State for Home Department, ex parte Evans Medical Ltd and Macfarlan Smith Ltd (Case C-324/93), paragraph 42; Judgment of the Court (Fifth Chamber) of 18 October 2001 – SIAC Construction Ltd v County Council of the County of Mayo (Case C-19/00), paragraph 42; Judgment of the Court of 17 June 2002 Concordia Bus Finland Oy Ab, formerly Stagecoach Finland Oy Ab v Helsingin kaupunki and HKL-Bussiliikenne (Case C-513/99), paragraph 59; Judgment of the Court (Fifth Chamber) of 18 October 2001 – SIAC Construction Ltd v County Council of the County of Mayo (Case C-19/00), paragraph 36.

contract documents or the tender notice in their ranking and/or weighting order so that economic operators are in a position to be aware of their existence and scope.[23]

The use of policy criteria for public procurement procedures in the space sector has to be handled very cautiously under EU law. Criteria linked with the origin of the economic operators are definitely not admissible. Accordingly, the geographic distribution system of ESA would not be compatible with EU law already for reasons of public procurement law (aside from conflicts with regard to state aid).

The principle of transparency

The principle of transparency forms the substantial basis for procurement procedures in a regulated environment. It requires the contracting authority to document the entire procurement process in real-time and in an objectively conceivable manner. This documentation starts with the authority clearly stating and defining its procurement needs as detailed as possible before initiating the procurement process *vis-à-vis* third parties. The contracting authority is not only required to clearly specify the desired procurement object, but also to state the conditions for awarding the contract, including the weighting of evaluation criteria or – should a weighting not be possible – at least their ranking to each other. On this basis, the tenderer has to be able to ascertain all substantial conditions for submitting its proposal.

Understanding the different procurement procedures Under the EC financial regulation (EU-FR) and implementation rules (EU-FRIR), EU bodies in principal apply four different procurement procedures – namely the open, the restricted, the negotiated procedure and the competitive dialogue.[24] One additional procedure, the contest, plays no significant role in procurements in the space sector and will therefore not be discussed in further detail.[25]

The open procedure and its relevance in space projects

Rules for conducting procurement under application of the open procedure are mainly found in Article 91 EU-FR and Articles 122, 140, 141, 143, 146, 147, 148, 149, 158a EU-FRIR.

In an open procedure, the contracting authority publishes a contract notice and every interested economic operator may then request the tender conditions and the respective draft contract to be provided. Sometimes, these documents are already included in the contract notice or may be downloaded from the internet. There is no pre-selection process in the open procedure.

The open procedure does not allow any negotiations between the tenderer and the contracting authority. Consequently, it is less suitable for complex procurement objects, which is why the open procedure is scarcely used for procurement projects in the space sector.

The restricted procedure and its relevance in space projects

Rules for the restricted procedure are located mainly in Article 91 EU-FR and Articles 122, 123, 128, 130, 140, 142, 158a EU-FRIR.

---

23 Judgment of the Court (Fourth Chamber) of 20 September 1988 – Gebroeders Beentjes BV v State of the Netherlands (Case C-31/87) paragraphs 31 and 36; Judgment of the Court of 26 September 2000 – Commission of the European Communities v French Republic (Case C-225/98), paragraph 51.

24 See Article 91 EU-FR.

25 The Contest is a procedure which aims to enable the contracting authority to acquire, mainly in the fields of architecture and civil engineering or data processing, a plan or design proposed by a selection board after being put out to competitive tender with or without the award of prizes. See Article 122 No. 4 EU-FRIR.

In the restricted procedure, calls for tenders may be restricted to a minimum of five economic operators which satisfy the pre-defined selection criteria published in the contract notice.[26] Such proceeding has to be clearly announced in the contract notice. Non-discriminating criteria are to be applied in order to achieve the reduction of tenderers, should more than the announced number apply.

Accordingly to Article 123 No. 3 EU-FRIR, the contracting authority may nevertheless continue the procedure should less than the announced number of candidates have applied and fulfilled the required capacities to submit tenders. Including additional economic operators – who did not ask to take part in the procurement procedure or candidates who do not have the required capacities – is not permissible.

Again no negotiations with the tenders are permitted under the restricted procedure. Consequently the problem of proper definition of the procurement objective and the contract conditions remain, making the restricted procedure not significantly more attractive for application in complex procurement objects.

The negotiated procedure and its relevance in space projects

The negotiated procedure is regulated mainly in Article 91 EU-FR and Articles 122, 123, 124, 126, 127, 130, 140, 142, 158a EU-FRIR.

The negotiated procedure may only be applied under enumerated conditions and generally only with prior publication of a contract notice.[27] A deviation from this principle is only permitted in the number of cases laid down in Article 126 EU-FRIR.

Similar to the restricted procedure, the contract notice for the negotiated procedure may set a maximum number of economic operators to be selected for participation as candidates. In case a sufficient number of economic operators fulfil the selection criteria, not less than three should be selected.[28] The selection criteria have to be fully disclosed in the contract notice in accordance with the principle of transparency. Neither the requested nor any other selection criteria may be further regarded in the evaluation of the criteria for establishing the best value for money regarding the different tenders.

It is established judgment of the European Court of Justice that the criteria for selection of economic operators and the criteria forming the basis for the award of the contract have to be clearly separated. Selection criteria may only be regarded in the selection process and award criteria may only be regarded in the evaluation process.[29] Selection criteria typically concern the personal traits and characteristics of the economic operator important for its ability to perform the contract at all; award criteria are tender-related with regard to establishing the quality and price of the offered goods, service or works necessary for determining the best value for money.

---

26 See Article 123 No. 1 EU-FRIR.

27 See Articles 126 and 127 EU-FRIR.

28 See Article 123 No. 2 EU-FRIR.

29 Judgment of the Court (Fourth Chamber) of 20 September 1988 – Gebroeders Beentjes BV v State of the Netherlands (Case C-31/87) paragraphs 18, 35; Judgment of the Court of 28 March 1995 – The Queen v Secretary of State for Home Department, ex parte Evans Medical Ltd and Macfarlan Smith Ltd (Case C-324/93), paragraph 42; Judgment of the Court (Fifth Chamber) of 18 October 2001 – SIAC Construction Ltd v County Council of the County of Mayo (Case C-19/00), paragraph 42; Judgment of the Court of 17 June 2002 Concordia Bus Finland Oy Ab, formerly Stagecoach Finland Oy Ab v Helsingin kaupunki and HKL-Bussiliikenne (Case C-513/99), paragraph 59; Judgment of the Court (Fifth Chamber) of 18 October 2001 – SIAC Construction Ltd v County Council of the County of Mayo (Case C-19/00), paragraph 36.

In case the number of economic operators fulfilling the selection criteria exceeds the maximum number announced in the contract notice, the contracting authority has to find a non-discriminatory means of further reducing the number of operators.

The contracting authority may chose to perform the negotiations in consecutive stages. Following each stage, economic operators may be eliminated from further participation by application of the award criteria published in the contract notice or the specifications. When making use of this possibility it has to be clearly announced in the contract notice or the specifications.[30] Also, genuine competition has nevertheless to be ensured, insofar as the number of appropriate solutions or candidates allows.

Following the selection of the economic operators in accordance to this procedure, the contracting authority may approach the selected economic operators for negotiations. The negotiations have to be conducted within the main cornerstones set by the contracting authority in the contract notice or the specification.

The contracting authority must not disclose any of the information exchanged with one competitor to the other competitors and it has to ensure that no contact is made between the competitors themselves as otherwise the secrecy of the competition may be harmed. This starts with observation of small details, such as arranging the schedule of negotiation rounds with sufficiently spaced time intervals in order to avoid that competitors accidentally meet on the premises of the contracting authority. It also requires especially careful keeping of minutes in order to uphold the principle of transparency. Economic operators should, for their own best interest, insist that exact minutes are handed out to them after every negotiation meeting with the contracting authority.

The competitive dialogue procedure and its relevance in space projects

Rules for the competitive dialogue procedure can be found mainly in Article 92 EU-FR and Articles 122, 123, 125b, 130, 140, 158a EU-FRIR.

The competitive dialogue procedure may only be applied under certain conditions, namely for 'particularly complex contracts'[31] where the contracting authority considers that the use of the open or the restricted procedure will not allow the contract to be awarded offering best value for money. In this sense the negotiated procedure and the competitive dialogue procedure may be chosen under similar circumstances under the contracting authority's discretion.[32] Article 127 No. 1 (b) and (c) EU-FRIR for the negotiated procedures is quite similar to the definition of the term 'particularly complex contracts' in Article 125b No. 1 EU-FRIR. Both allow its application in cases where the nature or the risks of the procurement objective do not permit prior overall pricing by the tenderer or where the nature of the service to be procured is such that contract specifications cannot be established with sufficient precision to permit the award of the contract by selecting the best tender in accordance with the rules governing the open or the restricted procedures.

---

30 See Article 124 EU-FRIR.

31 For the definition of the term 'particularly complex' refer to Article 125b No. 1 EU-FRIR: 'A contract is considered to be "particularly complex" where the contracting authority is not objectively able to define the technical means capable of satisfying the needs or objectives or able to specify the legal or financial make-up of the project.'

32 See Article 127 No. 1 (b) and (c) EU-FRIR for the negotiated procedures which quite similar to the competitive dialogue procedure allows its application in cases where the nature or the risks of the procurement object do not permit prior overall pricing by the tenderer or where the nature of the services to be procured is such that contract specifications cannot be established with sufficient precision to permit the award of the contract by selecting the best tender in accordance with the rules governing open or restricted procedures.

Similar to the negotiated procedure, the competitive dialogue procedure may be structured in consecutive phases in which the candidates enter into a dialogue, for example negotiations, with the contracting authority about the tender. Again, the number of candidates may be reduced after each dialogue phase while maintaining a sufficient number of candidates in order to ensure genuine competition. This approach has to be clearly announced in the contract notice or in the specifications. Once the contracting authority decides that one or more of the proposed tender solutions could fulfil its procurement needs, it may request the candidates to submit their best and final offer (BAFO) for evaluation in accordance with the pre-defined criteria. During the BAFO phase – like in the restricted procedure – no further negotiations between the candidates/tenderers and the contracting authority are allowed. There is still the possibility to request clarifications; however, this cannot change the pre-set parameters of the procurement process.

Special contract type – the framework agreement In public procurement procedures, the use of framework agreements offers great advantages to contracting authorities.[33] A 'framework agreement' is an agreement between one or more contracting authorities and one or more economic operators, with the purpose to establish the terms which are to govern contracts to be awarded during a given period, in particular with regard to price and, where appropriate, the quantity envisaged.

Framework agreements hold the benefit of flexibility for the contracting authority while at the same time making additional purchases easier, less costly and less time-consuming. However, a contracting authority's strong buyer power may have especially severe consequences in connection with framework agreements, all the more in the public dominated space sector. Misuse of this power may shift the commercial balance to the suppliers' disadvantage outside proper competitive aspects, as they may place an excessive and unjustified demand on the supplier.

A framework agreement may leave the supplier uncertain whether and when specific work orders under the framework agreement may be issued. At the same time, the supplier may be obliged to maintain its respective work capacities ready for the entire duration of the agreement. This weighs especially heavy in framework agreements concluded on a firm fixed price basis. A remedy may be the use of price escalation clauses aligning the agreement again with interim market developments. Such clauses, however, have to be part of the initial procurement process and thus have to be concluded in the framework agreement itself.

Framework agreements may also be chosen in a multi-supplier variant. Multi-supplier frameworks include first- and second-stage competition.[34] The first stage of competition determines the suppliers with whom the contracting authority will conclude the framework agreement. The second stage of competition allows the contracting authority to achieve the best possible bargain from the selected suppliers with regard to individual work orders.

33 See Arrowsmith, S. 2009. *Reform on the UNCITRAL Model Law of Procurement: Procurement Regulation for the 21st Century*. Eagan: West, § 2:2, p. 98.

34 See Arrowsmith, S. 2009. *Reform on the UNCITRAL Model Law of Procurement*, § 2:7, 2:8, p. 107; Frenz, W. 2007. *Handbuch Europarecht, Vol. 3, Beihilfe und Vergaberecht*. Berlin, Heidelberg, 924, # 3062 et seqq.

New ESA Procurement Regulation

The revised ESA-PR was adopted on 17 December 2008 during the 207th Council Meeting and is accessible to the public.[35] Approval of the ESA-PR by the ESA Council was given on 10 June 2010 and the regulation is open for review on the ESA EMITS website.[36]

The new ESA-PR – procurement principles The ESA-PR is based on the general principles laid down in Article 10 ESA-PR. According to Article 10.1 (a) ESA-PR, the ESA-PR as well as the placing of contracts shall always be interpreted so as to ensure transparency and fair and equitable treatment of all economic operators. Article 10.1 (d) ESA-PR. ESA therein[37] ensures the prerogative of the industrial policy and the implementation of the geographical return principle of Article VII and Annex V of the ESA-Convention. This may have an impact on the principle of equal treatment, which could experience a somewhat restricted interpretation in the light of the ESA's industrial policy as well as the Convention's geographical return principle.

Many public bodies, such as public research organisations or national space agencies, participate frequently as tenderers in ESA projects. In this respect, Article 10.1 (c) ESA-PR explicitly implements the principle 'that the participation of a Tendering Body does not cause any distortion of competition in relation to private economic operators'. As the term 'Tendering Body' – according to the regulation's list of definitions in Article 2 ESA-PR – is understood as 'a public body (including intergovernmental organisations) acting as potential contractor', the principle in Article 10.1 (c) ESA-PR requires the participation of such public bodies in ESA procurement procedures to be restricted to cases in which competition in relation to private economic operators is not distorted.

The new ESA-PR – supplier lists and prequalification According to Article 18 ESA-PR, ESA under the new ESA-PR continues to maintain a supplier list. While no further details are given, it can be expected that the system to which the new ESA-PR relates will be the existing EMITS (Electronic Mail Invitation to Tender System). Accordingly, prior registration in the electronic supplier list will remain a pre-condition for participation in any ESA procurement process. The supplier list in principle will be open to all economic operators who are considered to belong to one of the Member States, Associate Member States or Cooperating States of ESA with which the Agency may have made respective arrangements and who also fulfil a number of other requirements.

The question whether an economic operator belongs to one of the mentioned states may be determined by reference to Article II.3[38] of Annex V of the ESA Convention according to the therein mentioned criteria.

35 ESA/C (2008)202, Paris 17 December 2008.

36 To review the new ESA Procurement Regulation go to http://emits.esa.int/emits/owa/emits.main – folder 'Reference Documentation', subfolder 'Administrative Documents' – file 'Procurement Regulations' (pdf-format) [accessed: 30 April 2011].

37 Article 10 – Principles ESA-PR: '1. Provisions in these Regulations and in any instructions concerning the placing of contracts shall always be interpreted so as to ensure: […] d) the implementation of the defined industrial policy and to guarantee a distribution of work among Member States which is consistent with the prescriptions of Article VII and Annex V of the Convention.'

38 Article II.3 of Annex V of the ESA Convention: '3. The question whether an enterprise should be considered to belong to one of the Member States shall be settled in the light of the following criteria: location of the enterprise's registered office, decision-making centres and research centres, and territory on which the

Economic operators are obliged to update their entries in the supplier list at least once a year and in any case immediately should changes occur with regard to the criteria listed in Article 18.1 (d) to (h) ESA-PR.[39] A failure to update the information results in the contract not being awarded, Article 19.2 ESA-PR.

The new ESA-PR – procurement methods The new ESA-PR in its Part II enumerates the four procurement methods which may be employed in ESA procurement procedures.

Article 13 – competitive tendering

According to Article 13 ESA-PR, the term 'competitive tendering' encompasses the so-called open competitive tender as well as the so-called restricted competitive tender.

Concerning the open competitive tender, Article 13.1 ESA-PR merely states that it '[...] shall be the normal procedure for the placing of contracts'. When looking into the glossary of the ESA-PR, it becomes clear that the open competitive tender is meant to be open to any economic operator, underlining the resemblance to the EU's open procedure. Accordingly and following the provision in Article 27 ESA-PR, any economic operator registered in the ESA's electronic tool dedicated to procurement should have the possibility to access the proper invitations to tender and to submit a tender. This is, however, subject to the principles laid down in Article 10 ESA-PR, most notably ESA's industrial policy, the overarching principle of geographic return and, possibly, restriction of the participation of public bodies as tenderers in cases where this may lead to a distortion of competition toward the private economic operators.

The new ESA-PR does not mention a restriction of participation in the open tender under application of the so called 'C-Groups', as was the case under the former ESA procurement rules. The application of the C-groups for open competitive tenders formerly offered the possibility to strengthen the participation of small and medium-sized enterprises (SMEs), as in these groups either no 'primes' were allowed to participate at all (group C(1) and C(3)) or 'primes' had to include a significant number of SMEs in their offer (group C(2)), or at least had to demonstrate their serious endeavour to do so (group C(4)). It remains to be seen whether ESA may re-introduce this or a similar grouping-tool in future implementation rules.

The restricted competitive tender may be applied under the conditions enumerated under Article 13.2 ESA-PR.[40] Additionally, the provision provides the possibility to restrict the number

---

work is to be carried out. In doubtful cases the Council shall decide whether an enterprise shall be considered to belong to one of the Member States, or not.'

39 Article 18.1 ESA-PR – an economic operator is obliged to inform ESA immediately about changes to the following criteria concerning its electronic registration as ESA supplier: d) they are not bankrupt or being wound up, are having their affairs administered by the courts, have not entered into an arrangement with creditors, have not suspended business activities, are not the subject of proceedings concerning those matters, or are not in any analogous situation arising from a similar procedure provided for in national legislation or regulations; e) they have not been convicted of an offence concerning their professional conduct by a judgment which has the force of res judicata; f) they have not been guilty of grave professional misconduct proven by any means which the Agency can justify; g) they have fulfilled their obligations relating to the payment of social security contributions or the payment of taxes in accordance with the legal provisions of the country in which they are established or those of the country where the contract is to be performed; h) they have not been the subject of a judgment which has the force of res judicata for fraud, corruption, involvement in a criminal organisation or any other illegal activity detrimental to the Agency's interests.

40 Article 13.2 ESA-PR: '2. Restricted competitive tender may be applied: a) for supplies or services the special nature of which limits the capacity to procure them from a limited number of economic operators; b) for general procurements which have no industrial policy implications where the time and cost required

of economic operators to at least three. Article 13.4 ESA-PR requires that the reason for applying the restriction and the choice of the economic operators is recorded.

Article 14 – non-competitive tendering

Article 14.1 ESA-PR[41] provides the requirements for initiation of non-competitive tendering. As can be deduced from the non-application of Article 42 ESA-PR in accordance with Article 14.6 ESA-PR, negotiation in non-competitive tendering may be conducted without restriction. Nevertheless, the non-competitive tendering is not ESA's pendant to the EU's negotiated procedure, as the latter requires the contracting authority to maintain a measure of competition.

It should be noted that Article 14.1 (b) ESA-PR – in contrast to the EU procurement law – does not restrict the use of the non-competitive procedure in cases of urgency, having its cause outside ESA's sphere of influence. Accordingly, ESA is not prevented from invoking the waiver of competitive tendering in cases of urgency caused by the Agency itself.

Article 16 – two-stage tendering

The two-stage tendering is essentially a competitive dialogue procedure and ESA consequently uses this term in the text further describing the process. Two-stage tendering may be chosen in cases where ESA considers that it is not feasible to formulate detailed specifications for the supplies or where necessary inputs from economic operators are needed to detail these specifications.

The process of two-stage tendering provides for the possibility to enter into a dialogue with selected candidates and to thereby improve the tender specifications for which the selected candidates may then submit their offers. It also allows ESA a staggered approach during which the number of candidates may be consecutively reduced as the definition of the procurement object progresses through successive tendering rounds.

---

to examine and evaluate a large number of tenders would be disproportionate to the value of the supplies or services to be procured; c) for supplies or services procured by the Agency in the frame of international agreements entered into by the Agency with public bodies (including intergovernmental organisations), if expressly foreseen in the said agreements; d) where the supplies or services are procured by the Agency by means of a Framework Agreement as defined under Article 15.3 of these Regulations; e) for supplies or services classified secret or whose performance must be accompanied by special security measures in accordance with the Agency's regulations in force or when the protection of the essential interest of the Agency so requires; f) if the Industrial Policy Committee has given a directive or a guideline to that effect to the Director General, in particular in application of Article VII of the Convention and Articles IV.5, IV.6, IV.7 and V of Annex V to the Convention'.

41 Article 14 – Non-Competitive Tendering ESA-PR: 1. Competitive tendering may be waived in one or more of the following cases: a) if only one source for the supplies or services exists; b) in a case of extreme urgency resulting from compelling operational needs; c) where for scientific, technical or economic reasons contracts for additional or supplementary supplies or services cannot be separated from a previous contract; d) if the supplies or services required are the subject of intellectual property rights and can, as a consequence, only be procured from one particular source; e) where the supplies or services are procured by the Agency by means of Framework Agreement as defined under Article 15.4 of these Regulations; f) if the expenditure involved does not exceed 100,000 EURO; g) if the Industrial Policy Committee has given a directive or a guideline to that effect to the Director General.

Article 15 – framework agreements
With the new procurement regulation, ESA has introduced detailed rules concerning framework agreements.[42] Such framework agreements have a maximum duration of five years.[43] An exception to this rule may be possible subject to a contract proposal.[44] While the wording is not entirely clear, with regard to Article 43 ESA-PR a prolongation of a framework agreement may require the approval of the Industrial Policy Committee (IPC).[45]

Important aspects of the tendering proceedings
Details on the ESA procurement process itself are provided mainly in Part IV Tendering Proceedings. The provisions describe the process on a general level and apply to any of the ESA tendering proceedings unless provided otherwise. This gives the economic operator the possibility to analyse whether the procurement is following the rules of the regulation.

The ESA tendering proceedings hold a number of specialities and deviations from the EU procurement rules.

Regarding Article 24 and especially Article 38 ESA-PR, it becomes apparent that the ESA-PR do not clearly differentiate between selection and evaluation criteria. The EU rule, according to which selection criteria may no longer be regarded in the evaluation process,[46] does not appear to apply in ESA procurements. Accordingly, professional, technical, financial and other qualifications may be evaluated far into the procurement process and eventually lead to the respective economic operator's exclusion from the procedure.

According to Article 32 ESA-PR the ESA Directorate General (ESA-DG) may cancel an 'Invitation to Tender' at any time with no claim to compensation. The Glossary of the ESA-PR defines the term 'Invitation to Tender' as a formal communication to economic operators containing the conditions for the submission together with specifications and requirements and inviting them to submit tenders for a contract. It is also questionable whether such an extensive waiver would stand under applicable national law with regard to pre-contractual relations.

Article 17 ESA-PR, concerning the selection of subcontractors in connection with the selection of an industrial consortium, may be misleading under certain national legal systems. The provision requires the tenderer to procure subcontracts in accordance with the 'Best Practices for the Selection of subcontractors by Prime Contractors in the frame of ESA's Procurements' as was already the case under the old ESA procurement rules. The selection may not be understood as requiring the formation of a consortium of tenderers acting on an equal horizontal level to be subject to the Best-Practices-Rules.

42 See Article 15 ESA-PR.

43 See Article 15 No. 6 ESA-PR.

44 See Article 15 No. 7 ESA-PR.

45 See 'PART V: AWARD OF CONTRACT, ARTICLE 43 – SUBMISSION OF CONTRACT PROPOSAL AND INFORMATION NOTE TO THE INDUSTRIAL POLICY COMMITTEE.'

46 Judgment of the Court (Fourth Chamber) of 20 September 1988 – Gebroeders Beentjes BV v State of the Netherlands (Case C-31/87) paragraphs 18, 35; Judgment of the Court of 28 March 1995 – The Queen v Secretary of State for Home Department, ex parte Evans Medical Ltd and Macfarlan Smith Ltd (Case C-324/93), paragraph 42; Judgment of the Court (Fifth Chamber) of 18 October 2001 – SIAC Construction Ltd v County Council of the County of Mayo (Case C-19/00), paragraph 42; Judgment of the Court of 17 June 2002 Concordia Bus Finland Oy Ab, formerly Stagecoach Finland Oy Ab v Helsingin kaupunki and HKL-Bussiliikenne (Case C-513/99), paragraph 59; Judgment of the Court (Fifth Chamber) of 18 October 2001 – SIAC Construction Ltd v County Council of the County of Mayo (Case C-19/00), paragraph 36.

Third Element: Writing a Successful Tender

Writing a successful tender is often a very demanding task which should not be underestimated. The demands regularly increase with the applicable procurement procedure, whereas the negotiated procedure and the competitive dialogue usually require the greatest amount of resources. The required resources for submitting the tender should be carefully considered best before entering into the procurement process.

Meticulous and Systematic Analysis – Allocation of Resources

After becoming aware of a procurement project of interest, the respective economic operator has to obtain and meticulously and systematically analyse all tender documents. This is best done by persons having much experience with public procurement procedures. Should such expertise not be available in-house, drawing on external support is generally advisable already in this early stage as the later rectification of a tender process gone wrong usually proves extremely time consuming and demanding on the budget, if possible at all.

The applicable procurement procedure has to be identified and all relevant time periods and deadlines (for submission of application documents, for example) have to be put down in a diagram/timetable. All information and documents to be submitted, as well as the required manner of submission, have to be identified and laid down in a table. On this ground it should be possible already to estimate some basic demands of the procurement at hand and to plan for adequate resources both with regard to personnel as well as budget. With regard to personnel, the team for preparation of the tender and subsequent negotiations has to be built up and made available when needed.

Also important, especially for larger procurements, is a careful and efficient document management. It has proven beneficial for the preparation of a tender to implement an efficient document management system right from the beginning of the tender process.

A careful analysis of the contract notice and specifications often identifies questions concerning what is demanded by the contracting authority. In such cases, clarification should be sought by directly approaching the contracting authority in a timely manner. It may prove very risky to refrain from demanding clarifications and instead to try to solve suspected uncertainties with one's own interpretations. The same is generally true for suspected violations of the applicable public procurement rules. Also here, the contracting authority should be directly approached and asked to remedy the situation. Any undue delay on the side of the economic operator in this respect may block him from seeking effective legal remedy at a later stage.

Negotiations

In case the applicable procurement process allows negotiations, the negotiations team has to be carefully selected sufficiently ahead of time and their availability for the meetings ensured. The negotiations team should be structured with experienced members from all relevant disciplines which may become a topic in the respective negotiations. It is advisable to always have a person experienced in public procurement regulations, as well as contractual matters, participate in every negotiations meeting. In negotiations the economic operator should always insist on the keeping of official minutes and, if possible, should keep minutes itself in order to provide a cross reference in case of disputes.

Submission of the Tender

When acting in an open or a restricted procedure, as well as the competitive dialogue procedure, the submission of the tender always marks the point of no return. The tender leaves the economic operator's sphere of influence and changes are no longer possible. This obviously requires an extra-careful last check of all the tender documents to be submitted. Attempts to save resources in this crucial stage may well be ill-fated and result in the loss of all previous investments. In this respect it has to be kept in mind that any non-submission of required documents or declarations, and even the slightest mistake in formal requirements, can lead to the rejection of the tender. Accordingly, this last stage should be especially carefully planned.

Once the entire tender is placed in the properly labelled container, which fulfils all the contracting authority's requirements, the last but nonetheless crucial step is the timely submission of the tender to the designated address. If in any way possible, the tender should best be hand-delivered to the designated address and it should be insisted that the delivery is documented for later proof. In case a third party is tasked with the delivery, the economic operator should immediately verify the timely delivery by inquiry at the contracting authority.

Defending the Own Interests – Legal Remedies and Review Procedures

Legal Remedies in EU Procurement Procedures

The EU procurement law[47] requires the Member States to establish effective legal remedy provisions for review of public procurement procedures. Due to their legal nature as directives, these provisions are only binding for the Member States and only applicable to their respective national contracting authorities. The directive on procurement reviews is not applicable for procurement procedures by EU bodies.[48] Economic operators therefore only have recourse to the general remedies against actions of EU bodies provided in the Treaty on the Functioning of the European Union (TFEU). Accordingly, the economic operator may initiate proceedings for annulment[49] against decisions of the EU body responsible for the respective procurement. If the action is well founded, the act subject to the proceedings may be declared void.[50] This offers the possibility for annulment of any contract that has been awarded under breach of the EU procurement rules.

Also possible, but subsidiary to the proceedings for annulment, are the proceedings for failure to act.[51] These may be appropriate in cases where for example the EU body may not have followed its duty to observe the actions of a procurement agent and did not intervene against breaches by the agent.

Finally, a claim for compensation may be brought before the Court of Justice for any damage caused by the EU's institutions or by its servants in the performance of their duties.[52]

---

47 See Directive 2007/66/EC of the European Parliament and of the Council of 11 December 2007 amending Council Directives 89/665/EEC and 92/13/EEC with regard to improving the effectiveness of review procedures concerning the award of public contracts, OJ 2007 L 335, p. 31.

48 See Prieß, H.-J. 2005. *Handbuch des Europäischen Vergaberechts*, 3rd ed. Cologne, Berlin, Munich: Heymanns, 512.

49 See Article 263 TFEU (ex Article 230 TEC).

50 See Article 264 TFEU (ex Article 231 TEC).

51 See Article 265 TFEU.

52 See Article 340 TFEU.

Obviously, the general remedies of the TFEU were not specifically designed for public procurement procedures and may lack the efficiency of the remedies under public procurement rules of the EU Member States. Most noteworthy, actions brought before the Court of Justice of the European Union have no suspending effect.[53] A procurement process may therefore continue after an action is filed and the contract subject to the contested action already be awarded before a judgment is passed. This can only be prevented by interim measures of the Court suspending the contested action.[54] This is, however, not as prompt and therefore not as effective as a suspension automatically initiated with the filing for remedies.[55]

Under the TFEU, the plaintiff is granted a period of two months after actual knowledge of the respective action to initiate the proceedings of annulment. This time period is exceptionally long when applied in procurement procedures.

The proceedings for failure to act require the plaintiff to grant to the contracting authority a period of two months to define its position. Only if such a definition is not given within the time period can the plaintiff initiate corresponding court procedures and demand the desired action. Should the contracting authority react in an undesired way, the plaintiff has to change its action to a claim for annulment. Should the contracting authority not react to the request, the plaintiff may file an action for failure to act. In all these cases, the plaintiff has another two months to initiate the action.

Legal Remedies and Reviews in ESA Procurement Procedures

The ESA-PRS provides economic operators with the possibility to call for a review process for alleged breach of the procurement rules. Located in Part VI of the Procurement Regulations, the review is designed as a multi-step process.

Structure of the ESA review process The Head of the Procurement Department (HPD) is acting as a first instance for any review process.[56] Where a decision by the HPD is challenged, the claim may be directly referred to the Industrial Ombudsman. In other cases, the Ombudsman may be contacted if the HPD has not made a decision for a period of ten days after the claim has been brought before it. However, the Ombudsman does not act as a second instance, but may only be requested to give recommendations for measures to be taken by the HPD in the review process.

Article 54 ESA-PR establishes the Procurement Review Board (PRB) as second instance. The PRB consists of three independent members external to ESA and three corresponding alternate members, with one member and his or her alternate being selected by the ESA-DG, one member and his or her alternate being selected by industry and one member and his or her alternate being selected by the Chairman of the IPC. The ESA-DG is requested to establish detailed implementing instructions concerning the establishment and the proceedings of the PRB to be approved by the IPC. The instructions are available on the internet under the same link[57] as the procurement regulation. Of particular interest for procurement procedures are the “Implementing Instructions

53 See Article 278 TFEU (ex Article 242 TEC).

54 See Article 278 TFEU (ex Article 242 TEC); Article 279 TFEU (ex Article 243 TEC).

55 See detailed Sladič, J. 2007. ‘Einstweiliger Rechtsschutz im Gemeinschaftsprozessrecht’, *Schriften des Europa-Instituts der Universität des Saarlandes – Rechtswissenschaften*, Vol. 71, Saarland.

56 See Article 51 No. 1 ESA-PR.

57 To review the Implementation Instructions to the new ESA Procurement Regulation go to http://emits.esa.int/emits/owa/emits.main – folder ‘Reference Documentation’, subfolder ‘Administrative Documents’ – file ‘Procurement Regulations’ (pdf-format) – Annexes [accessed: 30 April 2011].

Concerning the Establishment of the ESA Procurement Review Board", constituting Annex V of the implementing instructions, providing additional details on the constitution and the work of the PRB.

According to Article 55 ESA-PR the PRB shall take its decision within 15 calendar days, with extension to 30 calendar days possible. The decisions of the PRB are final and binding on the parties.[58]

Personal right to review The right to review (Article 48 ESA-PR) is open to any economic operator who is not merely acting as a subcontractor (Article 49 ESA-PR), who can demonstrate a direct interest in the particular ESA procurement, and who claims a potential loss due to an alleged breach of the ESA-PR by ESA.

Exclusion of certain decisions from review Aside from excluding certain groups from the right to review, ESA also declares a number of material decisions which may not be subject to review procedures.[59] Most notably not open to review is the choice of the applicable procurement procedure, the decision to suspend the procurement process and generally any decisions of the IPC with regard to the award of the contract.[60]

Duration of a review process and deadlines The ESA-PR provide extremely short time periods for reaction and filing against violations of the ESA-PR.

According to Article 50 ESA-PR, any alleged breach of ESA-PR apparent prior to the closing date and time stated in the invitation to tender (ITT) must be filed prior to that date and time, and, if the breach was not apparent, no later than 10 calendar days after the breach became apparent. The use of the term 'apparent' suggests that the error does not need to be positively known to the individual economic operator in order for the deadline to start. It may instead be sufficient if the circumstances were sufficient for a knowledgeable objective observer to detect the breach.

Following the opening of the tender, another 10 calendar day deadline for claims based on an alleged breach of the procurement regulation is set in motion on the day the claimant knew or should have known the basis for the claim.

The HPD is given a period of 10 calendar days after having received a claim to issue his or her decision. Following the HPD's decision the claimant has another five calendar days to decide whether to challenge it. The decision is then transferred to the Ombudsman who will offer a written recommendation within 10 calendar days. Following, the HPD has another 10 calendar days to issue a written decision to the claimant who may – again within five calendar days following its receipt – challenge this decision by submitting it to the PRB. The PRB may make a final decision within 15 to 30 calendar days.

In sum a procurement review under the new ESA procurement regulation may take from 55 up to 70 calendar days if all stages of the review process are involved.

Before the initiation of a review process in order not to miss any of these very short deadlines, the economic operator should draw up a timeline according to when he has to make decisions and when statements, etc. have to be submitted. It should also be ensured that all required personnel are available according to the timeline.

58 See Article 55 No. 5 ESA-PR.

59 See Article 49 No. 2 ESA-PR.

60 See Article 49 No. 2 a), b) and c) ESA-PR.

With regard to the provision in Article 50.2 ESA-PR it has to be noted that ESA's aim to accelerate the review procedure may be contravened. According to this rule, to file a claim for an alleged breach following the opening of tenders, the claimant is granted merely 10 calendar days. However, this period only starts after the claimant (positively) knew or should have known of the basis for the claim. Consequently, the claimant may only be prohibited from filing for a breach that occurred following the opening of tenders, if a situation existed from which the claimant would have been objectively possible to notice the alleged breach. However, ESA is not obliged to publish the award of a contract in any manner freely accessible to the public. Accordingly, an economic operator, in the sense of Article 48 ESA-PR,[61] may not even become aware of the contract award, let alone any possible breach of the procurement rules after the opening of the tenders. Until an economic operator becomes aware of an alleged breach, a considerable amount of time may pass only then starting the 10 calendar day period of limitation. It remains to be seen how this possible loop-hole in the ESA-PR will be dealt with in the future and whether it may indeed allow for initiation of review procedures in excess of the original time frame of the 10-day deadline.

Suspension of the contracts award The initiation of a procurement review under the new ESA-PR does not by itself suspend the contracts award process.[62] Instead, the suspension has to be proposed on a case by case basis to the ESA-DG by the HPD, the Industrial Ombudsman or the PRB.

For a suspension of the procurement process by the ESA-DG, the claimant must demonstrate that it will suffer irreparable injury in the absence of a suspension, that there is probability of success, and that the granting of the suspension would not cause disproportionate harm to ESA.[63] As Article 1 No. 4 of Annex V of the ESA-PR further clarifies, a decision by the ESA-DG not to follow an interim measure recommended by the PRB shall in no case constitute the basis for a further claim, making the ES-DG's decision final.

Costs reimbursement and compensation Costs incurred by ESA in the course of a procurement review are regularly not levied on the claimant, unless the claimant was acting in bad faith. This is regardless of the outcome of the process.[64] In case the decision of ESA is upheld by the PRB, the claimant will not be reimbursed for costs.

Compensatiing costs to the claimant, should it succeed, is capped by Article 57 ESA-PR. Accordingly, the claimant may only receive up to EUR 100,000 as compensation for the loss or injury suffered due to a procedural breach of the procurement regulation. This includes costs for tender preparation and costs incurred for the review procedure.

The low limit for compensation may effectively discourage economic operators from initiating review procedures, as they may at the end leave them with even greater costs. This, however, underlines the importance of a motion for suspension of the procurement process, by which the economic operator may not only prevent the award of the contract to its competitor, but ultimately maintain its own prospect of being awarded the contract.

According to Article Rule 23.2.1 of Annex I forming part of Annex V to the ESA-PR, the claimant will receive no compensation should it decide to withdraw its claim, before a decision on

61 See ESA-PR 'Article 48 – Right to Review: Subject to Article 49 of these Regulations any economic operator demonstrating a direct interest in an Agency's procurement and that claims a potential loss due to an alleged procedural breach of these Regulations by the Agency may seek review in accordance with Articles 51, 53 and 55 of these Regulations.'

62 See Article 49 No. 3 ESA-PR.

63 See Article 56 No. 2 ESA-PR.

64 See Article 55 No. 7 ESA-PR.

the initial claim is made. The ESA review procedures do not provide the possibility to withdraw the initial claim and filing merely for a compensation of the incurred review expenses. This is particularly important, should motions for suspension of the procurement process be rejected and the contract awarded to a competitor during the review process.

Conclusion and Outlook

Both the EU and ESA employ complex rules for their procurement efforts, however acting on very different backgrounds, with historically different policies.

ESA is very much driven by the industrial policy of its Member States and acting on the background of the geographical distribution principle. In contrast, the EU – in all its actions – operates on the background of the EC Treaties, is bound by the goal of creating and sustaining the functioning of the common market, most notably under the principle of fair and non-discriminating competition. These different backgrounds strongly influence the two organisations' procurement regulations. Accordingly, the ESA procurement regulations underline the prerogative of the IPC and the influence of policy decisions. In contrast, the EU procurement rules are focused on controlling the contracting authorities' buyer power and in this sense calls for the adherence of strict rules in all stages of the procurement process.

A thorough understanding of the procurement rules of both organisations is not easily obtained and the complexity of the procurement regulations may be overwhelming, even for the contracting authorities. While both procurement regimes offer some measures of protection for the tenderers' interests through review procedures, none of these procedures are particularly effective. This is especially true with regard to the extremely short decision-making periods under the ESA rules and the cap for possible compensation. But also the necessity under the EU rules to employ the general legal procedures provided by the TFEU may lead to unsatisfactory results with in turn – for public procurement procedures – extremely long time periods for court actions and, as in the ESA rules, the lack of automatic suspension of the review process. This underlines that any larger procurement project requires meticulous planning by both the contracting authorities and the candidates/tenderers in order to avoid mistakes from happening and allow an effective use of resources.

With the increase of space activities by the EU under the evolving European Space Policy, it can be expected that the EU's procurement actions in the space sector will steadily increase. It will be interesting to observe how the EU procurement regime may likewise evolve in order to deal more efficiently with the specialities of this sector.

List of References

Arrowsmith, S. 2009. *Reform on the UNCITRAL Model Law of Procurement: Procurement Regulation for the 21st Century*. Eagan: West.

COM(2005) 208 final, Brussels, 23 May 2005, Communication from the Commission to the Council and the European Parliament, 'European Space Policy – Preliminary Elements'.

COM(2008) 748 final, Brussels, 12 November 2008, Communication from the Commission to the European Parliament, the Council, and the European Economic and Social Committee, and the Committee of the Regions,: 'Global Monitoring for Environment and Security (GMES): We Care for a Safer Planet'.

Council Resolution of 13 May 2003 on 'The Development of an Overall European Space Policy', *Official Journal* C 149, 26 June 2003.
Council Regulation No. 1605/2002 amended by Council Regulation No. 1995/2006 – Financial Regulation applicable to the general budget of the European Communities, OJ 2002 L 248, 1 (referred to as EU-FR).
Commission Regulation No. 2342/2002 last amended by Commission Regulation No. 478/2007 laying down detailed rules for the implementation of the Council Regulation (EC, EURATOM) 1605/2002 on the Financial Regulation applicable to the general budget of the European Communities, OJ 2002 L 357, 1 (referred to as EU-FRIR).
Council Directive 2000/78/EC of 27 November 2000 establishing a general framework for equal treatment in employment and occupation.
Directive 2004/18/EC of the European Parliament and of the Council of 31 March 2004 on the coordination of procedures for the award of public works contracts, public supply contracts and public service contracts, OJ 2004 L 134, 114.
Directive 2004/17/EC of the European Parliament and of the Council of 31 March 2004 coordinating the procurement procedures of entities operating in the water, energy, transport and postal services sectors, OJ 2004 L 134, 1.
Directive 2007/66/EC of the European Parliament and of the Council of 11 December 2007 amending Council Directives 89/665/EEC and 92/13/EEC with regard to improving the effectiveness of review procedures concerning the award of public contracts, OJ 2007 L 335, 31.
ESA Convention for the establishment of a European Space Agency and ESA Council Rules of Procedure, ESA SP-1271 (E), March 2003 (ESA-Convention).
European Space Agency Procurement Regulations (Adopted on 17 December 2008), ESA/C (2008) 202, Annex 1 (ESA-PR).
Frenz, W. 2007. *Handbuch Europarecht, Vol. 3, Beihilfe und Vergaberecht*. Berlin, Heidelberg, 2007.
Hobe, S., Heinrich, O., Kerner, I. and Fröhlich, A. 2009. 'Entwicklung der Europäischen Weltraumagentur als 'implementing agency' der Europäischen Union: Rechtsrahmen und Anpassungserfordernisse', *Kölner Schriften zum Internationalen und Europäischen Recht*, Vol. 17, Berlin.
Hobe, S., Heinrich, O., Kerner, I. and Schmidt-Tedd, B. 2009. 'Ten Years of Cooperation between ESA and EU: Current Issues', *German Journal of Air and Space Law*, 1, 49.
Judgment of the Court (Fourth Chamber) of 20 September 1988 – Gebroeders Beentjes BV v State of the Netherlands (Case C-31/87).
Judgment of the Court of 3 June 1992 – Commission of the European Communities v Italian Republic (Case C-360/89).
Judgment of the Court of 28 March 1995 – The Queen v Secretary of State for Home Department, ex parte Evans Medical Ltd and Macfarlan Smith Ltd (Case C-324/93).
Judgment of the Court of 26 September 2000 – Commission of the European Communities v French Republic (Case C-225/98).
Judgment of the Court (Fifth Chamber) of 18 October 2001 – SIAC Construction Ltd v County Council of the County of Mayo (Case C-19/00).
Judgment of the Court of 17 June 2002 Concordia Bus Finland Oy Ab, formerly Stagecoach Finland Oy Ab v Helsingin kaupunki and HKL-Bussiliikenne (Case C-513/99).

Judgment of the Court (Sixth Chamber) of 12 December 2002 – Universale-Bau AG, Bietergemeinschaft: 1. Hinteregger & Söhne Bauges.mbH Salzburg, 2. ÖSTU-STETTIN Hoch- und Tiefbau GmbH, and Entsorgungsbetriebe Simmering GesmbH (Case C-470/99).

Judgment of the Court (First Chamber) of 24 January 2008 – Emm. G. Lianakis AE, Sima Anonymi Techniki Etairia Meleton kai Epivlepseon, Nikolaos Vlachopoulos v Dimos Alexandroupolis, Planitiki AE, Aikaterini Georgoula, Dimitrios Vasios, N. Loukatos kai Synergates AE Meleton, Eratosthenis Meletitiki AE, A. Pantazis – Pan. Kyriopoulos kai syn/tes OS Filon OE, Nikolaos Sideris (Case C-532/06).

Judgment of the General Court (Third Chamber) of 2 March 2010 – Evropaïki Dynamiki – Proigmena Systimata Tilepikoinonion Pliroforikis kai Tilematikis AE v European Maritime Safety Agency (EMSA), (Case T-70/05).

Prieß, H.-J. 2005. *Handbuch des Europäischen Vergaberechts*, 3rd ed. Cologne, Berlin, Munich: Heymanns.

Proposition for the Resolution of 25 April 1979 on the Community's participation in space research, OJ C 127 of 21 May 1979.

Regulation (EC) No. 683/2008 of the European Parliament and of the Council of 9 July 2008 on the further implementation of the European satellite navigation programmes (EGNOS and Galileo), OJ 2008 L 196, 1.

Resolutions adopted at the 206th Council meeting, held at ministerial level ESA/C-M/CCVI/Res. 4 (Final).

Sladiĉ, J. 2007. 'Einstweiliger Rechtsschutz im Gemeinschaftsprozessrecht', *Schriften des Europa-Instituts der Universität des Saarlandes – Rechtswissenschaften*, Vol. 71, Saarland.

Chapter 17
Economics of the Procurement Process[1]

Vasilis Zervos

Introduction

In assessing the impact of funding space activities, it is essential to assess the efficiency by which the budgetary appropriations and funding profiles achieve their objectives. Procurement policy, which defines these profiles, is a 'derived' policy; it is best thought of as a tactical set of policies that, alongside export and industrial policies, serve higher-tier national strategic policies. The successes of national procurement policies are thus measurable against their optimality in achieving the strategic goals.

Strategic policy-makers for space most often are politically appointed agents and institutions. The relevant agent or institution responsible for the strategic policy has the choice of assigning the design and implementation of such tactical policies to specialised agents, or doing so in-house. This is the first of a set of choices made by the government, followed by the choice of contractors, type of contract and awarding process, but also by the monitoring process and assessment.

This chapter analyses the different types of contracts, and discusses the procurement processes, employed by space agencies. It assesses their efficiency, provides insights for the contractor wishing to interact with these agencies and, finally, offers some recommendations for the agency that might wish some day to re-evaluate the efficiency of its procurement process.

Appointment of a Specialised Space Agency by the State

Given the specialised nature of the sector and the technical requirements that are often not very well understood by the strategic policy-makers, specialised space agencies tend to undertake the task of making recommendations to the government regarding strategic space policies and then overseeing their implementation. This means that the government appoints a specialised agent to manage public space programmes.

The European Space Agency (ESA), for example, must consider the strategic setting of the space policy in Europe and work with the European Union and its members towards:

1 Acknowledgements for this chapter are attributed to an ASI project on the economic return of space activities (2009).

- establishing a European space programme and the coordination of national and European level space activities, with a user-led focus;
- increasing synergy between defence and civil space programmes and technologies, having regard to institutional competencies; and
- developing a joint international relations strategy in space.[2]

The presence of an agency in an industrial sector invokes the concept of a regulated industry with substantial public involvement and controls. Civil space agencies are multi-faceted public organisations: they are promoters of scientific discovery and exploration, promoters of space applications, knowledge creators and diffusers, supporters of the national industry and capabilities, prudent spenders of public money and iconic visionaries. Multi-national space agencies, like ESA, are also concerned with positively compromising differing national objectives into exciting and sensible programmes that attract financial contributions from Member States. The multiplicity of objectives and tools is often seen as beneficial, but there is always the danger that some objectives might conflict with each other.

The political representatives responsible for the creation and sharing of the 'pie' of public money – government budget – appoint the space agency to deliver prudently funded inspiring programmes: thus the political representatives are ultimately regulating and care-taking the expenditure of public funds to the space industry. This is an often implied objective: the space agency is expected to be prudent with public money, though this is not regularly emphasised. This objective is at the core of the agency's existence and at times can conflict with the space-industry political complex. It is perhaps easier to envision this process by looking at the two steps that evolve around the timing of a space programme:

1. To begin with, the space agency advocates the space programme to the political 'supervisors' for approval; at this stage, the interest of the space agency largely coincides with the interests of the industry that is to benefit from the resulting contracts.
2. Once the funding appropriations are approved and the space agency is given the budget and mandate to deliver the space programme, the space agency's objectives are expected to differ from the industry in that the former is supposed to control costs, effort and profitability.

This two-step process takes place within the space agency and complicates the analysis: for each programme, the behaviour of the agency is time and phase-inconsistent, complicating the setting of Laffont and Tirole's approach in terms of incentives and choices[3] as follows: during the submission stage of the proposed programme, the space agency is a bureaucratic budget maximiser (both in terms of size and number of projects) along the lines of Niskanen (1971).[4] Therefore, the agency is likely to have little incentive to scrutinise unreliably low cost estimates of each programme's costs. Game theory analysis shows how the military, for example, induces the US Congress to fund a larger than first-best production level, by suggesting a larger than first-best production plant.[5] In

2 ESA 2007. Resolution on the European Space Policy-ESA Director General's Proposal for the European Space Policy. [Online]. Available at: http://www.esa.int/esapub/br/br269/br269.pdf [accessed: 25 October 2010].

3 Laffont, J. and Tirole, J. 1993. *A Theory of Incentives in Procurement and Regulation*. London: MIT Press, 540–50 Ch. 13.

4 Niskanen, W.A. Jr. 1971. *Bureaucracy and Representative Government*. Chicago, IL: Aldine Atherton.

5 Rogerson, P.W. 1991. 'Incentives, the Budgetary Process, and Inefficiently Low Production Rates in Defence Procurement', *Defence Economics*, 3, 1–18.

this case, the introduction of a fixed-budget policy by the policy-maker can resolve the problem, but at the expense of high development costs.

The second stage begins after the decision by the policy-makers to fund the programme. Here the space agency has the role of managing the contract and process. At this stage, the interest of the space agency might well be in conflict with the interest of the contractors. This means that the space agency's objectives now call for cost-minimisation and programme schedules running on time with minimal overruns. As a result, in the space sector, of the three interest groups (politicians, bureaucrats and producers), only two of them (politicians and producers) have consistent objectives: politicians, who are trying to minimise programme costs, and producers, who are trying to maximise rents. Space agencies, on the other hand, exhibit a 'time inconsistent' set of objectives, which coincide with the producers prior to budget approval, while after the budget is determined coincides with policy-makers.

The impact that the recently (1990s) introduced objective of the space agency, to enhance the competitiveness of its domestic space industry, has had on the 'traditional' aims of the space agency, for rent and cost minimisation, needs to be considered. This recent objective is likely to clash with other objectives, or result in a situation where policies in support of one objective conflict with others.

There are a number of choices the government (or the principal-space agency) has to undertake with respect to procurement in step two. Clearly the choice of programme is the most important, often related to the strategic objectives of the government. The procurement process is a 'tactical level' process, where the most important decisions are with regards to the choice of contract, process and monitoring. These are key choices relating to the role of the agency *vis-à-vis* the private industry in delivering the final goods or services the government sets out to achieve, and are examined next.

Choice of Contract and the Economics of Contracting

Space projects that are contracted by the government are often high-technology and R&D intensive, but also enjoy a high degree of asset specificity (one-off space science and exploration programmes). These characteristics make the investment risky because a market transaction would not take place and, further, there would be no other potential direct user besides the government to share the costs in case the government were to pull out. This support by the government entails transfer of public funds in a variety of ways, besides direct procurement, such as R&D subsidies, government guaranteed loans, tax exemptions, etc.[6]

On the other hand, with the introduction of commercial markets, government funded programmes can lead to commercially viable products and customers, resulting in profits for the firm, thus raising the issue of the firm absorbing some of the costs associated with the risks of government funded space programmes. In such a case, the government might bargain not to refund the full cost of a project, discounting the project-linked future profit stream to the firm. The choice of contract and the bargaining power of the firm and the agency are essential factors in determining the success with which the government can implement its policy and objectives.

The significance of the type of contract employed is that it determines the power of the incentives the government uses to control the profit performance, costs, prices and effort of the space industry. Thus, for example, the profit of the firm undertaking a risky space project on behalf

6 Laffont, J. and Tirole, J. 1993. *A Theory of Incentives in Procurement and Regulation*, 10.

of a space agency is a function not only of the estimated profitability agreed by the government at the beginning of the project, but also of the cost overrun at the completion of the project and who will fund such overruns.[7] The profit of the firm from a space project can thus be represented in algebraic form as follows:

$$P = P_e + s(C_e\text{-}C) \qquad \text{(E1)}$$

where P = realised profit by the contractor
P_e = estimated profit of the firm (government determined profit margin)
C_e = estimated costs of contracted space project
C = actual costs of space project
s = sharing coefficient. The value of the sharing coefficient for the firm reflects the rate at which the difference between estimated costs and realised costs is spread between the agency and the contractor. The value of s is between zero and one (0 £ s ³ 1) and the implications of its value are discussed below.

The value of the sharing coefficient in (E1) is a crucial element of any procurement arrangement. The sharing coefficient reflects the trade-off between incentives and rent extraction the space agency agrees with the firm. Assuming that the space agency's primary objectives are the minimisation of the costs of space projects, as well as the rent the space firm receives, it is easy to see why these objectives are in conflict by assessing variations of the value of the sharing coefficient in contracts used by ESA and NASA.

Fixed Price Contracts (s=1)

In the case of s = 1 the firm has a very strong incentive to minimise costs through increased effort, since costs have a full impact on realised profits. On the other hand, the agency has no profit control and the firm can realise substantial rents (or losses). This type of contract is a 'fixed-price' contract. NASA and ESA have similar categories of fixed-price contracts. The first category is common to both and is the most straightforward application of the concept of fixed-price, namely firm-fixed-price contract. This type of contract is the simplest and most accurate form of a fixed-price contract, where no variation of price is allowed. This price is not flexible and is not subject to changes due to changes in the costs of the firm's inputs.[8] 'The price of the contract is not subject to any adjustment or revision by reason of the actual costs incurred by the contractor in the performance of the contract.'[9] In addition, both ESA and NASA also use fixed price contacts with variation for cases of lengthy supply periods.

Hybrid Contract with Ceiling Price to be Converted into Fixed Price

This type of contract employed by ESA aims to deal with uncertainties and risk at the time of the contract signing, not by endorsing a cost-plus type of contract, but by developing a hybrid scheme

7 Sandler, T. and Hartley, K. 1995. *The Economics of Defense*. New York: Cambridge University Press, 137.

8 *Annual Procurement Report, Fiscal Year 1983*. 1998. Washington, DC: NASA.

9 ESA 2009. General Clauses and Conditions for ESA Contracts, ESA/C/290. [Online]. Available at: http://esamultimedia.esa.int/docs/industry/SME/2004-Training/WGP/Annex1_General_Clauses_and_Cond_Rev_6.pdf [accessed: 25 October 2010].

where a ceiling price is initially set, similar to a cost-plus contract (see later section). In later stages when there are fewer uncertainties surrounding the project deliverables, the contract is converted into a fixed-price contract. This in effect poses a number of difficulties, notwithstanding the fact that for some contracts such information becomes available close to the completion of the contract. Given the efforts going into this type of scheme, advantages are not clearly defined, versus a well-monitored cost-plus contract scheme.

Cost-Reimbursement/Cost-Plus Contracts (s=0)

There are a number of different cost-reimbursement (or cost-plus) contracts, whose use was seen earlier to allow the agency to control the rent of the contractor, but also potentially resulting in low effort levels and high costs. Cost-reimbursement contracts are used under conditions of uncertainty and serve as a risk-spreading agreement between the firm and the government, where the government typically absorbs most, or all risks. This type of contract requires monitoring of the performance, costs and effort levels of the firm hence such costs must also be added to the total costs of the space project. Given that at the first stage of the budget formation process the space agency interests coincide with the interests of the contractors (see above section, 'Appointment of a Specialised Space Agency by the State'), space agencies have an incentive to relax their monitoring and assessment of cost estimations, making it easier for Congress, or other decision maker, to finance what appears to be inexpensive space projects. This would imply that the agency is largely responsible for cost overruns, in that its behaviour with cost-plus contracts could well encourage underestimation of project costs. A solution to this problem faced by the US Congress is to provide NASA incentives for accuracy, involving financial penalties, or a fixed-budget policy. It is clear that a major problem of cost-plus contract schemes is that the management of the firm has an incentive to inflate costs.[10] ESA's policy aims at lowering the percentage of cost-plus (or cost reimbursement) type contracts. Monitoring of contracts and associated costs are reduced in this way, and so are continuous funding negotiations between ESA partners. However, it must be acknowledged that in contracts relating to developing new and risky technologies, it is highly challenging to use instead fixed-price type contracts efficiently despite the use of tools used to verify costs, or hybrid cost types.

Incentive Contracts (s between 0 and 1)

Incentive contracts could be closer to a cost-reimbursement contract, or to a fixed-fee contract. This type of contract must clearly specify the targets on which the incentives are linked and use appropriate incentive schemes that minimise inefficiencies. Such incentives usually involve a formula that links project-specific performance indicators and costs to rewards and/or penalties ('the carrot and the stick'). They, therefore, require monitoring and costs associated with the setting of such detailed and technical contracts and potentially higher provisional legal costs in cases of disputes, compared to fixed-price contracts.

For the agency, the optimal value of 's' largely depends on the level of information the agency possesses *vis-à-vis* the contractor. In the case where space agencies have access to information about the contractors' technology, the optimal regulatory contract is the fixed price contract.[11]

10 See Lichtenberg, R.F. 1995. 'Economics of Defense R&D', in *Handbook of Defence Economics*, edited by K. Hartley and T. Sandler. London: Elsevier Science BV.

11 Laffont, J. and Tirole, J. 1993. *A Theory of Incentives in Procurement and Regulation*, 40.

Varying the information level means that the optimal contract is an incentive contract (where the value of 's' varies between zero and one). In negotiating non-competitive contracts, the agency and the firm have to agree on the limited price liability, but also the value of 's' and C_e.

Diagrammatically, the relationship between the project price (P) and the project cost (C) for cost-plus, fixed-price and incentive of contracts are examined in Figure 17.1.[12] Cost-plus type of contracts are assumed to include the profit to the firm in the form of a mark-up on costs (as a percentage for example), and are, therefore, illustrated in the diagram as a straight line above the costs = price line. Fixed price contracts are a straight parallel to the costs-axis line, since cost variations do not affect the price paid, while the incentives contracts are represented by a straight line with a slope in between cost-plus and fixed-price, reflecting the range of the sharing ratio values between one and zero.[13]

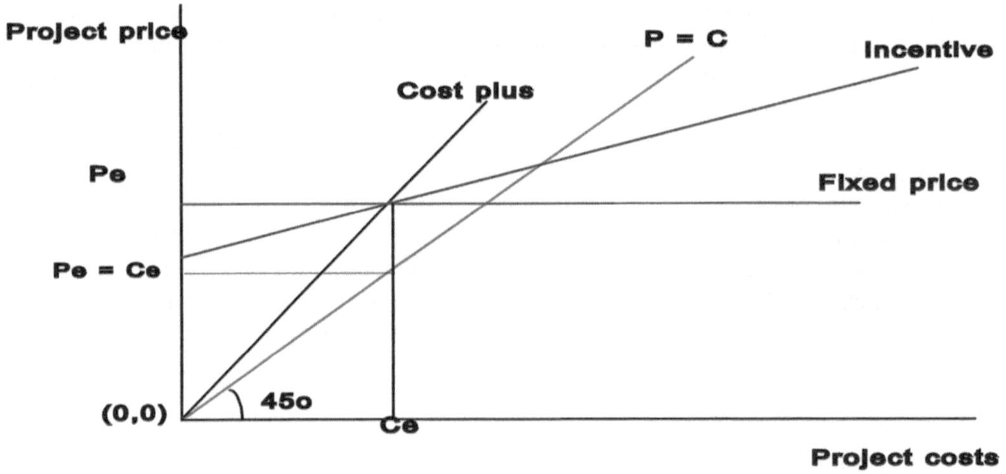

Figure 17.1 Project price and cost relationships

Source: Adapted from Sandler and Hartley (1995)

Space agencies have their own idiosyncrasies in mixing the generic types described above with a customised spectrum of contract types to fit their specific needs. In addition, it is important to note ESA's recommendations for potential bidders: that they first ensure the conformity of their proposal with their national space agencies, since in the event of a conflict it would be unlikely that they would be chosen. This is an obvious limitation imposed on bidders, as national support is a prerequisite for the awarding of ESA contracts within a *juste retour* system. The national

12 From Sandler, T. and Hartley, K. 1995. *The Economics of Defense*, 139.

13 A cost-plus contract implies a sharing coefficient of zero, which makes the project price dependent on actual costs. When actual costs are less than estimated costs, the price paid for the project is less than the target price. When actual costs equal estimated costs, from equation (E1), actual profit equals expected profit, and the target price equals expected costs plus expected profit (as in the fixed-price case), shown in Figure 17.1 as the point of intersection between the fixed-price and cost-plus lines.

governments are thus not losing out on their leverage over the local industry, on the contrary, the keys to the pool of ESA contracts are held by the national authorities.

A further conflict in agency procurement objectives can also occur when then agency has the added objective to promote industrial competitiveness in commercial markets. The most obvious conflict there relates to the competitive mode of awarding. Competitive tendering in bidding is generally sought by agencies, however the presence of a large pool of competing contractors can be in conflict with enhancing competitiveness in commercial markets (see later). The choice of contract type has also some implications however, as the government can in effect cross-subsidise the operations of space firms in commercial markets using competitive award schemes, but cost-plus contracts.

Monitoring of Contracts

Much of the monitoring costs and efforts by the agency and project managers of the contractors relate to cost controls. A widely used method of assessment of project progress is the earned value method system (EVMS), which is extensively applied to the majority of sizeable US programmes in general.[14] The US Department of Defense (DoD) is a pioneer in the development of such techniques and in their applications since the 1960s. Such mechanisms allow the monitoring and assessment of programme performance, benchmarked against the initial plan, allowing corrective actions (if available) and accurate estimates of expected completion in terms of time and cost during various phases of the programme. It must be noted, however, that following indications of over-use of detailed EVMS practices, which can result in sizeable costs themselves in terms of monitoring and bureaucracy, the threshold of programme value and type of EVMS application of surveillance is modified.[15]

NASA has delegated much of the authority for surveillance of its contracts to the DoD,[16] in particular the Defense Contract Audit Agency, following Federal Agency requirements to monitor contracting activities via a scalable EVMS approach.[17]

Fixed-price contracts are generally well-received by agencies as they are perceived as hassle-free and with low monitoring costs. In reality, the need to effectively re-negotiate fixed-price contracts simply postpones and often augments the effort and contract-specific risks of the agency. Cost-plus contracts are less popular owing to their more discretionary nature and monitoring costs, despite the fact that they may be optimal for specific cases. We examine a tool to illustrate

14 NASA 1999. NASA Policy Directive, NPD 7120.4C. Washington DC: NASA.

15 Office of the Secretary of Defense 2004. *Business Case Analysis for Proposed Revision to DoD Earned Value Management Policy*. US Office of Acquisitions. [Online]. Available at: www.acq.osd.mil/pm/historical/business_case.doc [accessed: 5 November 2009].

16 See NASA 2009a. Procurement Notice PN04-19, NASA procurement regulations. [Online]. Available at: http://www.hq.nasa.gov/office/procurement/regs/pn04-19.html [accessed: 25 October 2010]; NASA 2009b. Memorandum of Understanding between National Aeronautics and Space Administration (NASA) and Defense Contract Management Agency (DCMA) for Earned Value Management System Acceptance/Surveillance and Earned Value Management Project Surveillance. [Online]. Available at: http://evm.nasa.gov/mou.html [accessed: 25 October 2010].

17 Navy 2009. *EVM Contract Requirements Toolkit*. Centre for Earned Value Management US Navy. [Online]. Available at: https://acquisition.navy.mil/content/download/4820/21638/file/CEVM%20EVM%20Contract%20Requirements%20Toolkit%20rev3-20080319.pdf [accessed: 25 October 2010].

how linking pricing with contract management can be examined within a systemic approach that integrates the two elements, rather than treating them as separate and discreet.

Figure 17.2 assumes a linear relationship between cost and price and augments the EVMS analysis with price implications (EVMS-P). In effect, Figure 17.2 combines EVMS analysis with the pricing analysis of Figure 17.1 seen earlier. The EVMS schedule is illustrated in the right quadrant, while the left quadrant is identical to Figure 17.1's illustration of type of contracts. A 'Planning Box' (PB = TpABPp) connects the points where planned time of completion (Tp) meets the planned value of the programme (A: budgeted cost) and meets the planned price to the left of the 45° line (B), thus resulting in planned profit. At time T1 (current time), the project is reassessed by the earned value method to be heading for delays and over-budget at completion. The new 'Planning Box' that takes account of the delays (PBd) is defined by TdCDPp, or TdCEPd, depending on whether the contractor makes a profit on the part of the programme that is delayed and over budget.

Assuming acceptance with no additional penalty of the project at a later than planned time, a firm fixed price contract at current time is expected to result in zero profits for the final deliverable, while for a 'pure' cost-plus contract (such as profit being a percentage of cost), a proportional profit to the cost is achieved. Assuming re-negotiation at current time, the renegotiation line is defined as ED, where the agency aims for point D, while the contractor for point E. In cost-plus with a ceiling, the contractor receives no profit after a certain point defined by budget overrun and/or time.

Asymmetry of information is likely to exist because the agency, at current time, has information only about the left hand side of the diagram, while the contractor enjoys the full picture. In this case, the contractor can decide whether to share this information with the agency, depending on the type of contract and expectations.

NASA and ESA Procurement Policies and Trends

NASA's effective surveillance of much of its cost-plus contracts with the Department of Defence, owing to the latter's experience, has profound implications for the fragmentation process of assigning and monitoring contracts. The heavy burden placed upon agencies in terms of cost of surveillance, when following an EVMS approach for cost-plus contracts, results in a step-wise process of surveillance depending on the value of the contract.[18] It is clear that dis-economies of scale in contract surveillance kick-in for sizeable agencies like NASA that have to follow numerous contracts while maintaining a centralised process. Calls for a shift towards fixed-price contracts in the US follow an arguably smooth process followed in Europe, where according to industry sources about 90 per cent of ESA contracts and other major space agencies are on a fixed-price basis. Centralisation of surveillance processes is possible following trends and patterns in the execution of contracts, but is not an exact science, as the underlying reasons for such patterns are not always understood and common amongst high-technology projects. One of the important drawbacks of centralisation is the unfamiliarity and the potential growth of the asymmetry of information gap between the surveillance officers and the contractors.

NASA's trend in terms of its approach to competition is depicted in Figure 17.3. The percentage of awarded value under non-competitive contracts (%NASAnc) seems stable and close to the 40 per cent mark from 1997 to 2004, while if follow-up contracts are included the respective

18 NASA 2009c. *Earned Value Management Regulations and Requirements*. [Online]. Available at: http://evm.nasa.gov/regulations.html [accessed: 25 October 2010].

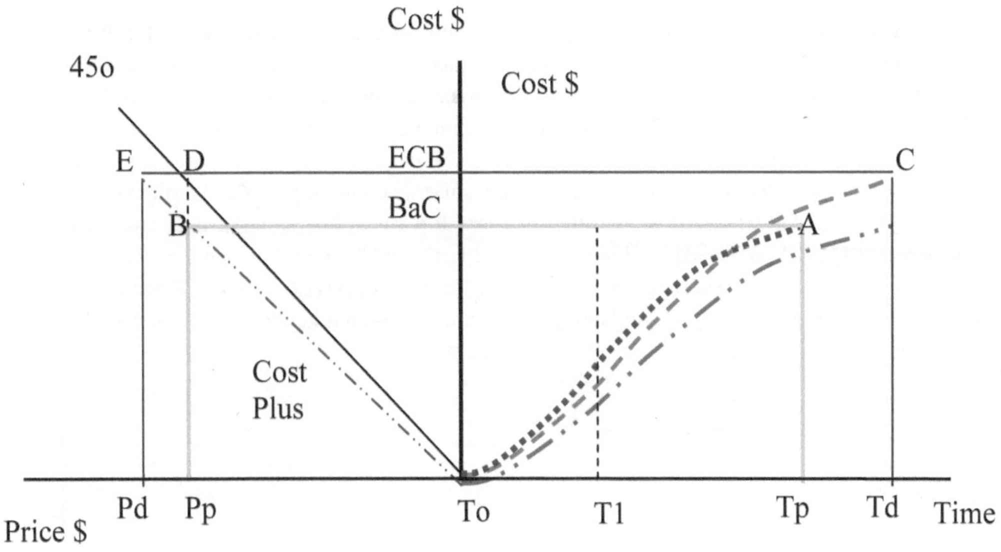

Notes:
Earned Value (EV) = budgeted cost for work performed = — · · — · ·
Planned Value (PV) = budgeted cost for work scheduled = ▪▪▪▪▪▪▪▪▪▪▪▪
Actual Cost (AC) = actual cost of work performed = — — — — — ·
Budget at Completion (BaC) = A = expected completion budget at time To
Estimated Completion Budget (ECB) = C = estimated budget at time T1
Schedule Variance (SV) = EV – PV
Cost Variance (CV) = EV – AC
To = starting time of project
T1 = current time
Td = expected completion time at T1
Tp = expected completion time at To
Pp = project price planned at time To
Pd = project price estimated at time T1
Cost-plus contract = .._.._.._.._

Figure 17.2 Augmented earned value management system with price (EVMS-P)

figure rises to over the 40 per cent mark (%NASAnc+fo). The value of contracts awarded under competitive procedures shows a slow rising trend over the same period, but is notably under the 60 per cent mark, in contrast to the period directly following the Apollo programme and up until the mid-1990s. This trend is attributed at large to the consolidation of the US space industry following the 'last supper' in 1993, where the government officially invited the industry to consolidate and re-structure:[19]

19 Zervos, V. 2008. 'Whatever Happened to Competition in Space Agency Procurement? The Case of NASA', *Journal of Applied Economics*, 11, 221–36; Aerospace Industries Association (AIA) 2009. *The Unseen Cost: Industrial Base Consequences of Defense Strategy Choices*. [Online]. Available at: http://www.aia-aerospace.org/assets/report_industrial_base_consequences.pdf [accessed: 25 October 2010]; Stockholm International Peace Research Institute (SIPRI) 2009. *Concentration in the Arms Industry*. [Online]. Available

In 1993 DoD leadership hosted a dinner at the Pentagon for a dozen executives of the largest defense companies. The executives were informed that there were twice as many defense suppliers as expected in the next five years and that the government was prepared to watch some go out of business. This event, dubbed the "Last Supper," precipitated a tidal wave of consolidation – in less than a decade more than 50 major defense companies had consolidated into only six. As part of this consolidation, what had been six aircraft primes narrowed to only two as Martin Marietta, General Dynamics' fighter division, North American, Rockwell International and McDonnell Douglas merged into or were acquired by Lockheed Martin and Boeing. Well-known companies such as GTE, Lucent, Hughes, Magnavox, TI, IBM, Eaton, GE, AT&T, Unisys, Westinghouse, Tenneco, Ford, Chrysler, Teledyne and Goodyear left the defense market entirely. Others sold off their defense and space assets.[20]

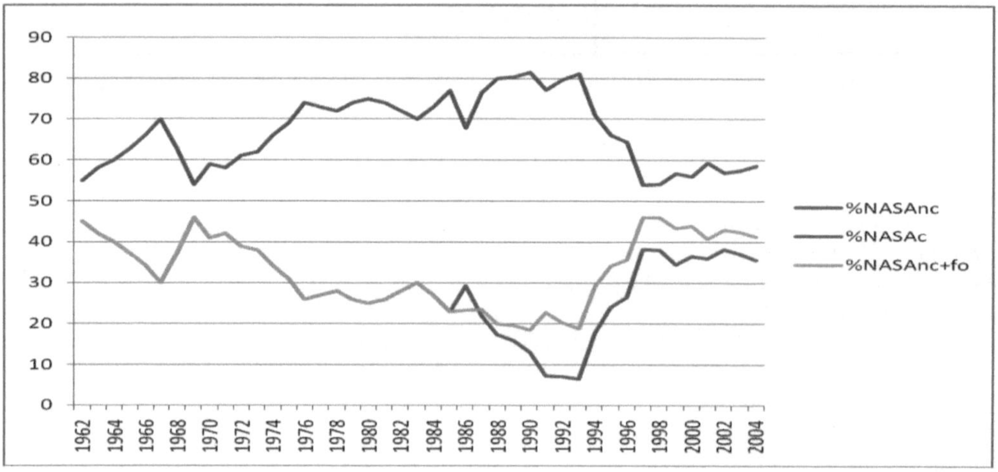

Figure 17.3 NASA's percentage distribution of competitive contracts through time
Sources: APR 1991; 2006; 2008

Furthermore, the relatively low competitive framework of the NASA awarding process is coupled with high and rising percentages of cost-plus contracts (%CPAF) and, to a lesser extent, firm-fixed-price (%FFP) contracts, which do not seem to be changing the pattern of contracting in favour of cost-plus. This is illustrated in Figure 17.4. Both factors of absence of competition and cost-plus contracting point towards expectations of higher contractor profitability, as opposed to a firm-fixed-price and competitive process.

---

at: http://www.sipri.org/research/armaments/production/researchissues/concentration_aprod [accessed: 25 October 2010].

20 Aerospace Industries Association (AIA) 2009. *The Unseen Cost: Industrial Base Consequences of Defense Strategy Choices*.

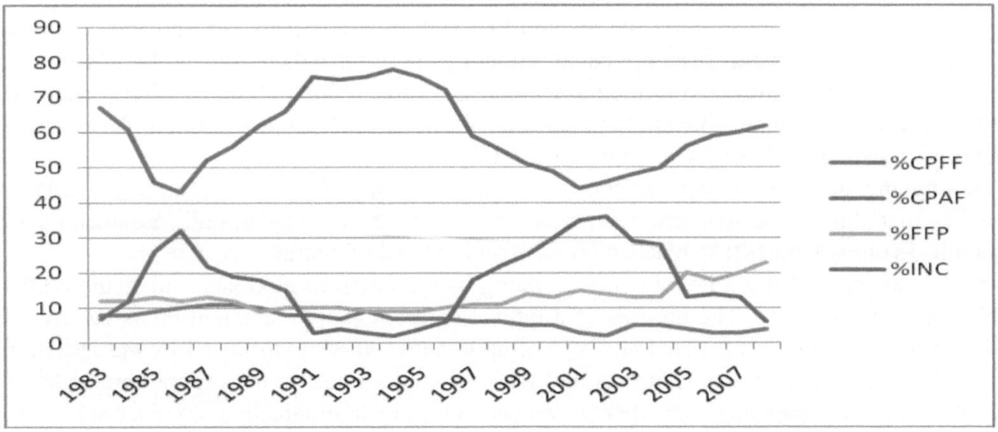

Figure 17.4 NASA's percentage distribution of contract types through time

Sources: APR 1991; 2006; 2008

NASA's publicly available information is well documented online with specific information provided for type of contract employed, detailed information on small and medium-sized-enterprises (SMEs) appropriations, efficiency in contracting, etc., and constantly monitors contractual performance against expected benchmarks.

Given the US federal nature of NASA's policies with regards to publicly available information and monitoring of performance, the administration follows and releases information on programmatic efficiency. These are quite indicative with ratings generically defined given the scope of the programmes involved.

Table 17.1 illustrates a rather exceptional case of poor performance in the case of overruns in astronomy and astrophysics. The target overrun is less than 10 per cent ('Target' column), while the actual is much higher (at times approaching 85 per cent).

Table 17.1 NASA overruns in astronomy and astrophysics

Year	Cost overrun (%)		Schedule overrun (%)	
	Target	Actual	Target	Actual
2005	< 10	42.9	< 10	35.7
2006	< 10	83.9	< 10	76.1
2007	< 10	51.4	< 10	57.8

Source: White House. 2009b. *Detailed Information on the NASA Astronomy and Astrophysics Research Assessment*. [Online: US White House]. Available at: http://www.whitehouse.gov/omb/expectmore/detail/10002316.2007.html [accessed: 25 October 2010].

European contractual efficiency and the benefits of fixed-price contracts are, however, hard to assess, as for Europe, the picture is complicated further by the fact that there is no publicly available information on the efficiency and outcome of such contracts. Much of the publicly available information serves as an invaluable guide on how to follow the procedures regarding placement of contracts and assisting the industry in placing well-drafted bids.

Regarding the distribution and outcome of contracts, there is far less publicly available information. In addition, high-risk projects are, in effect, not subject to the initially assigned fixed-price regime, as once changes take place, it is customary to have a Contracts Change Notice (CCN), which re-defines parts of the original contract, being incorporated as auxiliary and changing the original profile and funding. The process of a typical contract can be summed up as follows: a firm-fixed-price contract is negotiated and agreed upon between ESA, followed by the initiation of the programme's early phases (Phase A and B).[21] At a later point in the programme's phases (during Phase C, or D for example),[22] where advancements in technologically risky/uncertain areas have developed, an Engineering Change Proposal (ECP) is put forth and subjected to a technical evaluation by the programme manager who then needs to put it through a cost-assessment and approval process, following which, a CCN is added as a new clause to the contract.

For example, in 2005 ESA placed 778 contracts and 353 work orders, but over 2,300 contract change notices.[23] Despite the fact that most of those programmes were placed under a firm-fixed-price regime, the change notices that occurred cause de facto variations relating to the original contract scheme. In addition, Reynaud reveals that the direct negotiation contracts (251) are less than the open competition ones (238).[24] Competition is a challenge for ESA and European national space agencies, given the consolidated national and European space industrial base, coupled with the fair return principle. This is highlighted by the cases where lack of competition in contracting is justified by ESA's guidelines.[25]

Despite the lack of publicly available information on time-series of type of contracts used and efficiency, there seems to be qualitative and quantitative indication that competition in contracting appears rather weak. Unfortunately the lack of publicly available information does not allow the assessment of the contractual and procedural efficiency of the European space agencies at large and is a point requiring further attention so as to comprehensively evaluate the efficiency of the relevant processes.

Given the consolidated image of the European space industry, ESA also seems increasingly to favour an approach that will nullify negative effects from this consolidation to the SMEs in Europe. Specifically, ESA places subcontracting contracts directly with the subcontractors, but as the prime contractor is responsible for the programme as a whole, this can cause grey areas of accountability.

---

21 See NASA 2007. NASA Spaceflight Program and Project Management Requirements NPR7120 5D. [Online]. Available at: http://nodis3.gsfc.nasa.gov/npg_img/N_PR_7120_005D_/N_PR_7120_005D_.pdf [accessed: 25 October 2010].

22 *Ibid.*

23 Reynaud, P.M. 2005. *ESA Tendering Process and EMITS System*. ESA Procurement Department, Sinequanet Workshop. [Online]. Available at: http://esamultimedia.esa.int/docs/industry/SME/SineQuaNet-workshops/Darmstadt-8feb07/08_REYNAUD_The-Tendering-Process-and-ESA-EMITS-System.pdf [accessed: 25 October 2010].

24 *Ibid.*

25 ESA 2008. Procurement Regulations, ESA Director General's Office, ESA/C (2008)202. [Online]. Available at: http://emits.esa.int/emits-doc/ESA_HQ/EIO-PROCUREMENT_REGULATIONS.pdf [accessed: 25 October 2010], 23–5.

In addition, it appears that SMEs have limited scope in negotiating an ECP, as opposed to a main contractor/integrator. The ECP itself is often applicable to the high-technological components supplied by SMEs that absorb the associated risks in the early stages with a promise of an ECP to follow.[26] Similar approaches and challenges are faced by national space, since national agencies enjoy a more direct approach to their contracting, than the collaborative nature of ESA allows.

This issue is directly linked with the industrial policy of the fair return coefficient, as new smaller Member States, in particular, but also SMEs from larger European space-faring nations, which are not part of the consolidated Space Industrial Base (SIB), are contracted directly by ESA for programmes where the main contractor has the main responsibility for the deliverables.

Another key issue regarding the fair return coefficient and the relevant ESA industrial policy is that, with the number of countries joining ESA increasing, and the structure of the European SIB becoming increasingly complex, owing to national military space programmes, it becomes increasingly inefficient to manage *juste retour* on an annual basis. Hence ESA is following an evolutionary path towards a more flexible application of this quantitative return approach. It is, however, not necessary to restrict fair return to quantitative measurements; a qualitative dimension would add flexibility to inter-ESA negotiations, as it would allow for individual members to be satisfied with low quantitative returns, but perhaps returns of a more rewarding nature for the national industrial base.

Key Implications from Usage of Contracts for Efficiency

The use of cost-plus contracts has received much attention in the US as being of substantial benefit to the industry, while resulting in higher than optimal payments from NASA. This is, however, not a foregone conclusion, as the process of appropriations is such that it allows for renegotiation on an annual basis. This is due to the fact that the programme is not completely defined at the start of the contracting period. It is likely that for such risky projects, it will be even more challenging to set a fixed-price contract, or even to convert ESA's ceiling price to a fixed price scheme.

A cost-plus contract typically allows for the contractor to spend a proportion above the expected value, but on this overrun there is no profit, hence no incentive for such overruns. However, when successfully negotiated if a contract does not 'lock' in terms of its funding profile, by full commitment of the funding authority, then the contractor effectively is facing an annual re-negotiation process for each incremental funding period. In effect, the cost-overruns become part of next period's profile and thus are never treated as overruns. The overrun is real in terms of the overall project, but has little impact on the contractor's profitability, or incentives.

The same can be said about ESA's contract with ceiling price to be converted into fixed price (CP-FP). To illustrate this, what would be considered contract overruns under a well-defined, cost-plus, or fixed-price contract at the signing of the contract, become 'additional information' leading to a de facto re-drafting of the contract terms. For NASA, this takes place on an annual basis, for ESA's CP-FP contracts this institutionally is supposed to happen once. This means that, in fact, despite the labelling of a contract as 'cost-plus', the completion path of the contract is often best described as a 'set of renegotiated cost-plus contracts'.

---

26 Fuchs, M. 2001. *Presentation on the Occasion of the Industry Open Days*. SMESpaceAlliance, ESA, ESTEC, the Netherlands. [Online]. Available at: http://conferences.esa.int/isd2001/21.pdf [accessed: 25 October 2010].

In addition, during the phase where the contract is not yet finalised, there is little incentive for the industry to exert maximum effort. Indeed, for NASA one of the problems rests within the pricing of programmes during the inception and development phase, where the profit margin is the same as for the hardware production. Little attention is paid to the fact that the equality of profit margins results in the contractor having every incentive to extend the early phases, where paper projects are developed. The justification on the part of the government is that a programme well-designed from its early stages is an investment for the programme's lifetime, so funds spent in development are funds well spent, but this can be easily abused by the contractor. However, it makes perhaps less sense for the government to provide an equal proportion of profit during those stages as it does for the hardware phase, where reconfiguring takes place and hardware is manufactured at high risk with significant capital invested.

Conclusions

Space agencies are complicated bureaucratic organisations that are often faced with conflicting objectives regarding their policies *vis-à-vis* the industry. What is more is their contractual processes and fund-seeking procedures potentially result in behaviours that dynamically differ in terms of their compatibility with the objectives of the space industry.

In this framework, the use of 'simple' contractual approaches is often preferred, given the complexity associated with all other decisions. ESA for example shows a clear preference for fixed-price contracts. Simple solutions are, however, not always optimal for risky and dynamic environments. It appears that there is a tendency for fixing the terms of a contract initially, but this is nominal, as evidenced by the use of 'ceiling price to be converted to fixed price' type of contracts and the large number of ECPs/CCNs.

The approach ESA appears to follow with the direct placement of subcontracts appears to be nullifying some of the negative effects of industrial consolidation towards restoring the balance of power in negotiations between the prime contractors and the SMEs. The implications of this for ESA's industrial policy of fair return are not clear. In addition, this process results in ESA indirectly managing subcontractors in programmes facing challenges of complexity and accountability, as the main contractor has the responsibility for the overall programme's performance.

Cost-plus contracts seem to be primarily disadvantaged by the constant need to monitor and in the case of ESA, perhaps renegotiate during the course of the contract payments amongst different members. Overall, there appear to be substantial costs associated with surveillance of contracts, which especially for the cost-plus types employed by NASA leads to the use of specialised agents within the DoD to monitor and manage relevant processes with the use of sophisticated tools such as the EVMS.

Key Recommendations

It must be noted, that the lack of publicly available information in procurement contracting in the European space sector makes the relevant analysis and assessment of efficiency a challenging task; more transparency would facilitate the relevant evaluation. It is suggested that the addition of a qualitative element would complement the quantitative aspects of the fair return coefficient in the relevant negotiations, providing increasing degrees of freedom. Given that implementation is often more important than design for efficiency, it is important for novel tools to be developed to take into account such qualitative aspects, as well as low-cost monitoring of cost-plus contracts.

In this direction, cost monitoring analysis must be complemented by the relevant pricing implications that take into account the profit and payment incentive scheme of contracts. A step in this direction is the augmented earned value management system with price implications (EVMS-P, see Figure 17.2). European applications of such schemes would perhaps result in a more balanced distribution of contracts, increasing use of cost-plus arrangements, and limit the use of ECPs/CCNs that can change the initial nature of the contract and are frequently used.

References

Aerospace Industries Association (AIA) 2009. *The Unseen Cost: Industrial Base Consequences of Defense Strategy Choices*. [Online]. Available at: http://www.aia-aerospace.org/assets/report_industrial_base_consequences.pdf [accessed: 25 October 2010].

Annual Procurement Report, Fiscal Year 1983. 1998. Washington, DC: NASA.

Annual Procurement Report, Fiscal Year 1991. 1991. Washington, DC: NASA.

Annual Procurement Report, Fiscal Year 2006. 2006. Washington, DC: NASA.

Annual Procurement Report, Fiscal Year 2008. 2008. Washington, DC: NASA.

ESA 2007. Resolution on the European Space Policy-ESA Director General's Proposal for the European Space Policy. [Online]. Available at: http://www.esa.int/esapub/br/br269/br269.pdf [accessed: 25 October 2010].

ESA 2008. Procurement Regulations, ESA Director General's Office, ESA/C (2008)202. [Online]. Available at: http://emits.esa.int/emits-doc/ESA_HQ/EIO-PROCUREMENT_REGULATIONS.pdf [accessed: 25 October 2010].

ESA 2009. General Clauses and Conditions for ESA Contracts, ESA/C/290. [Online]. Available at: http://esamultimedia.esa.int/docs/industry/SME/2004-Training/WGP/Annex1_General_Clauses_and_Cond_Rev_6.pdf [accessed: 25 October 2010].

Fuchs, M. 2001. *Presentation on the Occasion of the Industry Open Days*. SMESpaceAlliance, ESA, ESTEC, the Netherlands. [Online]. Available at: http://conferences.esa.int/isd2001/21.pdf [accessed: 25 October 2010].

Laffont, J. and Tirole, J. 1993. *A Theory of Incentives in Procurement and Regulation*. London: MIT Press.

Lichtenberg, R.F. 1995. 'Economics of Defense R&D', in *Handbook of Defence Economics*, edited by K. Hartley and T. Sandler. London: Elsevier Science BV.

NASA 1999. NASA Policy Directive, NPD 7120.4C. Washington DC: NASA.

NASA 2007. NASA Spaceflight Program and Project Management Requirements NPR7120 5D. [Online]. Available at: http://nodis3.gsfc.nasa.gov/npg_img/N_PR_7120_005D_/N_PR_7120_005D_.pdf [accessed: 25 October 2010].

NASA 2009a. Procurement Notice PN04-19, NASA procurement regulations. [Online]. Available at: http://www.hq.nasa.gov/office/procurement/regs/pn04-19.html [accessed: 25 October 2010].

NASA 2009b. Memorandum of Understanding between National Aeronautics and Space Administration (NASA) and Defense Contract Management Agency (DCMA) for Earned Value Management System Acceptance/Surveillance and Earned Value Management Project Surveillance. [Online]. Available at: http://evm.nasa.gov/mou.html [accessed: 25 October 2010].

NASA 2009c. *Earned Value Management Regulations and Requirements*. [Online]. Available at: http://evm.nasa.gov/regulations.html [accessed: 25 October 2010].

Navy 2009. *EVM Contract Requirements Toolkit*. Centre for Earned Value Management US Navy. [Online]. Available at: https://acquisition.navy.mil/content/download/4820/21638/file/CEVM%20EVM%20Contract%20Requirements%20Toolkit%20rev3-20080319.pdf [accessed: 25 October 2010].

Niskanen, W.A. Jr. 1971. *Bureaucracy and Representative Government*. Chicago, IL: Aldine Atherton.

Office of the Secretary of Defense 2004. *Business Case Analysis for Proposed Revision to DoD Earned Value Management Policy*. US Office of Acquisitions. [Online]. Available at: www.acq.osd.mil/pm/historical/business_case.doc [accessed: 5 November 2009].

Reynaud, P.M. 2005. *ESA Tendering Process and EMITS System*. ESA Procurement Department, Sinequanet Workshop. [Online]. Available at: http://esamultimedia.esa.int/docs/industry/SME/SineQuaNet-workshops/Darmstadt-8feb07/08_REYNAUD_The-Tendering-Process-and-ESA-EMITS-System.pdf [accessed: 25 October 2010].

Rogerson, P.W. 1991. 'Incentives, the Budgetary Process, and Inefficiently Low Production Rates in Defence Procurement', *Defence Economics*, 3, 1–18.

Sandler, T. and Hartley, K. 1995. *The Economics of Defense*. New York: Cambridge University Press.

Satellite Industry Association (SIA) 2008. *State of the Satellite Industry Report*. Bethesda, MD: Futron Corporation.

Stockholm International Peace Research Institute (SIPRI) 2009. *Concentration in the Arms Industry*. [Online]. Available at: http://www.sipri.org/research/armaments/production/researchissues/concentration_aprod [accessed: 25 October 2010].

White House 2009a. *National Aeronautics and Space Administration Programs*. [Online: US White House]. Available at: http://www.whitehouse.gov/omb/expectmore/agency/026.html [accessed: 25 October 2010].

White House 2009b. *Detailed Information on the NASA Astronomy and Astrophysics Research Assessment*. [Online: US White House]. Available at: http://www.whitehouse.gov/omb/expectmore/detail/10002316.2007.html [accessed: 25 October 2010].

Zervos, V. 2008. 'Whatever Happened to Competition in Space Agency Procurement? The Case of NASA', *Journal of Applied Economics*, 11, 221–36.

Chapter 18
Security Rights over Satellites: An Overview of the Proposed Protocol to the Convention on International Interests in Mobile Equipment on Matters Specific to Space Assets

Dietrich Weber-Steinhaus and Deirdre Ní Chearbhaill

Introduction

The evolution of the space industry from one which was purely government funded towards a flourishing private industry means that one of the key challenges faced by industry participants today is how to access affordable financing for commercial space projects. From a lender's perspective, financing space projects involves many considerations including crucially, what security or collateral the borrower might be able to provide to ensure an adequate remedy is provided to the lender should the borrower fail to meet its repayment obligations or become insolvent.

The space industry operates internationally. Financing may be obtained from more than one financial institution, export credit agencies, the capital markets, private investors or a combination of some or all of these. The borrower's business and its assets are likely to be located in more than one jurisdiction, including, in the case of a launched satellite, in orbit. How then can the lenders ensure that their investment can be recouped should the borrower default or, worse, go into liquidation?

The Convention on International Interests in Mobile Equipment[1] (the 'Cape Town Convention' or 'Convention') seeks to facilitate the acquisition and financing of economically important items of mobile equipment, specifically aircraft equipment, railway rolling stock and space assets, through the creation of a *sui generis* security interest which will be recognised and enforceable in all contracting states to the Convention. It creates a new harmonised legal regime for the creation, registration and enforcement of these 'international interests' and related rights.

The draft Protocol to the Convention on Matters Specific to Space Assets (the 'Draft Protocol')[2] would in turn widen the scope of the Convention to space assets so that it applies to financing such assets. The Draft Protocol is being drafted under the auspices of UNIDROIT by a group of lawyers,

---

1 The Convention on International Interests in Mobile Equipment 2001. The full text of the Convention is available at www.unidroit.org.

2 Text of the revised Preliminary Draft Protocol to the Cape Town Convention on Matters Specific to Space Assets as it emerged from the fifth session of the UNIDROIT Committee of governmental experts for the preparation of a draft Protocol to the Cape Town Convention on Matters specific to Space Assets, held in Rome from 21 to 25 February 2011. Appendix XV of Document: UNIDROIT 2011 C.G.E./Space Pr./5/Report available on www.unidroit.org. The Governing Council of Unidroit decided at its meeting in May 2011 to convene a diplomatic conference for the end of February 2012 on the basis of the preliminary draft.

academics and industry experts. This chapter will look at the principal matters covered by the Draft Protocol and how, if the Draft Protocol enters into force, the new legal regime would work.

Unique Problems with Financing Space Assets

There are a number of issues relating to the transfer of ownership and control of a satellite that give rise to problems which would not arise with traditional earth-based asset financing. The Draft Protocol attempts to provide solutions to most of these matters with a view to facilitating financing within the sector, by adapting and expanding the Cape Town Convention to cover these concerns.

Repossession

If a lender has been granted security over an asset, its primary recourse in a default situation will usually be to the asset itself. A lender would take possession of, and sell or manage the asset so as to recoup any amounts due to it. A lender cannot, however, physically repossess a space asset once it is in orbit. In order to obtain constructive possession of the spacecraft, as well as obtaining title and control over the spacecraft itself, the lender or third party purchaser will require all necessary permits, licences and authorisations (including authorisations connected with the use of orbital positions and frequencies where applicable), know-how, intellectual property, ground infrastructure and command codes necessary in order to operate the spacecraft. A rights lender will also wish to have step-in rights to the operator's commercial contracts and in particular to have access to the receivables and income generated though the borrower's contracts with its customers. Unlike more traditional terrestrial assets, a defaulting borrower cannot simply 'hand back the keys' to a spacecraft and leave the lender to operate or sell it. The borrower's cooperation and active involvement is required in order to allow for the orderly transfer of the satellite to a new owner. If the borrower is in liquidation, this may be more difficult.

Lex situs

The conflicts of law rule of *lex situs* provides that the creation of an interest in property must be valid in accordance with the applicable law where the property is located at the time of the creation of the interest. It is extremely relevant to space assets as title to a satellite often transfers in orbit or at launch and an owner may also grant a mortgage over a satellite after it has been launched. What law could be deemed to govern the creation of such interests in orbit? How can the lender be assured that its interest is validly constituted?[3]

3 According to the public international law regime governing Outer Space, including the Treaty on Principles Governing the Activities of States in the Exploration and Use of Outer Space, including the Moon and Celestial Bodies, 27 January 1967 ('Outer Space Treaty') outer space is an area which cannot be subject to national appropriation. Article VIII of the Outer Space Treaty provides that the state upon whose register a space object is carried 'shall retain jurisdiction and control over such object … while in Outer Space or on a celestial body. Ownership of objects launched into Outer Space, including objects landed or constructed on a celestial body, and of their component parts, is not affected by their presence in outer space or on a celestial body or by their return to the Earth.' These provisions were not intended to be substantive rules of private law and should not be construed as covering which national laws might govern ownership and security interests created in outer space. Moreover, the term 'space objects' as used in the Outer Space Treaty would not include intangible assets.

State Responsibility and Liability

International public law[4] obliges the 'appropriate state' to authorise and continuously supervise the activities of non-governmental entities (including private companies) in their activities in outer space. States bear international responsibility for national activities in outer space[5], whether such activities are carried on by governmental agencies or by non-governmental entities. Furthermore, a launching state is internationally liable for damage caused by its space object.[6] A launching state is defined as a state which launches or procures the launch of a space object or from whose territory or facility a space object is launched[7] and for any one spacecraft, there may be more than one launching state. A launching state's liability is not extinguished by time or by a change of ownership or control. While this is appropriate when the relevant state is in a position to supervise and control the activities of a private company, and to subject it to national legislation governing its activities, upon transfer of title, operation and control of the object to an entity beyond the jurisdiction of the original launching state, the original launching state continues to be liable for incidents, which it is not in a position to control, prevent or regulate.

National Security

If possession and control of a satellite is transferred to a lender or third party, this may also raise national security, technology transfer and export control concerns.[8] These will need to be addressed by the new operator of the spacecraft and could even prevent certain entities or corporations from particular jurisdictions from taking control of the spacecraft.

The Cape Town Convention

Objectives

The objectives of the Convention are:

> to facilitate the acquisition and financing of economically important items of mobile equipment by providing for the creation of an international interest which will be recognised in all contracting states

4 The international public law regime governing space activities is contained in five international treaties – the Outer Space Treaty, Agreement on the Rescue of Astronauts, the Return of Astronauts and the Return of Objects Launched into Outer Space, 22 April 1968 ('Rescue Agreement'), Convention on International Liability for Damage Caused by Space Objects, 29 March 1972 ('Liability Convention'), Convention on the Registration of Objects Launched into Outer Space, 12 November 1974 ('Registration Convention'), Agreement Governing the Activities of States on the Moon and Other Celestial Bodies, 18 December 1979 ('Moon Agreement'), together with declarations and resolutions of the United Nations General Assembly.

5 Article VI Outer Space Treaty.

6 Article VII Outer Space Treaty and Article II and III Liability Convention.

7 Article I(c) Liability Convention.

8 See further Chapter 24 of this volume.

to provide the creditor with a range of basic default remedies and, where there is evidence of default, a means of obtaining speedy interim relief pending final determination of its claim on the merits

to establish an electronic international register for the registration of international interests which will give notice of their existence to third parties and enable the creditor to preserve its priority against subsequently registered interests and against unregistered interests and the debtor's insolvency administrator

to ensure through the relevant protocol that the particular needs of the industry sector concerned are met

by these means to give intending creditors greater confidence in the decision to grant credit, enhance the credit rating of equipment receivables and reduce borrowing costs to the advantage of all interested parties.[9]

Approach

The Cape Town regime uses a two document approach. The Convention itself is a general framework convention which sets out the rules applicable to all assets covered by the Convention. Each category of equipment (aircraft, rolling stock and space assets) has its own distinct protocol which must be separately ratified by each contracting state. The Protocol on Matters specific to Aircraft Equipment (the 'Aircraft Protocol') entered into force on 1 March 2006 and has been ratified by over 30 states.[10] A Protocol on Matters specific to Railway Rolling Stock (the 'Luxemburg Protocol') was opened for signature on 25 February 2007 but has not yet entered into force.[11]

The Convention and each protocol (once it has entered into force) are to be read as one instrument and in the event of inconsistency, the relevant protocol prevails.[12] The Convention may only apply to a category of equipment to which a protocol has entered into force and may only be enforced as between contracting states to that protocol, subject to the terms of the protocol.[13] As such, the protocol is the controlling document. The Convention establishes the fundamental regime, including the concept of the international registry, defines the security interests and establishes basic rules of priority and enforcement, while the protocols expand and modify these rules, where appropriate, to the individual categories of equipment.

What Interests are Covered?

The Convention provides for a new *sui generis* security interest called an 'international interest'.

An international interest is defined in Article 2(2) of the Convention as an interest:

9 See Goode, R. 2008. *Official Commentary to the Convention on International Interests in Mobile Equipment and Protocol Thereto on Matters Specific to Aircraft Equipment*, 2nd edition. Rome: International Institute for the Unification of Private Law (UNIDROIT), 14.

10 For an up-to-date list of the status of the Convention and its protocols, please see www.unidroit.org.

11 Four states must ratify the Protocol and the International Registry in respect of Railway Rolling Stock must be fully operational before the Protocol can come into force.

12 Article 6 of the Convention.

13 Article 49 of the Convention.

(i) granted by the chargor under a security agreement;
(ii) vested in a person who is the conditional seller under a title reservation agreement; or
(iii) vested in a person who is the lessor under a leasing agreement.

In addition, certain provisions of the Convention may apply to the interests of a seller of object pursuant to a contract of sale.[14]

A security agreement is defined as

> an agreement by which a chargor grants or agrees to grant to a chargee an interest (including an ownership interest) in or over an object to secure the performance of any existing or future obligation of the chargor or a third person.[15]

The Convention also covers assignments of international interests and of 'associated rights' (being all rights to payment or other performance by a debtor under an agreement which are secured by or associated with the object).[16]

Application of the Convention

The Convention will only apply where the debtor is situated in a contracting state at the time of the conclusion of the agreement creating the international interest. For the purposes of the Convention, a 'debtor' is (i) a chargor under a security agreement, (ii) a conditional buyer under a title reservation agreement, (iii) a lessee under a leasing agreement or (iv) a person whose interest in an object is burdened by a registrable non-consensual right or interest[17] and will include, insofar as the Convention applies to a contract of sale, the seller under a contract of sale.[18] The jurisdiction where the creditor is situated is irrelevant.

Provided a security agreement is in writing, relates to an object of which the chargor has power to dispose, enables the object to be identified (in accordance with the relevant Protocol), and enables the secured obligations to be determined[19] and the debtor is situated in a contracting state, then an international interest is created and the rights which the Convention gives to the chargee arising out of that international interest exist irrespective of the provisions of the domestic law in the jurisdiction the asset is in at the time the interest is created. It is thus intended that the *lex situs* rule will not apply to the creation of international interests.[20]

International Registry

The key feature of the Cape Town system is an international registry (one in respect of each category of equipment). International interests in mobile equipment may be registered on the relevant international registry which is accessible online 24 hours a day, seven days a week.

---

14 Article 41 of the Convention.
15 Article 1 (ii) of the Convention.
16 Article 1 (c) of the Convention.
17 Article 1 (j) of the Convention.
18 See for example Article III of the Aircraft Protocol, Article IV of the Draft Protocol.
19 Article 7 of the Convention.
20 See Goode, R. 2008. *Official Commentary to the Convention on International Interests in Mobile Equipment and Protocol Thereto on Matters Specific to Aircraft Equipment*, 2nd edition, § 2.42, 35–7.

The International Registry established pursuant to the Aircraft Protocol has been a proven success. Since the International Registry went live in 2006, over 236,000 registrations have been made against approximately 77,000 objects.[21] While the space assets register would not achieve the same number of registrations, it is clear from the success of the aircraft registry that an online register can be effective and acceptable to the international financing community.

The basic rules in the Convention in respect of priority are as follows:

> as between two registered interests, the first in time has priority;
> as between a registered and an unregistered interest, the registered interest takes priority;
> registration of an interest in a national registry is irrelevant to the order of priority.[22]

An international interest does not have to be registered in order to benefit from the remedies provided for under the Convention. However it must be registered to avail of priority.[23]

Enforcement

Party autonomy is respected with regard to the establishment of default on the part of the debtor. Parties may (and usually will) agree in writing as to what circumstances may bring about default.[24] Should the parties have no agreement in this regard, a default which gives rise to rights and remedies under the Convention is one which substantially deprives the creditor of what it is entitled to expect under the agreement.[25]

A distinction is drawn between the remedies available to a chargee[26] and those which are available to a conditional seller or lessor.[27] Upon the occurrence of an event of default, a conditional seller or lessor may terminate the agreement, take possession or control of the object and seek a court order to affect all of the above. A chargee may take possession or control of the charged object, sell or grant a lease of it, collect or receive any income or profits arising from the management of the object, apply for a court order ordering the above, or take ownership of the object in satisfaction of the debt. However, there are certain limitations placed on the exercise of these remedies. The chargee must inform and notify all 'interested persons'[28] of its actions, and must seek either their or the court's permission before ownership may be vested in it in satisfaction of the debt. The parties

21 Cowan, R. 2010. 'The International Registry'. Presentation to the Cape Town Treaty Forum – Rome 2010. Rome, 10 November 2010. [Online]. Available at: http://www.capetowntreatyforum.com [accessed: 16 June 2011].

22 Interests that pre-date the coming into force of the Convention will retain their priority under their applicable law, unless the Contracting State makes a declaration to the contrary on ratification (Article 60 of the Convention).

23 Goode, R. 2008. *Official Commentary to the Convention on International Interests in Mobile Equipment and Protocol Thereto on Matters Specific to Aircraft Equipment*, 2nd edition, § 2.43, 37.

24 Article 17 (1) of the Convention.

25 Article 17 (2) of the Convention.

26 Articles 8 and 9 of the Convention.

27 Article 10 of the Convention. The applicable law of the contract will determine its categorisation (Article 2 (4) of the Convention).

28 Article 1 (m) of the Convention defines interested persons as '(i) the debtor; (ii) any person who, for the purpose of assuring performance of any of the obligations in favour of the creditor, gives or issues a suretyship or demand guarantee or a standby letter of credit or any other form of credit insurance; (iii) any other person having rights in or over the object'.

to a secured transaction may agree to derogate from and have recourse to other remedies than those available under Chapter III of the Convention, subject to certain mandatory provisions.[29]

All remedies exercised under the Convention and the Protocol must be exercised in a 'commercially reasonable manner'. The parties' own agreement in a security agreement as to what is commercially reasonable is conclusive (save where the provision is manifestly unreasonable).[30]

Should the debtor become insolvent, contracting states may, if they make a declaration, choose from two alternative regulations aimed at improving a secured creditor's rights.[31] If no declaration is made, the national laws of the contracting state will be applied. Under Alternative A, the insolvency administrator is compelled to give possession to the creditor or cure all defaults and undertake to perform all obligations under the relevant security agreement within a certain waiting period, which must be laid down by the contracting state at the time of making the declaration. Under Alternative B, the insolvency administrator is requested to give a statement, saying whether the administrator will cure all defaults or allow the creditor to take possession after a certain period of time. If the administrator does not make this statement, a court order may be sought to obtain repossession.

While the Convention and Protocol seek to harmonise the law in respect of international interests, as far as the insolvency procedure and the rights of insolvent companies are concerned, the contracting state's ability to 'opt-in' and 'opt-out' of various provisions, through the use of declarations on ratification, and the discretion granted to national courts means that the remedies available on enforcement following the insolvency of the debtor/borrower are less than uniform across contracting states.

Draft Space Assets Protocol

The success of the Aircraft Protocol indicates clearly that the Cape Town regime can work for international asset financings. For example, the Export-Import Bank of the United States of America and other export credit agencies offer a reduction on their exposure fee for aircraft transactions if the Aircraft Protocol applies to the transaction.

The Draft Protocol seeks to apply and adapt the Convention to the financing of space assets and the unique environment in which they operate. The drafters of the Draft Protocol had a difficult challenge in trying to ensure that the Draft Protocol sufficiently adapts the core provisions of the Convention to the requirements of the space industry and its financiers. They have expanded the Convention to cover new interests not envisaged by the Convention and have broadened the ambit of the Convention. The most significant aspects are discussed below.

What is a 'Space Asset'?

Space assets are currently defined in the Draft Protocol as:

> "space asset" means any man-made uniquely identifiable asset in space or designed to be launched into space, and comprising

29 Article 15 of the Convention.

30 Article 8 (3) of the Convention.

31 Article 23 of the Convention.

> (i) a spacecraft, such as a satellite, space station, space module, space capsule, space vehicle or reusable launch vehicle [in respect of which a registration may be effected in accordance with the regulations], whether or not including a space asset falling within (ii) or (iii) below;
>
> (ii) a payload (whether telecommunications, navigation, observation, scientific or otherwise) in respect of which a separate registration may be effected in accordance with the regulations; or
>
> (iii) a part of a spacecraft or payload such as a transponder, in respect of which a separate registration may be effected in accordance with the regulations,
>
> together with all installed, incorporated or attached accessories, parts and equipment and all data, manuals and records relating thereto.

The scope of the definition was discussed in detail at each meeting of the drafting committee, who debated amongst other things whether, and to what extent, components, such as transponders, and assets in the course of manufacture or assembly should be included. The above definition is intended to cover any assets which would usually be capable of being separately financed and it covers both completed spacecraft and high value parts. The reference to "the regulations" in the definition is a reference to such regulations as may be made by the Supervisory Authority.[32]

Each space asset must be uniquely identifiable. Article XXX of the Draft Protocol sets out how a space asset should be described, being by its manufacturer's name, manufacturer's serial number and model designation, and which description must also satisfy any other requirements as may be established in the regulations as necessary and sufficient to identify the space asset for the purposes of registration on the International Registry.

Deferring to the regulations which may be passed by the Supervisory Authority in both the definition of space assets and Article XXX expands the role of the Supervisory Authority beyond that initially envisaged under the Convention as it would allow the Supervisory Authority's regulations, rather than the Draft Protocol itself to determine the application of the Convention to certain assets.

International interests are registered on the international registry against specific assets (and not against debtors) and so in order for the international registry to work, it must be possible for third parties to carry out searches against identifiable assets to ensure that priority is properly afforded to the party so entitled. The Draft Protocol in deferring to regulations (which will be amended from time to time) does not appear to set out sufficiently clear, uniform identifiers for the objects against which international interests will be registered.[33]

---

32 The Supervisory Authority is the allocated a range of powers and duties under Article 17 of the Convention, including the establishment and ongoing supervision of the international registry, the appointment of the registrar and the publication of regulations dealing with the operation of the international registry. The Supervisory Authority for the Aircraft Protocol is ICAO. It is not yet decided who the Supervisory Authority for the Space Assets Protocol shall be.

33 Compare, by way of example, that aircraft objects are registered on the international registry by make, model and manufacturer's serial number. Every airframe, engine and helicopter are (and historically have been) allocated a serial number and when the international registry was established, the manufacturers provided this information to the registry and have continued to update the registry as new aircraft are delivered.

Interests Protected Under the Draft Protocol

The Protocol and the space assets registry once it is created, will cover international interests as defined in the Convention as well as sales of space assets.[34]

In order to deal effectively with receivables due to a debtor in relation to the space asset, the Draft Protocol introduces a novel concept to the Cape Town regime namely that of rights assignments and debtor's rights. 'Debtor's rights' means 'all rights to payment or other performance due or to become due to a debtor by any person with respect to a space asset'.[35] This would include for example, rentals payable due to an operator under a transponder lease. A 'rights assignment' is defined as

> a contract by which the debtor confers on the creditor an interest (including an ownership interest) in or over the whole or part of existing or future debtor's rights to secure the performance of, or in reduction or discharge of, any existing or future obligation of the debtor to the creditor which under the agreement creating or providing for the international interest is secured by or associated with the space asset to which the agreement relates.[36]

A transfer of debtor's rights is constituted as a rights assignment where it is in writing and enables the debtors' rights the subject of the rights assignment, the space asset to which the rights relate and, in the case of a rights assignment by way of security, the obligations secured by the agreement, to be identified and determined.[37]

In essence, the rights assignment provides the creditor with the ability to take an assignment of the debtor's rights in respect of payment and performance of its third party contracts.

The Convention provides for the assignments of international interests and assignments of associated rights thereto and for such assignments to be registered on the international registry. The rights assignment provisions in the Draft Protocol go one step further by not limiting registrable assignments to assignments of international interests and by expanding the rights assignment to cover other contracts connected with the satellite and third party's performance of such contracts.

This should permit creditors to take security assignments of a debtor's commercial contracts with third parties and have such assignments registered as international interests.

International Approvals and Licences

In order to operate a satellite, certain licences and approvals must be obtained from (potentially) a number of governmental and intergovernmental agencies and sources in various jurisdictions. This places a restriction on the ability of a lender to transfer or exploit a space asset upon the enforcement of its security and accordingly raises issues for the Draft Protocol.

The current draft of the Draft Protocol proposes two alternatives to address this issue. Both proposals permit a Contracting State to restrict or impose conditions on the exercise of remedies under the Convention where such exercise would involve or require the transfer of controlled goods, technology, data or services, or would involve the transfer or assignment of a licence, or the grant of a new licence. The second alternative would also allow a Contracting State to impose

34 Article IV of the Draft Protocol.

35 Article I (2) (a) of the Draft Protocol.

36 Article I (2) (i) of the Draft Protocol.

37 Article IX of the Draft Protocol.

restrictions on the constitution of an international interest or a rights assignment for reasons of national security, international peace and security or in order to regulate controlled goods.

'Controlled' in this context means 'that the transfer of the goods, technology, data or services is subject to governmental restrictions'.

While these proposals have their merits, it means that contracting states may still place restrictions on the transfer and use of space assets with the resultant uncertainty that a creditor will be able to enforce its security upon a default.

Remedies

The Draft Protocol adopts the remedies of the Convention and contracting states retain the ability to opt for one of three possibilities in an insolvency situation (for example apply domestic law, Alternative A or Alternative B). The Draft Protocol provides that the holder of a rights assignment may exercise the remedies under the Convention as if the rights assignment were an international interest. It also specifically provides for the placing of command codes in escrow by the parties (although this provision is subject to restriction by contracting states).[38]

Conclusion

The Draft Protocol certainly provides a platform from which a final text may be developed, but still has some way to go before the text of it can be finalised. Prior to the publication of the first draft of the Aircraft Protocol, a comprehensive independent economic analysis was carried out to ascertain whether a uniform approach to the creation of security over aircraft would stimulate and facilitate the aviation industry.[39] An equivalent analysis does not appear to have been made in relation to space assets and so it is not certain that a uniform regime would stimulate the industry or that the lack of a uniform regime has hindered financing space projects to date. Critics of the Draft Protocol have suggested that rather than facilitating financing, the Draft Protocol might actually increase the risk associated with financing and accordingly make it more expensive.[40]

The Draft Protocol also envisages security packages which rely on the rights of creditors and owners over the physical asset and focuses on contractual rights, the debtor's rights to receivables, and the assignment of such contractual rights. While this type of security is covered, to some extent, in the Cape Town Convention, the Convention was conceived with the intention of addressing problems relating to cross-border recognition and creation of property rights in the asset itself. The parties involved in sophisticated space financings are arguably well capable of obtaining and negotiating contracts for the financing of space assets without the need for an international convention to govern the terms of such contracts.

---

38 Article XIX Draft Protocol.

39 Saunders, A. and Walter, I. 1998. 'Proposed Unidroit Convention on International Interests in Mobile Equipment as Applicable to Aircraft Equipment through the Aircraft Equipment Protocol: Economic Impact Assessment (September 1998)', 23 *Air and Space Law* 339 (1998).

40 'Assessing the Support for the Space Assets Protocol to the UNIDROIT Cape Town Convention', Report of the International Institute of Space Commerce (Reference no: IISC-09-P.12.1), 16 December 2009. [Online]. Available at: http://www.iisc.im/documents/IISC_-_09_-_P.12.1[2]_1.pdf [accessed: 1 December 2010]. See also International Consultation with representatives of the International Commercial Space and Financial Communities (Rome, October 2010), Report by Unidroit Secretariat, Unidroit Document CGE// Space Pr/5/W.P.4 at paragraphs 8-11.

Finally, it would appear that the key constraint to the prompt enforcement of security rights over a satellite will be the requirement to have access to the regulatory licences required to operate or sell the asset. While admittedly the Draft Protocol cannot change this, or the liability regime created by the Outer Space Treaties (which increases the regulatory burden by obliging states to exercise oversight of the activities of private companies), the failure to find a solution to this may mean that the Draft Protocol and Convention regime would probably provide very little added value on a practical level to the way financing is done today.

List of References

Agreement Governing the Activities of States on the Moon and Other Celestial Bodies, 18 December 1979.

Agreement on the Rescue of Astronauts, the Return of Astronauts and the Return of Objects Launched into Outer Space, 22 April 1968.

'Assessing the Support for the Space Assets Protocol to the UNIDROIT Cape Town Convention', Report of the International Institute of Space Commerce (Reference no: IISC-09-P.12.1), 16 December 2009. [Online]. Available at: http://www.iisc.im/documents/IISC_-_09_-_P.12.1[2]_1.pdf [accessed: 1 December 2010].

Convention on International Liability for Damage Caused by Space Objects, 29 March 1972.

Convention on the Registration of Objects Launched into Outer Space, 12 November 1974.

Cowan, R. 2010. 'The International Registry'. Presentation to the Cape Town Treaty Forum – Rome 2010. Rome, 10 November 2010. [Online]. Available at: http://www.capetowntreatyforum.com [accessed: 1 December 2010].

Goode, R. 2008. *Official Commentary to the Convention on International Interests in Mobile Equipment and Protocol Thereto on Matters Specific to Aircraft Equipment*, 2nd edition. Rome: International Institute for the Unification of Private Law (UNIDROIT).

Report of Unidroit Committee of Governmental Experts for the Preparation of a Draft Protocol to the Convention on International Interests in Mobile Equipment on Matters Specific to Space Assets, Fourth session, Rome, 3/7 May 2010 (Unidroit 2010, C.G.E./Space Pr./4/Report).

Saunders, A. and Walter, I. 1998. 'Proposed Unidroit Convention on International Interests in Mobile Equipment as Applicable to Aircraft Equipment through the Aircraft Equipment Protocol: Economic Impact Assessment (September 1998)', 23 *Air and Space Law* 339 (1998).

Treaty on Principles Governing the Activities of States in the Exploration and Use of Outer Space, including the Moon and Celestial Bodies, 27 January 1967.

Chapter 19
Research and Development Contracts

Martin J. Mittelbach

Introduction

The aerospace industry is one of the significant high-tech sectors in the EU. About 650,000 employees generate an annual turnover of approx. EUR 133 billion.[1] The share of industrial research and development (R&D) is comparably high. Across Europe, about EUR 11.3 billion were invested in research and development in 2008. This corresponded to about 11 per cent of the turnover. About 69 per cent of the costs for research and development were financed by industry; the remaining 31 per cent of the costs come from public funds.[2] The partners of contracts in this sector are states, international organisations (such as the European Union or the European Space Agency), the space agencies and other public institutions as well as industry, research organisations and universities.

The form of the agreements in this sector vary. The most frequently occurring agreements are the research and development contract, the co-operation contract and the consortium agreement. In the case of a research and development contract, the contractor (for example a research organisation or a university) obliges itself to render a research service in return for a financial counter performance and grant access rights to the results to the customer.[3] There is thus a performance and counter performance relationship. This type of contract will be dealt with in the following section ('Research and Development Contracts') of this chapter. In the case of co-operation agreements (see below, 'The Co-operation Agreement'), several partners collaborate to meet a mutual purpose, the achievement of a mutual success in development.[4] It is not typical for there to be an exchange of performance and counter performance in this case. If the co-operation is related to public funding, the term 'consortium agreement' is used, which will be addressed in the section below entitled 'The Consortium Agreement'.

Research and Development Contracts

The Legal Nature of the R&D Contract

The purpose of the research and development contract is the carrying out of the pre-defined development performance and the granting of access rights to the research results in return for

1 European Commission. 2010. *Analysis and Market Data.* [Online]. Available at: http://ec.europa.eu/enterprise/sectors/aerospace/market-data/index_en.htm [accessed: 30 April 2011].

2 The AeroSpace and Defense Industries Association of Europe. 2008. *Facts and Figures.* [Online]. Available at: http://asd-europe.org/site/fileadmin/user_upload/publications/ff2008-2009-01564-02.pdf [accessed: 30 April 2011].

3 Winzer, W. 2006. *Forschungs- und Entwicklungsverträge.* Munich: C.H. Beck.

4 *Ibid.*

remuneration. The research and development contract underlies various legal provisions depending on the underlying law order and content of the performance owed.[5] The difficulty with research and development contracts is that their specifications of performance are only seldom success- or purely performance-related. For this reason, it is being discussed in jurisprudence and literature what criteria can be drawn on to make differentiations. The German Federal Court of Justice (Bundesgerichtshof – BGH) dedicated itself to this issue for the first time with its judgement dated 16 July 2002.[6] In the judgment, the BGH points out that for the differentiation between contracts for services and contracts for work, the intention of the parties as per the contract should be decisive, whereby all circumstances of the individual case are to be taken into consideration. For determining the performance owed according to the intention of the parties in each individual case, the BGH names several criteria: the fact that the parties have clearly defined the task to be performed and the extent of the work would speak in favour of a contract for work. The agreement on a performance-related remuneration is also evidence that the parties have concluded a contract for work. In return, remuneration particularly depending on time and personal effort can also be evidence of a contract for services. It could also be significant, in determining whether the parties intended for one of them to be responsible for success, to know how probable the parties imagined success to be. The greater the imponderability related to the activity, the less probable it would appear to an expert customer that the performer intended to assume the risk of success. The agreement on milestones, however, was not drawn on by the BGH as evidence of a contract of work.

Other approaches can be found in literature. In a few cases, reference is made to whether the contract is a research contract (thus a contract for work) or a development contract (then a contract for services).[7] Further criteria for differentiating are also drawn, for example by Koch (2009)[8] who presents such factors as the type of remuneration,[9] the allocation of risk and obligations to assume liabilities,[10] or the agreement on warranty and rectification clauses analogue to the regulations of the contract for work.[11]

The Essential Contents of the Contract

Preamble Particularly in view of the problems of differentiation as previously described, it is recommended that the parties briefly outline their interests and the spirit and purpose of the contract in a preamble. In doing so, the insights and results previously gained should be particularly

---

5 The research and development contract cannot be allocated to any legally standardised type of contract under German law. In literature and jurisdiction, it is debatable whether it is a mere contract for work (*Werkvertrag*), or a mere contract for services (*Dienstvertrag*) or whether it is a *sui generis* contract. This differentiation is significant because law has formed both of these types of contracts in different ways.

6 Bundesgerichtshof. 2002. *Neue Juristische Wochenschrift*, (2002), 3323.

7 Möffert, F.J. 2008. *Der Forschungs- und Entwicklungsvertrag*. Munich: C.H. Beck.

8 Koch, T. 2009. *Die Haftungsfreizeichnung in Forschungs- und Entwicklungsverträgen*. Baden-Baden: Nomos.

9 Möffert, F.J. 2008. *Der Forschungs- und Entwicklungsvertrag*.

10 Ullrich, H. 1998. 'Zum Werkerfolgsrisiko beim Forschungs- und Entwicklungsvertrag', in *Festschrift für Wolfgang Fikentscher*, edited by B. Grossfeld et al. Tübingen: Mohr Siebeck, 298–328.

11 Plander, H. and Schieck, D. 1990. Forschung als Gegenstand von Werkverträgen, *Recht der Arbeit*, 219.

described.[12] In the case of a dispute, this presentation can be drawn on to interpret the mutual intentions of the parties.

Subject matter The subject matter of the contract can differ completely depending on the objective and form of the project. It can be merely related to tasks (for example carrying out a series of measurements) or merely performance-related (the development of a prototype for instance). In most cases, however, the subject matter is a combination of both elements (for example carrying out a series of measurements and valuating the results in the scope of a report). The description of performance, which is exported to an attachment to the contract in most cases, should be written as precisely as possible, in order to avoid later disputes about the subject matter.

Carrying out the work The individual steps of work are usually divided into time frames and milestones. Depending on the type and scope of the project, the conclusion of the contract is bound to duties to warn and control, as well as duties to report and deliver milestones.[13] In the case of extensive projects, the project is often additionally divided into phases that are supposed to enable the customer to cancel the project in the case of implicative failure.

Remuneration In the field of remuneration, several types of remuneration come into question. The instruments range from non-binding estimation of costs with a subsequent remuneration on a time and material basis, the determination of a programme budget with predetermined breakpoints for the discontinuation or continuation of the project and the reimbursement price with an upper limit, up to a fixed all-inclusive price.[14] Besides these, there are rules to be complied with in the field of awarding public contracts.[15]

When research organisations collaborate with companies to structure prices, the EU Funding Guidelines and particularly the Community Framework for State Aid for Research and Development and Innovation[16] are to be considered.[17]

The rights to the research results Results are usually divided into so-called 'protected' or 'protectable' results and so-called 'non-protected' or 'non-protectable' results. Protected (and protectable) results are primarily those rights that protect intellectual property rights, which cover not only industrial property but also copyright and related protection rights.[18] The area of unprotected

12 Möffert, F.J. 2008. *Der Forschungs- und Entwicklungsvertrag.*

13 Koch, T. 2009. *Die Haftungsfreizeichnung in Forschungs- und Entwicklungsverträgen.*

14 Ullrich, H. 1998. 'Zum Werkerfolgsrisiko beim Forschungs- und Entwicklungsvertrag'.

15 For example, the 'Verordnung PR Nr. 30/53 über die Preise bei öffentlichen Aufträgen vom 21. November 1953 (BAnz. 1953 Nr. 244), die zuletzt durch Artikel 289 der Verordnung vom 25. November 2003 (BGBl. I S. 2304) geändert worden ist' (Regulation PR No. 30/53 about the prices of open contracts), is a public price regulation applicable to public funded contracts in the Federal Republic of Germany. Similar regulations may exist in other European countries.

16 Community framework for state aid for research and development and innovation (2006/C 323/01).

17 According to 3.2.1. of the Community Framework, research contracts that a research organisation carries out on behalf of a company are not to be evaluated as indirect state aid in favour of the company, if one of the following conditions is fulfilled: (1) the research organisation provides its service at market price; or (2) if there is no market price, the research organisation provides its service at a price that reflects its full costs plus a reasonable margin. The consequence of these conditions is that any partial financing on the part of the research organisation within the framework of an R&D contract is prohibited.

18 Götting, H.P. 2007. *Gewerblicher Rechtsschutz*. Munich: C.H. Beck.

results is to a large extent covered by the so-called 'know-how'.[19] Furthermore, one differentiates between 'foreground' and 'background'. 'Background' covers all protected and unprotected knowledge that was already available at the conclusion of the contract. The 'foreground' describes the results developed within the scope of the contract.[20]

An initial question is which rights to the development results the customer should acquire. The customer can acquire either the property and/or a licence. However, it must be determined in advance the extent to which the contractual partners can freely dispose of the development results, if at all.[21] When drawing up the contract, it must also be kept in mind whether, when utilising the development results at a later point in time, the contractor's background will be needed and which rights the contractor should itself maintain, in order to continue to be active in the research sector.[22] When granting access rights, aspects like exclusivity, compensation, time limits, as well as fields of application and spatial limits are to be considered.

Warranty and liability Carrying out R&D projects involves various risks. Regulations concerning warranty and liability initially depend on the legal character of the contract and the underlying statutory law. Besides the warranty rights, the contractor also sees itself exposed to the danger of various claims for damages.[23] Apart from claims for damage due to late fulfilment of the contract, liability relating to the infringement of industrial property rights of third parties or tort claims for damage (for example from the product liability law) are particularly relevant. Whilst the contractor makes an attempt to negotiate a limitation of liability,[24] however, legal restrictions are often to be considered.[25]

Non-disclosure Almost every R&D project requires the non-disclosure of certain confidential contents. As statutory legal protection might still be considered insufficient[26] for the project, it is

19 The definition of the Act (EG) No. 772/2004 of the Commission dated 27 April 2004 has asserted itself as the generally recognised definition. 'Know-how' means a package of non-patented practical information, resulting from experience and testing, which is: (i) secret, that is to say, not generally known or easily accessible, (ii) substantial, that is to say, significant and useful for the production of the contract products, and (iii) identified, that is to say, described in a sufficiently comprehensive manner so as to make it possible to verify that it fulfils the criteria of secrecy and substantiality. In practice, however, the terms are not frequently used in a legal manner. 'Know-how' is then understood as the generic term for 'protected and non-protected' results.

20 Sometimes one also speaks of 'sideground'. This means the results, which were not available prior to the conclusion of the contract, but that were developed fully independently of the project (for example in another institute or a parallel project).

21 In Germany, among others, one must remember §42 of the 'Gesetz über Arbeitnehmererfindungen in der im Bundesgesetzblatt Teil III, Gliederungsnummer 422-1, veröffentlichten bereinigten Fassung, das zuletzt durch Artikel 7 des Gesetzes vom 31. Juli 2009 (BGBl. I S. 2521) geändert worden ist' (Employee Invention Act). This law contains some special regulations for university employees as a consequence of the stated freedom in research and teaching in Article 5 of the Constitution of the Federal Republic of Germany.

22 Winzer, W. 2006. *Forschungs- und Entwicklungsverträge.*

23 See Koch, T. 2009. *Die Haftungsfreizeichnung in Forschungs- und Entwicklungsverträgen.*

24 With research organisations, this is partly obligatory according to statutory stipulations, partly according to ministerial stipulations.

25 See Koch, T. 2009. *Die Haftungsfreizeichnung in Forschungs- und Entwicklungsverträgen.*

26 In Germany, the protection of business and trade secrets is regulated in §§17et seq. of the 'Gesetz gegen den unlauteren Wettbewerb vom 3. Juli 2004 (BGBl. I S. 1414), das zuletzt durch Artikel 2 des Gesetzes vom 29. Juli 2009 (BGBl. I S. 2413) geändert worden ist' (Act against Unfair Practices).

recommended to regulate this area in the contract. In doing so, it must be defined which information is confidential and how the information to be treated as confidential is to be handled. The non-disclosure obligation should also be limited in time.

Other contractual regulations Further, the R&D contract also typically contains regulations on publishing research results, the organisation of the project, as well as termination. Further elements relate to the coming into effect and duration of the contract, applicable law and dispute settlements.

The Co-operation Agreement

Introduction

The trend towards concluding research and development contracts has increased since the middle of the 1980s. The reason for this is the pressure on innovation caused by globalisation, to which companies are exposed. Besides the compelling global motivation, companies primarily expect to save costs and time as well as a dispersion of the possible risks of an R&D co-operation. In addition, especially in co-operations with research organisations and universities,[27] knowledge can be exchanged and foreign innovative potential can be increased and, in turn, the efficiency of the R&D project.[28] If co-operation agreements are concluded by companies on the same economic level, these are summarised as 'horizontal' co-operations. In contrast, agreements between companies on differing production or trading levels are termed 'vertical agreements'.[29] The standard case of this co-operative relationship is the further development of products under the involvement of suppliers. In addition, the co-operation between companies and universities and research organisations represents an exception, because these are usually neither competitors nor suppliers. The form of this type of co-operation is varied. It can be co-operation agreements, syndicates or consortiums. Furthermore, the consequence of such a co-operation can also be a joint venture or the mutual establishment of a company.

Anti-trust Assessment

In contrast to research and development contracts, co-operation agreements regularly contain competition agreements, such as the exclusivity of the co-operation in a certain field of research. National and European anti-trust laws must therefore be taken into consideration. Based on Article 83 Section 3 TEC (now Article 101 Section 3 of the Treaty on the Functioning of the European Union), the EU Commission has passed some Block Exemption Regulations, which are relevant for research and development contracts. Here, horizontal and vertical R&D co-operations are differentiated: Block Exemption Regulation No. 2659/2000[30] on R&D contracts is applicable to horizontal co-operations. Block Exemption Regulation No. 2790/1999 for vertical agreements[31]

27 In Germany several model contracts exist for such kinds of co-operations: 'Vertragsbausteine Berliner Vertrag'; 'BMWi Mustervertrag für Forschungs- und Entwicklungskooperationen'.

28 Heidinger, F. and Karre, M. 2008. *Forschungs- und Entwicklungsverträge*.

29 Winzer, W. 2006. *Forschungs- und Entwicklungsverträge*.

30 Commission Regulation (EC) No. 2659/2000 of 29 November 2000 on the application of Article 81(3) of the Treaty to categories of research and development agreements.

31 Commission Regulation (EC) No. 2790/1999 of 22 December 1999 on the application of Article 81(3) of the Treaty to categories of vertical agreements and concerted practices.

and Regulation 772/2004 on technology for transfer agreements,[32] are relevant for vertical co-operations whereby the R&D Block Exemption is regarded as applicable to all types of R&D contracts.[33]

The Essential Contents of the Contract

Subject matter The objective of the R&D co-operation is to be defined by the parties. The result of the co-operation can be a product, a process or even simply to gain scientific knowledge.[34]

Implementing the co-operation Besides the assignment of the work to be done, the mutual work programme, as well as a time frame for the individual steps of development, the co-operation agreement contains regulations on the organisation of the consortium. These cover the designation of co-ordinators and sub-project managers and where necessary, regulations covering bodies and their competencies and decision-making.

Non-disclosure The co-operation agreement should contain clear non-disclosure regulations. There are three categories. The first category covers the background the parties brought into the co-operation. Especially when an application for the protection of industrial property rights is taken into consideration, the non-disclosure provisions should be very restrictive. A second category covers the knowledge gained by each party on its own in the course of the co-operation. The third category is the knowledge that both parties have developed jointly.[35] It should also be defined what publications and under what conditions, be it scientific or for marketing reasons, may occur.[36]

Regulations on know-how The property rights to the development results have to be regulated. Should the parties not reach a contractual agreement, then the statutory provisions of company law may apply.[37]

The rights to know-how and to intellectual property are divided into several categories: the 'background', 'foreground gathered by each party separately' and 'mutually developed foreground'.[38] The first two categories are relatively simple to regulate. The party that brought background into the co-operation should generally retain all rights to it. Likewise, the party that

---

32 Commission Regulation (EC) No. 772/2004 of 27 April 2004 on the application of Article 81(3) of the Treaty to categories of technology transfer agreements.

33 Rosenberger, H-P. 2010. *Verträge über Forschung und Entwicklung*. Munich: Heymanns.

34 Federal Ministry for Education and Research. 2009. *Umgang mit Know-how in internationalen FuE-Kooperationen*. Bonn, Berlin.

35 *Ibid.*

36 Winzer, W. 2006. *Forschungs- und Entwicklungsverträge*.

37 Usually the partners of a research and development co-operation form a private partnership under the German Civil Code ('Gesellschaft bürgerlichen Rechts – GbR'). According to the provisions of the BGB, the contributions of the partners become joint assets. This means that no partner acquires the sole ownership of the development results. According to §719 BGB, the company assets underlie a jointly held commitment (*Gesamthandseigentum*). The parties can therefore only dispose of the company's assets mutually. No one partner can dispose of its share of the company's assets and the individual items belonging to them alone. This joint property, together with the solely joint utilisation of the development results, only rarely corresponds with the mutual will of the parties. The statutory regulations can, however, be waived in a contract.

38 See the sub-section of this chapter entitled 'The rights to the research results' for the definition of 'background' and 'foreground'.

came to a development result alone should become the sole owner.[39] In contrast, the regulation of mutually developed knowledge is problematic. In this case, the parties can agree that either the knowledge solely belongs to one partner according to certain criteria or it should belong to both parties involved. The latter case is extremely difficult particularly in the case of mutually existing patents and demands extreme contractual precision, above all when considering possible consent and mutual powers of disposal.[40]

The question about which access rights which party should be given must be isolated from the question of the transfer of ownership. On the one hand, the use during the scope of the project and the use after completion of the mutual project should be differentiated. On the other hand, it must be differentiated whether the use is regulated by the background or by the individually or mutually developed foreground. In this case, primarily the terms of the licence for using the background and the non-mutual foreground by the other partner – as well as by affiliates – need to be regulated.[41]

Liability Normally, the parties waive all claims for damage that could arise in correlation with the activities in the scope of the co-operation, unless the parties act intentionally or grossly negligently.[42] Furthermore, the parties also frequently exempt each other from indirect damage like loss of profits, and so on, whereby, the breach of non-disclosure regulations is often excluded.

Cancellation The contract should also contain terms concerning under which conditions the co-operation and participation of a partner can be voluntarily or involuntarily cancelled. Apart from the definition of grounds for cancellation, all rights and duties of the partners after cancellation of the co-operation should be defined in the contract, in order to prevent disputes after the co-operation has ended. This applies not only to the use of the results, but also to the aspects of absorption of the costs and liability.[43]

Other contractual regulations Further elements of the contract relate to regulations about the coming into effect and duration of the contract, applicable law, as well as dispute settlements.

The Consortium Agreement

Introduction

In order to differentiate the consortium agreement from the co-operation agreement just described, only those co-operations are addressed here that are concluded in operational relationship to public funding. The basis for the government to grant a benefit is an approval letter or a grant agreement, which regulates the rights and duties of the recipient of the grant in return for receiving public funds. In the grant conditions, which are part of the grant agreement, the individual beneficiaries

39 Federal Ministry for Education and Research. 2009. *Umgang mit Know-how in internationalen FuE Kooperationen.*

40 Winzer, W. 2006. *Forschungs- und Entwicklungsverträge.*

41 In the framework of co-operations, the Community Framework for State Aid for Research and Development and Innovation (2006/C 323/01) is to be adhered to in the case of collaboration of companies and research organisations.

42 Winzer, W. 2006. *Forschungs- und Entwicklungsverträge.*

43 Federal Ministry for Education and Research. 2009. *Umgang mit Know-how in internationalen FuE Kooperationen.*

of a promoted project are frequently required to regulate their mutual collaboration in the scope of the promoted total project with each other in a consortium agreement. In many cases, the funding body also influences the contents of the contract by means of auxiliary conditions. A large share of the European funding is awarded in the scope of the Seventh Framework Programme (FP7) of the European Union; at least the general conditions will be illustrated below.

Seventh Framework Programme (FP7)

Grant agreement The grant conditions and the process of awarding are stated in Regulation No. 1906/2006.[44] Besides that, the Commission also has several accompanying legal documents.[45] The grant is awarded by a bilateral agreement, the so-called 'grant agreement'. The grant agreement comprises a relatively short 'core contract' with three to seven annexes.[46] Annex I contains the description of work, Annex II the general conditions, Annex III specific provisions related to the funding scheme or activity, Annex IV and V accession of beneficiaries and new beneficiaries, Annex VI and VII financial statement and terms of reference for the certificate on the financial statements. In addition to that, the grant agreement can contain project-related special clauses, which are listed in the list of special clauses.[47] The grant agreement is only concluded between the Commission and the co-ordinator. The participants in the project, however, enter the core contract by signing a separate declaration of accession, 'Form C', which becomes part of the contract as Annex IV.

FP7 grant agreement – Annex II general conditions According to Article 24 of the Rules of Participation, all of those involved in the project should conclude a consortium agreement. This should primarily regulate

> (a) the internal organisation of the consortium; (b) the distribution of the Community financial contribution; (c) rules on dissemination, use and access rights, additional to those in Chapter III and to the provisions in the grant agreement; (d) the settlement of internal disputes including cases of abuse of power; (e) liability, indemnification and confidentiality arrangements.

Annex II of the Model Contract substantiates and explains these rules in more detail. Annex II begins with a definition, in part A, of the regulations on the implementation of the project, Part B contains the financial provisions of the implementation of the project, Part C contains the rules on intellectual property rights, use and dissemination, then the final provisions follow. The role of the co-ordinator is defined in II.2 Annex II. In Article 8 of the Core Contract, it is already stated that all communication between the consortium and the Commission goes via the co-ordinator. In addition, the co-ordinator must ascertain that all partners enter the consortium and assume all rights and duties arising from the grant agreement (Art. 1 Sec. 1 of the core agreement). The co-ordinator thus stands in the centre of the consortium and represents the bridge between the consortium and the Commission. The responsibilities of the beneficiaries are documented in II.2.4 of Annex II in the form of general provisions. Besides the obligation to conclude a consortium agreement, it is

44 Regulation (EC) No. 1906/2006 of the European Parliament and of the Council of 18 December 2006 laying down the rules for the participation of undertakings, research centres and universities in actions under the Seventh Framework Programme and for the dissemination of research results (2007–2013).

45 See http://cordis.europa.eu/fp7/find-doc_en.html [accessed: 30 April 2011].

46 http://cordis.europa.eu/fp7/calls-grant-agreement_en.html [accessed: 30 April 2011].

47 http://cordis.europa.eu/fp7/calls-grant-agreement_en.html#standard_ga [accessed: 30 April 2011].

stated that the partners fulfil the contract 'jointly and severally vis-à-vis the Union'. Furthermore, II.3 contains further specific performance obligations of each beneficiary.

Part B contains the financial provisions. It contains regulations about which costs of the project can be reimbursed, to what upper limit a project will be funded, which income is to be regarded as project income and how the financial contribution of the Community is defined. In addition, the Commission retains the right to carry out controls and sanctions, in order to safeguard the correctness of the settlement. As well as that, II 18.5 contains a right to a reduction if the project is not carried out or carried out poorly, only in part or late. To safeguard the claims for reimbursement, the Commission states in II 20, there is a guarantee fund that contains a share of the funding of every beneficiary. The Commission itself excludes all liability claims against the recipients of the funding.[48] Furthermore, the recipients are obliged to exempt the EU from liability towards third parties resulting from the use of project results. The same applies with regard to the breach of third party rights.[49]

With regards to the intellectual property rights, the following applies: as stated in the 5th and 6th Framework Programme, the party that developed the foreground compiled in the project is entitled to the ownership of it.[50] Insofar as the foreground was mutually developed by several parties, those project partners are entitled to it.[51] The parties should agree on regulations concerning the distribution and deployment of these mutual rights. Should the parties still not have agreed upon such respective regulations, then requirements are stated in II 26 No. 2 Annex II, according to which, every owner can award non-exclusive licences to third parties. The partners are obliged to protect the results to an appropriate extent. If they do not fulfil this obligation, then the commission has a subsidiary right to registration.[52] The parties are also obliged to use their foreground, whereby, however, commercial utilisation is only obligatory if it is meaningful from an economical point of view.[53] Furthermore, the parties are obliged to disseminate the foreground. However, in doing so, the protection of intellectual property rights should not be thwarted.[54] Therefore the other partners are to be informed of any measures of distribution 45 days in advance.

Every project partner must grant the other partners access rights to the foreground, if the requesting participant 'needs' that access in order to carry out the project. These access rights will be granted free of charge.[55] Accordingly, the same applies to the background, unless the contractual partner provided that the party concerned is entitled to grant them, or the parties have not come to any other agreement prior to accession.[56]

Insofar as the use of own knowledge and protection rights is necessary for the foreground of another party, the parties should grant them access to it. This right of utilisation shall be granted at fair and reasonable conditions, or free of charge, and requires the separate agreement in the consortium agreement.[57] The same applies to the background, insofar as it is necessary for the

48 II 42 No. 1 Annex II.

49 II 42 No. 2 and 3 Annex II.

50 II 26 No. 1 Annex II.

51 II 26 No. 2 Annex II.

52 II 28 Annex II.

53 European Commission. *Guide to Intellectual Property Rules for FP 7 Projects.* [Online]. Available at: http://cordis.europa.eu/fp7/find-doc_en.html [accessed: 30 April 2011].

54 II 30 No. 2 Annex I.I.

55 II 33 No.1 Annex II.

56 II 33 No. 2 Annex II.

57 II 34 No. 1 Annex II.

utilisation of the foreground.[58] This rule also applies according to Annex II 32 No. 3 for affiliates, whereby exceptions can be made for affiliates with domicile outside the EU and associated states.

Model consortium agreement The rules in the framework of Annex II give the partners a lot of freedom of disposition, which can be filled out in the framework of the consortium agreement. Some initiatives have thus developed model consortium agreements, which above all differ in relation to the intellectual property rights approach. In the aerospace sector, the DESCA (Development of a Simplified Consortium Agreement) model,[59] which was developed by several organisations from the research sector, and the IMG4 model,[60] which was generated by the aerospace industry, are to be named. The IMG4 model contract is based on the DESCA model and is, apart from a few IPR provisions, to a large extent identical with the DESCA model. Additionally, it includes an agreement to loan the material and equipment developed in the project.[61]

List of References

The AeroSpace and Defense Industries Association of Europe 2008. *Facts and Figures*. [Online]. Available at: http://asd-europe.org/site/fileadmin/user_upload/publications/ff2008-2009-01564-02.pdf [accessed: 31 April 2011].

Bundesgerichtshof 2002. *Neue Juristische Wochenschrift*, (2002), 3323.

European Commission 2010. *Analysis and Market Data*. [Online]. Available at: http://ec.europa.eu/enterprise/sectors/aerospace/market-data/index_en.htm [accessed: 21 February 2010].

Federal Ministry for Education and Research 2009. *Umgang mit Know-how in internationalen FuE- Kooperationen*. Bonn, Berlin.

Götting, H.P. 2007. *Gewerblicher Rechtsschutz*. Munich: C.H. Beck.

Heidinger, F. and Karre, M. 2008. *Forschungs- und Entwicklungsverträge*. Vienna: LexisNexis.

Koch, T. 2009. *Die Haftungsfreizeichnung in Forschungs- und Entwicklungsverträgen*. Baden-Baden: Nomos.

Möffert, F.J. 2008. *Der Forschungs- und Entwicklungsvertrag*. Munich: C.H. Beck.

Plander, H. and Schieck, D. 1990. Forschung als Gegenstand von Werkverträgen, *Recht der Arbeit*, 219.

Rosenberger, H-P. 2006. *Verträge über Forschung und Entwicklung*. Munich: Heymanns.

Ullrich, H. 1998. 'Zum Werkerfolgsrisiko beim Forschungs- und Entwicklungsvertrag', in *Festschrift für Wolfgang Fikentscher*, edited by B. Grossfeld et al. Tübingen: Mohr Siebeck, 298–328.

Winzer, W. 2006. *Forschungs- und Entwicklungsverträge*. Munich: C.H. Beck.

58 II 34 No. 2 Annex II.

59 The DESCA Core Group. 2007. *DESCA – The simplified FP7 Model Consortium Agreement*. [Online]. Available at: http://www.desca-fp7.eu/ [accessed: 30 April 2011].

60 ASD-IMG4. 2008. *IMG-4 Model Consortium Agreement*. [Online]. Available at: http://www.aerosme.com/news/article.asp?article=250 [accessed: 30 April 2011].

61 A comparison of all model consortium agreements is available on the website of the IPR Helpdesks: http://www.ipr-helpdesk.org/ [accessed: 30 April 2011].

Chapter 20
Contract Management

Mustapha Elriz and Peter Newman

General

This chapter examines contract management and how it is implemented. Contract management is the process which ensures that both the buyer and contractor fully meet their respective obligations as efficiently and effectively as possible, so as to meet the business and operational objectives required from the contract. It also helps the buyer achieve all of the benefits and expectations it envisioned when executing the contract.

In order for a buyer of a satellite to minimise programme risks, it implements controls on the contractor where such controls are delineated in the contractual documents. Most businesses limit their risks to areas that they can control; however, in the satellite industry the major items that form the significant part of the buyer's business are not always under the control of the buyer, namely the production of a very high technology product (the 'satellite') and a controlled explosion ('the launch vehicle'). To mitigate risks, the buyer implements controls on the contractor through the contractual documents. These controls are basically achieved by monitoring the contractor's performance at all times during the design, manufacturing, integration and testing of the satellite. The controls and monitoring regimes implemented by the buyer are the basis of contract management. However, in the case of the launch vehicle there is no such in-depth monitoring, as the Launch Services Provider (LSP) only provides a 'delivery service' for the satellite into orbit, which means that the buyer is not purchasing any hardware. It is possible to understand the launch services as a sophisticated courier service where the LSP is given a 'package' for delivery to a specific 'address' in space.

The foundations for contract management are laid out in stages prior to a contract award and include the procurement process and contract negotiations. For a satellite, the contract management plan starts with the 'Request for Proposal' (RFP) process in that the RFP includes a pro-forma contract and Statement of Work (SOW) as well as all the technical requirements. These documents should be prepared by those who will be required to monitor the contractor's execution of the contract, both technically and administratively, throughout the life of the contract. This is achieved by the inclusion of the pro-forma contract articles, among others, which lay out how the buyer intends to monitor the contractor's performance, make payments to the contractor, handle changes, deal with any disputes, expected warrantees, damages that may be assessed in the case of late delivery, a detailed acceptance criteria and, perhaps uniquely to a satellite contract, on-orbit performance incentives.[1]

The RFP process for the launch vehicle is very different from that of a satellite. In reality there is no reason to issue a formal RFP, as is the case for a satellite, as a letter to all the potential LSPs outlining the basic physical parameters of the satellite, the date that the launching services are

1 Performance incentives and warranty paybacks are basically the same. The difference is which of the buyer or contractor retains the amounts put at risk on the performance of the satellite over its contracted 'Operational Service Life'.

required and the satellite's final orbital location, is all that is required. Issuing a pro-forma contract to a LSP is unnecessary as each LSP has its own contract, all with similar terms and conditions, and SOW which are virtually non-negotiable except for some of the programmatical and commercial aspects of the contract and SOW.[2]

The Statement of Work (SOW) is a high-level narrative description of all the required work needed to be performed under the satellite contract or Launch Services Agreement (LSA). It stipulates and describes all the work elements, services and time frames required by the buyer and how the programme will be managed and monitored. It also defines the tasks to be accomplished by the contractor in a clear, concise and meaningful manner. It contains a detailed list of all documentation required to be provided during the manufacturing and on-orbit phase of the contract. This list of documentation is commonly known as the Contract Data Requirement List (CDRL). The SOW is normally prepared by the technical, commercial and administrative members of the buyer's team.

Prior to entering into satellite negotiations with the bidders, the buyer's programme team will define the contract management plan where such team should include the individuals who would be responsible for the various elements of the programme. In a satellite programme the buyer would appoint its programme manager who, as the title suggests, carries the buyer's responsibility for the success of the programme and who would normally report directly to senior management of the buyer's company. The programme manager is supported by technical experts who would report to the programme manager and assume programme responsibilities for monitoring the contractor's performance on the major elements of a satellite, which would include, as an example, the bus, payload, propulsion system, power subsystem, as well as a quality audit team. Administratively, the programme manager is supported by a contract administrator[3] who would assume responsibility for the day-to-day commercial aspects of the contract.

The programme manager for the satellite should also be the programme manager for the LSA as the launch services are a significant and integral part of the programme.

In order to have an effective contract management team, it is essential that the designated contract administrator be an integral part of the proposal evaluation team and a member of the negotiating team. By participating in negotiations the contract administrator will be in the position to establish relationships with the contractor's team and have insight into how the terms and conditions of the contract and the SOW were developed. This is essential as the contract administrator will have to manage the contract and from time to time will have to work with and explain the contract language and, being an active and integral member of the negotiating team, will have the understanding of the meaning behind the language and therefore will be able to act and interpret as the parties intended as and when required throughout the life of the contract.

For the buyers contract management team to be effective it is necessary that the contract administrator and the programme manager have a good working relationship and their areas of responsibilities and reporting are clearly defined. In the textbook case the contract administrator becomes the assistant to the programme manager and handles the commercial and contractual aspects of the contracts. The contract administrator must be aware of all the commitments and obligations made under the contract and must ensure that both the contractor and the buyer live up to those commitments and obligations throughout the life of the contract. The contract administrator

2 The launch services contracts provided by each of the LSPs are virtually identical in form and substance.

3 A 'Contract Administrator' is very often referred to as 'Contract Manager'.

should be involved in all official meetings held between the buyer and the contractor and be the buyer's note-taker for the meeting.[4]

As soon as the satellite contract has been executed, it is the responsibility of the programme manager to undertake the work associated with securing the launch services, as the satellite characteristics and delivery requirements required by the launch provider in order to make a bid for the launch services are defined in the satellite contract.

Access to Work

Included in the pro-forma contract of the satellite RFP must be language that clearly states the buyer's requirement of being able to access all work performed under the contract. This requirement is an absolute necessity and failure for a bidder to comply with this requirement could be sufficient reason to eliminate the bidder from any further consideration. The continual technical monitoring by the buyer of any satellite programme is an essential element in managing its technical and programmatic risk. This access to the work, either at the contractor's or sub-contractor's facilities, is an essential element of the buyer's contract management plan and this access can be either with its own experts or by technical experts retained by the buyer. In many cases the buyer's experts are supplemented with specialised technical consultants to cover areas where unique knowledge is required or where access restrictions, due to export controls, are imposed by the manufacturer. If access is prevented due to export controls, the contractor should be prepared to cover the cost of a consultant, selected by the buyer, to inspect specific work. It is understood that access by the buyer and its representatives to some of the contractor's facilities may be restricted due to security restrictions and/or government controls.

The buyer should also attain the right to attend all technical meanings and reviews of the contractor and its sub-contractors related to the project schedule and management, engineering, design, manufacturing, integration and testing of the work. All this allows the buyer's representatives insight into the status of the programme which is an essential part of contract management and risk mitigation.

In the case of the LSA, monitoring of the day-to-day performance of the LSP is not possible and would not be permitted. Launch vehicle technology is restricted for reasons of national security and other governmental restrictions and by the LSP for the reason that no hardware is being provided under the LSA to the buyer. It is also the case that launch vehicle sub-systems and component parts are procured in batches and it is not known until approximately six months prior to a launch which sub-system or component parts will be incorporated into the launch vehicle that will provide the launch services. However, there are many events during the LSA such as preparing and updating the Interface Control Document (ICD), Technical Interface Meetings (TIMS), Programme Review Meetings (PRM), coupled loads analysis and the delivery of several reports, all as defined in the LSA SOW, to be delivered to the buyer that will give an indication as to the progress of the LSA.

---

4 The official record of meetings are normally prepared by the contractor's contract administer, approved by the programme manager and submitted to the buyer for approval and/or comment.

Key Personnel

The bidder's proposal should identify the personnel, complete with résumés, who would be assigned to key programme positions such as the programme manager, chief technical authority, contracts manager/administrator, systems manager and so on. The buyer must have the right to request a change to the identified personnel, if it considers a particular position has been staffed with a person of questionable abilities or experience for that particular position. The contractor should, as soon reasonably possible, retain the initially identified and agreed team for the duration of the programme.

Notice

It is important that the contract identify the individuals to whom formal correspondence and notices should be addressed, as well as those who have the right to sign all formal correspondence on behalf of the buyer and the contractor. Any notice or correspondence received, signed by other than those identified individuals, cannot be considered formal correspondence and therefore would have no force or effect under the contract. The contract administrator would be responsible for maintaining a complete and comprehensive file of all correspondence and notices sent or received to or from the parties.[5]

Delivery

The delivery schedule is of critical importance in satellite and launch vehicle contracts. Should either the satellite or launch vehicle be delivered late, the consequences to the buyer could be so significant as to place the buyer into deep financial difficulties to the point where the buyer could be placed in receivership.[6] As an indication of the satellite contractor's confidence in its committed delivery schedule, the contractor should accept pre-agreed liquidated damages that would apply and be payable to the buyer, in the event that the satellite was delivered late. The percentage of the contract price that the contractor puts at risk on the delivery of the satellite varies from programme to programme. A low percentage could indicate a higher risk whereas a higher percentage may demonstrate the contractor's confidence in its delivery schedule. It is obvious that the liquidated damages may not totally compensate the buyer for its losses for the delivery of a late satellite, and the liquidated damages paid out by the contractor are minimal when one considers that an extended programme has a significant cost impact on the contractor.

LSPs do not normally accept liquidated damages in the LSA and do not apply them if the satellite is delivered late to the launch site. Getting the satellite and launch vehicle to be available to each other at the launch site at the time required by the overall programme plan is perhaps the most challenging aspect of any satellite programme.

The programme plan must take into consideration possible delays caused by either or both the satellite contractor and the LSP. Delays caused by the satellite contractor during the construction

5 E-mail is a convenient method of communicating but may not be acceptable in a strictly legal situation. The acceptability of e-mail communications should be determined prior to any formal correspondence being initiated.

6 This would be more applicable to a first time satellite buyer or to a small time satellite operator looking to replace an existing satellite.

and testing phase of the programme can result in the late delivery of the satellite to the launch site and a subsequent launch delay. A problem with the satellite can also develop at the launch site, requiring corrective action at the launch site. If the problem cannot be corrected at the launch site, the satellite will have to be shipped back to the contractor's plant. This particular delay, although quite rare, can result in a loss of the launch slot which can result in a significant and potentially disastrous delay to the entire programme.

Launch vehicle delays can also have serious implications to the programme. The most serious, and one for which there is no work-around plan,[7] is when there is a launch failure of a launch taking place one or two launches prior to the intended launch of the satellite. Following a failed launch, there is a detailed investigation into the cause of the failure and, until the cause is determined and any recommendations from the review board have been implemented, launches cannot resume. A launch delay can also be caused by the late delivery of a co-passenger satellite to the launch site.[8] A technical problem with a launch vehicle, launch vehicle ground equipment, range support or the weather can also result in a delay, but these tend to be less significant but do extend the satellite contractor's time at the launch site.

It is essential therefore to address the real possibility of a late delivery of either the satellite or launch vehicle in both the satellite and launch vehicle contracts and how the effects of such delays will be addressed.

Payment

The satellite pro-forma contract issued with the RFP should provide the bidders with information on how the buyer intends to make payments to the contractor. One of the best methods for monitoring the performance of any contractor is through achievement payment milestones. It is recommended that milestone payments be tied to the completion of a specific task and not to a specific calendar date, where no measurable task has been assigned to such date. The pro-forma contract should advise the bidders that it will only accept achievement payment milestones and that there could be up to, as an example, five milestone payments per month where the master programme plan identified completion of five specific tasks in any particular month. It may be that only one or two specific tasks will be completed in any one month, therefore only one or two milestone payments would be possible for that time period.

The bidder's payment plan will be based on a particular cash flow that it requires to remain cash neutral throughout the programme. During negotiations this cash flow will be discussed and modified to be acceptable to both the bidder and the buyer. The contract should contain a provision that prevents the contractor from ever exceeding the agreed cumulative cash flow in the payment milestones schedule. This is a positive provision for both the buyer and the contractor as should the contractor fall behind on a particular payment milestone, but complete a payment milestone scheduled to be completed after the current monthly period, it can be paid for the advanced milestone provided that the cumulative amount to be paid to the contractor at that particular monthly period does not exceed the negotiated cash flow for that point in time. This allows the contractor to be paid

7 Some LSPs have arrangements with other LSPs that if the selected LSP cannot launch the satellite for any reason the other LSP would launch the satellite. However, this arrangement must be delineated in the LSA and there is a cost for the back-up plan.

8 Some launch vehicles have the ability to launch more than one satellite at a time and the entire launch mission is designed for specific satellites and if one of the designated satellites is not available for its specific launch the launch may not take place.

for work that has been completed and, therefore, does not slow the programme down, which could be the case if the contractor placed additional programme resources on completing the outstanding milestone to the detriment of completing other parts of the work. This also assists the buyer relative to financing, as it can be determined at the outset of the programme as to how it can fund the programme and when monies may be required from a lender.

All invoices submitted following completion of a payment milestone should contain a certification by the contractor that the work associated with the milestone has been completed. The buyer will need time to verify the invoice and, if the work has not been completed to the reasonable satisfaction of the buyer, the buyer must notify the contractor that it does not consider the milestone complete, and advise the contractor in what ways the work is incomplete. Again, a timely response from the buyer will keep the programme on track.

When a payment milestone has not been totally completed, the buyer, at its sole discretion, could decide to make a partial payment of the payment milestone. The contractor should not have the contractual right to request a partial payment, however, if the situation should arise, making partial payments can help the relationship between the parties. Partial payments should never become the expected.

It is useful to show the contract price and delivery schedule broken down into major elements of the programme for both the benefit of the buyer and contractor's audit functions. In the case where a change to the contract is being made, and breakdown is included in the contract, the buyer can ensure that only that element where the change is being made is affected by such change.

In the case of the LSA, where a service is being provided, there are few, if any, achievement milestones. LSPs normally insist on calendar payments. It is sometimes possible to have a payment following launch, which is payable even if the launch is a failure.

Reports

The contractor's master programme schedule should be the vehicle by which the buyer monitors the contractor's performance and should be the basis of a monthly status report to the buyer. This master programme schedule must include all the activities, major and minor, that will occur throughout the entire production and testing phases of the satellite and up to final delivery. So as to understand the progress of the work, the monthly report should include the accomplishments for the month being reported, which would include all elements of the programme, such as product assurance, system engineering and design status, integration and testing, outstanding problems status, a listing of all meetings taken place in the reporting period and so on. A report on outstanding actions and their anticipated completion dates should be included together with other technical areas, such as link budgets and end to end performance of the satellite and so on. The list of payment milestones invoiced during the reporting period together with a list of payment milestones expected to be invoiced in the next reporting period should be included.

Senior management of the contractor should also be aware of the status of the programme and its problems. To ensure that this is the case, a quarterly senior management review should be convened where the attendees include both the buyer's and contractor's senior management.[9] This review would enable the contractor to explain to the buyer's senior management existing problem areas, or anticipated problems, and to obtain the contractor's senior management's commitment

9 For maximum exposure to the programme, the CEOs or equivalents of both parties should be in attendance for at least a part of the review.

to the programme in resolving the identified problems. It has happened that a programme management team has hidden certain problems from its senior management and, by convening a senior management review, this should be prevented. It also provides the buyer's management with some comfort in knowing that the contractor's senior management is involved and has an interest in the programme.

Change Management

A change or waiver/deviation request can be defined as any request made by the contractor, submitted in writing to the buyer, that identifies parameters or conditions detailed in the technical requirements or in the contract terms and conditions, which will add or delete work, affect the design of the satellite, time of delivery, or affect any other requirement of the contract. These change requests can range from minor changes to significant changes that may drastically alter the performance of the satellite.

A typical change request can request a change to a technical parameter or parameters, reduce the scope of testing, modifying procedures or processes and schedule adjustments. Change requests should only be made formally through the notification requirements, and should include a written proposal and description of the impact of the change to the deliverable item including any cost increase or decrease to the contract price. The contractor cannot proceed with any change that would affect the contracted satellite performance or any other requirement under the contract without prior written approval from the buyer.

There are normally two levels of changes – Class 1 (major) and Class 2 (minor) – that should be considered. Class 1 change signifies a change that impacts compliance with contractual requirements. Classification of a Class 1 change related to a satellite procurement contract could be, as an example, any baseline performance beyond specified tolerance, reliability and maintainability characteristics, weight, balance, moment of inertia, contract costs, incentives, fees, schedules, guarantees, or delivery schedule and so forth.[10]

A Class 2 change could signify any change to which the criteria governing Class 1 changes does not apply and must be made available to the buyer for review, but buyer approval is not required.

A deviation can be defined as a specific written authorisation, granted prior to the manufacture of a contract item, to depart from a specific performance or design requirement contained in an agreed specification, drawing or technical document for a number of units or a period of time. Major deviations can be those affecting performance, durability, reliability, inter-changeability, operation, mass, life and safety, and so on and must be submitted to the buyer for approval.

A waiver can be defined as a specific written authorisation from the buyer to accept a non-conforming item, which during manufacture or after having been submitted for inspection/test, is found to depart from specified requirements but is nonetheless acceptable for the satellite, or after rework by an approved method. Major waivers affecting a contracted item and performance must be submitted to the buyer for approval.

It is important to set deadlines in the contract related to the time frames that must be maintained for notification by the buyer of its acceptance or rejection of any contractor-proposed change or waiver/deviation. If there is a disagreement on the change or waiver/deviation, for any reason, the contractor must proceed with the contract as unchanged.

---

10 A Class 1 change should result is some benefit to the buyer as the satellite's contracted performance may not be achieved. This benefit will have to be negotiated and could be financial or programmatic.

The buyer always has the right to order work in addition to the work provided under the contract, provided the work is within the general scope of the work under the contract, or it has the right to dispense with or change the whole or any part of the work or schedules defined under the contract. If any buyer-instigated order causes an increase or decrease in the contract price, or the time required for the completion of the work, or affects any other provision of the contract, an adjustment must be made to the contract price, the delivery schedule or both as applicable, and to any other provisions as may be affected by such change.

Acceptance

The contract must make it clear that acceptance is only granted following final delivery of a satellite that meets the system performance requirements. At no other time in the programme should any form of acceptance be granted.[11] This may be unique to a satellite programme, but for a satellite to be delivered on-orbit, the only time that the buyer will be able to finally test the satellite will be in its on-orbit position. There will be a complete test of the satellite on the ground and the results presented at pre-shipment review. From these results it will be possible to extrapolate the test results expected on-orbit; however, until the measurements are performed, the satellite performance cannot be finalised.

In the case where the satellite is delivered on-ground, the results of the pre-shipment review will determine whether acceptance can be granted. In this case there must also be a test procedure in place for testing the satellite following launch.[12]

A clear process and prerequisite for acceptance of the satellite must be included in the contract, including a calculation to be applied in the event the satellite has less than its contracted performance and/or capacity.

There is no acceptance of the launch services. The launch is either successful or a failure. In the case of a failure the buyer will resort to the launch insurance for compensation.

Warranty

For reasons that are obvious normal warranty provisions for other types of equipment and products are not possible for a satellite after launch. Nonetheless, the contractor can implement some corrective action from the ground through software uploads; however, a repair to hardware is not possible. The RFP pro-forma contract should clearly state that the buyer expects the contractor to support the satellite throughout its operational lifetime. This support can be provided by the uploading of modified software and/or implementing a ground-based system solution and/ or making recommendations or implementing changes to satellite operational procedures. The contract documents should detail the procedures to be followed in the event of a problem with the satellite and the expected response time from the contractor. As the contractor will most likely

11 If an acceptance is given to any part of the work at any time prior to a final acceptance, and that part of the work should fail or provide less than expected performance following such acceptance, any recourse that the buyer may have had related to that part of the work may no longer be enforceable or applicable.

12 If the on-orbit testing of a satellite delivered on-ground and accepted on-ground does not meet the expected results, the buyer may not have any recourse to the contractor, but rather may be in a position to make a claim under any launch and on-orbit insurance policy.

benefit from any repair, through the performance incentive plan, the contractor's cost for any support after acceptance should not be passed on to the buyer.

Another part of the contract management responsibilities is to ensure that the satellite is designed, manufactured and tested to the latest industry standards. If an on-orbit satellite, similar to the satellite being manufactured for the buyer, exhibits a loss of performance or experiences any failures, the contractor must implement changes to the buyer's satellite prior to launch such that the problem does not exist on the buyer's satellite.[13]

Performance Incentives

As part of contract management, the buyer has to mitigate risks to the best of its ability. Satellite programmes carry a very high risk through the use of complex technologies, protracted deliveries and on-orbit performance. Performance incentives can be seen to address the uncertainty of the reliability and performance of a satellite. From the satellite buyer's perspective, performance incentives serve to incentivise the contractor to deliver a product that meets or exceeds contractual specifications and to provide on-orbit support. The performance of a satellite is determined during its on-orbit operation, but the ability of the contractor to repair any failure or non-conformance of an on-orbit satellite is extremely limited. Consequently, the incentive payments are meant to influence the contractor during the design and build process so as to produce a reliable satellite.

Through on-orbit incentives, the contractor must retain some responsibility and financial risk for the performance of their product and, thereby, have a direct financial incentive to construct and deliver a reliable satellite. All the time the contractor has money at risk during the operational phase, it will have a vested interest in providing adequate on-orbit support over the operational lifetime of the satellite.

Dispute Resolution

During the effective lifetime of the contract, which for satellites can be as long as 18 years, three years of construction and 15 years on-orbit, there will be disagreements between the buyer and the contractor that will need resolving so as to not jeopardise the delivery of the satellite or its performance on-orbit. It is therefore necessary to include a dispute resolution article in the contract, which clearly lays out a process and time frame for the resolution of any disagreements. One method to resolve these disagreements is through an escalation process ending with the buyer's and contractor's senior executives ultimately responsible for the programme finding an acceptable resolution. If a resolution to any disagreement cannot be reached within the timeframe allocated, an arbitration process, also to be defined in the contract, should be implemented.

Conclusion

There are many factors that go into the making of a successful satellite programme and clearly two of those factors are having a good programme management plan and team, and a contract that

13 If a known problem on an existing satellite, launched or unlaunched, is not rectified on the buyer's satellite, any launch and on-orbit insurance policy coverage may be restricted.

clearly defines the obligations of both parties. Both these factors require extensive planning from the time the programme is conceived up to the delivery of the satellite and continuing thereafter for the satellite's on-orbit lifetime.

A programme plan cannot be developed on the fly and the basis of the plan, with its details, should be included in the satellite RFP in order for the potential contractor to understand how the buyer plans to monitor the contractor's performance and the documentation the buyer will require the contractor to deliver throughout the programme in order to manage it. A master programme plan must be developed that addresses all aspects of the programme even if some of the items on the plan are not a contractual obligation identified in the satellite contract such as launch vehicle related issues and interfaces.

Communication and respect between the respective programme managers is a critical element toward the success of any programme. Frequent and meaningful meetings between key members of the parties' teams can add to the success of a programme and responding to and resolving action items in a timely manner will go a long way in achieving the delivery commitments.

As with the programme plan, it is necessary for the potential contractor to see the terms and conditions that the buyer plans to impose on the contractor prior to the submission of a proposal to the buyer in order for the bidder to address the risks that it will be expected to undertake should it be successful. Naturally these terms and conditions will be negotiated but the buyer must ensure that the final contract terms and conditions take the programme plan into consideration and provide the buyer with the necessary recourses should any problems arise during the course of the programme and to minimise programme risks.

It is essential that the SOW, technical requirements and the contractual terms and conditions are clear and unambiguous and that the parties understand the meaning and intent of each and every paragraph including the technical requirements. Buyers should not be afraid to add numerous definitions and clarifications throughout the documents that form the contract as this will help alleviate misunderstandings throughout the life of the contract and make for a successful and non-confrontational programme. This is especially important for satellite contracts where the contract can be in effect for 18 to 20 years as the team that conducted the negotiations are probably no longer involved in the contract or even employed by the parties involved. No matter how detailed the contract documents are, there will be disagreements between the parties, but if these disagreements can be controlled and kept unemotional and practical, a satisfactory resolution will be found without resorting to the external remedies available to the parties as provided for in the contract.

List of References

There is no list of references or bibliography for this chapter, nor is one possible. This is a rapidly evolving field dominated by practitioners and not academics. As a result, there is a lack of truly relevant academic literature on the specific area addressed herein. Rather than cite only tangentially related sources, or worse – out of date sources, the authors have chosen not to include a List of References for this chapter. However, the following is kindly offered as related material, in the event the reader wishes to pursue the general topic.

Bender, R. 1998. *Launching and Operating Aatellites: Legal Issues*. La Haye: Martinus Nijhoff, 350.

Droit des activités spatiales: adaptation aux phénomènes de commercialisation et de privatisation, Année 2004, volume 22, CNRS/ University of Bourgogne.

Le droit international de l'espace, Droit de l'espace – télécommunications, observation, navigation, défense, exploration, under the direction of Philippe Achilleas. Brussels: Larcier, 2009, 13–31.

Lyall, F. 1989. *Law and Space Telecommunications*. Aldershot: Dartmouth, 428.

Lyall, F. 2008a. 'Satellite Broadcasting', in *Max Planck Encyclopedia of Public International Law*. Oxford: Oxford University Press.

Lyall, F. 2008b. 'Broadcasting: International Regulation', in *Max Planck Encyclopedia of Public International Law*. Oxford: Oxford University Press.

Lyall, F. and Larsen, P.B. (eds). 2009. *Space Law: A Treatise*. Aldershot: Ashgate.

Ravillon, L. 1997. *Les Télécommunications par satellite – Aspects juridiques*. Dijon: Litec-CREDIMI, 509.

PART IV
Specific Aspects of Space Industry Contracts

Chapter 21
Performance and Warranty Articles in Space Industry Contracts

Ines Scharlach

From Research and Development to Commercial Contracts

Traditionally the space industry was focused on delivering complete satellites, launchers or subsystems (for example pay load, antenna, solar array) to very typical end customers like satellite operators, agencies or governmental bodies. But over the last years, a trend in the space industry has developed taking it beyond its traditional role to now focusing more on the delivery of services via the satellites themselves.[1] This can be seen in the business to business (B2B) and business to government (B2G) environment, but also in the business to private end customer (B2C) environment.

Performance and warranty (defects liability) contract clauses have always played an important role in the space industry, even though one may think they could be almost obsolete since there is not much one can do once the launch vehicle is launched or the satellite is in orbit. So one goal of the traditional space industry these days should be to define clauses about specific performances and processes and means for defects liability in a much more detailed way than ever before, since the customer structure is changing. Generally speaking, performance and warranty fall within the realm of what the other party is liable or responsible for and related questions, such as: can criteria (specific performances and processes) be well enough defined to mitigate sufficiently the risks for the involved companies? And, to what degree is internationalisation, as well as the change of the customer base, impacting those contract clauses or the mindset that was focused on governmental or agency but not on true commercial and competitive dealings?

In order to find an answer, this chapter first briefly covers the legal background of defects liability clauses, with a focus on England and Wales, France and Germany. A description of the contract clauses used today in the space industry then follows. At the end of the chapter a small selection of contract clauses that have been used over the years in the space industry in one way or another are presented.

Definitions and Background

Since the European space industry provides an environment in which English is the business language, but in most cases not the native language, it is quite common that, and mostly underestimated how often, misunderstandings occur due to translation. Similarly the impact of the different legal systems on the industry is often underestimated yet material. Notwithstanding

1 See also ASD-EUROSPACE. 2010. *The European Space Industry in 2009, Facts and Figures*, 14th edition, August 2010, 5.

this, generally speaking individually negotiated contract provisions will prevail over national legislation. But for the sake of completeness, a short and brief overview of the legal situation in England and Wales, France and Germany will be given, following the official definitions of terms often used in conjunction with defect liability.

Some terms are often used incorrectly in common parlance. In an attempt to clarify the situation with respect to correct interpretations, the correct definition of certain terms is given here.

Guarantee

This term means 'to pledge or agree to be responsible for another's debt or contractual performance, if that other person does not pay or perform'.[2] Very often this word is used in conjunction with financial dealings and, therefore, is a bit misleading since it is not limited to financial matters but includes performance guarantees.

Warranty

This term means 'a written statement of good quality of merchandise, clear title to real estate, or that a fact stated in a contract is true'.[3] The word can be used in different ways, e.g. in a real estate contract as well as in contracts where product warranty (product liability) plays a role. This term is generally correct but often misunderstood.

Defect Liability

This describes the situation wherein a defect causes some damage and the party who caused or is responsible for the defect is liable for the pecuniary loss as well as factual damage.

National Legal Regimes / Background

England and Wales English law (that is, the law that pertains to England and Wales) does not contain the concept of defects liability, as in France or Germany, but considers a person who has not performed as promised to be in breach of the contract.[4] The law does not require a faulty action, but a simple mal performance is sufficient to claim, for example, damages from the defaulting party.[5] Since in English contracts clauses basically define the recourse that can be taken, this also applies for defect liability remedies. Consequently one has to differentiate between a breach of a warranty and a breach of a condition.

The difference between a breach of warranty and a breach of a condition is basically that a breach of a condition entitles the infringed party to terminate the contract in total.[6] The defect (which would be the breach) would result in complete non-performance of the contract. Determining if the clause being infringed is a condition is possible because either it will be clearly stated in the clause

2 http://dictionary.law.com/ [accessed 30 April 2011].

3 http://dictionary.law.com/ [accessed 30 April 2011].

4 Bernstorff, C. Graf von. 2002. *Vertragsgestaltung im Auslandsgeschäft, 5. Auflage*. Frankfurt am Main: Fritz Knapp, 142 ff.

5 *Ibid.*, 142 ff.

6 McKendrick, E. 2003. *Contract Law*, 5th edition. London: Palgrave Law Masters, 215 ff.

or it can be interpreted as such. The next lower level of recourse is if the clause being breached is a warranty: then the only recourse for the party is a claim for damages.[7]

France According to French law, the first important differentiation to be made is to determine if there is an obvious defect or a vis caché (hidden defect), since the other party's rights depend upon this differentiation.

If the defect is obvious, the buyer can only either claim for the delivery of a conforming item or rescind the contract.[8] On the other hand, if it is a hidden defect – that is, though the buyer had checked the delivery the defect could not be detected – the buyer has rights, similar to the German defects liability right, which allow the buyer to ask for supplementary performance, to withdraw from the contract or to reduce the purchase price or claim compensation for damages.[9]

Germany Generally speaking, the German Civil Code offers various remedies in case of a defect occurrence e.g. § 437 ff BGB. The baseline for all claims is the fact that delivery of a conforming item is part of the claim for performance of the buyer according to § 433I2 BGB. The defects liability itself usually starts with transfer of the risk to the buyer. At the end of the day the German Civil Code considers a defect a non-conformity of the delivered item, as it was agreed upon during specification of the item.

The remedies in the case of a defect are outlined in BGB § 437 ff: if the item is non-conforming one can either claim supplementary performance, withdraw from the contract, reduce the purchase price or claim compensation for damage. Notwithstanding, German law also entitles the contractual parties to waive all rights with respect to defect liability.[10] Typically this has to be formulated and drafted very cautiously since the requirements are strict in terms of validly waiving or excluding those rights.

Space-Related Contract Types and Related Performance, Defects Liability Clauses and their Main Characteristics

It should be emphasised that a contractual agreement usually prevails over the legal regime. Therefore a short outline of the structure of contracts in the space industry as it exists today, as well as typical clauses related to defects liability, are given with a focus on commercial rather than governmental or institutional agency contracts.

Scheme of Typical Space-Related Contract Types

Contracts and their content vary first according to the legal definition of the type of contract, and then according to peculiarities of the deliverable.

Differentiation according to legal definition of contract:

7 *Ibid.*, 215 ff.

8 Bernstorff, C. Graf von. 2002. *Vertragsgestaltung im Auslandsgeschäft*, 152 ff.

9 *Ibid.*, 152 ff.

10 This is a consequence of the 'Vertragsfreiheit' principle in the BGB, which allows the contractual parties to agree in a contract on their own specific terms and conditions but in the boundaries of statutory law. § 145 BGB.

supply contract /sales contracts
development and research contract
service contract (e.g. maintenance, hotline, IT services)
licence contract
launch contract

Differentiation according to peculiarities of the deliverable:

satellite system including usage of satellite capacity equipment
smaller parts
ground system
launcher
launch start

Existing Schemes

Since defects liability claims are the preferred and most effective weapon if hardware is concerned, contracts in the space industry focus very much on such hardware items. However, due to the fact that contracts in the space industry are always a mixture of the contract types listed above, the defect liability clause may not always cover all instances of defects or non-performance that could occur, for example software and development defects.

Typical Content of Defect Liability Clauses

Warranty /defects liability This clause regulates what happens if a defect is found, i.e. rights regarding replacement, repair, turnaround times, compensation for damage, storage and the duration for which a defect can be claimed (usually in the space industry this is up to 36 months or until launch, whichever is earlier).

Maintenance of know-how Typically this enlarges the responsibility of the seller within the framework of the defects liability and extends to retaining expertise, as well as documentation, in-house longer than the agreed upon defects liability period. At first glance this seems not to be so critical, but when considering expertise in terms of knowledge that might not be written or archived, and given the life time of a satellite, this could cause enormous cost were the information not available.

Deficiencies noted on launched or not-launched hardware This clause outlines the right of the buyer if, for example, a spacecraft is already in orbit and an equipment item on that spacecraft is found to be defective. If the customer has bought several sets of that equipment for use on different satellites, or has information that there is a defect on such equipment found on a satellite of a different customer, then the customer has the right to require repair and/or rework, or at least an investigation followed by a correction. The result of such a defect is that all similar equipment that might still be on-ground must be reworked and repaired or replaced as well, usually at no cost to the customer. This obligation is usually for the defined lifetime of the spacecraft.

Acceptance – the start of the defects liability period Acceptance in the space industry is very often broken down into two different phases: pre-acceptance procedures (transit damages inspection, incoming inspection) and final acceptance. Typically the defects liability period starts at the conclusion of the pre-acceptance steps, which is usually called the 'final acceptance'.

What is interesting about this sequence is that, before the final acceptance, the seller is still in the position of potentially not having delivered according to the contract and, therefore, the burden of proof is still on the seller. Consequently, only when the final acceptance has taken place does the burden of proof shift. The burden of proof is a scheme which defines who has to prove that the defect is indeed a defect and that the deliverable is not in line with the contractual specifications.[11] This can incur huge additional costs, such as testing and transportation costs. The party claiming a defect has to prove, after acceptance, that the deliverable is not in line with the given specifications. As technical proof can usually only be obtained through extensive testing, this might incur costs for the claiming party. At the same time, it should not be forgotten that yet further transportation costs and risk can be incurred.

Service Level Agreement/ Incentives Schemes

Service Level Agreements (SLA) are typically annexes to service contracts wherein both parties agree on a certain level of performance (availability of the service, reaction times for repair, hotline services) and related measurements such as Key Performance Indicators (KPI). SLAs can be found within the space industry, but are not yet as widely known and used as in the IT industry, for example. Clauses that already move towards the use of performance measurements have been applied, but have been referred to as 'incentives'.

For satellites Incentive schemes are used to control the performance of the satellite once it is in orbit. Usually a certain amount of the contract price is withheld until:

launch or
successful in-orbit delivery and acceptance or
yearly performance of the mission or payload

So the incentive for the seller arises because the customer is not paying the full price at delivery or acceptance, and thereby always retaining a certain leverage over the supplier to force it to perform.

For services Typically the service provider is obliged to obtain all licences required for the provision and lease of satellite capacity, as well as to follow established practices and procedures for frequency allocation. One clause that covers the liability for non-performance is the 'Service Interruptions' or 'Service Levels' or 'Capacity Interruptions' clause. This defines the availability of the transponder capacity. Even so, these kinds of clauses do not bear the title 'defects liability' or similar, even though they cover exactly this topic. If the contract promised, for example, 99.8 per cent availability and that is infringed due to the service provider's actions, this constitutes a mal

11 Rebmann, K., Säcker, F.J. and Rixecker, R. 2006. *Münchener Kommentar zum Bürgerlichen Gesetzbuch, 5. Auflage*. München: C.H. Beck, § 640 RN 45–7.

performance and, therefore, would fall under the scheme of defects liability from a legal point of view.

Future Trends and Related Risks for the Industry

The focus of the space industry, as well as the understanding of the agencies, is increasingly the delivery of services in addition to the delivery of hardware (e.g. Galileo services, GMES/Sentinel data provision[12]). Consequently, the phrase 'one-stop shop for the customer' is being increasingly used by various companies of the European space industry. The following describes how this impacts the contractual set-up and the allocation of responsibility in the whole sales/supply chain.

The role of a prime contractor becomes more and more complex, since not only does the satellite need to be delivered, but maybe also services via the satellite, ground stations, billing engines and administrative environment. Although the traditional role of the prime contractor might still apply in some cases, there is an overall trend towards including value-added services, such as geo-information data provision. The legal community must be prepared for that change and should start inquiring and comparing contractual set-ups from industries with similar trends such as IT services.

At the same time, not only the services are changing but also the customer. Approximately 60 per cent[13] of orders placed within the European space industry are being placed by governments, European and national space agencies, or other institutional bodies. However, this will also change in the coming years.

GALILEO as well as geo data services are targeting the B2C sector and hence are moving away from a pure B2G or B2B business. This will certainly challenge the legal domain in the European space industry since apart from a few companies already dealing with services, most companies in the space industry, both large and small, are not used to serving a private end-customer. Furthermore, these companies are not sufficiently aware of the legal limitations that will result from serving such private customers.

Concerning the question of the impact of the international environment on the space industry, it is the author's opinion that this does not constitute a new challenge, but has been dealt with before, although it will nevertheless remain challenging for the industry.

The Way Forward

A logical step for the legal community in the space industry is to begin by understanding the new services that are soon to be provided by and to governments, space agencies, private companies and private end-customers. In-depth evaluation must be conducted to determine if the service levels such as are found in the IT sector would actually be of benefit.

The next consideration is the influence of the 'General Terms and Conditions' laws and the end-consumer protection laws worldwide, with obvious emphasis on European legislation. All these influences must be well understood and transformed into contracts or boilerplates that reflect the interest of the space industry and, at the same time, that of the customer, in a fair way whilst always being in line with the legal requirements.

---

12 See also ASD-EUROSPACE. 2010. *The European Space Industry in 2009, Facts and Figures*, 5.

13 *Ibid.*, 5.

Appendix 1 Check List for an SLA or Defects Liability Clause

turnaround times
defects liability period
repair costs
right to return or right to have goods reworked
compensation coverage
maintenance of know-how
spare parts management
defects liability period for spare parts on-ground (storage)
sample clauses in the space industry
availability
KPI (Key Performance Indicators)

Appendix 2 Sample Warranty Clauses

The following sample warranty clauses *must* – it should go without saying – be adapted to the specific case and reviewed by a legal counsel.

Parts

1. Rights of the Customer in Case of Defects

1.1 The Customer shall examine the delivery immediately upon receipt in order to identify any defects and in the case of any obvious defect, shall inform the Seller accordingly in writing within a period of two weeks. The Customer must notify the Seller of any defects that are not apparent within one year of receipt of the delivery at the latest. Where the Customer fails to provide notification within these exhaustive time limits, the delivery shall be deemed approved, with the result that the Customer loses its rights to assert defects in accordance with sections 1.2 and 1.4.

1.2 Where the delivery is defective, the Seller shall, at its discretion, be entitled to and repair the delivery or to deliver a defect-free item.

1.3 The Seller shall be entitled to make remedial action dependent on the Customer paying a reasonable proportion of the remuneration, having regard to the defect. The Seller shall be entitled to refuse repair or a new delivery where it can only be carried out at disproportionate cost.

1.4 Where repair by the Seller fails to remedy the defect on two individual occasions, the Seller refuses to effect subsequent performance or where the Seller fails to provide subsequent performance within a reasonable time defined by the Customer, the Customer shall be entitled to reduce the purchase price or withdraw from the contract and demand reimbursement of unnecessary expenditure, or compensation for damages instead of performance. The Customer's rights of withdrawal and compensation for damages instead of performance are excluded in the case of minor defects.

1.5 The Customer is not entitled to any remedies as a result of defects that are due e.g. to incorrect storage, operation, maintenance or excessive or inappropriate use of the delivery, to the use of unsuitable tooling and resources, construction work and construction sites or improper changes, corrective maintenance work and damage to seals in the delivery or by other breach of contractual specifications and product regulations on the part of the Customer or a third party.

1.6 The Customer's claims shall be subject to a limitation period of one year subsequent to delivery.

Equipment

1. Warranties

1.1 The Supplier warrants and represents that, notwithstanding prior inspection or Acceptance by the Customer:

(a) The Work shall conform with and meet the requirements and specifications of this Contract, its Annexes and Exhibits.

(b) Without limitation to above, each part of the Work shall be free from defects in materials and workmanship, and shall be manufactured and function in accordance with and fit for the purpose as in Annex 'Statement of Work'.

(c) The Work to be supplied hereunder shall consist of new, not used or reconditioned materials unless otherwise agreed herein.

1.2 The above warranties shall extend:

(a) in the case of all Work except that intended for flight, for a period of three (3) years from Acceptance;

(b) in the case of Work intended for flight, until Launch; and

(c) in the case of non-conforming Work, or a part thereof, corrected or replaced by the Supplier, for a period of three (3) years after the date of correction or replacement.

In the event that the Work is placed in storage, the above warranties shall be extended for a period not exceeding five (5) years, at no cost to the Customer.

Any claims for breach of warranty as a result of dishonesty, wilful misconduct, latent defects, fraud or wilful concealment shall be for the longest period of time permitted under applicable law.

1.3 The Customer shall have the right, at any time up to the expiration of the warranties set out in this Article and irrespective of prior inspections or Acceptance, to require that any Work not conforming to the requirements of this Contract or – relating to Software – the presence of any unauthorised corrupting or harmful piece of code, including but not limited to, viruses, trojans, worms, time or logic bombs, be promptly corrected, repaired or replaced at the Supplier's expense. The decision on whether to correct, repair or replace shall be the Supplier's but shall be made in consultation with the Customer. If the Supplier fails to correct, repair or replace such non-conforming Work within sixty (60) days or such time as deemed acceptable by the Customer after notification from the Customer, then the Customer may, at its option, either require the Supplier to repay such portion of the Contract Price as is equitable in all the circumstances in lieu of correcting, repairing or replacing such defective Work or have a third party correct, repair or replace such non-conforming Work and invoice the Supplier for all costs incurred in so doing.

1.4 The Customer shall give written notice to the Supplier of any breach of the warranties hereunder, after discovery of a defect.

1.5

1.5.1 When return for correction or replacement is required, the Customer shall return the Work and transportation charges and responsibility for such Work whilst in transit shall be borne by the Supplier who shall also bear the cost of delivering any repaired or replacement Work to the Customer. Where Work defects are repaired at the Customer's premises, all travelling or living expenses incurred by the Supplier or its employees and the cost of transporting any necessary material or equipment shall be borne by the Supplier.

1.5.2 During the warranty Period the maximum repair turnaround time, defined as the number of days between receipt at the Supplier's premises of a defective Work returned by the Customer under this Article 'Warranties' and Delivery of the repaired Work to the Delivery Location, shall not exceed TBD (to be decided) days or any other period mutually agreed in writing by the Parties.

In the event that any Work is not repaired and Delivered back to the Customer within the agreed repair turnaround time, defined as Annex 'Statement of Work' the provisions of Article 'Late Delivery' shall apply to that specific Work on an individual item basis from the first day after the expiration of the agreed repair turnaround time until the date of Delivery of that Work back to the Customer.

1.6 The Supplier shall assign to the Customer all warranties on goods or services given by its suppliers, manufacturers or subcontractors where such warranties exceed those given by the Supplier pursuant to this Article, or if such assignment is not possible, extend such given warranties to the Customer by reasonable alternative means.

1.7 Deficiencies noted on launched and not launched flight hardware.

1.7.1 Without affecting the rights, duties and obligations of the Parties under other provisions of this Contract, if the data available from a launched or unlaunched spacecraft containing Work similar to that to be Delivered hereunder or a launched or unlaunched spacecraft containing the Work shows that conditions exist which adversely affect or can be predicted to adversely affect the operation of the Work or that the performance of the Work departs significantly from that expected from the Contract documentation at any time during the period of the Work's in-orbit design lifetime, or that the Work does not meet all the requirements of Annex SOW, or can reasonably be predicted not to be able to meet the requirements of Annex SWO for the in-orbit design lifetime or that a parameter on an in-orbit spacecraft is moving towards its design limit prematurely and such degradation may jeopardise the in-orbit design lifetime, the Supplier shall advise the Customer and take prompt appropriate corrective measures at its sole cost in all of the unlaunched Work, so as to satisfactorily eliminate there from all the deficiencies noted in the launched and/or unlaunched spacecraft. The Supplier shall have the foregoing responsibilities with respect to all unlaunched Work regardless of whether the Supplier has previously delivered or the Customer previously accepted such Work, or whether title thereto has previously passed to the Customer. The Customer shall have the right to reject any such unlaunched deficient Work at any time. If the Supplier fails within a reasonable period of time, to take such corrective measures with respect to all unlaunched Work, the Customer may elect to have any and all such deficiencies corrected through other means, in which event, the Supplier shall make the Work available to the Customer, the Customer or their authorised representative(s) as required and shall pay all costs arising from such corrective measures.

1.7.2 The cost of such investigation shall be reimbursed by the Customer if the malfunctioning of the satellite is proved to be a consequence of malfunctioning of other items other than the Work.

The Supplier agrees that it will not withhold from the Customer any material information that it has or will have concerning anomalies, failures and deviations from the requirements of any satellites in the Programme for which the Supplier's Equipment is procured under this Contract. Notwithstanding any other provision of this Contract, the Supplier shall advise the Customer immediately by telephone and promptly confirm in writing immediately upon becoming aware of any event, circumstance or development which materially threatens (i) the quality of the Equipment or any component part thereof as well as any service or (ii) the quality of any Data to be provided hereunder.

1.7.3 Nothing in this Article shall require the Supplier to disclose the specific satellite or satellite owner affected by any deficiency and/or anomaly where such disclosure would be a breach of the Supplier's contractual obligations to the satellite owner.

1.7.4 The foregoing provisions 1.7.1, 1.7.2 and 1.7.3 shall apply mutatis mutandis to any Work that is not to be launched.

These terms shall in no way limit the Supplier's liability for damage or loss consequent upon any defect which is due to the negligence, omission or fault of the Supplier.

Maintenance of Know-How

The Supplier shall, on request of the Customer and at the Supplier's sole cost and expense, provide in a timely manner, expertise and support requested by the Customer to investigate the causes of malfunctioning of Work on board a spacecraft in orbit during its lifetime, to propose remedial measures and to perform trend analysis of the Work in orbit and over its in-orbit lifetime. The cost of such investigation shall be refunded by the Customer if the malfunctioning of the Work is proved to be the consequence of malfunctioning of items other than the Work.

The Supplier shall maintain the necessary expertise and capacity to rework the Work for as long as one or more of the spacecraft containing the Work are not yet launched in order to be able to implement changes to these spacecraft at the request of the Customer.

All drawings and design, manufacture and test Data and samples relating to the Work and necessary for the Supplier to meet its obligations under this Article shall be retained for the period of the in-orbit lifetime of the Work.

List of References

ASD-EUROSPACE. 2010. *The European Space Industry in 2009, Facts and Figures*, 14th edition, August 2010.

Bernstorff, C. Graf von. 2000. *Einführung in das englische Recht, 2. Auflage*. München: C.H. Beck.

Bernstorff, C. Graf von. 2002. *Vertragsgestaltung im Auslandsgeschäft, 5. Auflage*. Frankfurt am Main: Fritz Knapp.

McKendrick, E. 2003. *Contract Law*, 5th edition. London: Palgrave Law Masters.

Rebmann, K., Säcker, F.J. and Rixecker, R. 2006. *Münchener Kommentar zum Bürgerlichen Gesetzbuch, 5. Auflage*. München: C.H. Beck.

Sonnenberger, H.J. and Autexier, C. 2000. *Einführung in das französische Recht, 3. Auflage*. Heidelberg: Recht und Wissenschaft.

Chapter 22

Cost Overruns in Space Contracts: Mitigation Methods and Strategies

Walter Peeters

Introduction

Especially in public procurements, cost overruns are a recurrent issue. Contrary to some views, cost overruns have always existed, as is illustrated by the following example from Roman history, as quoted by Gibbon:[1]

> The young magistrate (Herod, son of Atticus), observing that the town of Troas was indifferently supplied with water, obtained from the munificence of Hadrian 300 myriads of drachmas for the construction of a new aqueduct. But in the execution of the works the charge amounted to more than double the estimate, and the officers of the revenue began to murmur, till the generous Atticus silenced their complaints by requesting that he might be permitted to take upon himself the whole additional expense.

Especially in cases of new projects that lack benchmarking possibilities, the risk for overruns realistically exists, hence early development projects in the space sector did not escape this fact. Holman reports that the total duration of the Mercury project was not less than 2.25 times the originally scheduled one, with a corresponding cost overrun of 120 per cent.[2] On the other hand, the Apollo project is reported to have had a cost overrun of only 25 per cent,[3] which is remarkably good in view of its complexity. This excellent result probably may be attributed to the fact that the schedule had to be adhered to strictly; it therefore also underlines the 'faster-cheaper' relation.[4]

In general, however, in times of economic welfare when year-to-year GDP increases regularly, such cost overruns for longer-term projects can be more easily absorbed (note that the early US human space programmes took place at times of yearly GDP growths around 7 per cent[5]). In general, cost scrutiny is more sever in times of lower economic growth. Another effect is the political necessities, as demonstrated by important studies conducted by the RAND Corporation and Harvard Business School in the late 1950s. They discovered that during the 1950s, and in particular during the Korean War, overruns by factors of 200 to even 800 per cent were noted. Owing to an increased degree of technological complexity, and to the need for rapid development

1 Gibbon, E. 1935. *The Decline and Fall of the Roman Empire*. London: Methuen, Vol. 1, 28.

2 Holman, M. 1974. *The Political Economy of the Space Program*. Palo Alto, CA: Pacific Books.

3 *Ibid.*

4 Johnson, S. 2002. *The Secret of Apollo: System Management in American and European Space Programs*. Baltimore, MD: Johns Hopkins University Press.

5 Source: http://www.whitehouse.gov/omb/budget/historicals/ [accessed: 30 April 2011].

occasioned by the war, a considerable number of cost-plus contracts were being issued without the possibility for appropriate control.[6]

Similarly, there are no strong records of budgetary investigations during the Apollo times in the 1960s, which could be explained by both the economic welfare, as well as the geopolitical, priorities at that time.

The situation has, however, drastically changed. Already in 2006, worries were expressed that the situation on cost overruns in NASA had not improved and NASA was instructed to:

> Notify the [Congressional] Committee 15 days prior to allocating funds, modifying, or extending existing contracts that are in excess of 15 per cent of the original contract value. Within this notification, the contractor, with the concurrence of NASA, shall justify the additional expenditure of funds, and NASA shall identify the source of any additional funds. It is critical that NASA be able to control costs for its activities. The Committee will not look favorably upon the use of contractors that repeatedly have cost overruns unless these cost overruns have been justified.[7]

At the end of 2008, the Government Accountability Office (GAO), the congressional watchdog, started an examination and reported to Congress on 5 March 2009 their findings. They came to the conclusion that only five out of the 40 major NASA projects came in on time and on schedule and that more than a quarter were at least costlier than anticipated.[8]

The conclusion of the survey was formulated as:

> GAO assessed 18 NASA projects with a combined life-cycle cost of more than $50 billion. Of those, 10 out of 13 projects that had entered the implementation phase experienced significant cost and/or schedule growth. For these 10 projects, development costs increased by an average of 13 per cent from baseline cost estimates that were established just 2 or 3 years ago and they had an average launch delay of 11-months. In some cases, cost growth was considerably higher than what is reported because it had occurred prior to the most recent baseline. Many of the projects we reviewed experienced challenges in developing new technologies or retrofitting older technologies as well as in managing their contractors, and more generally, understanding the risks and challenges they were up against when they started their efforts.[9]

In particular, the Mars Science Laboratory, from which the cost-to-completion has rapidly grown from 1.4 billion USD to over 2.3 billion USD (mainly due to a two-year launch delay), was a major target of criticism. Pursuing this project may even lead to cancelling or delaying other science projects under development.

There is little doubt that such increased cost overrun awareness will also affect the European space sector in this coming period of low, even negative, GDP growth.

6 Peck, M. and Scherer, F. 1962. *The Weapons Acquisition Process: An Economic Analysis*. Boston, MA: Harvard University Press.

7 US Senate. 2006. Senate Report 109-088 – NASA Appropriations Bill.

8 Lawler, A. 2009. 'Trouble on the Final Frontier', *Science*, 324 (3 April), 34–5.

9 US Congress. 2009. House Space and Aeronautics Subcommittee Hearing: Cost Management Issues in NASA's Acquisitions and Programs. Thursday, 5 March.

Can Cost Overruns be Mitigated?

An unfortunate reaction to cost overruns is to try to shift the budget. One of the traditional ways to shift the budget is to delay other projects, whereby these delays will, in their turn, lead to other cost overruns.

In an assessment report of the OMB (Office of the Management of the Budget) the following cost overruns and delays were noted on astronomy and astrophysics projects:[10]

- 2005: 42.9 per cent cost overrun (35.7 per cent in time)
- 2006: 83.9 per cent cost overrun (76.1 per cent in time)
- 2007: 51.4 per cent cost overrun (57.8 per cent in time)

These figures show the direct relation between schedule overruns and cost overruns. Such a relation is logical, as most space projects require highly-qualified project teams, both from the client as well as from the contractor, which teams form a very considerable portion of the cost. Extension of time will therefore automatically translate into extension of costs.

Presumably the biggest origin of such overruns is an initial underestimation of the complexity of the projects and their resulting cost. As an example, the previous report points out that most of the projects facing problems had an average weight increase of 40 per cent at the final design, a strong measure of the initially underestimated design problems.[11] Furthermore, the reuse of existing technologies or the use of Commercial off the Shelf (COTS) components is very often overestimated. As a NASA official expresses it, 'I won't call it lying or cheating. It's optimism.'[12]

We can, nevertheless, not ignore that there is a scientific-political component playing a major role in this:

> Most science managers have a scientific background and want to see some scientific programmes adopted, whatever it needs to convince administrators.
>
> The rules that 15 or 20 per cent overruns do not require any additional approval are inflatory in this respect.
>
> Many of the programmes have long lead times and cost overruns may be absorbed in the course of the project by other funding.
>
> Unfortunately often the 'momentum' theory is applied. Once a programme is sufficiently advanced and has already consumed funding, it is hoped that it will not be terminated at a later stage.

---

10 OMB. 2009. *Detailed Information on the NASA Astronomy and Astrophysics Research Assessment.* [Online]. Available at: http://www.whitehouse.gov/omb/expectmore/detail/10002316.2007.html [Accessed: 16 August 2009].

11 Lawler, A. 2009. 'Trouble on the Final Frontier'.

12 *Ibid.*

In their standard work on budgeting, Anthony and Young labelled this last technique 'Foot in the Door': sell a modest programme initially; conceal its real magnitude until after it is under way and has built constituency.[13]

It is evident, if such an approach is taken, that cost overrun mitigation is basically impossible and only damage control can take place. With greater transparency and more automated budget control techniques, however, budget overruns will be visible much earlier. Moreover, various programmes have been cancelled in the past, even when they have already reached a certain momentum. In this context we need only remember the cases of the European HERMES programme and the international X-38 project, both of which were terminated irrespective of the considerable funds already invested.

We have therefore to assume that an objective aim will be followed to initiate a programme with a minimum risk of cost overruns, without the intention of using one of these ploys.

A number of mitigation techniques have been suggested. One of them has been formulated as the 'Ten Commandments of Formal Methods';[14] based upon an analysis of successful projects, it is worth considering. The commandments are formulated as follows:

Thou shalt Choose an Appropriate Notation

We need to look at this in a broader context. Identifying applicable documents and the order of precedence, and further agreeing on standards, from the beginning of a project onwards are prerequisites even before the design phase starts, i.e. during the phase the requirements are being documented by the client.

Thou shalt Formalise but not Over-formalise

The strength of formal methodologies cannot be ignored, in particular at the start of projects, but the method on its own (reviews, documentation, minutes) often risks becoming a purpose, not a tool. Definitely in a later phase of the project, flexibility is required.

Thou shalt Estimate Cost

This point cannot be sufficiently stressed. Even if we are faced with projects with limited analogy, there are sufficient cost estimating tools available to give the client a reasonable feel for the final cost of a project when properly executed. Any client who does not have such pre-knowledge is bound to become the victim of over-runs.

Thou shalt Have a Forma- Methods Guru on Call

Irrespective of internal services, there is a definite advantage to bringing in experts from outside, in particular during reviews. Nobody is protected against project myopia, and being too deeply involved, in particular in calculations or project details, may lead to overlooking obvious solutions, possibly originated in other sectors.

13 Anthony, R. and Young, D. 1984. *Management Control in Nonprofit Organizations*. Homewood, IL: Irwin, 376.

14 Bowen, J. and Hinchey, M. 1995. 'Ten Commandments of Formal Methods', *Computer*, (April), 56–63, revised in Bowen, J. and Hinchey, M. 2006. 'Ten Commandments of Formal Methods: Ten Years Later', *Computer*, 39 (1) (January), 40–48.

Thou shalt not Abandon thy Traditional Development Methods

Many methods have been developed and have proven results, in particular in the project control phase. New methods regularly are coming on the markets which, however, often still need to be readjusted by feedback. A common mistake is to jump too early on such new methods, assuming they will assist more efficiently, and ignoring the fact that the traditional ones have a proven track record.

Thou shalt Document Sufficiently

Document control is undoubtedly one of the less creative tasks in project management, but highly important in order to be able to track changes and the originator thereof. Typical consequences can be reflected in contract change management but also in claims with insurance companies.

Thou shalt not Compromise thy Quality Standards

Some standards, such as ISO9000 or software standards, may seem to limit creativity, and the enthusiastic scientist or project engineer may have a tendency to take shortcuts. In the long term, such shortcuts may have serious consequences. Most launch failures, when *a posteriori* examined, have a link to a failure to respect a quality standard.

Thou shalt not be Dogmatic

The relation between a client and a contractor is based upon mutual understanding and respect. A dogmatic client will not create an atmosphere whereby the contractor will point out improvements or cost savings. The risk is that, even if a possible error is becoming apparent, the contractor will refrain from informing the client to avoid procedural issues.

Thou shalt Test, Test and Test again

Together with quality standards, this is a second area where false cost savings are often sought. Eliminating a development model, or replacing tests by simulations, will not only increase the risks but may moreover lead to compromising claims when insurance companies are involved.

Thou shalt Reuse

In a scientific driven environment, the 'not-invented-here-syndrome' is highly evident. Whereas the space world has been oriented to spin-offs, such realities as reduced budgets and considerably higher R&D budgets than those of other sectors (IT, pharma, biotech, etc.) should motivate the space sector to also search for 'spin-ins' at much lower costs than own developments.

Proposed Mitigation Method: The 5C Approach

While the previous method is strongly oriented towards cost overrun mitigation during implementation, the 5C mitigation method[15] is based more upon use of contractual instruments and can be described in five steps.

Step 1: Realistic Cost Estimation

Virtually all mitigation strategies will emphasise this point. If the client has no accurate cost estimate, it will not be able to conduct proper contract negotiation with a level of confidence, leading to a contract price in line with the real costs.

Step 2: Consideration on the Life Cycle Cost

Life cycle costs (LCC) are a much more common concept in other industries. Due to the fact that original space projects had relatively short operational lifetimes (compared to ships, planes and so on) the space industry has focused strongly on development costs. Longer lifetimes of, for example, telecommunication satellites are forcing rethinking in terms of LCC.

Step 3: An Appropriate Contractual Framework

The contract type is often chosen as a result of trends and seldom adapted to the particular features of a project. The strategic use of the right contract type is, however, a very important aspect of a cost overrun strategy and needs to be reiterated.

Step 4: Cost Control and Risk Management during the Project Phase

Even the best contractual agreement remains a baseline and needs to be monitored during contract execution. Here we enter the field of project control which, however, requires close interaction with the contractual agreements, depending on the contract type chosen.

Step 5: A Communication-managed Insurance Approach

Insurance can be seen as an ultimate cost mitigation instrument, in particular if public funding is involved. On the other hand, insurance rates are at such a level that the insurance cost is, after the launch, often the second highest cost of the project in terms of a subsystem. In case of a failure of documentation or communication, claims may be difficult to prove and thereby have a very considerable cost impact.

In order to forge a link between these mitigation techniques and the contractual process, we will discuss here a cost overrun avoidance strategy: the following steps are chronological:

---

15 Peeters, W. and Madauss, B. 2008. 'A Proposed Strategy against Cost Overruns in the Space Sector: The 5C Approach', *Space Policy*, (April), 80–89.

What has to be prepared before the contract negotiation?
What has to be included in the contract?
What needs follow-up during contract execution?

Steps to be Taken before Contract Negotiations

In order to be confident that the right price will be negotiated, it is important before the contract to have a convincing feeling about the cost of a project, taking into account its operational cost. The biggest cost engineering challenge and the main factor contributing to overruns is undoubtedly the original cost estimate of a project, as was again demonstrated in the aforementioned GAO findings and related discussions. This is not only linked to the technical problem on how to estimate novel projects, but also to the lack of project definition in the early project phases.

We consider four types of cost evaluation technique according to the following methodology:

- top-down methodologies
  - cost by comparison
  - cost by analogy
  - parametric costing
- bottom-up methodology
  - grassroots costing

Cost by comparison is the most risky technique. It basically means that the client does not estimate cost on its own, but relies on the offers it receives as a result of a tender. Undoubtedly, in the space environment, where oligopolistic market situations predominate, this method cannot be used, just as it cannot be used in general for major projects where only a few responses are received.

Cost by analogy requires the involvement of experts with extensive relevant experience to be able to provide an analogy between past and new project undertakings. In space development contracts this is often impossible as the technical and performance characteristics are in general very different, which can lead to very risky extrapolations (many cost factors are exponential). Moreover, one must ensure that the benchmark cost basis was accurate and known in detail.

Grassroots costing consists of dividing a project into very small fragments (like length of cables, number of different sensors, surface of solar panels) and putting an experience-based unit price on each element. This means that the final design needs to be known in minute detail, which most of the time is not the case in early phases of development contracts. Also, contrary to other sectors, such as the building industry, such unit costs are less known in the space sector due to the lack of serial production.

Parametric costing is one of the most popular and reliable tools for cost estimating in the space sector. PRICE[16] is the model which is most widely used in the space sector internationally, as it also provides good results for the operational cost phase.

Excellent work on parametric cost estimating is done by specialised organisations such as the International Society of Parametric Analysts (ISPA). They regularly update a comprehensive

16 PRICE, stands for Parametric Review of Information for Costing and Evaluation. Initially developed by the RCA Corporation in the 1960s, it is now marketed by PRICE Systems LLC.

handbook (which can be downloaded free of charge), entitled *Parametric Estimating Handbook* (3rd edition, Spring 2003).[17]

The advantages and disadvantages of these different methods are summarised in Table 22.1.

Table 22.1 Comparison of cost evaluation methods

	Advantage	Disadvantage	Applicability
Cost by comparison	No cost assessment needed	Only for open competition	Not recommended
Cost by analogy	Fast	Technical and cost sensitivity	Phase O or A only
Parametric costing	Reliable, also for operational cost	Technology sensitivity and assumptions	Mainly phases B/C/D/E
Grassroots costing	Most accurate method	Needs detailed design and time consuming	Only after phase B

If, referring to Table 22.1, we exclude cost by comparison for aforementioned reasons, it is clear, due to the nature of the methods, that:

we can only use cost by analogy for first, rough and early assessments;

grassroots methods are difficult and require very detailed design, most of the time not available before contract negotiations;

parametric costing is a reliable method which can be applied for most project phases, including the operational phase.

There are, therefore, no reasons why the client would not be in a position to make a reliable cost estimate internally before the contract negotiations, independently from the contractor. The use of the right tools will provide such an estimate and facilitate confidence in negotiations.

An element to be taken into account in this context is life cycle costing (LCC), which is becoming more important in the space sector. Indeed, whereas earlier satellites had very limited operational lifetimes, operational costs were only a fraction of the budgets in space projects.

While the operational phase (called phase E in space terminology) of the Apollo project accounted for roughly 20 per cent of the LCC,[18] this percentage doubled for the Space Shuttle programme. One of the important factors for this increase is the higher reusability of space shuttle elements, as well as the increasing operational life time.

There is, moreover, a considerable difference between the life cycle cost spent and committed. Studies on complex systems have demonstrated that already after phase A, when only a fraction

17 ISPA. 2003. *Parametric Estimating Handbook*, 3rd edition. [Online]. Available at: http://www.ispa-cost.org [Accessed: 30 April 2011].

18 Holman, M. 1974. *The Political Economy of the Space Program.*

of the budget is spent, approximately 70 per cent of the life cycle cost is fixed! This considerable difference can be illustrated as per Figure 22.1.

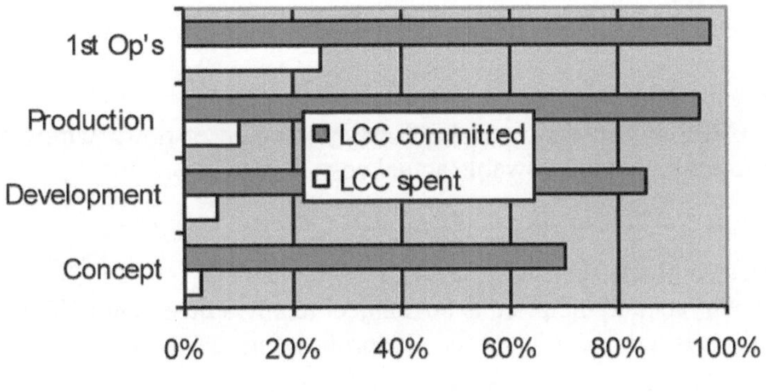

Figure 22.1 Commitment of life cycle cost per phase (Peeters and Madauss 2008)

Cost Overrun Measures during Contract Negotiations

Two elements need to be coupled during contract conclusion. The client needs to evaluate which price type it will propose (and *mutatis mutandis* which one it will reject) and, as a consequence, how a contractual change procedure will be implemented.

The relation between the contract type and the possible cost overruns has been underestimated. The decision on the right contract type should be based upon tailored considerations by the client, in a dialogue with the technical and the contractual department.

We will recall here the different types of contracts with their specific features:

Types of Contracts[19]

Basically we distinguish between two groups of contract types:

1. Cost-reimbursement contracts: in cost-reimbursement contracts the client is required to reimburse all allowable, allocatable and reasonable costs that the contractor can prove it has made.
2. Fixed-price contracts: in this case, the contractor has the obligation to deliver a final product for a specified price, as contractually agreed. (Note that, particularly in the construction industry, these types are also called 'lump-sum contracts'.)

Cost-reimbursement contracts
CPPF: cost-plus-percentage-fee contract
This is definitely the most straightforward type of contract, from a contractor's point of view. All justified costs are paid and the fee is added as a fixed percentage. The *target cost* is the estimated

19 See, for further details, Peeters, W. and In 't Veld, J. 1989. 'The Use of Alternate Contract Types in Europe as Protection against Overruns', *National Contracts Management Journal*, 23 (1), 23–34.

cost to completion, whereas the *target fee* is the fee payable if the actual cost equals the target cost. Note that under many contract regulations this cost type is not allowed.

CPFF: cost-plus-fixed-fee
In this case, costs are reimbursed but the fee remains constant, whatever the actual costs.

CPIF: cost-plus-incentive-fee
CPIF is similar to CPFF, but in this case the fee may vary up or down within set limits and in accordance with a formula tied to allowable actual costs.

Fixed-price contracts
FFP: firm-fixed-price contract
This is a one-price contract and the price is not subject to any adjustment unless there is a change in the scope of work required under its terms. The profit in this case can even become negative.

FPE: fixed-price-with-escalation contract
In this case the contractor is not required to estimate the escalation, but the contract price is linked to a certain date and payments are increased on the basis of mutually agreed (escalation) indices.

FPI: fixed-price-incentive contract
In this type of contract, a target fee is fixed, but the fee will be determined when actual costs are known. In this case, a ceiling price is determined, which is the maximum price accepted by the client for fee determination: for costs higher or equal to this ceiling price the profit equals zero. In general, also, a maximum fee is determined.

The difference between this type of contract and the CPIF contract is that, in this case, the upper limit is fixed (ceiling price); in the FPI case the contractor can suffer a considerable loss if its costs exceed the fixed ceiling prices. In the case of CPIF, the worst case for the contractor is no profit; its costs will be reimbursed anyway.

Some variants
Other incentives
We have so far only considered cost incentives in this chapter. We can also, however, consider other incentives, such as:

Performance incentives: a positive or negative fee is paid upon obtaining a certain technical performance. Imagine a satellite payload with a target mass of 50 kg; a performance incentive on mass reduction could be included.

Delivery incentives: in cases where delivery time is important (e.g. payload for a satellite with a predetermined launch date), (stepwise) incentives are often included.

AF: award fees: at the beginning of the contract, an amount is determined for awards, the award pool. This award pool is divided into evaluation events, and (subjective) measurement systems are developed and mutually agreed prior to the start of performance (e.g. rating system). At each event, the contractor can earn (part of) the attributed award. In general, a (low) base fee in the order of 2–3 per cent is added, independent of the performance. The most common form found in practice is a CPAF, costplus awardfee contract. In principle, however, award fees can be added to any type of contract.

Risk Distribution for the Different Contract Types

In global terms we can state that the risk for the client is higher in the case of cost-reimbursement contracts than in fixed-price contracts. Moreover, in terms of cost overruns, it can be shown[20] that in CPPF and CPFF cost-reimbursement contracts, there is no incentive for the contractor to stay within the budget, hence the attempts to remedy this by the introduction of incentive clauses, whereby the fee is shared between the client and the contractor on the basis of the actual cost.

Here, we have to stress again the importance of having an as accurate as possible estimate of the target cost, obtained via the types of contracts described above. Indeed, it is obvious that when the target cost is put too high, the contractor may easily obtain very high fees by staying considerably under this target.

Fixed-price contracts, and in particular FFP, may seem the safest from the client's perspective. We should, however, point out that:

> A fixed-price contract risks also resulting in cost overruns if too many changes are introduced, in particular by the client. Such Contract Change Notices (CCNs) are also difficult to negotiate as the contractor is often in a strong position, certainly in later phases of the contract, in particular when deadlines have to be met.
>
> Contractors may be driven, in view of cash-flow issues, to accept FP contracts even at price levels under the real cost. In the ultimate case, when a contractor goes bankrupt, the total costs for the client can be considerable. Indeed, it will be pretty much impossible for another contractor to take over work in an intermediate phase and, in general, the contract will virtually have to restart. The additional time pressure under such circumstances strongly reduces the possibility to negotiate the costs.

These considerations lead us to propose Table 22.2 for the appropriate choice of a contract type in general. More detailed selection criteria have been developed in the form of a decision chart.[21]

20 *Ibid.*
21 *Ibid.*

Table 22.2 Appropriate choice of contract type

Cost type	Specifications	Consequence on cost control	Other observations
CPPF	Subject to expected considerable changes	Requires strict and costly cost control	Not recommended
CPFF	Subject to expected considerable changes	Strict cost control	Only if the risk for such changes is high
CPIF	Subject to changes	Strict cost control	Requires mutual understanding of the mechanism
CPAF	Subject to changes	Strict cost control	Mainly for services which are difficult to qualify
FPI	Considered frozen	Incentive calculations	Rather complex cost type to control
FPE	Considered frozen	Limited efforts	Recommended in periods of strong financial fluctuations
FFP	Considered frozen	Minimal efforts	Stable and predictable financial situation

In Table 22.2 we represent the view that cost-reimbursement contracts should only be used in circumstances where the client assumes that there will be many changes in the specifications, for example in the case of an experimental satellite using new technologies.

The risk for overruns can be partially mitigated by incentive clauses, but this requires a good mutual understanding of the applicability thereof. The lack of objective benchmarks of an award contract, such as CPAF, has lead in the past to very subjective discussions and, therefore, has to be well considered before deciding on this contract type.

Fixed price contracts require the conviction that changes will be limited, as well as good mutual confidence that the right price level has been set as a target. Due to its nature, indeed, they can lead to considerable losses for the contractor and serious consequences for the contractual renegotiations.

There is no doubt that the wide variety of contract types and incentives will make the inexperienced user reluctant to enter into this unknown field. Furthermore, it is evident that no unambiguous solution can be found for each specific project; each contract type should be tailored to the specific requirements of the project. It is also evident that, for the same project, there will initially be differing views concerning the (preferred) contract type. Unfortunately, most interests are highly conflicting: an advantage for one party represents an equivalent disadvantage for the other party. This leads us to the conclusion that a contract type chosen is, in general, the result of a compromise, acceptable to both parties. Also the procedure to introduce the contractual changes needs to be linked inherently to this contract type choice.

As in most of these contract types, a target cost is taken as a basis for the negotiations and formulas. This underlines again the high importance of the first step to be taken, namely to commence the negotiations based on an as accurate as possible cost estimate.

Controlling the Project Cost during Contract Execution

Monitoring the cost evolution during the contract execution is in general the task of the project team. However, here it is important that a strong interaction between the contracts officer and the project controller is maintained.

A number of methods have been developed over the years in the space sector to monitor progress. One of the easy methods to follow visually, and to be advised for each project, is the Earned Value Method (EVM). As illustrated in Figure 22.2, this method shows if a project is still on track as far as time and cost are concerned (two closely interrelated parameters).

As shown in the example of Figure 22.2, this tool also makes it possible at an early stage to make a forecast of the probable time and cost overruns. This would facilitate not only taking timely remedial actions but ultimately also taking precautionary steps in terms of payment delays and budgetary carry forward.

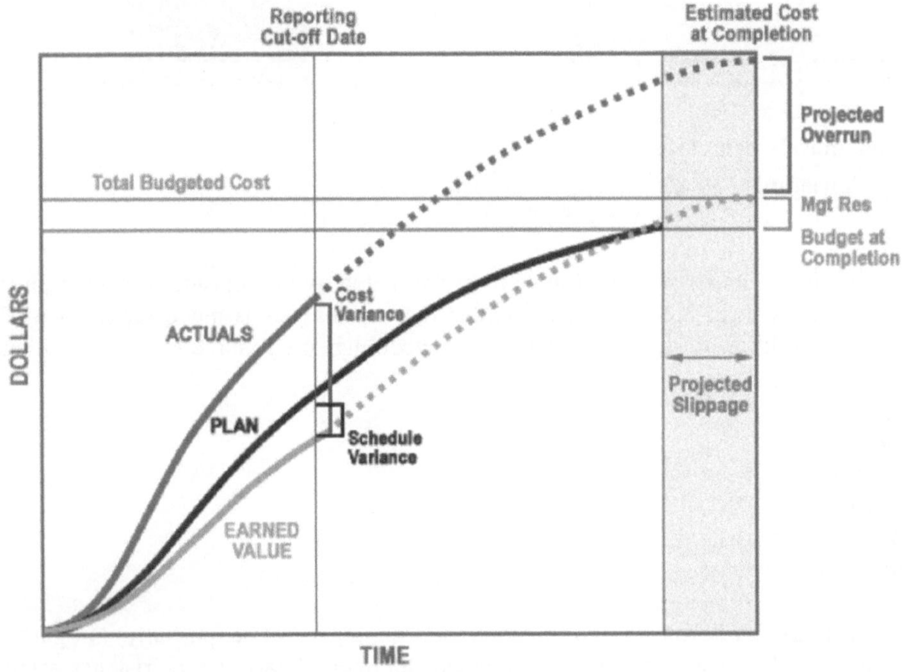

Figure 22.2 Earned value method (EVM 2010)

Risk management methods are often very technically oriented, but can equally be employed to detect other issues at an early phase. In principle, each risk will be evaluated in terms of the probability of occurrence and the consequences. This leads to three zones in a matrix as shown in Figure 22.3.

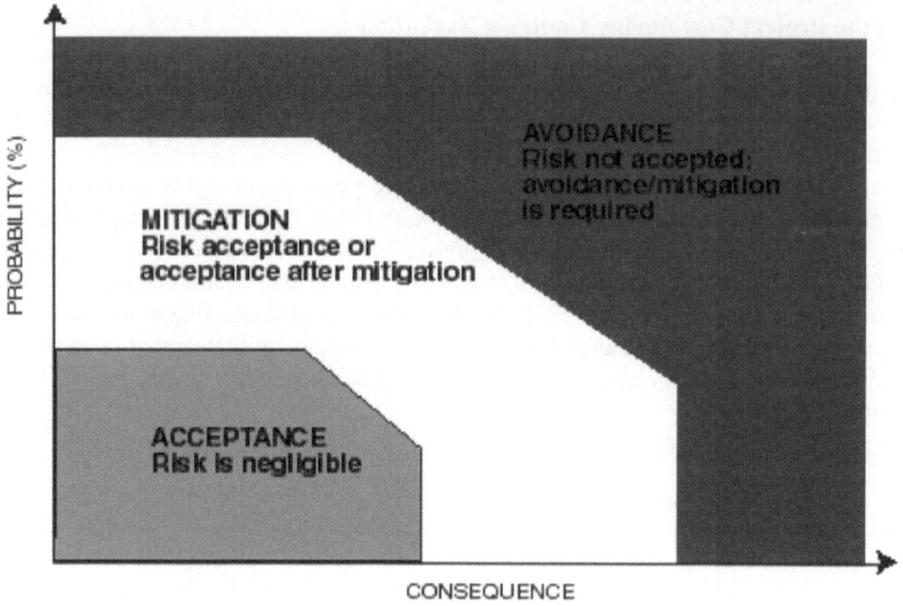

Figure 22.3 Risk matrix principle

Source: ESA, ECSS standard M-ST-80C

All risks falling in the upper zone will have to be mitigated by appropriate measures. In the context of cost overruns, it is strongly recommended that an analysis is made regularly of the following factors in addition to the usual technical, scheduling, programmatic and operational risks:

cost risks
financial risks
market risks
third-party liability risks
regulatory risks

Furthermore, these risks (if relevant for the specific case) can in general be (partially) mitigated if known well in advance. They should, therefore, be made an integral part of each risk assessment exercise.

Linked to this is the contractual relation with the insurance broker, whereby insurance can be considered as an ultimate risk mitigation method. Insurance brokers request to be fully informed on major changes, such as design changes and technical modifications – or important waivers. However, information on known problems is also an important factor in the relationship with the insurance company and often overlooked.

As an example, a generic series of problems occurred with a specific spacecraft bus (BSS702) leading to a number of spacecraft failures. On the basis that they were not fully informed by the clients of these failures, the insurance companies initially rejected and afterwards settled for partial repayment of claims,[22] which led to a loss for the client of over USD 100 million. Even after arbitration in one case, an operator failed to reach a compromise, as the claim was not considered to be justified.[23] All these important reductions in claims (some in the order of 50 per cent) could have been easily avoided by proper information exchange between the client and the insurance broker.

Conclusion

The space sector persists in having a reputation of project cost overruns. Certainly in periods of low GDP growth, as witnessed in Europe after the financial crash of 2008, we can expect higher public vigilance against cost overruns and the implementation of control measures in general.

The instruments to avoid cost overruns are available and well-known, all starting with cost analysis techniques enabling independent cost estimates. Unfortunately, this is often the crux of the problem. These independent cost assessments are either not respected under pressure of budget restrictions, or tend to underestimate the later phases of the life cycle cost (LCC). In such cases, a cost overrun is basically pre-programmed and unavoidable.

If a contractual agreement is based upon an accurate cost estimate, cost overruns can be mitigated by choosing the right contract type given the technical specificities of the project. Whenever a sound basis for cost overrun mitigation is established during the contract negotiation phase, it will clearly require diligent follow-up during the subsequent implementation phase. Project control methods can effectively assist in this, as can the notion of including cost aspects in the risk assessment exercises.

As long as the space sector is largely based upon public financing, it can only benefit from a better cost control image. All the tools to reach this goal are available; we just need the courage to apply them diligently.

List of References

Anthony, R. and Young, D. 1984. *Management Control in Nonprofit Organizations*. Homewood, IL: Irwin, 376.

Bowen, J. and Hinchey, M. 1995. 'Ten Commandments of Formal Methods', *Computer*, (April), 56–63.

Bowen, J. and Hinchey, M. 2006. 'Ten Commandments of Formal Methods: Ten Years Later', *Computer*, 39 (1) (January), 40–48.

EVM. 2010. *Earned Value Method Tutorial*. [Online]. Available at: http://evm.nasa.gov/tutorial.html [Accessed: 30 April 2011].

Gibbon, E. 1935. *The Decline and Fall of the Roman Empire*. London: Methuen, Vol. 1, 28.

Holman, M. 1974. *The Political Economy of the Space Program*. Palo Alto, CA: Pacific Books.

ISPA. 2003. *Parametric Estimating Handbook*, 3rd edition. [Online]. Available at: http://www.ispa-cost.org [Accessed: 30 April 2011].

---

22 Newton, D. 2005. *Satellite Insurance*. [Online: posted, 5 January 2005]. Report published under http://www.milliman.com [Accessed: 30 April 2011].

23 Orbicast. 2006. *XM Loses Satellite Insurance Arbitration*. [Online: posted 27 September 2006]. Available at: http://www.orbicast.com [Accessed: 30 April 2011].

Johnson, S. 2002. *The Secret of Apollo: System Management in American and European Space Programs*. Baltimore, MD: Johns Hopkins University Press.

Lawler, A. 2009. 'Trouble on the Final Frontier', *Science*, 324 (3 April), 34–5.

Newton, D. 2005. *Satellite Insurance*. [Online: posted, 5 January 2005]. Report published under http://www.milliman.com [Accessed: 30 April 2011].

OMB. 2009. *Detailed Information on the NASA Astronomy and Astrophysics Research Assessment*. [Online]. Available at: http://www.whitehouse.gov/omb/expectmore/detail/10002316.2007.html [Accessed: 16 August 2009].

Orbicast. 2006. *XM Loses Satellite Insurance Arbitration*. [Online: posted 27 September 2006]. Available at: http://www.orbitcast.com [Accessed: 30 April 2011].

Peck, M. and Scherer, F. 1962. *The Weapons Acquisition Process: An Economic Analysis*. Boston, MA: Harvard University Press.

Peeters, W. and Madauss, B. 2008. 'A Proposed Strategy against Cost Overruns in the Space Sector: The 5C Approach', *Space Policy*, (April), 80–89.

Peeters, W. and In 't Veld, J. 1989. 'The Use of Alternate Contract Types in Europe as Protection against Overruns', *National Contracts Management Journal*, 23 (1), 23–34.

US Congress. 2009. House Space and Aeronautics Subcommittee Hearing: Cost Management Issues in NASA's Acquisitions and Programs. Thursday, 5 March.

US Senate. 2006. Senate Report 109-088 – NASA Appropriations Bill.

Chapter 23

Space Insurance

Philippe Montpert

Introduction

'Space insurance' is defined as a specialised niche market in which fall all insurance contracts designed for protecting against the financial consequences of events occurring between the lift-off of the satellite and its end of life. This definition excludes insurance against the risk of damage on the launch pad or the risk of damage occurring while the satellite is being transported from its factory to the launch site. The liability incurred by a party while its satellite is launched or already orbiting is part of the space insurance domain.

Space Insurance

The start point for space insurance coverage is sometimes defined by the easy-to-understand expression: 'the point of no return', for example when the launch process is irreversible. This point varies depending on the launch vehicle technology.

For an Ariane 5 flight, for instance, it is the moment of ignition of the solid boosters followed by the physical lift-off of the rocket. It is indeed a point of no return as from that point in time, only two things can happen: a launch failure or a success. There is no way to shut down the engines and prepare for another trial.

If it is not an immediate launch failure, then, three distinct phases will occur in sequence:

the propelled launch phase (lasting about 20 minutes)
the transfer of the satellite on its final orbit followed by its functional testing (two months)
the operational phase (more than 15 years for the newest telecommunications satellites)

For each phase, the space insurers will allocate a certain premium rate as a function of the expected fail rate of the satellite during that phase. The premium level does not follow the duration of each phase, but rather the probability of having a satellite failure.

It is possible for a customer either to contract an insurance policy for one single phase or to combine several phases into one single insurance policy. In the latter case, the premium rates will be added up.

Space insurance is in principle available for all types of satellite applications: telecommunications (TV, internet), geo-localisation, deep space exploration, remote sensing or even military applications (as far as they are not considered weapons). In practice, the vast majority of the insurance policies are for covering commercial telecommunications satellites. These insurance policies are designed to protect the customer against the physical loss or the reduction in performance of the satellite – damage insurance – or against the consequences of the prejudice caused to third parties – liability insurance.

Liability Insurance

Third party liability insurance protects the satellite operator as well as all other participants to the space project against the financial consequences of a damage caused to a third party. The applicable legal regime is defined by Article 7 of the United Nations Outer Space Treaty of January 1967 and by the Liability Convention of 1972.

These conventions stipulate that the launching states[1] are responsible *in fine vis-à-vis* third parties for any damage induced by one of their satellites. To complement these very general conventions, most of the countries involved in space activities have passed specific laws to oblige space actors to procure from the commercial insurance industry third party liability insurance of a minimum specified level. This minimum level varies according to each different country. Above that level, the state is liable.

For instance, in France the state requires an amount of EUR 60,980,000 to be secured by satellite operators from insurance companies. France automatically becomes a launching state (but not necessarily the only one) for any satellite, whether foreign or domestic, launched by the Arianespace transportation system.

To simplify the process of securing liability insurance, and for commercial reasons as well, Arianespace includes such guarantee in all launch contracts. It provides a one-year guarantee after which the satellite operator will have to purchase its own insurance coverage. From that moment on, some satellite operators buy in excess of the minimum levels – sometimes up to USD 200,000,000 – because they consider that, should damage be caused by their satellite to another satellite in space, there is no certainty of immunity from any liability.

For instance, despite the UN rules, what could really prevent a third party from suing the satellite operator together with the launching state (by application of 'the principle of real life': a private operator is much better equipped to quickly indemnify the prejudiced third party rather than a bureaucratic state)? Hence, as prudent businessmen, they wish to protect the potentially huge defence costs associated with a law suit, together with any potential residual liability that they may have to carry.

History shows that there have been very few claims made to insurers with respect to third party liability coverage. There are only two publicly known cases:

> In 1978, a nuclear Russian satellite fell on Canada and produced potentially hazardous debris. There was no insurance, but Russia indemnified Canada for about CAN $3 millions.
>
> In 2007, the launch of JCSAT11 on Proton failed and some propellant contaminated the Kazakh ground. A claim of USD 1 million was filed.

When no claims are paid for a given specific protection, it is either because there is no risk at all or because the probability of occurrence is so low that not enough time has passed to encounter the first event. Satellite operators follow the latter argument and hence secure these insurance policies.

1 Launching state is defined in the 1972 Convention on International Liability for Damage Caused by Space Objects as (a) a state which launches or procures the launching of a space object (b) a state from whose territory or facility a space object is launched.

Damage Insurance

The term 'damage insurance' is somewhat misleading in the context of space insurance, as it could be understood as the term used in more classical ground property insurance definitions.

But the space insurance policy provides much wider protection than the pure 'physical damage' of satellite equipments. It covers the consequences of:

> Faulty design. For instance, the inadequate design of a propulsion system, leading to a leaking system and in turn to a massive reduction of operational lifetime, is insured. It does not matter whether the propulsion system was faulty before the lift-off. What is of importance it that the failure was discovered after the lift-off and that it could not have been detected before the launch by applying the usual industry standards tests and verifications.
>
> Ground operator mistake. The sending of a wrong command to the satellite by the operator sitting in the control station, leading to the complete loss of the satellite, is insured. By extension, the actions or inactions of the ground controller are equivalent to a space risk. Similarly the effects on the satellite of the unavailability of the ground station, because of its destruction by a fire for instance, are insured but not the cost of repair of the ground station itself (which could be insured by the traditional property and casualty insurance markets).
>
> Inadequate testing. An insufficient level of vibration during the ground testing, leading to a mechanical failure of the structure of the satellite during the launch phase, is insured. Again, the insured would have to prove that it could not have detected the under-testing of the satellite using the best standards of the industry. Similarly, an over-vibration level caused by the launch vehicle is insured as well.
>
> Performance reduction. A small deviation from the satellite performance specifications values, preventing the commercial mission from being fully fulfilled, is insured. However, this small deviation must be such that the satellite operator cannot fulfil its intended communication purposes.

This list is not exhaustive, but gives a flavour of the large range of failures or underperformances that are insured by space insurers.

It is important to note that there is no obligation to find the exact cause of the failure for the claim to be paid. The insured has nevertheless the obligation to use its best efforts to investigate the cause of the problem and to provide the insurers with an explanation. The counterpart of this unusual wide spectrum of coverage offered by this specialised branch of insurance is – along with high premium levels – a strict contractual obligation of information disclosure.

The insured has the obligation to disclose all pertinent technical and non-technical information to the insurers, whether before the insurance contract is signed or after, until the period of coverage has ended. This information is defined in the insurance policy under the generic term 'underwriting information' (UI).

The insurers have the right to request the renegotiation of the affected terms of the policy wording in the event the UI is materially amended. Failure to do so exposes the insured to the denial in part or in total of the claim. To deny the claim, the insurers may argue that the necessary information regarding the testing or the design was not provided to them at the right time (for example before they provided the insured with a formal insurance proposal) preventing them from including this additional risk in their quote.

One of the reasons of the importance of the information provided by the insured to the insurers is, unlike most other classes of damage insurance where an expert can be sent to evaluate the status of the goods, satellites cannot be reached once in orbit and can hardly be evaluated by another party other than the manufacturer or the satellite operator itself.

The last point of the above list made reference to the intended communication purposes. A loss is covered if the satellite status meets simultaneously two conditions:

1. the technical status of the satellite is such that the insurance loss definitions are fulfilled; *and*
2. the satellite or the affected portion of the satellite cannot be used for its intended communications purposes.

The second requirement, which seems to be redundant (if the insurance loss definitions are fulfilled, doesn't it mean that the satellite cannot be used?), was introduced by the insurers to try to overcome a specific issue. Satellites are designed according to technical requirements, which most of time are over specified to fulfil what the satellite operator intends to do. Each party in the chain introduces its own (hidden) technical margin. As a result, it could happen that, for example, a degraded amplifier can still properly serve the commercial market, even though it doesn't meet the specifications. Insurers are of the opinion that the claim is justified only if a situation leads to an impossibility to use the satellite for a commercial activity.

However, the satellite operators often procure their satellites to serve a larger commercial market than the ones existing at the time of the construction of the spacecraft. This causes some difficulty in precisely defining what the intended communications purposes are.

Who Offers Space Insurance Contracts?

There are only a few insurers worldwide that have started and maintained a specialised department to underwrite space risks. These are located in the USA, in the UK (Lloyd's), in France, Italy, Switzerland and Germany.

The space departments employ only a handful of specialists, most of whom spent the beginning of their carrier in the technical space industry.

Who Buys Space Insurance Contracts?

The party contracting a space insurance policy is the one having the 'risk of loss' which is most of the time – but not always – the owner of the satellite during that period of time. Depending upon the clause of transfer of title in the satellite procurement contract, this party could be either the satellite manufacturer or the satellite operator. The most common situation is when ownership (and the risk of loss) of the satellite is retained by the manufacturer until lift-off and then passed to the operator ('ground delivery'). In such a case, the satellite operator will be the insured under the launch insurance coverage.

In the event of a 'turn-key' contract, which stipulates that the manufacturer will hand over the property and the risk of loss of the satellite to the operator only after successful in-orbit acceptance testing, the manufacturer will secure insurance against the risk of loss of the satellite during the launch and test phase. There are fewer and fewer full turn-key contracts including the insurance. It is probably because the manufacturers cannot afford proposing a fixed price contract to the satellite operators including the space insurance premium, which may account for one-fourth of the total procurement cost, in particular in a very volatile market where the average premium rate can vary by a factor of two over a very short period of time.

Another reason is the much better protection offered to the satellite operator in the event of a ground delivery as the operator is indemnified directly by the insurers, rather than waiting to be contractually indemnified by the manufacturer who is in turn insured with the space insurers.

Finally, the duty of disclosure is easier to fulfil in the event of a ground delivery. Indeed, the operator can only pass to the insurers what it has received from its manufacturer and is not put in a position to chose which information to pass or not. To the contrary, the duty of disclosure imposed on the manufacturer in the event of a full turn-key contract is much more difficult to manage as the manufacturer is both at the source of the information and has to select the relevant information to be passed to the insurers.

How Much is Insured?

The sums insured under space insurance contracts are extremely diverse: they can span from USD 10 million to USD 450 million for heavy complex satellites.

The sum insured is usually equal to the book value of the satellite in the operator's financial statements, being the total of the value of the satellite, the launch cost and the insurance premium.

The sum insured is defined as an agreed value at the time of underwriting the risk. Once the risk has incepted, the sum insured cannot be disputed.

The premium costs vary considerably from one risk to another. To give a broad idea of the level of the premium percentages, the launch risks (including the first year in orbit) range from 10 per cent to 20 per cent and the in-orbit risks from 1 per cent to 2.5 per cent of the sum insured. High peaks and drops can be observed in this highly volatile market.

What is the Process to Secure a Space Insurance Contract?

Having selected the insurance broker, the future insured will, long before the launch date of its satellite, organise the disclosure of the technical information required by the space insurers.

The first step to obtain a space insurance policy is therefore to organise a technical presentation of the satellite and of its launcher to the insurance community – with a great level of detail. This will allow the insurers to evaluate the level of risk presented by the composite satellite/launcher. The technical presentation shall therefore contain enough information to allow that process to take place. As explained earlier, this technical presentation together with the following question and answer session is an extremely important piece of the process. Failing to disclose properly the risk to be insured may lead to significant problems in the event of a claim.

Then the insurers receive from the insurance broker a term sheet (the 'slip'), which summarises the main characteristic of the risk, like the sum to be insured, the duration of the risk period and the definitions of what is an insured loss.

Each insurer will then quote its own price for the risk, together with the proposed share of the sum insured it is willing to guarantee (the 'capacity'). The insurance broker will aggregate the capacities proposed by all space insurers up to the required sum insured, starting with the cheapest insurers. Once the targeted sum insured is reached, a line is drawn and the most expensive insurers are not selected to participate. This method is called 'vertical placement'.

Before making the final decision of where to draw the line, the wording of the insurance contract is discussed with all insurers with a view to obtaining one single set of insurance wording.

This is of course a simplified description of the process. There are many other factors than the price and the capacity in selecting or rejecting an insurer. For instance, the insurance companies financial security (as provided by the ratings agencies), the demand for specific clauses or amendments will play in favour or against that insurer. Moreover, it is also possible to apply a soft cut (an insurer can be asked to participate at half of the capacity it has offered) rather than a hard cut ('in or out').

What is Insured?

Any loss will be measured at the level of the satellite itself. Damage to the launch vehicle for instance is not insured, unless it causes the loss or the failure of the satellite.

The exact definition of the insured losses will be set according to the mission of the satellite. There are two main categories of insured satellites:

> Telecom satellites. Their mission is to transmit to the earth signals in certain frequency bands (Ku-band for direct transmission of television to personal dishes, C-band for transmission to large collective antennas, Ka-band for internet high-speed transmission) during the duration of the life. The quantification of the loss will follow these two main parameters: the insured loss will be calculated as a proportion of the number of amplifiers lost to the nominal ones, combined with a reduction of the life time. This is known as the 'transponder-years' method, which consists of multiplying the number of transponders by the satellite lifetime.
>
> Earth observation satellite. Its mission is to take images (in the visible band or other frequency bands) of the earth and download the collected data to specific gateways. The quantification of the loss will then take into account the capacity to take those pictures (number of working CCD captors for instance) at the right time (control of the altitude and attitude of the satellite) combined with the capability to store the data (functioning of the mass memory devices) and combined with the possibility to send the data on the ground without forgetting the life time duration.

If the satellite mission is only partially degraded, the quantification of the loss will be called 'partial loss' and the claim amount calculated as a direct proportion of the 'transponder-years' lost (in the case of a telecom satellite). On the other hand, an explosion of the rocket would evidently lead to a total loss of the mission and the payment of the full sum insured.

There is a unique point in between the partial loss and the total loss called the 'constructive total loss' (CTL) point. Satellite operators consider, because of the fixed operational costs of a satellite in-orbit, that beyond a certain degradation point a proportional indemnity is not financially sustainable. If a CTL occurs, they wish to be indemnified for the full value of the satellite in order to be able to launch a replacement satellite. The constructive total loss (CTL) point can be set anywhere between 75 per cent and 90 per cent.

In the event of a CTL, the insurers will pay 100 per cent of the sum insured, even if a small portion of the satellite mission is still operating and can in principle generate revenues. Once they have indemnified the insured for the full value of the satellite, insurers are entitled to take title to the satellite. While this possibility is not disputed by the parties, its application in the real life is most of the time problematic. The insurers becoming the owners of the satellite have suddenly to respect all ITU[2] rules and regulations, have to operate the satellite from their own orbital position (coordinated in frequency), pay for the control station services, pay for the third party liability insurance and so on. The only real accessible possibility is for the insurers to sell the damaged satellite to another operator with a back-to-back contract.

The insurers and the insured sign a full and final release agreement preventing any party to renegotiate the claim in the event later events prove that the claim amount evaluation was under or over estimated.

What is the Claim Collection Process?

The claim collection process is a two-step process. As soon as an abnormal event is recorded as potentially leading to a claim, the insured shall immediately (within a maximum of 30 days) send a short notice, the 'Notice of Loss', to the insurers. From that date, the insured has 180 days to characterise the loss, calculate the loss amount according to the insurance policy formulas and prepare all possible technical documents to justify and explain the failure. The final document, named the 'Proof of Loss', is then to be formally agreed by the insurers. The payment is usually done within 45 days from the insurers' agreement to the Proof of Loss.

Conclusion

Contracting space insurance coverage, whether damage insurance or liability insurance, is a relatively long and complex process.

The ill-named 'damage insurance' is in effect a 'performance guarantee' applied to a high-tech product, which is in many respects a prototype launched once and for all, and subjected during its lifetime to depressurisation, g-forces, high and low temperatures and so on. It is therefore somewhat surprising that through the years the insurance companies have succeeded in proposing to their clients comprehensive coverage structures and generic policy wordings, at premium levels which, until now, have allowed insurers to make a profit and the insureds to secure their commercial activities and make a profit as well.

Liability insurance is written in accordance with the UN treaties as well as the national laws when they exist, and aims at indemnifying the space operator from whom sums may be required to pay to third parties as damages for bodily injury or damage to property.

---

2 International Telecommunications Unit.

Chapter 24
Export Control Issues in Space Contracts*

Matthias Creydt and Kay-Uwe Hörl

Introduction

The management of export control issues is one ingredient of a successful space project and the allocation of associated risks is often hotly disputed during contract negotiations.

As export control law is a *lex specialis* of the foreign trade law, for the legal practitioner who is negotiating space contracts, and for whom it is important to avoid pitfalls during negotiations and throughout the lifetime of a contract, it is advisable to secure the detailed know-how of a specialised counsel.

Legal and Commercial Background of Export Control

For reasons such as the protection of national know-how and the avoidance of weapons proliferation, countries are concerned about the uncontrolled export of certain knowledge and technology. They have therefore agreed on rules at the international level and implemented them into national laws. However, many national space industries still depend on US suppliers and special attention must therefore also be paid to US (re-)export regulations. The cost and risk of non-compliance with these various rules are significant so there is also a commercial imperative to acquire good knowledge of the applicable rules as well as to implement appropriate export control management.

International Regulations

The unilateral actions of one state may restrict the export of dual-use equipment to critical states. Such actions are only effective, however, if those states cannot obtain the same supplies from third states. Hence, for export control purposes, different international regimes have been set up over time e.g. the Coordinating Committee for Multilateral Export Controls (CoCom), the Wassenaar Arrangement,[1] and the Missile Technology Control Regime.[2]

---

* The content of this chapter reflects the views of the authors and not necessarily those of their affiliated employers or institutions.

1 See The Wassenaar Arrangement on Export Controls for Conventional Arms and Dual-Use Goods and Technologies, as adopted by the plenary of 11–12 July 1996.

2 See Agreement on Guidelines for the Transfer of Equipment and Technology Related to Missiles of 16 April 1987 (MTCR), 26 I.L.M. 599 (1987).

National Regulations

United States

National interest in protecting unauthorised exports in the space sector is most apparent in US export law, as it requires re-export licences for many space-relevant products. Private space companies must comply with US rules regardless of where those firms are incorporated.

US Commerce Department regulations To facilitate the licensing of commercial telecommunications satellites, authority for certain communications spacecraft and components was entrusted to the US Department of Commerce (DoC). As a rule, the DoC controlled the export of all space hardware. In implementing the Export Administration Act (EAA),[3] the DoC incorporated such items into the Export Administration Regulations (EAR) and placed them on the Commerce Control List. In addition, the Missile Technology Control Act of 1990 implemented further international guidelines. In any case, obtaining a DoC licence was, and still is, considered easier than obtaining a US State Department licence.

The most important advantage of the DoC regime is that, instead of determinations being made on a case-by-case basis by the Bureau of Industry and Security (BIS) of the DoC, companies can determine for themselves whether their export is exempt from or subject to a DoC licence. Another considerable advantage under the DoC regime is the existence of a *de minimis* rule. Generally, items with a US content below the 25 per cent threshold are considered to be exempt from re-export licence requirements.

From a risk management point of view, these two advantages translate into fewer costs and schedule risks for a given space project. Today, however, the significance of the DoC jurisdiction for space has decreased since most dual-use items, for example most space items, are now subject to the authority of the Department of State.

US State Department regulations US export regulations were tightened after the Great Wall Industry incident.[4] For reasons such as the incident in China and political pressure on then-President Clinton, jurisdiction over certain space items, especially commercial communications satellites, reverted to the DoS on 15 March 1999.

The vexing DoS regulations complement the International Traffic in Arms Regulations (ITAR) administered by the Direction of Defense Trade Control (DDTC ex-ODTC) under the Arms Export Control Act.[5] More specifically, the regulations contain various articles aimed at items considered to be arms, ammunition or implements of war. These are listed in the United States Munitions List (USML), which was amended and now includes most space items. It contains, *inter alia*, launchers and satellites, as well as associated data. Consequently, the export of such items requires a licence. In other words, a positive authorisation is required and no self-determination by the industry is possible.

---

3 See Export Administration Act of 1979, 50 U.S.C. 2401–20 (lapsed 20 August 1994). It had superseded the Mutual Defense Assistance Control Act, 26 October 1951, Pub. L. 82-213, c. 575, 65 Stat. 644 (1951).

4 See generally Burnett, D.J. 1999. 'So what are the United States Government's Rules on the Export of Satellites and Launch Vehicles?' in Proceedings of the 10th International Conference – Commercial and Industrial Activities in Space – Insurance Implications (Florence, Italy, 25–26 March 1999), at 169–73.

5 Arms Export Control Act, as amended, 22 U.S.C. 2778, et seq.

Today, almost any space export needs a licence. The different types of DoS authorisations include Export Licences,[6] Manufacturing and Licence Agreements,[7] and Warehouse and Distribution Agreements.[8]

Moreover, technical discussions, as defined by ITAR, taking place on a space project are subject to prior submission of a Technical Assistance Agreement (TAA). Submitted to the DDTC, TAAs are reviewed by different DoS departments, as well as other agencies. Where no TAA is in place, the necessary application process can effectively slow down any trouble-shooting efforts, which can be particularly problematic for a project trying to stick to a tight schedule.[9]

Furthermore, Technology Transfer Control Plans (TTCP) are required for each company of a non-NATO country intending to launch a US-origin satellite or components.

In short, export control under the DoS regime can be burdensome and thus can raise additional costs.

Besides manufacturers, launch providers, operators and insurers are also affected by US export laws. Under the US regulation, any export of technical data is subject to a licence. This also applies to technical data which a company has to furnish to its insurer, making it that much harder to quote an insurance premium and to reinsure a space activity. In a way, applicable export regulations may run counter to a client's basic obligation of disclosure and the applicable policies and general rules of law.

There are plans by the current President Obama to reform the ITAR. The reason for this is to update the regulations and to adjust them to the threats and dangers the US is faced with today. The most important plans are: to introduce one single licence authority instead of having different jurisdictions within different departments; to combine the CCL and the USML into a single control list; to create a single IT system with a single point of entry for applicants, instead of having different systems of various administrations that are unable to communicate with each other; and to create a single enforcement agency, to replace the current loose coordination between the Department of State, the Department of Commerce, the Department of Justice, the FBI and so on. However, as expected, the plans are not without controversy. It is therefore unclear what the outcome of the reform plans will be, and when and if they will be enacted.

Europe

With regard to export controls in Europe, a uniform legal framework is still evolving. While common lists of dual-use goods, destinations and guidelines are essential elements for an effective European export control system, the content of those lists is of a strategic nature and thus falls within the competence of the Member States. Therefore, national export laws and regulations still exist. However, in order to ensure compliance with the international commitments and responsibilities of its Member States, the European Community realised the need for a common control system for exports from the European Community to third countries. Therefore, a European Council Regulation for a uniform and consistent application of the control of dual-use goods throughout

6 These DSP 5 licences (or DSP 119 for bulk exports) cover hardware, data and software as well as associated documentation, which is designated ITAR-controlled by the US government.

7 Under these agreements foreign entities are authorised to manufacture US defence articles or to perform certain services involving ITAR-controlled data.

8 These agreements allow the export of controlled hardware with the intention of reselling it abroad.

9 The same goes for changing previous authorisations on already exported goods, which are subject to a General Correspondence.

the European Union (EU) was established.[10] The aim was to promote EU and international security and to provide a level playing field for EU exporters.

For the export of arms, the relevant regulations are the European Union Code of Conduct on Arms Exports and the Common Military List of the European Union as well as the Directive 2009/43/EC[11] in regard to transfers of defence-related products within the EC.[12]

In addition, embargoes by means of Council Regulations against certain countries exist, as for example the so-called 'Iran Embargo'.[13]

Council Regulation (EC) No. 428/2009 for dual-use items The Council Regulation (EC) No. 428/2009 (Dual Use Regulation)[14] sets up a Community regime for the control of exports, transfers, brokering and transit of dual-use items.[15] The export control regime was established by Council Regulation (EC) No. 3381/94 and subsequent Regulation (EC) 1334/2000 of June 2000. However, since the Council Regulation (EC) No. 1334/2000 had been significantly amended on several occasions and further amendments were necessary, it was decided to have a complete recast in order to maintain clarity. This was done through Council Regulation (EC) No. 428/2009 of 5 May 2009 entering into force on 27 August 2009. The intention, to help complete the internal market and to coordinate a common European export control system, however, remains the same.

The Dual Use Regulation establishes a common EU applicable export authorisation. The scope of the Dual Use Regulation applies to all dual-use items, contained in the list of dual-use items of Annex I of the Regulation. The list of Annex I is based on the Wassenaar Arrangement. For all exports or brokering and transit activities in regard to such items, an authorisation shall be required.[16] However, for any intra-Community transfer of items listed in Annex I, an export authorisation is not required. Only for items that are listed in Annex IV of the Dual Use Regulation and that are considered especially sensitive is an intra-Community licence still necessary.[17] The term dual-use items includes goods as well as software and technology that can be used for both civil and military purposes.[18] In addition, in cases of existing embargoes or an intended end use concerning WMD, an end-user/end-use orientated authorisation is required.[19] The responsibility for deciding on such export authorisations lies with the national authorities. National provisions and decisions affecting exports of dual-use items, however, are to be taken in the framework of

---

10 EU, Council Regulation (EC) No. 3381/94 of 19 December 1994 Setting up a Community Regime for the Control of Exports of Dual-Use Goods, OJ L367 (31 December 1994) 000-0007, last amended by Regulation No. 2432/2001 of 20 November 2001. The second pillar of the legal framework is EU, 94/942/CFSP: Council Decision of 19 December 1994 on the Joint Action Adopted by the Council of the Basis of Article J.3 of the Treaty on European Union Concerning the Control of Exports of Dual-Use Goods, OJ L367 (31 December 1994) 0008-0163. The annex contains a common list of dual-use goods, which are subject to control when exported from the EU.

11 Directive 2009/43/EC of the European Parliament and of the Council of 6 May 2009 simplifying terms and conditions of transfers of defence-related products within the Community (OJ L 146, 10 June 2009, 1).

12 Since the role of such regulations is not of great importance for the space industry, there will only be a closer look at the Directive 2009/43/EC, due to its being more recent.

13 Council Regulation (EC) No. 423/2007 concerning restrictive measures against Iran.

14 Council Regulation (EC) No. 428/2009 of 5 May 2009 setting up a Community regime for the control of exports, transfer, brokering and transit of dual-use items (OJ L 134, 29 May 2009, 1).

15 Art. 1 Dual Use Reg.

16 Art. 3 (1) Dual Use Reg.

17 Art. 22 (1) Dual Use Reg.

18 Art. 2 (1) Dual Use Reg.

19 Arts 4 and 8 Dual Use Reg.

common commercial policy.[20] Further, the Member States may adopt additional export licence requirements for dual-use items not listed in Annex I for reasons of public security or human rights considerations.[21]

For all exports for which an authorisation is required, generally, such export authorisation shall be granted by the competent authorities of each Member State where the exporter is established.[22] Different types of export authorisations exist. Exports may be authorised through individual,[23] global[24] or general authorisation.[25] When a licence application is being reviewed for approval by a Member State, considerations to be taken into account are:[26]

a. obligations and commitments deriving from international treaties;
b. obligations under sanctions imposed by a common position, a joint action adopted by the Council, an OSCE decision or by the Security Council of the United Nations;
c. considerations of national and foreign security policy; and
d. considerations about intended end use and the risk of diversion.

The Dual Use Regulation further provides for co-operation with the Commission and the exchange of information between competent authorities with a view to decisions in regard to export authorisations.[27]

From a practical point of view, attention should be paid to the fact that the focus is increasingly on company compliance programmes and the ability of companies to avoid any non-compliances in the first place. Thus, according to the 428/2009 Dual Use Regulation, approval of a global authorisation will depend on the existence of an applicant's 'Internal Compliance Programme' as well.[28]

Any sanctions in cases of non-compliance are, however, subject to national legislation. Any provisions in this regard are therefore not part of the Dual Use Regulation.

Directive 2009/43/EC in regard to transfers of defence-related products within the EC With Directive 2009/43/EC of the European Parliament and of the Council of 6 May 2009, terms and conditions of transfers of defence-related products within the Community shall be simplified. The Directive applies to the defence-related products set out in its Annex[29] and aims at the establishment of a European domestic market for defence-related products, in order to enhance the competitiveness of the European defence industry. This shall be done through simplified rules and procedures applicable to the intra-Community transfer of defence-related products. In order to simplify the current licensing systems, provisions in regard to general transfer licences, global

20 Preamble (5) Dual Use Reg.

21 Art. 8 Dual Use Reg.

22 Art. 9 (2) Dual Use Reg.

23 Art. 2 (8) Dual Use Reg.

24 Arts 2 (10), 14 (1) Dual Use Reg., Annex IIIa Dual Use Reg.

25 Arts 2 (9) (11), 9 Dual Use Reg., Annex II of Dual Use Reg., Community General Export Authorisation No. EU001.

26 Art. 12 (1) Dual Use Reg.

27 Art. 19 Dual Use Reg.

28 Art. 12 Dual Use Reg.

29 Art. 2 of the Directive.

transfer licences as well as individual transfer licences are contained in the Directive.

Since the Directive does not become part of the national law of the Member States directly, it still needs to be converted by the Member States into their respective national law.

National Export Control Regulations

Although, as described above, national export control systems are generally driven by the same ideas and therefore are quite similar, there are also individual features in each of the national export provisions. Export control regimes of some the most important European states involved in the space business are thus briefly introduced here.

German Export Control Regulations

The main German export control regulations are the Foreign Trade and Payments Act (Aussenwirtschaftsgesetz, AWG) and the Foreign Trade and Payments Regulation (Aussenwirtschaftsverordnung, AWV), together with the Germany Export list (Ausfuhrliste, AL). For exports, BAFA (Federal Office of Economics and Export Control) is the central licensing authority. In a number of cases, and depending on how critical or sensitive a case may be, BAFA decides to grant or refuse an export authorisation only after political consultations with the Federal Ministry of Economics and Technology and the Federal Foreign Office.[30] Different types of export authorisations are available, such as Individual Licences, Maximum Amount Licences, Collective Export Licences and General Licences.

A unique German requirement for export transactions is the nomination of a person responsible for exports. This person must be a member of the board of directors or executive management and is personally responsible for the compliance with German export control regulations.[31]

French Export Control Regulations

The export control system of France is different from, for example, the German or the US systems. The main differences are: no licence agency exists, but rather the Ministry is assigned directly with the task of licensing; and a French exporter needs to obtain formal approval even to sign a contract with regard to the export of goods. The French Ministry responsible for the licensing process for export licences is the Ministry of Defence. Satellites and other space industry products are generally classified as Warfare Products and Assimilated Products (WPA). The export approval process for such items can be divided into two stages.

In a first step, before sending the proposal and signing a contract, the Agrément Préalable (Preliminary Approval) needs to be applied for. If approved, the Preliminary Approval is signed by the DGA and the restrictions are written by the Secrétariat Général de la Défense Nationale (SGDN) on behalf of the French Prime Minister following positive recommendation by the CIEEMG (Commission Interministérielle pour l'Etude des Exportations de Matériels de Guerre). The applicant is notified of the issuance of the Preliminary Approval by the Ministry of Defence.

---

30 A brief outline of German Export Controls can be found on the BAFA homepage at: http://www.ausfuhrkontrolle.info/bafa/en/export_control/publications/export_control_brief_outline.pdf [accessed: 10 October 2009].

31 The legal basis for this is 'Principles of the Federal Government on checking the reliability of exporters' of 10 August 2001.

There are different scopes or levels that can be authorised by a Preliminary Approval. A contract can only be negotiated once the Preliminary Approval level 'Sales or Negotiation' has been notified. Then the contract can only be signed once the next Preliminary Approval level, 'Sales', has been obtained.

In a second step, the actual export authorisation for warfare products known as the AEMG (Autorisation d'Exportation des Matériels de Guerre) needs to be obtained. Application for an AEMG also has to be submitted to the Ministry of Defence once the exporting company has produced proof that all restrictions have been respected. The export authorisation, however, is issued by French Customs, following approval by the Ministry of Defence, the Ministry of Foreign Affairs and SGDN on behalf of the French Prime Minister.

There are two different types of AEMG licence. The AEMG 'temporary export' licence (which is valid for one year and authorises the temporary export of goods mentioned in the Preliminary Approval) and the AEMG 'permanent exportation' licence (which is valid for two years and authorises the permanent export of goods mentioned).

UK Export Control Regulations

For the United Kingdom, the important export control regulations are contained in the Control Act 2002 together with the implementing legislation in the form of various orders. However, as of 6 April 2009, the Export Control Order 2008 consolidated and updated the Export of Goods, Transfer of Technology and Provision of Technical Assistance (Control) order 2003 (Amd 1863/2007), the Trade in Goods (Control) order 2003 as well as the Trade in Controlled Goods (Embargoed Destinations) order 2004 into one new single order. The UK licensing authority for strategic export controls is the Export Control Organisation (ECO) of the Department for Business, Innovation and Skills (BIS).[32] The ECO processes all military, nuclear and dual-use export licence applications. Licences are issued or refused after receiving advice from other Government departments, such as the Ministry of Defence, the Defence Export Services Organisation (DESO) or the Foreign and Commonwealth Office (FCO). Under UK law, the following types of export authorisation exist: a Standard Individual Export Licence (SIEL); an Open Individual Export Licence (OIEL), which is specific to an individual exporter, covering multiple shipments of specified goods to specified destinations and/or in some cases specified consignees; and an Open General Export Licence (OGEL), which allows the export of specified controlled goods by any exporter provided that the conditions are met and the shipment and destination are eligible.

Russian Export Control Regulations

The export control system of the Russian Federation has a lot in common with the German system. The reason for this is that the German system was to a large degree taken as a model by the Russian government. The export control regulations and the licensing process are administered by the Federal Service for the Technical and Export Control (FSTEK) which belongs to the Ministry of Defence. The main export control provisions are contained in Governmental Regulation No. 691 of 15 September 2008. Depending on how sensitive an export is, the FSTEK will also involve the Inter Ministry Council. Two types of licences can be applied for: the One-time Licence (which allows the export of a set amount of items) and the General Licence (which allows the export of a set amount of items, to specified countries, without the need for a specified end-user).

32 Formerly known as BERR (Department for Business Enterprise and Regulatory Reform).

Pitfalls for Practitioners

Export control managers are tasked with maintaining the legal integrity of their company by organising an export control process that complies with all applicable rules. While a good grasp of those rules is of paramount importance, it is equally necessary to install the appropriate documentation systems as well as manage the interface to suppliers and customers.

A number of IT-based tools enable the efficient management of export control licences and can easily be consulted for internal uses but also in cases of audits. Solutions are available that plug into the different existing IT environments. Obviously, it is not sufficient merely to store the relevant documentation, but companies must organise themselves to respect the various provisos of export licences. This necessitates, for instance, a reliable overview of foreign nationals working in a company. Thereby, those individuals can be kept away from a given project if they are not permitted under the relevant licence. At a time when employers are looking for maximum flexibility in the workforce, export control managers have to be concerned not only about the employees of the company but also about elements of the workforce that come from temporary employment agencies.

The minority of space companies are small or medium-sized enterprises. Often space companies operate in international structures with distinct legal entities in various countries. At a time when cross-border teams are ubiquitous, even within one company, the importance of covering from the start all necessary entities within the relevant licences, e.g. Technical Assistance Agreements, is more important than ever, especially when critical projects and application periods must be considered when drafting a project schedule.

One way to save time is by simplifying the signing procedures for TAAs. Often multiple companies are party to a TAA. Signatures can be obtained quicker if only one set of original TAAs is provided to the US supplier instead of as many sets of signatures as parties. In this context, it is also recommended that suppliers first send a draft of the proposed TAA to the customer to check for completeness and correctness. Only then should suppliers officially submit their TAA to the DDTC.

Flowing down export requirements to suppliers is relatively easy if dedicated subcontracts are concluded. The situation is quite different when it comes to purchasing from a large number of suppliers by way of purchase orders. In this case, it is recommended to have explicit and export control requirements within the general terms of purchase and to attach a questionnaire for classification of purchased goods to the purchase order. Buyers must then be instructed only to accept deliveries if the requested information is received prior to shipment. Regardless if purchasing by subcontract or by purchase order, clauses must be included whereby the supplier has to provide copies of export licences, agreements and respective provisos.

Vis-à-vis customers, it is recommended to include in proposal, and to negotiate for contracts, a caveat whereby performance is subject to export control authorisation. The argument here is that, granting a licence is a governmental act, which is not under the direct control of the applicant. If this is not negotiable, a compromise can be found under which the supplier has the obligation to duly submit its application. Essentially, it has to be decided if the obtaining of necessary export licences is of the essence for a contract. If yes, the appropriate remedies in case of failure need to be included (termination for cause, damages etc.). Alternatively, it may be agreed that the obligation consists only in filing the necessary applications in due time. Delays, refusal or licence revocation would then qualify as excusable delays or as *force majeure*.

A particular risk stems from 'non-ITAR' or 'ITAR-free' proposals. A change of jurisdiction of US parts could occur at any time, moreover parts could be incorrectly classified by a supplier and thus may turn out to be ITAR controlled after their delivery. Constant monitoring of the US export legislation is therefore necessary. Generally, therefore, it is wise to check very carefully, in each instance, if a company is really prepared to make such 'non-ITAR' or 'ITAR-free' proposals and wants to take the risks associated with such contracts. Similarly, licences may have to be adjusted due to changes of the original parameters, for example when a launcher and/or launch site for a particular mission changes or is first determined.[33] It is important to allow the necessary lead time to implement this on all levels of subcontracting.

If drafting a TAA for a US supplier or checking a TAA draft submitted by a supplier, it must be assured that the TAA text contains ITAR clauses that tackle the issue of foreign and contract employees. Pursuant to 22 CFR 124.16, access to unclassified defence articles and/or retransfer of technical data/defence services is authorised to individuals who are dual/third country national employees of the foreign licensee(s) and (its/their) approved sublicensees. The exclusive nationalities authorised are limited to NATO, the European Union, Australia, Japan, New Zealand and Switzerland. Further, all access and/or retransfers must take place completely within the physical territories of these countries or the United States.[34] Furthermore, in regard to contract employees, the following wording should be contained in the TAA:

> Contract employees to any Party to the Agreement hired through a staffing agency or other contract employee provider shall be treated as employees of the Party, and that Party is legally responsible for the employees' actions with regard to transfer of ITAR-controlled defense articles to include technical data and defense services. Transfers to the parent company by any contract employees are not authorized. The Party is further responsible for certifying that each employee is individually aware of his and/or her responsibilities with regard to the proper handling of ITAR-controlled defense articles, technical data, and defense services.

In order to take advantage of such relaxation, however, the respective company has to make sure to comply with these responsibilities and thus take all necessary actions.

Space companies having to observe export regulations face export risks. Measures like the described change of jurisdiction between US departments' change of classification result in uncertainty at the very least, and often in additional costs.

Export compliance programmes are costly and thus have repercussions on the (short-term) profitability of space projects. Non-compliance, however, is not an alternative as it may jeopardise a space project or even the entire space company. It is therefore recommended to comply with the letter and spirit of export control laws and take necessary organisational measures, including having:

5. dedicated export control staff
6. awareness programmes for relevant employees
7. defined processes for licence applications and administration
8. continuing and appropriate education for persons in 1 and 2
9. frequent audits of 1 to 4

---

33 For the level of compliance with end-use tracking: 2007. *End-Use Monitoring of Defense Articles and Defense Services Commercial Exports FY 2007*. [Online]. Available at: http://www.pmddtc.state.gov/reports/documents/End_Use_FY2007.pdf [accessed: 3 December 2010].

34 The US State Department was considering changing regulation of this issue of foreign employees of a party or sublicence to a TAA. However, at this point, it is not clear, if and in what way, the current regulation will be changed or adjusted.

In addition to these five company-internal measures, space ventures should also establish and maintain conducive relationships with the relevant export administrations.

Future Perspectives

In the future, it is likely that export control continues to play an important role in space contracts. This will especially affect those companies and industries that need to develop new markets and customers for which export restrictions are still applicable to certain extents.

It can be expected that some non-US companies will strive further towards ITAR-free space projects to escape the application of US export regulations. This is not only motivated by the associated cost of compliance but also an attempt to reduce risks, for example the risk of licence denials or delays. In parallel, American industry could increase its lobbying efforts to relax US export rules because they impair their export business or are inappropriate for new space applications such as space tourism.

As the legal framework is unlikely to change and due to its impact on space projects, export control should move more into the focus of space project management. As with other risks, a proper management of export compliance will translate into commercial advantages.

Conclusions

There are a number of valid reasons for the present export control regime. It creates a legal framework that prescribes certain rules that need to be abided by in space projects. As such projects are mostly composed of various partners, subcontractors and suppliers, regulating relations between them is necessary. This purpose can best be served by contracts that link the parties. Hence, it is recommended that with regard to such contracts responsibilities for export control risks are clearly allocated as early as in the pre-proposal phase to make those risks manageable.

A number of pitfalls can easily be avoided in export compliance. It is therefore important to have skilled and knowledgeable export control managers within the company. It is equally important that more attention is paid to the relevant rules.

As with other interfaces with governmental authorities, trustful cooperation should be pursued. This can be achieved by fully complying with their requirements and by maintaining maximum transparency to keep them informed of planed activities.

List of References

Author unknown. 2007. *End-Use Monitoring of Defense Articles and Defense Services Commercial Exports FY 2007*. [Online]. Available at: http://www.pmddtc.state.gov/reports/documents/End_Use_FY2007.pdf [accessed: 3 December 2010].

Burnett, D.J. 1999. 'So what are the United States Government's Rules on the Export of Satellites and Launch Vehicles?', in *Proceedings of the 10th International Conference – Commercial and Industrial Activities in Space – Insurance Implications (Florence, Italy, 25–26 March 1999)*, 169–73.

Epstein J.M. 2001. 'Exporting Commercial Satellite Technology: Coping in the Current Regulatory Environment', *Air and Sp. Lawyer*, (Fall), 17–20.

EU. 1994. Council Regulation (EC) No. 3381/94 of 19 December 1994 Setting up a Community Regime for the Control of Exports of Dual-Use Goods, OJ L367 (31 December 1994) 000-0007, last amended by Regulation No. 2432/2001 of 20 November 2001.

EU. 1994. 94/942/CFSP: Council Decision of 19 December 1994 on the Joint Action Adopted by the Council of the Basis of Article J.3 of the Treaty on European Union Concerning the Control of Exports of Dual-Use Goods, OJ L367 (31 December 1994) 0008-0163.

Jakhu, R.S. and Wilson, J. 2000. 'The United States Export Control Regime: Its Impact on the Communications Satellite Industry', *Ann. Air and Sp. L.*, 25, 157–81.

Johnson-Freese, J. 2000. 'Alice in Licenseland: US Satellite Export Controls since 1990', *Sp. Policy*, 16 (3), 195–204.

Nunn-Wolfowitz 2000. *Task Force Report: Industry 'Best Practices' Regarding Export Compliance Programs, 25 July 2000.*

Richter, A.K. 2009. 'Intra-EU-Ruestungsgueterrichtlinie, Zeitschrift für Außenwirtschaft in Recht und Praxis', *AW-Prax*, 294.

US State Department. ODTC. 2002. [Online]. Available at: http://www.pmdtc.org/processtime.htm [accessed: 26 February 2002].

Treaties/Acts

Agreement on Guidelines for the Transfer of Equipment and Technology Related to Missiles of 16 April 1987 (MTCR), 26 I.L.M. 599.

Export Administration Act of 1979, 50 U.S.C. 2401–20 (lapsed 20 August 1994).

Export Administration Regulations, 15 C.F.R. Part 730 et seq.

Export Control Act, 26 February 1949, c. 11, 63 Stat. 7 (1949).

Missile Technology Control Act of 5 November 1990.

National Defense Act, supra note XXX., 1511(1), 1511(2), 1513(a), 1514(a)(1), 1514(a)(2)(A), 1514(b).

National Defense Authorization Act, 101-510, Title XVII, ss. 1701–4.

Strom Thurmond National Defense Authorization Act for Fiscal Year 1999, 105-261, § 1513(a), 112 Stat. 2172, 17 October 1998 (United States: H.R.3616).

The Wassenaar Arrangement on Export Controls for Conventional Arms and Dual-Use Goods and Technologies. As adopted by the plenary of 11–12 July 1996.

(treaty / act) Arms Export Control Act, as amended, 22 U.S.C. 2778, et seq. authorizing the President to control exports. This authority was delegated to the Secretary of State by Executive Order in 1977 (42FR4311).

22 C.F.R. Parts, 120-130, § 120.6, § 121.1, category IV, category XV.

Chapter 25
The Use of Service Level Agreements in Space Projects

Ingo Baumann

Introduction

Service Level Agreements (SLAs) are widely used in the IT industry. They are part of contracts for a multitude of different data, internet and communications services. In recent years, SLAs have also become increasingly used in space projects. This chapter analyses the benefits this type of agreement has for the space industry. It describes what SLAs are and how they function. The chapter then looks into the question whether these characteristics make SLAs generally transferable to and useful for space projects. Some space projects, in which SLAs are already used, have been elected for more detailed analyses. Recommendations are then given for use of SLAs in future space projects. The chapter closes with conclusions and an outlook.

Service Level Agreements in the IT Industry

Service Level Agreements (SLAs) are a typical feature of many IT service contracts, especially in IT outsourcing projects.[1] The contractual structure of such outsourcing projects is often complex. In many cases, a modular structure is used comprising the main contract, one or more SLAs and a significant number of technical annexes. While sometimes the contract itself is defined as a 'Service Level Agreement', this term usually refers only to a specific set of terms and conditions being part of the overall contract.[2]

Background

The trend to use SLAs has arisen from the negative experience many customers gained in early outsourcing projects. They realised that the services provided did not match their needs and expectations. In addition, they had little ability to control or influence the contractual performance of the service provider for the outsourced services. A remedy for this situation was found in SLAs, which identify certain performance standards that the service provider must meet in providing its services.

---

1 For a comprehensive legal analysis of IT outsourcing agreements see Bräutigam, P. 2004. *IT Outsourcing – eine Darstellung aus rechtlicher, technischer, wirtschaftlicher und vertraglicher Sicht*. Berlin: Erich Schmidt. See also Söbbing, T. 2002. *Handbuch IT Outsourcing – rechtliche, strategische und steuerliche Fragen*. Frankfurt / Wien: Redline Wirtschaft; Burnett, R. and Klinger, P. 2005. *Drafting and Negotiating Computer Contracts*. Edinburgh: Tottel Publishing.

2 Bräutigam, P. 2004. *IT Outsourcing*, 802; Braun, H. 2006. *Die Zulässigkeit von Service Level Agreements – am Beispiel der Verfügbarkeitsklausel*. München: C.H. Beck, 3.

Structuring the Cooperation

During the negotiation phase, SLAs can be an excellent tool for helping the parties involved to improve their communications,[3] to understand and reflect their mutual abilities and expectations, to clarify contractual responsibilities and thereby to build the foundation for a long-term relationship. The SLA helps in structuring the discussions between customer and service provider about the details of the service, the requirements and expectations of the customer and the possible solutions the service provider can offer to meet these requirements and expectations. During the execution of the project, SLAs set the rules for constantly monitoring the quantity or quality of the service, for a fast resolution of technical problems and for measures to improve the service quality in the future. On this background, SLAs can also serve as a basis for effective dispute resolution.[4]

Divergent Aims and Failures

Practice shows that the parties often have different views about the role of the SLA and what it can realistically accomplish. Both sets of views may be valid, yet sufficiently different as to cause an early breakdown in negotiations. Before any development work on detailed contractual terms and conditions is done, it is advisable for the two parties to hold an open discussion to ensure that they have a basic level of mutual understanding and agreement. If they do not – and until they do – any further negotiation effort may prove futile.

With a view to the subject of this chapter, it is worthwhile to have a closer look at why negotiations on SLA-based contracts often fail in an early phase. In many cases, each party wants to use its own draft for the SLA and impose it on the other. This situation is comparable to the conflicting use of general terms and conditions, which always has high potential to create an impasse in negotiations. Other sources of conflict are different expectations regarding the purpose the SLA shall serve. The customer may have had a bad experience with previous projects and may want to use the SLA as a sledgehammer against the service provider each time the service does not meet expectations. This type of SLA tends to over-measuring and including every imaginable service level. On the other hand, the service provider may try to draft the SLA as vague as possible thereby reducing contractual consequences of non-performance to its maximum favour. In both cases, either negotiations are likely to fail or serious conflicts will arise later during the service provision period.

Intensive Negotiation Phase

The drafting and negotiation of an SLA require substantial time and effort of both parties. This is very often underestimated. It may take several months to conclude negotiations depending on the type of service to be provided, the parties' previous experience with SLAs, their familiarity with the key elements of an SLA, the demands of their other responsibilities and the state of the relationship between their respective organisations or companies. The effort is, however, strictly needed, as otherwise the SLA may produce more problems than it is supposed to solve. It is inadvisable to rush the negotiations on the SLA, because this process is designed to help the two parties build the

---

3 Blokdijk, G. 2008. *Service Level Agreements – 100 Success Secrets*. Newstead, QLD: Emereo Publishing, 28.

4 Braun, H. 2006. *Die Zulässigkeit von Service Level Agreements*, 5.

foundation for a successful long-term relationship. Imprecise or inadequate SLAs are reported to be one of the major reasons for failure of numerous projects.

Joint Negotiation Teams

SLAs are often regarded as purely technical documents. Negotiations are therefore held among engineers without involvement of legal and financial experts. Such approach, however, ignores that SLAs have strong interrelations and impacts both contractually and financially. SLAs are usually directly connected to contractual issues such as service obligations, warranty, liability, *force majeure*, termination and dispute resolution. Non-performance of SLA obligations may lead to serious financial consequences which, in some projects, are reported to have led even to insolvency of the service provider. It is, therefore, strictly advisable to involve the legal and financial experts as full members of the negotiation team for the SLA.

Features and Contents of the SLA

An SLA describes the quantity and quality standards of a service and, thus, makes the quality of the service measurable.[5] It is a key contractual document, setting out with certainty and precision descriptions of the services together with individual objective and realistically achievable performance levels and standards, in terms of quantity and quality in objective terms for the purposes of effective monitoring.[6] The SLA should therefore contain a detailed description of:

- the service
- the quantity and quality standards of a specific service
- the related services levels
- methods and procedures to control the agreed service levels
- sanctions for the service provider that does not meet the agreed service levels

Other standard elements of an SLA are the set-up of a User Help Desk (UHD), escalation procedures in cases of failures or non-performances and dedicated dispute resolution mechanisms.

Detailed definitions of the agreed service levels are at the heart of the SLA.[7] Most commonly, service levels refer to the service periods, the availability of the service, the mean time allowed between service failures, the mean time to repair, intervals of maintenance and, more generally, reaction and response times by the service providers.[8] What differentiates SLAs from standard Statements of Work is that the quantity and quality are defined in measurable terms. The service is broken down into sub-elements, parts of which are of a purely technical nature. Such technical elements may include the use of specific hard- or software, the performance requirements related to them (for example storage capacity) or the frequency for updates and replacements. Other elements are more related to the overall service quality and are usually expressed in relation to a specified time period.

5 See Bräutigam, P. 2004. 'SLA – in der Praxis alles klar?' *Computer und Recht*, 4, 248; Blöse, J. and Pechardschek, S. 2002. 'Die rechtliche Absicherung von IT-Outsourcing Projekten', *Computer und Recht*, 11, 788.

6 Burnett, R. and Klinger, P. 2005. *Drafting and Negotiating Computer Contracts*, 383.

7 Hörl, B. and Häuser, M. 2003. 'Service Level Agreements in IT-Outsourcingverträgen', *Computer und Recht*, 10, 715.

8 Söbbing, T. 2002. *Handbuch IT Outsourcing*, 164.

The most prominent example here is the criterion of service availability during a given time period. The time period may, depending on the individual case, either make reference to the usual working hours within the customer's organisation or be defined in relation to time intervals, such as hours per day or days per week. It is often overlooked that the fixation of a correct time reference is critical. Let us assume that the SLA requires a system availability of 98.5 per cent. Where the related time period is one week, this means that the respective system may have 2.52 hours of permitted outage. Where the related time period is one year, the system outage could, however, have duration of more than five days without constituting a breach of the respective SLA.[9] Especially from a customer perspective, it is therefore recommended to define reference time periods as short as possible.[10]

The definition of precise service availability provisions is especially important in case of complex technical systems. Where, for example, an overall system availability of 99 per cent is agreed in a SLA, actually each system component has to function without any failure over the whole reference time period. The service provider in such cases must be fully aware and must have control of all relevant factors influencing the system availability.

For each of the agreed service levels, the corresponding measurement method has to be defined along with the respective measurement times and intervals. Many technical systems offer the possibility of a 'log'; others require dedicated monitoring systems to be installed. Where a User Help Desk (UHD) is established, reaction and response time are usually measured by the time period between opening and closure of electronic trouble tickets. UHD services are grouped into categories established on the basis of the seriousness and criticality of a problem.[11]

An SLA further contains provisions on reporting. Usually, the service provider has to monitor all agreed service levels and to provide reports at regular intervals. Details concerning the times and intervals of reporting, as well as the requirements for the structure and content of the reports, should be laid down in the SLA. Where service levels are monitored solely by the service provider, the client should have special rights to conduct technical audits and review 'logs' or other technical monitoring data where available.

Once the service levels have been ascertained, the impact of the failure to meet them and the level of compensation has to be defined.[12] The provider is in breach of its contractual obligations when it is not providing the service within the agreed time, quantity and quality as laid down in the respective service levels. The customer is therefore entitled to receive compensation from the service provider. Negotiation should focus on a set of 'key service levels' instead of applying the compensation scheme to all possible service elements.[13] For some elements, it may be even appropriate to frame them as general 'targets' or 'objectives' within the overall service performance, without consequences for breach of contract if for some reason they are not achieved. In this way, the contractual remedies can be focused on the essential features of the service provision.[14]

Compensation for service level failure may technically be in the form of 'service credits', 'penalties' or 'liquidated damages'.[15] Attention has to be paid to the applicable national law and the different legal consequences associated to each of the above mentioned types of compensation.[16]

9 Bräutigam, P. 2004. 'SLA', 252.

10 *Ibid.*, 253.

11 Braun, H. 2006. *Die Zulässigkeit von Service Level Agreements*, 13.

12 Burnett, R. and Klinger, P. 2005. *Drafting and Negotiating Computer Contracts*, 384.

13 Braun, H. 2006. *Die Zulässigkeit von Service Level Agreements*, 12.

14 Burnett, R. and Klinger, P. 2005. *Drafting and Negotiating Computer Contracts*, 384.

15 *Ibid.*, 402.

16 For the German law see Braun, H. 2006. *Die Zulässigkeit von Service Level Agreements*, 15–19.

Engineers are often not aware that the terminology used is essential with regard to these legal consequences, especially for the application of the general liability provisions set out in the main contract. Considerable negotiation about the payment amounts and how they should be made, whether by actual sums paid by the provider to the customer or by a reduction in the sums paid to the provider by the customer, may be necessary before an agreement can be reached.[17] A balance needs to be struck so that the desired levels of performance can be secured for the customer without imposing too stringent restrictions on the service provider.[18]

Especially for large projects, a Service Level Management Board should be considered. It should be composed of representatives of both parties and meet regularly to discuss the service quality, any non-performance that has arisen during a given period, and the amount of compensation due to the customer. Such board would be the final step in the escalation procedure for resolution of problems and disputes. This function can ensure fast and cooperative conflict-resolution on the project management level, before applying the general rules of the main contract, for instance arbitration.

Usually, the amount of 'service credits' or other forms of compensation is capped to a certain percentage of the service fees, for example 5 or 10 per cent of the monthly invoice. Scheduled down-times of a system, especially during pre-agreed maintenance works, are taken out of the applicable compensation scheme.[19] Other details are subject to negotiation and depend on the individual services to be provided. In some cases, the parties may choose to identify not only a threshold level of acceptable performance for each service level, but also a level of 'increased impact' if the performance is at a certain level below the threshold service level. If the outsourcer's performance falls below the 'increased impact level', the service credit may increase substantially. An SLA should finally take into account that a system failure may affect a number of agreed service levels at the same time. In the absence of specific provisions in the SLA, the service provider would have to pay compensation for each of the service levels breached. In order to limit the financial risks for the service provider, it is therefore often advisable to introduce, for instance, a priority ranking among the service levels, or another balancing mechanism.

Where key service levels are not reached, or where the service provider constantly underperforms, the customer may have a right to terminate the contract for material breach. The interrelations between the respective termination clause in the main contract and the SLA have to be carefully drafted. Especially, the main contract should provide whether termination is related to the main contract or the respective service element only.[20] Attention should be drawn to the fact that the dependencies between the customer and the service provider can be very strong, especially in the case of long-lasting outsourcing services. In such case, termination by the customer may require a complex winding-up of the contract transferring the service provision back to the customer or to a new service provider.[21]

As the non-performance of service levels is connected to financial compensation or even termination of the contract, much attention should be drawn to the negotiation of effective *force majeure* clauses. Typically, service providers will seek a broad definition of *force majeure*, while customers seek a narrow, tightly defined provision restricted to general *force majeure* cases such as natural disasters.

17 Burnett, R. and Klinger, P. 2005. *Drafting and Negotiating Computer Contracts*, 404.

18 *Ibid.*, 383.

19 Bräutigam, P. 2004. 'SLA', 252; Braun, H. 2006. *Die Zulässigkeit von Service Level Agreements*, 10.

20 Bräutigam, P. 2004. 'SLA', 251.

21 See Burnett, R. and Klinger, P. 2005. *Drafting and Negotiating Computer Contracts*, 399, for a draft clause on exit management.

In typical IT outsourcing, customers expect the outsourcer to meet the agreed service levels without special incentives. In other cases, the service providers receives a bonus payment where all relevant service levels are fulfilled during a given service period. The bonus scheme can be a mirror of the compensation scheme with a cap relating to a certain percentage of the service fees. Bonus payments may sometimes apply in a more limited way as an incentive for the service provider to increase its service quality beyond the service levels agreed and to provide superior performance to the customer.

Conclusions

Although SLAs today form part of the IT industry's best practices, many customers and service providers still fail to negotiate an effective SLA. SLAs are not easy to design and require intensive exchange and detailed negotiations between the customer and the service provider.[22] A comprehensive, precise and fair SLA however provides an excellent tool for a successful, long-term relationship between the parties. It helps to create mutual understanding, to ensure effective project management and avoidance or structured resolution of conflicts. The following section evaluates under what circumstances Service Level Agreements may bring their benefit to space industry projects.

Pros and Cons of Using SLAs in Space Projects

Background

Space and related ground segments are basically IT systems with certain specific functions and characteristics. On-board computers used in spacecrafts face unique requirements such as extreme radiation resistance, high reliability and redundancy, limited space, weight and energy resources and the need for remote control and diagnosis capabilities. Once in space, spacecrafts cannot be repaired, at least not at reasonable costs. Software upgrades or new software must therefore be installed remotely in cases of changes to mission requirements, unforeseen situations, damaged components or software errors.

Due to the limited resources and extraordinary reliability requirements, the computing performance of a spacecraft is much slower than in comparable devices on earth. Today, space applications are in ever increasing need of more computing power and increased performance, supported by the trend to implement higher autonomy of spacecrafts (on-board multiplexing, on-board processing). In fact, information technology is the fastest changing discipline of space missions.[23]

The complex functionality of modern spacecrafts cannot be implemented without software.[24] Software is at the core of every space mission and the fastest growing component measured in

22 Blokdijk, G. 2008. *Service Level Agreements*, 20. The author reports that in more than one-third of projects the SLA does not work at all.

23 Ley, W., Wittmann, G. and Hallmann, W. 2009. *Handbook of Space Technology*. London: John Wiley & Sons, 363.

24 *Ibid.*, 372.

terms of complexity and development costs.[25] Where software aspects have been neglected at the beginning, this usually causes substantial schedule delays and higher costs.[26]

Growing Importance of IT Law for Space Projects

The importance of software for space missions is also a challenge for lawyers in the space industry. There is a growing need to look for best practices established in the IT industry and to adapt them for use in space industry contracts. Specific clauses in space industry contracts relate to the development, maintenance or upgrade of software. The European Space Agency (ESA) already regularly attaches Software Escrow Agreements to its contracts. IT law thereby adds to the growing diversification of international and national laws and regulations governing space activities.[27]

Potential for SLA in Space Projects

Within such an environment, there is certainly room for the use of SLA. However, their potential seems to be quite restricted. While being obvious from the terminology, it needs to be underlined that SLAs relate to services. In addition, due to their characteristics and the effort needed to conclude them, SLAs are only suitable for services provided over a certain period under fixed conditions. This considerably restricts their scope within the space industry. Service SLAs will generally not be suitable instruments for space projects relating to basic science, studies, or research and development work. They will also not be appropriate for typical supply contracts relating to hard- or software elements. For scientific satellite missions or for human spaceflight, the unique circumstances of such projects, the novelty of the technologies and the risks involved considerably reduce the possibilities for the implementation of SLA. However, their use could be considered in such projects for certain subcontracts, especially for maintenance and logistics services. It is reported that the European Space Agency has implemented SLAs for certain routine operational activities related to the ISS Columbus Module and the Automated Transfer Vehicle (ATV).

Use for Space Services

Even with the growing commercialisation of space activities, standard-type commercial services are still an exemption. Satellite communications was certainly the first branch of the space industry where such services were introduced, for example for the provision of basic telecommunications services or for the broadcasting of television signals. The closeness of satellite communications to the telecommunications industry in general supported the early commercialisation of this sector, leading to the eventual privatisation of the former international satellite organisations Intelsat, Inmarsat and Eutelsat in the late 1990s.[28] Earth observation has been the second branch of space industry subject to increasing private engagement and commercialisation. Today, geo-information data and images gathered by satellites are increasingly provided as an end-to-end service to the

25 *Ibid.*, 371.

26 *Ibid.*, 366.

27 See Baumann, I. 2005. 'Diversification of Space Law', in *Space Law: Current Problems and Perspectives for Future Regulation*, edited by M. Benkö and K.U. Schrogl. Utrecht: Eleven International Publishing, 47–74.

28 For a detailed description of these privatisation processes see Baumann, I. 2005. *Das internationale Recht der Satellitenkommunikation*. Frankfurt: Peter Lang.

customer. Satellite navigation may soon become the third branch of commercial space services provision.

Use of SLA during Operations and Services Phases

Even with regard to commercial space services, SLAs should be applied with great caution in the light of their suitability to the specific situation at hand. Space projects are usually of long duration and spanning many phases. These phases comprise early study work, detailed design and development, construction and testing, delivery to launch site, launch, early orbit phase, in-orbit testing and routine operations. Usually, an SLA will apply only for the routine operations phase. In certain cases, a transition or test phase can be implemented ahead to evaluate the system's performance, to test the suitability of the agreed service levels and to take corrective measures where necessary. Sanctions for not meeting the agreed service levels should, however, be applied only when the final service is provided under stable operational conditions.[29]

When considering the use of SLAs, one should also take account of the special risks related to space activities. These risks do not allow the typical risk allocation of a SLA to be applied without limitations. Even where end-to-end services are provided by operational satellites, these services might be affected by hardly foreseeable or controllable effects such as sun storms, atmospheric disturbances, space debris and so on. It would be unfair to oblige the service provider to compensate for non-performances in such cases of *force majeure* characteristics.

As a conclusion, it seems that the scope of application for SLAs is quite limited within the space industry. Most space projects are not suitable for their implementation, either due to their scope or due to the unique technologies and risks implied. The use of SLAs should therefore mainly be considered for well-established commercial space services as well as for certain subcontractor activities, such as for maintenance and logistics, for data up- and downlink services or for typical IT services associated to the space project.

Careful Preparation and Lessons Learned

In any case, the suitability of SLAs has to be carefully evaluated for each individual space project. It is useful to have standards and practices from the IT industry at hand. Project managers should be aware that SLAs often fail to provide their positive effect, mostly due to lack of time, understanding and resources for their drafting and negotiation. Lessons learned should be applied from precedents and experiences drawn from other projects, without, however, transferring them without due consideration. In the following section, some such precedents for SLAs in the space industry are presented and analysed.

Some Precedents for SLAs in Space Projects

Service Level Agreements are obviously not a common feature of space industry contracts. Until today, this instrument has been used only in a limited number of projects. This section describes these projects, their background and contractual structure. As far as information is available, details of the respective SLAs are reported and analysed.

---

29 Hörl, B. and Häuser, M. 2003. 'Service Level Agreements in IT-Outsourcingverträgen', 713.

Satellite Communications

Satellite communications has been the first and to date the most successful commercial use of outer space. It has significantly contributed to a general commercialisation and privatisation process within the space industry, making the construction, launching and operation of satellites a viable global business. Due to its economic importance and to its integration in the rapidly changing telecommunications markets, satellite communications leads the trends within the space industry and is an important indicator of future developments.

Not surprisingly, SLAs were first used within the satellite communications industry. Data from communications satellites are down- or uplinked from so-called teleports consisting of antenna and related hard- and software infrastructure. In the early years, teleports were typically operated either by the media and telecommunications companies or by the satellite operators themselves. Along with the privatisation process in the 1990s, these activities were outsourced to mostly smaller dedicated teleport operators. These operators now often provide their services under SLAs.

Even if not constituting true SLAs, the standard contracts of satellite operators for the lease of satellite transponders contain at least certain typical SLA elements, specifying the performance and availability of the transponder for use by the client and the consequences of non-performance or outages.

SLAs were then implemented on a large scale within two public private partnership projects in the European Space Industry, Skynet 5 and SatcomBw Stage 2.

Skynet 5 Skynet 5 was the first public private partnership project (PPP) ever contractually closed in the European Space Industry.[30] In 1997, the government of the United Kingdom (UK) conceived a military satellite communications system that would replace the Ministry of Defence's (MoD) current Skynet 4 satellites. The MoD chose the PPP route for the satellites because it believed that it would save the UK government about EUR 750 million over the life-time of the contract. Under the 15-year concession contract, Paradigm Secure Communications Ltd, a 100 per cent subsidiary of EADS Astrium Services, delivers core military satellite communications to the UK armed forces, with the ability to commercialise spare capacity to third parties. Paradigm took over the ownership and operation of the existing Skynet 4 infrastructure and deployed two new Skynet 5 satellites and the associated ground segment refurbishments from 2005 onwards.[31] Due to the military nature of the project, not much is publicly known about the contractual structure of the PPP or individual contract clauses. However, Paradigm's provision of services is measured against quality of service criteria and other performance standards as determined by respective service assurance mechanisms. In the event that Paradigm fails to meet these standards, deductions of service fees apply in respect of such service failure or under-performance in accordance with the applicable procedures.

SatcomBw As part of the military satellite communications programme, SatcomBw Stage 2, the German Armed Forces (Bundeswehr) are acquiring for the first time their own military communications satellites thereby laying the foundations for a secure information network for use by units on deployed missions outside Germany. The network supports the autonomous, global

30 Bertran, X. and Vidal, A. 2005. 'The Implementation of a Public-Private Partnership for Galileo Comparison of Galileo and Skynet 5 with other Projects' in *Proceedings of the ION GNSS 18th International Technical Meeting of the Satellite Division, 13–16 September 2005*, 390, 393.

31 *Ibid.*, 393.

transmission of audio and data as well as video and multimedia applications. The system went into operation in late 2010 and constitutes an important step in implementing the Bundeswehr concept for network-centric operations. The contract for the satellites communication programme was signed in July 2006 and runs for 10 years, with an option to extend it for a further seven and a half years. The customer is the Federal Office for Information Management and Information Technology of the Bundeswehr (IT-AmtBw). The contractor is MilSat Services GmbH (MSS), a joint venture set up specifically for the programme by EADS Astrium Services and the Friedrichshafen-based company ND SatCom Defence (NDD). Astrium owns 74.9 per cent of the shares in the joint venture, with ND SatCom Defence holding the remaining 25.1 per cent.

EADS Astrium is responsible for the space segment and will place two dedicated satellites in orbit. Thales Alenia Space has designed, manufactured, integrated, tested and delivered these satellites to Astrium. Astrium's German subsidiary, TESAT, manufactured the essential parts of the payload. The first satellite was launched in October 2009; a second identical satellite was launched in May 2010. Along with the in-orbit delivery of these two communications satellites for operations in military frequencies, the SatcomBw Stage 2 contract includes the associated operations, the delivery of a comprehensive ground user terminal segment and upgrading the management and control segment already installed with the Bundeswehr. MSS will also provide the Bundeswehr with commercial transmission capacities using Intelsat satellites to provide backup facilities and extra capacity. As in the case of Skynet 5, information on the contractual structure of SatcomBw Stage 2 is restricted. The project is not based on a pure public private partnership concept but on a mixture of standard supply service contracts with PPP elements. The underlying contract makes large use of SLAs, with a framework SLA – including the main principles and procedures – and a set of sub-SLAs describing the detailed service levels, time intervals and methods for measuring, reporting and escalation procedures, as well as the amounts of service credits linked to the non-performance of the respective service levels. Service Level Agreements concern the operation of a User Help Desk, the operation of a ground station, the routine operations of the two dedicated satellites, as well as the tasking of the commercial satellite capacities on the Intelsat system.

Both PPP projects show clear elements of typical service outsourcing and were therefore well suited for implementation of Service Level Agreements.

Satellite Navigation

Satellite navigation is increasingly used in almost all modes of transport, including aviation, road, rail and maritime transport, but also in other sectors such as communications, fisheries and agriculture. The annual global market growth rate for satellite navigation products and services has been substantial over the past years with predictions showing even more potential for the future.

The Galileo programme The two existing global systems, the US GPS and the Russian GLONASS, will be complemented by the European Satellite Navigation System Galileo in this decade. The system will consist of a constellation of 30 MEO satellites linked to control centres and a world-wide network of terrestrial stations. It will offer a set of services, including:

Open Service (OS): basic signal provided free-of-charge;

Safety-of-Life Service (SoL): enhanced signal including an integrity function that will warn the user within a few seconds in case of a malfunction. This service will be offered to the safety-critical transport community for example aviation. It will be certified according to the applicable standards, for example those of the International Civil Aviation Organisation (ICAO), and to the Open Sky regulations;

Commercial Service (CS): combination of two encrypted signals for higher data throughput rate and higher accuracy authenticated data;

Public Regulated Service (PRS): two encrypted signals with controlled access for specific users like governmental bodies;

Search and Rescue Service (SAR): Galileo will contribute to the international COSPAS-SARSAT cooperative system for humanitarian search and rescue activities. Each satellite will be equipped with a transponder transferring the distress signal from the user to the Rescue Coordination Centre and informing the user that his or her situation has been detected.

While the OS will be provided free-of-charge, the other services are intended to be provided for respective service fees. Originally, a concession scheme was set up with a private consortium operating the system and providing the services under the control of a supervisory authority (Galileo Joint Undertaking, GJU) established jointly by the European Union and the European Space Agency. However, negotiations failed and the European Union decided in 2007 to continue the deployment of Galileo based on more traditional procurements.[32] Currently two experimental satellites, Giove A and Giove B, are in orbit. Within the so-called IOV phase, a set of four operational satellites will be launched in 2011 together with the deployment of related ground infrastructure. In July 2008, a procurement process was started for the delivery and deployment of the remaining satellites and the complete ground infrastructure leading to the Full Operational Capability (FOC) phase of the system. Contracts have recently been signed for a first set of 14 satellites and the associated launch vehicles.[33] The system is supposed to be completed from 2014 onwards.

Galileo key performance indicators Galileo might be the first satellite navigation system employing SLAs on a considerable scale. Two kinds of SLAs have to be differentiated in the Galileo project. The first kind of SLA applies in the contractual relationship between the European Union as the owner of the system and the consortium of companies responsible for the operation of the system during the so-called Full Operational Capability (FOC) and later operational phases. The operator is responsible for the positioning, in-orbit-testing and the routine operations of the satellites, the operation of the control centres and the world-wide network of ground stations as well as for associated maintenance and logistics. Certain of these tasks will be monitored under SLAs whereby the respective service levels are referred to as Key Performance Indicators (KPI). The concept is inherited from the former concession scheme and is largely comparable to standards known from outsourcing projects.

The second set of service levels applies to the provision of the Galileo services to its users. As mentioned above, Galileo will provide a set of services beyond the free-of-charge Open Service,

32 See Heinrich, O. 2009. 'PPP-Verhandlungen im Projekt Galileo – ein gescheiterter Ansatz', in *Entwicklung der Europäischen Weltraumagentur als 'implementing agency' der Europäischen Union: Rechtsrahmen und Anpassungserfordernisse*, edited by S. Hobe, O. Heinrich, I. Kerner and A. Fröhlich. Berlin: Lit Verlag, 138–64.

33 European Commission Press Release IP 10-7: 'Commission awards major contracts to make Galileo operational early 2014'.

which is comparable to standard GPS and GLONASS signals. The Galileo commercial services will be provided to users against service fees and it is assumed that respective service contracts are to be signed between the future operator and the individual users. At this stage, there is very little information available on details of the future services provision. According to current schedules, early testing and service verification will start with the completion of the IOV phase in 2012. Based on the award of the contracts for the first order of FOC satellites, the European Commission announced that three of the five Galileo services will be provided as of early 2014: the Open Service (OS), the Public Regulated Service (PRS) and the Search and Rescue (SAR) Service. The Safety-of-Life Service (SoL) and the Commercial Service (CS) will be tested as of 2014 and will be provided as Galileo reaches Full Operational Capability with 30 satellites and a complete ground segment.

The European Commission released its Mid Term Review of the European GNSS programme in January 2011, providing information about the planned services.[34] The future service contracts will provide contractual guarantees to the users regarding the performance and quality of the services in terms of availability, accuracy, reliability and integrity. The guaranteed performance and quality standards of the services are to be defined by Key Performance Indicators (KPI) and non-performance will lead to compensation for the user.

Service guarantees will be the main differentiator of Galileo from the other global systems and will therefore be a decisive factor for its commercial success. SLA could play an essential role in the future set-up of Galileo services and the related service guarantees provided to the end-users.

Earth Observation

The market for earth observation (EO) data is still quite small and dependent on governmental support and engagement. Though most of the operators or distributors of earth imaging systems are private enterprises, still the vast majority of customers for data are public agencies. The operators/distributors usually have standard licensing terms for the distribution of their data and image products. However, EO products and services are characterised by an extensive customisation to the individual demands of the customer.[35]

The GMES programme Current policy developments may lead to a broader use of SLAS within the European earth observation industry in the future. GMES (Global Monitoring for Environment and Security) is a European initiative for the implementation of geo-information services dealing with environment and security.[36] Its objective is to foster better exploitation of the industrial potential of policies of innovation, research and technological development in the field of earth observation and to provide information services, which give access to accurate data and information in the field of environment and security under Community control and are tailored to the needs of a wide range of

34 European Commission Communication (2011) 5/3: Mid Term Review of the European Satellite Radio Navigation Programmes.

35 ECORYS Study on the Competitiveness of the EO Downstream Sector – Final Report (2008), 11. The Study can be found at http://ec.europa.eu/gmes/pdf/studies/gmes_ds_final_report.pdf [accessed: 6 April 2010].

36 Communication from the Commission to the Council and the European Parliament: Global Monitoring for Environment and Security (GMES): Outline GMES EC Action Plan (Initial Period: 2001–2003), COM (2001) 609 final, 23 October 2001.

users. Users include decision-makers at European, national, regional and local levels who develop and implement environmental and other relevant policies.[37]

Since 2008, four pre-operational GMES core services have been launched, including a land monitoring service, a marine service, an atmospheric composition monitoring service and an emergency response service. Other pre-operational core services are currently under development and concentrate on climate change and security. In addition, it is anticipated that a series of value added services will be developed by public and private entities, based on the above mentioned core services.

SLA within GMES user services After the completion of initial ESA GMES Service Element (GSE) projects, the further development and consolidation of these services is now under the responsibility of the EC, as an integral part of its space programme within FP7. The GMES services development under FP7 differs from standard research projects as it is foreseen to stimulate the establishment of operational downstream services, with the goal to be financially self-sustainable at the end of the project, ready to be based on non-R&D resources, including commercial revenues whenever appropriate.[38] Projects should be strongly user-driven and take into account user needs concerning the services and their quality specifications. Successful integration into current user practices and their working environment need to be demonstrated as part of the projects. To this end, the participants to the respective FP7 project consortia will – as service providers – deliver products and services to end-user organisations, which might be either formal project partners or not. An SLA is to be signed between the service provider and each end-user organisation (the User).

A template for such an SLA, to be adapted to the specific project, has been provided by the European Commission.[39] This GMES Service SLA is a committing agreement between the two parties, the service provider and the user, and specifies in transparent and measurable terms the quality, quantity and terms of access for the products and services to be delivered, as well as other obligations for the service provider and for the user respectively. The GMES SLA is to be concluded for a specified duration of at least one year. In case of conflict between the SLA and the project grant agreement with the European Commission, the provisions of the latter will prevail.

By the GMES SLA, the service provider agrees to provide the user with the service according to detailed service specifications. These specifications contain a list of the products to be delivered along with detailed product specifications, the geographical area to be covered, the service delivery modes, the service delivery schedules and the specification of other deliverables such as training, installation or maintenance. The specifications further include quality and accuracy specifications and related acceptance thresholds, applicable standards, service performance levels, back-up provisions and recovery procedures and timescales. The service provider is obliged to provide technical support to the user, to perform adequate quality control and to validate the service according to an agreed Validation Plan.

In turn, the user agrees to assess the utility of the service, to consolidate its requirements and to participate in the validation procedure. The user further agrees to integrate the service within its operational mandate as far as practically possible.

With a view to the envisaged commercialisation phase of the service, a target service delivery model has to be presented by the service provider. The model GMES Services SLA here differentiates

37 COM 223(2009): Proposal for a Regulation of the European Parliament and of the Council on the European Earth observation programme (GMES) and its initial operations (2011–2013), 12.

38 European Commission C (2009) 5893 of 29 July 2009, Work Programme Space 2010, 12.

39 The SLA template is available at http://ec.europa.eu/enterprise/policies/space/research/fp7-call-for-proposals/index_en.htm [accessed: on 5 April 2010].

between an outsourced service and an in-house service. In the latter, the service provider supports user capacity building in the project and plans for future revenues from maintenance and/or further development of the processing chain. For an outsourced service, the service provider would deliver the complete service to the user.

The model SLA for GMES services is only a template and considerable effort is necessary to adapt it to the specific characteristics of each individual service as well as to the requirements of users. Experience from previous phases has shown that this effort is often underestimated by the consortia elected for FP7 projects. As services are not yet provided under commercial terms, the SLA is considered to be merely one among several project deliverable documents to the European Commission. It remains to be seen whether this practice now evolves under the latest call of the space programme, building a sound basis for the future long-term service provision to end-users against commercially viable charges.

Recommendations for SLAs in Future Space Projects

As demonstrated in the section above, there are precedents for Service Level Agreements in all three main applications sectors of the space industry. It can be expected that the use of SLAs in space projects will increase in the future, especially as part of the operational phases of the European Galileo and GMES programmes. There is also potential for SLA in other space applications, for example for space-based telemedicine services.

From the above, the following recommendations can be made to decision-makers, project managers and procurement or contract officers when deciding about applying an SLA-based scheme to future space projects.

Choice of Space Projects

First, carefully consider whether an SLA is the right instrument for the specific project. Most space projects relate to basic science, studies, research and development, or to supplies of equipment or components. Clearly, an SLA is not suitable for such activities. For satellite projects, SLAs can generally only apply to the operational phases and, in most cases, standard clauses relating to performance, warranty and penalties are likely to serve the purpose as effectively as an SLA. SLAs can, however, be a good choice where a service is provided under certain standardised conditions and for a certain service period. Within the space industry, this restricts their application to well-established commercial satellite services and to sub-services of a typical IT character, such as hosting services, communications services, data services, maintenance and logistics. Even here, the implications of using novel technologies and of the risks inherent to space activities should be carefully considered.

Sufficient Time and Resources for Negotiation

Where SLAs shall be used, it is essential to plan for sufficient preparation and negotiation time. A good SLA requires substantial time and effort to be developed in close cooperation between the customer and the prospective service provider. Negotiations teams should include legal and financial experts and should build up knowledge based on standards and best practices in the IT industry and precedents and lessons learned from former space projects. As most space projects are subject to governmental procurement, tenderers may be required to quote and to contract on the basis of standard contract conditions with very limited freedom to negotiate. Non-compliances may lead to the exclusion from participating in the tender procedure. This does in principal not give room for a cooperative discussion on SLA terms and conditions. Where SLA-based services are to be procured, attention should therefore be drawn to the choice of the appropriate procurement procedure, for example the negotiated procedure or the competitive dialogue.

Where SLAs are to be used in space projects, the effort to manage the SLA during the contract's execution period should also not be underestimated. Appropriate resources should be foreseen, including positions of SLA managers and User Help Desk operators. In large projects, a Service Level Board should be established between the customer and the service provider to review the SLA, discuss changes, analyse reports, evaluate failures and non-performances, agree on compensation for non-performances, discuss measures to improve the service performance for the future and settle disputes.

Conclusions and Outlook

The spread of PPPs beyond the traditional transport and construction sectors into more strategic sectors such as the space sector has opened a new way of thinking.[40] Policy-makers, space agencies and national procurement agents now tend to have a more utilitarian, service-orientated approach. The industrial actors of the space sector have to adapt to this 'service paradigm', requiring a high level of reliability at an affordable cost.

This is drastically different from the traditional 'system paradigm', which was mainly promoting the use of the most advanced technology. The increasing use of SLAs in space projects is a remarkable sign of the new trend. Precedents can be found in two major PPPs for military satellite communications. The use of SLAs is also envisaged in Galileo and GMES as the two flagship programmes of the European Space Policy, following the general orientation of this policy towards space applications and the creation of innovative commercial downstream markets. It can be expected that SLAs will be used in more space projects in the future.

Service Level Agreements can provide a very valuable tool for certain space projects. However, their potential is limited due to the nature of most projects and the inherent risks of space activities. Generally, SLAs are only suitable where a service is provided under certain standardised conditions and for a certain service period. Within the space industry, this restricts the use of SLAs mainly to well-established commercial satellite services, to sub-services of a typical IT character as well as to maintenance and logistics.

The actors of the space industry have not yet collected sufficient experience with SLAs. Decision-makers, project managers and contract officers are recommended to carefully analyse standards and best practices available in the IT industry, as well as the negative lessons learned from previous projects. Decision-makers should refrain from using SLAs without due consideration. In most space projects, SLAs are either not suitable at all or the desired advantage can as effectively be reached by standard contractual solutions, such as performance obligations, warranties or penalties. In cases where SLAs are to be applied, sufficient time and resources need to be foreseen for detailed discussion and negotiation between the customer and the service provider, accompanied by the appropriate procurement procedures. The outcome could be a comprehensive, fair and effective SLA providing an excellent tool for a successful, long-term relationship between the parties involved in space projects.

40 Bertran, X. and Vidal, A. 2005. 'The Implementation of a Public-Private Partnership for Galileo', 398.

List of References

Baumann, I. 2005. *Das internationale Recht der Satellitenkommunikation*. Frankfurt: Peter Lang.

Baumann. I. 2005. 'Diversification of Space Law', in *Space Law: Current Problems and Perspectives for Future Regulation*, edited by M. Benkö and K.U. Schrogl. Utrecht: Eleven International Publishing, 47–74.

Bertran, X. and Vidal, A. 2005. 'The Implementation of a Public-Private Partnership for Galileo Comparison of Galileo and Skynet 5 with other Projects', in *Proceedings of the ION GNSS 18th International Technical Meeting of the Satellite Division, 13–16 September 2005*, 390.

Blokdijk, G. 2008. *Service Level Agreements: 100 Success Secrets*. Newstead, QLD: Emereo Publishing.

Blöse, J. and Pechardschek, S. 2002. 'Die rechtliche Absicherung von IT-Outsourcing Projekten', *Computer und Recht*, 11 (2002), 785.

Braun, H. 2006. *Die Zulässigkeit von Service Level Agreements – am Beispiel der Verfügbarkeitsklausel*. München: C.H. Beck.

Bräutigam, P. 2004. *IT Outsourcing – eine Darstellung aus rechtlicher, technischer, wirtschaftlicher und vertraglicher Sicht*. Berlin: Erich Schmidt.

Bräutigam, P. 2004. 'SLA – in der Praxis alles klar?', *Computer und Recht*, 4 (2004), 252.

Burnett, R. and Klinger, P. 2005. *Drafting and Negotiating Computer Contracts*. Edinburgh: Tottel Publishing.

Heinrich, O. 2009. 'PPP-Verhandlungen im Projekt Galileo – ein gescheiterter Ansatz', in *Entwicklung der Europäischen Weltraumagentur als 'implementing agency' der Europäischen Union: Rechtsrahmen und Anpassungserfordernisse*, edited by S. Hobe, O. Heinrich, I. Kerner and A. Fröhlich. Berlin: Lit Verlag, 138–64.

Hörl, B. and Häuser, M. 2003. 'Service Level Agreements in IT-Outsourcingverträgen', *Computer und Recht*, 10 (2003), 713.

Ley, W., Wittmann, K. and Hallmann, W. 2009. *Handbook of Space Technology*. London: John Wiley & Sons.

Söbbing, T. 2002. *Handbuch IT Outsourcing – rechtliche, strategische und steuerliche Fragen*. Frankfurt / Wien: Redline Wirtschaft.

Chapter 26

Space Contracts: The Legal and Financial Liability Regime under the New French Space Legislation

Mireille Couston

Introduction

In line with France's commitments under the framework of the 1967 Treaty and the 1972 Convention, the French legislation of 3 June 2008 establishes a third-party liability regime in case of damage caused by a space operation. It additionally sets up a liability regime relevant to persons participating in a space operation; innovative at the regulatory level but already long in existence at the contractual level.

These liability regimes have an impact on the whole of the contractual chain of the space sector and will be examined successively. But in order to grasp the context of these liability regimes and of their contractual consequences, it is necessary to explain the main tenets of the regime of authorisation of space operations established by the French space legislation.

Background

> The activities of non-governmental entities in outer space, including the moon and other celestial bodies, shall require authorisation and continuing supervision by the appropriate State Party to the Treaty.

It is strictly in line with this article VI of the 1967 Outer Space Treaty that the French legislation of 3 June 2008 implements a regime of authorisation for space operations.

The comprehensive list of authorities involved in the process is:

The minister in charge of space affairs: the minister grants authorisations by means of a by-law;

The Centre National des Etudes Spatiales (CNES – the national centre for space studies): it delivers a technical opinion of compliance to the Technical Regulation (RT), based on which the minister grants the authorisation; the minister may grant intermediary certificates during the development of a project;

The officers authorised to verify compliance with the legislative and regulatory obligations relating to space operations (they are empowered by the minister responsible for space affairs).

Any space operation falling within the ambit of the 3 June 2008 legislation must obtain an authorisation duly granted by the minister responsible for space affairs. The general regime is founded upon prior verifications and specific conditions for the grant of authorisations. It is organised according to two types of authorisations: a simple authorisation or a licence, but the criteria and the competent authorities are the same in both cases.

The grant of the authorisation for a space operation requires, on the one hand, that certain strategic and international aspects of the operation have been verified and, on the other, that a series of technical, moral, financial and professional guarantees are in place. The CNES must have also delivered an opinion on the compliance to the Technical Regulation. In brief, the three conditions for authorisation are: policy verification of the project, general verification of the business and technical verification of the project.

Policy Verification of the Project

Article 4, paragraph 2 of the legislation provides that no authorisation can be given for operations that could compromise 'the interests of national defence or France's undertaking of compliance to its international commitments'. This is a preliminary verification that must be done 'namely' in view of the proposed 'systems'.

General Verification of the Business

In addition to the information enabling the identification of the requestor (name, residential address, designation, corporate name, legal status, address, signatory's title, etc.), the documents submitted by the operator requesting the authorisation must prove that the operator fulfils the four warranties specifically mentioned:

absence of bankruptcy
sound management of the business
implementation of quality system and
training and qualification of the personnel

Documentary evidence of these four warranties is obligatory and applicable to each and every requestor; however, if a requestor has previously been granted a licence, it would only have to provide the elements supplementary to those already present in the licence.

The list of documents likely to prove the existence of the above warrantees is not exhaustive, and can also include elements such as:

social evaluation of the business
business reports
auditors' reports
certifications of compliance to international standards

The *ad hoc* financial guarantees requested for a particular operation can be insurances or, strictly speaking, financial guarantees. The law distinguishes between five possible types of financial guarantees, depending on their source:

financial institution
insurance company
joint and several guarantee
guarantee payable on first demand
current assets

The financial guarantees and/or insurances aim to cover the risk of having to indemnify against damage that may be caused to third parties during the space operation.

The application submitted by the requestor of an authorisation for a planned space operation must indicate the details of the financial guarantees envisaged 'namely' their nature, amount, lead set-up time. 'Namely' allows for a certain margin in the submission of the detailed documentation. The operator is, however, asked to prove the existence of these guarantees before the start of the operation.

The financial guarantees planned by the requestor must cover three entities explicitly specified by the law (Article 6.III):

the state (and its public bodies)

the European Space Agency/ESA (and its Member States) for the GSC (Guiana Space Centre) launches

the operator and the persons who participated in the production of the space object or who participated in the space operation

There are two cases of exoneration in which the operator will be exempted from the obligation of insurance (third party):

In the case of an operation aimed at maintaining a satellite in geostationary orbit. The operator must simply provide a document certifying its solvency.

In case it is impossible to find such guarantees because of the condition of the space insurance market. The operator then produces a document certifying its solvency.

It must be noted that in both cases, the exemption granted by the minister for space is limited: limited in time concerning issues of availability in the financial markets; limited in function in the first case mentioned above, since whenever there is an orbital manoeuvre, change of orbit and so on, the obligation of insurance applies.

Technical Verification of the Project

The CNES exercises control over the project in order to verify the compliance of the systems and procedures implemented by the operators with the 'Technical Regulation' previously defined in a bylaw. It will deliver an assessment of compliance. To render this possible, the requestor must provide a description of the planned project and of the systems and procedures envisaged. More specifically, it has the obligation to provide a certain number of documents which can be classified, according to their purpose, in three categories:

> In view of the 'safety of property, persons, public health and the environment', two series of documentation are required: internal organisation; study of the dangers and risk control plans.
>
> In the framework and conduct of the space operation, three series of documentation are required: internal rules and quality management norms; risk control; rescue measures.
>
> Six specific plans are required for the environment: prevention of risks in case of falling debris; prevention of environmental damage; debris limitation; collision prevention; nuclear safety plan (as applicable); planetary protection plan (as applicable).

The control of technical compliance relates to the exploitation phase of the project. However, an *optional system of partial certification*, based on each phase of the project under development is also provided. The CNES can thus, upon request and in line with the different phases of a project, certify the 'total or partial compliance with the technical regulation'.

The assessment of compliance to the Technical Regulation delivered by the CNES, and which is a condition for the grant of authorisation for a space operation, can be accompanied by additional requirements as provided in Article 5 of the legislation. These requirements tend generally to add some flexibility to the authorisation procedure, including for the partial certifications of Article 14. These requirements could also be helpful in any actions for indemnity.

A noteworthy closing remark to this introduction is that the authorisation regime briefly described above applies generally to space operations, but with procedural specificities in cases of transfer of control of space objects and of operations in foreign jurisdictions.[1] Notwithstanding these procedural differences in authorisation, the third party liability regime requires the systematic inclusion of the French state and the operator.

There are two distinct liabilities: first that of the French state, which is called upon at the international level and which can oblige the state to pay compensation for damage (see the section below entitled 'International Liability of the French State'); second that of the operator which comes into play at the internal level and which can cause the operator to indemnify a third party. In addition, the law has implemented a specific liability regime applicable to the contractual relationships between the operator and the persons participating in the operation (see the following section). The complexity of these regimes demands that comparative remarks be made (see the section below entitled 'Analytical and Comparative Remarks on the Liability of the State and of the Operator').

1 For a detailed analysis of the authorisation regime and procedural specificities, see Couston, M. 2009. 'La législation française sur les opérations spatiales [The French legislation on space operations]', *Jurisclasseur*, August 2009.

Operator's Liability to Third Parties and in the Framework of Relations with Persons Participating in a Space Operation

Third Party Liability

Principles established by the legislation of 3 June 2008

The principle of exclusive liability of the operator towards third parties

The 3 June 2008 Act (hereafter sometimes termed 'Act') provides the principle according to which: the 'operator is solely liable for damages caused to third parties'. This liability of the operator as provided under French law is according to the same mechanism as that provided by the 1967 Treaty and the 1972 Convention, namely:

1. absolute liability for damages caused on the ground or in the air (the operator can however lessen or set aside its liability and its financial burden by proving the victim's fault);
2. fault liability for damage caused in space.

Consequence of this liability: insurance policies

The fundamental consequence of the operator's financial liability resides in the obligation of holding adequate insurance policies and from which entities defined by law can benefit, as follows:

Nature: the operators must obtain insurance up to the amount for which they are liable according to the terms of the authorisation which they have been granted (Article 6). They may also hold financial guarantees of different types which would for instance result in: the written commitment of a financial establishment or an insurance company, joint and several guarantee or, even, an on-demand guarantee of disposable assets. In any case, the proof of these guarantees must be presented to the minister in charge of space affairs and to the finance minister *before* the space operation.

Beneficiaries: the insurance or financial guarantee must benefit the state and its public bodies, ESA and its Member States (if the operation is carried out from the GSC), the operator and the participants to the industrial production of the space object or to the space operation.

Limits to the insurance obligation: the minister in charge of space affairs can waive the obligation of insurance (or financial guarantees) for the operator if the operation consists of maintaining a satellite in its geostationary position. In this case, the operator only needs to prove that it is credit-worthy. This provision shows clearly that the risks involved in the presence of an object in geostationary orbit (which will never come back or only in several million years to earth) are less important than those involved with objects in low-earth orbit (which will fall back to earth in the medium term). Consequently, the operator's financial funds are deemed sufficient to face those risks. It is, however, stipulated that the operator must be in a position to show evidence of the above insurances or guarantees each time there is an orbital change or other manoeuvre that ends the maintenance in position of the object (thus increasing the risks of damages).

Specific Input of the Act: State Guarantee

Aim The exclusive burden of the operator's financial liability seen above is alleviated through the contribution of the state guarantee.

The *mechanism* of a state guarantee is provided at Articles 15 to 18 of the Act. It shows that the state guarantee benefits:

mainly the operator who has been granted authorisation for its space operation;

accessorily, 'as applicable' and only for damages caused during the launch phase, to persons who are 'non-third parties' to the operation, that is, the operator's co-contractors, clients, subcontractors, and subcontractors of the operator's clients.

Procedures

This mechanism functions according to two procedures for operators:

1. In case the liability of an operator is called into question in a given jurisdiction for space damage, it can request the competent administrative authority to exercise 'the defence rights in the proceedings' (Article 18).
2. In case the operator is found liable, the contribution of the state guarantee alleviates the exclusive financial liability of the former. The state pays the sum of the compensation in excess (if any) of the amount for which the operator was insured.

Elements conditioning the application of the French state's guarantee

It is not an unconditional guarantee. In the first instance, it can only be called upon under transparent circumstances where the operator would have informed the administrative authorities of any damage issues and of any pending legal action against it. Secondly, the operator can only benefit from the state's financial help under the five cumulative criteria below:

Liability of the operator – the operator must have been found liable for the indemnification of a third party. It is noted here that no requirement of the jurisdiction is mentioned, it can thus be equally in a French or foreign jurisdiction.

The existence of authorisation for the concerned operation – the damage must have occurred following a space operation authorised under French law.

Absence of the operator's intentional wrong – this point raises the problem of, on the one hand, interpreting and using the notion of intentional wrongdoing, to take into proper account the interest of the victims, the state and the operator and, on the other, to examine whether the terms of the granted authorisation have been complied with, including those of the supplementary conditions.

The absence of a serious disregard of the requirements of the authorisation – this condition has been specified in the 2008 Corrective Finances Act (Article 119). Such a condition that emphasises the supplementary requirements places the CNES (instigator of the said requirements) in a central, decision-making position.

The location of the operation – the operation must have been conducted
a. either from the territory
of France
or of another EU Member State
or of a state party to the agreement on the European Economic Area
b. or through means or installations
placed under French jurisdiction
or of another EU Member State
or of a Member State of the European Economic Area

Financial amounts of the guarantee
The French state will grant its guarantee to the operator on the basis of the amounts indicated in the Finance Act (and reproduced in the authorisation). Indeed, the ceilings indicated in the 2008 Corrective Finances Act are: EUR 50 million and EUR 70 million.

The amount of the guarantee granted by the state is determined on a case-by-case basis depending on three different phases (predetermined by law) during which the damage could occur:

damage caused during the launch phase
damage caused on the ground or in the air space after the launch phase
damage caused on the ground or in the air space during the object's return to earth

Towards Persons Participating in the Space Operation or to the Manufacture of the Object

What is striking since the middle of the 1980s is the growing presence of private interests and actors in the development of space activities. However, this is not without giving rise to novel legal precautions aimed at limiting or at least managing the risks and technological hazards inherent to space.

Indeed, due to the extreme technicalities of space objects and the risks inherent to space applications, the economic and industrial actors of the sector have long tried to reduce the legal and financial risks likely to be caused by any malfunction or unreliability of space objects. The principal tool they thus use is the contract. Space contracts, whether for satellite manufacture, launch or satellite exploitation, have hence seen certain specific and novel clauses, such as waivers of liability.

The 3 June 2008 Act provides a regulatory basis to this contractual precedent. It acts under the framework of two provisions related to 'liability towards participants to the space operation'. The topic of liability towards participants in a space operation is the subject-matter of chapter II (title IV) of the Act. It is developed in a more expeditious manner than that of damage to third parties. Only two articles are directly dedicated to it: Articles 19 and 20.

Definition of 'persons participating in a space operation' A reading of the two above-mentioned articles shows that, under the current regime, are concerned:

participants to a space operation
persons having participated in the production of the space object

In addition, the application of the regime can also be negatively determined, following the principle that it applies to persons:

who are not operators (article 1.2.)
who are not the primary users of the data of space origin (article 1.7.) and
who are not third parties to a space operation (article 1.6.)

In this case, *a contrario*, the definitions of operator, users and third parties given in Article 1 of the law will be used.

It can be then deduced that co-contractors, subcontractors and clients of the operator, and co-contractors and subcontractors of the operator's clients fall under the notion of 'persons participating in a space operation'.

Regime of waiver of liability The *principle*: in its Articles 19 and 20, the Act reproduces and highlights a principle already widely applied in space contracts: the cross-waiver of liability, which aims to reduce litigation.

Application
The law provides for such a waiver in two cases:

1. *In case of damages to a third party*: in this scenario and when the damage has given rise to a payment of compensation by the operator or to the application of the state guarantee, it is provided that the liability of participants to the operation or to the manufacture of the given object cannot be sought. The operator and the state thus abandon the possibility of any remedy.
2. *In case of damage to a person having participated in the operation* or in the production of the space object concerned: in this case, the law stipulates that the liability of other persons cannot be sought. It is the principle of mutual waiver of liability among participants to a space operation.

Exceptions
The principle of exclusion of liability is, of course, not applicable to third parties to the operation who may have the right to compensation, but the law provides for two other exceptions to the waiver of liability:

Intentional wrong: considering the above two cases, it is clear that the finding of liability of persons having participated in the operation or in the production of the object will be possible in case of intentional wrong. This double exception is founded on the necessary compliance with the Constitutional Council decision of 22 October 1982 on the Auroux laws, which does not allow this type of liability waiver mechanism without restriction, in order to preserve their purpose according to the principles of civil liability and equality.

Contrary provisions applicable to the manufacture or to the control of satellites: it must be highlighted that this is an exception that seems only applicable to satellites, since the launch phase is not mentioned. Indeed Article 20 of the Act provides that the waiver of liability among participants to the space operation or to the manufacture of the object would not apply in case of contrary contractual provisions:

- pertaining to damages caused during the production of a 'space object designed to be controlled in space';
- or pertaining to damages caused during its control in orbit.

In providing them a legal basis, the legislation of 3 June 2008 removes the threat of the judge possibly declaring null and void the waiver of liability clauses. The Act thus shows the will to establish the law in real-life situations in which the rules have been thought through and applied, taking concrete situations and practice in consideration. However, it is possible that conflicts may arise between the principle of waiver of liability provided in French law and certain contracts, where the reverse principle could be adopted. The judge would then have to find a balance between contract law and public law.

International Liability of the French State

International Rules

Nature and applicability of the international liability of the French state Under the terms of the 1967 Treaty (Article VII):

> Each State Party to the Treaty that launches or procures the launching of an object into outer space, including the moon and other celestial bodies, and each State Party from whose territory or facility an object is launched, is internationally liable for damage to another State Party to the Treaty or to its natural or juridical persons by such object ….

It is therefore the international liability of the launching state which is sought, with its application made via diplomatic means, and the victims' states representing them and exercising diplomatic protection for their benefit.

One can observe two limitations to the application of the international liability of the state: indeed the provisions of the 1972 Convention on international liability for damage caused by space objects apply neither to damage caused to nationals of the launching state nor to damage caused to foreign nationals participating in the space operation (Article VII of the 1972 Convention).

Specificity of French international liability
Automatic and joint and several liability in the following cases:

> For launches from GSC as a territorial state: France is systematically and jointly and severally liable for all launches from the GSC base. The 1972 Convention indeed provides that 'a State from whose territory or facility a space object is launched shall be regarded as a participant in a joint launch' (Article V.3).
>
> For the European Space Agency's space operations, as a Member State (with the exception of the qualifying flight and ESA's satellite launches).

Degrees of international liability of the French state
The international liability of the French state can be:

absolute liability for damage caused on the surface of the earth or to aircrafts in flight;

fault liability for damage caused elsewhere than on the surface of the earth. In this case, the French state is only liable if the damage is attributable to its fault or to the fault of persons for whom it is responsible.

Exonerations
The French state can be exempted of its absolute liability if the damage results from gross negligence or an act or omission committed with the intent to cause damage from the claimant state or from natural or juridical persons it represents.

Amount and nature of the compensation The compensation is essentially financial, but can be accompanied by material help.

Financial compensation: under the framework of international liability, the amount of the compensation is determined in accordance with international law and 'the principles of justice and equity', in order to restore the victims to the situation that would have existed if the damage had not been caused (*restitutio in integrum*).

Compensation and material assistance: if the state on whose territory the damage occurred – and if the damage presents a large-scale danger to human life or the functioning of vital centres – so requests, the French state as launching state could have to provide an 'appropriate and rapid' assistance (Article XXI of the 1972 Convention).

Addition of the 3 June 2008 Legislation: Action for Indemnity

Principle and conditions of the action in indemnity
The principle of the action for indemnity
Article 14 of the 3 June 2008 Act specifies that in case the French state would have to pay compensation under its international liability for damage caused by an operator (whether on the basis of the 1972 Convention or of international public law in general), it may take action for indemnity against the operator who caused the damage.

Conditions of the action for indemnity – there are two main conditions:

1. The action for indemnity is only engaged if the government has not benefited from the operator's financial guarantees and insurance (including those given by the foreign state in case of operations abroad) for the amounts indicated in the authorisation.
2. The action for indemnity cannot be started in case of damage resulting from acts targeting national interests (or example terrorism).

Financial amounts
Financial amounts requested in the action for indemnity
The framework provided for the amounts aims to limit these, depending on the circumstances:

They will be fixed and limited by the French Finance Act and will, in addition, be according to the phase of the space operation during which the damage occurred. The law thus distinguishes between damages occurring (and the related financial amounts):

during the launch phase
after the launch phase

In an action for indemnity, the French state is, however, not bound to these amounts and is able to request higher amounts in case of 'intentional wrong' of the operator who caused the damage.

Analytical and Comparative Remarks on the Liability of the State and of the Operator

The prime importance of the liability issue demands two series of complementary observations on sensitive points: on the one hand, the two mechanisms, which are the action for indemnity and the state guarantee, and on the other, the limits of liability and other commitments of the operator under various exemptions.

Interaction and Reach of the Action for Indemnity and of the State Guarantee

It must be here reaffirmed that in the first instance these are two distinct mechanisms as much in their nature as in their application by the 3 June 2008 Act, but that they function in a complementary fashion under the main framework of the obligation of insurance as seen above.

Their nature

The action for indemnity

This is a standard legal procedure, which consists of a legal action by a person who has had to perform an obligation that should have been performed by another (more often compensating a victim), against the real debtor or co-debtor of the obligation (responsible author of the damage) to obtain a judgment against the latter. It is therefore a legal action that aims to restore a balance between two or more parties to an obligation. In the framework of the French space law, the action for indemnity provided at Article 14 corresponds exactly to this model: the state being the only one able to take on international liability, it is the only one able to solicit compensation (and it will act according to the space treaties or the legal principles of international responsibility), but nonetheless without being in each case the author of the damage, which authorises it to turn to the said author in an internal legal action.

The financial guarantee

The financial guarantee granted by the state to a particular operator for an authorised space operation, but which has caused damages, is of a different legal nature. It is a financial facility granted to space operators ordered to pay compensation, in order to help them settle their debt by taking responsibility for part of the amount (the amount exceeding the sums indicated by the French Finance Act and for which the operator has necessarily taken out insurance). Here, the state is not jointly liable for the damaging activity, as in the previous case where it accepted its liability in the treaties. Indeed, the guarantee is alien to the idea of liability, and is linked to the notion of assistance from the state. The state brings financial help aimed at supplementing (if necessary) the insurance policies taken by the operator. The European Commission, referred to by notification from the French government, has upheld this assistance with regards to the Community provisions, on the basis of Article 87 paragraph 3(b)(c) which allows derogation from the prohibition of state help when the assisted operation is a sector of European interest or which favours the European industry.

Their application It is the difference in nature as seen above between the two mechanisms of the action for indemnity and of the financial guarantee that explains and justifies different applications, distinguishing between the different phases during which damages occur.

The 'launch phase'

The launch phase (and damage caused during this phase including to objects already on board the satellite) is a common phase mentioned in both cases. Hence, both the action for indemnity and the guarantee can be exercised for damages related to this phase, irrespective of their location.

'After the launch phase'

This is concerned in the case of the action for indemnity: damage caused 'after the launch phase', including at the time of the object's return to earth. The damages in this case are not localised and specific localisation is not required.

In the case of the guarantee, it is specified that damage caused 'on the ground or in the air space after the launch phase' includes the moment of return. This last notion localises the damage; it implies that the French government will only grant its financial aid in cases where space-unrelated actors are concerned (passengers of an aircraft, persons on the ground, etc.), meaning in the more serious cases affecting society. Here we see the principle of socialisation of certain risks, which by their collateral nature can legitimately be taken on by the taxpayers' money. However, in cases of damage caused between space objects cruising in outer space or orbital spaces, the state would not grant its guarantee: all the actors concerned having the knowledge of the hazards of space activities and having (usually) financially incorporated these in their activity plans.

Elements Limiting the Liability of the State and of the Operator

The respective liability of the operator and of the French government, which in the framework of space activities disappears in certain exemption models provided by the law, is also limited in the assumption of a wrong.

Fault The limitations to the responsibilities and obligations of the operator and of the French government are founded upon two essential notions: the notion of 'the victim's fault' and the notion of 'intentional wrong'. It is appropriate to define them and analyse the way in which they are used in the 3 June 2008 Act.

The 'victim's fault'

Article 13 paragraph 1 provides that the *ipso facto* liability of the operator for damages caused on the ground or in the air, can be lessened or set aside if the victim's fault is proven:

It must be understood that the operator is exempted from financial liability in case of an act or omission committed either by the state claiming compensation, or by physical or juridical persons claiming compensation.

But the law neither specifies if the negligence must be gross (one that largely departs from normal behaviour) or only slight (blunder, misdiagnosis), nor mentions whether this fault must be intentional. The role of the judge in the matter will be predominant in clarifying these elements. What is certain is that the burden of proof lies with the operator.

The 'intentional wrong'
This notion is used in Articles 13–15 with the three following legal and financial purposes:

The proof of an intentional wrong could allow the French state to be free of the financial limits in its action for indemnification. Thus, in case of the intentional wrong of the operator responsible for the damage, the government could, through an action for indemnification, demand sums higher than those indicated in the French Finance Act and reproduced in the authorisation.

The proof of an intentional wrong of an operator ordered to compensate a third party could allow the French government to be free of the duty to extend its financial guarantee to that operator.

The proof of an intentional wrong could allow the liability of the operator for damages caused to third parties (on the ground, in the air and in space) to be upheld, even when the obligations of the granted authorisation would have been fulfilled and the legal period of one year exceeded.

The exemption models The last paragraph of Article 13 of the legislation is thus drafted:

> Except in the event of an intentional wrong, the liability set forth in 1° and 2° ceases as soon as all the obligations set forth by the authorisation or the licence are fulfilled or, at the latest, one year after the date on which the obligations should have been fulfilled. The Government shall substitute itself for the operator for any damage occurring after that period.

Under the French Act of 3 June 2008, the liability of the operator ends in two possible circumstances:

when all obligations specified in the authorisation or licence are fulfilled;
or at the latest one year after the date at which these obligations should have been fulfilled.

In the latter case, it is indicated that the government substitutes itself as the operator for damages occurring after this period.

Here, five analytical remarks must be made.

First, it must be pointed out that the exemption of liability concerns liability for damages caused to third parties on the ground, in the airspace or elsewhere. It is therefore not related to liability towards participants of the space operations.

It is then noted that the principle of exhaustion of liability when the operator has fulfilled its obligations affords significant importance to the enforcement of the *supplementary obligations* provided by Article 5. These obligations are those that can be added namely in view of the compliance of the system to the technical regulation, and within the framework of partial certifications during the development of a system.

Consequently, this principle also tends to highlight, as a whole, the provisions relating to the inspections (Article 6) and to the agents who are competent and authorised to carry out the said inspection. The attention given to the issue of accreditation and swearing-in of the agents through the adoption of a decree specific to accreditation then becomes clearer. The inspections are likely to lead to the finding of a breach of obligation, or even of an intentional wrong, hence leading to the continuation of the operator's exclusive liability for damages to third parties (which results in the possibility for the state to file an action for indemnity).

In the fourth instance, it is noted that the one year period fulfils two specific functions, even though not expressly stipulated in the law:

> Indeed, this somewhat ambiguous provision can only be understood in light of the technical problem of certain space launchers, where one floor remains in orbit for a very long time after the launch. The law seems to have wanted, on the one hand, to protect the launch operators against any future liability actions and, on the other, to protect the satellite operators by being financially responsible for the damages in case of collision.
>
> In addition, this provision takes into account the financial limits of the space insurance market and tends to compensate for them.

Finally, the last sentence, which reads, 'the Government shall substitute itself for the operator for any damage occurring after that period', leads to the conclusion that the state will take on, *in lieu* of the operator, the compensation for damage caused to third parties. But it remains to be seen whether, in the case where the state has substituted itself for the operator as per the application of Article 13, it will be able to rely on Article 14 for the possibility of an action for indemnification. In this respect, the joint reading of Articles 13 and 14 shows that the action for indemnification (Article 14) is justified and based on Article 13 by mentioning that the operator is *solely* liable. It is therefore logical to then have the operator take on this liability through an action for indemnity.

However, in the situation of substitution, the state in turn should be 'solely' liable for the damages and in this case it is obvious that the action for indemnity against the operator is not possible. However, it must be highlighted that everything depends on the presence of the term 'solely', which would not be without uncertainty in case of litigation and interpretation by the judges.

General Conclusion

The new French space legislation adopted on 3 June 2008 is timely and helpful in a space context open to widening perspectives of commercialisation and privatisation and to novel international cooperation, such as the establishment of the Russian Soyuz launcher on the GSC base.

The principal points to remember (summarised in Tables 26.1 and 26.2), on the one hand, concerning the liability of the state and the operators and, on the other, the regime of persons participating in a space operation are as follows:

Liability of the State

1. It is an international liability that only the state is able to bear, but which can subsequently lessen by turning to the author of the damage through an action for indemnity.
2. The financial amounts likely to be demanded by the state under an action for indemnity are determined by the French Finance Law.
3. However, the claim of the state can go beyond the amounts indicated in case of intentional wrongdoing by the operator who caused the damage.
4. The state can be exempted from liability in case of gross negligence or of an act or omission committed by the claimant with the intention of causing damage.

Liability of the Space Operators

1. The operator is solely liable for damage to third parties.
2. In order to face this liability, the operator has the obligation to subscribe to insurance policies.
3. However, the system of the state financial guarantee alleviates the burden of insurance on the operator. The legislator has even foreseen that the burden of insurance could be removed in the event of control of a satellite in geostationary orbit.
4. The state guarantee is, however, only granted under certain conditions (operation having been granted authorisation; absence of intentional wrong).
5. The operator is exempted from liability either when all the obligations set by the authorisation have been fulfilled, or at the latest one year after the date at which these obligations should have been fulfilled.

Legal Regime for Participants to a Space Operation

For participants in a space operation or the manufacture of the object, the regime put in place by the 3 June 2008 Act establishes:

1. the principle of cross-waiver of liability;
2. this waiver is only valid in case of absence of intentional wrong of the concerned persons or of certain contractual stipulations to the contrary.

The space contracts which are covered by the French Space Act must comply with the different provisions, through clauses adapted to the requirements of this newly formalised legal order in French law.

Table 26.1 The liability regime

	State	**Operator**	**Participant**
International liability	Nature: absolute (air and earth) or relative (space) Type: payment of financial compensation / material assistance Exemption: gross negligence -------------------- Action for indemnity possible against the operator	-------------------- Payment of sums requested by the state, if any, through an action for indemnity	
National liability	-------------------- Possible grant of the financial and legal guarantee of the state to the operator (conditional)	Nature: absolute (air and earth) or relative (space) Type: Payment of financial compensation Exemptions: two cases (compliance with obligations / one year period -------------------- Mitigation: state guarantee	
Contractual liability			Legal regime for the exclusion of liability. Two exceptions: intentional wrong / contrary stipulations applicable to the manufacture or control of satellite

Table 26.2 The mechanisms of action for indemnity and state guarantee

	Action for indemnity (action of the state against the operator)	**State guarantee** (guarantee of the state granted to the operator)
Conditions of application	If compensation of a damage by the state under its international liability If the state has not already benefited from the operator's insurance If the damage does not result from an act targeting national interests (terrorism)	If the operator had a valid authorisation or licence If the operator is found liable for damage to third parties If absence of intentional wrong If the activity is localised or under jurisdiction foreseen by the law
Financial amounts	The financial amounts demanded under the action for indemnity are limited according to the damage occurred: • during the launch phase • after the launch phase. Possible that the action for indemnity is based on financial amounts higher than the limits indicated by the law, in case of the operator's intentional wrong	The financial amounts of the state guarantee are granted according to the time and place of the damage: • during the launch phase • on the ground or in the air space after the launch phase • on the ground or in the air space during the return to earth phase of the object

List of References

Clerc, P. 2008a. Gifas, 11 June 2008, Paris.

Clerc, P. 2008b. 3rd Eilene Galloway Symposium, 11 December 2008, New York.

Couston, M. 2008a. 'Note sur la loi sur les opérations spatiales', *Revue de Transports*.

Couston, M. 2008b. 'Commentaires sur la loi sur les opérations spatiales', *Revue Française de droit aérien et spatial*, III.

Couston, M. 2009a. 'La loi française sur les opérations spatiales', *Zeitschrift für Luft und Weltraumrecht*, I.

Couston, M. 2009b. 'Note introductive sur la loi française sur les opérations spatiales', *Space Law Basis*.

Couston, M. 2009c. 'La législation française sur les opérations spatiales [The French legislation on space operations]', *Jurisclasseur*, August 2009.

Etude du Conseil d'Etat. 2006. 'Pour une politique juridique des activités spatiales'. La documentation française.

Ministère de la recherche. 2003. 'Evolution du droit de l'espace en France'. Dossier.

Rapp, L. 2008. 'Commentaire sur la loi sur les opérations spatiales', *AJDA*, IV.

Rapport Labordes (Assemblée Nationale, April 2008), no. 775.

Rapport Revol (Sénat January 2008), no. 161.

Chapter 27

Intellectual Property Issues in the Use and Distribution of Remote Sensing Data

Lesley Jane Smith and Catherine Doldirina

Introduction

Outer space activities are inconceivable without the support of technology: it is used in all space segments and projects, in hardware and software, launchers and payloads, through to ground operations. The individual assets may be protected by one or more types of intellectual property (IP) regimes, ranging from patents on the technology utilised through to inventions made in outer space, and copyright over space data, known as remote sensing data. These IP regimes can be statutory or private. For a variety of reasons and particularly within international space projects, contractual regulation is predominant. Possibly the best known example of an international space project with its own specific IP regime is that of the International Space Station (ISS). Its inter-governmental regulatory framework provides for the protection of IP derived from inventions and experiments undertaken on board.[1]

Space projects generally involve collaboration with differing project partners, so there is an interest in ensuring both protection of the subject matter and constructing a feasible IP management regime within the project. This requires two steps: firstly, registration or acknowledgement of IP rights (IPRs) ownership; secondly, contracts regulating the terms of access, distribution and use, generally contained within IP licences, or appearing as IP clauses within the main body of the contract. For the most part, ownership of data in all forms lies with the national or regional space agency or public hand and is released for distribution and processing in a variety of fields, with an increasing demand for information that is relevant to the public sector. With the growth of private commercial activities in space, the scope for developing new markets in space data products and

1 The ISS consists of different modules owned by different partners; its use is governed by different national legal regimes. Article 21 of the Inter-Governmental Agreement (IGA) establishing the International Space Station (1998) provides for the jurisdiction of each partner state over its module. This in turn affects the applicability of the relevant national IP protection regimes. Certain limitations might be applicable, given the interpretation of Article 5 *ter* of the Paris Convention for the Protection of Industrial Property (1883) which limits the exclusive rights of a patent holder by requiring the freedom of transport to be guaranteed in the public interest (doctrine of temporary presence). With regard to space activities in general, the significance of this rule should be assessed, as it might be relevant where patented assets are transported to or from a space station through a launching site in a foreign country. Further details can be obtained from ESA, Patent and Space-Related Inventions, available at: http://www.esa.int. For an extensive overview of the legal issues relating to the International Space Station see von der Dunk, F.G. and Brus, M.M.T.A. (eds). 2006. *The International Space Station: Commercial Utilisation from a European Legal Perspective*. Leiden: Martinus Nijhoff and VSP.

services is expanding, with the search for the best business models for commercial products still underway.[2]

This chapter focuses on select aspects of IPRs encountered in commercial space projects, and remote sensing data in particular, and discusses how these are managed in practice. After an initial analysis of IP regulation for remote sensing activities, it briefly looks at the IP rules under the GEOSS project and the activities relating to the GMES Sentinel satellites.[3] Brief reference is made to the licensing practices of the French SPOT Image and the position of the German Infoterra GmbH, the latter as licensee under German legislation governing space data.[4] These are two examples of mechanisms designed for the distribution and use of remote sensing data by the private commercial sector.

Territoriality of IP Protection and the International Character of Space Activities

IP protection is *per se* territorially limited by virtue of existing international IP regimes,[5] so that the international nature of space activities constitutes a challenge to the legal protection of space-related IPRs. The principle of state jurisdiction over space activities under Article VIII of the Outer Space Treaty is used as a basis for securing territorial protection of space-related IPRs. Outer space is otherwise not subject to claims of sovereignty or territoriality.[6] Space activities, given their scope and financial dimensions, frequently take place in the form of collaborative missions between several partner-states or private entities, and agencies. This requires the creation of an IP management regime suited to the particular project or programme.[7]

Although harmonisation of certain IPRs within the European Union (EU) has advantages from a single market perspective,[8] an author/inventor/trademark owner remains tied to the territory of the state that first grants that owner IP protection. The variation in interpretation and enforcement

2 Smith, L.J. 2011. 'At What Price? IP-related Thoughts on New Business Models for Space Information', in Acta Astronautica, available online at http://dx.doi.org/10.1016/j.actaastr+o.2011.04.013.

3 There is a high level of international cooperation over the remote sensing data generated through GMES operations.

4 Gesetz zum Schutz vor Gefährdung der Sicherheit der Bundesrepublik Deutschland durch das Verbreiten von hochwertigen Erdfernerkundungsdaten (2007) *BGBl* I. 2590 (also, Satellitendatensicherheitsgesetz or SatDiG). An English translation is available online at the UN Office for Outer Space Affairs' website: http://www.unoosa.org. Both companies, Spot Image and Infoterra, now belong to the EADS Astrium group.

5 This principle is fundamental to any IP protection regime, be it patent, trademark or copyright law. See the Berne Convention on the Protection of Literary and Artistic Works (*1886*) 331 *U.N.T.S.* 217, the World Intellectual Property Organisation Copyright Treaty (1996) 36 *I.L.M.* 65 or Paris Convention for the Protection of Industrial Property (1883) 828 *U.N.T.S.* 305.

6 As prescribed in Articles I and II of the Treaty on Principles Governing the Activities of States in the Exploration and Use of Outer Space, including the Moon and Other Celestial Bodies (Outer Space Treaty, 1967), the exploration and use of outer space for the benefit of mankind and the non-appropriation of outer space by any nation are fundamental principles under international space law. See further, Abeyratne, R. 2003. 'The Application of Intellectual Property Rights to Outer Space Activities', *Journal of Space Law*, 29, 1.

7 This applies to the use of remote sensing data – the same data sets can be effectively utilised in different jurisdictions; data from several providers can also be combined to make one geographic information product.

8 It is now possible to register a Community-wide trademark at the Central European office for the harmonisation of trademarks, see the codified version of the Council Regulation on the Community trade mark (2009) OJ L 78/1.

of IPRs across differing jurisdictions can in practice lead to their dilution. It therefore serves as a reminder, particularly in relation to patents, that IPRs should be registered in all states where protection is sought, either individually, or through the applicable international procedure.[9]

The potential clash between territoriality as the basis of IP protection and the extra-territorial or international character of space activities, particularly those carried out in outer space (for example inventions made aboard the ISS), leads to a greater reliance on alternative management solutions for IPRs. These may take the form of international agreements that set up the space activities, or be part of the institutional or private licensing schemes that shape the behaviour of the actors on the relevant market. Competing or colliding IPRs in space-derived products and services is not uncommon and unauthorised use has lead to litigation over secondary products in the past, such as space imagery.[10] All this explains the high degree of private regulation of space-related IP through licensing, as seen in the relevant contract provisions governing IP in projects, and the reliance on data policies as the basis for the distribution and use of data resulting from, for example, scientific or remote sensing missions.[11]

Different Contractual Practices Addressing IP Issues in Space Business Markets

The approach to ownership and use of IP-protected systems in space projects is therefore largely determined by the space community itself.[12] In Europe, the relations between the various space sectors and markets take on a particular format that is influenced by the dominant role of the European Space Agency (ESA). This ensures a consolidated regulatory approach, including rules that contain standardised general conditions of contract and procedures. The result is an accessible and uniform approach within those contracts governed by ESA rules that contain provisions for IP ownership and control.[13] National space agencies acting for their governments, too, will generally impose a standardised contract governing the project structure under the applicable law, and include conditions for emergence of IPRs within the contract.[14] Exact details of IP retention (or title) and exchange depend on the particular form of funding for the individual project. Such a regulatory model exists at international level for inventions taking place on the Columbus module within the ISS. Article 21 Intergovernmental Agreement (IGA) and its corresponding Memoranda

9 In contrast to the European trademark, there is still no EU-wide single patent. The latest attempt to adopt the relevant regulation recently failed. See Extraordinary Council Meeting, Press Release. 2010 (Brussels). Available at: www.consilium.europa.eu [accessed: 30 April 2011].

10 Jakhu, R. 2003. 'International *Law* Regarding the Acquisition and Dissemination of *Satellite Imagery', Journal of Space Law*, 29, 65.

11 See below, section 'Remote Sensing'.

12 For an overview of the European space markets, manufacturers and customers, see the ADS-EUROSPACE, *14th Report*. 2010. Available at: www.eurospace.org [accessed: 30 April 2011].

13 The General Clauses and Conditions (GCC) for ESA Contracts, ESA/REG/002. 2010. Available at: www.esa.int [accessed: 30 April 2011]. Part II Option A contains the general Conditions Concerning Intellectual Property Rights for ESA Study, Research and Development Contracts, Option B contains a special regime for partly funded contracts.

14 It is not possible to provide full details of individual agency contract conditions. For a comprehensive overview of the parameters within which space projects take place, in German, see von Kries, W., Schmidt-Tedd, B. and Schrogl, K.-U. 2002. *Grundzüge des Raumfahrtrechts; Rahmenbestimmungen und Anwendungsgebiete*. Munich: C.H. Beck. The European Cooperation for Space Standardisation (ECSS) works towards achieving standardisation for project management.

of Understanding (MoUs) provide for registration of resulting IPRs at the agreement of the partner states involved.

The stakeholders in space involve public, private and other operators, including intergovernmental organisations, serving the interests of public and private clients. The particularities of a given market segment (be this launcher, satellites or services) determine – by contract – who is to benefit from the IPRs involved and under what conditions. Downstream satellite applications and services are contributing to a steadily expanding market, feeding diverse informational needs and purposes, such as remote sensing data, positioning, navigation facilities and more, all of which require access to and use of derivative products and services derived from original sources that are subject to some form of IP protection. Space-based data is generally processed into value-added qualitative information to serve specific market needs. Establishing title and ensuring the protection of IPRs, notably against unauthorised use, grow commensurate with demand.[15] Even if primary data are not subject to copyright under copyright law, the interest in securing title and recouping primary investments remains a paramount consideration in IP management.

The qualification and use of space equipment and information subject to an IP regime is therefore tailored to fit the category of customer in the light of the particular space (or earth-based) activity, and its individual ownership. The state or agency, as driver, generally controls title or ownership, while access may be subject to regimes ranging from free and open access, to fee-paying (commercial) mechanisms, and to no access (security[16]). Many jurisdictions impose some form of rules governing public access to (space) data.[17] The type of funding available for the particular project or programme is the major influence on details of the allocation of IPRs. This is why agency, inter-agency[18] and international policy guidelines and rules shape the relationships of those engaging in space activities, and their access to or use of IP protected assets. Sharing and distribution licensing mechanisms are in place over the particular subject-matter, with data access policies determining the general conditions for access and use. This can be best seen in the data policy provisions relating to access and use of data delivered by ESA under its Envisat and other related programmes.[19]

The details of the use of and access to IPRs, at least in Europe, therefore turn on which organisations' rules apply to the programme – ESA or the EU. The space programmes originally funded by the EU, notably prior to an established system for GMES, fell within the EU's research and development programmes governed by contractual rules that include provisions for IPRs.[20]

15 See ADS-EUROSPACE, *14th Report*. 2010. Available at: www.eurospace.org [accessed: 30 April 2011].

16 The increase in coordination relating to space technologies and information for security and defence purposes can be seen from acceptance of the Multinational Space-based Imaging System (MUSIS) as a programme within the European Defence Agency, see Council of the European Union, Competitiveness Council, 10500/09 of 29 May 2009.

17 See for example EU Directive 2003/98/EC of European Parliament and Council of 17 November 2003 on re-use of public sector information, OJ L 345/90 of 31 December 2003.

18 Inter-agency includes the framework of cooperation under the International Charter on Space and Major Disasters, as well as some parts of GEOSS. Participation in GEOSS is not limited to states, but is also opened to national GEOs and other organisations; some of these are agencies.

19 See for example ENVISAT Data Policy (1998), Earth Explorer Data Policy (2003), available at: http://eopi.esa.int/esa/esa. For a detailed analysis see Chapter 33 on ESA Earth observation policies in this book.

20 Details of the rules governing ownership and dissemination are available at: http://cordis.europa.eu/fp7.

Research funding continues to be available for EU space projects, notably through the latest Framework Research Programme 7 (FP7). This contains a schedule of the standard conditions applicable to projects implemented under its provisions. These contain generous rules on IP management and release. The ESA IPR conditions prescribe the retention of IPRs on the results of an activity, while indicating how these are to be made available, exchanged or shared. Where commercial distribution systems are to be developed, the data is generally available against a fee. In this respect, the practice of space data protection and access is one that ensures title and ownership, access to and use of data, subject to differing conditions. These may or may not be based on commercial models.

At another level, the space industry itself may benefit from framework research contracts, which can be placed with the appropriate national research institutions, with a view to securing valuable research results from studies and experiments in advance of further space activities. Here, a contractual IP regime will include provisions regulating exploitation of the research results, depending on the specific interests of the commercial partner. These may relate to space technology, an area where there is mutual interest between the industry and research institutions in carrying out the research studies. Agreement as to who is to secure IPRs over such results can be reached within the framework contract, and thereafter implemented within a space venture or project.

Finally, mention must be made of projects where parties introduce and rely on their existing IPRs within a new common venture. These so-called background IPRs must be demarcated against and set apart from the IPRs that are granted for the results of the joint effort. In general, therefore, the exact provisions for dealing with IPRs depend on the particular project and the rules applying to ownership and use.

Remote Sensing

Remote sensing has become an essential space activity and the significance of remote sensing and information derived from processing space data is growing, both at the EU and ESA level. Data transmitted to earth are essential in the fulfilment of many administrative functions, and there is a move to encourage commercial markets to develop products to serve local and national government needs, such as town and traffic planning, land management, public security and commercially operated navigation and tracking services.[21] The sharing and distribution of remote sensing data is regulated within the legal framework applicable to European remote sensing projects,[22] alongside licences used by commercial providers of remote sensing data and geographic information products. Current developments in devising the relevant space policies and rules confirm that there is a growing trend towards opening up access to remote sensing data and information in the states active in this field. This, in turn, paves the way for the successful development of commercial remote sensing activities, creating platforms from which space-based information and products can be accessed and made available.[23]As indicated, however, there is as yet no general consensus on how to construct the ultimate business model for commercial products, without some form of public funding.

21 For example, there is interest in extending the existing maritime automatic identification signal system to include developments from satellite signal information systems in the management and monitoring of shipping traffic and vessels.

22 'European' in this context refers to activities undertaken by both the ESA and the EU.

23 An overview of the types of products and services under development for satellite navigation systems can be accessed under the International Committee on Global Navigation Satellite Systems (ICGNSS).

Domestic Authorisation of Space Activities and Influence on IP

The increasing involvement of private entities in the space sector has lead to greater focus on IP issues. There are two differing dimensions to this and both are linked to the requirement that all space activities, including remote sensing, are subjected to authorisation at a national level.

First, the institutional dimension at national level determines the relationship between the state (or domestic space agency) and the private entities engaging in the space activities. The state is dominant and dictates its regulatory framework for remote sensing. This includes licensing mechanisms which impose particular conditions, including restrictions on how the activity should be carried out (for instance, restriction on territories that may not be remotely sensed, or on data that cannot be freely distributed), compliance with security regulations and quality standards.[24]

This has a direct impact on private companies undertaking remote sensing activities.[25] A case in point is the situation in Germany, where the licence to distribute high-resolution space data from its two particularly powerful government funded radar satellites, TanDEM X and TerraSAR X, has been awarded to a private company, Infoterra GmbH, a subsidiary of EADS Astrium GmbH. Infoterra has been awarded the licence by the responsible ministry to collect and distribute the data collected by these satellites. Infoterra must in turn ensure full compliance, by passing down the terms and conditions of the national remote sensing regulation within its own data access and use policies and licence agreements.[26] These conditions include ensuring that restrictions on handling data from territories appearing on the government's black list are applied.[27]

Second, the private dimension of regulation means that the activities of remote sensing entities in acquiring and distributing data remain subject to all other applicable domestic and international legal rules. These include the general law of copyright, IP and freedom of information legislation.[28] The last of these prohibits restrictions on access to particular categories of information. Space contracts are designed around the 'levels' of use and users in response to the degree of interaction between authorities and private entities. The focus of the regulations, at least in the case of remote sensing activities, is to provide a clear framework for the parties involved in generating data and processing information products. Licences include conditions upholding IP and mechanisms governing the transfer of data to end users. The approximation within the EU Member States of certain aspects of IP law is an advantage for the European market, in that specific aspects of IP such as the protection of data bases through copyright, and copyright term, are very similar.[29]

---

24 A great number of Member States have now passed space legislation to ensure that all space activities, including remote sensing, are subject to prior authorisation, see the recent overview in Jakhu, R. (ed.) 2010. *National Regulation of Space Activities*. Dordrecht: Springer.

25 See the German Satellitendatensicherheitsverordnung (SatDSiVG) of 26 March 2008 (*BGBl* I 508), the implementing regulations based on the same named statute, n. 4 above.

26 For further discussion, see Schmidt-Tedd, B. and Kroymann, M. 2008. 'Current State of Developments in the German Remote Sensing Law', *Journal of Space Law*, 34, 97–140.

27 See German Satellitendatensicherheitsverordnung, n. 25, above.

28 For instance, mandatory provisions such as compulsory licensing applicable to patents and trademarks, or provisions of the international agreements governing a specific activity, in the course of which protected subject-matter may be produced.

29 Patent law is less homogeneous within Europe at national level, see n. 9 above.

Typical Data IP and Policy Issues: The Transatlantic Paradox

A comparison between the treatment of remote sensing data in Europe and the US serves to demonstrate the diversity of the approaches to regulating and contracting in the field of IPRs. Europe favours the proprietary (property-based) approach for protecting primary remote sensing data.[30] This means that no distinction is made whether the data are generated by state-owned or by private remote sensing satellites or systems.[31] This position was adopted with a view to facilitating the development of commercial markets in space applications, and it differs greatly from that of the US.

The US prohibits restrictions on access to state-generated data that are based on copyright. In addition, it determines how and when private companies are required to submit primary data from their satellites to the national archive.[32] One of the major consequences of this political choice is that data can be accessed for commercial and non-commercial purposes under the same conditions in the US,[33] whereas in Europe, not only the conditions of access, but even the entities distributing data for commercial and non-commercial purposes are different. This applies, for example, to ESA's Category-1 and Category-2 users of remote sensing data.[34]

Another issue that is subject to different regulatory frameworks between Europe and the US is the protection of data and information during the different stages of processing. National regulations use inconsistent terminology, and the terms describing space data are often at odds with those adopted within the UN Remote Sensing Principles.[35] Some regulations differentiate between primary remote sensing data, processed data and information, while others refer only to one or two distinct categories of data. The divergences in terminology used and categories of processed space data create a risk of material differences developing in regard to their eligibility for copyright protection.[36] This explains why the contractual and regulatory regimes for space data have a high impact on the operation of private data markets.[37]

The benefits to be gained from accessing and using remote sensing data in support of governmental decision-making and international humanitarian purposes underline the interest in establishing data policies that govern their free and unrestricted use within specific defined

30 See e.g. European Space Agency (ESA) rules on ownership as per Article V ESA Convention (1975). Available at: http://www.esa.int/convention.

31 Domestic legislation of the European Union (EU) Member States and EU copyright rules allow public bodies to retain copyright over information they produce. See for example Directive 2007/2/EC of the European Parliament and of the Council establishing an Infrastructure for Spatial Information in the European Community (INSPIRE) (2007) OJ L 108/1.

32 This is required by the Land Remote Sensing Policy Act of 1992. H.R.6133.

33 Sec.105 Land Remote Sensing Policy Act of 1992. H.R.6133.

34 See ENVISAT Data Policy, n. 19 above.

35 UN Principles Relating to Remote Sensing of the Earth from Outer Space (1986) U.N. Doc A/RES/41/65.

36 The same concerns terms used in private data licences. See for example 'Derivative Works' and 'Value Added Products' (VAP) as per Article 1 Non-Exclusive License to Use SPOT Satellite Products Between SPOT Image Corporation and the End-User (available at: http://www.spotimage.fr [accessed: 30 April 2011]), and 'Derived Works' in paragraph 4(e) GeoEye Data Single or Multiple Organization License (available at: http://www.americaview.org [accessed: 30 April 2011]) that includes both 'Derivative Works' and 'VAP' of SPOT Image data and information products.

37 See for example Doldirina, C. 2010. 'Is the EU Legal Regime of Remote Sensing Data Protection Facilitating the Development of the Market of Applications?', in *Proceedings of the 51st Colloquium on the International Law of Space* (forthcoming); Smith, L.J. 2010. 'At What Price?'.

cases. This is best seen in international remote sensing activities, initiatives and projects like the International Charter on Space and Major Disasters, EU/ESA Global Monitoring for Environment and Security (GMES) or the Geographic Earth Observation System of Systems (GEOSS). GEOSS proposes the complete freedom and openness of data in its Data Sharing Principles,[38] with 'as few restrictions as possible', and 'with minimum time delay and minimum cost'. The Principles were endorsed by the GEO Ministerial Council in November 2010 and are in the process of being implemented.[39] However, this 'ideal regime' for data exchange, use and distribution might not become reality: adherence to its Principles is voluntary.[40] Differences between national regulatory environments are the major impediments: they constitute a risk of a conflict between the varying national treatments of data generated through independent missions, where these are combined and made available through GEOSS; the size of the system and the wide range of possible data use makes for difficult management.[41]

Trends in the Private Dimensions of Licensing Remote Sensing Data

Various studies already indicate that the current licensing mechanisms used by private remote sensing satellite operators and owners are over-restrictive, in that they 'lock up' information.[42] This is in part a reaction to the lower degree of legal protection, generally copyright, available for non-creative, automated processes, and a response to the development of new product and service markets across the value-added chain. Firstly, IPRs owners benefit from comparatively new rights with regard to their protected assets, such as the right of communication to the public under digital copyright law[43] and the *sui generis* database copyright protection for technology-geared software.[44] Secondly, since remote sensing data are usually licensed in the digitised form, they can also be

38 GEOSS 10-Year Implementation Plan (2005). Available at: http://www.earthobservations.org [accessed: 30 April 2011].

39 GEO, Beijing Declaration (5 November 2010) reads as follows: '3. *Commit* to (i) maximize the number of documented datasets made available on the basis of full and open access; (ii) create the GEOSS Data Collection of Open Resources for Everyone, a distributed pool of documented datasets with full, open and unrestricted access at no more that the cost of reproduction and distribution; and (iii) develop flexible national and international policy frameworks to ensure that a more open data environment is implemented, thus putting in practice actions for the implementation of the GEOSS Data Sharing Principles.' Available at: http://www.earthobservations.org [accessed: 30 April 2011].

40 The voluntary nature of GEOSS implementation was found by the GEO Executive Committee to be capable of adversely affecting its sustainability, see Mid-Term Evaluation of GEOSS Implementation (2010), 7–8. Available at: http://www.earthobservations.org [accessed: 30 April 2011].

41 See description of GEOSS. Available at: http://www.earthobservations.org/geoss.shtml [accessed: 30 April 2011].

42 See for example Stienstra, D., Watzke, J. and Birch G.E. 2007. 'A Three-way Dance: The Global Public Good and Accessibility in Information Technologies', *The Information Society*, 23, 149; Leys, C. 2001. *Market-Driven Politics: Neoliberal Democracy and the Public Interest*. London: Verso, 3; Trosow, S.L. 2003. 'The Illusive Search for Justificatory Theories: Copyright, Commodification and Capital', *Can. J.L. & Jur.*, 16 (2), 217.

43 First codified in the WIPO Copyright Treaty.

44 This right currently exists only in the EU, see European Parliament and the Council Directive 96/9/EC of 11 March 1996 on the legal protection of databases (1996) OJ L 77/20.

'over'-protected by technological protection measures, such as copy disabling.[45] The relevant licences often contain restrictive conditions, and extend ownership rights beyond what is therefore available under copyright legislation. Licences may limit the types of use and further distribution of licensed data or products,[46] many containing blanket provisions prohibiting all activities that are not expressly allowed. These are drafted on the basis of permitted uses, lists of activities that the user may perform with regard to the licensed data.[47] While the economic investment in such space information systems justifies creating restrictions on its use or access, these must not be such as to significantly impede the freedom to process data and to generate further information products.

Private entities distributing remote sensing data generally have greater freedom than the public hand or agencies to adopt licensing schemes that best suit their interests.[48] Nevertheless, apart from those jurisdictions with national data policies, there is little guidance as to what data licences should effectively contain and the limited effect of data policies on private actors only compounds the uncertainty. This has come about by conferring all stages of data with full copyright protection, and extending it through licence conditions down the value-added chain. Data licences usually contain a broad reference to the fact that the data are protected by copyright, by trade secrets and constitute confidential information. For those entities established in Europe, reference is generally made to protection of the data under the *sui generis* database protection right.[49]

Challenges Arising

This brief overview of the European and international framework for cooperative remote sensing satellite missions and the licensing practices of private companies in the use and subsequent distribution of remote sensing data shows that, for the time being, there are indeed differences in the rules and regulations applying to remote sensing activities and, particularly, to the distribution of space data. There is little sign that market developments are encouraging a coherent streamlined approach among international partners and stakeholder companies operating in the commercial management of remote sensing data and information.

One immediate difficulty is that the number of participants involved in cooperative missions increases the risk of conflict of applicable rules. This must be addressed in the founding framework agreements for the given project. GEOSS is a good example of an important cooperative project

45 Digital copyright was initially secured under the WIPO Copyright Treaty and subsequently adopted in national regulations across the globe. Disabling measures are computer programmes that prevent the user from doing anything that would impede the author's rights in terms of the copyright regulations. Often, licences create rights and obligations that do not exist within the relevant regulations. The problem with licensing remote sensing data is that it is unclear whether they are protected by anything other than economic copyright in the first place. The use of digital protection measures can easily cause an imbalance between the degree of protection conferred by law and that provided by contract.

46 Generally, only non-transferable, non-exclusive limited rights to use the remote sensing data or information are granted to the licensee. See 2.1. SPOT Image General Supply Conditions of Satellite Imagery Products (January, 2008). Available at: www.spotimage.fr [accessed: 30 April 2011].

47 See 2.1(c)(e) SPOT Image General Supply Conditions, n. 46 above.

48 See for example relevant provisions of Envisat Data Policy that *inter alia* state that the distributing entities of data for Category-2 Use enjoy freedom of price-determination for their services and products and have the right to market to users directly products and services that include satellite programming, acquisition of data, processing, archiving, cataloguing and dissemination.

49 2.2. SPOT Image General Supply Conditions, n. 46 above.

that may well face such difficulties. The system will not operate its own satellites, but is to be supplied with the necessary data by governments, their agencies and even private companies.

Recommendations

Greater standardisation in the use of and reference to IP regulations as they apply to space activities and their outcomes would serve the interests of all in achieving a consistent approach to IPRs in space projects.[50] National regulations should therefore strive for coherency, accommodating the various stakeholders and participants with differing interests, whether these are public or private. The recent extension of the EU's competences now to include the field of IPR could be a stepping stone towards removing at least those impediments caused by differing IP regulation.[51] The development of global initiatives such as GEOSS, as well as their regional counterparts, such as GMES, undoubtedly contributes to harmonisation of the laws and practices that shape the content of the relevant licensing mechanisms.

The need to protect IPRs is balanced by the need to create reliable commercial ventures serving both data providers and users. Licensing mechanisms must allow the industry and its customers to operate within accepted business models, if the commercial sector is to become fully established.

Conclusions

Contract is an effective mechanism for protecting activities that lead to the creation of IPRs over inventions, copyright in works or generation of space data. The international nature of the majority of outer space activities means that intellectual property protection and appropriate licensing regimes are generally addressed by framework cooperation agreements. This avoids additional ambiguities that could otherwise be caused by the conflict of laws applying to IPRs. Contractual provisions, particularly in relation to remote sensing activities, can deliver suitable formulae for workable solutions across the variety of applicable domestic laws and regulations governing copyright and freedom of information. This in turn, avoids artificial barriers on the generation, use and distribution of remote sensing data. The latter activities nevertheless still require discussion if, in the long term, feasible business models are to be developed by the industry to deliver the space-based products and services currently required as tools to support the demands for all types of information in managing modern society.

List of References

Abeyratne, R. 2003. 'The Application of Intellectual Property Rights to Outer Space Activities', *Journal of Space Law*, 29.

ADS-EUROSPACE. *14th Report*. 2010. [Online]. Available at: www.eurospace.org [accessed: 30 April 2011].

50 For recent proposals on a copyright regime for space, see Stirling, J.A.L. 2007, 2008. 'Space Copyright Law: The New Dimension', *Journal of the Copyright Society of the USA*, 54, 345 (update December 15, 2008 available online).

51 Article 118 Consolidated Version of the Treaty on the Functioning of the European Union (2010) OJ C 83/47.

Consolidated Version of the Treaty on the Functioning of the European Union (2010) OJ C 83/47.
Council Regulation on the Community trademark (2009) OJ L 78/1.
Council Resolution on The Contribution of space to innovative and competitiveness in the context of the European Economic Recovery Plan, and further steps, 10500/09 29 May 2009.
Description of GEOSS. [Online]. Available at: http://www.earthobservations.org/geoss.shtml [accessed: 30 April 2011].
Directive 2007/2/EC of the European Parliament and of the Council establishing an Infrastructure for Spatial Information in the European Community (INSPIRE) (2007) OJ L 108/1.
Doldirina, C. 2010. 'Is the EU Legal Regime of Remote Sensing Data Protection Facilitating the Development of the Market of Applications?', in *Proceedings of the 51st Colloquium on the International Law of Space* (forthcoming).
Earth Explorer Data Policy (2003). [Online]. Available at: http://eopi.esa.int/esa/esa [accessed: 30 April 2011].
ENVISAT Data Policy (1998). [Online]. Available at: http://eopi.esa.int/esa/esa [accessed: 30 April 2011].
ESA Convention (1975). [Online]. Available at: http://www.esa.int/convention [accessed: 30 April 2011].
European Parliament and the Council Directive 96/9/EC of 11 March 1996 on the legal protection of databases (1996) OJ L 77/20.
Extraordinary Council Meeting, Press Release. 2010 (Brussels). [Online]. Available at: www.consilium.europa.eu [accessed: 30 April 2011].
GEO, Beijing Declaration (2010). [Online]. Available at: http://www.earthobservations.org [accessed: 30 April 2011].
GeoEye Data Single or Multiple Organization License. [Online]. Available at: http://www.americaview.org [accessed: 30 April 2011].
GEOSS 10-Year Implementation Plan (2005). [Online]. Available at: http://www.earthobservations.org [accessed: 30 April 2011].
German Satellitendatensicherheitsverordnung (SatDSiVG) of 26 March 2008 (*BGBl* I 508).
Gesetz zum Schutz vor Gefährdung der Sicherheit der Bundesrepublik Deutschland durch das Verbreiten von hochwertigen Erdfernerkundungsdaten (2007) *BGBl* I. 2590. An English translation is available at: http://www.unoosa.org [accessed: 30 April 2011].
Inter-Governmental Agreement establishing the International Space Station (1998).
Jakhu, R. 2003. 'International Law Regarding the Acquisition and Dissemination of Satellite Imagery', *Journal of Space Law*, 29, 65.
Jakhu, R. (ed.) 2010. *National Regulation of Space Activities*. Dordrecht: Springer.
Leys, C. 2001. *Market-Driven Politics: Neoliberal Democracy and the Public Interest*. London: Verso.
Mid-Term Evaluation of GEOSS Implementation (2010). [Online]. Available at: http://www.earthobservations.org [accessed: 30 April 2011].
Non-Exclusive License to Use SPOT Satellite Products Between SPOT Image Corporation and the End-User. [Online]. Available at: http://www.spotimage.fr [accessed: 30 April 2011].
Paris Convention for the Protection of Industrial Property (1883) 828 U.N.T.S. 305.
Schmidt-Tedd, B. and Kroymann, M. 2008. 'Current State of Developments in the German Remote Sensing Law', *Journal of Space Law*, 34, 97–140.
Smith, L.J. 2011. 'At What Price? IP-related Thoughts on New Business Models for Space Information', *Proceedings of the 61st International Astronautical Congress*. American Institute of Aeronautics and Astronautics (forthcoming).

SPOT Image General Supply Conditions of Satellite Imagery Products (January, 2008). [Online]. Available at: www.spotimage.fr [accessed: 30 April 2011].

Stienstra, D., Watzke, J. and Birch, G.E. 2007. 'A Three-way Dance: The Global Public Good and Accessibility in Information Technologies', *The Information Society*, 23, 149.

Stirling, J.A.L. 2007, 2008. 'Space Copyright Law: The New Dimension', *Journal of the Copyright Society of the USA*, 54, 345 (update 15 December 2008 available online).

The Berne Convention on the Protection of Literary and Artistic Works (1886) 331 U.N.T.S. 217.

The General Clauses and Conditions (GCC) for ESA Contracts. 2008. [Online]. Available at: www.esa.int [accessed: 30 April 2011].

The World Intellectual Property Organisation Copyright Treaty (1996) 36 I.L.M. 65.

Treaty on Principles Governing the Activities of States in the Exploration and Use of Outer Space, including the Moon and Other Celestial Bodies (1967).

Trosow, S.L. 2003. 'The Illusive Search for Justificatory Theories: Copyright, Commodification and Capital', *Can. J.L. & Jur.*, 16 (2), 217.

UN Principles Relating to Remote Sensing of the Earth from Outer Space (1986) U.N. Doc A/RES/41/65.

U.S. Land Remote Sensing Policy Act of 1992. H.R.6133.

Von der Dunk, F.G. and Brus, M.M.T.A. (eds) 2006. *The International Space Station: Commercial Utilisation from a European Legal Perspective*. Leiden: Martinus Nijhoff and VSP.

Von Kries, W., Schmidt-Tedd, B. and Schrogl, K.-U. 2002. *Grundzüge des Raumfahrtrechts; Rahmenbestimmungen und Anwendungsgebiete*. Munich: C.H. Beck.

Chapter 28
Negotiating the Security Aspects of Satellite Communications Services Contracts

Tare C. Brisibe*

Introduction

Telecommunications networks serve as a tool for preserving national security and support law enforcement through intelligence gathering by legal interception and access to retained data. It is contended[1] in this regard, that interception of communications by governments has had a long history, for instance in the United States where law enforcement agencies (LEAs) have practised wiretapping since the invention of telegraph communication in 1844, and tapping of telephones since the early 1890s. The European Union (EU) approach is no different given the detailed regulatory framework requiring entities involved in the operation of satellite-based communications networks or delivery of electronic communications services to ensure compliance, after assessing the extent of their legal interception and data retention obligations, in accordance with national legislation. Whilst debate continues on issues such as what rules ought to govern surveillance alongside considerations of acceptable oversight mechanisms, there remains the much overlooked financial and operational implications of related regulatory obligations and the consequent assignment of contractual responsibility between various stakeholders in the delivery of telecommunications services. Funding the capital and operating costs of legal interception and data retention are a thorny issue. Although LEAs in a good number of EU countries may contribute[2] towards costs of meeting interception obligations by, for instance, reimbursing the relatively low variable costs associated with executing intercept requests, the more significant and onerous costs associated with installing suitable infrastructure and building interception capabilities are the fixed capital costs of deploying required hardware, software and personnel. Obviously, the high cost to new entrants and small communications service providers arising from compliance with interception obligations could cause these companies serious and irreparable financial harm. This chapter explores means by which binding and potentially onerous security-related regulatory obligations may be mitigated,

---

* This chapter is written as the sole opinion of the author and does not reflect, nor is it intended to reflect, the views of any organisation with which he is or has been affiliated.

1 Stoddart, J. (Privacy Commissioner of Canada). 2009. *Surveillance, Search or Seizure Powers Extended by Recent Legislation in Canada, Britain, France and the United States*, 13.

2 Examples of countries that provide for reimbursement of interception costs (for example costs of hardware and software design, acquisition and maintenance, and delivery of intercept related information to LEAs) include: Estonia (Electronic Communications Act, § 114), Finland (Communications Market Act, § 98), France (Post and Electronic Communications Code, Art. D98-7), Italy (Decree of 26 April 2001), Lithuania (Law on Electronic Communications, 2004, Chapter 11, Article 77) and the UK (Regulation of Investigatory Powers Act, 2000 § 14). See: International Chamber of Commerce. 2010. Doc. No. 373-492, *Global Business Recommendations and Best Practices for Lawful Intercept Requirements*, 7.

relying on the assignment of responsibility in the service delivery chain through the negotiation of suitable contractual terms.

Background

In the broad sense, it can be stated that activities undertaken in the European space industry range from satellite manufacturing to the supply of ground equipment and launch services. But a significant share of such activity, can be attributed to the satellite services sector,[3] which to the exclusion of earth observation (remote sensing), can be summarised as comprised of mobile (data or voice), fixed (broadband, private networks or transponder agreements) and broadcasting (television or radio) services. In the European regulatory context, Article 2 (c) of the Framework Directive[4], defines electronic communications services as:

> … a service normally provided for remuneration which consists wholly or mainly in the conveyance of signals on electronic communications networks, including telecommunications services and transmission services in networks used for broadcasting.

In addition, Article 2 (a) of the Framework Directive defines electronic communications networks as:

> … transmission systems and, where applicable, switching or routing equipment and other resources which permit the conveyance of signals by wire, by radio, by optical or by other electromagnetic means, including satellite networks, fixed (circuit- and packet-switched, including Internet) and mobile terrestrial networks, electricity cable systems, to the extent that they are used for the purpose of transmitting signals, networks used for radio and television broadcasting, and cable television networks, irrespective of the type of information conveyed.

These statutory provisions underscore the fact that regulation of communications technologies in Europe, including satellite services and networks, is currently subject to a number of legal instruments in force since 2003. Thus, it is the Authorisation Directive[5] that outlines the basis for licensing satellite services and, amongst others, dictates certain obligations to be transposed by EU Member States in the form of national laws, regulations and administrative provisions.

This chapter addresses the relevant obligations listed as conditions in an Annex to the Authorisation Directive, which include the obligation[6] to protect personal data privacy specific

3 For a definition of those activities falling within the scope of the term 'satellite services', see Article 1 of the International Telecommunication Union, *Radio Regulations*, 2008 edition, as adopted by the World Radiocommunication Conference (WRC) (Geneva, 1995) and subsequently revised and adopted by the WRC (Geneva, 1997), the WRC (Istanbul, 2000), the WRC (Geneva, 2003), and the WRC (Geneva, 2007).

4 Directive 2002/21/EC of the European Parliament and of the Council of 7 March 2002 on a common regulatory framework for electronic communications networks and services, OJ L 108, 24 April 2002, 33–50.

5 Directive 2002/20/EC of the European Parliament and of the Council of 7 March 2002 on the authorisation of electronic communications networks and services, OJ L 108, 24 April 2002, 21–32.

6 In conformity with Directive 97/66/EC of the European Parliament and of the Council of 15 December 1997 concerning the processing of personal data and the protection of privacy in the telecommunications sector, OJ L 24, 30 January 1998, 1–8. Directive 97/66 has since been repealed and replaced by Directive 2002/58/EC of the European Parliament and of the Council of 12 July 2002 concerning the processing of

to the electronic communications sector. The said Annex also lists, and this chapter addresses, the obligation[7] enabling legal interception by competent national authorities.

Whilst statutory legal interception obligations can be traced to the EU Council Resolution of 17 January 1995 on the Lawful Interception of Telecommunications, they have been brought into sharp focus since 2001,[8] when heightened security concerns requiring an expanded function for LEAs in tackling terrorism gave rise to greater investigatory and intelligence gathering mandates, relying heavily on the availability of legal interception systems.[9] Likewise, increased considerations on the use of retained telecommunications data for law enforcement led to the adoption of Data Retention Directives[10] in 2002 and 2006 respectively.

A combined effect of the regulatory framework described above, implies that alongside legal interception systems, additional facilities required to interrogate the network, such as data retention capabilities for collection and storage of interception-related information, or communications-related traffic, have to be installed by *both* network operators and service providers in accordance with a range of laws, regulations and administrative provisions applicable in EU Member States. These security-oriented capabilities come at significant financial cost and could sometimes constitute a barrier to market entry for the satellite services network operator or provider that is expected to bear the burden for making the same available. It is to the mitigation of potential financially onerous obligations through negotiated contractual obligations, that this chapter is dedicated.

Satellite-Based Communications and the Service Delivery Chain

It has been argued,[11] that since terrorist activity capable of endangering national security would require some form of organisation dependent on communications, effective counter-terrorism strategies require, amongst others, surveillance or analysis of communications. Communications in this respect would seem to stem mainly from internet access via computing systems and mobile communications by Satellite-Personal Communications (S-PCS) / cellular (GSM) terminals, which

personal data and the protection of privacy in the electronic communications sector, OJ L 201, 31 July 2002, 37–47.

7 In conformity with both Directive 97/66/EC (see note 6) and Directive 95/46/EC of the European Parliament and of the Council of 24 October 1995 on the protection of individuals with regard to the processing of personal data and on the free movement of such data, OJ L 281, 23 November 1995, 31–50.

8 See UN Security Council Resolution 1373, 2001, Threats to International Peace and Security Caused by Terrorist Acts, at Paragraphs 2(f) and 3(a). See also, Articles 1, 16, 17, 20, 21, 25(4) and (5) and 27, of the Convention on Cybercrime, 2001, Council of Europe Treaty Series No. 185, currently with 45 signatory states including non- EU members.

9 Defined as '...the statutory-based action of providing access and delivery of a subject's telecommunications and call-associated data to law enforcement agencies'. See Glossary to the EU Council Resolution of 17 January 1995 on the lawful interception of telecommunications, OJ C 329, 04 November 1996, 1–6.

10 Directive 2006/24/EC of the European Parliament and of the Council of 15 March 2006 on the retention of data generated or processed in connection with the provision of publicly available electronic communications services or of public communications networks and amending Directive 2002/58/EC, OJ L 105, 13 April 2006, 54–63.

11 Bobbitt, P. 2008. *Terror and Consent: The Wars for the Twenty First Century*. London and New York: Penguin, 55, 63 and 97; Taipale, K.A., 2007, 'The Ear of Dionysus: Rethinking Foreign Intelligence Surveillance', 9 *Yale J.L. & Tech*, 139.

rely on satellite services (fixed or mobile) for traffic backhaul over oceanic spaces and in remote areas devoid of communications infrastructure. Whilst the practice of intercepting communications content and collecting traffic data has been applied to traditional cable infrastructure or wireless networks, on the basis of the existing national infrastructure, legal interception of international communications transcending national borders gives rise to thorny questions of jurisdiction alongside practical problems associated with implementation and compliance due to the involvement of a variety of entities that may be involved in the typically fragmented service delivery chains underpinning satellite communications.

For instance, assuming each state retains sovereignty over telecommunications within its territory,[12] and because the location of an interception target or S-PCS / cellular user is not always fixed, it is vital to effective infrastructure monitoring, that a service area be determined. We will note that in terms of satellite footprints, a service area may cover up to one-third of the earth's surface by way of global beams or be restricted to smaller spot beams. Because a service area could establish the extent to which the jurisdiction of a state extends, it implies that should the satellite ground infrastructure managing the communication lie in the jurisdiction other than that where the end user terminal is operating, then notification of use, and any ensuing commands for interception of that user, will cross into a different jurisdiction, noting also that the eventual legally intercepted product (i.e. call content and interception-related information) will also traverse international boundaries.[13]

Furthermore, and particularly with regards to computer systems accessing the internet, it is noted[14] that more than one service provider may be involved in the transmission of a communication. Each service provider may possess some traffic data related to the transmission of the specified communication, which either has been generated and retained by that service provider in relation to the passage of the communication through its system or has been provided from other service providers. Placing the aforementioned practicalities in the context of satellite services as far as satellite-based infrastructure are concerned, although communications traditionally takes place through three major components or segments, the responsibility of ownership and / or operation of the respective components or segments – as well as the separate task of satellite service provision – does not always lie in the same entity. To be clear, with regards to components and segments, these would typically be comprised of the space segment (consisting of satellites in orbit), the ground earth station(s) and end user terminal(s). But with regards to ownership and operation, the following functions have been identified,[15] as including:

12 See Preamble to the Constitution of the International Telecommunication Union, Final Acts of the Plenipotentiary Conference (Antalya, 2006) Instruments amending the Constitution and the Convention of the International Telecommunication Union (Geneva, 1992) as amended by the Plenipotentiary Conference (Kyoto, 1994), the Plenipotentiary Conference (Minneapolis, 1998) and the Plenipotentiary Conference (Marrakesh, 2002).

13 Johnston, T.F. 1999. 'Security Issues in a Satellite Global GSM Network', *Information Security Technical Report*, 4 (1), 47–8.

14 See Explanatory Report to the Convention on Cybercrime, Council of Europe Treaty Series No. 185, 29 of 63.

15 Brisibe, T. 2006. *Aeronautical Public Correspondence by Satellite*. Essential Air and Space Law Series, Volume 3. Utrecht: Eleven International Publishing, 23; Henaku, B.D.K. 1998. *The Law on Global Air Navigation by Satellite: An Analysis of Legal Aspects of the ICAO CNS /ATM System*. Leiden: AST, 82.

owning and operating communications satellites by providing the capability for communications to be channelled through the satellites provided;

owning and operating a ground earth station through which satellite communications are routed to the terrestrial system or re-transmitted to a satellite;

owning and operating earth stations / user terminals which receive and transmit various forms of communications through the satellite;

providing satellite communications services, with or without an entity's own space segment, ground earth station or earth station / user terminal.

Given the contextual circumstances described above, it is imperative that two primary considerations be borne in mind when entering into contract negotiations aimed at apportioning potential lawful interception and data retention obligations on specific entities in the service delivery value chain. Firstly, the value chain for provision of satellite services needs to be clearly understood, because technical and / or commercial relationships with end user terminal(s) employed by individuals who constitute interception targets will probably not always be limited to the satellite service provider. Secondly, although legal interception and data retention obligations apply equally to both network operators and service providers, the deployment of any legal interception capability within a satellite-based system is closely linked to and dependent upon ownership and control of specific ground-based infrastructure.

Best Practices in Contract Negotiation

Explanatory notes to the European Telecommunications Standards Institute's (ETSI) technical specifications for the design of legal interception solutions recognise the fact that as the telecommunications market in Europe develops, more services will be provided across national frontiers, using terrestrial or satellite communication links. In order to address these circumstances, further technical requirements for the development of legal interception solutions have been recommended, taking into account questions of extra-territoriality. Thus, in contemplating the design and / or implementation of legal interception and data retention solutions, a network operator, service provider, or access provider, providing services to a home country (i.e. a state or territory where associated ground infrastructure is situated and required for managing communications) from a foreign territory, are expected to make arrangements, amongst others, such that firstly, legal interception is possible relating to activity of a target identity within a specific national domain; and secondly, if the legal interception interface lies in a foreign territory, then arrangements (both technical and organisational) are made such that interception is possible as if the interception interface were located in the home country.

The above requirement, deriving from the provisioning of national communications services in an international context by a practice known as 'roaming' (in terrestrial cellular parlance) or 'visiting terminals' (in the satellite context), applies equally to a network operator, service provider or access provider in the business of providing services to a home country from a foreign territory, including international space above earth by satellite operators, as well as those entities providing services via satellite facilities. Implementing, operating and maintaining security-orientated capabilities comes with a cost and could constitute a financial barrier to market entry for the satellite services network operator or service provider expected to bear the burden for making the same available. It is therefore prudent to carefully consider possibilities aimed at mitigating the assumption of obligations that could have significant financial consequences, when conducting contract negotiations. These possibilities include the following.

Firstly, one should identify and become thoroughly familiar with the nature of traffic data required to be retained and precisely where such data could reside in the network architecture and with which entity. This will allow for the proper assignment of contractual obligations to be relied upon when meeting security orientated regulatory obligations. For instance, the 2006 Data Retention Directive lists traffic data that should be retained in respect of both mobile and internet communications as follows:

a. data necessary to trace and identify the source of a communication
b. data necessary to identify the destination of a communication
c. data necessary to identify the date, time and duration of a communication
d. data necessary to identify users' communication equipment or what purports to be their equipment
e. data necessary to identify the location of mobile communication equipment
f. card holder data necessary for customer service and marketing purposes.

Whilst the above listed traffic data expected to be retained in respect of both mobile and internet communications appears straightforward, we will recall that more than one service provider may be involved in the transmission of a communication. Therefore one may also assume that each service provider could possess some traffic data related to the transmission of the specified communication, which has been generated and retained by that service provider in relation to the passage of the communication through its system, or has been provided from other service providers. It may also be the case that traffic data, or at least some types of traffic data, are shared among the service providers involved in the transmission of the communication for commercial, security or technical purposes. In such instances, any one of the service providers or network operators may possess the crucial traffic data that is needed to determine the source or destination of the communication.

As one of several examples, with respect to re-selling cellular services relying on satellite connectivity for backhaul, taping or monitoring of a communications session is done on a per user basis, where GSM users are registered to their respective GSM home network operator, as a consequence of which mapping a user name to ID (for example phone number) can only be carried out by the GSM home network operator. Whilst the cellular service re-seller transfers call roaming records to the respective GSM home network operators, using the Transfer Account Procedure (TAP) in order to transfer billing information, such TAP records would only include the IMSI,[16] IMEI[17] or cell ID of a chargeable subscriber roaming on the re-sellers' network, i.e. a calling party for a mobile originating call or the called party for a mobile terminating call. Traffic data categories listed above and required to be retained by telecommunications network operators and/or service providers for security purposes would indicate that such data can only be collated, retained and provided in an interceptable form by GSM home network operators. Such traffic data would normally be comprised of the IMSI (of the calling party and called party), MSISDN[18] (of

16 International Mobile Subscriber Identity.

17 International Mobile Equipment Identity

18 Mobile Subscriber Integrated Services Digital Network Number (or Mobile Subscriber ISDN Number).

the calling party), IMEI (of the calling party and called party), call duration, cell ID of the calling party, and traffic data displaying use of supplementary services by the calling party such as call forwarding or call transfer, as well as the number(s) to which the call is routed, etc. This is because the GSM home network operator is able to consolidate the TAP records with its own traffic data considering that certain data elements remain solely in the possession of the GSM home network operator, such as name(s) and address(es) of the subscriber(s) or registered user(s), subscription type and call data for non-roaming calls.

Secondly, it should be noted that the national laws, regulations and administrative provisions with which satellite service providers are expected to comply do not always make law enforcement agencies responsible for reasonable costs incurred[19] when making available operational assistance to carry out legal interception, seizure and preservation orders. It is therefore important that in contract negotiations, an attempt be made to work these costs out between each service provider.

Thirdly, in assigning contractual obligations, it is prudent to identify applicable regulatory obligations in the territories or countries with statutory requirements that call for the physical presence of satellite-related ground infrastructure required for managing communications. One should aim to assume responsibility for providing traffic-data-related information to that entity in which responsibility lies for operating such infrastructure, on the basis of appropriate financial compensation.

Finally, it may be possible, within technically feasible limits, to rely on statutory provisions[20] that facilitate mutual judicial assistance between EU Member States without having to re-invent the wheel by deploying one's own security capability at great cost. For instance, it is permissible for states to ensure that systems of telecommunications services operated via a gateway on their territory, which for the lawful interception of the communications of a subject present in another Member State are not directly accessible on the territory of the latter, may be made directly accessible for the legal interception by that Member State through the intermediary of a designated service provider present on its territory.

Conclusively, legal interception is actively practised worldwide, as well as in Europe, with an increasing number of applications. Whilst accurate international standards-based network forensics technologies for lawful interception, data retention and network management are needed[21] by satellite service providers in order to meet national requirements in the current security environment, it still remains possible to mitigate the financial burden by relying on negotiated and pragmatic contract terms.

---

19 Although it is also useful to explore the possibility of cost recovery mechanisms, albeit cost recovery mechanisms, at least where they exist, certainly differ between EU Member States such that the entity that bears or contributes to the cost may be either the government, law enforcement agency or service provider. See for instance Article 21 of the Annex to the Council Act of 29 May 2000 Establishing in Accordance with Article 34 of the Treaty on European Union the Convention on Mutual Assistance in Criminal Matters Between the Member States of the European Union. (Mutual Assistance Council Act). OJ C 197/1, 12 July 2000.

20 See generally, Articles 17, 18, 19 and 20 of the Mutual Assistance Council Act.

21 International Telecommunication Union. 2008. *Technical Aspects of Lawful Interception*, ITU Technology Watch Report no. 6, 6.

List of References

Bobbitt, P. 2008. *Terror and Consent: The Wars for the Twenty First Century*. London and New York: Penguin.

Brisibe, T. 2006. *Aeronautical Public Correspondence by Satellite*. Essential Air and Space Law Series, Volume 3. Utrecht: Eleven International Publishing.

Constitution of the International Telecommunication Union, *Final Acts of the Plenipotentiary Conference* (Antalya, 2006).

Convention on Cybercrime. 2001. Council of Europe Treaty Series No. 185.

Council Act of 29 May 2000. Establishing in Accordance with Article 34 of the Treaty on European Union the Convention on Mutual Assistance in Criminal Matters Between the Member States of the European Union. (Mutual Assistance Council Act). OJ C 197/1, 12 July 2000.

Directive 2002/20/EC of the European Parliament and of the Council of 7 March 2002 on the authorisation of electronic communications networks and services, OJ L 108, 24 April 2002, 21–32 (Authorisation Directive).

Directive 2002/21/EC of the European Parliament and of the Council of 7 March 2002 on a common regulatory framework for electronic communications networks and services, OJ L 108, 24 April 2002, 33–50 (Framework Directive).

Directive 2002/58/EC of the European Parliament and of the Council of 12 July 2002 concerning the processing of personal data and the protection of privacy in the electronic communications sector, OJ L 201, 31 July 2002, 37–47 (2002 Data Retention Directive).

Directive 2006/24/EC of the European Parliament and of the Council of 15 March 2006 on the retention of data generated or processed in connection with the provision of publicly available electronic communications services or of public communications networks and amending Directive 2002/58/EC, OJ L 105, 13 April 2006, 54–63 (2006 Data Retention Directive).

EU Council Resolution of 17 January 1995 on the lawful interception of telecommunications, OJ C 329, 04 November 1996, 1–6.

Henaku, B.D.K. 1998. *The Law on Global Air Navigation by Satellite: An Analysis of Legal Aspects of the ICAO CNS /ATM System*. Leiden: AST.

International Chamber of Commerce. 2010. Doc. No. 373-492, *Global Business Recommendations and Best Practices for Lawful Intercept Requirements*.

International Telecommunication Union. 2008. *Technical Aspects of Lawful Interception*, ITU Technology Watch Report no. 6.

International Telecommunication Union. 2008. *Radio Regulations*, 2008 edition.

Johnston, T.F. 1999. 'Security Issues in a Satellite Global GSM Network', *Information Security Technical Report*, 4 (1), 47–8.

Stoddart, J. (Privacy Commissioner of Canada). 2009. *Surveillance, Search or Seizure Powers Extended by Recent Legislation in Canada, Britain, France and the United States*.

Taipale, K.A. 2007. 'The Ear of Dionysus: Rethinking Foreign Intelligence Surveillance', 9 *Yale J.L. & Tech*, 139.

UN Security Council Resolution 1373, 2001, Threats to International Peace and Security Caused by Terrorist Acts.

Chapter 29

The Legal Framework for Space Projects in Europe: Aspects of Applicable Law and Dispute Resolution

Frans von der Dunk

Introduction

Space projects in Europe take place in a complicated environment involving many public, private and intergovernmental actors, where the participation of the private sector, as independent space operators or as sub-contractors to others, is usually subsumed under the label of 'the space industry', producing hardware, software and services to be used in outer space, in support of space activities, or using products, data or information generated with the help of space activities.

Such private, semi-private and quasi-private actors use contracts as the main mechanism to protect their interests, the freedom to contract within the rule of law being the paramount overarching legal principle. However, because of the large measure of governmental and intergovernmental activity and involvement in the space arena and the manifold public aspects of using space those governments might perhaps be expected to subject that freedom to contract to restrictions in the context of the space sector much more than in other sectors.

Moreover, in view of the almost inherent international character of most space activities in Europe,[1] such governmental interference with the private space sector would likely lead to many issues of potentially conflicting jurisdictions. The current contribution attempts to analyse some of these issues from the perspective of the national space laws that have been enunciated in European countries[2] and their intricate relationship to the international space law regime.

These national space laws have been drafted at least partly to implement the applicable international regime *vis-à-vis* the private sector (notably, in this context, the Outer Space Treaty,[3] the Liability Convention[4] and the Registration Convention[5]), which therefore also has to be kept

1 For example, most of the so-called 'primes', commercial entities sizable enough to serve as 'prime contractors' to ESA and the major national space agencies, are actually international consortia composed of companies from various Member States.

2 For the present purpose, 'European' is taken to refer to the Member States of the European Union and/or ESA; i.e. the Russian Federation and the Ukraine, though both European states in a geographical sense as well as having developed national space legislation, will not be taken into account.

3 Treaty on Principles Governing the Activities of States in the Exploration and Use of Outer Space, including the Moon and Other Celestial Bodies (hereafter Outer Space Treaty), London/Moscow/Washington, done 27 January 1967, entered into force 10 October 1967; 610 UNTS 205; TIAS 6347; 18 UST 2410; UKTS 1968 No. 10; Cmnd. 3198; ATS 1967 No. 24; 6 ILM 386 (1967).

4 Convention on International Liability for Damage Caused by Space Objects (hereafter Liability Convention), London/Moscow/Washington, done 29 March 1972, entered into force 1 September 1972; 961 UNTS 187; TIAS 7762; 24 UST 2389; UKTS 1974 No. 16; Cmnd. 5068; ATS 1975 No. 5; 10 ILM 965 (1971).

5 Convention on Registration of Objects Launched into Outer Space (hereafter Registration Convention), New York, done 14 January 1975, entered into force 15 September 1976; 1023 UNTS 15; TIAS 8480; 28 UST

in mind for the current purpose. At the same time, when enunciating their national space laws, the states that did so – Norway (1969),[6] Sweden (1982),[7] the United Kingdom (1986),[8] Belgium (2005),[9] the Netherlands (2007)[10] and France (2008)[11] – did not necessarily limit their scope to covering subject matter covered by the aforementioned treaties. States might well extend the scopes of their national laws to include other areas of the space arena, thus impacting contracts dealing with issues *not* addressed or impacted by the international space treaties.

The National Space Laws and the Scope of Jurisdiction over Private Entities involved in Space and Space-related Activities

The first part of the analysis concerns the definition of the scope of the six national space laws at issue to determine to what extent the respective authorities under these laws and their licensing systems, at least in general terms, could impact the freedom to contract. This analysis, on second view, has to address two connected issues: (1) which categories of activities are concerned *ratione materiae*; and (2) which categories of (private) actors undertaking them are concerned *ratione personae*. For it is contracts related to those activities, respectively undertaken by those actors, that would be most fundamentally concerned.

The Categories of Activities Falling within the Scope of the National Space Laws

As the title of the Norwegian Act of course implies, its requirement to obtain permission only applies to the launch of objects into outer space.[12] All five other national acts do essentially encompass all activities normally considered space activities: launching and satellite operations as well as, at least in principle, commercial manned spaceflight. Beyond such general coverage of what Articles VI and VII of the Outer Space Treaty and the Liability Convention are concerned with at the international level, each of them takes a slightly different approach on what is *also* requiring a licence under the relevant act.

695; UKTS 1978 No. 70; Cmnd. 6256; ATS 1986 No. 5; 14 ILM 43 (1975).

6 Act on launching objects from Norwegian territory into outer space (hereafter Norwegian Act on launching), No. 38, 13 June 1969; *National Space Legislation of the World*, Vol. I (2001), at 286.

7 Act on Space Activities, 1982: 963, 18 November 1982; *National Space Legislation of the World*, Vol. I (2001), at 398; *Space Law – Basic Legal Documents*, E.II.1; 36 *Zeitschrift für Luft- und Weltraumrecht* (1987), at 11; plus Decree on Space Activities, 1982: 1069; *National Space Legislation of the World*, Vol. I (2001), at 399; *Space Law – Basic Legal Documents*, E.II.2; 36 *Zeitschrift für Luft- und Weltraumrecht* (1987), at 11.

8 Outer Space Act, 18 July 1986, 1986 Chapter 38; *National Space Legislation of the World*, Vol. I (2001), at 293; *Space Law – Basic Legal Documents*, E.I; 36 *Zeitschrift für Luft- und Weltraumrecht* (1987), at 12.

9 Law on the activities of launching, flight operations or guidance of space objects (hereafter Belgian Space Law), 17 September 2005, adopted 28 June 2005; *Nationales Weltraumrecht / National Space Law* (2008), at 183.

10 Law Incorporating Rules Concerning Space Activities and the Establishment of a Registry of Space Objects (hereafter Dutch Space Law), 24 January 2007; 80 *Staatsblad* (2007), at 1; *Nationales Weltraumrecht / National Space Law* (2008), at 201.

11 Law on space activities (*Loi relative aux opérations spatiales*) (hereafter French Law on Space Operations); Loi no. 2008-518 du 3 juin 2008; 34 *Journal of Space Law* (2008), at 453, unofficial translation 34 *Journal of Space Law* (2008), at 453.

12 See Sec. 1, Norwegian Act on launching.

In Sweden, 'all measures to manoeuvre or in any other way affect objects launched into outer space' are thus included in the licence obligation, yet '[m]erely receiving signals or information in some other form from objects in outer space' is not, and neither is the launch of sounding rockets.[13] Under the UK Outer Space Act, not only 'any activity in outer space', but also 'procuring the launch of a space object' requires a licence.[14]

The scope of the Belgian Space Law *ratione materiae* encompasses 'the activities of launching, flight operations and guidance of space objects', where the last two terms are further defined as 'any operation relating to the flying conditions, navigation or evolution in outer space of the space object, such as the control and correction of its orbit or its trajectory'.[15]

The Dutch Space Law looks very identical: 'the launch, the flight operation or the guidance of space objects in outer space' as constituting 'space activities' all require a licence under the Law.[16] In addition, however, the scope of the licensing obligation *can* be extended to 'the *organisation* of outer space activities'.[17] The Explanatory Memorandum accompanying the Law indicated that the legislators especially eyed the possible desirability to include the organisation of space tourist activities in this phrase in the future.[18]

Finally, the French Law on Space Operations uses the key term 'space operation', meaning 'any activity consisting in launching or attempting to launch an object into outer space, or of ensuring the commanding of a space object during its journey in outer space ... and, if necessary, during its return to Earth', to determine the scope of the authorisation regime *ratione materiae*.[19] Furthermore, also the French Law includes the 'mere' procurement (as opposed to the 'real' space activity) of launching.[20] Finally, the Law deals with the activities of programming earth observation satellite systems and handling the resulting data in a special context designed to ensure protection of French defence interests.[21]

In sum: the six national regimes thus surveyed at the highest level offer a different mix of activities *ratione materiae* requiring a licence or authorisation. The only common denominator here would be that all those extensions still concern activities in the form of *services*; the manufacturing of *products* is not touched upon.[22]

---

13 Sec. 1, Swedish Act on Space Activities. See also Sec. 2.

14 Sections 1(c), resp. (a), 3(1), UK Outer Space Act. Whilst there is no uniform view on what 'procuring' precisely means, it is generally accepted to constitute a rather broad term encompassing at any rate the customer of the launch at issue. It may be noted, furthermore, that under Sec. 13(2), UK Outer Space Act, 'a person carries on an activity [in outer space] if he causes it to occur or is responsible for its continuing', which also constitutes a rather broad concept.

15 Sections 2(1), resp. 3(5), Belgian Space Law.

16 Sec. 1(b), Dutch Space Law. See also Sec. 3(1).

17 Sec. 2(2)(b), Dutch Space Law (emphasis added).

18 See *Tweede Kamer der Staten-Generaal, Vergaderjaar 2005–2006*, 30 609, nr. 3, discussion of sec. 2 at 17.

19 Art. 1(3), French Law on Space Operations. See also Art. 2.

20 See Art. 2(3), French Law on Space Operations.

21 See Arts 1(7), 23–5, French Law on Space Operations.

22 It should be noted that this is not altogether that self-evident; for example Russia and the Ukraine have principally included 'space research' and 'creation (including development, manufacture and test) of, as well as using and transferring space technics, space technologies, other products and services necessary for carrying out space activities' (Art. 2(1), (2), Law of the Russian Federation on Space Activities, No. 5663-1, 20 August 1993, effective 6 October 1993; *National Space Legislation of the World*, Vol. I (2001), at 101), respectively 'construction and application of space engineering' (Art. 1, Law of the Ukraine on Space Activities, No. 502/96-VR, 15 November 1996; *National Space Legislation of the World*, Vol. I (2001), at 36)

The French Law on Space Operations is the only national act that, in addition to a broad sweep of space activities properly speaking plus procurement of launches, makes reference to 'those [entities] taking part … in the *production* of the space object(s) the launch or operation of which is part of the [space] operation'.[23] It does so, however, only in the context of defining 'third parties', from which such manufacturers are excluded, and not of the licensing requirement; its main effect is thus to handle the liability aspects differently from those *vis-à-vis* third parties.[24]

The Categories of Private Actors Falling within the Scope of the National Space Laws

The scope *ratione personae* of the Norwegian Act on launching as a matter of fact is defined firstly by means of the territorial and quasi-territorial criteria: *anyone* launching from Norwegian territory, ships or aircraft requires permission under the Act.[25] Secondly, however, Norwegian national or permanent residents require such a permission also if they launch from '[a]reas that are not subject to the sovereignty of any state', so that no other state would be able to assert territorial jurisdiction over such activities.[26] Scandinavian neighbour Sweden has followed a more comprehensive approach: both relevant activities undertaken from Swedish territory and such activities undertaken by Swedish nationals require a licence.[27]

The United Kingdom in this context is the odd man out, in that the licensing requirement is limited *ratione personae* only to UK nationals.[28] At the same time, the UK Outer Space Act is the first European national space law consciously dealing with the possibility of competing jurisdictions. Firstly, the licence requirement *is* waived 'for activities in respect of which it is certified by Order in Council that arrangements have been made between the United Kingdom and another country to secure compliance with the international obligations of the United Kingdom', presumably including adherence to the licensing requirements or a comparable system of authorisation and supervision of such other country.[29] Secondly, more generally that requirement *may be* waived if the Secretary of State 'is satisfied that the requirement is not necessary to secure compliance with the international obligations of the United Kingdom'.[30]

Belgium uses both key criteria for establishing jurisdiction through the licensing requirement, albeit again in different fashion. Anyone undertaking the relevant activities from anywhere within Belgian territorial or quasi-territorial sovereignty, including the use of installations, personal or property of the Belgian state, requires an authorisation.[31] In addition, Belgian nationals, whether

---

in the key concept of 'space activity' to which these acts apply; although when it comes to licensing properly speaking this does not mean the licensing system and requirements automatically and/or comprehensively apply to those subcategories of space activities.

23 Art. 1(6), French Law on Space Operations (emphasis added).

24 Compare Arts 19–20, French Law on Space Operations, on liability towards persons taking part in the space operation with Arts 13–18 on liability towards third parties.

25 See Sec. 1(a), (b), Norwegian Act on launching.

26 Sec. 1(c), Norwegian Act on launching.

27 See Sec. 2, Swedish Act on Space Activities.

28 See Sec. 2 in conjunction with Sec. 3, UK Outer Space Act.

29 Sec. 3(2)(b), UK Outer Space Act.

30 Sec. 3(3), UK Outer Space Act. Such a satisfaction would most likely only be generated by another state exercising *its* jurisdiction in sufficiently serious fashion.

31 See Arts 2(1), 4, Belgian Space Law.

natural or juridical persons, require such an authorisation '[w]hen provided for under an international agreement ... irrespective of the location where such activities are carried out'.[32]

The Netherlands primarily focuses on territorial and quasi-territorial jurisdiction, requiring a licence from anyone undertaking space activities as defined from Dutch soil or Dutch-registered ships or aircraft.[33] It uses its personal jurisdiction in a subsidiary fashion, namely only where certain activities are undertaken 'from the territory of a State that is not party to the Outer Space Treaty or on or from a ship or aircraft that falls under the jurisdiction of a State that is not a party to the Outer Space Treaty' – thus primarily aiming to fill a potential gap in the application of the latter.[34]

Thus the Dutch Space Law to a limited extent takes into account complications arising from multiple licensing obligations, as application of personal jurisdiction and, as far as the organisation of space activities is concerned, territorial and quasi-territorial jurisdiction, is made subject to specific regulatory follow-up action. Unlike the UK Outer Space Act, however, it does not so much provide for a mechanism to *waive* a licence obligation in case other licensing obligations are applicable, but rather for an *a priori* gap of application of a licence which can then be filled – in particular if not filled by another state.

Also *ratione personae* the French Law on Space Operations is the most sweeping in scope. In the first instance, every French operator also if acting outside France would also require an authorisation, if launching, procuring launches of or commanding space objects.[35] Such an authorisation also brings with it certain benefits in terms of a limit on the reimbursement by the authorised operator of the French state should the latter be obliged to answer international liability claims under the Liability Convention.[36] Interestingly, such benefits are then extended to operators undertaking the relevant activities from the territory or quasi-territory of other Member States of the European Union or European Economic Area (EEA) if these activities form part of activities undertaken from France and are duly authorised as such.[37]

Taking into consideration that activities to be authorised under the French Law in Space Operations may also require licences from other states, leading to the most fundamental and substantial potential for competing jurisdictions, France allows for a quite sophisticated and tailor-made waiver mechanism.[38]

Summing up, the various national acts discussed indeed leave ample room for potentially conflicting jurisdictions, all except the United Kingdom applying both territorial (including quasi-territorial) jurisdiction automatically, and at least potentially (and not necessarily with due regard for the application of another state's territorial jurisdiction) personal jurisdiction as well. Of these,

32 Art. 2(2), Belgian Space Law. See also Art. 4.

33 See Sec. 2(1), Dutch Space Law.

34 Sec. 2(2)(a), Dutch Space Law. Cf. also the possibility for additional regulation for the *organisation* of space activities per Sec. 2(2)(b); also *supra*, at n. 17.

35 See Art. 2(2), (3), French Law on Space Operations.

36 Cf. Arts 14–17, French Law on Space Operations.

37 See Art. 15, French Law on Space Operations, in conjunction with Art. 2(1).

38 Thus, Art. 4(5), French Law on Space Operations, provides: '[w]hen an authorisation is solicited for an operation which is to be carried out from the territory of a foreign State or from means or facilities falling under the jurisdiction of a foreign State, the conditions in which the administrative authority may exempt the applicant from all or any part of the compliance checking mentioned in the first paragraph [of Article 4], when the national and international commitments made by that State as well as its legislation and practices include sufficient guarantees regarding the safety of persons and property and the protection of public health and the environment, and liability matters' may be established by a decree of the Council of State.

however, only the United Kingdom and (essentially) France have formally allowed for the waiver of licensing requirements focusing in fact on instances where multiple jurisdictions may be at stake.

The National Space Laws and Dispute Settlement

This brings analysis to the last issue to be discussed here: to what extent have the six laws at issue taken into account the possibility of legal disputes regarding rights or obligations under, or elaboration and implementation of the respective laws and their provisions? Answering that question for Norway is easy: the half-page, three-section Act does not contain any clause related to dispute settlement.

The Swedish Act on Space Activities refers to the Swedish Penal Code as the law largely applicable to severe violations of the Act and any licence granted under it for violations, and provides for jurisdiction of Swedish courts in such cases.[39] This explicitly applies also to persons responsible for such violations outside of Sweden, as long as they can be properly prosecuted in Sweden. Penalties imposed can be fines or imprisonment of up to one year. Only the Swedish Government is entitled to initiate prosecution, the details thereof as following from the Penal Code.

Also under the UK Outer Space Act violations of its provisions or of a licence granted under it committed outside of the United Kingdom would still be subject, in principle, to the jurisdiction of the UK court system.[40] Furthermore, the UK Outer Space Act makes brief reference to general criminal law provisions, in that a fine may be imposed, which on summary conviction may not exceed 'the statutory maximum'.[41]

The Belgian Space Law also addresses dispute settlement primarily in the context of licence applications, refusals thereof and counterclaims by the Belgian state in case of international liability compensation being paid – meaning: how such claims will be handled as between the Belgian state and the licensee.[42] There is no specific reference whatsoever to jurisdiction of the Belgian courts on such claims; consequently such claims will essentially fall within the general Belgian administrative law regime, with any potential international involvement being dealt with by the Belgian rules on private international law.

More or less the same could be said about the Netherlands, although in this case the reference to such an administrative law regime is made explicitly.[43] Furthermore, the possibility to institute criminal proceedings in the context of the Law or a licence granted under it, under either the Dutch Criminal Code or the Economic Offences Act, is not excluded.[44] Again, however, apparently no specific reference to jurisdiction of Dutch courts over relevant disputes is considered necessary. In case of involvement of non-Dutch entities the standard rules of private international law (in this

---

39 See Sec. 5, Swedish Act on Space Activities.

40 See Sec. 12(4), UK Outer Space Act, although, in view of the exclusively-personal scope of the licensing system, this can only concern UK nationals. Cf. also para. (6).

41 See Sec. 12(2), UK Outer Space Act.

42 See e.g. Art. 15, Belgian Space Law.

43 See e.g. Sec. 14(1), Dutch Space Law, where the government is empowered to use administrative orders to apply and enforce specific Sections of the General Administrative Law Act in the context of licensing or disaster investigation under the Dutch National Space Law. Cf. also further references to the General Administrative Law Act in Sections 14(2), 15.

44 See Sec. 16(2)(e), Dutch Space Law.

case of course the Dutch rules) would determine the extent of such jurisdiction just as if the dispute would concern another economic sector.

The French case is particularly interesting because of the explicit reference to operations not (primarily) conducted from French territory and by non-French nationals, as discussed before. Also the French Law on Space Operations, however, does not offer much detail on dispute settlement issues, beyond a general reference to the Insurance, Public Health and Penal Codes.[45] The President of the Tribunal de grande instance is only mentioned as the authority to enforce access to facilities of licensees and suchlike.[46]

The main conclusions to be drawn from this summary analysis on dispute settlement concern the general approach to economic and commercial space activities, from the perspective of jurisdiction, applicable law and dispute settlement: not to treat them any differently from other economic and commercial activities. Not even the much more fundamental likelihood of international involvement and complications here, of international state responsibility and/or liability being at issue, of security and other strategic interests being at stake, or indeed of the involvement of European organisations, were seen as calling for a special treatment. No doubt, such an approach largely follows from the character of the space laws investigated, being by and large general framework laws taking care primarily of governmental worries that private space activities conducted under their control might cause trouble and/or at the same time need to be stimulated appropriately for the greater public – but still, essentially, national – benefit. Normal administrative law or similar procedures would still be able to handle any disputes in this context appropriately, even as they may much more frequently come to be confronted with the involvement of intergovernmental organisations enjoying a certain level of functional immunities and/or of private entities from other jurisdictions and licensed in those.

Probably only with a more fundamental involvement of the European Union – in which respect the Treaty of Lisbon[47] does not represent as large a step forward as many would have liked it to represent – this might change. Fundamental pieces of EU legislation such as Regulation 44/1001/EC ('Brussels I')[48] and Regulation 864/2007/EC ('Rome II')[49] have shown the competence as well as the willingness of the EU institutions to harmonise the national regimes for private international law in several fundamental respects.

The Future Outlook

To sum up: the six national space laws all apply their own approach *ratione materiae* and *ratione personae* to the establishment and exercise of jurisdiction over the space industry – generally without much attention for the potential clashes of jurisdiction arising from, for example, the

45 See Art. 7(I), French Law on Space Operations; this is however in the context primarily of the competence to monitor certain of the requirements imposed by the Law. Cf. also Art. 10, referring to the Code of Criminal Procedure in this context; Arts 21, 27, referring to the Research Code and Art. 22, referring to the Intellectual Property Code.

46 See Art. 7(II), French Law on Space Operations.

47 Treaty of Lisbon amending the Treaty on European Union and the Treaty establishing the European Community, Lisbon, done 13 December 2007, entered into force 1 December 2009; OJ C 306/1 (2007).

48 Council Regulation on jurisdiction and the recognition and enforcement of judgments in civil and commercial matters, No. 44/2001/EC, of 22 December 2000; OJ L 12/1 (2001).

49 Regulation of the European Parliament and of the Council on the law applicable to non-contractual obligations, No. 864/2007/EC, of 11 July 2007, OJ L 199/40 (2007).

application of territorial jurisdiction of one state and the application of personal jurisdiction of other states to an essentially conglomerate space endeavour. This is done so, largely, for the purpose of establishing the necessary controls by means of a licensing system, and thus essentially relates to a state-private company relationship not altogether different from many such relationships covered already by general national law. As a consequence, also, little attention is being paid to specific dispute settlement questions that may arise.

A further factor to be kept in mind here is that 22 other EU Member States[50] do *not* have any national framework law specifically for licensing space industry participants, whereas the Union itself under the current regime is not entitled to take fundamental steps in this field, either. The general legal regimes of those states would certainly become involved, and likely invoked, however, once issues similar to licensing, responsibility and liability would arise in those states; in such scenarios the jurisdictional authorities would then have to do even without any summary guidance that the national framework space laws might provide.

Precisely for such reasons, it is likely that in at least a number of those 22 countries development of a national space law will become a serious issue soon. Once there would be considerably more than six national space laws in the EU Member State community, a need might arise, and initiatives may be actually undertaken, to harmonise them at least as to their effect in the private, commercial law areas – especially once the international consortia involved start complaining about being confronted with different, potentially even contradictory licensing requirements coming from a number of different Member States trying to assert authority for the sake of properly handling international responsibility and liability – which they then have to take into consideration in their contractual relations.

Conclusions

The next, final question arising from the above, consequently would be: what would be the impact of these conclusions, focused as they are on the area of licensing, on the field of contracting, whether between public entities and the private sector, or within the private sector as such?

Only in France, the contractual freedom of space industry participants was touched upon directly in one particular area. The obligatory insurance for third-party liability under Article 6 of the French Law on Space Operations has to include in its coverage 'the operator *and* the persons having taken part in the production of the space object or in the space operation', effectively a statutory boundary on how the various partners could handle such third-party liability claims amongst themselves.[51] As to inter-party liability, Articles 19 and 20 apply the cross-waiver as the default standard.[52]

50 Of course, of the six states discussed in the present contribution Norway is not an EU member; leaving only five out of 27 current EU Member States with a national framework space law.

51 Emphasis added.

52 Cf. Art. 19, French Law on Space Operations, which provides: 'persons having taken part in the space operation or in the production of the space object … cannot be held liable by another of these persons, except in case of a wilful misconduct', although in some cases parties are allowed to expressly deviate from such a cross-waiver.

With the above exception of France, no references to such a cross-waiver of liability between contractual partners is called for; and also beyond that cross-waiver the freedom to contract is certainly left intact by these national space laws.[53]

Still, in the context of contracts between national public entities (such as national space agencies) and private companies, several aspects of the national framework law and the licensing regimes will be taken very much into consideration. The most obvious example is the aforementioned one of liability, where in the absence of cross-waiver obligations other than in France and depending upon the liability reimbursement requirements provided for by the national law respectively the individual licence, the contractual partners will have to negotiate how to deal with those amongst themselves and/or with the involvement of the insurance industry.

At the 'head' of each contractual chain in Europe relating to space and space activities in each case is either a public space agency (whether ESA or a national space agency) or a private company or consortium. For company-to-company contracts drafted in the latter context, because of any licence itself required by the company at the head of the chain, obviously such elements will be flowed down as appropriate. To the extent that company-to-company contracts are concluded further down a chain headed by such a public agency-prime contractor relationship, ultimately the same will apply: in this case, the public agency will be required in contracting with private sector parties to ensure that relevant rules and obligations otherwise to be imposed through the licence will now be flowed down through the prime contract. And when it comes to any disputes, at the least companies may expect national authorities having enunciated national space laws to apply their respective jurisdiction to contracts along the same lines as defined *ratione materiae* and *ratione personae* by those laws, even if (of necessity) applying general systems of administrative law rather than a specific system of dispute settlement offered by the national space law. So, even if contractual freedom is, as such, hardly touched upon by the European national space laws discussed, if a certain activity under the national space law requires a licence, in subcontracting for (part of) that particular activity, inevitably the contractual partners will have to take the main elements of the law and the licence into consideration – whatever they might be in any specific given context and/or legal framework.

List of References

Belgium 2005. Law on the activities of launching, flight operations or guidance of space objects, 17 September 2005, adopted 28 June 2005; *Nationales Weltraumrecht / National Space Law* (2008), at 183.

Convention on International Liability for Damage Caused by Space Objects, London/Moscow/Washington, done 29 March 1972, entered into force 1 September 1972.

Convention on Registration of Objects Launched into Outer Space, New York, done 14 January 1975, entered into force 15 September 1976.

Council Regulation on jurisdiction and the recognition and enforcement of judgments in civil and commercial matters, No. 44/2001/EC, of 22 December 2000; OJ L 12/1 (2001).

53 In contrast, for example, to the United States, where the Commercial Space Launch Act provides for an obligatory cross-waiver of liability to be included in launch contracts; see Sec. 70112(b)(1), Commercial Space Transportation – Commercial Space Launch Activities, 49 U.S.C. 70101 (1994).

France 2008. Law on space activities (*Loi relative aux opérations spatiales*); Loi no. 2008-518 du 3 juin 2008; 34 *Journal of Space Law* (2008), at 453, unofficial translation 34 *Journal of Space Law* (2008), at 453.

Netherlands 2007. Law incorporating rules concerning space activities and the establishment of a registry of space objects, 24 January 2007; 80 *Staatsblad* (2007), at 1; *Nationales Weltraumrecht / National Space Law* (2008), at 201.

Norway 1969. Act on launching objects from Norwegian territory into outer space, No. 38, 13 June 1969; *National Space Legislation of the World*, Vol. I (2001), at 286.

Regulation of the European Parliament and of the Council on the law applicable to non-contractual obligations, No. 864/2007/EC, of 11 July 2007, OJ L 199/40 (2007).

Russia 1993. Law of the Russian Federation on Space Activities, No. 5663-1, 20 August 1993, effective 6 October 1993; *National Space Legislation of the World*, Vol. I (2001), at 101.

Sweden 1982. Act on Space Activities, 1982: 963, 18 November 1982; *National Space Legislation of the World*, Vol. I (2001), at 398; *Space Law – Basic Legal Documents*, E.II.1; 36 *Zeitschrift für Luft- und Weltraumrecht* (1987), at 11; plus Decree on Space Activities, 1982: 1069; *National Space Legislation of the World*, Vol. I (2001), at 399; *Space Law – Basic Legal Documents*, E.II.2; 36 *Zeitschrift für Luft- und Weltraumrecht* (1987), at 11.

Treaty of Lisbon amending the Treaty on European Union and the Treaty establishing the European Community, Lisbon, done 13 December 2007, entered into force 1 December 2009; OJ C 306/1 (2007).

Treaty on Principles Governing the Activities of States in the Exploration and Use of Outer Space, including the Moon and Other Celestial Bodies, London/Moscow/Washington, done 27 January 1967, entered into force 10 October 1967.

Tweede Kamer der Staten-Generaal, Vergaderjaar 2005–2006, 30 609, nr. 3.

Ukraine 1996. Law of the Ukraine on Space Activities, No. 502/96-VR, 15 November 1996; *National Space Legislation of the World*, Vol. I (2001), at 36.

United Kingdom 1989. Outer Space Act, 18 July 1986, 1986 Chapter 38; *National Space Legislation of the World*, Vol. I (2001), at 293; *Space Law – Basic Legal Documents*, E.I; 36 *Zeitschrift für Luft- und Weltraumrecht* (1987), at 12.

Chapter 30
The ITU Filing of Satellite Systems

Ingo Baumann and Hans Dodel

Introduction

This chapter describes the international procedures of the International Telecommunication Union (ITU) for the deployment of a satellite system and related earth stations. The procedure can only be initiated by the competent administration of a Member State. National laws and regulations set the conditions for the initiation of such procedure. The chapter aims to give practical advice for any company or institution intending to file for frequency rights related to a satellite system.

The ITU

The International Telecommunication Union (ITU) has its roots in the International Telegraph Union founded in 1865 and the International Radiotelegraph Union founded in 1906. It is thus one of the oldest international organisations.[1] At the 1932 Madrid Conference it was decided to combine the International Telegraph Convention of 1865 and the International Radiotelegraph Convention of 1906 to form the International Telecommunication Convention. It was also decided to change the name to International Telecommunication Union.

In 1947, after the Second World War, the ITU held a conference in Atlantic City with the aim of developing and modernising the organisation. Under an agreement with the newly created United Nations, it became a UN specialised agency on 15 October 1947, and the headquarters of the organisation were transferred from Bern to Geneva in 1948. Membership of the ITU is open to governments, which may join the Union as Member States, as well as to private organisations like carriers, equipment manufacturers, funding bodies, research and development organisations and international and regional telecommunications organisations, which can join as Sector Members. These members typically participate in and contribute to one of the three Sectors of the ITU; however, voting rights in the conferences are limited to the Member States. Today the membership of the ITU includes 191 Member States and about 560 Sector Members.

The legal framework of the ITU comprises, in particular, the following legal instruments with treaty status. These instruments are:

- The Constitution and Convention of the International Telecommunication Union signed on 22 December 1992 (Geneva) and entered into force on 1 July 1994. Since their adoption

1 For the history of the ITU and a comprehensive description of its structures and working methods see: Lyall, F. and Larsen, P. 2009. *Space Law: A Treatise*. Aldershot: Ashgate, 199; Lyall, F. 1989. *Law and Space Telecommunications*. Aldershot: Dartmouth; Tegge, A. 1994. *Die Internationale Telekommunikations-Union*. Baden-Baden: Nomos; Baumann, I. 2005. *Das internationale Recht der Satellitenkommunikation*. Frankfurt: Peter Lang; and Leive, D.M. 1970. *International Telecommunications and International Law: The Regulation of the Radio Spectrum*. Leiden: Sijthoff.

in 1992, the ITU Constitution and Convention have been amended by each subsequent Plenipotentiary Conference.

- The Administrative Regulations (Radio Regulations and International Telecommunication Regulations) which complement the Constitution and the Convention.

In addition to the Constitution and Convention, the basic texts of the ITU include the Optional Protocol on the Compulsory Settlement of Disputes, adopted in 1992 and not amended since, as well as Decisions, Resolutions and Recommendations of the Plenipotentiary Conferences.

In 1993, the ITU underwent reorganisation and as a result, the Union was streamlined into three Sectors, corresponding to its three main areas of activity: Telecommunications Standardisation (ITU-T), Radiocommunications (ITU-R) and Telecommunications Development (ITU-D). Each of the three ITU Sectors works through conferences and meetings, where members negotiate the agreements that serve as the basis for the operation of global telecommunications services. In each of the three Sectors, activities of the different bodies may concern space activities, but the Radiocommunications Sector is certainly of the highest interest. ITU-R plays an essential role in the management of the radio-frequency spectrum and of the geostationary and non-geostationary satellite orbits, finite natural resources which are increasingly in demand from a large number of space services such as fixed, mobile, broadcasting, amateur, space research, meteorology, global positioning systems, environmental monitoring and, last but not least, those communication services that ensure safety of life at sea and in the skies. World Radiocommunication Conferences (WRC), held every three to four years, review and, if necessary, revise the Radio Regulations. The WRC also adopts Resolutions and Recommendations strongly influencing space activities.

The engagement of the ITU in space activities started shortly after the launch of Sputnik 1 in 1957. In order to meet the challenges of new space communications systems, a study group was set up in 1959 for space radio-communications. In addition, an Extraordinary Administrative Conference for space communications was held in 1963 in Geneva to allocate frequencies to the various space services. Subsequent conferences made further allocations and put in place regulations governing the use, by satellites, of the radio-frequency spectrum and associated orbital positions. In 1992, allocations were made for the first time to serve the needs of a new kind of space service using non-geostationary satellites, known as Global Mobile Personal Communications by Satellite (GMPCS). Article 44.2 of the ITU Constitution contains the basic principles governing the use of radio frequencies and satellite orbits for space activities.[2]

The Radio Regulations have, among others, the objective to facilitate the equal access to and the rational use of the natural resources of the radio frequency spectrum and the different satellite orbits, geostationary and non-geostationary. The frequency spectrum is allocated to the different space services and the assignments of frequencies by national administrations to individual space stations[3] are subjected to advanced publication, coordination, notification and recording procedures applying the so-called 'first come, first served' principle. Due to the number of 'filings' for satellite systems and the increasing problem of filings not related to actually planned projects (so-called 'paper satellites'), four measures have been introduced during the last years:

2 Article 44.2 of the ITU Constitution reads: 'In using frequency bands for radio services, Member States shall bear in mind that radio frequencies and any associated orbits, including the geostationary-satellite orbit, are limited natural resources and that they must be used rationally, efficiently and economically, in conformity with the provisions of the Radio Regulations, so that countries or groups of countries may have equitable access to those orbits and frequencies, taking into account the special needs of the developing countries and the geographical situation of particular countries.'

3 In ITU usage, satellites are referred to as 'space stations' and operational satellites as 'space networks'.

- the administrative due diligence procedure
- cost recovery processing charges per filing[4]
- a limit of 24 months after date of receipt of the filing to submit the request for coordination
- a limit of 84 months after date of receipt of the filing to bring the satellite into operational use

For certain frequency bands, allotments have been made in an agreed plan for use by one or more administrations for space services in one or more identified countries or geographical regions under specified conditions. Those '*planned bands*' primarily concern direct broadcasting satellites, a service posing numerous problems of general international public law, space law and communications law.[5] The planned bands are specified in the Radio Regulations Volumes 1 and 2, in:

Appendix 30: for satellite broadcast services (BSS) limited to geostationary satellites
Appendix 30A: for feeder links (uplinks) for broadcast services (BSS) in geostationary orbit
Appendix 30B: for satellite fixed services (FSS) limited to geostationary satellites

The ITU Framework for the Filing of Satellites and Earth Stations

Introduction

The starting point to operate an earth station or to bring into use a satellite system is a specific communications demand in terms of:

- type of traffic (communications, data, multi-media, TV – the service type)
- traffic volume (bit-rate per link, bit-per-day, daily throughput, distribution of daily throughput, number of television programmes, etc.)
- traffic network, geographic distribution of terminals (the network topology – is it confined to national, regional or global coverage)
- desired quality of service (bit error rate and availability of service in per cent of time during the worst month of the year)

together with a system engineering outline and, particularly, a transmission plan. These planning documents are a prerequisite for the national and, subsequently, for the international registration of the satellite system or earth station to be established and used for commercial or governmental applications.

The ITU filing for a satellite is international by principle, even if the intended service region is limited to national boundaries. In addition to the filing for the satellite system, all earth stations to be employed in relation to the system need to be filed for as well. In case the earth stations make use of an existing and coordinated satellite system, a national frequency assignment and licensing procedure

4 In addition to the ITU cost recovery processing charges per filing, the national regulatory authority levies additional fees and charges.

5 See for more details Baumann, I. 2005. *Das internationale Recht der Satellitenkommunikation*; Fisher, D.I. 1990. *Prior Consent to International Direct Satellite Broadcasting*, Utrecht Studies in Air and Space Law, Vol. 8. Dordrecht: Martinus Nijhoff; Powell, J.T. 1985. *International Broadcasting by Satellite: Issues of Regulation.* Westport, CT: Quorum Books.

is sufficient. However, in case the radiation of the earth station in the horizontal (the coordination distance) exceeds the national boundaries, filing must also be made internationally through the ITU.

ITU Radio Regulations and Other Applicable Documents

The applicable rules and recommendations of the ITU are documented in the ITU Radio Regulations (RR, the *Red Books*).[6] Guidance in the application and the practical handling of the RR is given in the ITU Rules of Procedure (RP, the *Turquoise Book*).[7]

The Radio Regulations are structured in four volumes:

Vol. 1: The Articles, listing the frequency allocations from 9 kHz to 1,000 GHz (the edge of laser) plus the ITU terminology and the radio characteristics:

- terminology and technical characteristics
- frequencies, frequency allocations, special agreements
- coordination, notification, recording of frequency assignments and plan modifications
- interferences and international monitoring
- administrative provisions, secrecy, licences, ID of stations, service documents
- provisions for services and stations
- distress and safety communications

Vol. 2: The Appendices detailing the technical definitions, terms provisions, and methods, for example to compute the power of interference in a radio link, and so on.

Vol. 3: The ITU Resolutions and Recommendations as adopted by the World Radio Conferences (WRC), the '*ITU laws*' governing the use of the radio spectrum.

Vol. 4: The ITU recommendations incorporated by reference[8], technical and procedural details contributed by ITU Member States to support Volumes 1 through 3.

The Rules of Procedure (RP) complement the RR by providing clarification for the application of particular regulations or establishing practical procedures that may not be provided in the current RR. These rules shall be used by administrations and the Radiocommunications Bureau (RRB) in the application of the RR. The RP are built in three parts:

Part A: The rules that relate to one or more of RR provisions
Part B: The rules that relate to a process e.g. to a technical examination
Part C: Internal arrangements and working methods of the RRB

In addition to the RR and the RP, the ITU publishes a number of documents such as the Space Network List (SNL), containing a complete list of all satellites in all types of orbits, or the Space International Frequency Information Circulars (Weekly Circular) in which all new ITU inputs,

6 The current edition of the Radio Regulations 2008 can be obtained as a print copy or as a CD directly from the ITU at www.itu.int.

7 The current edition of the Rules of Procedure is of 2009.

8 Incorporation by reference is defined as the method of making a document of any kind become part of another separate document by referring to the former in the latter, and by declaring that the former shall be taken and considered as part of the latter the same.

particularly APIs (Advanced Publication Information), RCs (Requests for Coordination) and Notifications are listed. There are also ITU software packages available, notably the powerful information system 'The Space Query and Extract System' (Space Query). This software provides access to the Space Radiocommunications Stations (SRS)[9] database of the Radiocommunications Bureau, as well as to the electronic publications of the Space International Frequency Information Circulars (IFIC). It also provides full access to the related graphical data through the General Interference Management System (GIMS),[10] and enables printing of selected space networks and earth stations in the IFIC format.

The ITU Regions

While frequency allocations for services are preferably made on a worldwide basis ('*harmonised allocations*'), there are frequently regional differences in allocations. To this end, the ITU has defined three regions across the globe as depicted in Figure 30.1.

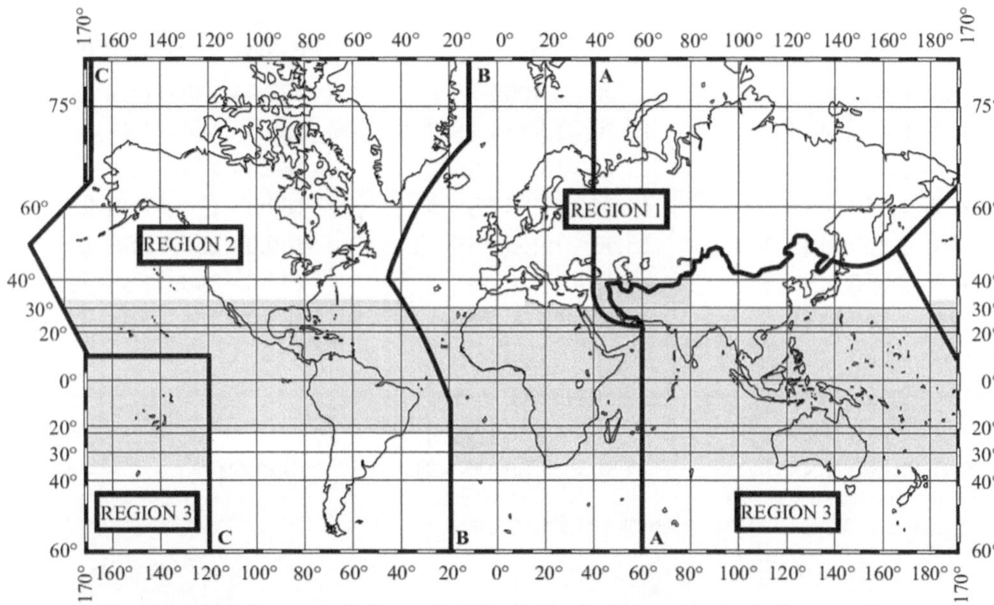

Figure 30.1 The ITU regions, (1) Europe incl. Russia, the Middle East, Africa, (2) the Americas and (3) the Rest of the World

---

9 The Space Radiocommunications Stations (SRS) is a service document published by the RB per Article No. 12489 RR; it contains alphanumeric and graphical information on satellite networks and earth stations.

10 The GIMS allows the capture and modification of graphical data (service areas, antenna gain contours and gain towards the geostationary orbit) relating to the electronic notification of satellite networks in the Space Radiocommunications Stations database. It also allows carrying out Power Flux Density calculations using graphical data captured via this product either by using the digitiser or by importing a file in the GXT format.

First Steps – Selection of Suitable Frequencies, Orbits, and Orbital Positions

The planning of a telecommunications satellite system starts with the assessment of the communications requirements, from which the applicable category of service follows (fixed, mobile, broadcast, planned/unplanned bands, etc.). On that basis, a suitable frequency band and associated orbital position(s) need to be selected.

Frequency allocations The ITU Radio Regulations allocate certain bands of the frequency spectrum to the different service categories. The frequency allocations for Mobile Satellite Service (MSS), Fixed Satellite Service (FSS), and Broadcast Satellite Service (BSS), Earth to space (↑) and space to Earth (↓), in the frequency range between 137 MHz and 1,000 GHz, are shown in Figure 30.2.

P	0.137 - 0.138 MSS ↓
	0.148 - 0.150 MSS ↑
	0.312 - 0.315 MSS ↑
	0.387 - 0.390 MSS ↓
	0.400 - 0.401 MSS ↓
	0.455 - 0.456 MSS ↑
	0.459 - 0.460 MSS ↑
L	1.452 - 1.492 BSS ↓
	1.525 - 1.559 MSS ↓
	1.610 - 1.660 MSS ↑
S	1.980 - 2.010 MSS ↑
	2.120 - 2.160 MSS ↓
	2.170 - 2.200 MSS ↓
	2.484 - 2.520 MSS ↓
	2.520 - 2.670 BSS ↓
	2.670 - 2.690 MSS ↑
C	3.400 - 4.200 FSS ↓
	4.500 - 4.800 FSS ↓
	5.150 - 5.250 FSS ↑
	5.830[1]- 7.075 FSS ↑
X	7.250 - 7.750 FSS ↓
	7.900 - 8.400 FSS ↑
K_u	10.70 - 12.75 FSS,BSS↓
	12.75 - 13.25 FSS ↑↓
	13.75 - 14.80 FSS ↑
	15.43 - 15.63 FSS ↑↓
K_a	17.30 - 21.20 FSS ↑
	21.40 - 22.00 BSS ↓
	24.75 - 25.25 FSS ↑
	27.50 - 31.00 FSS ↑
Q	37.50 - 43.50 FSS ↓
	43.50 - 47.00 MSS ↑↓
V	47.20 - 50.20 FSS ↑
	50.40 - 51.40 FSS ↑
W	66.00 - 71.00 MSS↑↓
	71.00 - 76.00 FSS ↓
	81.00 - 86.00 FSS ↑
	123.0 - 130.0 FSS ↓
	158.5 - 164.0 FSS ↓
	167.0 - 174.5 FSS ↓
	167.0 - 174.5 FSS ↓
	209.0 - 226.0 FSS ↑
	232.0 - 240.0 FSS ↓
	265.0 - 275.0 FSS ↑
	.
	.
	.
	1000 GHz

[1] starting at 5.725 in R1

Figure 30.2 Frequency allocations for MSS, BSS, FSS from P-Band to 1 THz (↑ = uplink, Earth to space, ↓ = downlink, space to Earth)

Note: 1 THz = 1 Tera-Hertz = 10^{12} Hertz = 1,000,000,000,000 Hertz.

Shared allocations Most allocations for satellite communications are shared with terrestrial communications services. Historically, these terrestrial services were in existence long before the advent of space communications and, thus, in the event of mutual interference, the terrestrial services have priority over satellite systems in geostationary earth orbit (GEO), which in turn, generally, have priority over systems in non-geostationary satellite orbits (NGSO), see Figure 30.3.

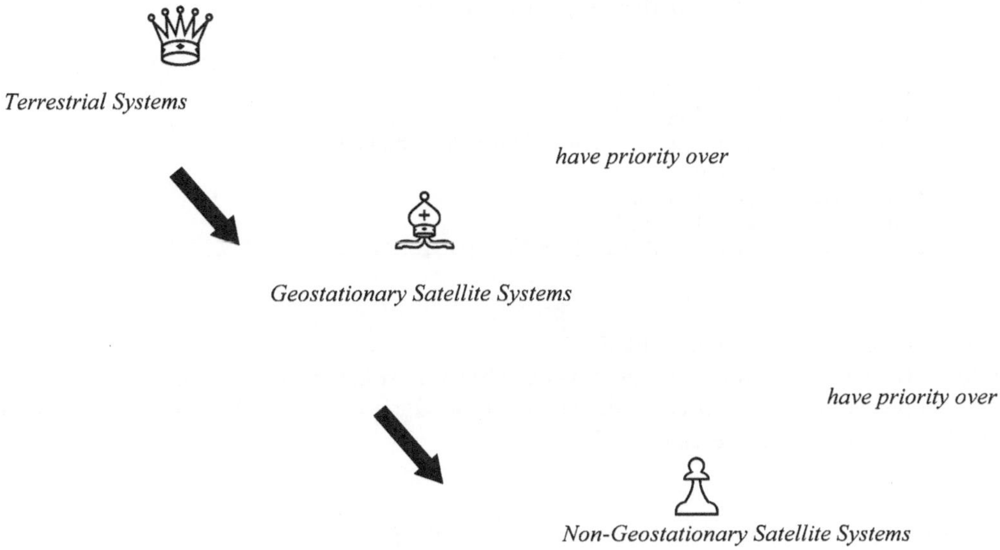

Figure 30.3 Priorities of radio systems

Wavelength allocations The administration of optical communications and related allocation of frequencies, referred to as wavelengths here, is also part of the electromagnetic spectrum and thus a task of the ITU, though this activity is still in its infancy. Aside from the fact that there are not as many links operational at this time it is also considerably easier to coordinate optical links as a result of their extremely high directivity, which clearly leads to fewer possibilities of interference (which for the same reason, leads to a substantially higher inherent degree of communications privacy).

Planned bands / national reservations In the WARC 1988 (ORB '88) the delegations to the ITU decided to introduce planned (frequency) bands for BSS (Broadcasting Satellite Service) and FSS (Fixed Satellite Service) as national assignments so that countries not active in space at this time could, at a future date, access the frequency spectrum, which, without this plan, could otherwise be saturated by then. The assignment of a geostationary orbit and the associated spectrum foreseen is reserved for that country. An application to use is formal and not subject to competition by other applications of other countries. However, once the filing is made, the satellite system must be operational within 84 months or the filing becomes null and void.

The Broadcasting Satellite Service plan

Appendices 30 and 30A of the ITU Radio Regulations establish arrangements for national use of the planned BSS bands, whereby, for each individual nation, there is an orbital position assigned for the use of the planned band (see Table 30.1).

Table 30.1 Planned bands for Broadcasting Satellite Services (BSS)

- 11.7 to 12.5 GHz (space to earth) Region 1
- 12.2 to 12.7 GHz (space to earth) Region 2
- 11.7 to 12.2 GHz (space to earth) Region 3 (region in which Australia is located)
- 14.5 to 14.8 GHz in Regions 1 and 3
- 17.3 to 18.1 GHz (earth to space) Regions 1 and 3
- 17.3 to 17.8 GHz (earth to space) Region 2

The Fixed Satellite Service allotment plan
Appendix 30B of the ITU Radio Regulations establishes arrangements for national use of the planned FSS bands, whereby, for each individual nation, there is an orbital position assigned for the use of the planned band (see Table 30.3).

Table 30.2 Planned bands for Fixed Satellite Services (FSS)

- 4.500 to 4.800 GHz (space to earth)
- 6.725 to 7.0250 GHz (earth to space)
- 10.700 to 10.950 GHz (space to earth)
- 11.200 to 11. 450 GHz (space to earth)
- 12.750 to 13.250 GHz (earth to space)

Coordination is not required for existing satellite systems or new satellite systems operating within the planned bands. All other frequency bands are unplanned and therefore applications for use have to go through the standard process of coordination and notification with the ITU.

Unplanned bands / first come first served For all bands listed in Figure 30.2, but not included in Tables 30.1 and 30.2, there are no national reservations of any kind. These unplanned bands and orbital positions are allocated on a demand-assignment basis upon application – the first come first served principle.

Applicants must coordinate with existing users who have already notified the use of the spectrum and an associated orbital position. In comparison to the planned bands, this leads to a far more efficient and effective utilisation of the spectrum as well as of the orbital positions.

Selection of orbits and orbital positions The first selection concerning the orbit position addresses the type of orbit, geostationary or non-geostationary. One geostationary satellite covers some 42 per cent of the surface of the world, whereas some 48 to 66 satellites in low earth orbit (LEO) might be required to reach the same coverage. The elevation angle (the angle over horizon to the spacecraft) and the associated rain attenuation (which is the worse the smaller the elevation angle), and signal latency (which is the smaller the lower the orbit) are often used to argue for LEO. However, satellites in LEO appear with varying elevation angles, down to the value incurred with geostationary satellites viewed from, for example, Europe, and signal latency, when handled judiciously, will not be noticed by the user. Thus, a LEO system bears no inherent advantage and, due to the large number of spacecraft, incurs substantially higher cost, so that the orbit of choice generally is the geostationary earth orbit (GEO).

The most relevant aspect for the selection of a specific position in GEO is the likelihood of successful coordination. To this end, the RR frequency allocations and the existing systems need to be analysed in detail.

In the GEO, the separation between two different satellite systems operating in the same frequency bands has to be some 5° at C-band, about 3° at X-band, 2° at Ku-band and 1.5° at the Ka-band in order to avoid mutual radio interference. However, national administrations have begun to reduce these orbital separations more and more, both to the disadvantage of the operators of adjacent spacecraft, as well as to their own disadvantage, in terms of increased risks of interference.

After an orbital position in GEO has been elected in the early phases of an ITU filing, but within the process of coordination is found to be unsuitable, the orbital position can be shifted up to 6 degrees right or up to 6 degrees left of the initial position while retaining the filing process.

Monitoring stations for the observation of the satellite spectrum Monitoring stations surveying the occupancy of orbits, including the geostationary earth orbit, and the use of frequencies are employed around the world. For example, the German BNetzA operates a surveillance station to monitor the frequency spectrum allocated to space services and to detect and evaluate cases of interference. The use of this station can be called upon by any applicant, to ascertain that the frequency spectrum and orbital position selected is reasonably free of interference.[11]

The Filing Process with the ITU

Procedural Steps and Time Schedule

The procedures for the API, Due-Diligence, Coordination and Notification underlie a rigid time sequence, as given in Figure 30.4.

As shown in the table, the first critical step is the filing of the Request for Coordination inside the first 24 months after receipt of the application at the ITU. This is a complete system description with all its parameters, including the spacecraft, the earth stations and the services. It is the basis for the frequency coordination with other systems. If this Request for Coordination is not received in time, the filing is null and void (and the moneys paid up to here lost). The often even more critical milestone in the filing process is, however, the time between the date the ITU RRB has received the API and the date of bringing into use (BIU) the first satellite. This time limit for bringing into use is now strictly limited to 84 months. There is no extension of that period under any circumstances whatsoever. If documented BIU is not notified to the ITU in time, the filing is null and void (and the moneys paid up to here lost). The applicant is free to submit a new application, however this would cause considerable costs and, even more significantly, the new application would be reduced in priority against all other applications meanwhile received by the ITU, due to the first come first served principle. Where delays in the bringing into use are incurred, the operator often acquires

11 The observation of the orbit and the radio frequency spectrum reveals spacecraft in orbit and radio carrier transmissions with their radio frequencies, power levels and bandwidths; it does not extend into the baseband signals transmitted by these carriers, so it is not an infringement of the communications privacy of these carriers. The information collected by monitor stations can be employed and utilised in coordination processes. More details can be found in the forthcoming publication: Dodel, H. and Woerfel, M. 2011. *Satellitenlizensierung*. Berlin: Springer.

another satellite, preferably already in orbit, and puts the satellite onto the position it has filed for. Such satellite serves as a placeholder until the launch of the operator's first satellite. It is to be noted that this measure is only feasible if the satellite purchased uses the same frequencies and power levels as the planned satellite, has the same transmission characteristics, and covers the same area on the earth.[12]

1	$t_{receipt}$	*Date of receipt of Advanced Publication Information*[1]
2	t_{ific}[2]	API appears in the ITU *Weekly Circular* Beginning of submission of objections by objectors
3	t_{ific} + 4 months	End of submission of objections
4	$t_{receipt}$ + 6 months	Earliest possible *Request for Coordination*[3] by applicant
5	$t_{receipt}$ + 24 months	Latest possible *Request for Coordination* by applicant If missed, filing is null and void (!)
6	$t_{receipt}$ + 24 months	Earliest possible *Bringing Into Use*[4] Earliest possible *Notification* by applicant
7	$t_{receipt}$ + 48 months	Latest possible *Bringing Into Use*[4] 24 months after *Notification* If missed, filing is null and void (!)
8	$t_{receipt}$ + 84 months	Latest possible *Bringing Into Use*[4] If missed, filing is null and void (!)

[1]'API' per Article 11A, Appendix 4, RR; [2]t_{ific} = '*IFIC Date*', typically a few weeks after $t_{receipt}$;
[3]'RfC' per Article 11, Appendix 3, RR; [4]*Bringing Into Use, BIU*, i.e., begin of operations

Figure 30.4 The chronological sequence of events of an ITU filing

Administrative due diligence To substantiate the seriousness of the filing, the applicant must submit information to the RRB in the frame of an Administrative Due Diligence in accordance with ITU Resolution 49. This information encompasses:

- the identity of the satellite network
- the name of the administration
- the country symbol
- reference to the Advance Publication Information or to the request for modification of the Region 2 Plan or for additional uses in Regions 1 and 3 under Appendices 30 and 30A; or reference to the information processed under Section III of Article 6 of Appendix 30B, if applicable
- reference to the Request for Coordination (not applicable for Appendices 30, 30A and 30B)

12 Practice here has not always followed these principles, but could have been realised only because no other administrations objected.

- the frequency band(s)
- the name of the operator
- the name of the satellite
- the orbital characteristics
- the name of the satellite manufacturer contracted to build the spacecraft
- the date of the contract to manufacture the spacecraft
- the date of delivery of the spacecraft
- the number of spacecraft under contract
- the name of launch provider contracted to launch the spacecraft into orbit
- the date of launch contract
- the contractual launch window within which launch is to take place
- the type and name of the launch vehicle under contract and
- the name of the launch site

The ITU RRB may request additional information and proof documenting the realisation of the satellite in the timeframe foreseen.

The coordination process After receipt by the ITU of the Advance Publication Information including the Due Diligence Information, coordination with existing systems commences and has to be achieved. Only in case both the examination of the Due Diligence documentation and the frequency coordination are successful, can the satellite system be formally notified to the RRB and will then be included in the Master International Frequency Register (MIFR).

Radio interference The reason for coordination of radio systems is to assure their compatibility. Radio signals, when handled negligently, interfere with adjacent systems. According to ITU Radio Regulations, such interference caused by an earth station to another earth station or to a satellite shall not exceed 6 per cent of the inherent thermal noise of the other system, per entry of interference. The ITU cannot and does not specify or limit how many sources and entries of interference might impinge on the earth station or satellite concerned. Today in Europe, a satellite in orbit might have as much as 50 per cent of its total noise power budget due to radio interference incurred from other systems.

The Advance Publication Information

On the basis of the above described planning and evaluation, the Advance Publication Information (API) is prepared and submitted to the national regulatory agency.[13] Generally, the national agency advises and supports the applicant in this process. It examines the application for technical correctness and conducts an audit to evaluate the conformity of the application with the ITU Radio Regulations, and, if found free of errors, submits it to the ITU. In some countries, the agency also scrutinises the business plan underlying the application to ascertain that the regulatory effort will not be wasted for a system that is not likely to be built and operated.

13 In Germany the Bundesnetzagentur für Elektrizität, Gas, Telekommunikation, Post und Eisenbahnen (BNetzA); in Austria the Telecom-Control-Kommission (TKK); in Switzerland the Bundesamt für Kommunikation (BAKOM); in the Netherlands the Agentschap Telecom; in France the ANFR (Agence nationale des fréquences) and the ANRT (Agence Nationale de Réglementation des Télécommunications); in the United Kingdom the OFCOM; in Ireland the COMREG; in Italy the AGCOM.

The API has to be submitted in the required ITU formats. The data to be included in the application contain, as a minimum, the parameters listed in Table 30.3.

Table 30.3 System parameters required for application

(01) Orbit	(02) Earth Station Polarisation
(03) Frequency Band	(04) Spacecraft Orbital Position
(05) Carrier Bandwidth	(06) Type of Service
(07) Carrier Power	(08) Carrier Frequency
(09) Carrier Power Spectral Roll-Off	(10) Type of Satellite Antenna
(11) Carrier EIRP	(12) Minimum Power Density
(13) Maximum Power Density	(14) Minimum Peak Power
(15) Maximum Peak Power	(16) Polarisation Isolation
(17) Carrier Modulation Technique	(18) Type of Earth Station Antenna
(19) Carrier to Noise Ratio	(20) E.S. System Noise Temperature
(21) Earth Station Type	(22) Coverage Area

These parameters are needed for the process of coordination, particularly for the identification of any risk of mutual interference with other systems.

The application is then submitted to the ITU RRB, whereby all communications have to go through the national agency.[14] The RRB publishes the Advanced Publication Information in its International Frequency Information Circular. This publication serves for the other Member States and their operators to identify early the potential of harmful interference caused by the planned system to its own existing systems. Objections need to be raised to the RRB within four months after publication in the weekly circular and the RRB forwards these objections to the national agency. The agency and the applicant must then seek coordination with the existing systems.

Frequency Coordination of Satellite Systems

Coordination of satellite systems In case one or more administrations of other Member States have raised objections against the API, the planned system has to be coordinated in order to avoid any harmful interference. The national agency has to send a Request for Coordination to the RRB and the other administrations having objected. Together with the request, the applicant has to prepare revised and detailed transmission data and system parameters.

The agency now conducts bi-lateral discussions and negotiations on the basis of the applicable provisions of the Radio Regulations. This discussion is based on an exchange of information and proposals: each administration presents its proposal(s) for coordination, and on this basis an

14 The Radio Regulations Board (RRB), comprised initially of nine part-time members, was established in 1994 following revisions to the Constitution and Convention and elections conducted at the Plenipotentiary Conference (Kyoto, 1994). The part-time Board replaced the previously full time International Frequency Registration Board (IFRB).

attempt is made to work out mutually agreed parameters and arrangements for the operation of the satellite systems under mutual non-interference. Upon request by one or more administrations, the RRB conducts a technical evaluation in order to identify and to analyse the risks of harmful interference. The RRB can also be used as a moderator of the coordination discussions, however without having any decision-taking power. The coordination results in bilateral agreements between the administrations involved. In some cases, these agreements are also concluded between the operators themselves, whereby a backing through the respective administrations is at least formally required.

Coordination procedures usually take quite some time, in some cases even years. The resulting agreement may force the operator to adjust or even re-design the intended satellite system:

1. to reduce some or all transmit powers, thus increasing size and cost of its earth stations;
2. to reduce its intended ground coverage to avoid or at least reduce interference;
3. to change the intended orbital position; or even
4. to resort to other frequency bands.

While measures (1) and (2) can be effected within the running application, measure (3) is limited to position shifts in the geostationary orbit by 6 degrees left or right of the applied position, and in measure (4), the smallest change in the frequency spectrum requires a totally new filing.

In some cases, technical solutions like frequency sharing or reduction of power density or other arrangements are conceivable if the interfered-with nation or operator so agrees. This might cause significant costs for the operator and reduce/endanger in extreme case the commercial viability of the system.

Coordination of earth stations The associated earth stations must also be filed independently of the satellite system. If the so-called 'coordination distance' of an earth station does not extend beyond the national boundaries, this filing is handled by the national regulatory authority only. If the coordination distance extends onto other nations, the filing is handled the same as satellite filings, for example, through the national regulatory authority with the ITU.

The coordination distance of an earth station

The coordination distance of an earth station is the geographical range from the earth station beyond which another earth station (sharing the same frequency band) cannot be interfered with. To this end, the permissible signal level is defined in the ITU RR, below which there is no undue interference. For earth stations outside this coordination distance the operator is not required to coordinate with them.

Atmospheric diffraction

To evaluate the level of mutual interference with earth stations inside the coordination distance, the straight path between the respective earth stations is transposed from a topographic map to an earth curvature profile on the basis of the terrain between the two points plotted on that profile.[15] If there is an unobstructed line-of-sight between the two points, the transmit power, the mutual antenna gains and the free space attenuation between the two points are used to compute the received power, for example the level of interference. If the connection between the two points is obstructed by terrain,

15 More details can be found in the forthcoming publication: Dodel, H. and Woerfel, M. 2011. *Satellitenlizensierung*.

say, by a mountain, then the signal will be diffracted over the mountain ridge. This diffraction loss is added to the straight line free space attenuation. This often suffices to reduce the level of interference to below the ITU limits so as to allow successful coordination of the earth station.

Tropospheric refraction
Electromagnetic waves refract off the troposphere, particularly at lower gigahertz frequencies. In this way, terrestrial radio relays can interfere with satellite earth stations. Therefore, the potential tropospheric refraction caused by terrestrial radio links must be evaluated for the potential site for an earth station. Vice versa, the potential interference caused by an earth station due to tropospheric refraction with another kind of radio relay station needs to be observed.

Site shielding
The preferred location for earth stations is not in remote mountain valleys, where there would be natural shielding from and against radio interference. Sites are preferably chosen close to the point of service, which is usually in an urban area. However, cities are also the node of many radio relays. In case there is no naturally shielded location nearby, a solution can be found by artificial site shielding such as digging a pit and submerging the earth station below ground level. In no case would one locate a satellite earth station on the rooftop of a building where it would be exposed to any and all radio interference.

Interference cancellation
In cases of natural or artificial site shielding, there are often very few cases of interference left exceeding the shielding effect and impinging on the earth station's reception of satellite signals. In these cases, small antennas can be mounted near the earth station. These antennas are directed towards the radio sources and thus receive the disturbing signals, which are then subtracted from the total sum of signals received by the earth station. Thereby, the interference is cancelled out and only the desired signal is left.[16]

Notification and Insertion into the Master International Frequency Register

After conclusion of the coordination process, the national agency submits the results to the ITU RRB. This formal notification must also contain the final technical description of the planned satellite system. As long as all requirements of the Radio Regulations are met, the RRB inserts the planned system into the Master International Frequency Register. Upon publication in this register, the system now enjoys priority over later systems (first come, first served). However, each operator and its competent national agency are required to actively observe the weekly circular and to analyse whether any new system might cause harmful interference. The ITU RRB does not itself raise objections in such cases but leaves it to the administrations and the operators to defend their rights. Objections, again, have to be raised within four months of API publication.

Summary

The ITU procedures for filing a satellite system and associated earth stations are well established. The preparation and execution of the procedures are, however, quite costly and time consuming;

16 More details can be found in the forthcoming publication: Dodel, H. and Woerfel, M. 2011. *Satellitenlizensierung.*

well-experienced experts need to be available for any operator applying. Due to the ever increasing use of frequencies and orbits, coordination with existing systems becomes more and more difficult. There is a high risk that the intended frequency bands and positions cannot be used as planned and that re-configurations of the technical planning have to be made. Due to recent changes in the ITU procedures, the time schedule for the filing is now extremely tight. Delays, namely for the bringing into use of the system, might make the filing process null and void, causing a considerable loss of investment and even more critical the loss of priority towards later applicants.

Conclusions

The establishment of a satellite system and associated earth stations requires the assignment of suitable frequencies and, for the satellites, of orbital positions. To obtain these assignments, highly complex national and international procedures have to be conducted by the operator. Only the competent administration of a Member State can submit an application to the ITU and, after successful coordination, can notify the satellite system for insertion in the Master International Frequency Register. National laws and applications provide for the conditions under which the competent agency will act and sets numerous obligations and responsibilities of the applicant.

The preparation and conducting of both the national and international procedures requires careful planning as well as sufficient financial and expert resources. Once the ITU procedures are initiated, there are strict time limits for bringing the satellite system into use. Therefore, the execution of the procedures must be planned in line with the schedule for the production and launch of the satellite(s) and the establishment of the associated ground segment.

List of References

Baumann, I. 2004. 'Die Novellierung des Telekommunikationsgesetzes – Auswirkungen auf die Satellitenkommunikation', *ZLW*, 532.

Baumann, I. 2005. *Das internationale Recht der Satellitenkommunikation*. Frankfurt: Peter Lang.

Baumann, I. and Gerhard, M. 2006. 'Neuregelung des Verfahrens zur Anmeldung von Satellitensystemen bei der ITU zur Übertragung deutscher Orbit- und Frequenznutzungsrechte', *ZLW*, 87.

Dodel, H. 2007. *Satellitenkommunikation*. Berlin: Springer.

Dodel, H. and Woerfel, M. 2011 (forthcoming). *Satellitenlizensierung*. Berlin: Springer.

Fisher, D.I. 1990. *Prior Consent to International Direct Satellite Broadcasting*, Utrecht Studies in Air and Space Law, Vol. 8. Dordrecht: Martinus Nijhoff.

Leive, D.M. 1970. *International Telecommunications and International Law: The Regulation of the Radio Spectrum*. Leiden: Sijthoff.

Lyall, F. 1989. *Law and Space Telecommunications*. Aldershot: Dartmouth.

Lyall, F. and Larsen, P.B. 2009. *Space Law: A Treatise*. Aldershot: Ashgate.

Powell, J.T. 1985. *International Broadcasting by Satellite: Issues of Regulation*. Westport, CT: Quorum Books.

Tegge, A. 1994. *Die Internationale Telekommunikations-Union*. Baden-Baden: Nomos.

PART V
Specific Aspects of Satellite Services Contracts

Chapter 31
Specific Clauses of Launch Services Agreements

Claude-Alain du Parquet

Introduction

Background

Space activities are relatively recent. The first launch of a satellite into earth orbit actually took place on 4 October 1957, hardly more than 50 years ago. For a long time, launch activities were carried out only by governments and the legal framework for space activities remained the domain of international conventions,[1] which established very broad principles, but did not address launch services marketing.

National space laws appeared later with only a handful of countries adopting such laws, among which are, this list not being exhaustive, Norway,[2] Sweden,[3] the United Kingdom,[4] the USA[5] and recently France.[6] However, the purpose of the legislation was to establish the conditions and modalities under which entities under the state's jurisdiction and control could conduct space activities, and to require such entities to assume a certain, not to exceed, part of the international liability assumed by the state as a 'launching state' under the various international conventions related to space exploration and exploitation.

In this context, the first launch services agreements (LSAs) that may be considered a commercial contract, that is to say those proposed for consideration by NASA to non-governmental customers, have been elaborated according to usual rules and practices applicable to contracts in general, even if they contained very specific clauses peculiar to launch activities.

These contracts have been used as models by the launch services providers (LSPs) that appeared on the market. Even if competition among them may have induced some adaptation, limited to commercial aspects, initial basics imposed by the nature and specificities of launch activities have been unchanged by the newcomers.

---

1 Treaty on Principles Governing the Activities of States in the Exploration and Use of Outer Space, including the Moon and Other Celestial Bodies (10 October 1967). Agreement on the Rescue of Astronauts, the Return of Astronauts and the Return of Objects launched into Outer Space (3 December 1968). Convention on the Registration of Objects Launched Into Outer Space (15 September 1976).

2 Norway: Act on launching objects from Norwegian territory etc. into outer space (1969).

3 Sweden: Act on space activities (1982); Decree on space activities (1982).

4 U.K.: Outer Space Act (1986).

5 USA: 49 USC Chapter 701 – Commercial space launch activities (2002); CFR 14 III Sec. 400–499 – Commercial space transportation (2003).

6 France: Loi 2008-518 relative aux opérations spatiales (3 July 2008); Décret 2009-643 relatif aux autorisations délivrées en application de la Loi 2009-518 (9 July 2009). Arrêté du 31 mars 2011 relatif à la réglementation technique en application du décret n° 2009-643 du 9 juin 2009 relatif aux autorisations délivrées en application de la loi n° 2008-518 du 3 juin 2008 relative aux opérations spatiales.

Launch Activity Specificities

Space activities imply a huge level of investment and expenses. Launchers (in the field of space activities, the term of launcher, or launch vehicle, is used rather than rocket) and satellites are very expensive. Carrying out launch operations also means having a launch base at one's disposal with launcher assembly and satellite preparation buildings, and a tracking stations network; all this also meaning a very high level of public investment. Last but not least, launchers are consumed during launch and therefore have no reuse value, making launch services even more expensive.

Launch activities are not only costly, they are risky. This is inherent in the technologies involved. The lift off mass of a launcher of the Ariane 5 class is about 750 tons, of which 650 tons is propellant, enabling the launcher to reach a speed, at its third stage satellite separation, of about nine kilometres per second. In addition, the one-shot nature of rocket launching does not allow corrective actions in case of problems during the launch phase insofar as, after take-off, the launcher is under the sole control of the on-board computer, which follows its flight program so that any problem occurring after launch inevitably results in a degradation of the targeted orbit or of the satellite operating capabilities or, even worse, in the satellite destruction or loss. All these constraints are reflected in the various clauses contained in LSAs.

Clauses Peculiar to Launch Services Agreements

This section presents the nature of LSAs and addresses the provisions or clauses dictated by the specifics described above.

Contracts for Services

LSAs are contracts for services. The customer does not procure a launcher but launch services performed by the LSP for the purpose of placing its payload, generally a satellite, into earth orbit. In a manner of speaking, the customer buys a *ticket* for a seat on a launcher by means of which the LSP will inject its satellite into the desired orbit.

Launch services comprise the manufacture or procurement, delivery and assembly on the launch base of the launcher used to perform the launch, this launcher remaining the property of the LSP. The services also include the performance of the mission analysis studies and tests aimed at demonstrating the capability of the launcher to achieve the launch mission and at predicting the environmental conditions met by the satellite aboard the launcher during the flight and the production of the flight software loaded in the launcher's on-board computer. In that respect, it is worth noting that due to the complexity of launchers, onus rests on the customer to arrange for and demonstrate the compatibility of its satellite with the launcher and not the contrary.

Launch services also comprise range services, such as transport and handling of the satellite inside the launch site until integration onto the launcher; putting at the customer's disposal installations, facilities and support necessary for preparing and fuelling the satellite before integration on the launcher.

Limitation of Liability

Considering the high level of risk involved in launch activities, LSAs never warrant the success of the launch.

The contractual obligation is deemed completed once the launch operations have attained the point beyond which they can no more be interrupted. To illustrate this, let us consider the Ariane 5 launcher. After the final 10-second countdown, at H0 seconds, the Vulcain core engine of the launcher is ignited. However, the sole thrust of the Vulcain engine is not sufficient to lift the launcher. For 7.2 seconds the launcher remains on the launch pad while the Vulcain engine keeps burning, and the on-board computer verifies all the engine's parameters (thrust, pressure, etc.). If no anomaly is detected, at H+7.2 seconds, the on-board computer will release the command for ignition of the solid boosters that will deliver the thrust allowing the lift off.

In this sequence, the contractual definition of launch corresponds to the order of ignition of the solid propellant boosters. In the event of anomaly during the Vulcain burn, the on-board computers will not release the command for ignition, and the Vulcain will be shut down. This is known as a 'launch abort'. In that case the launch has not been performed. The LSP has not fulfilled its contractual obligation and must proceed with a new launch attempt with the same launcher or with a new one if the launcher used for the first attempt has been damaged.

The precise definition of 'launch' of course depends on each launcher's ignition sequence, but in any case, although the launch mission begins at launch and aims at matching the launch specifications and injecting the satellite into the targeted orbit, as after *launch* the flight phase is automatically controlled by the on-board computers, the contractual obligation is deemed fulfilled at launch, irrespective of whether the launch mission thereafter resulted in a success or a failure.

As a consequence, the risk of launch failure is to be insured by the customer through launch insurance.

Allocation of Liabilities and Risks

In addition to the limitation of liability provisions mentioned above, LSAs provide a mutual no-fault no-subrogation inter-party waiver of liability adhered to by the parties by signing the agreement. The purpose of this inter-party waiver is to prevent any recourse by and between the parties involved in the activities related to the launch of a given satellite.

Those parties are numerous. Without being exhaustive, we may mention: the customer purchasing a satellite with a view to having it put into orbit by the LSP; the LSP operating the launcher used for the launch; the owner of the launch base (generally a government) consisting of various facilities, such as launch pads, launcher assembly buildings, satellite integration and preparation buildings; the contractors and sub-contractors of all the aforementioned persons; the customers of the satellite operator; the insurers of all those persons, and so on. All such parties are directly or indirectly involved in the launch of a given satellite and may cause or suffer damage, directly or indirectly arising from the execution of the launch services.

To illustrate this point, the LSP may destroy or damage the satellite during the launch campaign or during the flight phase; the satellite owner/manufacturer may damage the LSP's facilities during the preparation of the satellite for launch or its integration to the launcher. The satellite operator's customers may suffer losses of revenues in the event of delay in the availability of the satellite services if the launch is delayed or the satellite destroyed during flight phase. In all these cases, the liability assumed by a party could be far beyond its financial capabilities.

This is why, in signing a LSA, the LSP and its customer agree to bear any and all loss of property and bodily damages and all direct or indirect consequences each of them may sustain in connection with the performance of the said agreement. In addition, each of them undertakes to pass this waiver obligation along its chain of contractors and sub-contractors, or to hold the other party harmless in case of a claim from any member of its chain against the other party or any member of that other party's chain.

Without being exhaustive, the LSP chain encompasses all the firms that participated in the design, execution and manufacturing of the components of the launcher, including propellants, all the persons or entities (governmental or not) who put the launch facilities and installations at the disposal of the LSP, and all the insurers of all these persons and entities, and so on. The customer's chain encompasses the satellite manufacturer and all its contractors and sub-contractors, the customer's insurers, any clients to whom the said customer has sold or leased the satellite services, etc. In addition, in the event of shared launches, with two or more satellites on-board, the inter-party waiver is extended to all co-passengers launched on a same flight. It is worth noting that this inter-party waiver is extended by the parties to their insurers. Generally, most LSAs expressly exclude any liability of the LSP and its chain of contractors in case of launch failure, even though it is already induced by the generality of the above conditions.

The purpose of this system is to avoid redundant insurance coverage resulting from all parties seeking at the same time to cover direct and indirect losses, and financial consequences of the liability they might incur for damages caused to one another in connection with a launch operation. It contributes to reduce global costs and avoids saturating the insurance market capacity.

Third Party Liability Insurance for Damage Caused by the Launcher after Launch

LSAs provide for the obligation of the LSP to take out an insurance covering the liability assumed by states as launching states under the Convention on International Liability for Damages Caused by Space Objects (September 1972).

This insurance obligation is imposed by the launching state as a requirement of the launching licence or authorisation. It requires the said LSP to obtain insurance coverage for damage caused to a third party or parties by the launcher or the transported satellite. The insurance is intended to be the primary coverage used to indemnify the victims of such damage, the issuing state then covering damage in excess of such insurance.

The liability covered is limited to damages caused to third parties, defined as any third party other than the parties to the LSA and all the parties associated with the inter-party waiver of liability, described above.

The risk attaches at launch and the insurance remains valid for a certain time after separation. The validity period may vary depending on the launch services supplier and the law applicable to the launch operation. This insurance not only covers the parties to the LSA, but names additional insureds varying from one LSP to another, but basically covering the government of the LSP and of its customer, any launching state under the above mentioned convention, contractors and subcontractors, at any tier, involved in the manufacturing, preparation and launch of, the launcher and satellite, and the directors and employees of all these entities.

Criticality of these Clauses and Provisions

The clauses and provisions seen above are of paramount importance to LSPs. The financial and technical risks inherent to launch activities are such that without the clauses of limitation of the contractual obligation and allocation of liabilities and risks, the launch services market would never have been able to emerge and develop as it has. Therefore, each LSP has its own standard clauses addressing the issues seen in this section and has very few, not to say not any, margin within which to negotiate them.

Other Clauses

Apart from the clauses seen above, which are critical for LSPs, LSAs contain the same clauses as any other contract addressing price, schedule, delays and so on as adapted to the nature of launching activities.

Price and Payment Plan

Price and payments terms are commercial items negotiated on a case-by-case basis. However, two particularities are worth mentioning.

Launcher manufacturing and launch operation costs and expenses are fully borne by the LSP before launch. Therefore, the contract price is generally spread over a payment plan providing for full payment prior to launch.

Launch services have been at the origins commercialised by governmental bodies, which, as such, were not subject to sales taxes. The first private launch operators that entered the launch market have benefited from the same sales tax exemption from their tax authorities. Under the competition currently prevailing on that market, an LSP losing the benefit of such exemption would quickly be out of the market.

Launch Scheduling

Considering the time required to manufacture a satellite, which is rarely less than 24 months, LSAs are generally signed two years in advance. From time to time, there may be cases of LSAs signed closer to the launch date, but it is always on a case-by-case basis under special circumstances such as, for instance, launch failure of a given launcher forcing a satellite operator to urgently find a new LSP. This is why the system is usually retained to start from a launch period of generally three to six months, which is reduced to a one month launch slot, generally six months prior to the first day of the launch period, the launch day being fixed three or four months prior to the first day of the launch slot.

Such procedure is subject to mutual agreement of the parties. However, in case of conflict, the final decision rests with the LSP who has to accommodate the respective rights of all its customers

Launch Postponement

Satellite manufacturing and launch activities are subject to a wide range of contingencies.

Delays may be induced by the satellite as well as by the launcher. Launcher and satellite manufacturing is a long process that may be subject to delays. An LSP will not authorise a launch if it has any doubt as to the reliability of the launcher to be used for that launch.

In the same way, if a satellite has a failure in orbit, the satellite manufacturer will not authorise the launch of a similar satellite until it has identified and fixed the problem. But a satellite delay, especially if declared shortly prior to the launch, may also impact the whole launch schedule of the LSP. In all those cases, the party concerned will have to request a postponement. In that respect, customers may generally request a postponement for any reason, while LSPs may only postpone a launch for a limited number of reasons, mainly related to technical or reliability problems, or, for shared launches, co-passenger unavailability.

When the postponement is at the initiative of the customer, the principle is that the satellite cannot take the place of, or priority over, the satellite of another customer of the LSP. Therefore, the satellite of a customer requesting a launch postponement loses its ranking and is shifted to the first vacant launch opportunity, which, in the worst case, may be at the end of the rank. When the postponement is at the initiative of the LSP, the principle is that the latter must respect the ranking of all its customers, which results in the so called *domino effect*, well known to all persons involved in space activities.

There may be some exceptions, but in a very limited number of cases, for instance in the event of planetary encounters where there is one launch window every two, three or more years (for the 1986 Halley comet encounter the next launch window was 76 years later). Such a satellite will generally be granted a priority securing its launch window in case of domino effect, it being understood that, to be in a position to offer such a priority, the LSP must have included appropriate provisions in the LSAs executed with all its other customers.

In order to ensure an equal and fair treatment of all their customers, LSPs have elaborated standard clauses which they insert into all contracts they sign.

Regarding penalties, the situation may vary from one LSP to another. Experience has shown that during the implementation of an LSA, the probability of delay on the part of one party or the other was equal. The risk, when penalties are provided for, is that each party will dissimulate its own delays to the other with the hope that the latter will be late itself. This is particularly counterproductive. This is why LSAs often exclude penalties for delay, regardless of who the delaying party is.

Another reason for excluding penalties is that LSP's postponements often not only affect one but several customers, which makes the LSP's situation even worse. Therefore, when penalties cannot be avoided, they generally apply to both LSP and customer and are subject to a maximum cap of 2 or 3 per cent of the launch services price.

LSAs always provide for a maximum duration of postponement, generally 12 months, beyond which, if the postponement is at the initiative of the LSP, the customer may terminate the launch; and if it is at the customer's initiative, the launch services price is subject to renegotiation.

Termination

In the case of termination of an LSA, the LSP is left with a launcher for which it may have no other customer and loses a launch opportunity, which, considering the fixed costs associated with the maintenance of a launch system, may dramatically affect the company's annual results. Therefore, customer's termination for convenience is possible, but subject to termination fees increasing all along the implementation of the LSA up to a maximum generally as high as 45 to 55 per cent of the contract price.

In the event of postponement of the launch by the LSP in excess of a certain duration, generally 12 months, the customer is entitled to terminate the LSA with full reimbursement of the amounts paid to the LSP up to the termination date. Regarding termination by the LSP, most contracts only provide termination for the customer's payment default, which is treated as a termination for convenience.

Applicable Law and Disputes

Except in a very few cases, LSAs are governed by the LSP's domestic law. A certain number of reasons argue for this choice. The LSP's domestic law is usually the law prevailing at the place where the launch is performed and the law of the state which is the owner of the launch facilities used for the launch. As such, this state organises the authorisation and licence system to be satisfied by the LSP to run its launch activities and validating the inter-party waivers of liability contained in the LSAs.

Deviations to this principle are very rarely consented by LSPs, for instance when contracting with a sovereign government, and only after having obtained assurance that the limitation of liability and inter-party waiver of liability were valid under the customer's law.

Due to the nature of the project involved, disputes are naturally subject to international arbitration, the ICC being the preference in that respect. Arbitration enables the parties to designate arbitrators having experience and backgrounds in space activities and offers better confidentiality conditions.

Conclusion

Presenting the main features of launch services agreements in a few pages is a challenge and we have been obliged to simplify or ignore some aspects that would have required further development.

The clauses described above in the section 'Clauses Peculiar to Launch Services Agreements' are really the essence of LSAs and are far from usual practices prevailing in other industry domains. Clauses described in the section 'Other Clauses' are clauses that are common to commercial contracts and we have tried to explain to what extent they have been adapted to cope with the constraints imposed by the nature of launch activities.

This being said, LSAs are basically commercial contracts. Beyond the peculiarities pointed out above, LSPs are very creative as they strive to satisfy the customers and a number of variations have been proposed that could not be addressed here, among which, multi-launch agreements that allow big satellite fleet operators to adapt their satellite's launch rate to the evolution of their needs, contracts for satellite constellations or launch risk guarantees offered by certain LSPs, which provide for a free reflight in case of launch failure attributable to the launcher.

But to conclude on the basics evoked in this chapter, no significant changes are likely to occur within the respective parties' relations in launch service contracts as long as launcher technology status remains as it is.

List of References

Aubin, Y. and Portwood, T. 2001. 'Les clauses réciproques d'abandon de recours et de garantie contre les recours des tiers', *Revue de Droit des affaires internationales*, 6, Thomson/Sweet & Maxwell.

Balaam, P., Maroquene, F. and Parquet, C.-A. du. 2000. 'ASAP 5: Low-Cost Access to Space for Auxiliary Payloads', in *Selected Proceedings of the 2nd IAA International Symposium on Small Satellites for Earth Observation (12–16 April 1999, Berlin, Germany)*, published by Elsevier Science Ltd – Journal of the International Academy of Astronautics, *Acta Astronomica*, 46 (2–6), 127–33.

Droit des activités spatiales, adaptation aux phénomènes de commercialisation et de privatisation, under the direction of L. Ravillon, Université de Bourgogne – CNRS, Travaux du Centre de recherche sur le droit des marchés et des investissements internationaux, Volume 22, Edition LexisNexis Litec, 2004.

Lafferranderie, G. 1994. 'Responsabilité juridique internationale et activités de lancement d'objets spatiaux au CSG', *ESA Bulletin*, 80. [Online]. Available at: http://www.esa.int/esapub/bulletin/bullet80/laff80.htm.

Parquet, C.-A. du. 2004. 'Launch Services Agreement and Inter Party Waiver of Liability', in *Proceedings of the Project 2001 Plus-Workshop of 29/30 January 2004 in Berlin, Germany, on Global and European Challenges for Air and Space Law at the Edge of the 21st Century – 'Towards a Harmonised Approach for National Space legislation in Europe'*, 129–133, co-sponsored by the Institute of Air and Space Law and Chair for Public International Law, European Law, International and European Economic Law of the University of Cologne and Deutsches Zentrum für Luft- und Raumfahrt e.V. German Aerospace Center.

Parquet, C.-A. du. 2005. 'La gestion des risques dans les contrats de services de lancement', in *Le droit des activités spatiales à l'aube du XXI siècle*, sous la direction de L. Ravillon, Université de Bourgogne – CNRS, Travaux du Centre de recherche sur le droit des marchés et des investissements internationaux, actes du colloque des 10 et 11 Juin 2004, Dijon, Volume 25, Editions Lexis Nexis Litec, 2005, 179–86.

PROJECT 2001 (Working Group on Launch and Associated Services). *Legal Framework for Commercial Launch and Associated Services: Proceedings of the Project 2001-Workshop on Commercial Launch Activities, 19 Janvier 2000, Brême, Allemagne*. Deutsches Zentrum für Luft und Raumfahrt, 2000.

Ravillon, L. 2009. 'Le cadre contractuel des activités de lancement', in *Droit de l'espace: télécommunication, observation, navigation, défense, exploration*, under the direction of P. Achilleas's, collection droit des technologies. Bruxelles: Larcier.

Chapter 32
Specific Aspects and Characteristics of Satellite Capacity Agreements in the Satellite Communications Business

Oliver Huth and Rafaël Roelandt[1]

Introduction

Satellite capacity agreements (also referred to as transponder service agreements) are at the heart of any communication satellite operator's business. Today, these agreements still generate the major revenue of satellite operators that operate fleets of geostationary communication satellites for broadcasting and broadband services. The sales, finance and legal departments of such operators are thus fully focused on the conclusion and execution of such vital agreements.

This chapter focuses on certain contractual elements or characteristics specific to a communication satellite operator's business when contracting satellite capacity to its customers. It goes without saying that many elements are subject to negotiation between the satellite operator and its customers. The transponder contract clauses described below thus only reflect the mere fact that these subject matters are typically included in such agreements; the exact wording obviously varies and will be the result of negotiation skills and leverage between the parties. Moreover, it has to be stressed that, although satellite operators like any other company will seek to use their contract templates, many transactions are unique and require tailor-made legal solutions. This has to be kept in mind when reading this chapter. The categorisations and contract clauses set out hereinafter describe certain recurring elements when dealing with satellite capacity agreements concluded between satellite operators and their customers.

Types of Services

A satellite capacity agreement is characterised notably by the specification of the services to be provided, i.e. the type of service to be rendered to the customer.

A categorisation in types of services can be made as follows:

> Satellite capacity provision for broadcasting: the satellite operator provides satellite transmission services via specified transponder capacity to TV and radio broadcasters for Direct-to-Home (DTH) TV or for radio transmissions, respectively.
>
> Uplink/contribution link services: sometimes combined with the provision of satellite capacity, the satellite operator ensures the uplinking of the customer's signals to the satellite.

1 The views expressed in this chapter are our personal views and do not bind the companies we work for.

The operator can also establish connectivity as requested by the customer to feed certain uplink stations for further transmissions (contribution link services).

Occasional use services: the satellite operator provides satellite capacity on short notice for short time periods. These services are used for what is often referred to as Satellite News Gathering (SNG).

Broadband services: the satellite operator provides satellite capacity for establishing broadband connections for private internet use or for company networks (VSAT).

This typology cannot be considered exhaustive. A customer might wish to combine certain services (such as, for example, contracting uplink services together with satellite capacity).

The Role of the Regulatory Environment

The contracting of satellite capacity obviously needs to take into account the governing regulatory and licensing regimes. The licensing of the uplink and downlink stations is only one regulatory aspect to be considered by the contracting parties. Notably, the customer's uplink signal and its uplink facilities shall comply with the local regulations of the jurisdiction in which such uplink facility is located. Unless the satellite operator has contractually committed to provide uplink services using uplink facilities on behalf of the customer, a satellite transponder agreement will typically provide for a clause specifying the customer's responsibility for the compliance with earth station licensing requirements.

Another interesting issue to be mentioned is this context is the aspect of what is often referred to as 'landing rights'. 'Landing rights' can be described as permissions that operators must obtain for their satellite to be used in a particular country.[2] Certain jurisdictions require foreign satellite operators to apply for concessions or licences in order to be able to serve customers in these respective countries. Such concession is often linked to various requirements for the actual contracting of satellite capacity. As an example of such requirements, the Mexican and Brazilian regimes impose the obligation to incorporate or use local legal representative offices through which the contracting of satellite capacity to local customers is compulsory. From a contractual point of view, as a consequence, the local representative entity will serve as the entity contracting with the end customer for the provision of satellite capacity. For a satellite operator, this creates the necessity to establish local presences in the respective countries, which obviously generates costs and additional administrative and compliance work. The office of the US Trade Representative (USTR) has recently criticised certain countries for not meeting international commitments to open their domestic satellite services markets by putting up regulatory barriers[3] (burdensome landing rights requirements being amongst those). It goes without saying that satellite operators need to consider and adapt their contracting structure to the regulatory regime in place should they wish to serve the respective country.

---

2 Oberst, G. 2006. 'Landing Rights Resurfacing in Europe', *Via Satellite*, Vol. 21, p. 14. [Online]. Available at: http://www.viasatellite-digital.com/viasatellite/200611/?pg=14#pg14 [accessed: 20 June 2011].

3 De Selding, P. 2010. 'USTR Criticizes Closed International Satellite Services Markets', *Space News*, 16 April.

With regard to Europe, landing rights – generally speaking – were abolished in 1994 (however, the issue regularly resurfaces in different forms or under different names).[4]

Finally, every satellite operator is subject to its home licensing jurisdiction of its administrative and registered office with regard to the conducting of a satellite operations business. Such activity is subject to a licensing regime, the structure of which may differ between the countries. In the case of SES ASTRA S.A. operating out of the Grand Duchy of Luxembourg, these matters are dealt with under the Concession Agreement concluded between the Grand Duchy and SES ASTRA S.A. Under this Concession Agreement, SES ASTRA S.A. is granted the right to operate a satellite system with satellites positioned in specific areas of the geostationary arc as specified in the Concession Agreement. The existence of this concession is a *conditio sine qua non* for the provision of satellite capacity to SES ASTRA's customers. This explains another characteristic of transponder agreements: a satellite operator cannot control changes in the licensing or concession regime affecting its operations; it will thus insert a protective clause in its transponder agreements in case of, for example, a concession withdrawal.

Broadcasting Services – Specific Contract Clauses

For the provision of broadcasting services, satellite operators and their customers execute 'transponder agreements'. They form the legal basis for the provision of satellite capacity for the transmission of TV or satellite radio signals. The actual headings used in these agreements reflect their very nature in a more precise way: 'Agreement for the provision of satellite capacity' or 'Agreement for digital transmission services on the [X] satellite system'. The main object of these agreements is the provision of a specific *service*.

Providing Satellite Capacity

The satellite operator commits to provide transmission services for the customer. The customer obtains the right to use satellite capacity and pays a consideration for this right. The transponder agreement will specify the key parameters of the transmission, amongst others the orbital position of the satellite, the initial transponder number, the customer uplink and downlink signal frequency and polarisation, the capacity as well as the transmission hours. Further, the minimum transponder performances will be defined. Further technical specifications of the customer signals and regarding the customer uplink signal will also be detailed. The latter consist in certain ITU-T Recommendations,[5] ITU-R Recommendations[6] or ETSI standards, with which the customer's signals need to comply.

For Occasional Use services, certain satellite operators grant access to self-service online booking systems. This service is obviously offered due to the high demand and the requests to be served with capacity on very short notice, notably to cover unforeseen events or to cover major sports events such as the football World Cup.

But what exactly does provision of capacity mean? The customer is entitled to use certain uplink frequencies for transmissions to the satellite and relies on the satellite to transmit it back to the earth. The essential relay to 'bend the satellite pipe' to connect point A to point B is the

4 Oberst, G. 2006. 'Landing Rights Resurfacing in Europe', 14.

5 ITU-T is ITU's Telecommunication Standardisation Sector.

6 ITU-R is ITU's Radiocommunication Sector.

transponder.[7] A transponder (also called repeater) is 'the device that takes the received signal uplinked from an earth station, filters it, translates it to the down-link frequency and amplifies it for transmission to the receiving earth station.'[8] The main frequency bands used for commercial satellite services are the C band, the Ku band and the Ka band (it is spectrum attributed within these bands that is used for satellite communication). Each satellite will have transponders operating in a specific frequency band.

For pay TV services, the customer will want to encrypt its signals prior to uplinking them to the satellite. In order to be able to monitor signal and reception quality, the satellite operator needs to be able to decode the signals, and thus will want the customer to be contractually bound to provide decoding capabilities.

Control of Content and Liability for Content

Satellites in geostationary orbit (the main European operators Eutelsat S.A. and SES ASTRA S.A. each operate entire satellite fleets serving mainly European territories, but also Africa and the Middle East) transmit a multitude of TV and radio signals. For example, the ASTRA fleet currently allows for the transmission of over 2,500 TV and radio channels.[9] It is technically impossible to control each and every single channel with regard to its content. Not only is this impracticable for the satellite operators, but it is also the competence and responsibility of the broadcasting authorities to monitor and supervise the content of the channels broadcasted and to grant the respective broadcasting licences. It is – to a very large extent – the duty of the broadcasters to comply with these media law regulations. However, despite the fact that broadcasters are the direct addressees of European audiovisual media laws and regulations, the latter naturally have direct and indirect consequences and influence on the satellite communication business, be it through national laws, the law of the European Union, the case law of the European Court of Justice and the European Court of Human Rights as well as the Council of Europe conventions[10] (such as the European Convention on Transfrontier Television dated 5 May 1989, as amended).

Keeping the aforesaid in mind, a transponder agreement will typically include a clause specifying the customer's responsibility of compliance with all national or international laws, regulations or provisions relating to the content and obliging the customer to obtain and maintain all applicable broadcasting licences.[11] Before commencement of services, it is also good practice, or in some cases a requirement, to request the broadcaster to provide evidence of its broadcasting licence; the transponder agreement will contain a corresponding obligation of the customer.

The most important legislative instrument amongst the audiovisual media law regulations in Europe is the 'Television without Frontiers Directive', as amended and restated through the Audiovisual Media Services Directive (hereinafter referred to as 'AVMSD').[12] This Directive, together with the European Convention on Transfrontier Television, constitutes the fundamental

7 Pelton, J.N. 1995. *The 'How to' of Satellite Communications*, 2nd edition. Sonoma: Design Publishers, 50.

8 *Ibid.*, 49.

9 SES ASTRA website information. 2011. [Online] Available at: http://www.ses-astra.com/business/en/index.php [accessed: 20 June 2011].

10 Baumann, I. 2005. *Das Internationale Recht der Satellitenkommunikation*. Frankfurt: Peter Lang, 469.

11 White, S., Bate, S. and Johnson, T. 1996. 'Satellite Transponder Contracts', in *Satellite Communications in Europe: Law and Regulation*. 2nd edition. London: FT Law & Tax, 366.

12 Directive 2010/13/EU of the European Parliament and of the Council of 10 March 2010 on the coordination of certain provisions laid down by law, regulation or administrative action in Member States

framework rules for many political and legal issues related to direct broadcasting via satellite in Europe.[13] Satellite operators will refer to these important rules in their transponder agreements and make the customers aware of their compliance obligations in this regard.

This being said, there have been cases of satellite operators being caught in the middle of content related disputes between media supervisory authorities/governments and broadcasters.[14] Content transmitted via satellite can also be disturbing for certain state regimes, and satellite communication has been accused of violating the sovereignty of receiving states and of serving as a vehicle to divulge illicit content.[15] These conflicts are also, but not exclusively, due to the fact that still today, there is no international binding legal regime in place which adequately or comprehensively regulates direct television via satellite.[16] In this context, the UN General Assembly Resolution 37/92 adopted on 10 December 1982 (which encompassed, as an Annex, the 'Principles Governing the Use of Artificial Earth Satellites for International Direct Television Broadcasting') has '... just remained a mere recommendation to the international community'.[17]

In order to cope with the event of direct action by authorities *vis-à-vis* a satellite operator on the grounds of illegal content being transmitted, a transponder agreement will contain clauses permitting to terminate the agreement and to seek indemnification from the customer for damage caused. Contractually, this can be achieved by introducing a termination right with immediate effect (or subject to a cure period) in the event of a breach by the customer of the terms of the transponder agreement (in this event: breach by the customer of audiovisual law provisions for which it is responsible under the transponder agreement). The national licensing regimes governing the relationship between the satellite operators and the governmental authorities will usually provide for the legal basis to act towards the operators. Satellite operators, when providing capacity only, are not 'media service providers' as defined in the AVMSD;[18] the provisions of this Directive addressed to these media service providers thus obviously cannot apply to a satellite operator.

Transponder Availability and Interruption of Services

The uninterrupted and flawless transmission of the signal is vital for any customer. Unfortunately, transponder or satellite malfunctions affecting customer traffic may occur.[19] In order to avoid any signal disruption, transponder agreements may provide for the obligation of the satellite operator to ensure back-up services through spare transponders available on the same satellite or on other

concerning the provision of audiovisual media services (Audiovisual Media Services Directive), codified version, OJ L 95, 15 April 2010, 1.

13 Baumann, I. 2005. *Das Internationale Recht der Satellitenkommunikation*, 476.

14 See the decree by the French Conseil d'Etat dated 13 December 2004 regarding the case of Al Manar (text of the decision available at: http://www.conseil-etat.fr/cde/node.php?articleid=1096 [accessed: 20 June 2011]).

15 Detailed analysis of this problematic area by: Achilleas, P. 2002. 'Globalization and Commercialization of Satellite Broadcasting: Current Issues', *Space Policy*, 18 (2002), 40–43.

16 See, regarding the situation in 1993, Peyrefitte, L. 1993. *Droit de l'Espace*. Paris: Dalloz, 327.

17 Diederiks-Verschoor, I.H.Ph. and Kopal, V. 2008. *An Introduction to Space Law*, 3rd revised edition. Alphen an den Rijn: Kluwer Law International, 58.

18 Article 1. 1 (d) of the AVMSD defines a media service provider as 'the natural or legal person who has editorial responsibility for the choice of the audiovisual content of the audiovisual media service and determines the manner in which it is organized'.

19 See the case of Intelsat's Galaxy 15 in: De Selding, P. 2010. 'Intelsat, SES Safely Negotiate Passage of Wayward Craft', *Space News*, 3 June 2010. [Online]. Available at: http://www.spacenews.com/satellite_telecom/100603-intelsat-ses-negotiate-wayward-craft.html [accessed: 20 June 2011].

satellites. In such a case, the capacity available will not always be sufficient to serve all customers affected. The transponder agreements will thus establish an order of priority between the customers, ranging from the status of 'non-pre-emptible' to 'pre-emptible', with different possibilities to establish priorities between 'equally protected' customers (for example seniority of service). The protection level is often subject to negotiation between the parties. Technical parameters will set the framework for such negotiations (for example availability of capacity on the transponder, on the satellite or on other, possibly co-located satellites). The pricing of the services will obviously be influenced by the protection level.[20]

A satellite operator will preserve the right to interrupt the customer's signal for operational testing, maintenance, monitoring, preventive or curative repair or adjustment to be carried out either with respect to the satellite as a whole or part thereof.

In the event of unjustified signal unavailability, a transponder agreement will contain compensation rights of the customer (sometimes referred to as 'Outage Credits'). The agreement will exactly define as of when and under which circumstances the customer is entitled to compensation (for example signal power specifications and thresholds, duration of the interruption).

Termination Provisions

A transponder agreement usually will provide for termination rights for both sides. Typically, each side may terminate the agreement by written notice if the other party commits a material breach and fails to remedy such breach within a specified period of time after the receipt of a written notice requesting such breach to be remedied.

The agreement will further typically include a termination right of the customer in the event of a transponder unavailability lasting for a specified longer period of time.

Liability and Indemnification

As for any commercial contract, the issues of liability, its limitations and the correlating indemnification provisions are a central element of a transponder agreement. Each party will obviously seek to negotiate the most favourable regime for its own benefit. As mentioned above, the satellite operator has no editing control over the content transmitted and will thus seek to obtain an indemnification by the customer in the event of third party claims arising, notably, from the customer's non-compliance with licensing obligations or other audiovisual media law provisions.

Broadband Services

Increasingly, communication satellites provide internet related, broadband access services or other data transmission or relay services. The business models for these data transmission services differ from one satellite operator to another. Different customer needs and profiles will trigger different kinds of services. Again, there is a multitude of service types offered, ranging from broadband internet access services, over Internet Protocol (IP) trunking services (providing backbone connectivity) to the establishing and operating of corporate Very Small Aperture Terminal (VSAT) networks. Voice over IP services can also be found.

---

20 White, S., Bate, S. and Johnson, T. 1996. 'Satellite Transponder Contracts', 372.

In Europe, the provision of a bi-directional satellite internet service[21] is only one example from amongst this large variety of services. End-users are connected to the internet using forward and return channels via satellite. Downstream and upstream Internet Protocol (IP) traffic is transmitted according to data rate limitations agreed upon between the parties. For these services, the satellite operator often does not contract with every individual end-user. The contracting partners of the satellite operator are the broadband service/access providers, who commit to deliver these services towards the individual users sitting at home in front of their PCs. Distributors will often be used to sell these types of products to the end-customer. The individual user needs specific equipment, such as a satellite antenna with a specific receive/transmit radio front-end as well as a satellite modem equipped with a demodulator and a return link modulator.

Similar to the broadcasting agreements, the agreement to provide broadband services will contain a provision stating that the satellite operator shall not be held liable for the content (data, images, sound recordings for example).

For unjustified unavailability of services, a similar refund concept as provided for under the broadcasting agreements will typically be included as well.

Concluding Remarks

In times of fast information technology developments, changing media formats and consumption behaviour (for example 3DTV), satellite payload architecture and the services offered using satellite infrastructure constantly will have to adapt to this changing environment. They can, however, also play the role of an innovating force. The requests and demands of the customer will play a decisive role in this context. Certain elements and characteristics described above, such as the responsibility of the customer for the transmission's content, will be one of the key issues to be addressed in an agreement. Finally, the legal and regulatory teams of both satellite operators and their customers will closely monitor all regulatory and legal developments on a global, European and on a national level, in order to ensure full compliance with all laws and regulations applicable.

List of References

Achilleas, P. 2002. 'Globalization and Commercialization of Satellite Broadcasting: Current Issues', *Space Policy*, 18 (2002), 40–43.

Baumann, I. 2005. *Das Internationale Recht der Satellitenkommunikation.* Frankfurt: Peter Lang.

De Selding, P. 2010. 'USTR Criticizes Closed International Satellite Services Markets', *Space News*, 16 April.

De Selding, P. 2010. 'Intelsat, SES Safely Negotiate Passage of Wayward Craft', *Space News*, 3 June.

Diederiks-Verschoor, I.H.Ph. and Kopal, V. 2008. *An Introduction to Space Law*, 3rd revised edition. Alphen an den Rijn: Kluwer Law International.

Oberst, G. 2006. 'Landing Rights Resurfacing in Europe', *Via Satellite*, Vol. 21.

Pelton, J.N. 1995. *The 'How to' of Satellite Communications*, 2nd edition. Sonoma: Design Publishers.

21 Today, Eutelsat's service is called 'Tooway'; SES ASTRA currently markets this type of service under the name of 'ASTRA2Connect'.

Peyrefitte, L. 1993. *Droit de l'espace*. Paris: Dalloz.
White, S., Bate, S. and Johnson, T. 1996. 'Satellite Transponder Contracts', in *Satellite Communications in Europe: Law and Regulation*, 2nd edition. London: FT Law & Tax.

Chapter 33
ESA Earth Observation Data Policies: Principles, Current Status and Reforms

Gisela Süß*

Data policies for earth observation satellites are crucial for the exploitation of the products and the success of the programme. Over the last decades different trends can be observed regarding data policies. In the past, even public data providers like national and international space agencies showed some interest in using the data for commercial purposes.[1] Recently, there is a shifting trend towards open data policies motivated by the conviction that this will stimulate the downstream market and lead to the creation of value-added products and setting up of new services. The evolution of the data policies of the European Space Agency (hereinafter referred to as 'ESA' or the 'Agency') over the last years reflects this tendency. The following contains a description of ESA's earth observation missions, their data policies and the relevant legal aspects.

Data Policies for ESA Earth Observation Missions

The legal framework applicable to the data policies for the Agency's missions is provided by the ESA Convention[2] and the Rules concerning Information, Data and Intellectual Property, adopted by the ESA Council on 19 December 2001.[3] The following provisions of the Convention have particular relevance for data policies:

> Article III (Information and Data) and especially III.2: 'In carrying out its activities under Article V, the Agency shall ensure that any scientific results shall be published or otherwise made widely available after prior use by the scientists responsible for the experiments. The resulting reduced data shall be the property of the Agency.'
>
> Article VII.1b provides that one of the Agency's industrial policy goals is to improve the world-wide competitiveness of European industry.

The IPR Rules address data policy issues in Section III of Chapter III, whereby:

---

* This chapter reflects exclusively the personal opinion of the author.

1 Gabrynowicz, I. 2007. *The Land Remote Sensing Laws and Policies of National Governments: A Global Survey*, Report for the US Department of Commerce/National Oceanic and Atmospheric Administration's Satellite and Information Service Commercial Remote Sensing Licensing Program, January 2007, Section V.B.4; Clerc, P. 2002. 'The State of Remote Sensing Law: French Regulation and Practice', in *Proceedings of the First International Conference on the State of Remote Sensing Law*. University, MS: National Remote Sensing and Space Law Center.

2 Convention for the establishment of a European Space Agency, entry into force 30 October 1980.

3 ESA/C/CLV/Res.4 (Final) attached to ESA/C(2002)3.

data produced by the Agency by analysing data resulting from an ESA programme shall be the property of the Agency;

the access, use and dissemination of the data shall be decided by the participating states to the programme concerned within a clear and coherent policy;

the commercial use of the data delivered by the payload may be allocated by the Agency to third parties, on conditions to be approved by the participating states to the programme concerned.

The data policies for satellite missions normally contain provisions defining (i) what data are obtained, (ii) how they are processed and distributed, (iii) under what terms and conditions (in particular regarding pricing) the data are received and used, and (iv) what archiving arrangements are to be made.[4] From a legal point of view, the terms and conditions applying to recipients of the data are of particular interest. At ESA, an evolution from more restrictive towards 'open access' data policies started several years ago already and has now been formally recognised in the relevant texts. The following sections describe these data policies and their evolution.

ERS, Envisat, Earth Explorer Data Policies before the 2010 Revision

The data policies applicable to ESA's various scientific earth observation activities were all driven by the concepts developed for the Envisat mission. Envisat is the largest earth observation satellite ever built. It carries 10 sophisticated optical and radar instruments to provide continuous observation of the earth's land surface, atmosphere, oceans and ice caps. Important discussions on data policy took place in the context of this mission.

The Envisat Data Policy objectives were (and still are) to maximise the beneficial use of Envisat data and to stimulate a balanced development of science, public-utility and commercial applications, consistent with the mission's objectives.[5]

This data policy was based on the fundamental distinction between scientific use (Category-1 scheme) and all other uses (Category-2 scheme). Category-1 use was defined as: 'Research and applications development use in support of the mission objectives, including research on long-term issues of Earth system science, research and development in preparation for future operational use, certification of receiving stations as part of the ESA functions and ESA internal use.' Category-2 use: 'All other uses which do not fall into Category-1 use, including operational and commercial use'.[6]

ESA retained overall policy and programmatic responsibility for the distribution of Envisat products for Category-1 use. These products were disseminated in accordance with the Utilisation Terms and Conditions, which determined the licensing arrangements and rights of use and further distribution. The price set by ESA for Category-1 products corresponded, or was near, to the date reproduction cost. For projects approved by ESA's Earth Observation Programme Board, data were provided free of charge.

4 Harris, R. 2002. *Earth Observation Data Policy and Europe*. Lisse: Balkema Publishers, 4–5.

5 See the introductory statements of the former and current Envisat Data Policy, ESA/PB-EO(1997)57 rev. 3 and ESA/PB-EO(2010)54.

6 Envisat Data Policy, version attached to ESA/PB-EO(1997)57 rev. 3.

For Category-2 use, ESA delegated to distributing entities the task of distributing Envisat products and thus the responsibility for market and service development. In order to ensure competitive market conditions and user choice, two consortia with overlapping world-wide distribution rights were selected. The contracts concluded between ESA and these distributing entities included mutual commitments on investment, market-development activities, delivery times and success-oriented discount schemes to increase sales. The price for Envisat standard products and services provided by ESA to its distributing entities was set at levels comparable to the pricing for Category-1 use.

The Earth Explorers Data Policy,[7] which was first approved by the states participating in the Earth Observation Envelope Programme in 2002,[8] took into account the specificity of the scientific objectives of these missions, which are research-driven and experimental. A single, simple and fully transparent mechanism for accessing all Explorer mission data for all uses, based on established procedures (Announcements of Opportunity and unsolicited Category-1 proposals), at or close to reproduction cost or completely free of charge (if price waived by ESA's Earth Observation Programme Board) was considered best to meet these objectives. Accordingly, the Earth Explorers Data Policy provided that the same data policy principles are applicable to all Explorer missions as those applied for Category-1 use of ERS and Envisat data.

The dissemination of data for Category-1 use under these data policies has worked successfully over the past decade overall, and hundreds of research projects have been accepted under this scheme. This has contributed to the promotion of scientific research and to the competitiveness of the European industry in accordance with the objectives of the ESA Convention, set out above.

The results for the Category-2 scheme are less impressive: while the volume of data disseminated by the distributing entities has increased, the expectation of a broadened market and user base has not materialised as was expected. With an increased quantity of data being distributed, only a limited amount of sustainable services has been put in place. Despite the low cost at source, only a few private firms have taken advantage of this scheme and the pricing scheme for Category-2 use has led to some major disparities.

As a consequence, the ESA data distribution scheme had been rethought and the results of the new approach are reflected in the data policy prepared for the GMES Sentinels .

GMES Sentinel Data Policy

Besides these ESA-only missions described above, the Agency is developing specific satellite missions in the framework of Global Monitoring for Environment and Security (GMES), the initiative led by the European Union. The objective of GMES is to support Europe's goals regarding sustainable development and global governance of the environment, to mitigate the effects of climate change and ensure civil security by providing timely and quality data, information and services.

---

7 Following the successful deployment of the ERS satellites and Envisat, which address earth science issues on a global scale, the Agency is now developing under its Earth Observation Envelope Programme the 'Earth Explorers' series, smaller-scale research missions focusing on specific aspects of our terrestrial environment. So far, three Explorer satellites have been launched: in 2009, GOCE (Gravity Field and Steady-State Ocean Circulation Explorer) and SMOS (Soil Moisture and Ocean Salinity), observing soil moisture over the earth's landmasses and salinity over the oceans; and in 2010, CryoSat 2, which measures floating sea-ice thickness to detect seasonal and inter-annual variations.

8 ESA/PB-EO(2002)79 rev.3.

Whilst the EU is responsible for the overall initiative, defining the requirements and granting continuity of data and services, ESA is the development and procurement agency for the dedicated GMES Sentinel missions[9] and the coordinator for the whole GMES Space Component,

The data policy for the Sentinel missions developed by the Agency under the GMES Space Component, carried out in cooperation with the European Union, will not be decided by ESA alone, but together with the EU. The orientations adopted on 29 May 2009 by the Space Council[10] underline the importance of the Commission and of the Agency, defining the Sentinel missions' data policy and ownership in a manner consistent with the INSPIRE Directive and the GMES Space Component Programme Declaration.

The Sentinel Data Policy will become part of the overall GMES Data and Information Policy, which is dealt with in Article 9 of the Regulation of the European Parliament and the EU Council on the European Earth monitoring programmes (GMES) and its initial operations (2011–2013).[11]

Article 9.1 contains a list of objectives of the GMES Data and Information Policy, i.e. (i) promoting the use and sharing of GMES information and data; (ii) full and open access to information produced by GMES services and data collected through GMES infrastructure, subject to relevant international agreements, security restrictions and licensing conditions, including registration and acceptance of user licences; (iii) strengthening Earth observation markets in Europe, in particular the downstream sector, with a view to enabling growth and job creation; (iv) contributing to the sustainability and continuity of the provision of GMES data and information; and (v) supporting the European research, technology and innovation communities. The objective of full and open access is of particular importance.[12] This relates to the Ten-Year Implementation Plan of the Global Earth Observation System of Systems (GEOSS),[13] which affirms this principle in section 5.4.

Taking into account the objectives of the overall GMES Data and Information Policy, as set out in the proposed GMES Regulation, the states participating in the ESA GMES Space Component programme sent out a strong signal for an open GMES Sentinel data policy by adopting on 30 September 2009 'Joint Principles for a GMES Sentinel Data Policy.[14] According to this text:

> Anybody can access acquired Sentinel data; in particular, no difference is made between public, commercial and scientific use and between European or non-European users. However, restrictions may be based on applicable security rules and regulations.

9 The GMES Space Component comprises six series of earth observation Sentinel missions, which include radar and super-spectral imaging for land, ocean and atmospheric monitoring. The first satellite is planned to be launched in 2013.

10 Attached to ESA/C(2009)64 and 10500/09 COMPET 308.

11 Regulation EU No. 911/2010 of the European Parliament and the EU Council of 22 September 2010 on the European Earth monitoring programme (GMES) and its initial operations (2011–2013) L 276, 20 October 2010, 1–10.

12 Mantl, L. 2009. 'The Commission Proposal for a Regulation on the European Earth Observation Programme (GMES) and its Initial Operations (2011–2013)', *ZLW*, 3, 421.

13 For the Resolution of the Third Earth Observation Summit of 16 February 2005 and the Ten-Year Implementation Plan, see the website of the Group on Earth Observations http://www.earthobservations.org/, which is coordinating efforts to establish a Global Earth Observation System of Systems.

14 ESA/PB-EO(2009)98 rev.1; the principles are called 'joint principles' since they were prepared together with the European Commission.

> The Sentinel data will be made available to the users via a 'generic' online access mode, free of charge. Generic online access is subject to a user registration process and to acceptance of the generic terms and conditions.

Given the cooperative nature of the ESA GMES Space Component Programme, these Joint Principles will only enter into force once they are also approved by the EU as part of the overall GMES Data and Information Policy. According to Article 9.2 of the GMES Regulation of the European Parliament and of the Council on the European Earth monitoring programme (GMES) and its initial operations (2011–2013), details of this policy will be contained in a delegated act adopted according to Article 290 TFEU. This delegated act may comprise, in particular, measures establishing registration and licensing conditions for GMES users and measures defining criteria for restricting access to the information produced by the GMES services and to data collected through the GMES dedicated infrastructure.

2010 Revision of ERS, Envisat, Earth Explorer Data Policies

The Agency's ERS, Envisat and Earth Explorer Data Policies were revised in May 2010, with a view to granting open and free-of-charge access to most of the earth observation data provided by these missions.[15] This revision was also intended to adapt ESA's existing data policies to the Sentinel Data Policy Joint Principles adopted by the states participating in the GMES Space Component in September 2009 and to consolidate the data policy provisions for different ESA missions, hitherto set out in separate documents.[16]

The revised data policy aims to maximise the beneficial use of the earth observation data provided and to maintain balanced use of these data for a variety of applications, be they scientific, for the public good, or commercial.

The revised ESA Data Policy is based on the distinction between two categories of datasets: 'free' and 'limited'.

'Free datasets' covers the majority of data, which are available online without any attached technical or financial constraints. This notably includes the data from the Earth Explorer missions as well as the atmospheric chemistry and altimetry (ATSR, MERIS) data from ERS and Envisat. There is full and open access to the datasets, free of charge. The access is granted electronically by online registration and user acceptance of ESA's standard Terms and Conditions.

'Limited datasets' includes the Synthetic Aperture Radar (SAR) data from the ERS and Envisat missions, where priorities are managed via categories of use due to technical and financial constraints, since most SAR products are generated in response to specific user requests and operating this instrument in different modes leads to conflicting user demands. The priorities conflict concerning limited datasets is solved by implementing a Category-1 use/Category-2 use scheme adapted from previous data policies. Category-2 use has higher priority in the case of conflict with Category-1.

15 New ESA Data Policy for these missions: ESA/PB-EO(2010)54.

16 Envisat's in ESA/PB-EO(1997)57 rev.3, ERS in ESA/PB-EO(1999)16 and Earth Explorers in ESA/PB-EO(2006)35.

Legal Aspects

The evolution of ESA's Data Policies described in the previous section shows a trend away from restrictive licensing/charging conditions and towards open data policies that aim to increase the use made of the data. This development reflects a broader trend more generally apparent in favour of making earth observation environmental data more easily accessible and freely available, which is being supported by international and European legislation, as shown in the next section.

Availability of Data

On an international level, the basic text is the United Nations Principles on Remote Sensing of the Earth from Space, which was adopted by consensus on 3 December 1986.[17] This contains a set of non-binding, yet agreed and therefore politically relevant, principles applying to the remote-sensing activities of UN Member States. These principles promote data sharing on a non-discriminatory and reasonable-cost basis.[18] ESA's Data Policies for earth observation missions have always been based on open and non-discriminatory access, in accordance with these UN Principles.[19]

The GEOSS Ten-Year Implementation Plan mentioned above,[20] which was endorsed via the Resolution adopted on 16 February 2006 by nearly 60 governments and the European Union, sets out (in section 5.4) the following data-sharing principles, which are – although likewise non-binding – another important instrument documenting international consensus in this sector:

> There will be full and open exchange of data, metadata and products shared within GEOSS, recognising relevant international instruments and national policies and legislation.
>
> All shared data, metadata and products will be made available with minimum time delay and minimum cost.
>
> All shared data, metadata and products being free of charge or no more than cost of reproduction will be encouraged for research and education.

The GMES Information and Data Policy and the revised ESA Data Policy refer to this principle of 'full and open' access. Such access means that data and information derived from publicly-funded research are made available with as few restrictions as possible, on a non-discriminatory basis, for no more than cost of reproduction and distribution.[21] It is only one step from a 'full and open' policy to a 'free-of-charge' policy.

In its Communication of 28 October 2009, entitled 'Global Monitoring for Environment and Security (GMES): Challenges and Next Steps for the Space Component',[22] the Commission

---

17 UN Resolution A/RES/41/65.

18 See in particular Principle XII. For a detailed analysis, see von der Dunk, F. 2002. 'United Nations Principles on Remote Sensing and the User', in *Earth Observation Data Policy and Europe*, edited by R. Harris, ch. 4.

19 See for example the former Envisat Data Policy ESA/PB-EO(1997)57 rev.3 and the revised Data Policy for ERS, Envisat and Earth Explorer missions ESA/PB-EO(2010)54.

20 See the section on the GMES Sentinel Data Policy.

21 Uhlir, P.F., Chen, R.S., Gabrynowicz, I. and Janssen, K. 2009. 'Toward Implementation of the Global Earth Observation System of Systems Data Sharing Principles', *Journal of Space Law*, 35, 201 (206).

22 COM(2009)589 final.

suggests following a free and open-access data policy for the Sentinels through a 'free-of-charge licensing and online access scheme, subject to security aspects'. Such an approach it motivated by the objective to maximise the beneficial use of Sentinels' data for the widest range of applications and is intended to stimulate the uptake of information based on earth observations data for end-users.

In Europe, this movement towards open data policies is also being driven by the implementation of several EU directives encouraging Member States to adopt open data policies. Under the provisions of the directive on the re-use of public sector information (PSI Directive),[23] environmental information must be disseminated to the public on request. The INSPIRE Directive lays down general rules to establish an infrastructure for spatial information in Europe for the purposes of EU environmental policies.[24]

Spatial datasets are subject to the data-sharing obligation set out in Article 17.[25] Accordingly, public authorities may charge and licence each other and EU institutions, provided this creates no obstacle to sharing. Where charges are made, these are to be kept to the minimum required to ensure the necessary quality and supply of spatial data sets and services, together with a reasonable return on investment, while heeding where applicable the self-financing requirements of public authorities supplying them. In accordance with Article 14 of the INSPIRE Directive, discovery and view services for spatial data sets must be made available to the public free of charge. This INSPIRE Directive is an important reference text for the overall GMES Data and Information Policy and the Sentinel Data Policy and is recalled in the relevant texts adopted by the European institutions and ESA respectively.[26]

This trend also reflects changing user expectations as to the accessibility of earth observation data and the increasing demand for them. Upgraded information technology systems supporting the data access – especially over recent years – have led to increased take-up for the earth observation data. A growing number of earth observation datasets is available online and provided free of charge. In the US, the approach is that government information is considered to be a valuable resource and that open exchanges of such scientific and technical information foster research excellence and effective use of funds. Accordingly, the NASA Earth Science Enterprise follows a policy of full and open sharing of earth science data obtained by US government funding, as soon as the data become available. This policy is based on the view that the greater the availability of data, the more quickly and effectively the user community can use the information to address basic earth science questions and provide the basis for developing innovative and practical applications to benefit the public at large.[27] Past studies have shown that high prices for data are a major obstacle to the development of downstream services. Full and open access to satellite data and information is therefore expected to give the earth observation sector the boost that is precisely one of the main objectives of GMES.

---

23 Directive 2003/98/EC of 17 November 2003.

24 Directive 2007/2 of 14 March 2007 establishing an Infrastructure for Spatial Information in the European Community.

25 INSPIRE covers 34 Data Themes laid down in three Annexes. Annex II refers in section 3 to 'Ortho-Imagery Geo-references image data of the Earth's surface, from either satellite or airborne sensors'.

26 See Recital 27 of the Regulation on the European Earth Monitoring Programme (GMES) and its initial operations (2011–2013), as per note 11, and the Joint Principles for a Sentinel Data Policy as per note 14 above.

27 Harris, R. 2003. 'Global Monitoring for Environment and Security: Data Policy Considerations', *Space Policy*, 19, 265 (276).

Whilst there are strong legal and socio-economic arguments in favour of openness of public data, there are also some legitimate reasons for limiting access. These reasons may be especially related to (national) security concerns or the need to protect copyright or personal privacy.

Security

Access to satellite data may be restricted for security reasons. This is of particular importance for high-resolution images and 'dual-use' technologies, which are relevant to both civil and military applications. Whilst the security aspect has generally no importance for ESA's earth observation research missions, it may become relevant for the Sentinels developed as part of the GMES Space Component. The very name 'Global Monitoring for Environment and *Security*' itself points to the significance of the security dimension here.

The security restriction is mentioned in several texts: the Joint Principles for a GMES Sentinel Data Policy;[28] the Commission Communication of 28 October 2009 entitled Global Monitoring for Environment and Security (GMES): Challenges and Next Steps for the Space Component;[29] and the text of the Regulation on the European Earth monitoring programme (GMES) and its initial operations (2011–2013), adopted by the European Parliament on 16 June 2010.[30] At this stage, it is, however, not yet completely clear how this security provision will be implemented. The GMES Regulation provides in this respect that the Commission may adopt, by means of delegated acts within the meaning of Article 290 TFEU, measures 'defining criteria for restricting access to the information produced by the GMES services and to data collected through the GMES dedicated infrastructure'. These measures shall be taken 'without prejudice to national rules and procedures applicable to space and in situ infrastructures under national control'.[31] In practice, national legislation may apply to observation systems (whether space-based or *in situ*), which contribute to GMES. An example is the German Satellite Data Security Act,[32] the provisions of which must be heeded for national 'high grade' systems like TerraSAR-X. The French Law on space operations[33] also takes account of security aspects and authorises restricting operational space activities at any time on the grounds of fundamental national interest, international commitments or foreign policy.

Copyright

It is questionable whether satellite data may be subject to copyright protection. Copyright is the set of exclusive rights granted to the author or creator of an original work, including the right to copy, distribute and adapt it.

Turning to the definitions of data given in the UN Principles Relating to Remote Sensing of the Earth from Space, there appear to be varying degrees of statutory intellectual property protection. According to the definitions contained in Principle I:

> The term 'primary data' means the raw data that are acquired by remote sensors borne by

28 See note 15.

29 See note 23.

30 See note 12.

31 Article 9.2 of the Regulation on the European Earth monitoring programme (GMES) and its initial operations (2011–2013), see note 11.

32 Gesetz zum Schutz vor Gefährdung der Sicherheit der Bundesrepublik Deutschland durch das Verbreiten von hochwertigen Erdfernerkundungsdaten (Satellitendatensicherheitsgesetz – SatDSiG), of 23 November 2007, *BGBl* I, 2590.

33 Loi no. 518-2008 relative aux opérations spatiales du 3 juin 2008.

a space object and that are transmitted or delivered to the ground from space by telemetry in the form of electromagnetic signals, by photographic film, magnetic tape or any other means.

The term 'processed data' means the products resulting from the processing of the primary data, needed to make such data usable.

The term 'analysed information' means the information resulting from the interpretation of processed data, inputs of data and knowledge from other sources.

In general, primary or raw data produced technologically without any act of human intellectual creativity are not protected by copyright law. Higher-level data and products requiring creativity and originality in their production or 'analysed information', as per the above principle, may be copyright.

The issue of copyright is generally covered by the data's licence conditions. Thus, as regards ESA earth observation data and products, the utilisation of 'Terms and Conditions', which must be accepted by the user – generally by a mouse click on the online registration form – state that ESA is the owner of its mission data products, that the user must recognise ESA's title and ownership of the data/products by properly marking them, and that any onward distribution requires ESA approval. This does not prevent the user from acquiring its own copyright protection, which may arise as a result of its own interpretation of ESA processed data, data inputs or knowledge emanating from other sources.

Privacy

High-resolution satellite data can potentially interfere with personal privacy rights. An example is Google's Street View programme, a feature on Google Maps that offers free access via the internet to panoramic, navigable views of streets.

In one well-known case, *Boring v. Google*, the US courts had to weigh the delicate balance between the right to freely publish and access images, on the one hand, and the individual's right to privacy, on the other. The Borings, who live on a private road in Pittsburgh, discovered that Google had taken 'coloured imagery of their residence, including the swimming pool, from a vehicle in their residence driveway months earlier without obtaining any privacy waiver or authorisation'.

The Pennsylvania Western District Court dismissed the invasion-of-privacy claim because the claimants were unable to prove that Google's conduct, for example the publicity given to their private life through a photograph of the outside of a residential structure, was highly offensive to a person of ordinary sensibilities.[34] This decision was upheld by the Court of Appeal.[35] One of the grounds for the claim's dismissal was the fact that no people were visible in the images.

Whilst it is relatively easy to imagine that aerial photography may violate privacy rights, it is more difficult to envisage intrusions into private life being perpetrated by satellite data/products. However, satellite images may display features relating to pieces of land and construction works prompting certain conclusions about the owners and therefore potentially intruding on their privacy; thus, satellite images may reveal certain characteristics of land or buildings that may

34 Boring v. Google, Inc., 598 F. Supp. 2d 695, 699–700 (W. D. Pa. 2009).

35 United States Court of Appeals for the Third Circuit, No. 09-2350, see http://www.ca3.uscourts.gov/opinarch/092350np.pdf [accessed: 1 May 2011].

aid the government, for example the exploitation of a plot of land, or the emissions from a plant. These examples point to another legal issue arising from privacy considerations: the use of earth observation (satellite) data for law enforcement purposes or as evidence in administrative and judicial proceedings.[36]

Privacy issues are unlikely to arise under typical research missions such as ESA's Earth Explorers, which monitor specific environmental data and evolutions of major scientific interest. They are more likely to arise under operational programmes like GMES, which is carried out in cooperation with the European Union. It is interesting to note that the list of EU policies, with which initial GMES operations are to be implemented consistently,[37] includes protection of personal data. The EU's rules in this area are set out in the Data Protection Directive.[38] The INSPIRE Directive[39] (Article 13.1 (f)) addresses the potential conflict between open data access and privacy: Member States may limit public access to spatial data sets and services where access would adversely affect the confidentiality of personal data and/or files relating to a natural person, where that person has not consented to public disclosure of the information and where such confidentiality is covered by national or Community law.

Liability

For sake of completeness the issue of liability is addressed in this section, even if its relevance is limited. The following questions may be raised: who can be made liable for damage arising from possible satellite malfunctioning (from errors in collected or processed data for example) which may affect the quality of the resulting services (in the case of GMES for instance)? What would the legal basis for any such claim be? Claims for compensation for loss of satellite performance are less likely to occur in the earth observation area than in that of navigation or telecommunications, where commercial services are at stake. Nevertheless, there are still cases imaginable where public or private entities could seek to claim damages for non-delivery of observation-satellite services due to technical malfunction.

Even if the provisions of the Convention on international Liability for Damage caused by Space Objects entered into force on 1 September 1972 (hereinafter referred to as the 'Liability Convention') apply to ESA.,[40] they are not relevant in this context. Pursuant to Article 1 of the Liability Convention the term 'damage' means loss of life, personal injury or other impairment of health, or loss or damage to property; the term damage covers only the consequence of direct physical impact of space objects, but not damage that may arise from malfunctioning of the payload of the satellite or from errors in the collected or processed data.

In these cases, compensation on the basis of civil-liability claims could be sought in theory from the satellite's designer, manufacturer, owner, operator or added-value service providers. Depending on the nature of the relations between claimant and defendant, such claims could be

36 On this aspect, see Mayence, J.-F., 'Use of Satellite Data for Law Enforcement', a presentation given at the 'Current Legal Issues for Satellite Earth Observation' conference organised by the European Space Policy Institute on 8–9 April 2010.

37 See (14th) recital of the preamble to the Regulation on the European Earth Monitoring Programme (GMES) and its initial operations (2011–2013), see note 11.

38 Directive 95/46/EC of 24 October 1995 on the protection of individuals with regard to the processing of personal data and on the free movement of such data.

39 See note 24.

40 The provisions of this Convention apply to ESA since it has declared on 23 September 1975 the acceptance of its rights and obligations in accordance with Article 22.

based on remedies existing under contract or tort law. However, their chances of success are rather limited. It would seem difficult to rely on Directive 85/374 on the Liability for Defective Products[41] (and its implementation provisions under national law), since the entities involved in the satellite's development and construction are normally not acting as product-makers, for example labelling products with their name.[42] Furthermore, the licensing terms, which the receiver of the data (and services) must accept, generally exclude all data-provider liability for the data's suitability to a specific project or any damage derived from their use.

A specific liability issue arises under public international law which deserves attention. Satellite data may reveal crisis situations and thus be critical to humanitarian relief operations. In which case, is the satellite operator obligated to transmit the data to national authorities? And do those authorities have a 'responsibility to protect'?[43] While the latter concept has, since the 2001 Report of the International Commission on Intervention and State Sovereignty (ICSS),[44] attracted some criticism,[45] the general reception has been remarkably positive.[46] Regarding any legal obligation to disclose critical environmental information, the relevant provisions are to be found in the UN Remote Sensing Principles (X): 'States participating in remote sensing activities that have identified information in their possession that is capable of averting any phenomenon harmful to the Earth's natural environment shall disclose such information to States concerned.'

Conclusion

Observations from space and satellite data are making an important contribution to our comprehension of the earth system, its weather, climate (change), oceans, atmosphere, land, natural resources and human-induced hazards. Understanding the earth's ecosystems is crucial to improving human health, safety and welfare, alleviating human suffering including poverty, protecting the global environment, limiting major-disaster impact and achieving sustainable development.[47] Modern science is increasingly data-driven, while science and research are in turn crucial drivers of economic growth. And with modern technologies allowing almost unlimited access to information and knowledge, restrictive data policies would seem to be somewhat outdated.

In this context, certain 'soft law' instruments have proved to be powerful tools for demonstrating and driving international consent. Although legally non-binding, the GEOSS Ten-Year Implementation Plan, with its principles of data-sharing and 'full and open' data policies, is

---

41 Directive 85/374/33C of 25 July 1985 on the approximation of the laws, regulations and administrative provisions concerning liability for defective products.

42 Furthermore, as an international organisation, ESA is not subject to EU regulations or directives (see FN.59).

43 Ribbelink, O. 2008. 'Another Responsibility to Protect? Changing Perceptions of Sovereignty and Human Rights', *Essays in Honour of Cees Flintermann*. Antwerp/Oxford/Portland, OR: Intersentia.

44 ICSS. 2001. *Report of the International Commission*. Ottawa: IDRC.

45 See e.g. Weiss, T.G. and Hubert, D. 2001. *The Responsibility to Protect: Research, Bibliography, Background*, Supplementary Volume to the Report of the International Commission on Intervention and State Sovereignty. Ottawa: IDRC; Stahn, C. 2007. 'Responsibility to Protect: Political Rhetoric or Emerging Legal Norm?', *American Journal of International Law*, 101.

46 See e.g. the Secretary-General's High-Level Panel Report, 'A More Secure World: Our Shared Responsibility', A/59/565(2004), § 201–3; General Assembly Resolution, 2005 World Summit Outcome, A/RES/60/1, 24 October 2005; SC Res. 1674(2006).

47 See GEOSS Ten-Year-Implementation Plan.

exerting considerable influence on the data policies of public providers. It builds on and further develops past practice based on other soft law instruments, such as the UN Principles on Remote Sensing and the Disaster Charter.

The development of ESA's Data Policies over recent years shows the organisation's capacity to adapt and to take due account of changes on the international and European scene. Technical progress, with its ever-increasing possibilities, is constantly creating new challenges for earth observation, which are relevant to data policies. The increasing precision of earth observation data and the higher resolution inevitably raise – especially for operational programmes such as GMES – the question of access restrictions on security and privacy grounds.

The example of the GMES Space Component, a programme that is being carried out on the basis of cooperation between the Agency and the European Union, demonstrates the growing influence of European law on ESA's Data Policies, even if the Agency itself is not directly subject to EU regulations and directives.[48] With the entry into force of the Lisbon Treaty giving the EU explicit competence for space (Article 189 (1)), the influence of the European Union as legislator and decision-maker in the space sector has increased yet further and must be taken into account by ESA and by the other sector players.

List of References

Boring v. Google, Inc., 598 F. Supp. 2d 695, 699–700 (W. D. Pa. 2009).

Brachet, G. 2004. 'From Initial Ideas to a European Plan: GMES as an Exemplar of European Space Strategy', *Space Policy*, 20, 11 f.

Charter on Cooperation to Achieve the Coordinated Use of Space Facilities in the Event of Natural or Technological Disasters. [Online]. Available at: http://www.disasterscharter.org/charter [accessed: 1 May 2011].

Clerc, P. 2002. 'The State of Remote Sensing Law: French Regulation and Practice', in *Proceedings: The First International Conference on the State of Remote Sensing Law*, edited by G.I. Gabrynowicz. University, MS: National Remote Sensing and Space Law Center.

Communication from the Commission to the European Parliament, the Council, the European Economic and Social Committee and the Committee of the Regions on Global Monitoring for Environment and Security (GMES): Challenges and Next Steps for the Space Component, COM(2009)589 final.

Convention for the establishment of a European Space Agency approved by the Conference of Plenipotentiaries held on Paris on 30 May 1975 and entered into force on 30 October 1980. [Online]. Available at: http://www.esa.int/convention/ [accessed: 1 May 2011].

Convention on International Liability on Damage caused by Space Objects, UN/GA Res. 2777(XXVI).

Directive 85/374/33C of 25 July 1985 on the approximation of the laws, regulations and administrative provisions concerning liability for defective products.

Directive 2003/98/EC of 17 November 2003 on the re-use of public sector information.

Directive 2007/2 of 14 March 2007 establishing an Infrastructure for Spatial Information in the European Community.

48 Hobe S., Kunzmann K. and Reuter T. 2006. 'Forschungsbericht ESA – EU: Rechtliche Rahmenbedingungen einer zukünftigen kohärenten Struktur der europäischen Raumfahrt', *Kölner Schriften zum Internationalen und Europäischen Recht*, Bd. 13. Berlin: LIT Verlag, 394.

Earth Explorer Data Policy, ESA/PB-EO(2006)35.

Envisat Data Policy, ESA/PB-EO(1997)57 rev.3.

ERS Data Policy, ESA/PB-EO(1999)16.

Fifth Space Council's Resolution 'Taking forward the European Space Policy', adopted on 26 September 2008 (ESA/C-M/CCII/Res.1) (Final); see also 289th Competitiveness Council meeting, Brussels, 26 September 2008.

Gabrynowicz, I. 2007. *The Land Remote Sensing Laws and Policies of National Governments: A Global Survey*, Report for the US Department of Commerce/National Oceanic and Atmospheric Administration's Satellite and Information Service Commercial Remote Sensing Licensing Program, January 2007.

Gesetz zum Schutz vor Gefährdung der Sicherheit der Bundesrepublik Deutschland durch das Verbreiten von hochwertigen Erdfernerkundungsdaten (Satellitendatensicherheitsgesetz – SatDSiG), of 23 November 2007, *BGBl* I, 2590.

Harris, R. 2002. *Earth Observation Data Policy and Europe*. Lisse: Balkema Publishers.

Harris, R. 2003. 'Global Monitoring for Environment and Security: Data Policy Considerations', *Space Policy*, 19, 265.

Hobe, S., Kunzmann, K. and Reuter, T. 2006. 'Forschungsbericht ESA – EU: Rechtliche Rahmenbedingungen einer zukünftigen kohärenten Struktur der europäischen Raumfahrt', *Kölner Schriften zum Internationalen und Europäischen Recht*, Bd. 13. Berlin: LIT Verlag.

ICSS. 2001. *Report of the International Commission*. Ottawa: IDRC.

Joint Principles for a GMES Sentinel Data Policy, ESA/PB-EO(2009)98 rev.1.

Kohlhammer, G. 2001. 'The Envisat Exploitation Policy', *ESA Bulletin*, 106 (June 2001).

Loi no. 518-2008 relative aux opérations spatiales du 3 juin 2008.

Mantl, L. 2009. 'The Commission Proposal for a Regulation on the European Earth Observation Programme (GMES) and its Initial Operations (2011–2013)', *ZLW*, 3, 421 f.

Orientations adopted on 29 May 2009 by the 6th Space Council, ESA/C(2009)64 and 10500/09 COMPET 308.

Proposal for a Regulation of the European Parliament and the EU Council on the European Earth Observation Programme (GMES) and its initial operations (2011–2013) COM(2008)748/4.

Regulation of the European Parliament and the EU Council on the European Earth Observation Programme (GMES) and its initial operations (2011–2013) see 2009/0070 (COD). [Online]. Available at: http://register.consilium.europa.eu/pdf/en/10/pe00/pe00022.en10.pdf [accessed: 1 May 2011].

Resolution of the Third Earth Observation Summit of 16 February 2005 and Ten-Year Implementation Plan. [Online]. Available at: http://www.earthobservations.org/ [accessed: 1 May 2011].

Revised ESA Data Policy for ERS, Envisat and Earth Explorer missions, ESA/PB-EO(2010)54.

Ribbelink, O. 2008. 'Another Responsibility to Protect? Changing Perceptions of Sovereignty and Human Rights', *Essays in Honour of Cees Flintermann*. Antwerp/Oxford/Portland, OR: Intersentia.

Rules concerning Information, Data and Intellectual Property, adopted by the ESA Council on 19 December 2001 ESA/C/CLV/Res.4 (Final), ESA/C(2002)3.

Stahn, C. 2007. 'Responsibility to Protect: Political Rhetoric or Emerging Legal Norm?', *American Journal of International Law*, 101 f.

The Secretary-General's High-Level Panel Report, 'A More Secure World: Our Shared Responsibility', A/59/565(2004), § 201–3; General Assembly Resolution, 2005 World Summit Outcome, A/RES/60/1, 24 October 2005; SC Res. 1674(2006).

Uhlir, P.F., Chen, R.S., Gabrynowicz, J.I. and Janssen, K. 2009. 'Toward Implementation of the Global Earth Observation System of Systems Data Sharing Principles', *Journal of Space Law*, 35, 201f.

United Nations Principles on Remote Sensing of the Earth from Space, UN Resolution A/RES/41/65.

United States Court of Appeals for the Third Circuit, No. 09-2350. [Online]. Available at: http://www.ca3.uscourts.gov/opinarch/092350np.pdf [accessed: 1 May 2011].

von der Dunk, F. 2002. 'United Nations Principles on Remote Sensing and the User', in *Earth Observation Data Policy and Europe*, edited by R. Harris. Lisse: Balkema Publishers.

Weiss, T.G. and Hubert, D. 2001. *The Responsibility to Protect: Research, Bibliography, Background*, Supplementary Volume to the Report of the International Commission on Intervention and State Sovereignty. Ottawa: IDRC.

PART VI
Conclusions and Outlook

Chapter 34
Conclusions and Outlook

Lesley Jane Smith and Ingo Baumann

The European space industry is a niche sector, embedded in the wider European Aerospace and Defence industrial complex. A few large industrial holdings are directly responsible for more than 70 per cent of the total space industry employment.[1] Growth in this sector depends heavily on public budgets and the cyclical demand of commercial satellite communications operators. Nearly half of the overall market is placed with public customers, such as the European Space Agency and national space agencies. Given its strategic importance and interdependencies with the defence sector, political intervention is strong.

The space industry is governed more extensively by public international law than most other industrial sectors. Various treaties set the basic principles for space activities, with the Outer Space Treaty laying down the principle rules for activities in outer space at international level, followed by the Registration Convention, the Liability Convention, the Rescue Agreement and the Moon Treaty.[2] In addition to these basic documents, a number of bi- and multilateral agreements provide for cooperation in space activities, such as providing earth observation data in case of disasters or establishing and maintaining the ISS.[3] Many intergovernmental organisations are active in the space sector. Before their privatisation, the intergovernmental organisations Intelsat, Inmarsat, Eutelsat and Intersputnik monopolised the market in international satellite communications services.[4] The provision of satellite meteorological services in Europe falls under the responsibility of the Eumetsat organisation.[5] The International Telecommunications Union (ITU) provides the regulatory framework for the use of frequencies and related orbital positions for all types of space systems. Satellite communications have been liberalised on a global scale through agreements of the World Trade Organisation (WTO). The direct influence of the public international law framework on contract practice and contract clauses is, however, relatively low.

According to Article VI of the Outer Space Treaty, states are responsible also for private space activities under their jurisdiction.[6] With the increase in commercialisation and privatisation of space

---

1 ASD Eurospace. 2010. *The European Space Industry in 2009: Facts and Figures*, August 2010. [Online]. Available at: http://www.eurospace.org [accessed: 30 April 2011].

2 The full texts of the treaties are available at: http://www.un.ooosa.org.

3 Charter On Cooperation To Achieve The Coordinated Use Of Space Facilities In The Event Of Natural Or Technological Disasters. [Online]. Available at: http://www.disastercharter.org [accessed: 30 April 2011]; Intergovernmental Agreement concerning cooperation on the Civil International Space Station (ISS Agreement).

4 Baumann, I. 2005. *Das internationale Recht der Satellitenkommunikation*. Frankfurt: Peter Lang; Lyall, F. and Larsen, P. 2009. *Space Law, A Treatise*. Aldershot: Ashgate, 319.

5 Information. [Online]. Available at: http://www.eumetsat.int [accessed: 30 April 2011].

6 Article VI sentence 1 Outer Space Treaty: 'State Parties to the Treaty shall bear international responsibility for national activities in outer space, including the Moon and other celestial bodies, whether such activities are carried on by governmental agencies or by non-governmental entities, and for ensuring that national activities are carried out in conformity with the provisions set forth in this Treaty.'

activities, the number of countries implementing national space legislation in order to fulfil their treaty obligations is increasing. Only recently, the French national space legislation entered into force.[7] This legislation is likely to have far-reaching effects on the whole of the European space sector, as the main European launch service provider Arianespace falls under French jurisdiction. Germany is expected to enact national space legislation in the near future, with other European countries likely to follow. Small jurisdictions such as the Isle of Man meanwhile have succeeded in attracting space business by implementing space legislation with a low and flexible degree of regulation for industry.[8]

The licensing of satellite communications services and the corresponding frequency assignments falls under another set of national laws and regulations, with specific provisions governing the conditions under which the national authority secures the international filing of frequencies with the International Telecommunications Union (ITU). While technically forming part of telecommunications law, these provisions are essential for any satellite project.[9] Suitable frequencies are scarce resources, especially for satellite communications and navigation, and are increasingly subject to disputes about priority rights as well as to complex coordination procedures. Operators have to undergo due diligence checks and time limits for '*bringing into use*' the assigned frequencies have considerably been shortened. The ITU was among the first organisations to establish guidelines for the avoidance or handling of space debris.[10]

Other international and national regulations are linked to the strategic dimension of space activities and its inherent dual-use character. An important part of space technology is subject to export control, including arms control and non-proliferation.[11] The applicable national laws to different degrees limit world-wide commercialisation and cooperation with non-European states or companies. Contractual clauses for space projects assign the responsibility for obtaining the corresponding licences and authorisations among the parties and may, in some cases, define their refusal by the competent authority as a case of *force majeure*. Encryption of satellite commands and signals is already the subject of specific legislation and may require detailed contractual regulations for access to keys or control rooms, treatment of classified documents or personal security clearance.[12] Generally, IT security is of increasing importance to all kinds of space projects.[13]

Until today, military or dual-use systems still fall within the national domain of the ESA Member States. Article II of the ESA Convention provides that the Agency undertakes its activities '*for exclusively peaceful purposes*', a provision that was interpreted strictly in the past. Attempts to establish a multilateral military satellite communications system failed several times, and recent agreements on the exchange of classified earth observation data also failing to meet expectations.[14] In response to increasing political and programmatic demands by the EU and the Member States, ESA now engages more in dual-use systems and technologies and has concluded

7 Cross reference Couston, M., Chapter 26.

8 Cross reference Aganabe, T., Chapter 13.

9 Cross reference Baumann, I. and Dodel, H., Chapter 30.

10 Cross reference Achilleas, P. and Loubeyre, R., Chapter 9.

11 Cross reference Hörl, K.-U. and Creydt, M., Chapter 24.

12 Germany enacted the Satellite Data Security Act in 2007 governing the treatment of the TerraSAR and Tandem-X high resolution radar satellites. The purpose of the Act is to safeguard the security and foreign policy interests of the Federal Republic of Germany in connection with the distribution and commercial marketing of satellite-acquired earth remote sensing data especially on international markets.

13 Cross reference Baumann, I., Chapter 25.

14 Commentary 'With or without MUSIS', *Space News*, 21 (49), 13 December 2010, 18.

a cooperation agreement with the European Defence Agency (EDA). Both flagship programmes of the European Union, Galileo and GMES, include security service elements providing navigation and geo-information services to public security authorities, including the military. Plans for future programmes, namely for Space Situational Awareness or Automatic Vessel Identification, are also strongly characterised by dual-use aspects. European dual-use programmes are likely to increase in the future, with a corresponding effect on the legal framework and contract practice.

The engagement in security-related space projects is not the only challenge ESA faces. The Agency has initiated comprehensive reforms that include its financial, procurement and contract management. The latter two have significant effects for the contract practice in the European Space Sector. Tenderers now have the possibility to challenge procurement decisions of the Agency, even if the mechanisms are quite restrictive and provide limited remedies.[15] The new ESA General Clauses and Conditions (GCC) provide for a more balanced risk sharing, including limitations of liability for certain aspects, but they also include for the first time performance penalties.[16] A number of other new clauses reflect the growing orientation of ESA projects towards service-related aspects.

The biggest challenge for ESA comes from intensified relations with the European Union. The EU competence in space established through the entry into force of the Treaty on the Functioning of the European Union (TFEU) significantly strengthens the influence of the EU on space policy and programmes. EU and ESA closely cooperate on the basis of a Framework Agreement signed in 2004 and align their policies by resolutions of the joint Space Council and other instruments of governance. As a result of the growing cooperation between the EU and ESA and under the terms of delegation agreements for the Galileo and GMES programmes, ESA has to observe and apply financial and procurement regulations of the EU. Most significantly, ESA acts as procurement agent for the Galileo Full Operational Capability (FOC) applying EU competitive dialogue procedures and specific procurement conditions foreseen by the relevant EU regulations. For the participating industry, the application of the EU framework led to significant uncertainty and unusual costs and efforts.

The experience from the Galileo FOC tender has also shown that the application of the EU legal framework for the procurement of large space systems has significant limitations, namely concerning the required flexibility to adapt budgets, schedules and technological solutions. There is now a growing demand for the EU to implement suitable budgetary mechanisms as well as specific procurement and contract conditions for its space programmes. The 7th Space Council Conclusions recognise 'that the development and operation of space programmes, which are by nature long-term and high risk activities, require specific financial means and implementing rules, as well as long-term commitments'.[17] The EU may implement specific rules as part of the next revision of the applicable financial regulations in a few years time. Further steps in European Space Policy will certainly bring ESA closer to the EU, whatever the future governance model might be. From a contractual perspective, political decisions about the future application of the ESA's geo-return principles will be of special importance and effect.[18]

Many space technologies and applications have reached a high degree of maturity and deliver essential services, among which car navigation, television broadcasting and weather forecasting are the most prominent. The range of applications encompasses merely all aspects of policy and society,

15 Cross reference Heinrich, O., Chapter 16.

16 Cross reference Stjernevi, G. and Katsampani, E., Chapter 15.

17 See the Conclusions of the 7th Space Council, 'Global Challenges: Taking Benefit of European Space Systems', 25 November 2010.

18 Cross reference Schmidt-Tedd, B., Chapter 3.

including telemedicine, location-based services, monitoring of climate change, environmental protection, precision farming or vessel identification. From a contractual perspective, regulations applying to specific applications sectors, such as data protection obligations regarding medical patient data, may need to be reflected in specific clauses. Links to numerous sectors for applications increase the overall complexity of space industry contracts further.

The broad scope of applications and their direct or indirect economic benefits were among the main drivers for the European Union to deal with space activities and are of highest priority today within the European Space Policy. The strategy focuses on bringing '*space down to earth*' and to exploit space as an enabler for the delivery of EU policies, provider of services to citizens and contributor to overall economic growth and innovation.[19] Space technology should respond to public policy objectives and user needs at regional, national and European level. This 'Service Paradigm' remains a challenge for the industry, already having concrete effects in contractual practice. The new General Clauses and Conditions of ESA require industry to undertake performance guarantees related to the continuity, quality and reliability of space services.[20] Not surprisingly, Service Level Agreements are now a feature within an increasing number of ESA and other space industry contracts.[21]

At first hand, contract practice in the European Space sector does not seem to differ much from practice in other high-technology industrial sectors. Negotiations circle around the typical major legal issues such as IPR, warranties, liability, applicable law or dispute settlement. However, certain contractual solutions are particular to the space sector, taking into account the characteristics of the space environment and the high risk associated with the launch and operation of space objects. Launch Service Agreements contain far-reaching waivers of liability and detailed risk-sharing mechanisms between the launch service provider and its customers.[22] To cover the risk of launch or in-orbit failures, operators take out space insurance provided by a small number of highly specialised brokers and insurance companies and with high and volatile premiums.[23] Under in-orbit delivery schemes, the risk of launch failures is increasingly attributed to the satellite manufacturers. Standard warranty clauses would be meaningless for operational phases of space projects, as a component of a satellite cannot be repaired or replaced once it is in orbit.[24] Malfunctions can then only be corrected by software uploads and complex operational contingency procedures. Inventions made in outer space, namely on board the International Space Station, require a dedicated legal regime.[25] A whole part of ESA's General Clauses and Conditions deals with IPR issues, including the use of existing background know-how, and are generally dominating negotiations of research and development contracts. The individual aspects of each project may require further specific contractual solutions.

Contracts in the space sector therefore show a low degree of standardisation, with individual negotiations generally prevailing over the use of general terms and conditions. The interdependence of the main industrial players is so strong that disputes are usually solved either on project or management level, with more serious conflicts involving national space agencies and ministries. There is little case law available to the practitioner, when compared to other industrial sectors.

---

19 See the Conclusions of the 7th Space Council 'Global Challenges: Taking Benefit of European Space Systems', 25 November 2010.

20 Cross reference Stjernevi, G. and Katsampani, E., Chapter 15.

21 Cross reference Baumann, I., Chapter 25.

22 Cross reference du Parquet, C., Chapter 31.

23 Cross reference Montpert, P., Chapter 23.

24 Cross reference Scharlach, I., Chapter 21.

25 Cross reference Smith, L.J. and Doldirina, C., Chapter 27.

Privatisation and commercialisation at the end of last century had important effects on the space industry. Large parts of the space sector, namely satellite communications, now work under liberalised market conditions and operators are faced with strong international competition. Business trends and models of other industries were also introduced in the space sector. Instead of establishing own infrastructures, public customers increasingly relied on commercial services. In some cases, models of public private partnerships or outsourcing have been successfully implemented, surprisingly even to satisfy military needs. In other cases, such models have failed due to the lack of proven technology, calculable risks, reliable revenue expectations or a workable risk sharing mechanism between the public customer and the private service provider. Galileo is the most prominent example for a failed public private partnership concept.[26]

Galileo and GMES are the two flagship programmes of the European Space Policy and reflect most of the current challenges for both public and private stakeholders of the European space sector. They also enable some prediction as to future developments, especially in procurement and contract practice. Not surprisingly, numerous chapters of this volume therefore make reference to these programmes and analyse specific legal or contractual aspects. While the overall political governance of the new European Space Policy is already quite advanced, programme governance for Galileo and GMES is still characterised by significant trial and error.[27] Programme governance structures were given up or changed soon after their implementation and are today in a transitional status. For the long-term operational and service phases of the programmes, suitable governance, budget and management instruments are still to be developed. The 7th Space Council has only recently underlined the importance of

> rapidly identifying, on the base of agreed governance schemes, the required operational schemes for the flagship programmes in the long-term, which are essential to ensure the proper interface between the space agencies, service-providers and end-users, to take the responsibility for long-term operations and adaptation of the infrastructure, to ensure the delivery of continuous data and services to users and to maximise opportunities for the development of commercial services.[28]

Development of the European space sector is guaranteed to continue and *Contracting for Space* can therefore only review the current state of play in procurement and contract practice, as well as underlying laws and policies. Important changes will arise from the further development of the European Space Policy and the increasing cooperation between EU and ESA in setting up space programmes providing services for numerous policies. Future financial, procurement and contract conditions dedicated to EU space programmes will have important effects on industry and project practice.

Specialised European agencies and institutions, such as EMSA, EASA, EDA, EEA or the EU Satellite Centre may, within their respective domain, soon become new procurement entities for space services and infrastructures. These are likely to employ own specific procurement procedures and contract conditions and practices, adding to the overall complexity of project practice.

---

26 See European Court of Auditors, Special Report, No. 7, 2009: 'The Management of the Galileo Programme's Development and Validation Phase'. [Online]. Available at: http://eca.europa.eu [accessed: 30 April 2011].

27 See European Court of Auditors, Special Report, No. 7, 2009: 'The Management of the Galileo Programme's Development and Validation Phase'.

28 See the Conclusions of the 7th Space Council 'Global Challenges: Taking Benefit of European Space Systems', 25 November 2010.

The increasing number of actors in the European space sector will also require new models of governance ensuring close coordination and cooperation.

A large part of future public spending for space activities will be assigned to services and infrastructures of a dual-use character. A steadily growing awareness of the need for shared space assets for security has been expressed in several European policy documents. Space services are relevant across the whole spectrum of security issues, from environmental monitoring to conflict prevention and maritime surveillance. Exploitation of space for security purposes will increase the demands on industry to provide highly secure, reliable and continuous services and is likely to influence contract practice significantly. Participation of the military in dual-use projects may necessitate handling of classified documents, encryption of communication and personal security clearance.

The developments are challenging for the legal practitioner in the space industry. The overall legal framework for space projects is highly complex and new actors, laws and regulations constantly add to this complexity. Depending on the specific project, lawyers will have to deal with a broad range of legal regime spanning from international treaties, national space legislation, telecommunications law, export control, IPR, IT law, insurances, security regulations to standard international commercial law and contract issues. Negotiations for larger projects sometimes takes years and require the early setting up of internal project teams with the full-time participation of legal experts. During the project execution phase, Change and Claim Management are demanding strong legal support. These developments are calling for new practices of legal project management.

Contracting for Space has brought together a significant number of practitioners of European space law and policy, with specialist contributions on current developments in key aspects of the space industry. The editors are hopeful that this book lends some support to the further development of contract practice and serves as a useful guide in negotiations and legal project management.

List of References

ASD Eurospace 2010. *The European Space Industry in 2009: Facts and Figures*, August 2010. [Online]. Available at: http://www.eurospace.org [accessed: 30 April 2011].

Baumann, I. 2005. *Das internationale Recht der Satellitenkommunikation*. Frankfurt: Peter Lang.

Charter On Cooperation To Achieve The Coordinated Use Of Space Facilities In The Event Of Natural Or Technological Disasters. [Online]. Available at: http://www.disastercharter.org [accessed: 30 April 2011].

Commentary 'With or without MUSIS', *Space News*, 21 (49), 13 December 2010, 18.

Conclusions of the 7th Space Council, 'Global Challenges: Taking Benefit of European Space Systems', 25 November 2010.

European Court of Auditors, Special Report, No. 7, 2009: 'The Management of the Galileo Programme's Development and Validation Phase'. [Online]. Available at: http://eca.europa.eu [accessed: 30 April 2011].

Information. [Online]. Available at: http://www.eumetsat.int [accessed: 30 April 2011].

Intergovernmental Agreement concerning cooperation on the Civil International Space Station (ISS Agreement).

Lyall, F. and Larsen, P. 2009. *Space Law, A Treatise*. Aldershot: Ashgate.

Index